THE NEW WORLD

THE
NEW WORLD

PROBLEMS IN
POLITICAL GEOGRAPHY

By
Isaiah Bowman, Ph.D.
Director of the
American Geographical Society
of New York

ILLUSTRATED WITH 215 MAPS
AND WITH 65 ENGRAVINGS FROM
PHOTOGRAPHS

33240

Yonkers-on-Hudson, New York
WORLD BOOK COMPANY
1921

WORLD BOOK COMPANY

THE HOUSE OF APPLIED KNOWLEDGE

Established, 1905, by Caspar W. Hodgson

YONKERS-ON-HUDSON, NEW YORK
2126 PRAIRIE AVENUE, CHICAGO

In an autocracy a very small political group may take the most fateful decisions respecting peace and war. In a democracy the citizen participates in this grave task. It is therefore the pramount duty of all citizens who wish to see our civilization preserved and advanced, to know the peoples about them, their problems, their desires, their resources, their possibilities, and their spirit, — in short, the political and geographic as well as the historic and economic bases of their life. Yet such information concerning the different peoples and countries of the world is often hard to come by, and its interpretation usually requires an acquaintance with the sources of knowledge that few people possess. *The New World* is designed to provide for the average citizen the background of information that is necessary to understand the main international questions of our time and to follow their development

PREFACE

WHETHER we wish to do so or not we are obliged to take hold of the present world situation in one way or another. Though that situation is based upon a group of international problems of extraordinary complexity, opinions respecting these problems must in many cases be translated into immediate action on the part of government executives. In an autocracy the people are asked to accept unquestioningly the judgments of officials reputed to be wiser than they; in a democracy like ours we periodically ask the voters (suddenly doubled in number by the extension of the suffrage to women) to express an opinion and commit the government to a policy.

No one can contemplate our relation to affairs with equanimity in view of the state of political education in the United States. Our hitherto domestic point of view, our century-long and uninterrupted success in territorial expansion, the high and false values set upon material wealth, even our view of party politics and the responsibilities of party leaders, all alike increase the difficulties of a time beset by perils of a new order.

To grasp the full meaning of questions which involve other powers that like ourselves have patriotic pride and the means to defend their honor, requires something more than native common sense and a willingness to deal fairly. For these questions have a geographical and historical setting and require scholarly consideration. It is to the roots of wrong that the voters and the constructive statesmen of our time must address themselves. In England and France the government leaders can depend upon a body of specialists and experienced administrators. In America we have never had a trained and permanent foreign-office staff; and however lofty our intentions, we work, so far as scholarship goes, on administrative principles little different from those of a hundred years ago.

It is therefore unnecessary to elaborate an explanation for a book that deals with so many political questions as this one. As a general review it is likely to display many faults of judgment and emphasis. It goes without saying that no one could hope to present a wholly balanced account of present political conditions. However, the attempt has been made to avoid all but the most necessary expressions of editorial opinion, leaving the facts on the two sides of a given question to speak for themselves. Where this principle has been set aside, it has been for the purpose of pointing more explicitly than could otherwise have been done to the gravest of existing dangers.

There are some questions that can hardly be said to have two sides, and there are other questions of a debatable character that require a judgment now and not later.

The text has been illustrated at every turn by maps, many of th specially perpared for the purpose, because maps are particula current problems of political geography. Furthermore, not only are many valuable published maps difficult to find, they are still more difficult to interpret. It seemed that a real service could be rendered by assembling them and commenting upon the facts that they display.

The large number of maps required and the many boundary changes taking place have made it impossible to represent the latest boundaries on every map, in spite of the fact that some of the maps have been engraved several times in order to have them include more recent decisions. Liberal cross-references are therefore given in the figure inscriptions and in the main text. A few of the maps represent conditions that may not actually be carried out, as, for example, the maps illustrating the treaty of Sèvres between Turkey and the Allied Powers, a treaty still awaiting ratification. In fact, many of the conditions set forth in other treaties now in force may be altered by later negotiation.

There are three personal acknowledgments which I take pleasure in making: to Mr. John Storck, Miss Gladys M. Wrigley, editor of the *Geographical Review*, and Miss M. A. Purcell, editor for the publishers, all of whom gave the most intelligent and constructive assistance. In addition I wish to thank Mr. Storck for his help in assembling the statistics and in the preparation of the maps. Thanks are due the officers of the American Geographical Society for interest in the work and for permission to use many of the original drawings, as well as plates, of maps which first appeared in the *Geographical Review*. I wish also to record my great obligation to former members of the Commission of Inquiry, an exceptionally able group of scholars who coöperated with the American Geographical Society in forming an organization which had for its object the systematic collection of data for the use of the American government in the conference for the establishment of peace, thus rendering an important public service in time of need. Further acknowledgments are made in the form of bibliographic notes at the end of the volume and in the inscriptions beneath the maps.

ISAIAH BOWMAN

2 April 1921

CONTENTS

THE NEW WORLD

PROBLEMS IN POLITICAL GEOGRAPHY

CHAPTER ONE

MAJOR PROBLEMS

THE effects of the Great War are so far-reaching that we shall have henceforth a new world. Shaken violently out of their former routine, people everywhere have created or adopted new ideas and new material arrangements. Yet the student of history sees in this period of change but a step in an age-old process; to him the effects of the war are as new ingredients dropped into the caldron of humanity. The world is not new in the sense that war has ceased, that all political and social problems will be promptly settled, that present international boundaries and economic arrangements will forever remain unchanged. The qualities of selfish ambition and envy are deep-seated; they will pass away only when human life itself is extinguished. So long as they exist there will be war, with its revotionary effects upon political, social, and economic life.

Man's mental qualities and reactions change but little; they repeat certain effects from age to age. Almost every event of our time has its counterpart in history. The officials of the Roman Empire faced problems strikingly like our own, whether they relate to land ownership and distribution, the burden of taxes, the drift of country folk to the city, growing love for material wealth and pleasure, or the rise of political problems of a magnitude beyond the power of individual rulers. Each age has had its grand catastrophe, its great war. We call the late war Armageddon, but historians have long called the battle of Leipzig (1813) the "Battle of the Nations."

After each crisis humanity has set itself vigorously to work recasting its world. This it is now struggling to do after the years of war just left behind. Like the great geologic eras of earth history, the new age dates from a period of general change in habit of life. Our political and social environment has been revolutionized. We now look out upon world problems and alien peoples, almost unknown to us until yesterday, in a spirit akin to that of Europeans four centuries ago, when they stood at the threshold of the Age of Discovery. Everywhere men have been stirred by new ideas. The new era will

date from the years of the World War just as medieval Europe dates
from the fall of Rome, or as the modern democratic era dates from the
Declaration of Independence.

What are some of the new problems of the world?

New world
problems

Whatever the faults of the old world, it was at least what a business man would call a "going concern"; can the *new* world be
set going in an orderly manner?

How much of the old world is left?

What new boundaries, concessions, colonies, mandataries, spheres
of influence, and protectorates now appear on the map of the world?

What kind of people compose the new states?

Will the new democracies survive, — in Poland and Jugo-Slavia
and Austria, for example, — or are some of the experiments in
self-government likely to fail?

What elements of economic strength and weakness has each of
the new states, and also each of the old states whose resources
have been either increased or diminished by treaty?

*The large and powerful states — the "great powers" — have, from
this time forward, a new set of rights and responsibilities. How will
these responsibilities be met?*

Will the strong states administer their colonies or protectorates
in the interest of the natives?

Responsi-
bilities of
the great
powers

Could the grip of the large "western" powers be loosened without
anarchy following in the "protected" or "occupied" regions
of the world, like Egypt (British), Santo Domingo (United
States), Morocco (French)?

Can the terrible burden of armaments be reduced by common
agreement?

Has the day of deliverance come for the oppressed minorities of the
earth, those who have hitherto been persecuted because of differences between themselves and the majority or ruling class in race,
religion, or social customs?

How far can the protection of minorities be carried? Can the so-
called minorities treaties stand, or do they threaten the integrity
of the unwilling signatory states — Poland, Czecho-Slovakia,
Rumania, Jugo-Slavia, and Greece?

Will strong nations continue the struggle for trade privileges, raw
materials, and strategic zones, with the prospect of war between
them if they cannot realize their commercial and political ambitions otherwise?

In short, will the changes in the political and economic geography of the world spell peace or war, strength or weakness, in the years immediately before us?

These are vital problems for every nation. By reason of some of them war may come, not in a generation, but in a few years. The danger spots of the world have been greatly increased in number, the *zones of friction* lengthened. Where there were approximately *8000 miles* of old boundary about the former states of central Europe, there are now *10,000 miles*, and of this total more than 3000 miles represent newly located boundaries. Every additional mile of new boundary, each new location, has increased for a time the sources of possible trouble between unlike and, in the main, unfriendly peoples. Nor have neighboring peoples yet learned to look upon the new boundaries as final limits; for it takes time to adjust a nation's thought and life to a new frontier.

Zones of friction lengthened

Hatreds have been intensified by the cruelties of the war, and one of the chief problems is that of restoring a state of friendship in the world. This will be difficult for all, but especially for weak, ignorant, and quarrelsome people. In some countries conditions of life and morality are even worse than before. A Syrian recently expressed this state of things in striking terms: "Once I wept all day long: now I weep for that day."

When the lovely windows of Rheims cathedral were broken into thousands of pieces and scattered through the streets, the people at once began collecting the pieces. Every fragment that could be found, no matter how tiny, was carefully laid aside against the day when the pieces would be fitted together again and the windows restored.

Rheims cathedral a symbol of the world

Rheims cathedral and its broken windows are a symbol of the world. A few years ago the world was orderly. To be sure, it was not perfect; some of its problems were exceedingly difficult and perplexing. Then like a thunderclap came the war and the terrible suffering and wreck of war. About some of the world's peoples now lie the ruins of their former life, and they are trying to piece them together again. Even in the United States, remote though it be, the evil effects are manifold. No American, however secluded his life, however distant his home from the big cities and the coasts, is free from the consequences of the World War. The world is broken; its international life is disrupted; it is in a state of general economic disorder.

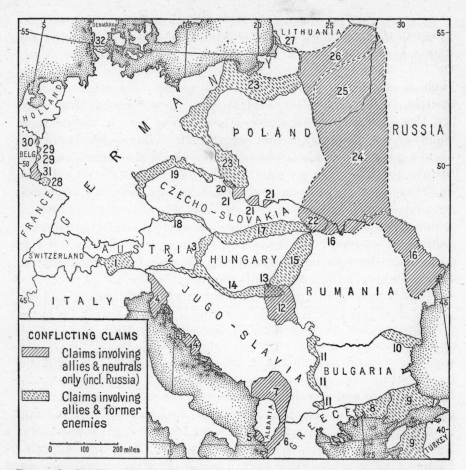

Fig. 1. Overlapping territorial claims in central Europe. Claims are represented not in their most extreme but in their more conservative forms; in general, therefore, the ethnic line is taken as the limit of the claims of Austria and Hungary; the eastern limit of Poland's claim as shown on the map is some distance west of her boundary in 1772 (see Figure 166), etc. The districts are numbered as follows:

1. Part of Austrian Tyrol
2. German-Slovene borderland
3. German Hungary
4. Istria and Dalmatia
5. Valona
6. Northern Epirus
7. Serbo-Albanian zone
8. Western Thrace
9. Eastern Thrace and the area claimed by Greece in Asia Minor
10. Southern Dobrudja
11. Western Bulgaria (See Fig. 153)
12. Southern Banat
13. Northern Banat
14. Southern Hungary
15. Western Transylvania
16. Eastern Ruthenia and Bessarabia
17. Southern Slovakia
18. Southern Bohemia
19. German Bohemia
20. Czech districts in German Silesia
21. Teschen, Orawa, and Spits (named in order from west to east)
22. Ruthenia
23. Upper Silesia, Posen, Danzig, Marienwerder, and Allenstein
24. Polish-Russian border zone
25. Lithuanian-Polish-Russian border zone
26. Polish-Lithuanian border zone
27. Trans-Niemen territory
28. Saar basin
29. Malmédy, Eupen, and Moresnet
30. Southern Limburg
31. Luxemburg
32. Northern Slesvig

THE NEW MAP OF THE WORLD

A map of the new world is a picture of one of the most important results of the war. Most people think of a map as a fixed thing. On the contrary it is almost as changeful as mankind itself. Two kinds of changes are constantly taking place, the first of which is brought about by scientific explorations. It was only a short time ago that the south-polar region and much of central Africa were blanks on the map. Thus the map grows with our knowledge of the world's geography. The second kind of change is brought about by the changing fortunes of nations. The boundaries of the different countries have never long remained fixed in history. "Frontiers are snapshots of the life of nations." It was with a great deal of astonishment and anxiety that many people saw the old landmarks suddenly disappear in 1919. The world was at one of the turning points of its career; new nations sprang up; men began to talk about a New Europe.

Maps as pictures of the new era, changing with history

SOME BASIC CAUSES OF THE COMPLEX PROBLEMS OF THE WORLD

So far as Europe and western Asia are concerned, the current problems would be much easier to solve if people of different kinds were not so intimately mixed in broad belts on their common frontiers. Sharp lines of division between groups differing in race, religion, or language are the exception, not the rule. Thus arise disputes as to the disposition of mixed zones, each side claiming to have a majority. These areas have often been referred to as the "twilight zones," or "gray zones," phrases expressing doubtful character. Eastern Galicia (Fig. 167) is such a region of mixed population; in general the Poles live in or near the towns and the Ruthenians occupy the country districts. Another region of mixed population is Macedonia (Fig. 159); another is the Dobrudja (Fig. 143). In a portion of Transcaucasia, Armenians and Tatars are so intermingled that to avoid the rule of one people by another they signed a special treaty in 1919 providing for joint administration of certain mixed zones.

The "twilight zones"

For many years we had almost forgotten that religion forms one of the world's major problems, not merely because there is a contest between the various religions for supremacy, but also and chiefly because religion, from its nature or through its use by ambitious rulers or peoples, may become a political force. Mohammedanism, for example, has always been feared in this respect, because its followers are taught to carry its message to unbelievers even by fire and sword.

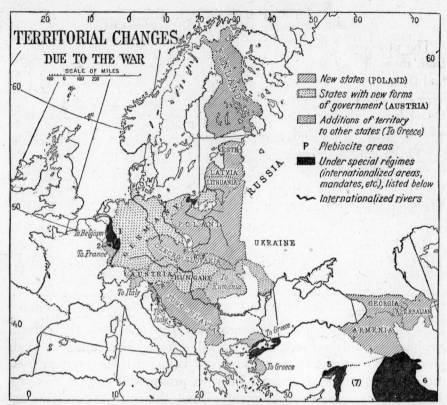

Fig. 2. The territorial reorganization of central Europe and the Near East. The numbered areas are as follows: 1, Left Bank of the Rhine; 2, Saar district; 3, Danzig Free City (or State); 4, Zone of the Straits; 5, Syria, under French mandate; 6, Mesopotamia, under British mandate; 7, Zone of possible Arab state extending southward into Arabia and related to both French and British spheres of interest. For more detailed maps on larger scales see the appropriate chapters that follow. For the boundaries of the Free State of Fiume see Figure 139. The original plebiscite arrangements for Teschen, Orawa, and Spits on the northern border of Czecho-Slovakia were later set aside (Fig. 179). For the Tripartite agreement (southern Anatolia) see Figure 48.

Religion also a world problem

It is a religion of force and political authority, and we have nothing with which to compare it in the Christian religion except the forcible conversion of the American Indians in the days of Spanish colonization or of the barbarians of the eastern Baltic lands by the Teutonic Knights. In Russia, the national religion (Greek Orthodox) and the state were long inseparable ideas, and the Czar was the head of the church; but there was little politico-religious proselytizing and no fanatical spirit. Religious motives in the Mohammedan world are important in relation to French and British policy in the eastern Mediterranean and particularly along the road to India (pages 54 to 57). Islam, to use another name for Mohammedanism, is a religion that has millions of converts each year, chiefly among low-grade populations, such as the negroes of central Africa.

THE FORM OF THE PRESENT PROBLEMS

The problems following this war are very much more complicated than those of any preceding time. The old causes of trouble, which had their roots in the unequal geographical conditions and in the jealousies of different dynasties, are complicated by a general desire for better living conditions and by a universal unrest and dissatisfaction with present social and political forms. There has been growing, chiefly in Russia, an internationalist movement, and we have seen it in the form of Bolshevism carry devastation and fear into every corner of old Russia. It has sent its agents abroad to carry its revolutionary beliefs into peaceful communities and even into the democracies of the western world.

Old problems now complicated by new desires

In addition we have local problems that, put together, give the leaders of each nation the greatest concern. Everywhere throughout the world labor is demanding shorter hours and larger pay. In

Even the local problems serious

RELIGIONS

▨	Protestant
▧	Roman-Catholic
⣿	Greek Orthodox
■	Mohammedan
☐	Heathen

Fig. 3. Note the religious differences between Russians and the people of the western border states that have broken away to form independent national units. The creation of Poland adds a powerful unit to the Roman Catholic bloc. International boundaries as in 1920 (for eastern Poland, Finland, and Rumania see Figures 182, 144, and 188 respectively). Boundaries of religions after Debes, *Handatlas*.

many countries peasants are taking possession of the large estates and dividing the land. Nations large and small are anxious about their frontiers and the stability of the arrangements resulting from the treaties following the World War. There is fear of trouble from the unlike populations that are included with the majorities of many states. Everywhere there is general anxiety lest the present disorganization of the world should lead to still greater economic distress.

New and broader issues in place of the old The early issues of the war have long since changed their aspect. Only to mention the outstanding persons and events of the years of war is to see how little concern there is with them at the present time. Their place is taken by larger and more enduring interests. The new interests consist of geographical, social, and political problems that affect the entire world. They may be thought of as due, at least in large part, to world disorganization. From a state of high idealism maintained during much of the war, men have passed into a state of realism. They are not seeking an opportunity for service so much as an opportunity for gain. The spirit of team-play that prevailed during the war has in too many instances changed to a spirit of extreme and dangerous individualism. Too many men are fiercely impatient with the necessary routine of life. On them the lessons of the war have been largely lost. Until a new atmosphere has been created, the world will remain disorganized, unstable, dangerous.

Varying and entangled causes of change In studying the changes that take place in the map of the world, we shall do well to keep before us at all times how complicated are the current causes of change in national boundaries. In the past these causes have been hardly less complex. Sometimes it was the personal ambition of a king or of the nobility that altered the frontier of a nation. Sometimes it was the pressure of a hungry population. Sometimes it was one of those great periodic migrations or waves of people that have swept from Inner Asia into the eastern and central districts of Europe. Sometimes it was religion, as in the spread of Mohammedanism from the 12th to the 15th centuries. And sometimes, as in the recent war, it was a great group of complicated factors very difficult to disentangle.

Causes of the World War of 1914–1918 It was not the death of a Grand Duke at Sarajevo or the invasion of Belgium, nor was it the ambitions of the German ruler or the Pan-German dreams of the German Junkers — it was not any one of these things that produced the war. It was a combination of all of them, colored by a desire to control the seats of production and the channels of transportation of all those products, like coal and oil and hemp and cotton and iron and steel and manganese, that are the founda-

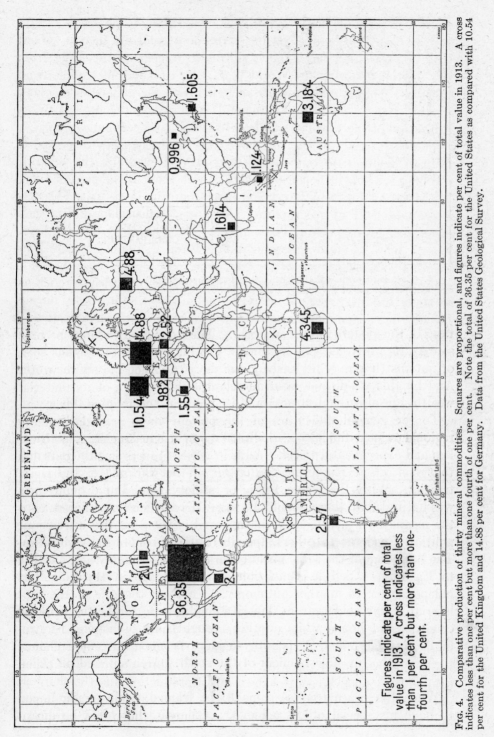

FIG. 4. Comparative production of thirty mineral commodities. Squares are proportional, and figures indicate per cent of total value in 1913. A cross indicates less than one per cent but more than one fourth of one per cent. Note the total of 36.35 per cent for the United States as compared with 10.54 per cent for the United Kingdom and 14.88 per cent for Germany. Data from the United States Geological Survey.

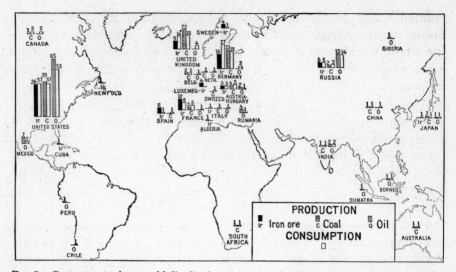

Fig. 5. Cartogram to show world distribution of the three leading industrial minerals. Figures represent percentages of the world's total in 1913. Data from the United States Geological Survey.

tions of the modern industrial world. These commodities may become sources of unrivaled power, and in the hands of unscrupulous men or nations they may be used for the devastation of the entire world. And by this we do not mean merely the destruction of its material wealth, but also the destruction of its political and religious liberty.

Lack of agreement as to the objects of the war and the peace treaties

To the general difficulties of the present there are added many regional or local difficulties, which have now reached a climax in a restless and experimental world. Added to these causes is the confusion that has arisen respecting the *objects* of the war and of the peace treaties. With the whole fabric of society torn and disfigured, it was natural that there should be many divergencies of opinion as to the means by which it could be restored. To some the war meant political freedom; to others, the liberation of oppressed minorities. The "freedom of the seas" meant one thing to Germany and another to England. "Self-determination" to one group in Russia meant independence, to another autonomy, to a third the rule of the proletariat. One soldier from America might hope for better working conditions at home, while another thought only of helping France, or beating Germany, or possibly a glorious adventure, or a chance to follow the invisible banners of the spirit. Men suffered and died for different objects.

When the peace treaties came to be framed, each person hoped to have his special object achieved; otherwise he would be disappointed. Add to the numerous disappointments the growing confusion resulting from the bitterly contested war that involved nearly the whole world, and it is not hard to understand that any settlement would have a far greater number of unfriendly critics than supporters. This will be true also of many of the international policies, agreements, and treaties of the immediate future, whether they relate to frontiers, commercial opportunities, or the forms of government.

Because it is inhabited by imperfect human beings, the world has always had its causes of friction and its downright wrongs. These things the wise men of all times have tried to adjust. But complete success will never be attained. The evolutionary struggle that marked the rise of mankind from the primitive to the present state will long continue. Taking it by and large, this is a *competitive* world, and to the costs of ordinary competition must be added the cost of the supreme competition of war. National and racial ambitions, hatreds, and rivalries will continue to the end of time, though they may be reduced in scope and intensity.

While it is important to face these facts, it is far more important that men's minds should be turned to experimentation in the field of coöperative plans. The world has had many leagues of nations in principle. The present proposal is set in high relief by the colossal losses of the war. For example, we had a working league of nations when practically the entire world combined against Germany and her associates; and in the future, whether or not the League of Nations in its present form continues, new leagues will have to be formed when new needs arise. The great practical value of an international court of justice and of experiments in the field of international labor, international postal regulations and patent agreements, the international exchange of data on statistical sources and agriculture, and other modes of promoting international exchange of ideas has been demonstrated. By slow stages, through more general education, and especially through the influence in each generation of a few wise, far-seeing, and practical men, sound coöperative plans may be further developed to the point of reducing the causes of international trouble. But the world's peoples are still fundamentally unlike, and the road to success passes through a wilderness of experiment.

Practical value of existing international agreements

CHAPTER TWO

PROBLEMS OF IMPERIAL BRITAIN

English-
speaking
peoples
and the
new map
of the
world

DESPITE the great colonial empires once held by France and Spain and the wide distribution of their holdings, it is the people of English speech who have been the most persistent colonial organizers of modern times. Though they have frequently abused native rights, they have nevertheless been the most successful in their use of native help in managing the affairs of colonies of different race. This is true of American rule in the Philippines and Porto Rico as well as of the government of British colonies. Their sense of responsibility is alert. It is because their navies are powerful that the sea is free. In the common language they speak and write there is a bond of political significance. Both have a traditional tendency toward liberal government.

Ultimate
protection
may de-
pend upon
naval
strength

Among English-speaking nations the two most powerful commercially, the United Kingdom and the United States, have a combined naval strength which comprises nearly 75 per cent of the world's total. This is a matter of the gravest importance, for in the past few years we have seen much of the world thrown into a state bordering on anarchy, and if the process continues or at some future time recurs, it may be that the sea lanes and distant strategic points on the rim of civilization can be held only if there be a powerful and mobile fleet. For these reasons, we shall wish to see first of all how the World War and the peace treaties have affected lands governed by the English.

Dangers of
territorial
inflation

The territorial inflation of Great Britain as a result of the World War is a source of real danger to her. So widespread and varied are British possessions that commercial, racial, and religious convulsions, no matter in what part of the world they take place, impinge upon the interests of Britain. Even before the war her territory was sufficiently widespread to test her capacity for government; and in the past few years she has assumed new obligations which involve enormously heavy financial and military expenditures. The treaty with Persia requires Great Britain to give military advice and other aid to that country. Holding Mesopotamia and Egypt and Palestine means cultivating good relations with the Arabs. Thus in the Near East alone Britain has added to her former responsibilities an area of 800,000 square miles, with a population of 12,000,000.

The favor-
able geo-
graphical
distribu-
tion of
British
possessions

British possessions are so distributed that they lie chiefly about the borders of the Atlantic and Indian oceans, and it is on these two oceans that British commerce is of greatest importance (Fig. 7).

12

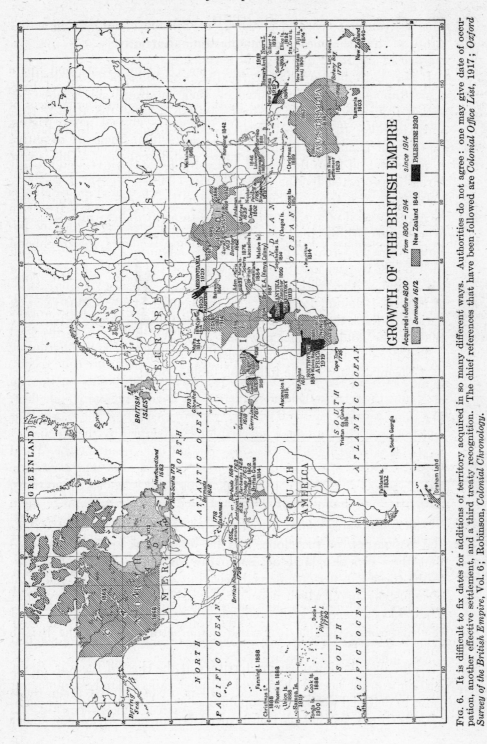

Fig. 6. It is difficult to fix dates for additions of territory acquired in so many different ways. Authorities do not agree: one may give date of occupation, another effective settlement, and a third treaty recognition. The chief references that have been followed are *Colonial Office List, 1917; Oxford Survey of the British Empire*, Vol. 6; Robinson, *Colonial Chronology*.

This distribution has also given Great Britain advantages in naval strategy, since the lines of communication are relatively short and are marked by an admirable series of harbors.

Protecting features on the landward side of British territory

It is remarkable to what degree the possessions of Great Britain, a maritime power, are protected on their landward side against invasion from continental interiors. In the case of the British Isles and Australia, this protection comes from insularity. In India the continental frontier is formed by a great mountain barrier; Egypt is in part set off from the rest of Africa by desert country; and South Africa is protected by the great Kalahari Desert, north of which is the barrier of a tropical forest thrown halfway across the continent. As a great naval power, Japan might be thought to have an advantage over Great Britain in Australasia and India, which are nearer to Japan than to Great Britain. But this advantage of nearness is in turn offset by the maritime supremacy of the British Empire as a whole and of the British Isles in particular. Finally, the territories of France, Belgium, Portugal, and the United States — four friendly nations — flank the possessions of the British Empire more extensively than do the lands of other powers.

The size and population of the British Empire have trebled in the past seventy years, as the following table shows:

GROWTH OF THE BRITISH EMPIRE

DATE	AREA IN SQUARE MILES	POPULATION
1800	1,500,000	20,000,000
1850	4,500,000	160,000,000
1900	11,300,000	390,000,000
1919	13,700,000	475,000,000

Extraordinary growth of the British Empire in a hundred years

The empire now contains well over one quarter of the land surface and population of the globe, and its possessions are so distributed that they give England access to raw materials vital not merely to the success of her commercial fleet, but vital also to the great host of industries upon which depends the welfare of the British people. The table on page 15 gives a comparative view of the great stock of raw materials available to British manufacturers within the British Empire.

In the distribution of enemy territory at the close of the war, Great Britain won the largest share, and with her gains in land go important gains in material wealth. Mesopotamia has rich oil deposits. Tanganyika Territory, as that part of former German East Africa now under

RAW MATERIALS WITHIN THE BRITISH EMPIRE, 1914[1]

The figures given are the approximate averages for four (or five) normal pre-war years.

Commodity[2]	Annual consumption of United Kingdom (with % from British Empire)	Annual **production** within the empire	Annual **consumption** within the empire	Chief sources of supply within the empire
Antimony (metal)	6000 tons (10 %)	1000 tons		Australia (output curtailed by development of Chinese deposits). Mexican supply (2000 tons) in British hands.
Asbestos . . .	160,000 cwt. (60%)	1,784,000 cwt.		Canada furnishes 80% of world's supply, and more than enough for the empire.
Borax	10,000 tons		12,000 tons	British corporation controls important fields in Argentina and Peru.
Butter	6,500,000 cwt. (55%)			The supply is insufficient. Australia and New Zealand are the chief producers.
Cheese	2,900,000 cwt. (80%)			Canada supplies 50% of consumption of U. K.
Chromium (ore) .	No data			Rhodesia supplies over 40% of world's production.
Cobalt	No data			Canada is chief source of world's supply.
Copper (metal) .	120,000 tons (25%)	87,000 tons	150,000 tons	Australia (50%); Canada (40%).
Cotton	1,000,000 tons (20%)	1,250,000 tons		India produces over ⅔ of total, but much of her production is not suitable for the British industry. Egypt produces high-grade cotton.
Fertilizers . . .	600,000 tons		850,000 tons	No important empire sources.
Graphite . . .	16,000 tons (45%)	31,500 tons	17,000 tons	Ceylon produces the world's best graphite.
Iron (pig) . .	8,600,000 tons (70%)	5,800,000 tons	10,000,000 tons	United Kingdom (80%); Canada (15%).
Lead	180,000 tons (25%)	155,000 tons	212,000 tons	Large resources in Burma are being developed.
Manganese (ore)	430,000 tons (45%)	600,000 tons		India could easily supply the empire's needs.
Mercury . . .	600 tons		850 tons	No important empire sources.
Nickel	No data	22,000 tons		Canada can supply the empire's needs, though her deposits are controlled by American capital.
Platinum . . .	35,000 oz.		37,000 oz.	No important empire sources.
Sulphur . . .	370,000 cwt.		1,750,000 cwt.	No important empire sources.
Thorium . . .	35–50 tons	120 tons		India produces 100 tons, formerly in German control.
Tin	20,000 tons (60%)	81,500 tons	27,000 tons	Straits Settlements (80%); Nigeria, United Kingdom, Australia (about 5% each).
Tungsten (ore) .	No data	3,700 tons		India and Australia each produce about 30%, and the Malay States a little less.
Wheat	195,830,000 bu. (50%)	705,000,000 bu.	736,000,000 bu.	India (50%); Canada (25%); Australia (10%); United Kingdom (5%).
Wood pulp . .	844,000 tons (10%)	1,260,000 tons		Practically all from Canada.
Wool	566,000,000 lbs. (80%)	1,246,000,000 lbs.	650,000,000 lbs.	Australia (60%); New Zealand (15%); South Africa (10%); United Kingdom (10%).
Zinc	194,000 tons	235,000 tons	200,000 tons	Australia is by far the most important (90%); promising deposits in India also.

[1] Coal and petroleum are not included. See Figs. 4 and 5.

[2] The commodities of the table are indicated in three styles of type: **boldface**, representing those which are produced in quantities sufficient to supply the needs of the empire; *italics*, those which could be developed to the point of supplying the needs of the empire; and ordinary type, those for which the empire will have to depend in part upon outside sources.

a British mandate is called, has a large labor supply and valuable fibers, oils, cereals, and cattle ranges. Those parts of Togoland and the Cameroons gained by Great Britain have rich resources in palm oil. Nauru, in the Pacific, has valuable phosphate deposits. Kaiser Wilhelm's Land, now added to British New Guinea, has petroleum, copra, and pearl fisheries. With all these assets go strategic and political advantages, as well as increased coaling and cable station facilities of direct benefit to the entire British trade organization.

In the industrial revolution that changed western Europe completely, England took the lead, and she has held it in the hundred-and-fifty-year period since the beginning of that revolution. This she could not have done if she had not had within the boundaries of the empire a large part of the raw materials that she required. Trade became the life blood of the British Empire.

Before the period of colonization, England was drawing the principal material for shipbuilding from northern Europe, and it was always a matter of anxiety to her that her sources of supply might be taken away. This was one of the strong reasons for colonizing America, where she could find an abundant supply of materials for shipbuilding. "Her shipping was to England like the hair of Samson, the secret of her national strength." The extension of this policy led England into the adoption of political principles of most far-reaching consequences, for in seeking raw materials of every sort Great Britain's activities and claims collided at many points with those of the other industrial nations of the world.

(A) Trade Organization of the Empire

To pay the
huge war
debt indus-
trial reor-
ganization
required

There is a particular aspect of the British economic and political situation that we need to examine before taking up the problems of the empire in detail. How is the organized commercial life of Great Britain to be continued under the great strain of feeding and clothing England's industrial millions at the same time that an enormous war debt is paid? The map of the United Kingdom (Fig. 8) shows how remarkably concentrated is the industrial population, and how closely dependent upon coal. The people engaged in agriculture in England compose but 6 per cent of the population, while in France they form 40 per cent, in Italy 35 per cent, in Russia 72 per cent, in Jugo-Slavia 80 per cent. In general, the people of the British Isles live in dense agglomerations, and their welfare is bound up with coal, iron, and steel, the freedom of sea routes, and the right to trade wherever they choose.

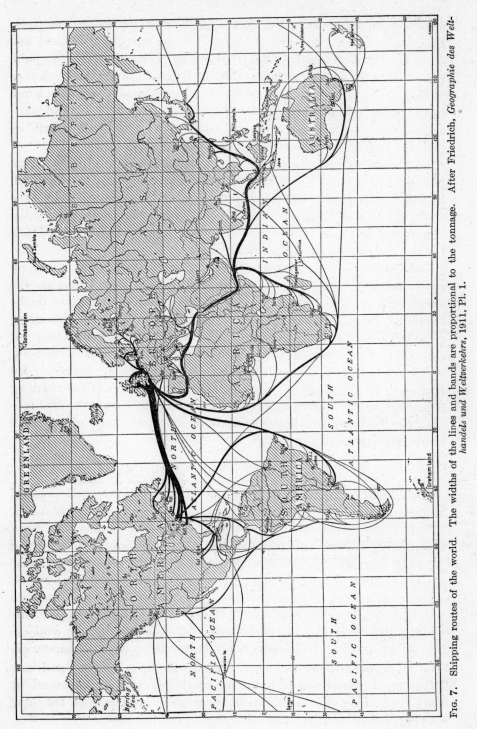

FIG. 7. Shipping routes of the world. The widths of the lines and bands are proportional to the tonnage. After Friedrich, *Geographie des Welthandels und Weltverkehrs*, 1911, Pl. 1.

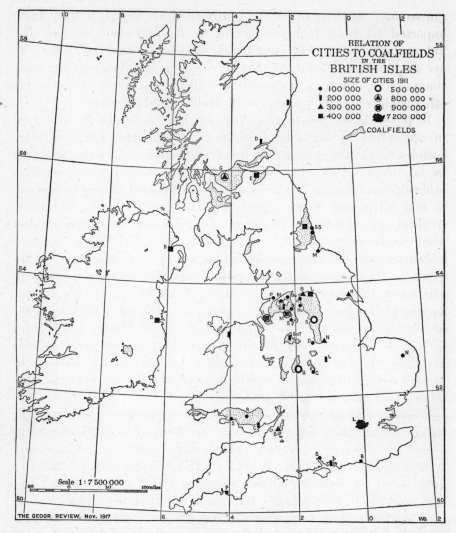

FIG. 8. Outline map showing the relation of cities to coal fields in the British Isles. From Mark Jefferson, in the *Geographical Review*, Vol. 4, 1917.

PREFERENTIAL TARIFFS

Conflict of trading principles

One of the most acute problems of Great Britain grew out of her attitude toward tariffs. England maintained throughout the modern commercial period a free-trade policy to which her whole commercial system became adjusted. It had aspects of serious international importance. England wished to see her goods admitted into the world's trade areas, regardless of political ownership, on terms of equality with those of all other powers. In carrying out this policy her interests ran counter to those of other countries, which impose a tariff upon imported goods for high revenue, or for the protection of their own industries, or for the exclusion of the trade of commercial rivals. In her own colonies Great Britain threw open her doors to the merchants of all countries on terms more liberal than those of any of the other great colonizing powers except Holland and Germany.

In pursuing her free-trade policy, England at length found herself in opposition to her own colonies. For example, the Australian colonies fought the principle of free trade, and in 1873 were permitted by law to make such tariff arrangements as they deemed best with other British colonies. While the colonies found it almost impossible to take advantage of the opportunity this created, owing to mutual rivalries and differences in degree of economic development that would make any tariff law bear unequally upon the different regional industries, yet the principle had been won, and it was never relinquished. It became part of a general plan for winning equality of privilege with the mother country, and eventually it led to the acceptance by British leaders of the fact that a general preferential agreement, or commercial union of the empire on terms of absolute equality for each of its parts, was the one sure way of keeping the empire intact. To allow the self-governing dominions to continue to make tariff treaties with foreign states would be to invite in some degree discrimination against English trade. *Colonial opposition to British tariff regulations*

England's general policy as well as the nationalistic policies of its self-governing units have both been modified. After full discussion, a plan was put into force, called the British Finance Act, effective on 1 September 1919. This act applies the new preferential rates of duty to all the British dominions outside of Great Britain and Ireland and also to British India, the Indian native states, and all British protectorates. Any territories that may have come under the protection of the British government subsequently to the date of going into force of the act, or any territory which Great Britain may administer under a mandate of the League of Nations, may have the act in question applied to it by an Order in Council. The preferential rates apply to almost all goods subject to customs duties which are proved to be consigned from, grown, manufactured, or produced within the British Empire. *The new British Finance Act*

In the same way American goods have preferential treatment in Porto Rico and the Philippines; that is, they are admitted duty free or with only a light import tax, while those of other nations pay a heavier tax. According to the British plan, a country that is willing

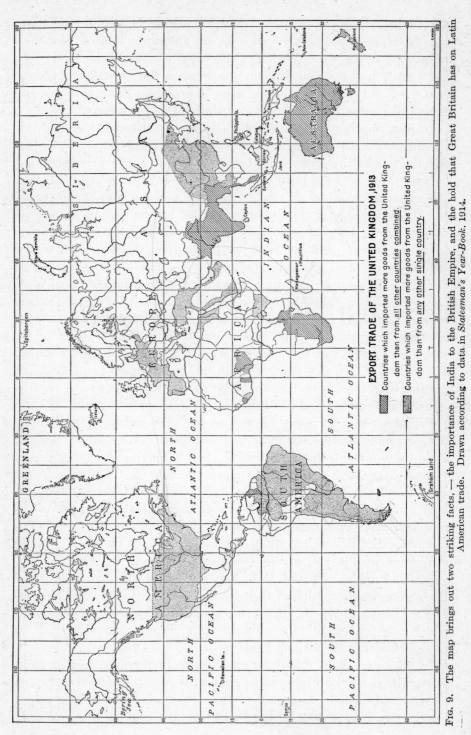

FIG. 9. The map brings out two striking facts, — the importance of India to the British Empire, and the hold that Great Britain has on Latin American trade. Drawn according to data in *Statesman's Year-Book*, 1914.

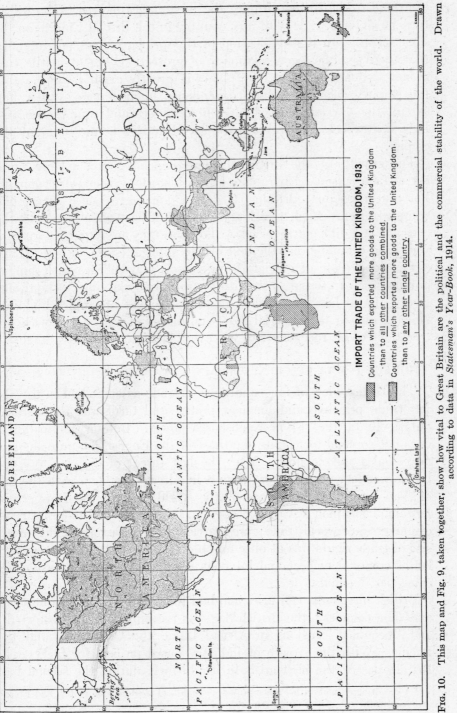

IMPORT TRADE OF THE UNITED KINGDOM, 1913

Countries which exported more goods to the United Kingdom than to all other countries combined.

Countries which exported more goods to the United Kingdom than to <u>any other single country</u>.

Fig. 10. This map and Fig. 9, taken together, show how vital to Great Britain are the political and the commercial stability of the world. Drawn according to data in *Statesman's Year-Book*, 1914.

to extend to the British Empire the advantages of free trade, will in turn be able to trade with any country in the British Empire on the same terms.[1] In the application of this principle it is not intended that there shall be a general policy of protection, except in the case of new industries. The new plan will greatly expand trade within the empire, decrease British dependence upon foreign states, and extend the development of internal resources and communications. It is also expected to increase the social and economic unity of the empire.

The process of empire building The growth of the British Empire depends upon a large number of factors, some geographic, others historic or social or economic. For centuries Great Britain has been gaining experience in colonial administration. Each year large numbers of her young men enter the consular and diplomatic service. To do so they are required to pass a very rigid examination; the best of the applicants are chosen. Thus is formed a caste of officials from schools and colleges with similar purposes. A fraternal spirit with a strong imperial tinge is the result. Every official has been drilled in the principles of empire building. He goes out to the imperial frontiers, his mind well stored with the traditions of his race, eager to win every possible trade advantage.

THE SEA POWER OF GREAT BRITAIN AND IMPERIAL DEVELOPMENT

World trade a vital matter to Great Britain The British view of fair conditions of trade as embodied in the old free-trade principle and the new preferential tariff was the natural outgrowth of the rise of English sea power. Bolivia, for instance, does not contend for claims like those of the English, because she has no colonies and no fleet. After the last threat of disaster to English power had passed, more than a hundred years ago, with the fall of Napoleon, the coast lines of the world became the frontiers of Britain. The men of England came to think more and more in terms of universal or world trade; any barrier to the freest and fullest exercise of trade rights was at once an object of concern; the larger England's commercial fleet and interests became, the more inclusive became her demands.

British capital, industry, and trade in the colonial possessions British merchants centuries ago had founded numerous plantations and then colonies; the British flag was recognized over "protected" and "occupied" regions in Africa, India, the Caribbean, and the Pacific. With the growth of industry based on coal for fuel, Great Britain passed the next crisis in her history, during the second half

[1] A recent agreement with France provides equality of treatment of British and French investors in the colonies of either power.

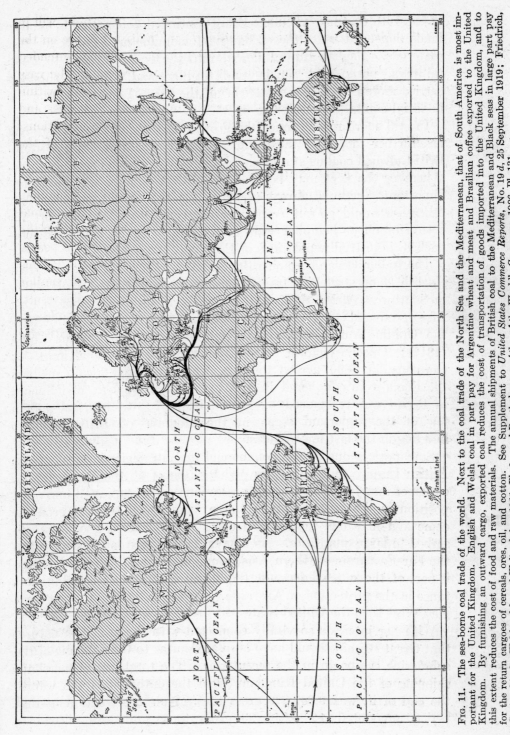

Fig. 11. The sea-borne coal trade of the world. Next to the coal trade of the North Sea and the Mediterranean, that of South America is most important for the United Kingdom. English and Welsh coal in part pay for Argentine wheat and meat and Brazilian coffee exported to the United Kingdom. By furnishing an outward cargo, exported coal reduces the cost of transportation of goods imported into the United Kingdom, and to this extent reduces the cost of food and raw materials. The annual shipments of British coal to the Mediterranean and Black seas in large part pay for the return cargoes of cereals, ores, oil, and cotton. See Supplement to *United States Commerce Reports*, No. 19 *d*, 25 September 1919; Friedrich, *Geographie des Welthandels und Weltverkehrs*, 1911, Pl. 6; and Bartholomew, *Atlas of the World's Commerce*, 1906, Pl. 131.

of the 19th century, when successful continued occupation of remote
lands depended upon the exchange of manufactured goods for raw
materials. English capital flowed into the trade regions, to build
railways, ports, and canals, and to buy land. English shipping
carried more than half the trade of all the seas. London became the
financial capital of the world.

The coal fleets of Britain

In still more recent times the growth of the coal export business
has further increased the commercial and naval power of Britain.
British-owned coaling stations are located at scores of strategic points.
Wherever the fleet may be, there is always fuel for it; and, more
important, there is always a cargo for the freight steamer that
otherwise would go out empty, or nearly so, to a distant port for
cotton or oil or hemp or wool or food to bring back to the close-
packed, industrial populations of England.

British power extended from the Atlantic to the Pacific

The Indian Ocean became a British lake. There was forged a great
English chain stretching from Gibraltar to Nigeria, past Walvis Bay
in Southwest Africa, down past Cape Town, up to Zanzibar in East
Africa, onward to the coast of Arabia and Baluchistan. After
the Opium War, Great Britain obtained Hongkong from China
(1842); Queen Victoria was made Empress of India in 1876;
Germany in 1890 agreed to recognize British rights in Zanzibar;
the Boers were conquered in 1902; the British sphere of influence
in Persia was recognized by Russia in 1907 — to mention only a
few of the important steps in the progress of British empire
building in the last few decades.

Singapore is one of the commercial and strategic outposts of the
British Empire that illustrates perhaps best of all the significant location of many outlying British possessions. It occupies an unrivaled
position in the center of a vast area from which tropical products
come and in which textiles and other manufactured goods are absorbed in large quantities. As a naval base it guards the sea road to
the Far East from southern Asia, commands the Dutch East Indies,
is part of the outer defense of India, and is of almost equal importance in the protection of Australia. Strategically it is to Asia what
Key West is to the United States.

With her interests so vitally connected with the sea, it is natural
that Great Britain should have been anxious as to the outcome of the
submarine campaign in the recent war. The total loss of merchant
shipping of the United Kingdom, from the outbreak of the war to
the end of it, was 9,031,828 gross tons. New construction in that
period amounted to 4,342,296 gross tons, purchases abroad to

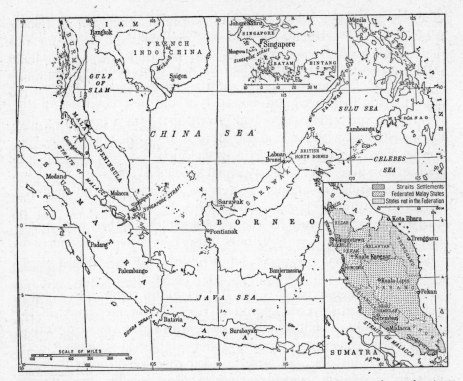

Fig. 12. Focus of American, British, French, Dutch, and Japanese interests in southeastern Asia. Burma, the Straits Settlements (including Singapore), the Federated Malay States, Sarawak, Brunei, and British North Borneo are the principal British possessions. The Dutch own the greater part of Borneo in addition to Java, Sumatra, and other islands near by. French interests are concentrated in French Indo-China, and in the corner of the region stand the Philippine Islands, an American possession. Japanese interests are both strategic and commercial and are related chiefly to trade with India, Java, and the Philippines, a trade which developed rapidly during the World War.

530,000 gross tons, and enemy tonnage captured to 716,520, making a net loss of 3,443,012 gross tons. In addition more than 14,000 lives were lost on ships sunk at sea.

These losses have been a great strain upon the energy of the British people. To a limited extent they are offset by the gains of Great Britain in the division of the German merchant marine. Of 2,550,000 tons surrendered to the Allies by Germany, the larger part was given to Great Britain. Likewise in the division of the ships sunk at Scapa Flow by Admiral von Reuter and later salvaged, 70 per cent were delivered to the British. As a penalty for the sinking, Germany also agreed to deliver to the Allies 275,000 tons of tugs, lighters, floating cranes, and dry docks, the greater part of which goes to Great Britain. Of the shipping that Germany has agreed to build for the Allies (in amount not to exceed 200,000 tons a year for five years),

Losses and gains of the British merchant fleet

Great Britain is also to receive a share. The predominance of British shipping is still as strongly marked as ever, in spite of the large losses of the war.

The basis of British trade policy

With a road opened to India and the Far East, colonies planted in the Caribbean, islands annexed in the Pacific, ports obtained in China; with British capital invested in the new countries of the world wherever trade centers had grown up; with a protecting fleet developed; and with cable and coaling stations to support and control her fleet, Great Britain has a special interest in the conditions of trade everywhere. As long as special trade privileges are restricted to the possessions of a single power, no objection can be made by Britain or any other power. Should they be established by force or otherwise in one country by the goverment of another, and in discrimination against Great Britain, they may become a source of danger. Herein lies the basis for disputes in which America and France may have a vital interest.

Conflict of American and British interests in Latin America

It is in Latin America that the United States comes into sharpest conflict with British trade interests. Recently the merchants of the United States have built up a large trade with Latin American states; they have purchased many railways and established steamship lines, banks, and industries, and have invaded zones of business once exclusively in British control. America also upholds the Monroe Doctrine, especially in relation to the weak states of the West Indies and Central America. Should the United States greatly extend its political influence into South America also, and should it gain through political effort any special trade privileges, there would be conflict of one sort or another with the British Empire.

Britain's alliance with Japan

In 1902 Great Britain made an alliance with Japan, another sea power with an island for a base. It turned out to be a wise alliance, for in the World War it brought Japan into the camp of the Allies. When, in 1920, the time had come to renew it, objections were raised by Japan on the ground that her subjects did not enjoy equality of privilege in British dominions. Against Japan's plea for equality the most vigorous protests were made by Australia, New Zealand, and Canada. If Japanese subjects were let into those countries in large numbers and were permitted to acquire every kind of property, especially land, then British subjects in India would also insist on admission to the dominions, with the result that the white populations there would be submerged beneath a mounting wave of color.

Had Japan won the hoped-for concession from Great Britain, she could then have brought pressure to bear upon the United States for the freer admission of her subjects and the removal of special restrictions on Japanese settlers in California, which state now contains nearly half the Japanese in the United States. In closing their gates to Asiatic immigration into the white man's lands of the Pacific, the people of the British dominions and of the United States find themselves drawn into a closer understanding, which is the strongest present guarantee for the peace of the Pacific.

The alliance between Japan and Great Britain did not endanger the United States, for provision was made against the use of the alliance to force Great Britain into war upon the United States at the wish of Japan. The alliance kept Japan in active and necessary touch with western political ideals, but this result is now accomplished by Japanese participation in the affairs of the League of Nations. Without the alliance or the League, Japan's rapid encroachments upon her neighbors, as in China, Korea, and eastern Siberia, might well alarm Americans for the security of the Philippines.

Effect of the alliance on the United States

Great Britain has incurred a net war debt of more than $26,000,000,000, in addition to $9,000,000,000 loaned to her weaker allies. For a small country this is a colossal figure. The dominions have incurred their own huge debts, and cannot help except through the special channels of trade. It will tax British financial power to the utmost to keep the nation solvent. The interest alone is a staggering sum to pay each year. There are three principal ways in which it can be met:

How Great Britain can pay her huge debt

(1) By increasing production through harder and more effective work.

(2) By developing important resources of food and raw materials in new colonies where land is cheap and labor abundant, as in former German East Africa.

(3) By capitalizing railroads and extractive industries, like agriculture and grazing, in under-developed non-industrial regions like South America, the East Indies, Australia, and South Africa.

The two last-named means imply political activity in every land where British capital goes, in order that investments may be safe and that they may grow in importance. Unless wise coöperative plans are developed for the regulation of investment interests among rival powers, the present struggle may be found more keen than the trade struggle before the war, because of the impulse of high taxes that are the necessary consequence of vast national debts.

(B) The Empire in Relation to Its Parts

The problems of the British Empire

With this general view of the British Empire, we may now turn to regional conditions that in a measure threaten its existence or limit its contribution to human welfare. Other empires have been great in their day, and the Roman Empire, in many respects the greatest of all, was for long periods in a state of comparative peace and was finally overwhelmed only after centuries of proud history. The Mohammedan Empire was at one time the greatest in existence (8th century). At the beginning of modern times, the colonial empire of Spain was the most remarkable. In a century Spain had pioneered a way into the western world, built up a powerful navy, and developed a system of colonial government. But all these empires failed, partly by reason of their vast extent and the inclusion of alien peoples in large numbers, but partly and chiefly because of the decay of national character, or at least its failure to develop in proportion to the growth of its responsibilities. When men became corrupt or soft at the same time that they ruled subject peoples selfishly, or neglected their own internal economic affairs, then each empire collapsed under the strain.

Need for a new orientation of British imperial policy

Seeing their problems in the light of historical experience, the British have sought to anticipate the causes of decline and to provide against them by the adoption of coöperative plans whereby there is achieved a greater degree of local self-government. The collapse within a few years of four other empires now makes the faults of the British Empire stand out in clearer perspective; for its past beneficence was but relative, and its record was bright in part by reason of its contrast to the record of the autocratic empires of Germany, Austria, Russia, and Turkey. It must be said to the credit of the British that they have learned to develop, even in remote and diverse communities, a capacity for self-government in a manner and to a degree never before known in history. It must be admitted also that the British have dealt with a greater diversity of peoples and conditions than have the other colonizing nations of the modern world.

While a marked devotion to high political ideals is evident in the present attitude of the British government towards its possessions, it was not the compelling force of such ideals that was responsible for the extension of British power. Political administration was assumed only because it was found necessary for the development of trade, and with each new development went the necessity for new conquests to protect the frontiers of the trade regions into which British merchants had penetrated.

In spite of the many differences between them, the parts of the British Empire, outside the British Isles, may be grouped into three great divisions :

(1) The five self-governing dominions, — Canada, Australia, South Africa, New Zealand, and Newfoundland, — units which are in general of the same stock and the same speech as the United Kingdom, each with a political consciousness that has led to the development of what amounts to separate nationality.

(2) That part of the empire in which Great Britain governs peoples of race and speech different from her own. Some regions, like India, are complex countries with a wide range of civilization ; others — the Anglo-Egyptian Sudan, for instance — are undeveloped tracts sparsely inhabited by people of a low order of social development ; and there are dependencies or protectorates in varying stages between these two groups (1 and 2).

(3) Military posts and calling stations, like Malta, Aden, and Gibraltar.

THE DOMINIONS

During the war we had the rare spectacle of devotion to the common cause of the empire on the part of each one of the colonies and dominions, but withal a keen anxiety as to the political changes needed thereafter to give the dominions a larger degree of independence. The most striking statement on the subject came from General Smuts of South Africa, whose address in London on "The British Commonwealth of Nations" was a daring exposition of the views of the distant subject who desires a larger share in the control of his provincial affairs, and who at the same time wishes the "commonwealth of nations" idea to displace the old "imperial" idea within the British Empire. *Colonial objects in the war*

The natural political drift of a people in a new geographical environment is toward independence. Rarely can the mother country long maintain its hold unless it adapts itself to this tendency. In addition, settlers of diverse views and nationalities become merged into a group with common aims and with plastic habits of thought. A national spirit is developed that cannot fail to exhibit original and independent tendencies. Here we have the essence of the colonial problem of every nation that attempts to rule distant peoples of the old stock in the interests of home commerce and industry and the general safety of the sea routes. Great Britain lost the United States, but she has never lost the lesson which the American Revolution carried with it, and her five self-governing dominions are now in *Virtual independence of the dominions* all practical respects free and independent, except as to foreign policy. The sole restriction is that they shall not have independent foreign relations. The dominions make their own laws, impose their own taxes, and even decide how much they shall contribute for the defense of the empire. Finally, the Peace Conference of Paris accorded to each of the dominions representation in the Assembly of the League of Nations, as if they were wholly independent states.

Imperial unity or eventual separation now in the balance

It is plain that a choice must soon be made between complete separation and a still closer union on the basis of equality. "Daughter am I in my mother's house, but mistress in my own" seemed the expression of a liberal doctrine when it was written, but it does not satisfy present aspirations. The dominions are no longer content to be without a share in the direction of imperial policies, in support of which, as well as for their own security, they have incurred colossal debts and given thousands of their best men on the battlefields of Europe. Since 1887, the prime ministers of the self-governing colonies have met from time to time with the British secretary of state for foreign affairs (and in later years with the British premier) to discuss matters of general interest. The latest of these imperial conferences was held during the World War, and was by far the most important. On 4 May 1917 it recommended the convocation of a special conference after the war to consider the entire question of constitutional relations within the empire.

Special problems of Ireland, Egypt, and India

But the most acute political problems confronting Great Britain arise, not from the dominions whose independence is now virtually complete, but from those portions of the empire where a fierce nationalism threatens to end in revolution — Ireland, South Africa, India and Egypt. These four have been long-standing sources of trouble, and they will continue to vex the statesmen of England for many years to come. Each one of these possessions is related to a particularly vital interest of the empire.

IRELAND

Two opposing views of Irish independence

We will take the case of Ireland first. The Irish complain of long centuries of oppression, and no one can deny that unjustifiable and oppressive measures are the chief historical source of the present trouble. But the world has grown tremendously more complex since the Irish question first took shape. In its present form it is to Englishmen less a matter of control by the British army or the civil officers, than of the security of the British Empire as affected by a change in the political government of Ireland. Irishmen are now demanding, not home rule, but complete independence. This apparently simple political program is opposed by two vital conditions:

(1) The division within the country itself between industrial Ulster and the rest of Ireland, chiefly agricultural.

(2) The religious bitterness between Protestant England and Catholic Ireland, which is half the trouble in the case of Ulster also.

It has been well said that the key to the misfortunes that have overtaken Ireland is the geographical situation of that country, which is near enough to England to enforce connection and yet far enough away to discourage intimacy. St. George's Channel, which separates Ireland from England, is three times as wide as the Straits of Dover. Had it been narrower, Roman power might have been extended to Ireland; and thus there might have been achieved in early times a unity of people in the British Isles out of which might have grown, if not a permanent union, at least a sympathetic understanding. A recent writer, contrasting the apparently insoluble Irish question with the progress of imperial policy in Canada and Australia, remarked: "The dominions are geographically remote and morally near — the Irish are geographically near and morally remote." *(margin: Effects of Ireland's geographical situation)*

After the fall of Rome in the 5th century, Ireland remained a *secluded* island, and there grew up an indigenous culture, especially marked by the rapid development of a distinctive Celtic literature and art. From Ireland, where Christianity was introduced in the 5th century, Christian teaching spread to England and to northern Europe. In spite of its cultural progress, however, Ireland kept its tribal system of government. In contrast to this system was the more highly developed English government, and out of that fundamental contrast and what it stood for in the way of English power in trade and land tenure was born much of the trouble that devastated Ireland in the bitter centuries that followed. The foci of trade would inevitably be also the foci of trouble. It was on the eastern coast that English settlements were made, through which flowed such mutual commerce as the two peoples had developed, and here, all through the 12th and 13th centuries, armed contests took place. *(margin: Differences between political development in England and in Ireland)*

There was chronic trouble between the Irish chiefs on the one hand and the British government on the other, and advantage was taken of the difficulties of the time to devastate the lands of the chiefs and to

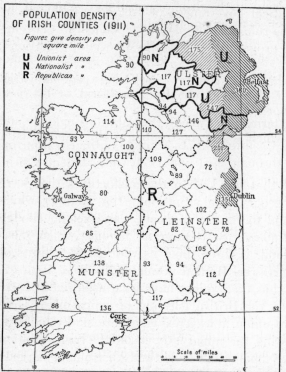

POPULATION DENSITY
OF IRISH COUNTIES (1911)

*Figures give density per
square mile*

U   *Unionist area*
N   *Nationalist "*
R   *Republican "*

Fɪɢ. 13. The distribution of population in Ireland by counties (1911). The shaded counties represent denser population and are the only ones in which manufacturing is important. Note the evenness of distribution elsewhere. The Unionist, National, and Republican areas are represented according to the returns of the election of 1918.

plant upon them English tenants. Not more than one eighth of the soil of Ireland finally remained in native hands. Many Irish proprietors were executed without due process of law. Nothing less than the destruction of the Irish people was contemplated.

Added to the differences between the two peoples was the fact that the Irish were mainly Catholics and as such were regarded as representatives of autocracy, for it must be remembered that in England the Reformation was closely associated with the cause of political freedom. Strongly influenced by a religious motive, the people of Ireland regarded law and government as opposed to the religion which they practiced and revered. This was the condition in Ireland throughout the 15th, 16th, and 17th centuries.

Oppressive measures taken in the 17th century

To add to the difficulties of the problem, James I encouraged the colonization of Ulster, in the north of Ireland (Fig. 13), by Scottish settlers (Presbyterians), and thus a division on religious grounds was established on the soil of Ireland itself that has made Ulster a symbol throughout the world. Whenever in recent years there has been an approach to a solution of the general question, Ulster asserts its adherence to England and refuses to accept union with the rest of Ireland. To compel it to go seems to Ulster to be denying it the freedom that the rest of Ireland seeks.

Believing that Irish industry competed with that of England in English and continental markets and that the naval defense of the British Isles was solely an English responsibility, England im- posed her commercial system upon Ireland. In 1665 and 1680 Ireland was forbidden to send to England live stock and the products of live stock. In 1663, 1670, and 1696, acts were passed excluding Ireland from trade with the colonies. The only way in which Irishmen could meet these restrictions was by emigration or by rising against the British authorities.

Outbreaks against the British government were resumed after the conquest of Ireland by Cromwell in 1652 and continued, from one cause or another, down through 1761 and 1771, each difficulty being marked by cruel repressions, continued confiscation of the land, and a swelling stream of emigrants. It was to America that most of the emigrants went, and during the period of the American Revolution the Irish in America gave it the fullest support, happy to fight in a distant land and under another flag the forces which they and their ancestors had been unable to overcome in the homeland.

In this fact and in the subsequent large emigration to America of Irish people, Catholic in religion, bitterly hostile to England, and with a history marked by cruelties of every kind, is to be found the reason for the development of strong pro-Irish sentiment in America which has led, among others, to such actions as the Congressional resolutions (1920) favoring the independence of Ireland and the insertion, in the reservations to the League of Nations as originally discussed in the Senate, of a provision that the adhesion of the United States would be conditional upon Irish independence.

Amidst all the complexities of Ireland's later relations with England there is one episode which stands out in strong relief, and that is the development of an Irish Parliament, which tended more and more strongly toward independence. The significant date in this movement was 1782, when the British Parliament at length gave to the Irish Parliament practically the full measure of power that the American colonies had sought before the War of the Revolution. It might be thought that this would have marked the end of the Irish question; as a matter of fact the question only entered a more intense phase.

The Irish Parliament and the British Parliament were united under the British Crown and were to coöperate for common purposes. Instead of coöperating, each sought to increase its authority over the other. Irish people talked more and more about the "independence" that they had gained in 1782. Englishmen, on the other hand, pointed to the common union of the two countries under the Crown and assumed an attitude of authority over the weaker state. During this period of political trouble, the religious differences were never forgotten, and from time to time they led to disorders in various parts of Ireland. The end of the experiment was marked by the dissolution of the Irish Parliament and the union of Great Britain and Ireland (1801).

A principle of settlement

The Irish problem will never be settled until Irishmen are given a fair chance to manage their own affairs. And yet it is difficult to give them that chance under conditions of disorder, such as prevail at the present time, — disorder whose roots run deep into the soil of hatred prepared by past wrongs. It is upon the historical facts that the Irish have long dwelt, looking backward to the misdeeds of past generations of English rather than forward to the practical business of securing such conditional freedom as they can. The whole of Irish and English relations is one long sequence of mismanagement. It was an English scholar who wrote, "Ireland is the one spot in the British Commonwealth where anarchy has continuously flourished."

Nor have the Irish people responded to the provisions of the Irish land purchase acts of 1903 and 1909, whereby a huge sum was made available to redeem for peasant cultivation the estates of the landed proprietors. In its later phases the long and complicated history of agrarian reform is primarily political rather than geographical. Too much attention has been paid to grazing; primitive agricultural methods are still in vogue on the small peasant farms. To overcome the difficulty of supporting a dense population under these conditions and in the general absence of industries, the government in the past few years has fostered the growth of coöperative societies, only to find its work opposed at the most critical moment by the country traders, who found that the coöperative movement threatened their livelihood as middlemen. The Irish leaders also opposed the development of better economic conditions on the ground that these diverted the public mind from Home Rule.

Attitude of the English toward the Irish question

To Ireland's arguments Englishmen reply by saying that in time of war the strongly indented coasts of Ireland might furnish bases for hundreds of submarines that could blockade the English coast. British leaders argue that if Ireland were given complete independence, Scotland and Wales might well follow with similar demands for separation. They believe that the empire would fall away; that the industrial power of Great Britain would be broken; that her naval preponderance could no longer be maintained.

Whatever one may think of these arguments respecting Ireland, it cannot be assumed that *outlying* portions of the Empire, like South Africa, India, and Egypt, if lost to British control, would merely change flags and live peacefully on without trouble. If England's grip is loosened there, one of two things will happen — independence or possession by some other strong power. If the latter, shall it be Japan or Russia or Germany or Turkey? If the former, will a given people have peace or anarchy? To run a country, there are required strong men, experience in government, the organized collection of revenue, and a proper scheme of civil administration. These things do not spring up full-grown in a moment.

Fate of possessions lost to England

THE SOUTH AFRICAN REALM

Among more distant possessions of the empire, the question of local government in relation to British sovereignty is always colored by problems of race and often of religion and land tenure as well. In these respects South Africa presents complications of as serious import as those encountered in any other British imperial possession; hence it will serve to illustrate both the range of British interests and the way in which problems at first chiefly of local interest may become critical for the imperial scheme.

When England first became interested in South Africa as a way station on one of her imperial roads, she found the region in the hands of the Dutch. In 1806, during the Napoleonic Wars, Great Britain captured Cape Colony, and the Congress of Vienna formally recognized her position there. In 1820 a fairly heavy stream of English emigration to South Africa began. The rest of the 19th century was filled with a bitter struggle for mastery between the English and the Dutch settlers, or Boers, which finally ended in the Boer War (1899–1902).

English beginnings in South Africa

In her development of the resources of South Africa and in her efforts to strengthen her political and military control of its populations, England found herself confronted with three prime difficulties:

Problems of government

(1) Possession of the unoccupied land had been acquired by people of Dutch descent, called Boers.

(2) The richest regions had long been occupied by native blacks, who constituted a dense population fringing the eastern coast.

(3) The distances that had to be covered were so great and the means of transportation so feeble that English control of the region could at first be only nominal.

Control by
natives and
by Boers
displaced
by English
control

The development of gold and diamond mining in South Africa led to a heavy investment of capital in the region and a natural influx of white labor. Parallel with these developments went the displacement of both natives and Boers by English immigrants, or — what amounted to the same thing — the extension of English political control over unwilling peoples. At first Great Britain's success with the natives was far greater than with the Boers. She could make treaties with the native chiefs establishing conditions of trade, and by securing the coöperation of men of different race she could manage to extend her control over millions of blacks along the eastern border of the territory. It was the Boers who gave her the most trouble. As English colonists came in, the Boers moved farther and farther north, penetrating at last to Lake Ngami at the northern edge of the Kalahari Desert, whence considerable numbers of them "trekked" still farther northward, into the interior of central Africa, cutting across the grasslands to the edge of the tropical forest, and westward almost to the Atlantic coast in Angola (Portuguese West Africa).

The journeyings of some of these early Boer colonists occupied years, and their settlements were temporary, being maintained only until news came of richer prospects ahead. The largest compact body of Boers settled permanently in the Transvaal, the country across (north of) the Vaal River. Toward the English they maintained an attitude of aloofness and independence, and they regarded their own country as one in which discriminatory laws could be framed to the disadvantage of the foreigner. Naturally the English felt that the ensuing contest was not so much for political ownership as for equality of commercial opportunity, since the Boer republics frankly sought to keep out the British trader. After the Jameson raid (December 1895 to January 1896) and other less important episodes, the contest between the English and the Boers ended in the Boer War of 1899–1902. There were heavy losses on both sides, and altogether it was an expensive enterprise for Great Britain.

The world has seen no more remarkable feat than the one that Englishmen and Boers accomplished at the close of the war. Sincerely trying to forget the hostility and the bitterness natural to war, the leaders of both sides adopted a policy of conciliation. The Union of South Africa was formed in 1910, consisting of Cape of Good Hope, Natal, Orange River Colony, and the Transvaal. General Botha, who had been fighting the British less than ten years before, became the first premier of the new dominion, with a cabinet composed entirely of Boers. Since then, political and economic problems have been squarely

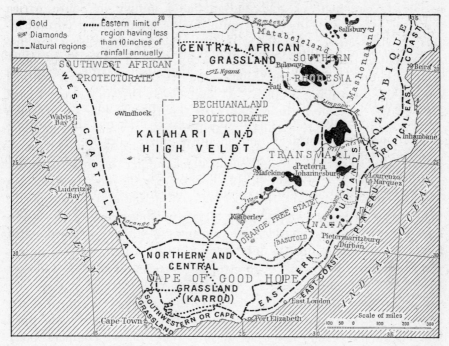

Fig. 14. The political divisions and plant regions of South Africa. From *The Guide to South and East Africa*, 1916, map opp. p. 101, supplemented by Bews, *The Grasses and Grasslands of South Africa*, 1918, and by Bartholomew and Lyde, *An Atlas of Economic Geography*, 1914, Pl. 39. See also the map and illustrations accompanying Evans, "The Veld: Its Resources and Dangers," *South African Journal of Science*, Vol. 17, 1920, pp. 1–34.

faced. South Africa has won a larger and larger measure of independence. During the recent war the Union of South Africa played a notable part. General Botha invaded German Southwest Africa and in the course of a few months conquered the entire region. A long campaign ensued in German East Africa, ending with the total collapse of German power. But it was not chiefly of the British Empire that the South Africans were thinking. It was the consolidation of a nation that they sought, and German East Africa and German Southwest Africa were regarded as a menace to the security of the Union rather than of the Empire. Naturally, South Africa was opposed to the return of these colonies to Germany, and early in February 1921 the Council of the League of Nations approved the terms of a mandate whereby German Southwest Africa is to be administered by the Union of South Africa.

South African campaigns against the German colonists

South Africa may be a union, but it is by no means a unit. Even before the federation (1910), the colonies quarreled with each other over customs arrangements, railways, legislation respecting native black labor, and immigration from India. The Transvaal govern-

Separatist tendencies caused by racial questions

ment favored the foreign port of Lourenzo Marquez (Portuguese) rather than Cape Town and Durban (British). Fearing the effects of education and industrialization upon the natives, the Boers wished to keep the blacks "in their place"; they disliked the English for treating blacks and whites upon a basis of equality. It must be admitted that their fear was based upon some significant historical facts. The Basutos once annihilated an English army; they can now put thousands of armed and mounted men into the field at a moment's notice. On one occasion they welcomed an English crown governor with an escort of many thousands of horsemen.

The disposition of whites by political divisions is as follows:

WHITE INHABITANTS IN THE UNION OF SOUTH AFRICA [1]

POLITICAL DIVISION	WHITE POPULATION	DENSITY PER SQ. MI.
Cape of Good Hope	619,000	2.1
Orange Free State	182,000	3.2
Transvaal	499,000	4.0
Natal	122,000	3.5
Southwest Africa	14,000	.003
	1,436,000 [2]	

South Africa's desire to reserve her lands for the whites
There are four and a half times as many blacks as whites in South Africa; the numbers are 7,000,000 and 1,500,000 respectively. The whites are increasing the more slowly; and with the use of colored labor, the percentage of "poor whites" is increasing. Troubled as the whites are by these considerations, their attitude toward Asiatic labor (Indian and Malay) may be understood. They do not want it, and they care little for the effect upon the British Empire as a whole should trouble be created by infringement of Indian rights. They point out that few regions are left in the temperate zone for the expansion of white populations. The black, on the other hand, is acclimated to low, hot countries with a high level of productiveness and need not feel cramped if he is kept in them.

Problem of the native
At one time the race problem assumed a most dangerous form. This was in 1913, when there was a great miners' strike on the Rand, accompanied by disturbances on the lines of transportation from Bloemfontein to the sea. The possibility of a general collapse of

[1] The density of native population is 3.8 per square mile in Rhodesia, 18.7 in Basutoland, and 9.2 in the Union of South Africa. Data from *Statesman's Year-Book*.

[2] This total would be increased by 45,000 if we included all British possessions in South Africa. The largest single unit is 37,000 in southern Rhodesia.

transportation threatened to result in a native uprising. While the danger from the natives was temporarily averted, it continues to form one of the chief problems in South Africa.

Parallel with the troubles between blacks and whites run the diffi- culties due to the presence of Indian laborers, who have migrated from India. The Indians were first brought in about fifty years ago to work as indentured laborers on sugar and tea plantations. Thus to the already serious problem of the blacks of Natal and Basutoland there was added the problem of the Indians, who now number 150,000. For the blacks, there was no mother country to raise questions that in- volved political interests or the integrity of the British Empire. The Asiatics, on the other hand, had the active support of the political leaders of India, who could make serious trouble for the empire. To settle the question, the Parliament of the Union of South Africa in 1919 passed the Asiatics Trading and Land Act. The two principal provisions of the act are: Special difficulties raised by the Indian population

(1) No new trading licenses may be issued to Indians after 1 May 1919, except in the case of a business which was licensed by an Indian before that date.

(2) After the above-mentioned date, no Indian may acquire fixed property in the Transvaal.

This act has aroused the indignation of Indian subjects throughout South Africa, though it involves treatment of the Indians no different from what they already have experienced in Basutoland and Bechuana- land, where they are under the direct administration of Great Britain, or in Rhodesia, where they are subject to the regulations of the British South Africa Company.

From the standpoint of the whites, the problem of the Asiatics in South Africa is frankly stated to be that of a struggle between the white and colored races for predominance in Africa, the case being the same as that of the blacks, as described above. The Indians bring in a very low standard of living and thus displace the European in labor and in trade. If the white race in South Africa can absorb a large white immigrant population in the next few years, it will be able to resist the colored races and occupy the land effectively; but the more abundantly colored labor is brought in, the smaller will be the stream of white immigrants. The effect of colored immigration in the large cities, particularly Cape Town, is socially and morally deplorable. Where Indians have competed with the white in business and industry, A " white man's country "

Indian
merchants
displacing
whites

they have largely displaced him. The competition of the Indian trader presses heavily on the European in the veldt country of northern Natal, where the principal industries are coal mining, cattle farming, and the cultivation of maize. It presses upon him in the Vitwatersrand and in the towns of Pietermaritzburg, Dundee, and Ladysmith, where some European firms have been rendered bankrupt and residence property has depreciated in value in the vicinity of the Indian quarter. There is a large Indian population on virtually all plantations owned by white men.

Objects
of the
present
government

The Union of South Africa, torn by these perplexing problems, is divided into a number of political parties in violent opposition to each other. It was by a relatively narrow margin that General Smuts became premier. He and the party of which he is the leader, the South African party, have three main principles as the basis of national unity and security:

(1) The maintenance of South Africa's place in the British Empire as opposed to complete independence.

(2) Fair and hearty coöperation between the various branches of the white race, particularly the Boers and the English.

(3) Concentration of the national energies upon a policy of industrial development.

By the election of February 1921, the South African party of Smuts commands a working majority in the South African Parliament. The success of his moderate policy has yet to be assured, however, for opposed to him is the powerful Nationalist party, which stands for disunion and a narrow racial policy.

The development
of South
African
resources

Under the Union of South Africa the economic development of the country has been carried on far more effectively than in the days of rivalry and disorder. Comprehensive irrigation schemes have been developed that will reclaim much of the desert land of which South Africa is in large part composed. Also there have been drilled throughout the dry veldt country, where grazing is the principal industry, a large number of deep wells which furnish the necessary water for stock, thus greatly extending the range of South African herds. Geological explorations have been carried forward to the point of making known the varied mineral wealth of South Africa, which includes gold, diamonds, iron, coal, copper, platinum, manganese, and building stones.

Agricultural and industrial development could be greatly developed in the eastern and southern coastal strip. In a belt of mountain and upland country near the coast, 1000 miles long and at least 15 miles wide, there is a rainfall exceeding 40 inches a year. If the run-off were regulated, forest growth encouraged, and waterpower developed, the region would in time vastly increase its agricultural production. It could also expect to become a center of industry in the manufacture of the raw materials of tropical East Africa.

RHODESIA AND THE ADJACENT PROTECTED ZONES

Lying north of the Union of South Africa is Rhodesia, the immediate government of which is in the hands of the British South Africa Company. At the present time the political and commercial affairs of Rhodesia are in a state of change. Some of its people would like to see established a crown colony government, similar to that of Nigeria; others would prefer to have the colony included within the Union of South Africa; some advocate autonomy, which would place Rhodesia in a position in the imperial family similar to that of Newfoundland or New Zealand; and still others, chiefly merchants, wish the continuation of the present régime. *A possible change of policy*

The difficulties in the way of autonomy or of union with South Africa spring chiefly from the fact that the company which has developed the region has invested a vast amount of money, and were this to become a charge against the people now inhabiting the region, it could scarcely be borne by them. Equally difficult is the proposal to have the imperial exchequer pay the bill, to the advantage of the population of Rhodesia. *Costs of development to be defrayed*

The company is now confronting the very serious criticism that it is exploiting the native population, whereas Great Britain has always prided herself upon her strict adherence to the principle of maintaining the rights of the natives in the colonies under her control. In Canada and Australia she has done this by special reservations, and corresponding attention was given to the same subject in New Zealand in 1840, in Fiji in 1874, in Papua in 1888. Moreover, Great Britain agreed to the insertion in the League of Nations covenant of Article 22, which accepts the principle that the well-being and development of peoples not yet able to stand by themselves shall be a trust of civilization. *Native rights*

It has been otherwise in Rhodesia, where the native is not allowed to live securely upon his land, and this in a region where landownership is a matter of particular importance because of the settled agri-

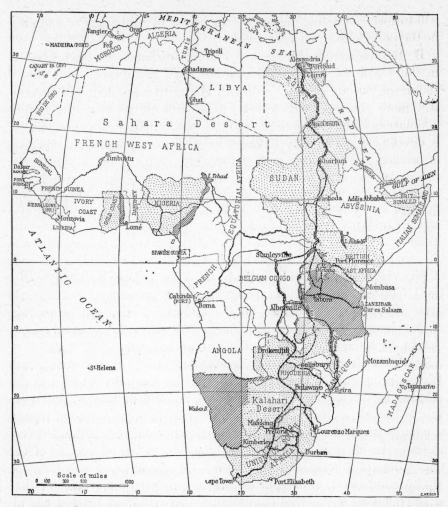

Fig. 15. British possessions in Africa, and the Cape-to-Cairo railway. Except for a short section southwest of Albertville, the railway is completed from Cape Town to Lake Tanganyika. The principal unfinished section is in the Anglo-Egyptian Sudan. British possessions in Africa that were held before 1914 are stippled; those gained as a result of the World War are crosslined. Note that the new name for British East Africa is Kenya Colony; also that the new boundary between that colony and Italian Somaliland is not shown on this map (for this see Figure 271).

Land situation seriously affects the native farmer

cultural life of the people. Great Britain knows perfectly well how to handle the problem. In Nigeria, for example, all the land is native-owned. But in contrast to this happy state of affairs, in southern Rhodesia the natives have lost landownership as tribes and as individuals. Until the radical concession of the British South Africa Company is revoked, the native put in possession of his lands, and economic restrictions removed, the relation of natives and whites will furnish a standing menace to the people of South Africa, and may be the prelude to a race catastrophe.

If Bechuanaland, Basutoland, and Swaziland are incorporated in the Union of South Africa rather than maintained as a direct charge of the imperial government, the native problem will become still more complex. It will be more difficult to keep the native population within its present confines, seeing that race consciousness is developing a tendency to press for a nearer approach to equality of privilege. But as the cost of the white man's living is constantly rising, his impulse is to secure himself in a position of relative economic advantage. This position he tries to gain by becoming a member of the Labor party, which seeks special privilege, or of the Nationalist party, which stands for race exclusion.

Extension of boundaries has increased the white man's problem

THE INDIAN EMPIRE

For Great Britain, the question of peace or anarchy wears some of its gravest aspects in India, where there are religious, economic, and international problems of the first order. Here are 66,000,000 Mohammedans who, with their brethren of the Arab world, threaten British hold on southwestern Asia; and were that hold broken at one place, it would immediately be relaxed at all others. Moreover, the trade of India is altogether essential to Great Britain's hold on general Asiatic trade. The British exports to India are greater than to any other country except France. Let us look at the historical relations of this dependency of imperial extent and importance.

Under the Portuguese, in the early years of the 16th century, there was developed a trading and governmental system which first brought European wares and political ambitions into the Indian field. Later came the East India Company, which was organized at London in 1600. The Portuguese were easily displaced, and the Dutch were driven to concentrate their efforts in the East Indies. The French, however, offered a more effective resistance, and a long struggle was waged that finally resulted (1757) in victory for the English company. During the hundred years that followed, the East India Company gradually lost its valuable monopolies, and after the Company had proved itself incapable of handling the great revolt of 1857 (the Sepoy Rebellion), Parliament assumed full control of the government of India.

Colonial rivalry and the establishment of English power

The problem of England is twofold — to control the 325 millions of India and to develop British trade, and to do both in such a manner as to keep the peace. For India has always been a difficult coun-

The diffi-
culties of
govern-
ment

try to dominate. Alexander the Great reached it in 327 B.C., but his empire did not remain. Many later invasions took place across the northern frontier: there came Mohammedans, congregated chiefly in the northern part; Afghans, who waged an almost continual border warfare; and Turks, who sought to extend their power into the dense masses of India and of China as well. In large measure India has absorbed the invader. With the British, however, this has not been true; they came for trade, not for conquest.

India long
in a state
of anarchy

As in so many of the protected regions of the world, the question is one not merely of trade, but of order. Many of the most progressive and intelligent Indians believe that were Great Britain to leave India to her fate, the land would fall into disorder and there would be rivers of blood. For when India ruled herself, there was incessant warfare between her many local rulers; each one sought an extension of his realm and an increase of power; intrigue, bribery, and war followed n logical sequence. Under British rule the country has been in the main peaceful. But as in Egypt, there is a nationalist movement, and its followers regard the British as exploiters who lack real sympathy for the native. They wish to see Great Britain driven out and native rule restored.

Recent dis-
orders in
northern
India

The Moslem Indian population was more or less disorderly throughout the World War. The last serious trouble occurred in April 1919, when nearly four hundred natives of Amritsar were killed by General Dyer's troops for assembling in a public square. Thereupon Indian feeling was greatly inflamed everywhere and the whole national movement was much intensified. The Indian National Congress selected the site of Amritsar for its 1919 session and sought to promote Indian independence; but the more moderate Indian representatives had a separate conference at Calcutta and were concerned chiefly with reforms in the present government.

Unruly
border
peoples

On India's northern frontier, adjacent to the Afghan border, there is great difficulty with unsubdued mountain tribes — *e.g.* Wazirs and Mahsuds. The British government has respected the independence of the tribes and has protected the area by maintaining garrisons at strategic points. These tribes can put 30,000 armed men in the field and, as they are fanatical Moslems, they are easily tempted to hostilities through the influence of their religious leaders. In May 1919 they invaded northern India, burned villages, cut telegraph lines, and carried out raids against the Indian population. Through the summer and autumn of 1919 the British, in the face of

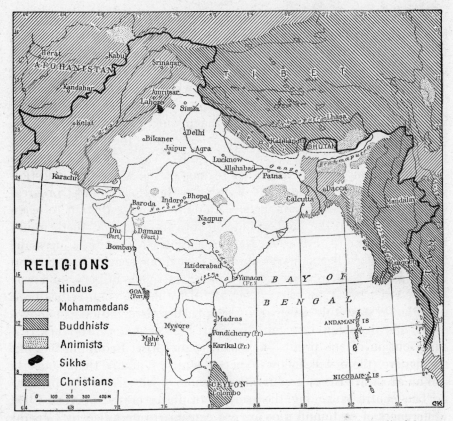

RELIGIONS

☐ Hindus
▨ Mohammedans
▧ Buddhists
▨ Animists
◆ Sikhs
▨ Christians

FIG. 16. The widespread effects of the caste system of the Hindus may be realized from a study of this map. Note the large Mohammedan population of northwestern India. From *Imperial Gazetteer of India*, Vol. 26, 1909, Pl. 15.

strong resistance, sent military forces into the mountain region where the unruly tribes live, and partly subdued them.

Disorder in India is a particularly grave matter, since it affects not only the control of the country but also the distribution of food and the whole modern system of trade that has become established there. India now has 112,000 square miles of irrigated land and the irrigation works require coöperative control and an orderly government. Were the railroads and the irrigation works, the ports, and the whole machinery of commercial life to be disorganized, India would be ripe for a great disaster. The famines of the past would be repeated, millions would be killed by starvation and war, and misery and anarchy would spread from India to the adjacent lands. If an Indian policy can be developed which will give autonomy to the local Indian governments, fair treatment to the natives, and an equitable

Danger of famine in general disorganization

FIG. 17. Dekka, near the northwestern frontier of India, where the British have fought Afghan and other tribesmen.

distribution of the profits of business enterprise among natives and foreigners, there will follow a better state of affairs than could be obtained under the rule of rival princes.

Diversities of race, religion, and caste prevent a unified native government

The contrasts among the peoples of India are very great. The differences of caste and race are too extreme to permit any real unity of the population for a long time to come. But what is of more present practical interest, the diversities are so great that there is no such thing as general public opinion. Each section of the country, each part of a religious sect, each caste, has its own ideas and has no respect for those of another. The contrasts and animosities of feeling could not be more marked if the various groups were separated by great distances and lived under quite different conditions. "India" is not in their minds when they find fault with British rule; they think only of the autonomy of their own district.

Effects of a complicated historical and racial development

The contrasts between the different races, languages, and religions of India have been increased through a long history involving many different kinds and degrees of civilization. Moreover, three fourths of the people are agricultural and live in small villages and on farms. In general, the better types live in the cooler regions of the north. The hotter the climate, the denser the population and the greater the ignorance. Climate and physical environment, as well as racial characteristics, have produced a degree of diversity almost incomprehensible, so that India is not to be thought of as a country of common characteristics or as presenting to its leaders and rulers a problem of a simple nature. Its 325,000,000 people are composed of 45 different races speaking 170 languages and divided into 2400 tribes or castes. They are scattered over an area almost precisely half that of Europe. Of this population three fourths are under British rule, but only half of one per cent use English effectively.

Of the total population, 217 millions are Hindus and 60 millions are composed of descendants of the original Turanian tribes. The latter form the lowest grade of inhabitants in the country. Many of them are outcasts doing the lowest and most menial work; others have kept their freedom by living in the mountains, in the deserts, in the forests. All of them hate the Hindus bitterly.

From long before the Christian era a most to 1000 A.D., the Hindus came from the north in wave on wave of conquering hordes that, crossing the high passes of eastern Afghanistan, subdued the land only after long and bloody struggles. After the conquest of the aboriginal populations, the Hindus fought each other and a state of anarchy prevailed. Finally there came the perfection of the caste system to disunite the Hindus still further, reduce the warlike class, make the people pacifistic, and lay India open to invasion and conquest. Of these invasions, the one that produced the greatest visible effect ended in 1206 A.D., when the Moslem hordes poured into India; during the next three hundred years the Mohammedan kingdoms were formed. With the coming of the British, the rivalries which had formed the basis of past anarchy subsided. But even now the number of castes, the prejudices of the people, the restraints which their religions put upon their treatment of animals, all greatly retard the economic development of the country.

The Hindu conquests and the caste system

In all India there are some 700 feudatory states, each jealous of the others' rights and privileges. They include two fifths of the land of India and have a population of about 75,000,000. There are states of every size, scattered from one end of the land to the other. The largest is Haiderabad, with a population of 13,000,000. Some of the states are of ancient origin; others are recent; some were formed out of the fragments of the Mogul Empire (1526–1761). When the British government took over the management of the country, it guaranteed the integrity of existing states and the dignity and privileges of the rulers, making treaties with them which have persisted down to the present time. The rulers are not sovereign, but are subordinate to His Majesty the King-Emperor and to his repre-

Problem of the feudatory states

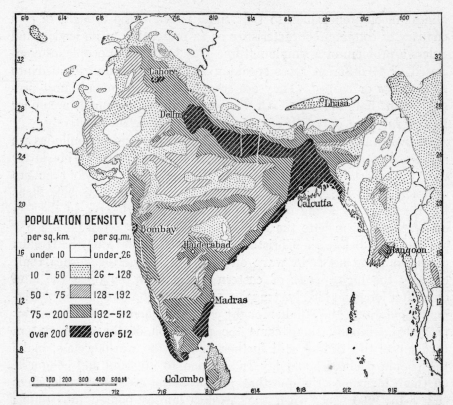

Fig. 18.   The importance of the monsoon rains is suggested by the denser populations of the eastern and western coasts; and the Ganges valley is marked by a population density greater than that found in all but a few other regions in the world.   After Bartholomew, *Advanced Atlas of Physical and Political Geography*, 1917, Sheet 65.

sentative the Viceroy, or Governor-General, of India.   Were the people warlike, they would present to Great Britain an impossible problem of race, religion, and general order.   But only 25,000,000 can be said to have any military spirit, and these are widely scattered.

Village organization the basis of self-government

The society of India has its basic feature in the village organization.   Through all the long and complicated history of India, varied by conquest, by interstate rivalries, by famines, by calamities such as plagues of locusts and epidemics of disease that carried off millions, the village organization and confederations of village communities have been maintained.   These confederations have been the most durable organization in India, and the improvement of Indian conditions can be carried on only if attention is paid to the value of the village community as the basis of self-government.

India is fundamentally agricultural; less than 10 per cent of the population is urban, as compared with 78 per cent in England and

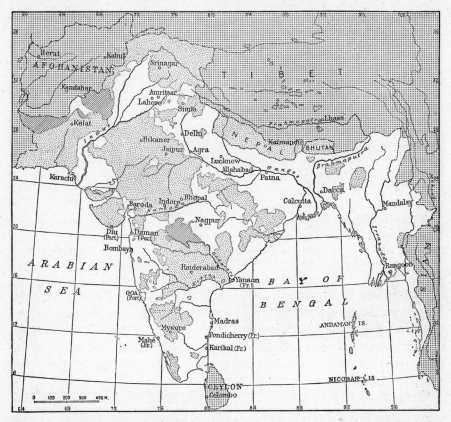

FIG. 19. The native states and territories are shown in light stipple and the territories permanently administered by the government of India with diagonal ruling, while British India is left white. From *Imperial Gazetteer of India*, Vol. 26, 1909, Pl. 20.

Wales and 48 per cent in Germany. In Bombay, 18 per cent of the population is urban, the high percentage being due to the presence of cotton mills; while in Assam, where the country is broken and the people lead an unsettled life, only 3 per cent live in cities. India as a whole has but thirty cities of more than 100,000, while the United States, with one third the population, has sixty-eight cities of more than 100,000. Only two of India's cities, Calcutta and Bombay, have more than a million people each. The population, completely dependent on agriculture, is crowded on the flat lands of India, where a rainfall of seventy nches is needed to insure crops. As a consequence, terrible famines ensue when the rains are light.

So long as India depends upon minor crops, such as form the basis of her present food supply, her condition will be slow to improve commercially. The more remunerative crops are wheat and cotton,

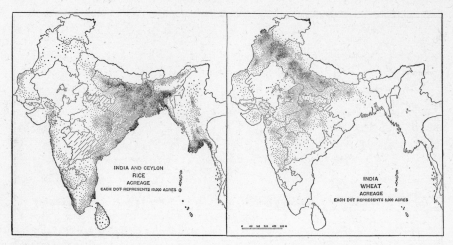

FIG. 20. Distribution of wheat and rice crops in India. Compare with Figure 18. From Finch and Baker, *Atlas of American Agriculture*, 1917, Figures 25 and 58.

and these are to a large degree dependent upon artificial irrigation. Moreover, increased irrigation would make the people more independent of the uncertain rains. The rains of India are seasonal in character — the so-called monsoon rains — and have great variations from year to year and from district to district in the same year.

Recurrent famines and the famine service

When the rains fail altogether, famine results unless there is artificial irrigation. Formerly these famines were accompanied by terrible loss of life; but with increase of railway lines and better facilities for the transportation of food by motor and otherwise, and especially by the organization of a "famine service," the loss of life is now largely averted. The ensuing poverty is still very great, however, on account of the loss of cattle, which strip the grazing grounds and migrate from place to place, dying in large numbers and thus wiping out the peasant's capital.

Small irrigation works or tanks

Much has already been done to further irrigation; but the task is only begun. The irrigation service in India includes not only great modern engineering works but also an immense system of artificial reservoirs, the most extensive of their kind in the world. Some of them are of great antiquity. They consist of earthen tanks formed by building a series of banks around a depression in the ground or across the outlet of a small valley. Their extent is from a few square rods to several acres. Some of the more modern ones have dams made of masonry. When one reservoir is filled with sediment, another is constructed above or below it. The floor of the former reservoir

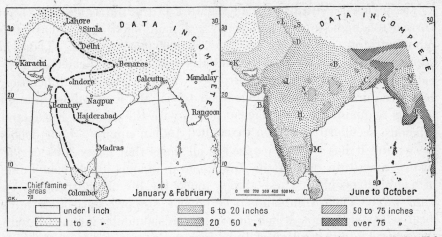

FIG. 21. Rainfall and famine areas in India. Rainfall from *Imperial Gazetteer of India*, Vol. 26, 1909, Pl. 10. Famine areas from Andree, *Geographische Handbuch*, 1899, p. 579; id., *Geographie des Welthandels*, Vol. 2, 1913, p. 552; supplemented by Digby, *The Famine Campaign in Southern India*, 2 vols., 1878; Merewether, *A Tour through the Famine Districts of India*, 1898; Scott, *The Famine Land*, 1904.

is then converted into cultivated fields. Figure 22 shows the reservoirs in a small portion of the province of Haiderabad; the minute distribution gives an idea of the large number of people of India that live in villages and on small holdings of land, and makes one realize the full meaning of the statement that three fourths of the people of India are agricultural.

Among the larger works is the Punjab system (at the northwestern corner of the northern famine district, shown in Figure 21), whereby nearly 2,000,000 acres of land once arid have been placed under irrigation, in addition to more than 9,000,000 acres previously irrigated in the Punjab district. This was done by turning river water into three great canals that, with their main branches and smaller tributaries, have a total length of 3000 miles. The irrigated area lies in a region whose average rainfall is from 7 to 25 inches, and where agriculture would always be precarious without artificial help. *The great Punjab system*

The fault which almost all classes of Indians have to find with the British government is based upon the cumbersome workings of the India Office and the Indian administration in general. The rural people, who form three fourths of the population, pay the greater part of the revenues in the land tax; yet they are without representation in the legislative bodies, and have no way of expressing their grievances. The revenues are not employed to suit their local needs. Great irrigation works and railroads are built and harbors are improved, but the lot of the farmer is unchanged. *Indian complaints of British administration*

The policy of centralization of the work of the India Office has been carried to a high state of inefficiency.   A mere handful of 3000 British administrators are trying to rule 325,000,000 subjects.   Those in supreme authority are overloaded with work.   The officials are critically selected, but they are confronted with overpowering difficulties, being required to make rulings upon trivial and local affairs, though lacking acquaintance in sufficient detail, with the climatic, racial, and religious peculiarities of the diversified Indian empire   Long delays ensue, and it has been recognized in all times that delays in securing justice constitute one of the fundamental and justifiable complaints of a subject people.   These things touch the life of the people in a vital way.   Their complaints will not be stopped until they have local self-government, which in some form should be integrated with the general admin stration of India by provinces and as a whole.

Pressing upon the people of India in a manner to produce great distress is the land tax, in addition to which is the water tax in the irrigated areas.   The land tax keeps the mass of the population in a state bordering on slavery.   Millions cannot get sufficient food.   At the end of his year of labor, the farmer finds his crop divided between the landlord and the government.   He has to go into debt to the village shopkeeper, getting credit for food and seed in the ensuing year.   Since 240,000,000 people in India are connected directly or indirectly with agriculture, this means that a large majority of them, probably two thirds, are living in a state of squalor.

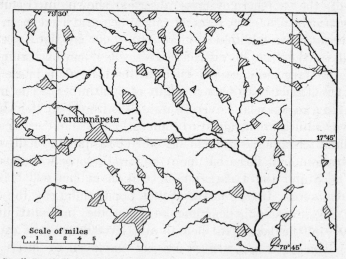

Fig. 22.   Small "tanks" containing surface water impounded behind earthen dams and used for local irrigation.   They occupy 1580 square miles in British India.   Reduced section from the topographic map of India, scale 1: 253,440, Sheet 56–0, 1914.

This does not mean that many Indians are not living under better conditions. Thirty millions of them, many of whom are town-dwellers, have prospered by the general increase of trade and through the benefits of the Indian administration. There are many rich bankers and merchants. But the position of the peasant remains the same, and it cannot be improved until the land revenue system is changed and the heavy land tax reduced. The most serious of the social and economic problems of India were not created by the British, but the people of India look to their British rulers for a solution. Here, as in Ireland, there is an economic problem of great magnitude that is constantly involved with political issues. As in all times and places, a government remote from the common people is blamed for disaster and appealed to for relief.

What has England done to meet the complaints of her Indian subjects?

The revised government of India

On 20 August 1917, the Secretary of State for India announced in the House of Commons that the British government was in favor of gradual development of self-governing institutions in India. To this end there was introduced into Parliament the Government of India Bill, which was passed in 1919 as the so-called Reforms Bill. In each of the eight major provinces (excluding Burma) administration will be divided between the governor, who retains power over questions that are "reserved," and the ministers, who deal with questions that are to be "transferred" to them. Among the transferred subjects are local government, agriculture, industrial development, public health, education, and public works. The governor will continue to be appointed by the Viceroy or by the Crown, and will be assisted by an Executive Council, of whom one must be an Indian. The ministers are chosen from the elected members of the Legislative Council. Not more than one fifth of the Legislative Council may be officials (*i.e.* British). Three seats on the Viceroy's Executive Council are assigned to Indians.

Financial matters now largely under Indian control

This dual form of government has not been applied to the central administration, but there has been created a second chamber, the Council of State, and a majority of both assemblies will be elected by popular vote. India's financial policy will be largely in her own control. By this bill the franchise has been extended to more than 5,000,000 persons, out of a total of 60,000,000 who might be eligible. The franchise was previously exercised by some 33,000 persons. The bill is avowedly transitional, and itself provides for a commission to investigate its results after the expiration of ten years.

Opinion with respect to the new form of government varies widely. Some objection has been raised on the ground that the Brahmins, a powerful caste despising all other Indians and constituting but 5 per cent of the population, may win fresh political and administrative power in addition to the vast social, religious, and official powers which they already possess.

THE EMPIRE AND THE MOHAMMEDAN REALM

We have viewed India's problems mainly from the political and economic standpoints. While the religious aspect is important, its importance springs chiefly from the relation of the whole Mohammedan question to the maintenance and security of the road to India. We shall first discuss the power and geographical extent of Islam. No matter where that realm might be placed in the world, it would interest thinking men.

Mohammedanism is in substance a political as well as a religious matter. Although its adherents are widely distributed (Fig. 23), every Mohammedan every day turns in prayer toward Mecca, his Holy City; only from Mecca can be proclaimed a Jihad, or Holy War, to which all Mohammedans must respond; it is the religious capital of 250,000,000 people and has been the center of Mohammedanism for more than a thousand years. The pilgrimage to Mecca draws thousands of picked men from every part of the Moslem world, and thus is practically an annual Pan-Islamic congress where all the interests of the Moslem world are discussed. Mohammedanism is the most fanatical religion in the world. To the Mohammedan, the Christian is "a dog of an infidel." To die for the Prophet is to save one's soul.

The extraordinary fact about Mohammedanism is its strong hold upon its followers. No people once Mohammedan has ever been converted to the Christian religion. The power of Islam is persistent. There is scarcely anything like it in the world, and it is growing with terrific speed, not only among the crowded populations of the East, but also and chiefly among the millions of negroes in central Africa. Brown and black and yellow respond to its teachings. On all these races the white man has laid the hand of political control and is correspondingly feared or hated. Mohammedanism therefore represents a fanatical religion whose political power will try the tact, and it may be the military strength, of the western powers.

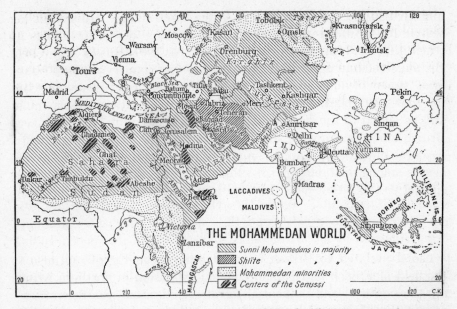

FIG. 23. A study of the map suggests the extent to which colonial government and commerce are affected by religious considerations in the East Indies, northern Africa, and the Near East. There are many Mohammedan sects, but only the powerful Senussi sect is shown here in its chief centers of influence. After Schrader, *Atlas de géographie historique*, Pl. 51; Senussi localities after Debes, *Handatlas*, 1913. Area *A*, in northern India, represents a locality inhabited by both Shïite and Sunni Mohammedans; *B*, in the Balkans, represents Bosnia.

The heart and center of the Mohammedan realm is on the eastern side of the Red Sea. On the western side of the Red Sea is Egypt, sometimes called the "wasp-waist" of the British Empire. Great Britain's interest in Mohammedanism is therefore vital. At the northern end of the Red Sea is the Suez Canal, on the direct route to India from the whole Mediterranean region and from England. Of the 325,000,000 people of India 66,000,000 are Mohammedans. During the recent war it took 250,000 Anglo-Indian troops to hold in control the Mohammedans and the border tribes. For Great Britain, Egypt and India and Mesopotamia and the gateway of the Mediterranean Sea all hang together joined by their common association with Great Britain's road to India and by the presence of a Mohammedan element. The problems of these regions have long had vital and sinister aspects for the men of England.

With the break-up of both the Turkish and the Russian empires, Great Britain's relations to the Mohammedan world and the Near East have been altered in many respects. Turkey was always able to threaten trouble among the Mohammedan populations of the British Empire, not only in the Near East but also in Zanzibar

The road to India through the Mohammedan realm

Turkish
and Rus-
sian inter-
ests no
longer
a menace to
Britain

and British East Africa, South Africa, and India. Russia, in her search for a warm-water outlet, was making desperate efforts to reach the head of the Persian Gulf. In 1907 Russia and Great Britain signed an agreement giving the former country political rights, or a "sphere of influence," down to the line shown in Figure 230. But for that agreement, the probable ambitions of future Russia might still be added to the force of the dominant religion in Turkey to keep British statesmen uneasy about the safety of their far-flung empire. A source of anxiety, however, remains in the activities of Bolshevist agents among unstable British subjects, whence may spring results as sinister as those that had their origin in the imperialism of the Czar.

The Religious Confraternities

Closely related to British imperial interests in Egypt and also to the field of French and Italian colonial expansion in northern Africa, are the powerful and influential secret societies, or "confraternities," among the Mohammedan populations. This is a general or collective name for the various religious societies of the Mohammedan world, of which there are from fifty to one hundred distributed all the way from Morocco to Bagdad. Almost every adult male Moslem is a member of one of these societies.

The confraternities came into existence in an interesting way. After Mohammed's death, Mohammedanism changed its aspect. It reached into the field of law and gave religious authority to the words and decrees of the lawyers. The rulers on their side also sought to control the church and make it an instrument of military and political conquest. In addition, the Turks and the Arabs developed strong racial and then political animosities. In reaction to all these changes, pious men of strong character founded sects or fraternities, withdrew to remote regions, gathered disciples, and built monasteries.

Some of these societies were active and reached from one end of the Moslem world to the other; others were very obscure and local. Some have lived for a long time; others went out of existence almost with the death of the original founder. Some were military in spirit; others were pacifistic. Some of them have become great missionary agencies whose chief goal has been the vast interior of Africa, where they would be far from the arm of European authority, and where there are millions of ignorant, superstitious negroes to convert. Some were devoted to poverty, and others amassed great wealth with which they could fit out small military expeditions. These extended Mohammedan authority and provoked border tribesmen to make trouble for European governors about the borders of the Sahara as well as in the Anglo-Egyptian Sudan, Libya, French Equatorial Africa, and elsewhere.

The most powerful of the African societies is the Senussi, which has been in existence for about eighty years and has a quite special character. Its founder claimed to be a direct descendant of the Prophet. He traveled from Mecca all through northern Africa, founding fraternity centers, and for a time became so powerful that the Sultan of Turkey feared loss of prestige as Caliph. He finally settled down in Cyrenaica (Fig. 74), where he was almost out of reach of the Turkish authorities and where he could travel among his own people by convenient caravan routes. *The most powerful religious sect, the Senussi*

Though at first free from all political influence, the Senussi gradually were drawn into political relations which have affected their later development. They resisted the coming of the Italians after the Italo-Turkish War (1911–1912), feeling that with Italian control over northern seaports, the lucrative trade in slaves would be suppressed or heavily taxed, and ordinary trade diverted. Between 1912 and 1914 they were supplied with arms, ammunition, and money by the Turks, and thus were able to resist successfully the Italian advance into the interior of Cyrenaica down to the end of the war. *The Senussi in international politics*

With the outbreak of war in August 1914, Turkish agencies became active in Libya (Tripoli), and the Italian forces were driven back nearer the coast. As the war progressed, the leader of the Senussi became more and more ambitious, and desired to make himself sovereign of the Moslem wor d. He attacked the Egyptian border from three points, the central one being the oasis of Siwa, but the British drove him out in February 1917, and so completely defeated him that his forces made no effort to return. *The attack in Lower Egypt*

The central stronghold of the Senussi is the oasis of Kufra (Fig. 74), in the heart of the Sahara, more than five hundred miles west of the Nile. It is surrounded by absolute desert, and the caravan routes to it are known only to Senussi guides. From this point the influence of the leader of the sect extends over most of the Sahara country. Occupying a central position, he has a convenient system of communications. Tilho has given a fascinating account of his long struggle during the World War with desert tribesmen under Senussi influence in the Tibesti region northeast of Lake Tchad on the border of French Equatorial Africa. *Central stronghold of the Senussi*

THE EGYPTIAN PROTECTORATE

Egyptian rising of 1919

Ever since the beginning of the World War, political storm signals have been flying in the Near East, and it is worth while to see what they mean. The most recent was the threatened revolution in Egypt in March 1919. Egypt asks for freedom : can she be trusted with it ? The British government had its hold on Egypt confirmed by the treaty of peace with Turkey (1920) : why did Egyptians resent this?

Growth of an Egyptian nationalist party and violent measures in 1919

The Egyptian leaders, who are intellectually alert, developed a strong nationalistic movement at the time England occupied the Nile valley (1881). In 1882, the nationalist party asked for "independence," and England undertook repressive measures. In 1914, as a result of the World War, England abolished the shadow of Turkish overlordship which had existed since 1882, and declared Egypt a protectorate of the British Empire. Thereupon the nationalists became more active than ever, again demanding independence. Failing to reach the Peace Conference at Paris, they broke into insurrection. From one end of the lower Nile valley to the other, property was destroyed and shops were looted ; a number of British soldiers were killed.

Egypt cannot be allowed to become disorderly

The rioting of 1919 was one of many proofs of the limitations of British policy in Egypt and of that violence which marks the character of the small nationalist groups of Egypt. If the Egyptians lived at the South Pole, the organized world could forget about them and let them trouble each other as much as they chose ; but instead they live near one of the great world thoroughfares, the Suez Canal ; this is England's road to the East, her direct road to the most important of her possessions — India.

A deep religious motive underlying political disorder in Egypt

Moreover, whatever the faults of British rule in Egypt, — and they are many, — the whole world is interested in these disorders because behind them lies a far deeper motive than desire for political independence: the hatred of the Moslem Egyptian leaders for Christian rule. The outbreaks in Egypt have been supported largely by Turkish gold ; the leaders have often been incited or inspired from Constantinople. The British assert that the test of capacity for self-government by Egyptians is not to be found in the violent spirit and phrases of the extreme nationalists, nor in their policy of assassination and intimidation.

The nationalism of Egypt is unworthy of consideration in so far as it is the work of agitators of mixed allegiance, like Syrians, Turks, and Albanians, and of religious fanatics. In so far as it is the honest expression of the Egyptian people, it is a matter of serious import. It is futile to point to the benefits of British occupation, for in all lands and times the benefits of alien rule have been considered incapable of balancing its disadvantages. It is axiomatic that a second-rate government under native control is better than a first-rate government under foreign control.

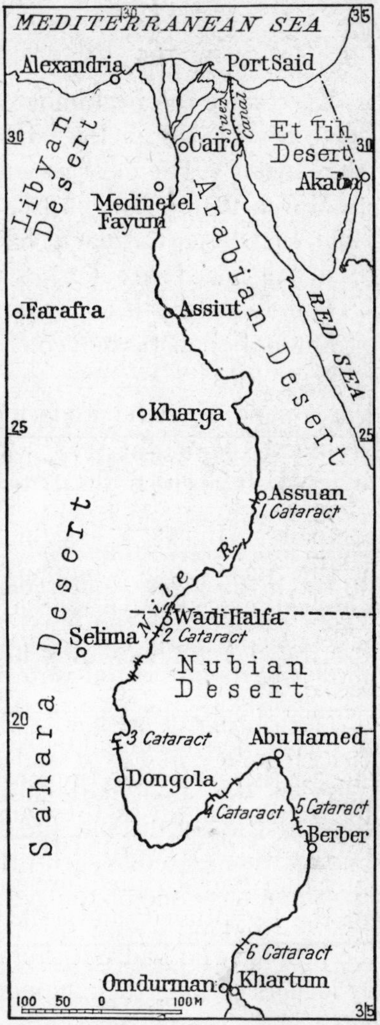

While nationalist sentiment has made a deep and wide penetration, of which account should be taken, it must be realized that the alternative to British occupation is the return of the country to the mixed people, chiefly Moslems, who constitute the leaders of the nationalist movement. It would not mean turning the country over to the Copts, or true Egyptians, who form the bulk of the population; it would bring Egyptian control of the restless negro populations of the Sudan and would reënforce intolerant Mohammedanism throughout the Arab world.

The trouble in Egypt can be understood only if we know the way in which the British came to control the country. The Turks were the nominal rulers, having conquered the country in 1517, when — as now — it was weak and disorganized. During the Napoleonic

Fig. 24. Map of Egypt showing the principal towns, the bordering deserts, and the cataracts of the Nile.

Wars there was military occupation by both the British and the French. After the withdrawal of the British there followed a fierce war of factions ending in the complete victory of Mehemet Ali, who was practically independent ruler of Egypt till his abdication in 1848. Although Mehemet Ali continued to acknowledge the nominal suzerainty of the Sultan, he succeeded in having the pashalik made hereditary in his family and his fourth successor, Ismail, was called Khedive. Both British and French commercial interests in Egypt increased, especially after the completion of the Suez Canal in 1869 by a French

Universal dislike for alien rule a deep-seated motive

The alternative to British control

Beginnings of British control

Fig. 25.   Entrance to the Suez Canal at Port Said.   This narrow ribbon of water is vital to the integrity of the British commercial and political empire.

company.   In 1875, needing money, the Khedive sold his shares of the Suez Canal Company to the British, who since then have watched every move in that part of the world.   Would America, or France, or Italy not take the same interest in a disorderly country bordering its most vital waterway?

French and British Dual Control   Since the greater part of the huge debt which the successive rulers of Egypt had accumulated in the 19th century was borrowed from the British and the French, those two powers established a condominium, known as the Dual Control (1876–1883).   The Egyptian leaders bitterly resented the interference of the foreigners; but only after they had accepted foreign money did they raise the cry of "Egypt for the Egyptians" and seek to organize a general revolution among the people, who had not shared in the original loans now squandered by leaders seeking their support against the foreigner.   France having declined to use military force, the British took the field and crushed a rebellion engineered by Arabi Pasha, an army officer.   To maintain order Great Britain kept in Egypt an army of occupation and named herself "adviser" to the new Egyptian government.

The Mahdi and trouble in the Sudan   Directly thereafter trouble arose in the Sudan, where the Mahdi, who had proclaimed himself as the "deliverer" of his people, appealed to the fanaticism of his followers (1881), defeated the Egyptian troops, massacred General Gordon and 11,000 men at Khartum (1885), and for about twelve years held the region in his grasp.   Finally, in 1898 General Kitchener completely annihilated the armies of the Mahdi at the battle of Omdurman.   As a war measure the Sudan, as well as Egypt, was declared annexed to the British Empire in 1914, with the status of a "protected state." Moreover, the treaty of Sèvres between Turkey and the Allied powers (1920) recognizes the British protectorate in Egypt, and Turkey renounces the tribute formerly levied on Egypt.

But a treaty which is not signed by the representatives of the people whom the treaty affects does not in itself settle disorder or kill political ambition. The Egyptian nationalist program calls for nothing less than independence from British control, neutrality of the Suez Canal, the recession of the Sudan to Egypt (it was never under effective Egyptian control), and a parliamentary form of government. Egypt protested that she would keep on struggling to be free as she understands freedom; the British government renewed its determination never to relinquish its hold. *The program of the Egyptian nationalist party*

The resulting disorders forced Great Britain to attempt a wholly new orientation of her Egyptian policy through the Milner mission of 1920. After a conference between British and Egyptian representatives, a tentative agreement was drawn up, promising self-government in the immediate future, with moderate British control and special reserved rights in relation to the Suez Canal. While Egypt would secure "independence," Great Britain would reserve the following rights:

(1) To guarantee Egypt from outside aggression and to have access to Egyptian territory in case of war.

(2) To maintain a garrison in the Suez Canal Zone.

(3) To control the foreign policy of Egypt and to represent Egypt in countries where no Egyptian representatives are appointed.

Great Britain would also agree to abolish the capitulations which granted special privileges to foreigners, and to have no more "advisers" in the different government departments. The expected adoption of this preliminary agreement would alter the British protectorate declared in 1914 and recognized by the treaties of Versailles, St. Germain, and Sèvres.

The population of Egypt now numbers 13,000,000. The people are mostly farmers living on the delta and on narrow strips of fertile land on either side of the life-giving Nile. There

Fig. 26. The ribbons of irrigated land along the Nile River, including the broad irrigated expanse of the Nile Delta. From *Annuaire statistique de l'Egypte*, 1914.

is a well-educated and wealthy class in the towns eager to secure political control, though a limited number see and acknowledge the benefits of British supervision and work with British officials in maintaining order.

THE ANGLO-EGYPTIAN SUDAN

South of Upper Egypt there is a vast extent of country known as the Anglo-Egyptian Sudan, extending from Wadi Halfa to Uganda in the Victoria Nyanza region. It was formerly a source of great difficulty to the British administration of Egypt. Unruly tribes inhabit its semi-arid western sections, and their fanatical religion (Mohammedanism) has led them to oppose bitterly the authority of Christian rulers. It was in 1898 at Omdurman, opposite Khartum, that Kitchener defeated the Mahdi, or "Deliverer" (page 60), and restored order. The climax to the events since that time was reached in July 1919, when the Golden Sword of the Mahdi was surrendered to the Imperial Sovereign of the British Empire.

The land and the people The country lies partly in the basin of the Nile and partly in the interior-basin drainage of the Sahara. The portion lying in the east and south is fertile and has great possibilities for agriculture and cattle breeding, while the northern and western portions are arid or semi-arid.

Three types of distribution Negroes and Arabs comprise the bulk of the population. They fall into the following groups:

(1) Cattle-owning nomads who occupy the watered and more luxuriant country toward the south. In the region of the Nile the country is thickly settled.

(2) Sedentary peoples of mixed type (as in central Kordofan); these live in villages of a dozen or several score huts, the size of each village depending upon the quantity of ground that can be conveniently cultivated and upon the supply of water.

(3) Camel-owners living chiefly in the northern desert districts; these own also large herds of cattle, sheep, and goats, and cultivate the soil.

The Nuba tribes as an example of colonial difficulties As an example of the sedentary type we may take the case of the Nuba tribes of Kordofan, since they illustrate also the difficulties that confront British officials in these remote sections of the world. The Nuba tribesmen occupy the Nuba Hills in central Kordofan. Each community is restricted to a given hilly district whose boundaries are naturally defined. Cultivation is limited to the terraced slopes

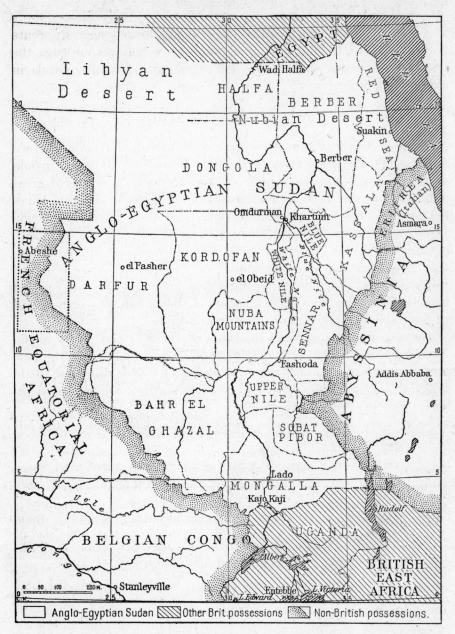

Anglo-Egyptian Sudan · Other Brit. possessions · Non-British possessions.

Fig. 27. Six hundred miles in a straight line south of the Nile mouths the Anglo-Egyptian Sudan begins, to extend nearly fifteen hundred miles farther south. Much of it is desert. Part of its population is difficult to manage. Its control is one of the many difficult tasks which the British have undertaken in the field of colonial government. New boundary (between Wadai and Darfur) in the area of the dotted rectangle, left center, from *L'Afrique Française*, February 1920. The boundary between Egypt (British) and Libya (Italian) is still indeterminate. So far as it has been defined in preliminary agreements it is shown in Figure 74.

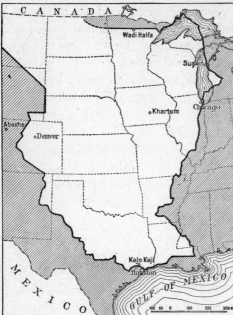

Aridity of the western desert portions has led to water storage in trees

FIG. 28. The difficulties in the way of management of the Anglo-Egyptian Sudan may be judged by studying this map of comparative distances. A single main railway line runs from Wadi Halfa southward through Khartum to El Obeid, 230 miles southwest of Khartum. This line has but one important branch, to the Red Sea coast near Suakin.

of the hills. Some grain is produced and vegetables, cotton, and tobacco also are grown. The Nuba tribesmen own considerable herds of cattle, sheep, and goats. They have long defended their hills by stone walls built across the valleys and by a system of water, grain, and even cattle storage in the caves found in the more inaccessible heights.

One of the most remarkable of the features of the region is illustrated in Dar Hamar, southeastern Kordofan, where the natives are dependent for most of the year on the supply of water stored in the enlarged natural cavities of the tebeldi trees in sufficient quantities to last through an entire dry season. The diameter of the trees varies from 10 to 15 feet, and the interior reservoir is often 20 feet high. The trees form valuable property and are let or sold with the adjacent land. It is estimated that there are at least 200,000 of them in the district. When the local water supply becomes inadequate, certain families break away and form a new village.

The better land and denser populations border the Nile

The best agricultural land of the Anglo-Egyptian Sudan is in the Kordofan region, but the crops are limited by the amount of rainfall, except locally along the river, where river floods or irrigation from the Nile make possible a larger extent of cultivated land and a denser population. Swarms of migratory locusts occasionally visit the district and devour the crops. Cotton and cereals are grown, and a variety of grains. Cattle form the principal basis of the export trade to Egypt. Ivory is imported from southern districts, and ostriches are kept in some of the villages. Gum arabic forms a principal article of commerce.

Protection from the various Arab tribes and sub-tribes of the plains round about has been secured by payment of a regular tribute

Military expeditions against the Nuba hill-men

of grain and slaves. Among themselves, the more powerful hill communities of the Nuba tribes have always made war upon the weaker communities, an intertribal conflict stimulated by the protection from Arab invasion which the English government gave to the hill communities. In 1908 a military expedition was sent into the country to storm the principal strongholds and bring the natives to a state of submission, and again in 1909, 1910, and 1911 successive expeditions had to be sent to maintain order.

Darfur, west of Kordofan province, remained semi-independent until 1916, when, following the rebellion of the sultan Ali Dinar, the country was conquered and later incorporated as the fifteenth province of the Sudan. This measure led to the settlement of the long-postponed frontier question of Wadai and Darfur.

Pacification of the region on the western frontier

Great Britain and France have now agreed upon the boundary line shown in Figure 27. It is a settlement of importance to the peace of the Sudan by reason of the fact that until it was made neither the British nor the French could effectively pacify the more remote peoples on their common borders, the British operating from Khartum and the French from the forts along the Shari River, the principal feeder of Lake Tchad.

BRITISH INTERESTS IN ARABIA

Interior Desert Tribes and Coastal Settlements

British power in Arabia has been exercised hitherto chiefly on the borders of the country and in places accessible to naval vessels. With the advance of the Turkish armies on Egypt by way of Syria and Palestine in 1916, British forces had to win and hold the allegiance of the Arabs. The enormous difficulties of this task were overcome with marked success.

Physical geography of Arabia as an isolating factor

To understand the political problems of Arabia, let us look first at the physical geography. Arabia is a huge desert peninsula. Placed over the United

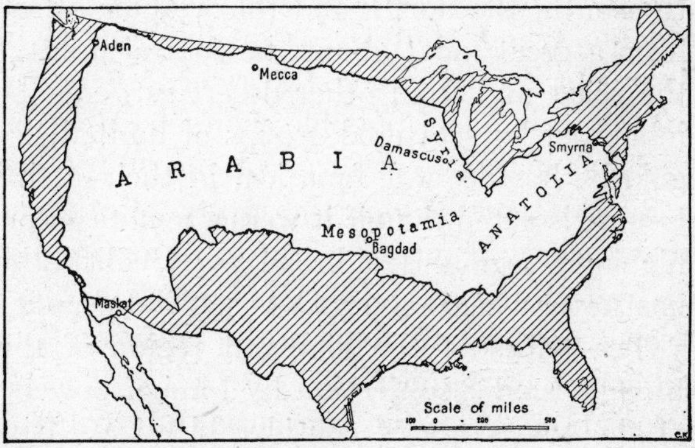

FIG. 29. Anatolia and Arabia in terms of American locations.

States, it would extend from San Diego, California, to Chicago, and from Canada to Mexico (Fig. 29). Every part of this vast region is more or less a unit in itself. It is bordered on at least one side by a broad and nearly impassable desert. The isolation of the country is still further marked by the absence of good harbors and improved roads.

The fanatical and intolerant character of the desert tribes

The country is broken into strongly marked physiographic units, and its people have always been divided into primitive organizations, in which the tribal idea is paramount. The tribes are all fiercely fanatical and have excluded the intruder to a remarkable degree, being helped in this respect by the inaccessibility of the country. Even the Turkish officials and the Turkish tribes have been kept out. Though the desert interior is sufficiently high to make the climate possible for white men, no white men — not even explorers — have penetrated the innermost districts until recent times. The nomadic tribes live within a limited space, and the persistent feuds, especially between the northern and southern tribes, have intensified their isolation. This is the more remarkable when we consider that the general mode of life and the language of the whole nomadic group are the same.

The Nejd the heart of Arabia; its people never conquered

The population groups lying in the heart of Arabia are very strikingly located. They occur at oases scattered along the valley floors of a drainage system associated with a belt of highland known as the Djebel Tuwaik (Fig. 30). This highland — the backbone of central Arabia — is in the form of a long ridge extending roughly north and south for a distance of nearly 400 miles, with an average breadth of 20 miles. Its western border is a relatively steep and regular scarp 400 to 600 feet high. Its eastern slope descends by broad steps to the desert wastes that flank it on this side. On the south, the north, and the west lie other sandy desert tracts that form a great moat about the central uplift, which, far removed from the coast and from other desert settlements, having small resources, inhabited by scattered groups of limited size, and with a people singularly hostile and fanatical in their attitude toward the stranger, is more isolated than if it were a remote oceanic isle. Southeast of the highland region is a broad tract called the Empty Quarter, which has never been traversed by a European.

The tribes of the highland region of the Nejd have never been brought under subjection by foreign powers in modern times. Some of the towns are of considerable size. Riyadh has a population of 12,000 to 15,000. The inhabitants of this district form the Wahabi group of Arabs, who live under Ibn Saud as ruler. The latter has maintained a rather high state of military efficiency and religious ardor, and by favoring the development of the principal towns and villages is able to preserve the integrity of his desert empire.

It is an interesting fact that the traders of Yemen and Koweit send part of their wares through this belt of oases in the heart of Arabia. Hither comes coffee from the Yemen in exchange for the tea, sugar, and other goods of the Persian Gulf coast.

The Mohammedanism of these desert tribes is much diluted. There is a great variety of religious tendencies,

SOUTHERN NEJD

Scale of miles

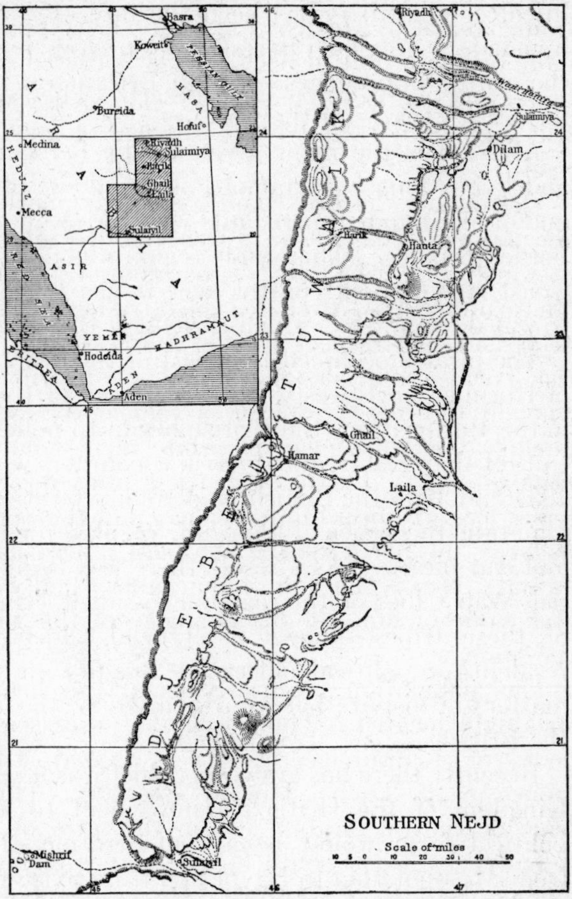

Fig. 30.   The heart of the Arabian desert and home of the independent Wahabis. After Philby, *Geographical Journal*, March 1920.

expressed in various sects, and there are even primitive pagan and semi-pagan forms involving the worship of rocks and mountains.

Arabia has a northern border of watered country, often called the Fertile Crescent, where the nomadic Arab has become a sedentary tiller of the soil.   Mesopotamia and Syria, like the Hedjaz, Yemen, and Oman, are settled by branches of the Arab people.   The government of the outer coastal states, the commerce, and the customs of the people as well, are quite different from those of the inner desert tribes.   In many places the latter are peaceful enough; in others they periodically raid the rich valleys of the fertile border, or they take to piracy, as on the shores of the Persian Gulf.

Owing to the lawlessness of its people and their disorganized po-

The Fertile Crescent and the divisions of Arabia

Foreign control of Arabian gateways

litical condition, it has been the fate of Arabia to have its borders invaded by foreign interests. Non-Arab powers have controlled all the water approaches — Great Britain on the south and east and formerly Turkey on the west.

Al Hasa is the name given to the Persian Gulf border of Arabia, and it has long been famous as the home of pirates or slave traders and of evil-minded merchants who thrive on the sale of guns to unruly border peoples. This whole region was once described as the Pirate Coast, and British control over it has its foundation in an attempt to put down piracy, which throve on British commerce.

British control of the Trucial Coast, or Pirate Coast

The pirates occupied the coast of the Katar peninsula at the strait of Hormuz, northwestward to the head of the gulf (Fig. 230). Early in the 19th century the British began to police the gulf, and from 1805 to 1821 they had frequent naval encounters with the pirates. Between 1835 and 1856 the British made many treaties with the Arab chiefs to maintain the peace of the gulf, regulate or abolish the slave traffic, and end piracy. As a result there was formed among the six principal Arab tribes of the region a so-called Trucial League. The chiefs of these tribes, known as Trucial Chiefs, deal with the British resident, or political officer, at Bushire on the Persian coast in all matters in dispute between themselves, the Turks, the Persians, and the British.

Opposition to a great Arab confederation

Recently there has grown up, chiefly as a result of the newly-created Kingdom of the Hedjaz, a movement to secure Arab unity. The political form would be a confederation of Arab states extending from Mesopotamia to Egypt and from Syria to the Red Sea, including the whole Arabian peninsula. In fact, the religious or learned doctors of Mecca have already (1916) proclaimed the Sherif Hussein, of Mecca, King of the Arab Nation. But the great powers have never recognized this action; their interests, no less than the weakness of the Arabs themselves, will prevent real confederation.

Difficulties of control of the Arab world from desert Arabia

Also opposed to the desired Arab union is the physical geography of the Arabian peninsula. The detached tribal states are widely separated on the margin of the great Arabian desert. It is nearly a thousand miles from Damascus to Mecca. While the Hedjaz is the strongest state, with a population of several hundred thousand, its military power is feeble and its political experience small. Nor do all the Arab states welcome control by the King of the Hedjaz, who rules his tribes like a patriarch. Added to the opposition of the chieftains of the inner desert tribes is that of the sheiks of Asir and Yemen on the coast, farther south.

FIG. 31.   General view of Jiddah, an Arab town, chief port of the Kingdom of the Hedjaz.

Even before the recent war, the Arab half of the Turkish Empire was interested in the founding of a separate Arab empire.   Among the Arabs there has never been any real interest in the famous Pan-Turanian movement of the Turks (page 435).   Here we have a very interesting fact: there was a division of the Ottoman Empire along lines of nationalism rather than religion.

The local differences of culture and history likewise oppose confederation.   Syria and Arabia have unlike customs, traditions, and habits.   Damascus has an age-old ambition herself to become the head of an independent Arab kingdom. *Sectional rivalries*

While the movement for Arab independence made rapid headway during the World War, it has now taken on very artificial forms.   As soon as the war was over, the traditional disputes of the Arabs were revived.   They ended in an armed conflict between Ibn Saud, leader of the Wahabis of the Nejd, and King Hussein of the Hedjaz.   The former represents the most extreme elements of Mohammedanism; the latter stands for a more reasonable and orthodox view of his religion.   The quarrel grew out of a question of boundaries, but it rests in large part also upon deep-seated religious differences that illustrate the difficulties of Arab unity, whether we consider Arabia itself or northern Africa, or the Sudan, or Syria and Mesopotamia, the other principal territorial divisions of the Arab realm. *Struggle between the interior tribes and those on the border*

If France and Great Britain have their way, the Arab state will not be formed of the parts which the Arabs have claimed, nor even of Syria combined with Palestine or Mesopotamia. At most it would consist of interior territory southeast of coastal Syria, and it is not expected that the French will permit it to include the railroad and cities east of the Sykes-Picot line, — Homs, Damascus, Hama, and Aleppo. (See Figure 209 for the Anglo-French agreement of 23 December 1920.)

Protection of foreign interests

The border regions of Arabia will stay in the hands of the European powers as long as these powers remain strong. Only by becoming orderly and self-governing can the Arab tribes expect at last to be measurably free from foreign control, because disorder would threaten not only the trade and lives of foreigners; it would threaten also England's road to India, besides stirring up trouble in Egypt and among the Mohammedan peoples of India itself.

Hedjaz and the annual pilgrimages

Because of its relation to the Pan-Arab movement, the Hedjaz will continue to be important in international affairs in spite of its small size. It is only about 700 miles long and 150 miles wide, and lies between the highlands of the plateau of Arabia and the Red Sea coast. The name "Hedjaz" means *barrier*, which refers to the wall of high mountains on the edge of the tableland. The largest city in the Hedjaz is Mecca, with a population of 80,000, and next to it is Medina, with 40,000. The principal traffic is related to the pilgrimages made by many devout Mohammedans from all parts of the Moslem world. From 80,000 to 100,000 people annually visit the holy cities of Mecca and Medina. Most of them come by sea, but many come by caravan and, more recently, by rail as far as Medina. Only Mohammedans may enter either city.

Oman and the illegal trade in firearms

Of special interest in a study of Arabia is the principality of Oman. The eastern Oman is one of the most advanced districts of Arabia. The population of the entire province is estimated at 500,000. First in importance is the town of Maskat, with a population of 10,000 and a fine harbor, the seat of extensive trade with India and East Africa.

One of the long-standing difficulties at Oman has been the illicit trade in firearms. In 1912 the British compelled the Sultan to promulgate a law prohibiting this trade; but French vessels, down to the time of the Hague arbitral decision of 1905, had entire freedom of commerce in the waters of Oman and could not be searched by British gunboats. It is probable that Great Britain will assume a protectorate over the region. Everywhere else in the vicinity she has increased her power, in line with her policy to control the approaches to the route to India.

Since 1885 the various sultans or emirs of the small Arab states along the southern coast of Arabia have virtually recognized British protection. The British have also annexed the Kuria Muria Islands and assumed a protectorate over Bahrein Island in the Persian Gulf (Fig. 230). A treaty concluded with Turkey in 1909 recognized as a British sphere all of Arabia south of a line drawn between Yemen and Aden and extending northeastward to the Katar peninsula, on the Persian Gulf. *Extent of the British sphere of influence in Arabia*

The two border provinces of Yemen and Asir remain to be considered. Yemen is the small province at the southwestern corner of the Arabian peninsula. The strip near the coast s barren country with a few oases. Toward the east, at the edge of the tableland with local mountains exceeding 10,000 feet in height, there is greater rainfall and high production. The people are mostly town dwellers and fairly industrious. It is believed that the population numbers at least 1,000,000, but no census has ever been made. Europeans in the region number less than 1 per cent of the total population. The largest city is Sanaa on the edge of the plateau, with a population of 25,000; Hodeidah is the principal port. Paying little heed to Turkish overlordship, Yemen was a virtually independent country up to 1914 and will probably remain so, provided it enters no alliance that threatens the welfare of the great powers. *The geography of Yemen*

In length the province of Asir (Fig. 30) is about 230 miles, in width about 150 miles. Like the Hedjaz, it has for eastern boundary a rugged mountain belt, with well-watered and fertile valley floors that produce dates and coffee known for their quality throughout the world. Shells, skins, and salt also are exported. There are no navigable waterways. All inland communication is by caravan. Asir has unexplored regions inhabited by warlike tribes. Ghizin is the principal port. In 1912 the ruling sheik declared his country autonomous. In 1914 Turkey sent warships to the coast, but the World War prevented further military measures. *The unruly country of Asir*

With a mandatary for Palestine and Mesopotamia, Great Britain has almost encircled the Arabs (the French remain in Syria), and need fear no immediate difficulties in protecting her sea route from the Suez Canal to India unless there should come about a general union of Mohammedan peoples. *British penetration of the Arab world*

There is a particular spot near the border of Arabia that deserves notice because of its critical relation to the Aden and Red Sea outlet on the British road to India, at the Strait of Bab el Mandeb. This is the port of Sheikh Said, which the French have claimed for more than half a century. It lies on the eastern shore and *French and British interests in conflict at the Strait of Bab el Mandeb* directly opposite the British-owned island of Perim in the strait itself. It is between Perim and Sheikh Said (Fig. 271) that ships take their course, and if the place were fortified it would menace the Indian and eastern Asiatic commerce that passes this way. The British look longingly at it, for with this and Sokotra‿ Island — which they already own — in their hands, every part of the Indian route would be amply protected. The small French colony of Somaliland exists near by, but it is so completely overshadowed by British Somaliland and the British Aden colony that it can never become a menace to legitimate British interests, either commercial or naval.

A British
protecto-
rate on the
southern
coast of
Arabia

East of the port of Aden is an undefined area on the Gulf of Aden which is a British protectorate known as the Makalla Sultanate. The region exports raw tobacco, skins, coffee, honey, and shells, and has a total annual trade of about $2,000,000, nearly equally divided between exports and imports.

MESOPOTAMIA

In Mesopotamia Great Britain confronts two matters of special political concern to her, in addition to the general problem of responsibility toward the native Arabs:

(1) The country flanks Great Britain's land route to India.

(2) In southeastern Mesopotamia Great Britain has built great oil refineries and docks for handling the rich petroleum yield of regions near by, both in Mesopotamia and in southwestern Persia.

British
interests
and prob-
lems

Great Britain's sense of responsibility to the native is not unmixed with other motives; for Mesopotamia, as a part of it (Irak) was in ancient times, might become part of a general Arab confederation and would then be lost to Great Britain. A British company controls transportation on the Tigris-Euphrates river systems, and British capital has been invested in the railroad from Basra northward (now extended almost to Mosul as part of the Bagdad system). British surveys of the irrigation possibilities of Mesopotamia have shown the enormously productive capacity of the soil when properly watered. Cotton, tobacco, silk, and other subtropical products could be grown on a huge scale and might give the region extraordinary commercial importance. The possible value of these products to industrial England is almost incalculable. Originally interested in the region chiefly because of the pirates that infested the Persian Gulf and preyed upon British shipping, England established political residencies and

Fig. 32. Drainage, population, and boundaries of Mesopotamia. After Map of Eastern Turkey in Asia, Syria, and Western Persia (Ethnographical), scale 1 : 2,000,000, British General Staff, No. 2901, 1915. Lake and swamp areas in the Euphrates valley are shown by diagonal ruling. For boundary with Syria see Figure 209.

trading posts about the shores, and extended her commercial and political penetration until she is today in secure hold of the chief resources, which are growing in value with the rapid increase of the world's industrial population.

Ambition to control the Berlin-Bagdad route — as part of the Pan-German scheme — was one of the causes of Germany's hostility to England before the war. The rich trade of India and the Orient, including the East Indies, makes the possession of these regions a commercial advantage. Together, India and China possess more

International rivalry for the wealth of Mesopotamia

than 40 per cent of the world's population. China also has vast untouched resources of iron and coal, and were they to be developed and the population industrialized, these resources would become a source of economic power with which an ambitious nation could control virtually the whole world. Mesopotamia, by reason of its position between the industrial nations of the West and the undeveloped populations of the East, becomes a critical region, a true problem area.

England's occupation of the region, including her development of its resources and her relations with the native, will be challenged by her rivals, the more so because her control of Mesopotamia will not end with this territory alone. To the north lies Kurdistan; to the west lies the Arab realm; to the east lies Persia. In each one of these regions other powers have what they regard as vital interests, and they will not stand by and see the region exploited for the benefit of British capital only. The English have been enterprising and successful hitherto in many of their political ventures, but they have here a problem that will fully test their administrative powers.

Those who challenge the British claim to the occupation of Mesopotamia have to recognize, however, that if Great Britain's hold were relaxed, rival ambitions and native intrigue would surely make this a field of disorder, to the injury not only of Great Britain but of France and Persia as well. At least until affairs become orderly again, the peace of the world demands that the region be held, if not by England, at least by some other strong power.

The oil of Mesopotamia and the British commercial fleet

While irrigation may furnish the basis for the chief riches of Mesopotamia, the immediate wealth of the country lies principally in trade and in the development of the oil resources (Fig. 230). The production of the Persian and Mesopotamian fields is small at the present time, but the reserve is great, and this is a matter of prime importance to Great Britain, whose navy depends chiefly upon oil for fuel, and whose commercial carriers are being turned into oil burners at a rapid rate. Late in 1919 plans were made calling for the development of huge oil refineries at Swansea in southern Wales, and already large refineries have been established at Abadan on the Shatt el Arab (Fig. 32). The control of the world's oil supply is a matter of great concern, and it will form the basis of one of the keenest commercial rivalries of the next fifty years. Thus Mesopotamia means not only problems of land, frontiers, natives, railroads, and river steamers; it is also vitally related to one of the many life streams that support the British commercial fleet.

In many respects the occupation of Mesopotamia is an exception to the established British policy of keeping to islands, as in New Zealand and Jamaica, or to relatively detached areas, like Australia or Egypt, or to strategic ports, as at Walvis Bay and Aden, or to peninsulas partly shut off from the interior by mountains or forests or deserts, as India, the Straits Settlements, and North Borneo. Mesopotamia is an alluvial basin bordered by tablelands and mountains inhabited by restless, unruly, nomadic, and fanatical Moslem peoples who, both far and near, have overrun the basin time and again, and who will not leave Great Britain to occupy peacefully a rich land which is their traditional prey. Like India, Mesopotamia will have its problem of a northwest frontier, and in an equally dangerous and costly form. *Occupation of Mesopotamia a departure from traditional British policy*

" THE GOSPEL OF EMPIRE IS THERE OIL IN MESOPOTAMIA? "

In this headline from a London paper [1] we have illustrated the opposition between two divergent theories of political control for British protected areas and mandates. *Two opposing views of British expansion*

(1) There is the principle that, taking advantage of mandatory power assigned to it, Great Britain may encourage the development of resources of special interest to British citizens. The British public would thereby pay what might be called the overhead charges in maintaining opportunities and privileges which would be of financial benefit only to the private trader. Once accepted, this policy leads naturally to the strongly developed tendency to give protection and special benefits to the British trader, since British taxpayers are paying the costs of government and desire to see concrete financial compensation. To a like degree there would develop a tendency to give special favors to the British trader rather than to the native trader, who by himself is incapable of organizing a strong government.

(2) Opposed to this principle is the theory of protection for the benefit of all, the native and the non-British subject to have equal opportunities with the British trader. This clearly requires altruism on the part of the British taxpayer, who reaps no advantage in holding the territory, except the indirect benefits conferred upon the British citizen due to the increase of trade. To put into practice such a policy is an uphill task.

The enduring wealth of Mesopotamia is the extraordinary fertility of the soil. It is competently estimated that the average combined

---

[1] *The Daily Herald*, 26 March 1920.

discharge of the Tigris-Euphrates rivers would irrigate 7,000,000 acres in winter and 3,000,000 acres of varied crops in summer. Half of this area could be immediately reclaimed if the ancient system of canals and drains were restored, and the Euphrates water turned into the land west of the Tigris, while the Tigris and its tributaries were made to irrigate the land east of the Tigris. It is even suggested that for the better utilization of their waters for irrigation purposes, the rivers should not be used for navigation, but should be superseded by railways for the transport of cereals and cotton.

CHAPTER THREE

POLITICAL AND COLONIAL AIMS OF FRANCE

(A) READJUSTMENT AND REORGANIZATION

HAD it not been for the temperamental flexibility of her people, the war of 1914–1918 might have ruined France. Almost the whole world eventually came to her aid, but it should not be forgotten that she also helped herself through a courageous expenditure of her energies and resources that now brings her a crop of after-war troubles of the gravest import. More than 1,400,000 of her soldiers were killed. Of these about half came from French farms, and almost all of them were young men, whose death resulted in a heavy capital loss to the state. Her soil and forests were devastated in a large part of the occupied region; her mills were destroyed in the most highly industrialized part of her territor ; and her coal mines were damaged so seriously that it will take several years at least to restore them to productivity. She lost 30 per cent of her shipping. Three million head of cattle were taken by Germany in the occupied region. Every Allied army operating in France had to get a large part of its mine-timber and railway ties as well as road metal in France. Her ports, never large enough for her own normal needs had to be occupied in large part by British and American engineers. Her farming and industrial populations were displaced. In consequence, the whole economic life of France must be made o er, owing to the disturbance caused by the abnormal arrangements of the war.

What the war cost France

To be sure, there was some financial return to France during the war, in that more money was spent by the Allied armies in France than in any other country. On the other hand, she had so little coal, her industrial machinery was so badly deranged, her manufacturing energies had to be spent so largely on big guns, ammunition, and the repair and replacement of the material wastage of war, that she was compelled to make a large part of her purchases for her ordinary needs and for much of her ammunition in the United States and in England.

Reconstruction a difficult and costly problem

The problems of France are therefore largely those of reconstruction — to set going again her national machinery. To develop her own mills and factories to the pre-war point and to turn back into their old channels the forces of labor and capital will require years of patient adjustment. Remaking her industrial organization will also create new social and political problems that may threaten the internal peace of France.

77

THE BURDEN OF WAR COSTS

The effect
of the dis-
covery that
Germany
could not
pay war
costs

    In the first place, every Frenchman took for granted what Lloyd George felt obliged to promise the British people in December 1918 — that Germany could be made to pay the costs of the war; it was in that expectation that many men had toiled and fought during four years of war. It was likewise expected that the bill to Germany should include compensation for all the damage done to civilian property. When the war ended and a settlement came to be made, it was discovered that Germany had destroyed so much that she could never pay the damage in addition to the costs of war. This was a terrible blow to France. The effect on the French spirit was not unlike that of a great military defeat.

    People had lost sight of the fact that the war had cost the Allies more than twice Germany's total wealth before the war and much more than the combined national wealth of all the enemy powers. If absolutely everything in Germany could have been confiscated and sold for what it was normally worth, the total would have amounted to less than one half the war expenditures of the Allies alone. In addition, Germany's own debt amounted to one half her total wealth. In short, the costs of the war could not be repaid.

Impossi-
bility of ad-
minister-
ing the
whole of
Germany

    But there were other reasons than its inadequacy against such a confiscation of German wealth. It would have reduced the German people to economic slavery, and the administration of Germany under such conditions would have cost much more in trouble and money than the value of the goods produced. It was impossible to escape the fact that, in the last analysis, only those reparation payments would be of value which were made in *goods* or in *services*. To confiscate immovable German property would not have helped at all, since only those goods (or their equivalent in sound, not inflated, money) which could be moved to Allied countries could be of the slightest value to the Allies.

    In other words, if reparation payments were to be of value they must be made outside of Germany — at London, Paris, Rome, or New York; for as long as either money or goods remained in Germany they could be of use only to Germans. This meant, of course, that reparation payments must be made over a term of years, since Germany's national income in any single year would amount to but a very small percentage (about 5 per cent) of the total costs of the war. It also meant that Germany must produce a great deal more than she consumed, if large payments were to be made. That is, Germany must

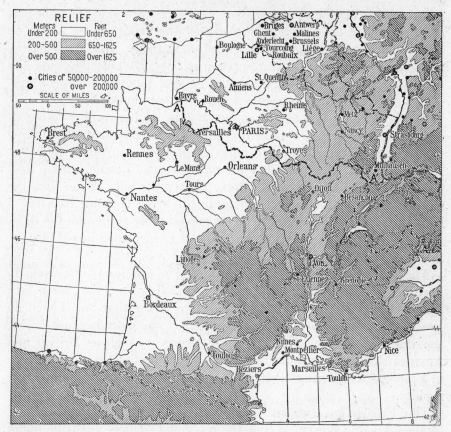

Fig. 33. Relief map of France, based on Vidal Lablache. North of the line *A-A'*, one third of all persons engaged in gainful pursuits are employed in industry (as derived from *Album graphique et statistique de la France*, 1907, p. 82). This is the chief industrial region of France and was the seat of the German invasions of 1870 and of 1914–1918. The plains of Belgium are continuous with those of northern France. It was by way of Liége, Brussels, and Lille that the German armies invaded France in 1914, reaching in a few weeks a point within a few miles of Paris. Note the position of Alsace-Lorraine and the defensive value of the Rhine.

be allowed to prosper in order to pay a large indemnity, and of course a certain part of this prosperity could be won only at the expense of the nations with whom Germany would compete for world trade.

Finally, the Allies saw that even to confiscate Germany's gold reserve would be unwise. Paper money has no value in itself; its value depends upon the willingness of people to accept it, and that in turn depends upon the ability of the government to redeem it in gold or silver upon demand. When the Germans occupied Poland and Serbia and Rumania, they issued floods of paper money based upon their small gold reserve. This paper money would be worthless if there did not exist the possibility that it could be exchanged for gold.

Why Germany's gold reserve had to be left in Germany

For the Allies to take away Germany's gold reserve would mean the ruin of thousands of people who had accepted the paper money (based on that reserve) or who had had it forced upon them. Furthermore, the amount of Germany's gold reserve was only $700,000,000, and the estimated war costs of the Allies are several hundred times as large.

Reluctantly French economists came to see that it would be best to leave Germany's gold in her own hands, let her run her own government, including her railways, and obtain payments by taking from her the products of her industry or their equivalent in value. In other words, German labor for many years to come, rather than present German capital, would have to pay the bill. Even then the money that could be extracted and still leave German industry a basis on which to continue would be enough only to restore the damage to civilian property. The war costs of France must be paid by the French people themselves.

The realization of these facts produced a profound impression in French labor circles, where it was at last clearly seen that for a long time there will be heavy taxes to pay for a war that was forced on France by Germany. Laboring men object the more because during the war French capital did not pay nearly so high as British and American capital; income taxes and excess-profits taxes were lower in France. Yet during all that time the cost of living was mounting rapidly.

The French government therefore tried to avoid labor troubles by demobilizing slowly, so that the returning soldiers might be found employment as rapidly as they became free from army discipline. Societies were organized to assist locally. The government lent its aid to rebuild the devastated regions of northern France. These measures, with the granting of small pensions for temporarily unemployed soldiers, made the return to normal conditions of life easier than it would otherwise have been, and also safer for the country.

PROBLEMS OF THE EASTERN BORDER

One of the largest territorial gains made by France as a result of the World War was due to the recovery of Alsace-Lorraine (5600 square miles). These provinces were taken away in 1871, following the Franco-Prussian War. They are inhabited chiefly by Germans in the central and eastern portions, and by French on the west. Nearly half of Lorraine is occupied by a French-speaking majority, but only 6 per cent of the area of Alsace. As a whole the people are unquestionably French in sympathy. To have these provinces held by Germany was intensely irritating to French pride, and their return became one of the objects of the war. Resentment toward Germany was the more bitter because the iron ore of Lorraine was one of the bases of German industry, and possession of it proved to be a marked advantage in a war largely based on machinery and steel.

The return of the provinces adds to France a population of 1,900,000. It gives her also the richest iron-ore beds of Europe, thus enabling her to become a great producer of iron and steel to provide for her

FIG. 34. The narrow belt of country between France and Germany is an old zone of friction. It was once held as a separate kingdom, as shown above. The idea of creating a line of buffer states in the same general position was advanced during the World War. After Putzger.

own normal needs, to restore the devastated areas, and to export to her colonies and elsewhere. It was from Lorraine that Germany derived 75 per cent (21,000,000 long tons) of all the iron mined in the empire. Alsace has oil wells at Pechelbronn, and at Wittelsheim there is one of the two greatest potash deposits in the world, the other being at Stassfurt in Germany. The Saar basin coal deposits extend into northern Lorraine, and there are also valuable salt deposits. In contrast to the mineral resources of Lorraine, and the industries dependent upon them, is the great agricultural production of Alsace. Its soil is a marked addition to the wealth of France.

The return of Alsace-Lorraine brought up an interesting religious problem, seeing that during the period of their occupation by Germany these provinces did not share with the rest of France the rupture between church and state. And in Alsace-Lorraine the clerical party is quite as strongly religious and Catholic as it is Francophile. This situation has led French leaders to take steps to restore diplomatic relations with the Vatican, a plan which received great impetus in the administration of Millerand, following Clémenceau. The result will be to weld the provinces still more firmly to France, while at the same time French foreign problems will receive far more sympathetic consideration in Spain and Italy, where powerful clerical influences are important in the management of political relations. France will benefit also by the support that the Vatican may give her in the settlement of the Turkish problem, for the Vatican is concerned in the treatment of the Christian populations in Asia Minor and Syria, and in the disposition of the shrines of Palestine.

The religious leaning of Alsace-Lorraine

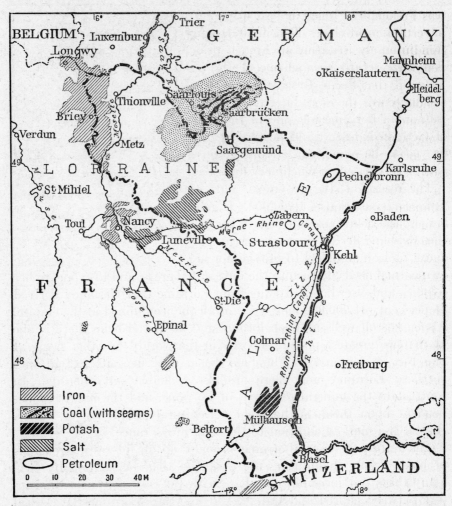

Fig. 35. Mineral resources and principal water communications in the Alsace-Lorraine region. By taking these two districts from France in 1871, Germany deprived France of the strategic frontier of the Rhine and won for herself immense iron-ore resources that were of increasing value in Germany's modern period of industrial development and overseas commerce. A new well at greater depths than hitherto reached has located large reserves of petroleum at Pechelbronn (1920). Petroleum products to the amount of 50,000 tons are now derived annually at this locality. After Gallois, the *Geographical Review*, August 1918.

The Left Bank of the Rhine as a buffer state

It will be a great temptation to the French people to interfere in the affairs of the region called the Left Bank of the Rhine, for it is here that French military men would like to create a buffer state in which there should be no danger of German military preparations against France. The idea is a tempting one, though we must remember that the people are German and not French. For twenty years before the treaty of Vienna (1815) made it Prussian, the Rhineland

was French, and there is still
a certain pro-French element
mindful of the prosperity and
democracy of the days when it
was a part of France. Many
people hoped to see the region
become self-governing or in
some way attached to France.
If local self-governing geographical divisions are set up
in a future Germany, the
Rhineland will probably become one of the principal divisions.

When a few of the people
in the region started a separatist movement at the end of
the war and proclaimed the
"Republic of the Left Bank of
the Rhine," they immediately
won French sympathy. At the
peace conference it was urged
by some Frenchmen that Allied, or at least French, military occupation of the region
was necessary for a long time
to come. This should not be
hastily branded as mere imperial design; for more than four
years the sound of artillery fire
could be heard at Paris; it
takes but an hour to drive from
the city to the nearest battle-

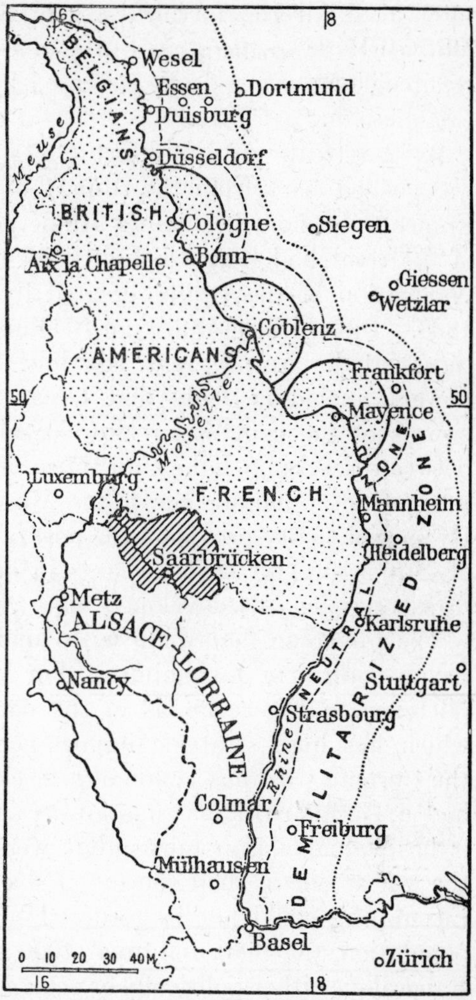

FIG. 36. The Saar district (diagonally ruled); the Left Bank (stippled area west of the Rhine); and the bridgeheads and adjacent territory east of the Rhine, subject to temporary Allied control and to demilitarization.

fields of the war; there was almost nightly danger of air raids; the
nerves of the French people had been strained to the limit of endurance,
and the effect on many French children will last throughout their life-
times. With victory in her hands, France passionately desired to be
free from the long-standing menace of German invasion.

France has gained important advantages in the region of the Left
Bank. The Allied armies are to occupy it for fifteen years, withdrawing their troops from each of three successive zones at five-year

intervals. All the fortifications in the region are to be destroyed, likewise those in the strip thirty miles wide, east of the Rhine. The occupied territory is to be governed by an Interallied Rhineland High Commission.

Control of
Rhine navi-
gation

By the treaty of Frankfort (1871) the eastern frontier of France was pushed back from the Rhine; by the treaty of Versailles (1919) France once more becomes a Rhine power. Regulation of the traffic of the river had been conducted by the Central Commission for the Navigation of the Rhine created by the Mannheim Convention of 1868. But neither France nor Belgium, and not even Switzerland, was represented. France now has four representatives, and the other powers, including Italy and Great Britain, have two each. The powers of the commission are extended to include the upper Rhine between Basel and Lake Constance, if Switzerland agrees, and, in the interests of Belgium, the lower Moselle with its connecting canals. By special treaty provision the port of Kehl (Fig. 35) is joined to that of Strasbourg for seven years, in order that the port facilities of Strasbourg may be developed more conveniently.

Luxem-
burg also
a buffer
state, long
under Ger-
man in-
fluence

The foregoing facts help us to understand why France wished to secure control of Luxemburg. For Luxemburg, as may be seen by reference to Figure 36, is in the narrow frontier belt, every part of which has high strategic importance. This duchy was taken into the German Customs Union almost eighty years ago; its ruling house had a German origin; its railways were built by German capital; it has valuable iron mines that were used by the Germans during the war as one of their sources of steel for shell and cannon. Clearly Luxemburg could not be returned to German control, and its small population (260,000) and area (1000 square miles) do not permit it to stand alone either politically or economically. It had been taken from Belgium in 1839, but in the plebiscite of September 1919 it voted to enter the French Customs Union. French control of its iron mines and blast furnaces is inevitable. The small duchy is virtually a dependency of France.

Inter-
national
status of
the Saar
region

There remains the problem of the Saar. This region consists essentially of a coal basin from which, before the war, Germany obtained about 9 per cent of her total coal supply, or more than 17,400,000 metric tons. The coal reserves of the Saar are 17,000,000,000 tons, or a thousand times the annual production and 22 per cent of the total reserves of Germany in 1913. France was poor in coal and had practically no petroleum at all. What she wished to secure was outright ownership of the region. Eventually she obtained outright

FIG. 37. The Marne-Rhine canal at Lutzelburg, its most elevated point, where it crosses the Vosges Mountains. It was completed in 1854 by the French. See Figure 35 for the course of the canal.

FIG. 38. The Saar district of the treaty of Versailles. It includes by far the larger part of the Saar coal basin (Fig. 35).

ownership of the mines (which were also placed in the French Customs Union), as compensation for the damages inflicted by the Germans on the French mines at Lens and Valenciennes, where the shafting was blown out by dynamite and the galleries were flooded. At the end of fifteen years a plebiscite must be held in the Saar region, and the inhabitants will then be permitted to vote on their future ownership, whether by France or by Germany. But provision is made for the exclusion of immigrants, whether French or German, from the privilege of the plebiscite. Only those may vote who will have attained the age of twenty and who resided in the Saar district when the treaty with Germany went into effect.

Temporary military control of the Saar basin

Until the treaty of Versailles went into effect on 10 January 1920, the control of the Saar basin was in the hands of the military authorities. There was a short period of strikes, together with general disorder and some pillage. This disturbance proved to be the work of persons from outside the region, more than seven hundred of whom were arrested. Eight of these were condemned to twenty years of forced labor, and others to five or ten years; one was executed. By the terms of later French decrees the expulsion of political agitators ceased; some already sent away were invited to return; and a larger degree of self-government was promised the people, most of whom have offered no active opposition to French occupation.

French political and military interests on Germany's frontiers

France is indeed beset by problems that arise because of her contact with Germany. Practically all of France's mineral resources (Fig. 40) and most of her great manufacturing cities (Fig. 33) are grouped along the German frontier — and Germany will always be in need of all the coal and iron she can get and may again be tempted to seize a neighbor's supply just over the border. Is it surprising that many French statesmen are anxious when they look towards the future?

This anxiety as to possible future action by Germany is most clearly seen in the eagerness with which French diplomats have reached understandings with Rumania and some of the new states created by the Peace Conference of Paris, especially Czecho-Slovakia and Poland. The French detailed well-known generals to help develop the armies of these states, and appear to have succeeded in effecting friendly alliances with their governments. With their support France would naturally feel more secure. In this connection it is necessary to add that in acting as guide and friend to the young and untried nations France has assumed a very real responsibility. Each of the new states will often find its position difficult, and the possibilities of friction with neighboring states will be many; it will often be tempted to resort to force to gain its ends. The peace of Europe may well depend chiefly upon the kind of advice and support that France gives to the new states of central Europe.

THE GREAT NEEDS OF FRANCE

France needs two things to put her on terms of equality with Germany, her ancient foe. She needs a higher birth rate, and she needs a complete awakening and reorganization of her economic life.

As long as the population of France remains at a standstill and that of Germany increases, there will be a steady ethnic penetration by German-speaking people, against which France cannot effectively contend. Germany has a population of 60,000,000; France has less than 40,000,000. The birth rate of France just offset the death rate in 1913; in 1918 the population of France declined 190,000, not counting the war losses and the deaths due to an epidemic of grippe. In Germany there was persistent increase in the years before the war period. Unless the situation in France improves, the French people, declining relatively in numbers, will decline in power also. To study the problem more effectively and provide practical measures, a national bureau was created in January 1920, dealing with the question of the birth rate. The acquisition of the Saar coal and the Lorraine iron may take on a new significance in relation to the future population of France. A recent writer has argued the close relation between coal production and the birth rate; he points to the fact that it was the coal and iron districts of Germany that had the greatest increase of population since 1871.

The lowering birth rate of France

The second of France's great domestic problems is how to place her industries on a pre-war basis. During the war her manufacturing energy was turned largely to the making of guns for herself and her allies, while England built ships and created great reserves of ammuni-

The shipping problem

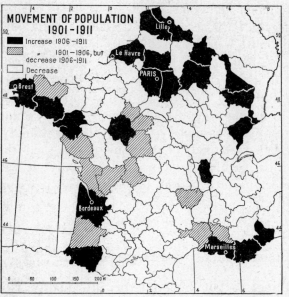

MOVEMENT OF POPULATION
1901 - 1911

■ Increase 1906 -1911

▨ ,, 1901 - 1906, but
decrease 1906-1911

□ Decrease

Lille

Le Havre

PARIS

Brest

Bordeaux

Marseilles

0   50   100   150   200ᴹ

FIG. 39. The large established centers of population and most of the industrial regions show increase of population. Rural France shows general decrease. From map in the *Geographical Journal*, Vol. 40, 1912.

The economic problems of France

tion. By the treaty of peace England has her merchant marine nearly restored ; France, however, gets relatively few ships as a result of the division of the German merchant marine. Even before the war France had a ship deficit, and now she needs raw materials more than ever. At the present time the cost of building ships is excessively high, and the difficulty of France is correspondingly great.

To awaken the economic life of France is perhaps less difficult than to solve the problem of the lowering birth rate, but it is only slightly less difficult. France is an old country, with life adjusted to her resources and to modes of thought and work against which modern ideas have long beaten in vain. This adjustment has some advantages : the life of such a nation is steadier. But the disadvantages also are great, and of this fact the ports of France furnish an example. Control of a given port is divided between more than half a dozen different government authorities. For example, at Havre the Ministry of Public Works can build the docks, but the French Ministry of Marine controls the pilot service, the Minister of Commerce is responsible for the warehouses, the Minister of Finance collects the dues and regulates the hours of work, and the Minister of the Interior polices and lights the quays. Whereas in most of the world's ports it takes but a few years to carry out improvements, here it takes many years. All French ports, even Paris, the largest of all, have obsolete rules for their regulation and are years behind the ports of America and Great Britain in administration. Even before the war these rules interfered in the most serious manner with the development of French trade.

Turning to the industrial field, we see that French iron and steel plants need more coal than France herself will be able to supply for Increased coal and iron assets of France several years, even with the addition of the Saar fields. Part of the lack will be supplied from Germany under the clauses of the treaty of Versailles relating to the importation of coal, but this is a temporary measure. A sound solution requires efficient handling of the whole coal and iron problem of the region of which Lorraine and the Saar are a part.

Since several tons of coal are needed to smelt one ton of iron, it is in Relation of German coal to French iron ore general cheaper to carry iron to coal. To reverse the process would be to increase the cost of iron and steel goods and diminish the chances of successful French competition in foreign markets. But the coal fields are still chiefly in Germany, Westphalia having the largest reserves of coking coal in continental Europe. In 1913 Westphalia produced 69 per cent of the coke used in reducing the Lorraine iron ore, the Saar only 15 per cent, and France 12 per cent. If we look into the future the story is the same. Of estimated reserves of coal in fields tributary to the Lorraine iron districts, Westphalia has 62 per cent, the Saar only 19 per cent. The Rhine valley and Belgium offer cheap canal and rail transportation. Though some iron ore can be economically smelted in France with imported coke from Germany, Belgium, and England, some also would naturally be shipped to western Germany for smelting, since the Saar coking coal is inferior in quality and offers only local competition to German coke. The result of shipping iron ore to Germany for smelting and manufacture would be improvement of German industry and quicker reparation payments to the Allies. These facts will help in understanding future agreements between France and Germany relating to iron and coal shipments and industries. Such agreements are bound to come in time, for they are distinctly to the advantage of both parties.

In this connection it may be noted that France has obtained large interests in Luxemburg blast furnaces, and that whatever her arrangements with Germany, she will have an excess of iron and steel above her ordinary needs. This will help her foreign trade in China, South America, Asia Minor, Italy, and the Balkans, and it will also help in the rebuilding of the devastated and occupied areas of northeastern France.

One of the current questions of more than local interest relates to The necessity for political and economic decentralization the internal administration of France and the effect upon the national spirit. Partly by reason of its geographical position, partly through sentiment and the influence of the national capital, partly because the functions of government have been centralized there ever since the

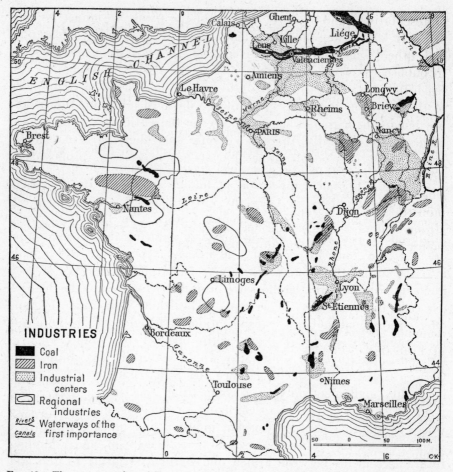

FIG. 40. The concentration of France's mineral resources and industries on her northeastern frontier is shown. Though iron and coal deposits are rather generally distributed, those of greatest commercial value are in the eastern districts, where more than half of the iron and steel products are manufactured. According to *United States Commerce Reports* for 1919 and 1920, the central districts of France produced in 1919 but 12 per cent of the steel, the southwestern 4 per cent, the western 3 per cent, and the southeastern 3 per cent. Alsace-Lorraine in the first six months of 1919 produced 32 per cent of all the steel manufactured in France. The total water-power development by 1921 will be 1,500,000 horsepower, or 20 per cent of the total available. The Alps, central France, and the Pyrenees are the chief centers of development. By "Regional industries" are meant industries based upon products derived directly from the soil. After Vidal Lablache, supplemented by *World Atlas of Commercial Geology*, Part I, *Distribution of Mineral Production*, United States Geological Survey, 1921.

days of Napoleon, who used this method to consolidate his personal power, Paris has played a part in the economic life of France out of proportion to her industrial advantages. The ninety administrative units of the country — the *départements* — are artificial divisions, with few geographical or economic bases. Nearly all the local functionaries are appointed by the central government or by its local representatives, and even the mayors of the towns are under its control. In later years, however, the increase in the speed of telegraphic and other communication has enabled the provincial newspapers to publish the world's news long before the Parisian newspapers can reach the provinces. Thus the provinces have come to have opinions of their own on the happenings of the day. In addition, the people are demanding a greater share of power in the settlement of their local affairs. Consequently, there is a strong movement for a measure of governmental decentralization, and it has even been proposed to divide the country into a number of geographical regions, each several times the size of the existing *départements*, for purposes of local administration. It is thought that such regional capitals would become strong centers of intellectual and political life and would increase the political strength of the country as a whole.

RELATIONS WITH THE COLONIES

Unlike England, France has no problem of satisfying the growing demands of self-governing dominions. All the overseas possessions of France are directly dependent upon the central French government. Very heavy responsibilities remain, nevertheless, because France had rapidly expanded her colonial possessions before the war and now gains additional territory. She has acquired a mandatary over Syria, has divided with Great Britain the Cameroons and Togoland as mandatory colonies, and has had her status in northern Africa confirmed by the great powers. Figure 49 shows her new territorial gains in Africa as a result of the war. *French colonial responsibilities*

It may be safely predicted that French colonial rule will be of a high order. The example of Morocco is heartening. Under the wise administration of able army officers, assisted by a few civilian officials, the country has become safe and orderly, and every advantage has been given the native to help him improve his lot. Development has not merely produced railways, automobile and wagon roads, and mines; it has also improved public health and education. *Morocco as a sample of what France can do in her colonies*

It is the thought of some of her wisest leaders that it would be greatly to the interest of France if she were to make no further efforts in the field of imperial expansion. The world has now been parceled out nearly to the limit of vacant "political space." France formerly opposed British expansion in Africa and in the Persian Gulf region, and German expansion in central Africa and Turkey. Further possible gains are not worth the price of diplomatic quarrels and perhaps *Advisability of discarding the old imperial program* war. Of diverse peoples in widely scattered lands, France now has all that she can well manage. To her at this time is applicable in a peculiarly strong sense the principle that "the test of mastery is restraint."

(B) Special Colonial Interests of France

With this general view of the problems of the French people, we may now look at their special colonial interests as developed by the results of the war. We shall not examine each colony in detail, but shall select for consideration only those that present political or commercial problems of the first rank. Among them two are predominant, — Syria and French North Africa.

SYRIA

Historical importance of Syria

From every standpoint the problem of Syria is the more vexatious of the two, partly by reason of the strong dislike for the French among the native Syrians (Arabs chiefly), partly because French and British interests intermingle in a complex and even dangerous manner. Here we have an echo of the past. "Nowhere else has so much history run into or through so narrow a space," it has been said, and "The military history of Syria may be pictured as the procession of nearly all the world's conquerors" — from Thothmes to Tamerlane and Napoleon.

While the Turk has administered Syria, he has been an alien there. He has not settled upon the land in any numbers, and separate Turkish colonies do not exist in Syria. There are few social and family ties between Turks and Syrians. The removal of the Turk from Syria therefore involves no important social or economic readjustments.

The racial mixtures of Syria

Syria is one of the most densely populated portions of the former Turkish Empire. Though a mere coastal strip, barely fifty miles wide and three hundred miles long, it has nearly 3,000,000 people, of whom two thirds are Moslems. There are also nearly 500,000 Christians and 125,000 Druses. Racially the Syrians are of highly mixed origin: Hittites, Egyptians, Greeks, Romans, Arabs, Turks, and Assyrians, not to mention lesser folk. In the mountain valleys of the Lebanon itself and in central Syria live the Druses, warlike tribes sharing the Lebanon with the agricultural Maronites, whom they frequently raid. On the grassy seaward slopes of the mountains bordering the Gulf of Alexandretta are the settlements of the Ansarirebs.

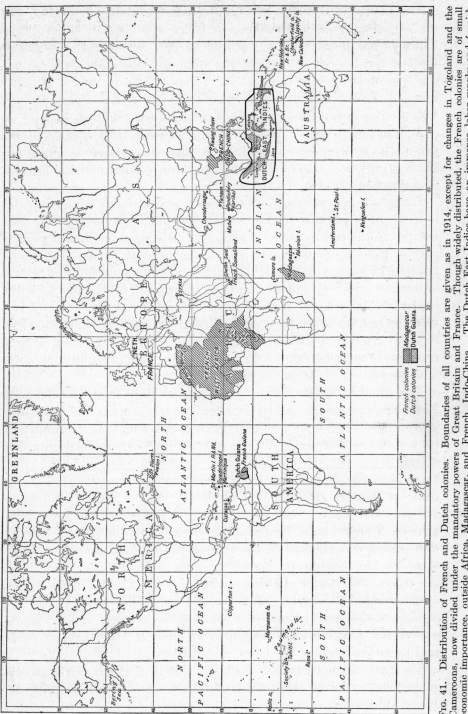

FIG. 41. Distribution of French and Dutch colonies. Boundaries of all countries are given as in 1914, except for changes in Togoland and the Cameroons, now divided under the mandatory powers of Great Britain and France. Though widely distributed, the French colonies are of small economic importance, outside Africa, Madagascar, and French Indo-China. The Dutch East Indies have an immense labor supply and furnish heavy exports of raw materials — fibers, rubber, coffee, spices, etc.

The Taurus ranges shut Syria off from the Anatolian plain (Fig. 42), for the great pass in the Taurus, called the Cilician Gates (Pylæ Ciliciæ), has long been in Turkish hands. The effective northern frontier has been the ranges of the Amanus Mountains, with a passageway at the Syrian Gates (Pylæ Syriæ). The mountains of Lebanon terminate Syria on the south, though the Syrian claims include Palestine and even the peninsula of Sinai on the Red Sea.

A desert separates Syria from Mesopotamia. On the eastern border of the better-watered coastal strip are the sown lands, the grain-growing regions. One of the richest of these is Damascus and the belt of country south of it.

Damascus lies well out in the desert, and a desert strip separates it from the sown land on the west. It is far from the sea and does not lie on a natural route of commerce. Yet it has endured from the earliest times by reason of its advantageous situation on the alluvial deposits of a river that runs eastward from the mountains and waters a hundred and fifty square miles of otherwise desert land. It is the oldest, the largest, the richest of the cities of Syria, an object of empire throughout its history, and of sufficient political importance to draw to it much of the through trade that would follow other natural courses if topographical considerations only were taken into account. The population of Damascus exceeds 250,000.

The interests of France in Syria do not date from recent times. From the days of the early Phœnician traders, long before the Christian era, Marseilles in southern France had maintained commercial intercourse with Syria, and the relationship has remained unbroken to this day. During the Crusades, France took the lead in the effort to redeem the Holy Land from Mohammedan conquerors. It was quite a natural thing that Frenchmen should thereafter become the rulers of Syria. Antioch and Tripoli had French princes, Jerusalem a French king. France, "the eldest daughter of the Church," had played a noble part in the redemption of lands sacred to Christians, and in recognition thereof the Pope conferred on French kings the title of "Protector of Oriental Christians." Castles in the French style were built in Syria; Marseilles, in competition with Genoa and Venice, established commercial and political ties. Silks, pearls, spices, and camphor were brought from India to Palestine and Syria, and thence to France, Germany, and England.

The material aspects of French interest in northern Syria are displayed chiefly in the silk industry and the railroads. Excepting the Hedjaz line, every railroad in the country has been financed by French

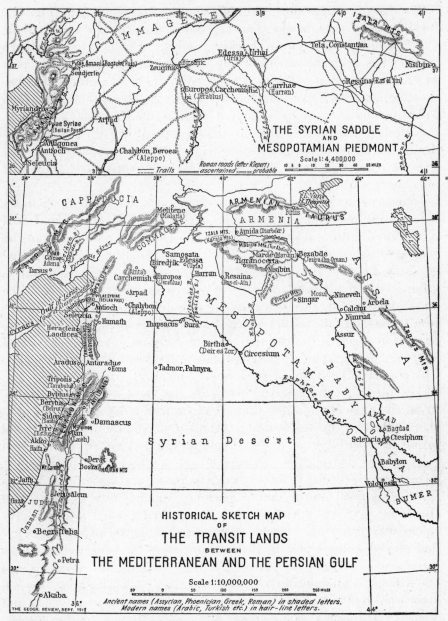

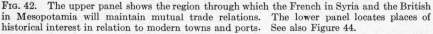

FIG. 42.   The upper panel shows the region through which the French in Syria and the British in Mesopotamia will maintain mutual trade relations.   The lower panel locates places of historical interest in relation to modern towns and ports.   See also Figure 44.

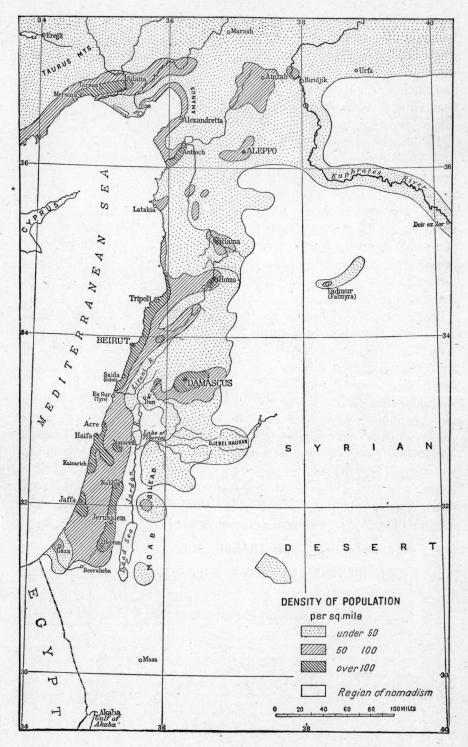

DENSITY OF POPULATION

per sq. mile

under 50

50   100

over 100

Region of nomadism

0   20   40   60   80   100 MILES

capital. The silk factories of
Lebanon, the most important
single industry in the country,
were founded by Frenchmen,
and their annual product, estimated at a million pounds of
silk, is exported to France.

To all these long-standing
causes of interest in the political affairs and trade of the
Syrian coast, there has been
added the effect of French
thought and life on the people
of Syria. French schools are
more numerous throughout the
former Turkish territories than
those of any other nation.

There is need of France in
Syria and elsewhere in the
Near East, in the interests of
western civilization and as a
barrier against anarchy and
Mohammedanism. England
alone is unequal to the task.

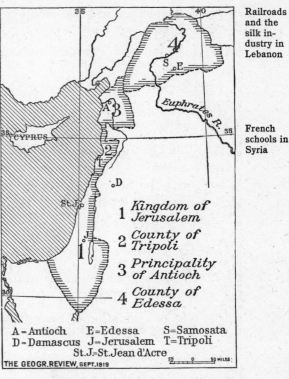

Railroads
and the
silk in-
dustry in
Lebanon

French
schools in
Syria

1 *Kingdom of
Jerusalem*

2 *County of
Tripoli*

3 *Principality
of Antioch*

4 *County of
Edessa*

A = Antioch   E = Edessa   S = Samosata
D = Damascus J = Jerusalem T = Tripoli
St.J.= St.Jean d'Acre

THE GEOGR. REVIEW, SEPT. 1919

FIG. 44. Syria under French princes, after the
Crusades. After Shepherd.

The growth of the desire for independence among the Syrians, as
opposed to French control, is shown in a specific way by the action of
the General Syrian Congress held at Damascus on 2 July 1919. This
congress is one of the most important political events in the past
several years in Syria. The principal features of its program (the
so-called Damascus program) are as follows:

The Damas-
cus pro-
gram

(1) Complete political independence.

(2) Constitutional monarchy with the rights of minorities guaranteed.

(3) Assistance from the United States for twenty years in financial
and technical matters.

FIG. 43. The Damascus population group is dependent upon irrigation. The city is a central
point in the caravan trade of the desert of Syria. Djebel Hauran, Gilead, Moab, and the
plateau of Judea are foci of heavier rainfall and population. The coastal fringe of population
also corresponds with a belt of heavier and more dependable rainfall. The nomad of the Syrian
desert has always coveted the crops and raided the villages of the settled oases dwellers. See
also Figure 45. From *L'Asie Française*, February 1920.

(4) A protest against the creation of a Zionist state, which is considered a grave menace to the bulk of the people.

(5) Lebanon and Palestine not to be separated from the rest of Syria.

(6) Complete independence for Mesopotamia.

(7) The annulment of all agreements previously made by France and Great Britain for dividing Syria or establishing Zionism.

A still bolder step was taken in March 1920. Another Syrian congress was held at Damascus and the independence of Syria was declared, with the Emir Feisal as King. The text of the Declaration of Independence adopted by the Syrian Congress is as follows:

"The Conference declares:

(1) The complete independence of Syria within its natural boundaries, from Sinai to the Taurus, and from the Syrian desert to the sea, without any protectorate, mandate, or other form of foreign interference.

(2) The proclamation of Emir Feisal (son of the King of Hedjaz) as King of Syria.

(3) Compulsory military service.

(4) The notification of the representatives of the European powers, and of the Peace Conference at Paris, of this decision."

The matters in dispute between Great Britain and France on the one hand and the Arabs on the other are still in process of negotiation. In the meantime, the aggressive attitude of Emir Feisal has led to French military action. In July 1920 Damascus was taken; a heavy fine was levied against the city, and Feisal was driven away.

Moslem opposition to Zionism

In the summer of 1919 an American commission was sent into the country to inquire into the wishes of the people of Syria and the needs of the country. It was found that if the people of Syria had a free choice, they would undoubtedly prefer Emir Feisal as ruler. They wish also to see Syria extended southward to include Palestine, as in the days of the Crusades. They certainly do not wish Palestine to become a Jewish state, since the Jews constitute only a little more than one tenth of the total population. They believe that in a Zionist state the Jews would secure political control and would not respect the holy places as impartially as would an outside, established

Fig. 45. Relief map of Syria to serve as a reference in the study of Figures 42 and 43, which show respectively the historic routes and the density of population.

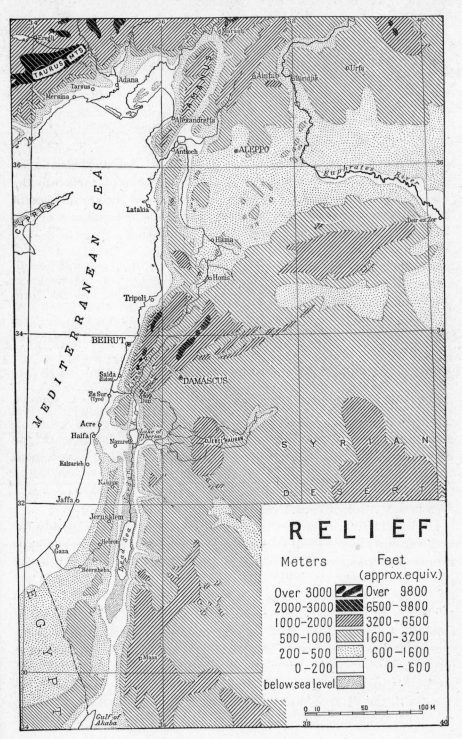

RELIEF

Meters   Feet
(approx.equiv.)

Over 3000   Over 9800
2000-3000   6500-9800
1000-2000   3200-6500
500-1000   1600-3200
200-500   600-1600
0-200   0-600
below sea level

0   10   50   100 M

power, for the so-called "holy places" include places sacred to the Christian and to the Moslem as well as to the Jew.

The Catholics of the Lebanon, as well as the Maronites, prefer French ownership or protection, and in using the word "Lebanon" they mean really a greater Lebanon outside of Syria. On the other hand, the Moslems wish American or British assistance, combined with political independence. The Druses are everywhere opposed to France.

The Lebanon

The Lebanon was set off from Turkey in 1861 under the nominal protection of six European powers, with a Christian governor. The population is composed chiefly of Maronites, who are attached to the Roman Catholic Church. After an international régime was established, there was an almost complete change in the conditions of life, military service was abolished, the taxes were reduced, a great deal of wealth was accumulated, roads were built, orchards were planted. The population of the Lebanon is more than 200,000, or 160 to the square mile, while the rest of Syria has but 30 to the square mile; about 350,000 are Christians, about 50,000 Druses, and the small remainder is Mohammedan. On 1 September 1920 General Gouraud proclaimed the autonomy of the Lebanon. Beirut is the seat of government. From Palestine the district given autonomy extends northward to the River Kebir, which empties into the Mediterranean due west of Homs.

The Jews have sought to include the southern Lebanon within the new boundaries of Palestine. To this arrangement is opposed the fact that the Phœnician coast shows practically no influence traceable to Jewish culture and has never been under effective Jewish occupation. Nor was the civilization of eastern Palestine, beyond the trench of the Jordan and the Dead Sea, ever Jewish: it was Greek, Roman, Byzantine, or Christian Arab. Over it the Jew has never exercised control, except temporarily after conquest.

The Sykes-Picot agreement

During the World War, the British and French diplomats framed the so-called Sykes-Picot agreement, which was designed to give France permanent rights in Syria and to delimit French and British power in Armenia, Mesopotamia, and Syria. Of great importance for a time, this agreement has now been set aside.

British troops replaced by French in 1919

Though all of Syria was overrun by the British troops under General Allenby, it was agreed, before the task of occupation was begun, that military success or failure should have no bearing upon the future political control of that region. Therefore when it became necessary to provide a somewhat more permanent form of government until the Turkish treaty could be arranged, the British troops evacuated not only Syria but Cilicia, and their place was taken by the

FIG. 46. West of Damascus are the mountains of southern Lebanon, from which descend toward the east a number of small streams that water a large tract of very dry country. Damascus has been proclaimed the capital of the Arab nation, but the Allies have not recognized Arab independence, and French military forces hold the town.

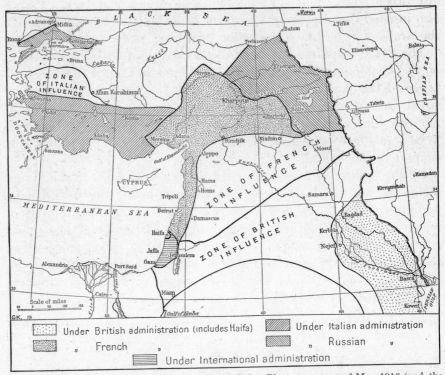

Fig. 47.　Division of Turkey according to (1) the Sykes-Picot agreement of May 1916 (and the later Italian agreement); (2) the secret treaty of London of 1915 as it affected the Straits Zone at Constantinople, the Italian sphere of influence in southern Anatolia, and the Russian sphere in Turkish Armenia.　From maps and text in the *Manchester Guardian*, 8 and 10 January 1920. International boundaries as of 1914.

French (November 1919).　French occupation was to extend eastward only as far as the Sykes-Picot line, but it was specifically agreed that this arrangement in no way prejudged the question of mandates or boundaries to be determined in the future.

It was agreed also that British troops should occupy Palestine up to the ancient boundary — that is, from Dan to Beersheba — and Mesopotamia, including Mosul.　It was further agreed that France should protect the Armenians; and that the cities of Damascus, Homs, Hama, and Aleppo were to be garrisoned by Arabs.　When these arrangements were put into effect, Arab hostility to French occupation obliged the French to proceed against Feisal and take Damascus, as already described.　The French also seized Aleppo and thus held the gateways to the desert.

French position respecting Syria　　The French insisted that the basis of any new plans for the disposition of Syria should be the Sykes-Picot agreement.　This meant that they could not see Mosul and Palestine go to Great Britain or to any other power, unless France got concessions in return.   France also insisted that she should have the same status and relations with the Arabs of Syria that England had with the Arabs in Mesopotamia.

The Syrian situation had been further complicated by the creation of the kingdom of Hedjaz in 1915.   Through Emir Feisal and his father, King Hussein, special agreements had been made between Great Britain and the Arabs, and the Emir long received a large monthly subsidy from the British government.   France did not wish to be bound by any of these British-Arab agreements, all of which lent support to the idea of Arab independence. French opposition to Emir Feisal

By the Sykes-Picot agreement the eastern boundary of the Syrian region lay west of the Damascus-Medina railroad; this would have permitted France to hold only the coastal portion of a broad group of regions, and France wished to control the interior pastures, farms, and cities of Syria from Aleppo to Damascus and beyond.   France insisted on the frontiers of 1916, with rectifications based on geographic and ethnographic grounds.   She also sought concessions at Mosul for petroleum and pipe lines, claiming these on terms of equality with British oil

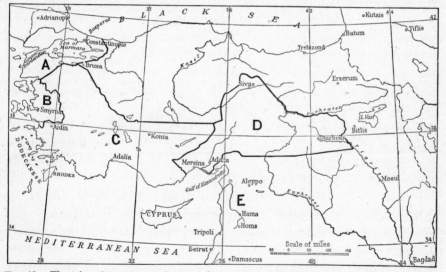

Fig. 48.   The tripartite agreement between Great Britain, France, and Italy (10 August 1920) regarding equality of commercial privileges in the respective spheres of influence of the signatory powers.   This agreement displaces the provisions of the secret treaty of London of 1915, the Sykes-Picot agreement, and certain other special agreements and promises.   By its terms Italy gains recognition of her special interests in Zone C, and France in Zone D; the three powers give each other diplomatic support in their respective spheres; provision is made for the capitalization on terms of equality by British, French, and Italian bankers of the Bagdad railway and other lines; the coal basin of Heraclea (on the north coast of Anatolia, east of the Bosporus) is to be exploited by Italy with French and British reservations.   On the map, A represents the southern, or Asiatic, part of the Zone of the Straits, B represents the Greek zone at Smyrna (Fig. 161), and E represents Syria.

interests in Mesopotamia and Kurdistan, as France is in great need of petroleum in her home territory. Matters were finally settled when France relinquished claims upon Mosul, where her sole interest was petroleum, in return for the privilege of getting one fourth of the oil that Great Britain secures in Mesopotamia. This was good policy for Great Britain, because it gave her unrestricted control of the Tigris and easier access to central and western Kurdistan. France also grants to the British the right to build oil pipe lines to the Mediterranean, across the French sphere of influence in Syria, in return for the privilege of buying one fourth of the oil that may be piped in this way from Persia.

Present possibilities of a united Syria

There can be little hope that a greater or united Syria will be established, owing principally to the unwillingness of Great Britain and France to withdraw from their respective spheres of military occupation. Yet if Syria should break up into small units, the effect would unquestionably be to perpetuate the old religious differences. This is one of those rare times when men's minds and plans are in a state of change, a time of political experiment. Some statesmen think that before new habits of intrigue and religious rivalry are formed, it would be well to make a united state out of these diverse religious and racial elements — one in which religious hatreds would become lessened in the common thought that men would give to political experimentation and a new economic life.

The Arabs of the desert wish to hold the settled coastal strip, but there is one clear historical argument against such an arrangement: the desert Arab has never long held or effectively governed the people of the settled lands. There are strong ethnic reasons also. We commonly think that the pure-bred Arab nomads of the desert typify the Arabian population. But they have little in common with the Arabs settled on farms or in towns, as in Mesopotamia and Syria. In addition there is considerable variation among the Arabs in the matter of racial purity. Those in Syria have become modified in part by invading stocks; those of the Yemen have probably as much east African as Semitic blood in their veins.

Many political writers see only selfish aims in the efforts of the strong powers to maintain themselves in some of the most important localities in the world. But one thing is tied to another politically in such a way that many motives, rather than one, control the actions of the powers. Hedjaz could not rule Syria. It is far away; the new kingdom is poor and weak; and the leaders on whom the King of the Hedjaz could call for help are few in number and quite without the necessary experience. The business of governing is not simple; it is difficult and costly. Left to themselves, the people of backward countries become the prey of strong and selfish nations, or create disorder, or join with other weak people and make first political and then military trouble for neighboring nations.

FRENCH INTERESTS IN NORTHERN AFRICA

Morocco

French popular interest in northern Africa has long been keen, and the economic development of the region has been steadily promoted. Morocco is first in importance and is of international interest because it in part controls access to the Mediterranean. The country is divided into three zones (Fig. 50):

(1) Tangier, under international control.

(2) The narrow Spanish Zone, south of Tangier.

(3) The French Protectorate, including most of Morocco.

By international agreement Tangier has been administered by the resident diplomatic corps. It is probably the most instructive example of the difficulties and penalties of joint government of a town by representatives of the great powers. Until it is put into the hands of a single power, or until the authority now exercised by different men is consolidated in the hands of a single administrator, the people of Tangier will be subject to unjust treatment and the commercial possibilities of the region will not be developed. The trouble dates back to 1856, when, by the terms of the British-Moroccan treaty of that year (later supplemented by the Spanish-Moroccan treaty of 1861), a "system of capitulations" was established, which has lasted down to the present day and which exists in modified form in the Spanish Zone as well as in the area of the French Protectorate. In 1880 the capitulations were codified, and any benefits under them were to be equally enjoyed by the subjects of all foreign powers. In 1904 England and France exchanged forms of recognition, the one declaring that she abandoned all political interests in Morocco, the other making a similar declaration respecting claims in Egypt. Each nation, furthermore, undertook to support the other's policy.

Unsatisfactory status of Tangier

In the same year France and Spain came to terms as to their spheres of influence in Morocco, and this date (1904) therefore marks the beginning of the division of Morocco into three distinct spheres.

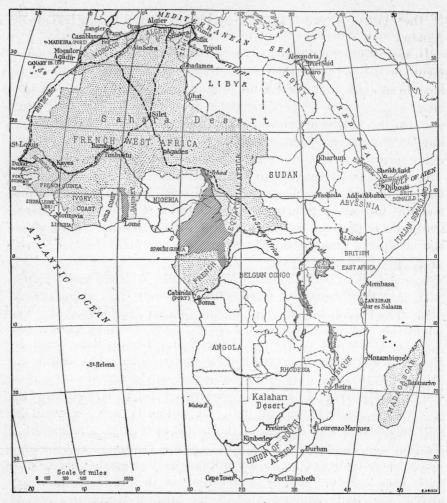

Fig. 49.   French possessions in Africa.   The dotted areas were acquired before 1914; the cross-lined areas are under French mandate.   Two small areas north and south of Ghat in Libya were ceded to Italy by France in 1919 in pursuance of that article of the secret treaty of London, 1915, which stipulated that Italy was to have grants of territory in Africa from both France and Great Britain provided these two powers gained territory in that continent.   Great Britain made similar frontier adjustments on behalf of Italy in Libya and Somaliland (Fig. 74).   The map also shows existing and proposed railways in French Africa.   Most interesting are: (1) the trans-Saharan projects, which would link North Africa with British South Africa and the Guinea region; (2) the coast project from Morocco to Dakar, which, if connected with the Spanish system by a Gibraltar tunnel, would cut the time from Paris to South America by nearly a week.

— Tangier, the Spanish Zone, and the French Protectorate, — though the treaty with Morocco providing for the French Protectorate was not signed until 1912.   France's treaty of 1912 was signed with the Sultan, Mulai Hafid.   It was the outgrowth of difficulties with Germany, following the conference of Algeciras in 1906, and especially of the threat of war in 1911 in connection with the events at Agadir.[1]

It was also in 1912 that the French and Spanish came to an agreement on the limits of their respective spheres. Since then, efforts have been made to frame a rational government for Tangier, but they have so far failed. The diplomatic agents of the various powers are also the judges in the courts, and citizens of each of the powers have extraterritorial rights, because it is impossible for a foreigner to enjoy security of life or property under a Moroccan administration. The Sultans of Morocco have delegated to the foreign representatives matters of trade, public health, and general administration, and this fact has still further complicated life for the native. Public works are neglected; the population continues to suffer from a shortage of water; commercial efforts are not organized; social legislation is practically unknown. *French penetration and extension of political power*

So much the greater part of Morocco lies in the French portion that the administration of the whole region may fairly be considered as a French problem, in spite of the other foreign interests. The population of French Morocco is between 5,000,000 and 6,000,000, and the area is 220,000 square miles. If the arid lands were irrigated, forests protected and replanted, and the locust plagues controlled, the population might be increased as much as 500 per cent. *The present status of the French in Morocco*

To control Morocco might today be easier were it not that for several centuries the descendants of the Moors expelled from Spain have been spreading fanatical hatred of the European; and until recently, when the French began effective intervention, they defeated every effort to hold their land in European subjection. The long contest between Moors and Europeans is marked by more than one historic episode. One of the decisive battles in world history was that of Kasr-al-Kabir in 1578, when the Portuguese king and army suffered a terrible defeat with the most destructive consequences upon Portugal's future colonial history. For a few years (1661–1684) the British held Tangier, but eventually were forced to evacuate it. *A long and bitter contest*

Within the past fifty years France has intervened more and more often in Moroccan affairs. She has governed with rare ability,

[1] The Agadir crisis took place in 1911, when the German gunboat *Panther* was dispatched to the port of Agadir in Morocco, ostensibly to protect the commercial interests and the lives of German nationals, but really to check the French policy of expansion in Africa. At the moment of the crisis unexpected sympathy developed between France and England, and Germany was obliged to withdraw her demands under cover of the grant by France of extensive territory in French Equatorial Africa on the southern and eastern borders of the Cameroons.

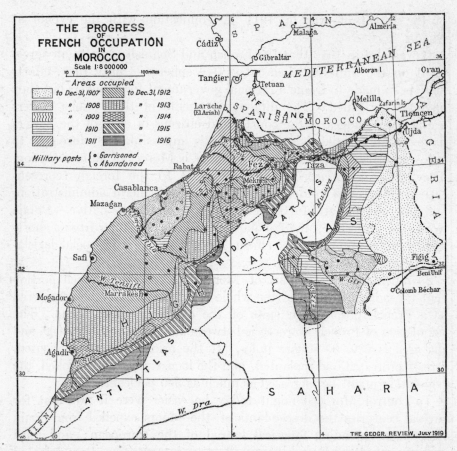

Fig. 50. Note the location and number of French military posts. From map in *Annales de Géographie*, January 1917.

though she would find her problem much easier if she could get rid of the Spanish Zone, which is a refuge of brigands and political agitators. This she cannot do, for Spain considers her Moroccan territory of special political value, possibly of ultimate commercial value, and will not relinquish it (page 154).

New international agreements respecting Morocco

The French government has declared the policy of the open door in Morocco, which guarantees commercial and industrial equality to all the Allied nations. The attitude of the French government is based upon the willingness of the Allied nations to surrender all special privileges of an international character which they formerly enjoyed. That is, the Moroccan people and rulers are not under special obligation to any nation other than France ; all outstanding obligations to other nations are canceled. German interests in Morocco have long been

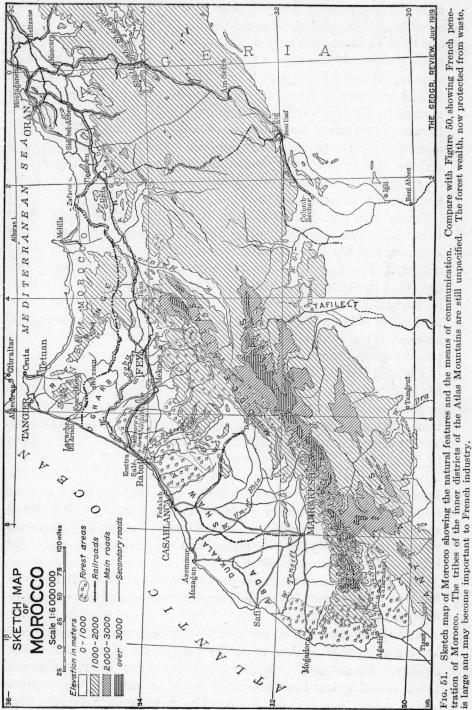

Fig. 51. Sketch map of Morocco showing the natural features and the means of communication. Compare with Figure 50, showing French penetration of Morocco. The tribes of the inner districts of the Atlas Mountains are still unpacified. The forest wealth, now protected from waste, is large and may become important to French industry.

of little consequence; but Germany pressed her claims upon every occasion, not because she hoped to control Morocco, where the French and Spanish interests had been longer established than her own, but because she wished to have a pawn in disputes with France elsewhere, as in Equatorial Africa (page 107). The treaty of Versailles carries a provision requiring Germany to abandon all rights and privileges granted by the General Act of Algeciras of April 1906 and the Franco-German agreements of February 1909 and November 1911. Germany further renounces all treaties and agreements between herself and the Moroccan Empire, abandons the régime of the capitulations (carrying servitudes in favor of European nations, including herself), and gives up all mining rights.

French supervision over Moroccan government affairs

Before the period of European intervention that began about 1875, the Sultan of Morocco had absolute power, both political and religious, and his immediate officers controlled all the affairs of the country. The French have continued this form of government, except that the French resident-general has become a kind of minister of foreign affairs. The French have also added such departments as those of public works, public lands, finance, agriculture, and postal service. Thus France exercises supervisory power over the sources of production and the means of exchange.

French development of ports, roads, and a good civil administration

Through her intelligence officers and her military and civil administrators, France has conducted her relations with the natives in the most delicate manner and with fine respect for the native customs, though sufficiently firm in carrying out the pacification of unsettled regions. In short, she has extended the best of her policies in Tunis and Algeria throughout all Morocco. She has developed the ports of Morocco, not only Casablanca as the major port, but also local ports like Kenitra and Mogador. In the matter of railroad building France was handicapped by the agreement of 1911, which required construction of the international Tangier-Fez line — on which work has only recently begun — to take precedence over other lines. Several narrow-gauge lines have been constructed, however, and an impetus has been given to road building. More than twelve hundred miles of metaled roads are open to traffic, and about the same mileage of other roads.

Agriculture and forestry encouraged

Agriculture has been encouraged by teaching the native Moroccan the advantages of modern methods and the use of agricultural machinery. Agricultural experiment stations have been established. Stock breeding has been taught in order to improve the strain of sheep, cattle, horses, and mules. The French have taken strong

Fig. 52. Casablanca, one of the seaports of Morocco. An airplane photograph showing the Place de France and the European quarter. From the *Geographical Review*, 1919.

measures for the protection of both the cork-oak forests of the littoral and the beautiful cedar forests of the Middle Atlas.

Algeria

Including the Saharan district administered with it, Algeria has nearly a million square miles, or four times the area of France; but it is only the coastal belts that are of present economic importance (Fig. 55). It is divided into four physiographic zones which run parallel to the Mediterranean coast:

(1) The Little Atlas, or maritime, mountain and valley belt called the Tell.

Physiographic divisions of the country

(2) The intermediate plateau of the Shat, marked by failing streams and salt lakes.

(3) The Great, or Saharan, Atlas range, with peaks that exceed six thousand feet in height.

(4) A second interior piedmont belt with intermittent streams, broad mud and salt flats, and the gravelly and sandy wastes of the northern Sahara.

The people are distributed chiefly in the coastal belt and in scattered oases in the interior. Their lot has been made easier in places

Figs. 53 and 54. The old and the new in Moroccan agriculture. To the primitive plow are harnessed any available animals — and even women. "It is not unusual to see a camel, an ass, and a woman drawing the plow," says Bernard (*Le Maroc*, 1913, p. 170). The introduction of modern agricultural machinery is, however, beginning to transform Moroccan agriculture.

by the good results of French irrigation, which has involved the
building of two large water-storage basins.

French control in Algeria dates from 1830, when the occupation of
several coast towns was carried out and negotiations with native
chieftains were begun. The effect of French occupation has been
to stabilize the social and business life of the people, remove the control of military chiefs who ran the country under nominal Turkish
sovereignty, and put an end to depredations upon Mediterranean
commerce by the Barbary pirates.

These results France was able to achieve only after a long struggle.
There was practically continuous native opposition to her control
from 1830 to 1847. Again in 1851, 1864–1871, and 1881, insurrec-
tions were put down. From that time on the country was sufficiently
quiet to enable the French to press inland step by step, until by 1905
their control of Algeria was extended also over the whole desert
interior. It is interesting to note that by the treaty of Sèvres
Turkey is to recognize the French protectorate in Morocco as of
1912, and in Tunis as of 1881, thus confirming French occupation of
northern Africa from Libya westward to the Atlantic, except Tangier
and the northern Spanish Zone.

There are about 4,750,000 native inhabitants in Algeria and in
addition 30,000 non-European whites and 750,000 Europeans (chiefly
French and Spaniards). Berbers form three fourths of the total
population. The present tendency is toward a decline of the European population, in spite of port improvements, the construction of
several thousand miles of railway, and the building of an equal mile-

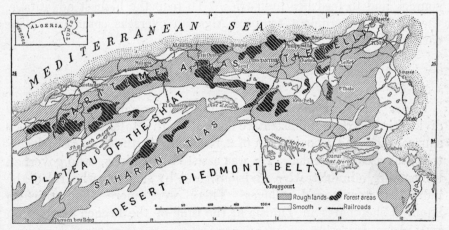

FIG. 55.   Generalized relief belts of Algeria and Tunis.   Forests from M. Marc, *Notes sur les
forêts de l'Algérie*, 1916.

age of first-class roads, besides telegraph lines and other modern facilities of commerce.

Decline of European population

The decline of European population is in part due to a bad system of land tenure. Boundaries are ill defined, titles are insecure, and much of the land is held in common by individual tribes. Though the French authorities have delimited many tribal boundaries and passed laws permitting the sale of family as opposed to tribal property in land, the tribesmen have not responded to the opportunity, chiefly because they saw the demoralizing effects upon families that, having sold their land, dissipated the proceeds and fell into a state of poverty. Those French colonists who have purchased state lands, hitherto unoccupied, have been compelled to live for a term of five years upon their holdings, and this obligation has further diminished the zeal of intending colonists.

The land of Algeria is capable of high production. The hilly maritime belt (fifty to one hundred miles wide), known as the Tell, grows cereals — chiefly wheat, barley, and oats — in abundance, especially since the increase of water supply brought about by the drilling of artesian wells. Olives, tobacco, and wine are produced in nearly all the cultivated oases of the interior valleys. Nearly a half-million acres are devoted to the production of grapes for wine.

Importance of Algerian products in French trade

A review of these and other exports of Algeria, like horses, sheep, oxen, wool and skins, fruits and oils, and a consideration of their total value,— which with imports now exceeds $250,000,000 annually, — will show the practical basis of French interest in the territory. The products are such as France needs to supplement her own resources and to feed her industries. To reap the highest advantage, the French government requires Algerian overseas commerce to be carried wholly in French ships.

Tunis

Plan of government under Turkish rule

Under Turkish rule and before the French occupation, Tunis was divided into sixty administrative districts with a total extent of 42,000 square miles and a population of 2,100,000. At the head of each district was a caid, or ruler. He was assisted by caliphs, who governed the smaller administrative divisions, and by sheikhs, who ruled the individual towns and villages. There were more than thirteen hundred sheikhates in Tunisia at the time of the French occupation in 1881.

The French in general retained the old system, except that they

Fig. 56.   A city of the Tell, Constantine in Algeria.   For location see Figure 55.

FIG. 57.   Oasis in the gorge of Kantara, Algeria, located in the Maritime Atlas (Fig. 55).

Changes introduced by the French

divided the country into territorial divisions, rather than according to tribes, and themselves reserved the privilege of appointing the tribal chiefs, or caids.

Semi-nomadic tribes of Tunis

The various tribes of Tunis numbered from a few hundred to many thousands in each district. Originally they were practically all semi-nomadic, and some of them were wholly so. Wherever there was good pasture, there they grazed their herds and flocks, and the size of the tribe was largely controlled by the size of the pasture, the nearness of towns or the sea coast, and their military strength, the purely nomadic tribes preying upon passing caravans or upon more settled people in the towns of the oases.

Unruly spirit of the Tunisian tribes

The French occupation was largely to prevent raids of the Khroumer tribes on Algeria.   There was a great deal of trouble in 1881 and also in 1887, but since then these tribes have devoted themselves more steadily to cattle-raising and agriculture. They number probably about 7000.   Some Tunisian tribes, such as the Drid and the Ouerten, composed of hard-working people who raise cereals, cattle, and sheep, have submitted peacefully to French occupation; others, like the Chaihia, have never become reconciled to it, and are ready for revolt at almost any time. Some of them were extremely unruly during the Turkish occupation, as for example the Souassi, who at one time

FIG. 58. Scene in the desert interior of French Algeria. Photo by Gautier in the *Geographical Review*, January 1921.

Brown Bros.

FIG. 59. In the northern sand dune belt of the French Sahara.

were obliged to flee into Tripoli, but returned to Tunis as a result of famine. They number about 37,000 and at present are engaged in agriculture. The Neffet, who are warlike and fanatical, have more than once revolted against the Turkish government. They are occupied chiefly as shepherds, but own some palm groves in the oasis of Gabes (Fig. 55).

The native way of life

In the Nefzaoua district there are nearly fifty villages scattered among the oases and surrounded by sandy soil and sand dunes. The population is engaged in the cultivation of date palms and numbers about 10,000. Formerly the villages bought protection from nomad raids; but with French occupation and the pacification of the wild frontier tribes this is no longer necessary.

A large number of the tribes of Tunis live in a confederation called Overghemma. They are supposed to number nearly 50,000. Some of these have fixed dwellings; others are nomads. For a time after the French occupation they kept the border districts in a constant state of turmoil; but gradually they were driven out or subdued, and the frontier regions are now kept in order by a string of fortified posts.

Difficulties of administration over these people have been most admirably met by France. Tunisia, indeed, is often held out as a model in this respect. In the present state of the country and the future prospects there is promise of reward to France for the drain upon her military and economic resources entailed by occupation and pacification.

CHAPTER FOUR

BELGIUM AS A EUROPEAN FOCUS

THROUGHOUT recorded history Belgium has been a battle ground of rival tribes and nations. As early as the middle of the 17th century she had been called "the military arena of Europe" — and since that time she has continued well to deserve the name. For more than two hundred years previous to the War of the Spanish Succession (1702–1713), Belgium was ruled by the Spanish Hapsburgs. As a result of that war she was handed over to the Austrian Hapsburgs, the dynasty which continued to rule Austria-Hungary until that country surrendered to the Allies in November 1918. In 1792 an army was sent by France, then in the midst of her great Revolution, ostensibly to free Belgium from Austrian rule; but before long Belgium found herself annexed to France, and French domination continued until 1814. *Belgium as a European battle ground*

At the Congress of Vienna in 1815 the wishes of the Belgian people were again ignored; for instead of becoming independent, Belgium was joined to Holland to form the Kingdom of the Netherlands, in order to improve the defenses against France. But there were differences of language, religion, and economic interests between the two peoples that could not be reconciled after a separation of one hundred and thirty-five years, especially as the Dutch took care to enforce the use of the Dutch language and to occupy the best offices of the government. In 1830, when the news reached Belgium that Charles X, the Bourbon king of France, had been deposed by his subjects, the country was profoundly stirred. Petitions were sent to William I, king of the Netherlands, asking for the administrative separation of Holland and Belgium. William replied by sending an army to put down the ensuing disorders, whereupon Belgium declared and won her independence. Her final status, however, was not settled until 1839, when Holland accepted the treaty of London, which, in 1831, had established Belgium as "an independent and perpetually neutral state." This was the treaty which was broken by Germany when she invaded Belgium in August 1914. *Winning of independence*

Thus the World War saw Belgium affected by only the latest and most grievous of a long succession of servitudes and disasters. The reason for her melancholy history is clear: she stands upon the great world highway that joins central and western Europe. She has suffered, not because of her own ambitions, but because of the ambi- *The dissipation of human energy on the battlefields of Flanders*

119

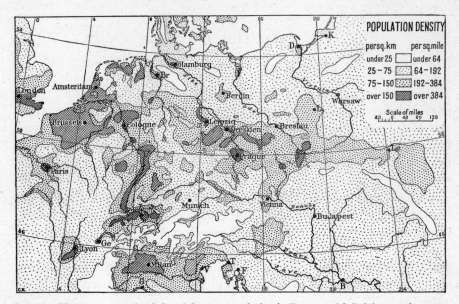

FIG. 60. The two converging belts of densest population in Europe, with Belgium at the meeting place. Cities with a population exceeding 500,000 have their names spelled in full; those with a population less than 500,000 are indicated by initials only. Based on Andree, *Handatlas*, Sheet 31.

tions of others who have struggled for supremacy on her soil. Her shattered hopes have been the evidence of her neighbors' greed. It would be difficult to measure the human energy that has been dissipated and perverted upon the fields of Flanders; it is imperative that means be devised for preventing a recurrence of so terrible an expenditure.

Growth of industrial power

If the position of Belgium has brought her tragic consequences in times of war, it has nevertheless given her prosperity in times of peace. During the 19th century, and in spite of her small size, Belgium became a great industrial nation. In 1910 her population (7,500,000, or more than 650 to the square mile) was comparable to that of Pennsylvania, whose area is four times as great. She was the third greatest industrial nation of the continent, mined considerable coal of her own, and had other valuable mineral resources, although her iron supply was wholly insufficient for her needs.

THE TASK OF REBUILDING

Present handicaps

The German occupation and the general effects of the war require that the industries of Belgium be rebuilt from their foundations. It is estimated that from 1914 to 1918 the country suffered damages totaling $7,600,000,000. Although she will receive 8 per cent of the

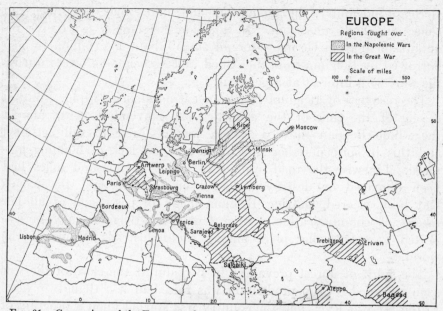

FIG. 61. Comparison of the European theaters of war a hundred years ago and today. The Napoleonic Wars are taken from Putzger, *Historische Schul-Atlas.*

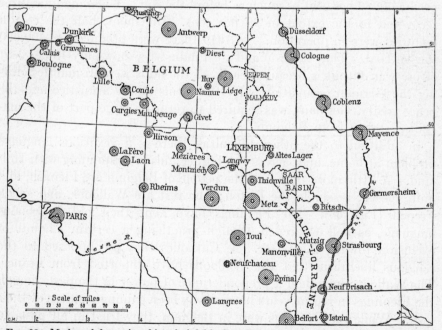

FIG. 62. Modern defenses in a historical field of conflict. Note the chain of German defenses on the Rhine, the belt of forts close to the French frontier, and the great forts of the intervening country, — Strasbourg, Metz, Namur, Liége, and Antwerp. There is a large industrial population between Paris and the northeastern frontier (Fig. 33). A dense industrial population also occupies the frontier zone of Germany on both sides of the Rhine. From map entitled *Guerre Européenne*, 1914, 1 : 1,200,000.

German indemnity, the amount of indemnity that the Allies can collect is wholly uncertain. In addition Belgium is to receive reimbursement from Germany for all sums (about five billion francs) borrowed by Belgium from the Allied and Associated Powers during the war, with interest at 5 per cent.

The work of restoration

The recovery of Belgium has been extraordinarily rapid. Within a year of the time of the armistice (11 November 1918), almost the whole Belgian railway system was restored to full activity, and this in spite of labor difficulties and the lack of building material. Likewise the road system, of which a thousand miles had been damaged or destroyed, had been restored and the canals had been cleared, putting Belgium again in possession of all her means of communication. In a few years Belgium may be expected to recover her place among the industrial nations of the world.

Revival of industry

The spirit of unrest prevailing in Belgium at the close of the war soon subsided. Crop production was raised in less than two years to the pre-war level, and the country was started upon a program of real economic revival. By the end of 1920 Belgium's industries were producing 80 per cent as much as before the war. Glass manufactures recovered to the extent of 98 per cent. In Ghent, half the cotton factories were in operation. In 1919 there were produced 18,500,000 tons of coal. That the iron and steel industries show only 18 per cent of pre-war output is because nearly all the mills were dismantled during the German occupation. By the terms of the armistice and the peace treaty, Germany was required to return a large part of the machinery taken from Belgium.

Flemish-Walloon problem

In addition to the other difficulties there is a vexatious language problem at home, and, across the border, misunderstanding with Holland. A little more than half the people of Belgium are Flemish, and quite closely resemble the Dutch; the rest are Walloons, and speak French (Fig. 63). The Flemings have kept their old indigenous language, as well as French, though practicing a certain amount of exclusion toward the latter. As Catholics they are opposed to the religious liberalism that the Walloons have imported from France. The Walloons have had a preponderance of power in the past, though the Flemings in recent years have slowly been gaining a status of their own. While the Germans were in Belgium, they tried in all possible ways to foster a separatist movement, and even promised the Flemings to guarantee their independence. But the Flemish people remained loyal to the idea of national unity.

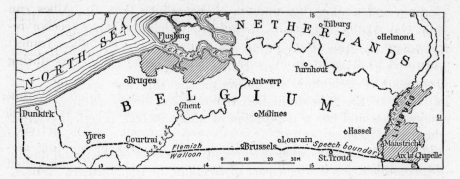

FIG. 63. The shaded areas represent the districts in Holland which Belgium would like to have. Possession of the one on the left would permit Belgium to improve the Scheldt and thus remove long-standing restrictions on the growth of Antwerp; possession of southern Limburg would increase the defensive strength of Belgium's eastern frontier. The Flemish-Walloon speech boundary is after Vidal Lablache.

BELGIAN CLAIMS TO ADJACENT TERRITORY

Belgium's misunderstandings with Holland arise out of her claims to Dutch Limburg and to the left bank of the lower Scheldt (Fig. 63). The Limburg region is inhabited by Dutch people and was given to Holland by the powers in 1839, greatly to the dissatisfaction of Belgium. Belgium would now like to have it back, chiefly on account of (1) its coal deposits, (2) its strategic value in the military defense of the country, and (3) its relation to the eastern water transportation routes. With the coveted strip in her hands, she could connect the Meuse and the Rhine by canal. This is an almost vital matter in a country having the densest population in Europe and the highest per capita mileage of railways and canals. Belgium feels that Holland cannot defend the region in time of war and calls attention to the fact that German troops retreating into Germany after the armistice of November 1918 crossed Dutch territory, thus violating the neutrality of Holland. Under the treaty of Versailles, however, Germany is not allowed to maintain armed forces in the region known as the Left Bank of the Rhine, and Belgium is therefore fully protected against a sudden attack from this side. *Limburg question*

As for the problem of the Scheldt, Belgium claims that the growth of her great port, Antwerp (on the Scheldt, 50 miles from its mouth), is largely at the mercy of Holland, which controls both banks of the river for a distance of 40 miles. By the treaty of 1839, regulations regarding pilotage, buoying, and dredging of this river must have the joint consent of Holland and Belgium. Holland, however, has prevented or delayed improvements of the river in order that Rotterdam might *Belgium's desire to share control of the Scheldt* profit at the expense of Antwerp. The negotiations between Belgium and Holland had for their object a guarantee to Belgium of the full use of the river in time of peace and of its improvement to meet Antwerp's growing needs; but Holland refused to yield, and no improvement of Belgium's status on the Scheldt was secured. The left bank of the Scheldt in Dutch possession covers an area of 275 square miles and has a population of about 80,000, practically all of whom are Dutch.

Relations with Luxemburg

Belgium has always wished to regain possession of the grand duchy of Luxemburg, for it was a part of Belgium, or the Southern Netherlands, until the French Revolution. In 1839 the western, or Walloon, portion was assigned to Belgium and the eastern, or German, portion became the grand duchy of Luxemburg as we know it today. Though its neutrality had been guaranteed in 1867, the duchy was occupied by Germany throughout the World War. Ever since 1842 it had been a member of the German Customs Union, and its railroads have been under German control. Both of these conditions are now set aside by treaty. The country is rich in iron and has some coal. France, to which the upper classes of the duchy have been very partial, has also been interested in the possession of Luxemburg. A plebiscite held on 28 September 1919 favored a customs union with France and a continuation of the rule of the reigning family. The grand duchy is a little smaller than Rhode Island, having an area of 1000 square miles, and it has about 250,000 inhabitants.

EUROPEAN AND COLONIAL ACQUISITIONS

Territorial gains in Europe and Africa

Belgium's territorial gains as a result of the war are very small. They include the following:

(1) Small additions of territory along the German frontier, in the Eupen, Malmédy, and Moresnet regions, with an area of 382 square miles and a population of 64,000 (Fig. 64).

(2) Ruanda and Urundi, a minor but agriculturally valuable part of former German East Africa (see Figure 65 and also page 125).

The additions on her eastern frontier were made in order to strengthen Belgium from a military standpoint. In 1839 the defensive strength of her frontiers was not thought a matter of great importance; but the invasion of Belgium by Germany, one of the powers that had guaranteed her neutrality, made it clear that the country is not safe as a neutral and must be given the means of defending herself in case of attack. Before the war Germany had built military railways leading to the border and along it that were a menace to Belgium's peace. One of Germany's famous concentration camps was at Elsenborn, near the Belgian border.

Strong dissatisfaction was expressed in Germany with the terms of the treaty of Versailles that provided for the disposition of the Eupen and Malmédy districts. Under Belgian supervision, all voters were permitted to express a preference for German ownership, but because voting took the form of signing an open register, the arrangement prevented the free expression of opinion. Only a few hundred persons registered a desire to have the districts return to Germany.

The Ruanda and Urundi districts in eastern Africa were assigned to Belgium in return for the help given by the Belgians in the

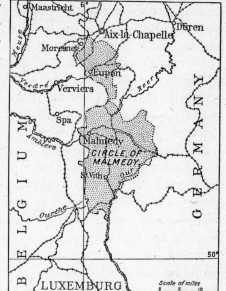

FIG. 64. The "circles," or administrative districts, of Eupen and Malmédy, which Belgium gained in 1920 by the terms of the treaty of Versailles. With these two industrial districts there was included, by treaty, the small tract of Moresnet which had been overlooked in the treaty of 1815 and was thereafter subject to international administration. The delimitation of the exact boundaries had not been completed by the boundary commission down to the end of 1920.

campaign for the conquest of German East Africa (1917). Belgium is to act as mandatary of the League of Nations. In ceding the two districts, Great Britain reserved small portions on the eastern side in order to have a practicable route for a railroad which shall join Tanganyika Territory (as former German East Africa is now designated) to Uganda. This portion of the line is a link in the Cape-to-Cairo railroad (Fig. 15). In return for these important concessions to the British, Belgium obtains valuable economic advantages, as follows:

(1) A free outlet for the produce of the east-central portion of the Belgian Congo by way of Lake Tanganyika to Dar es Salaam on the Indian Ocean. African concessions to Belgium

(2) Concession areas at Kigoma (on Lake Tanganyika) and Dar es Salaam on the eastern coast for the storage of goods.

(3) The right to transport merchandise from Lake Tanganyika to the Indian Ocean in Belgian freight cars.

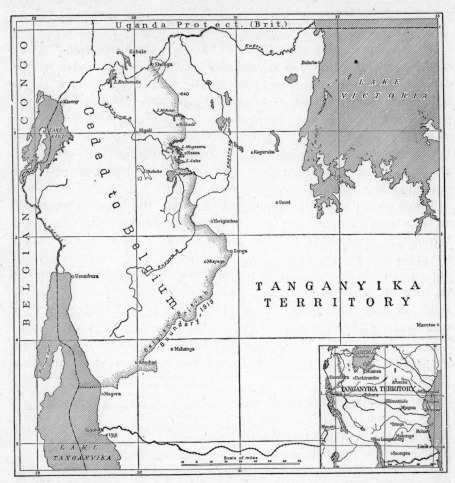

Fig. 65. The northwestern corner of former German East Africa, allotted to Belgium. It is densely populated and has a considerable extent of upland suitable for white settlement (Fig. 263). The part ceded to Belgium (districts of Ruanda and Urundi) has an area of 18,000 square miles and a population estimated at 3,500,000, or about half the total of former German East Africa. Agriculture and grazing are the chief native occupations.

Belgium thus gains in former German East Africa 18,000 square miles of territory of great economic value, to be added to the 1,000,000 square miles she already possesses in the Belgian Congo. Ruanda and Urundi are high plateau regions, the former culminating in the volcanic mountains northeast of Lake Kivu, the latter bordering on Lake Tanganyika. While climatically suitable for a white man's country, the territory has a dense native population, intelligent and independent. The soil is fertile and native agriculture is well developed; it is one of the most important cattle regions in Africa. Its mineral wealth is still unexplored.

THE BELGIAN CONGO

The economic value of the Belgian Congo is still unrealized. Most of the territory lies far inland, and this location has imposed a handicap upon both settlement and trade. The white, or European, population numbers only about 6000 persons; of these 3000 are Belgians, more than two thirds of them officials. The region is in great need of white colonists, chiefly planters and traders; and it needs capital to develop its resources. Its native population is variously estimated at from 7 to 15 millions, chiefly negroes in a low state of social and economic development.

Taken as a whole, the colony now involves the home government in little expense over revenues, which have been greatly increased through an improved but still unsatisfactory census that extended the application of the native tax. Cotton planting is done on a growing scale and has only begun to be developed in large regions favorable to very extensive production. The chief item of export is copper. Palm oil and rubber also figure in the export list. Katanga, the comparatively healthy upland rim of the basin in the southeast, is highly mineralized. The copper deposits are known to be among the largest in the world; already copper is exported to the amount

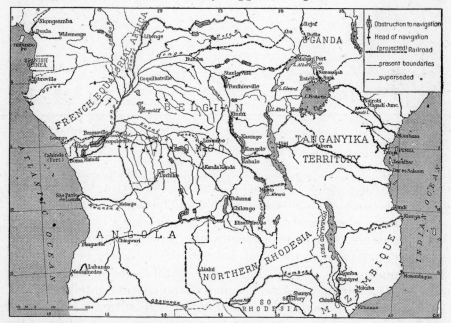

Fig. 66. Rail and water transportation in the Belgian Congo. Railroads from 1 : 2,000,000 map of Africa; data on navigability of rivers from G. Kaeckenbeeck, *International Rivers*, Publications of the Grotius Society, I, 1918.

of 27,000 tons, and the export of tin has begun. Diamonds (in the Vasai basin) and gold (in Welle) are other exploited mineral resources.

The state-built roads now aggregate more than 6500 miles in length. More than 1200 miles of railway have also been built, the existing roads being as follows:

Matadi-Leopoldville	240 miles
Stanleyville-Ponthierville	75 miles
Kindu-Kongolo	150 miles
Kabalo-Albertville	165 miles
Katanga Railway (completed to Bukama)	435 miles
Mayumba Railway	84 miles

These are supplemented by a water-transport system of many thousands of miles and by a series of wireless stations, at Boma, Stanleyville, Albertville, Kilo, Kindu, etc., which link the coast with the more important inland towns.

CHAPTER FIVE

THE ITALIAN SITUATION

No one of the other powers allied against Germany in the World War has come out of the struggle with so many threatening internal and external questions and so little increase of national territory in proportion to area, population, national debt, and war effort as Italy. The internal difficulties were bound to come; the external problems are chiefly of her own making.

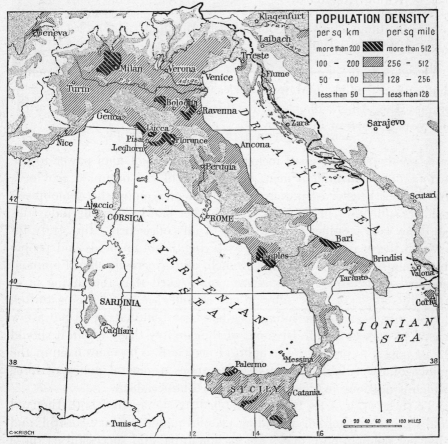

FIG. 67. Italy is about twice as large as the New England states and contains five times as many people. Only a few districts in the United States have a density of agricultural population as great as the cross-lined areas on the map above. From Agostini, *Atlante geografico metodico*, 3d ed., 1913. The line of the treaty of London, 1915, is shown by heavy dashes on the eastern border of the Adriatic. By the treaty of Rapallo between Italy and Jugo-Slavia, signed in November 1920, this line has been modified to form an international boundary, after a dispute that lasted for two years and frequently threatened war, owing to D'Annunzio's seizure of Fiume. See pages 259–270 for a discussion of the Adriatic question and a map of the new boundary (Fig. 138). The total Italian gains in Europe as a result of the war embrace an area of 8900 square miles and a population of 1,600,000.

Fig. 68.   The harbor of Trieste, western side of the Istrian peninsula.   While
chiefly by Jugo-Slavs.   The city

AMBITIONS FOR EXPANSION IN EUROPE

**Imperialistic
program of
Italy**

A great debt and small means to pay it, loss of man power to the
extent of a half-million men, devastation of the occupied provinces
on the northeastern frontier, unemployment among the demobilized
soldiers, difficulty in obtaining coal for her slowly reviving industries
— these were troubles grave enough in all conscience.   But Italy increased the anxieties of the time by trying to obtain lands and people
to which, according to British, French, and American official opinion,
she had no right.   These governments argued that the taking in of
unwilling aliens of quite different speech and race has in the past often
led to war, because the ruling race has been tempted, in all but a few
cases, to persecute and drive out of the country those whom it should
be its policy to protect; the habit of persecution becomes fixed in the
minds of the ruling class, and there arises a general policy of force
which is not long in changing into naked imperialism.

To these arguments Italy has replied by saying that both England
and France are holding unwilling peoples under military control, and
that her colonial enterprises are as honorable and successful as those
of her neighbors.

**Promises
made to
Italy in
1915**

If we study the situation of Italy in the light of Italian arguments,
we shall have a great deal of sympathy for her.   She entered the war
in 1915 with the distinct understanding that she was to gain large
territories.   On the north especially she sought territory to remove
the historic menace of Austria.   That power had crossed the great

Brown Bros.

the city is inhabited chiefly by Italians, the surrounding country is inhabited
was formerly Austria's chief seaport.

northern mountain wall and held the heads of the valleys that drain
the southern, or Italian, Tyrol; a first concentrated rush would bring
her down into the densely populated and fertile northern Italian plain
(Fig. 67). In this region, at least, Italy's expectations have been
realized. Elsewhere she has not been so fortunate. France and
Great Britain both promised her additional territory in Africa if they
gained African territory themselves. But in the final settlement
France was long unwilling to make any territorial concessions to Italy
in Africa, though the British government eventually surrendered
considerable tracts of territory in western Egypt and British Somaliland. In this matter, whatever reasons may have guided her, France
was clearly delaying a proper settlement of Italian problems. A
basis for final agreement was laid in 1920, when France and Italy
agreed upon a Libyan boundary, as shown in Figure 74.

In 1915 the French and British (and the Russian government of that
time) had agreed also that on the eastern side of the Adriatic Italy
was to gain territory as defined by the treaty of London line (Fig.
67). This agreement was made at a time when the old diplomatic
methods of settling a dispute were still in vogue; the powers thought
of themselves as victors rightfully taking spoils from the vanquished. With this point of view no one would disagree when the
vanquished had sinister designs on the nations they forced into a
terrible war, were it not for the fact that such a policy would merely
lead to another war. Now it was the thought of many of the soldiers
who died for their ideals that this was a war that should end war:

Purpose of the war

That could only be if the peace that followed the war were a just peace. Otherwise, as one statesman remarked, it would be "a peace that would end peace."

The dilemma of the political leaders

To grasp this principle in its full significance took a long time, and the idea was especially slow in gaining a place in the thought of the Italian political leaders. They felt that they had nothing tangible to show their people for the sacrifices of the war. A successful fight had been waged, but all they had to exhibit was a *moral* victory, and a moral victory will not buy coal and raw materials for factories, nor will it buy machinery and ships. For a long time the Italian mind dwelt on the practical rather than the idealistic aspects of the victory. The Allies, whether rightly or wrongly, came to distrust Italian political judgment and became anxious about her influence in Turkey and northern Africa.

It was asserted also that although Italy agreed to fight all the enemies of the Allies (treaty of London, 1915), she never made war upon Turkey, and declared war upon Germany only after she had been fighting with Austria for a year. She was to have a protectorate over central Albania only; but she really took control of all Albania. Fiume was outside the treaty of London line; but she claimed that also. Finally, she landed troops in southwestern Anatolia (Scala Nuova) without the authority of the other Allied and Associated Powers, and in fact against their strong protests. In many quarters it was said that the action of the Italian government in Anatolia was no less radical and unauthorized than that of D'Annunzio at Fiume. As a result of Allied protests, the Italians at last agreed to stay behind a demarcation line in Anatolia.

Italy obliged to give up conquered territory

Italy was requested to give up the things she coveted. She had taken the Dodecanese, a group of islands off the coast of Asia Minor, in 1912 at the close of the war with Turkey; but the islands are Greek in speech and race, and the Allies insisted that they be turned over to Greece. The Dalmatian coast is solidly Jugo-Slav, and this also Italy was urged to give up, though possession of it was promised in 1915 as an inducement to her to enter the war. Outside of Europe she made important but not large gains: additional territory in Libya (Fig. 74), a sphere in southern Anatolia (Fig. 48), ownership of the island of Castelorizzo near Rhodes, and Rhodes itself for a term of years. She also won the Trieste region and the Istrian peninsula besides a large tract in the Trentino as far north as the Ötzthaler Mountains, a district whose northern part is inhabited chiefly by German-speaking people who do not welcome Italian rule.

FIG. 69. Arco, on Lake Garda, in the southern Trentino. Part of the territory inhabited by Italians which was held by Austria until 1914, when it was "redeemed" by Italy as a result of the World War and the treaty with Austria.

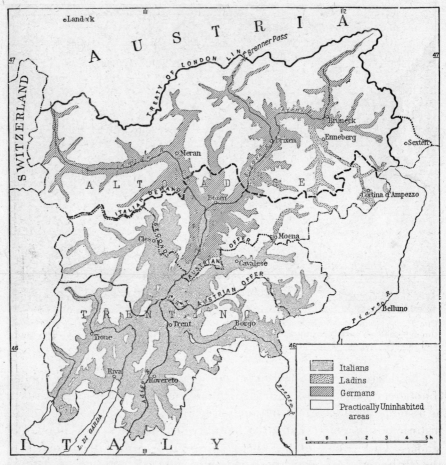

Fig. 70. The disputed territory of the southern Tyrol. Austria made two offers in 1915, the second of which would have given Italy most of her "unredeemed" people in the Trentino. Austria refused to make further concessions, and at length Italy went to war. By the treaty of St. Germain (1919) between Austria and the Allied and Associated Powers, Italy was given what she called her natural, or geographical, frontier in the Brenner Pass region; but it should be noted that she thus gains nearly 230,000 German-speaking people who are likely to create an irredentist problem as serious as that before 1914. From C. Battisti, *Il Trentino*, 1917, Pl. 3; O. R. Torniolo, *L'Alto Adige*, 1917, Pl. 1. Legend applies only to that portion of the map included within the limits of the Tyrol gained by Italy.

It was in the Trentino that Italy made her chief effort to win territory by diplomatic means after the war started in 1914. To keep Italy out of the war, Austria offered in 1915 to give her that part of the Tyrol ethnically Italian (Fig. 70). Italy refused the offer, entered the war, and by the treaty of St. Germain-en-Laye obtained all the territory south of the Brenner Pass, thus adding to her population about 230,000 German-speaking people. The irredentist problem of the Tyrol is not settled; it is simply transferred from Italy to Austria.

Fig. 71. View in the Brenner Pass region on Italy's present northern frontier. Southward through the pass have come the Teutonic invaders, again and again, to occupy the valley lands and threaten the rich northern plains of Italy.

The desire for territorial expansion and the increase of her foreign commerce is not a new thing in Italian life. It should not be taken as a sudden expression of national greed. It flows naturally from the historic position of Italian cities, notably Genoa and Venice, in oriental trade. They were among the greatest of Mediterranean marts of the 12th and 13th centuries, and only entered a period of definite decline when the Turk reached the coast of the Near East in the 15th century and the Portuguese in the early years of the 16th century developed the commerce of the route to India by way of the Cape of Good Hope. In the long period from the 10th to the end of the 18th century, Venice held the Dalmatian Islands and a large part of the coast. When the western European powers were pushing on to new colonial fields in America, the Far East, and Africa, Italy still moved in a Mediterranean orbit. Trade, not territory, was the limited ambition of her regional leaders. *Historical basis of Italy's program*

In modern trade, however, territorial ownership is a vital matter. Tariffs, consular service, coaling and cable stations, spheres of influence, capital investments, and emigration, all have greater or less relation to diplomatic exchanges and advantages that spring from *Benefits of distant territories* actual ownership of exploited land and people. Italy has been slow and vacillating in building this idea into her national policy. Her present effort is designed to prevent her latest opportunity from escaping.

That Italy has pushed for advantages with her allies is also not strange when we remember her traditional enmity toward France. Up to 1915 Italy was still formally allied with Germany and Austria (the Triple Alliance). Suddenly she changed friends. Limited in her demands by the counter proposals of France, Great Britain, and the United States, her leaders were not sure of those practical advantages that they had expected. There was for a time, after the war, a growth of pro-German feeling. Thus Italy finds herself again in the middle of the road. Her future diplomatic and commercial orientation can scarcely be predicted.

INTERNAL POLITICAL AND INDUSTRIAL PROBLEMS

Union of Italian peoples

The domestic problems of Italy are large and menacing. It was only sixty years ago that she became a unified modern state, and the forces of disunion that long kept her the prey of foreign powers and that fostered the petty quarrels between neighboring states of the Italian peninsula have not yet been destroyed. The long struggle between the Vatican and the Court has kept her people divided. The good of the country demands a strong, unified government, and this can develop only if her domestic problems are solved.

Annual loss of population

Italy is one of the most densely populated states of Europe. The climate is sunny and the soil fertile; the crops are varied and abundant, the people industrious. But each year thousands of Italians emigrate to newer lands in the United States and South America. While many of them, having acquired a modest fortune, return to stay, and many others return for a season only, a greater number remain in the new lands. The children of Italy to a large extent become the citizens of the Argentine or the United States.

Lack of fuel for Italian industries

In part, this emigration is due to the lack of coal and petroleum. Without native fuel, Italy can develop certain manufactures only to the extent to which she can import coal. She must purchase coal from America and from England chiefly. While seventy-seven million tons of coal are to be exported to her by Germany in the ten years ending 1929, it is almost certain that this amount will be diminished. Not only does the lack of coal in Italy increase the cost of her manufactured wares to her own people;

it tends also to make her import her manufactured goods from abroad. The northern mountain regions will enable her to develop water power to take the place of coal in some degree; but this is a possibility of the future rather than a remedy for present problems.

Sulphur and mercury are the only minerals produced in large quantities in Italy. Italy held the mercury mines of Idria (Fig. 138) from the armistice of November 1918, and these, finally allotted to her by treaty with Jugo-Slavia, place her in the first position in the world in the production of mercury. Of the world's total of 4000

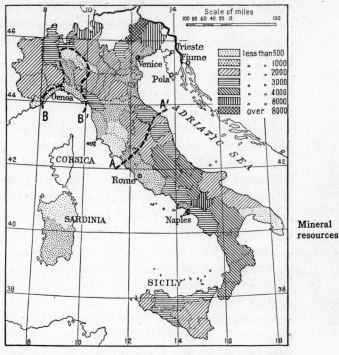

Mineral resources

FIG. 72. Average annual emigration of Italy's population for the years 1902–1906. Figures represent losses per hundred thousand. Below the lines *A-A'* and *B-B'* the emigrants go chiefly to the United States and South America. Elsewhere the emigrants go chiefly to other European countries. There are also migratory elements that return annually to the homeland. From Guido Assereto, *L'Italia e le sue colonie*, 1912, Pls. 30–31. For the final boundary between Italy and Jugo-Slavia as determined by the treaty of Rapallo, see Figure 138.

tons of mercury, Italy produced during 1919 nearly 1700 tons. The sulphur of Italy comes chiefly from the volcanic region of Sicily and constitutes 47 per cent of the world's total production. But it is a minor mineral, and its total value is not sufficient to make it the basis of such great industries as arise in the iron and coal fields of the world. At best, Italy is a poor country industrially.

The need for developing industries is the more serious for Italy at the present time because she has not the ready means, found in England and France, for absorbing her unemployed in factories and mills. Her people are poorer than before they entered the war, and for a long time to come the channels of trade and development will be clogged because of the abnormal conditions, and especially because of the waste produced by the war. This is bound to lead to general internal disorder, which in turn increases the number and

Strikes and the demobilization of large armies

seriousness of her problems. The strikes prevalent during the late months of 1919 and throughout 1920 have disarranged the machinery for coal importation and reduced fuel production at home, thus making heavy inroads upon Italy's limited supply of valuable timber. In some cities revolutionary workmen have taken over factories without opposition from the military forces, to the still further disarrangement of industrial life.

General lack of interest in politics, except in the cities

The government of the country is the result of struggles between determined leaders of the various parties or factions. The mass of the people have little voice in important decisions. For example, the labor party of the cities, the so-called proletariat, denounced D'Annunzio's adventure at Fiume and opposed the effort of the ruling class to make it fight for imperial ambitions. In a few cases, notably at Trieste, there was even a demand for a republic.

The greater number of the Italian people are farmers, who are on the whole without education and who take little interest in politics. (Figure 73 shows the distribution of illiteracy in Italy.) They are against communism; that is, they wish to keep the principle of private ownership. But in 1919 they did demand, and secure to some extent as a result of the fear of the government, the use of uncultivated lands on the large estates, the *latifundia*. There appeared to be no choice for the government in this matter, for early in October 1919, agrarian disorders, especially in the south, grew in intensity and in scale, and at one time reached a point that threatened civil war. They were especially marked in Sicily, where, in the first two weeks, thirty persons were killed and a hundred wounded. Peasants went about in armed bands, taking forcible possession of uncultivated estates. The disorders began to decline at the end of a month, stopped in less than three months, and revived for a time in 1920.

Italy financially hard hit by the war

The per capita wealth of Italy is lower than that of Great Britain, France, or the United States. She had just finished the costly war with Turkey in 1912 when she had a new war to face. Only by importing coal, iron, and cotton in order to increase her industrial production can she hope to pay her staggering war debt. At best it will be difficult for her to meet current expenses and the interest on her debts, to say nothing of paying the principal.

Altogether praiseworthy have been her efforts at financial reconstruction thus far. By practicing economy and by taxing her people heavily to pay for current expenses, Italy has shown a disposition to meet her obligations. If she continues in this course, her credit will be good, her money will rise in exchange value, her trade will

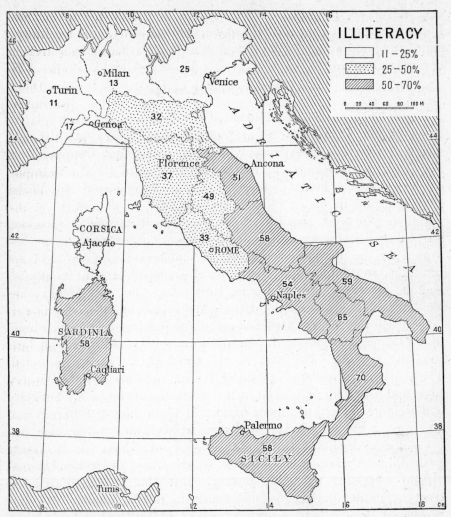

Fig. 73. Compare with Figure 72 to see how Italian illiteracy affects the character of the population of the United States. European neighbors of Italy get the largest number of emigrating literates, but character and literacy are not necessarily related. All territory outside the boundaries of 1914 is cross-lined downward and to the right. Compiled from data given on sheet 15 of Mori, *Nuovo atlante de geografia fisica, politica ed economica*, Vol. I, 1918.

increase. It will be a real test of Italian national character to come out of the present difficulties without throwing the country back into the state of disunion and poverty from which it rose only after so long and painful a struggle.

Europe and the world need a strong Italy. The genius of her people, their industry and strength, should be developed, not impaired. Relieved from the prolonged threat of invasion from the north, she can afford to reduce her army and navy to small size and

Reduction of armaments a boon to Italy

thus throw off one of the chief burdens of the past. The capital formerly spent in preparation for war will build dynamos, railways, ships, and factories, and will put her on the road to becoming a stronger commercial nation.

ITALIAN COLONIAL INTERESTS

Figure 74 shows the distribution of Italian colonies. Their relative poverty and unimportance are noteworthy. Every step in the direction of colonial expansion has been costly and disappointing. But Italian ambitions will not be satisfied until there are Italian colonies in the lands bordering the Mediterranean — in Adalia (Turkish) and in Africa (Berber and Arab).

Feeble and artificial colonial efforts
Italian efforts at expansion have been wholly artificial. Lacking internal political cohesion, without colonial experience, having no capital for the development of colonial enterprises, yet proud of her traditions and entertaining the hope of a revival of military powers and the ancient glories of Rome, Italy could take only feeble steps along the road by which Great Britain and France had passed to power.

Assab on the western Red Sea coast was purchased in 1870, whereupon Italian colonial ambition declined until 1885, when it was suddenly revived. The port of Massowah (Fig. 74) was occupied. The vast and continuous stream of Italian emigration, due to heavy taxes and a hard life, was to be turned into colonial channels. Yet Italy had no large modern merchant marine, and was obliged to import coal and iron for the manufacture of raw materials from possible colonies.

Colonial expansion took its most active form in East Africa. Italy pushed into Abyssinia, and in 1889, by the treaty of Ucciali, claimed virtual suzerainty over the country. But Menelik repudiated the treaty, claiming that it read differently in the Abyssinian text, and in 1896 at the battle of Adowa a force of 12,000 Italians was almost annihilated by an army of 80,000 Abyssinians. Italy was forced to give up her idea of an Abyssinian protectorate, and in addition she had to pay a heavy indemnity.

Only the Eritrea and Somaliland regions remained, with their arid climate and poor soil. A poor late-comer in the colonial field, Italy had only the crumbs that fell from the British and French tables. Yet the Italians have taken intelligent and energetic action with respect to the resources in their possession. They have built roads, trained native troops for police purposes, drilled artesian wells, built lighthouses, established schools, encouraged immigration, and regulated the water supply.

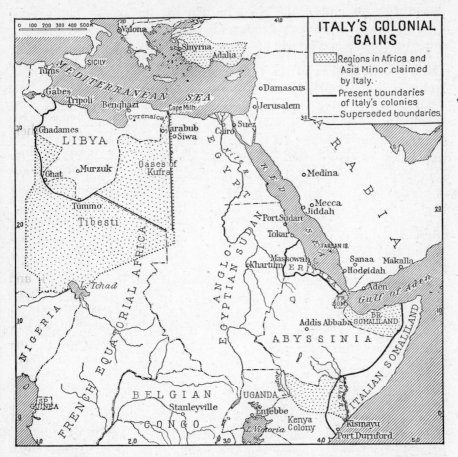

FIG. 74. Italian colonies. To Italy were assigned the islands of Rhodes and of Castelorizzo near the mainland of Anatolia. (See Figure 158.) Additions of territory, at British expense, were made west of Egypt and in the eastern part of Kenya Colony, and the French agreed to a rectification of the Libyan boundary. Based on *L'Afrique Française*, January 1920, p. 10; March 1920, p. 89; *Mouvement Géographique*, 15 August 1920, p. 438.

Of far greater importance to Italy than her own dependencies are Italian "colonies" established under other flags. Wherever the Italians have gone in large numbers — America, Argentina, Brazil — they have formed settlements of great benefit to Italian trade. Italian merchants have established branch houses, Italian newspapers have kept up interest in the homeland, Italian banks have facilitated the flow of credits. Returning emigrants, with large aggregate funds, have enriched Italy's national treasury and promoted home industries. It is in such colonies in large and rich commercial nations rather than in the poor national possessions in Africa that Italy has reaped real commercial benefits.

Libya (Tripoli)

In northern Africa, Italian interests center in the province of Libya, which became a part of the Italian realm as a result of the Turkish-Italian war of 1911–1912.

The Berbers and Arabs of Libya

Libya is the great region between western Egypt and Tunis. It is inhabited by Mohammedan Berbers and Arabs, both of which stocks are strongly mixed with negro blood, owing to the continual flow of slaves northward from central Africa. Slaves are still kept, and, until the Italian occupation, were exported from those parts of northern Africa that were in the control of Turkey. In Libya the Berbers have been pushed back into the mountains by the Arab invaders. In the large towns the Arabs are also mixed with Berbers, Jews, Egyptians, and natives of Algeria, Tunis, and European countries.

Mode of life of Arabs and Berbers

The Arabs came into Libya as a result of the Mohammedan conquest of the country in the 7th century. In the 11th century there came a still stronger inflow of Arab robber tribes. Their conquest of the coastal region was complete; but they were never able to extend their control far inland. They live in tents, own flocks and herds, and raise dates and other tropical products in the oases scattered along the depressions or along the upland borders where a little water is available. The Berbers are almost altogether sedentary, cultivating the soil and living in permanent habitations. The oases of the coast are fertile and well-watered in Libya, and these draw to them, in the harvest season, many nomadic tribes of the desert.

Division of the land into tribal territories

The nomadic tribes of Libya have a patriarchal organization, and property within the tribe is collective. Each family lives by itself in a group of fifteen or twenty tents, and a collection of families constitutes a tribe with particular ownership of oases and pasture land, beyond which it cannot go. The boundaries are clearly marked and recognized in the oases, but rather badly marked in the pastures, and quarrels are frequent. Even the largest towns are not big cities in the American sense of the word. Tripoli has about 73,000 people, Benghazi 35,000, and the others are much smaller.

The warlike Tuaregs

One of the most interesting tribes of northern Africa are the Tuaregs. They are warlike and engage chiefly in raiding caravans that traverse the desert. While a few live in Libya, most of them live farther west in the French colonies of Tunis, Algeria, and Morocco. They are treacherous and revengeful, and they have been brought under control by the French only with extreme difficulty. The Senussi (page 56) have some of their chief centers and strongholds in Libya, whence they wield great political and religious influence over Saharan tribes of Mohammedans, both near and remote.

During the World War, the interior of Libya and some of the coast line was recaptured from Italy by Arabs, Turks, and Germans working in coöperation. A final armistice with the Arab chiefs was not signed until 24 April 1919, when they agreed to recognize Italian sovereignty over the country. Operations in Libya during the World War

During the last few years the value of the trade leaving Libyan ports has steadily declined. Goods worth more than $3,000,000 were exported from Benghazi, the second port of the country, in 1905. In 1908 the exports amounted to a little more than $1,500,000, and in 1913 they had fallen to less than $200,000. This decline in trade was caused by the unrest and brigandage which prevailed in the interior, and by the success of the British and French in deflecting the trade of the Lake Tchad region to Egyptian and Tunisian outlets. Decline of Libyan trade

The interior of Libya does not seem capable of important development. In many places it is impossible to build railroads or construct roads, since in this portion of the Sahara the desert sand shifts to an unusual degree before the driving winds. Agriculture is possible only in the oases, and irrigation elsewhere is out of the question. To these natural difficulties must be added the fact that Italy has assumed a privileged position with respect to her colony, and foreign merchants must pay double the customs duties and anchorage charges collected from Italian shipping.

Under the Romans, Libya and Cyrenaica had a far larger population than they now contain. With the invasion of the Islamic Arab, the country was depopulated and large sections reverted to the desert. To control the population of 600,000 Berbers and Arabs, to reconcile the natives to European ideas and culture, to reëstablish the irrigation works, to destroy the locusts, — or at least to diminish their numbers, — and to carry out sanitary and educational measures, will be no easy task for Italy. Difficulties confronting Italian officials in Libya

The administration of Libyan peoples calls for adaptation to the spirit and needs and way of life of strange and hostile tribes. For years to come a considerable military force will be required merely to pacify the country. Moreover, the colony will not pay. It will not be possible to expand into adjoining fertile regions having a rich trade. Libya is a liability that will test Italy's interest in difficult colonial problems and her power of handling them.

Italian Interests in Asia Minor and Albania

After her war with Turkey in 1912, Italy sought privileges on the Turkish mainland opposite her new-won archipelago of the Dodecanese. Italian bondholders of the Ottoman Public Debt obtained a concession from the Turkish government for a railway line to run from Adalia on the coast to the inland town of Buldur at the southeastern end of the Aidin railway. By this means Italy hoped to win the trade of a rich coastal lowland region and its tributary valleys, whence subtropical products are exported, like rice, tobacco, opium, cotton, and fruit.

Italian operations in Asia Minor More recent advances of the Italians have emphasized their eagerness to win a foothold in Asia Minor. They occupied the harbor of Marmara as a coaling station and landed troops at Adalia in April 1919, when all that had been agreed to by the Allies was that Italy should have a battalion in Turkey. They also sent battleships to Smyrna and landed 500 men at Scala Nuova.

These operations of the Italians, taken independently of the other Allies, were a source of anxiety to the Greeks about Smyrna and to the French in Syria, and also caused grave unrest among the Mohammedans, who feared that even temporary occupation by the Italians would mean a loss of sovereignty or of important commercial advantages.

The final result of Italian ambitions in Asia Minor is conditional possession of the island of Rhodes. At the time of signing the Turkish treaty (treaty of Sèvres, 1920), Italy also agreed to relinquish the Dodecanese to Greece, except for Rhodes, which is to have a plebiscite in a few years. If the people of Rhodes vote for union with Greece, Italy will retire, provided Great Britain also retires from Cyprus — which Great Britain will probably never do.

The Albanian venture Equally disappointing to Italy has been her Albanian venture. Beginning with the occupation of large parts of Albania and claims to all of it as a protecting or mandatory power, she retired her troops to Valona, only to be driven out of this port by Albanian forces. On 3 August 1920 she signed an agreement with Albania by the terms of which she abandons Valona (much overestimated as the naval key to the Adriatic), but retains the island of Saseno, which commands it, and the use of the bay of Valona when necessary for shelter or refitting. Italy also has the right to occupy and fortify the two points of land that inclose Valona on the north and south, and to have freedom of action if the integrity of Valona and Albania is threatened. She recognizes the independence and unity of Albania, and hopes in this way to neutralize anti-Italian influence in both northern and southern Albania,

CHAPTER SIX

THE DEMOCRATIC DRIFT IN SPAIN

THOUGH Spain neither gained nor lost territory as a result of the World War, her international relations have taken on new aspects by reason of her participation in the fulfillment of the treaties that closed the war. She is a member of the Council of the League of Nations, and her representatives sit on several important commissions. She also enjoys a new status in the Spanish Zone of northern Morocco. Her financial condition is so greatly improved as a result of her active trade as a neutral during the war that she has entered upon a new period of industrial development. The features of Spanish life that may counterbalance these favorable conditions are the social instability of the people and the political instability of the state. In recent years there has been a rapid development of the radical, or socialist, movement in Spain, and the revival of a separatist tendency on the part of the provinces, a tendency which has manifested itself repeatedly in Spanish history, despite the unifying influence of the long struggle against the Moor.

RADICALISM IN SPAIN

The period of recent socialist activity corresponds roughly with the reign of Alfonso XIII, since his coming of age in 1902, though the impelling causes of unrest do not lie in the character of the king, who is popular, or in his influence in government, which has always been conciliatory and constructive. A few months before his coronation there were serious riots at Barcelona and Saragossa. In 1903 riots took place at Salamanca, Barcelona, and Madrid. Stimulated by a crop failure and a famine in Andalusia, rioting occurred in southern Spain in 1905; disorders led to the proclamation of martial law in Catalonia; Seville, Granada, Oviedo, Bilbao, and Valencia were centers of serious disturbance. In 1908 martial law was proclaimed in Barcelona, and the restoration of order was followed by the passage of laws that improved living conditions — at least to a modest degree — in the industrial regions. *Social and political disorder*

The more liberal policy of the government following these various disorders might have had a happy outcome had it not been for native troubles in Morocco, which required the increase of the Spanish military forces and the calling out of the reserves. In Catalonia there *Causes of recent trouble*

145

Fig. 75. General view of Toledo, a town of great historic interest as a center of Christian military organization in the reconquest of Spain from the Moors.

were strikes and disorders as a protest against the government's policy in Morocco. These had their center at Barcelona, where in July 1909 a revolutionary mob, consisting among others of Spanish workmen and disorderly spirits from South America and eastern Europe, attacked the convents and churches and engaged in three days of street fighting. It was necessary to establish martial law throughout the whole of Spain on 28 July, and for two months the country was kept in order only by military means. Ferrer, an anarchist and leader in the disorder, was tried by court martial and shot.

On top of these difficulties came the news of the defeat of the Spanish forces in Morocco by the Rif tribesmen, who were subdued only after six months of hard fighting. Thereupon trouble broke out afresh. Constitutional guarantees had to be suspended in 1911, owing to a general strike on government-owned railways. In 1912 another strike was avoided only by putting the military in control of the train service. To the opposition elements the government has become the symbol of inefficiency.

That Spain should have continued its traditional form of government without a general revolution is a tribute to its democratic king, for the liberal agitation that started before the beginning of his reign has never ceased. While the loss of the last of her American and Asiatic colonies, in 1898, might have enabled her leaders to turn their attention to domestic problems, the action of the radical elements in industrial regions hastened the country into a series of bitter contests, the end of which is not yet in view.

In November 1919 a lockout was put into force at Barcelona by the employers, and the threat was made by the Spanish Employers' Association to extend the lockout to the whole of Spain if the government did not treat more fairly the two parties to the quarrel — employers and employed. Each accused the other of political motives. By January 1920 terrorism and bitterness had greatly increased, and strike agitation had extended to Madrid, Valencia, Vigo, and other cities from Barcelona. Closely connected with these disturbances were the perils of the army juntos, which exist for political and illegal as well as for professional purposes. Growing in power, they may menace the security of the state in times of internal disorder.

Internal disorganization

SEPARATIST TENDENCIES AND THEIR HISTORIC CAUSES

The World War of 1914–1918 divided Spain. Many Spaniards are jealous of French cultural influence in Latin America and resent French pressure on Spain in Moroccan affairs. Gibraltar is remembered against Great Britain. The liberal and many of the intellectual elements favored the Allies during the war; the conservative elements were in sympathy with Germany.

Running like a thread through all the political turmoil and the disturbed social and financial conditions of Spain is the vexed question of the relations between church and state, which reached its climax in the attempt of the government to control the religious orders. It was during a period of general protest against the corruptions and privileges of the ecclesiastical bodies, and specifically in the year 1836, that religious congregations had been banished from Spain. But in 1851 the law of 1836 was so far altered as to permit the reestablishment of certain orders. From that time down to the present, the growth in the number and power of the orders has been rapid, and their political and social influence is formidable. Every attempt to tax or control them has been met by violent clerical agitation. Exempted from taxes, they have been enabled to engage in commercial projects and industrial work in such a way as to compete unfairly with lay rivals.

Relationship between church and state

Troublesome as it already was, the problem presented a more serious aspect with the change from a monarchist to a republican form of government in Portugal in 1910, when the religious congregations expelled from Portugal came to Spain. There were also ecclesiastical

refugees from France that came to Spain at the time of the separation of church and state in France (1905).

In addition to the political factors, there are geographical conditions
that make it difficult to maintain the territorial integrity of Spain.
The Spanish peninsula is broken up into a number of natural regions
separated by formidable barriers which, in the past, exercised a
strong influence upon the local inhabitants, and later, upon their
social and judicial systems as well as upon their political forms and
solidarity. The great extent of the interior plateau, the broken
character of its borders, and the ruggedness of the more prominent
sierras, have made it more difficult to diminish those diversities of
speech, political thought, and social character which for a long time
kept the populations of Spain apart and which still threaten to turn
the country back into the state of disunion that has repeatedly prevailed. From the earliest times down to the union of Castile and
Aragon late in the 15th century, as well as in the period following,
princely rivalries have disfigured the political life of Spain.

The population of Spain numbers about 20,000,000, and the density is a little more than 100 to the square mile. Considering its geographical position and its natural resources, the country is very thinly
populated as compared with the rest of Europe. The long succession of military expeditions conducted against the Moors during their
occupation of most of the Spanish peninsula greatly decreased the
native population. On the other hand, the country never recovered
the loss sustained by the expulsion of the Moors in 1609. It was a
great blow to agriculture, for the Moorish peoples of the southern
semi-arid region were masters in the reclamation of arid lands. They
had built irrigation works and applied a system of cultivation far superior to that formerly in vogue. The Moors introduced sugar cane,
cultivated cotton rather widely, and in general improved the breeds of
live stock. Of less importance, but still a considerable factor, was the
expulsion of the Jews late in the 15th century. The whole colonial
period was marked by emigration and heavy loss of life in military
expeditions and in the struggles of the pioneers in new and unhealthful
conditions. It must be remembered that there was no such thing as a
science of tropical medicine in the days of Spanish colonial expansion.

The earlier history of Spain has some striking modern parallels.
Spain made great progress during the period of the Roman occupation
and possessed a certain unity, due to the general use of the Roman law
and the organization and almost universal influence of the Christian
church. When the Roman Empire fell apart with the onset of the

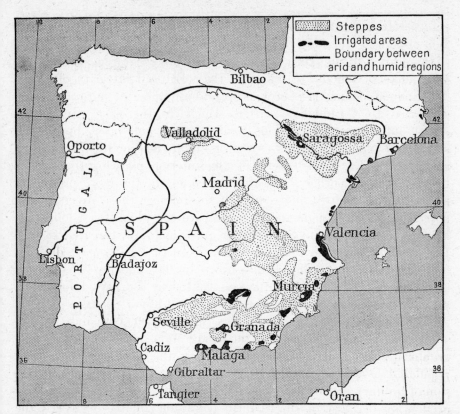

FIG. 76. The greater part of the plains and valley country of Spain is dry. The boundary between arid and humid regions is after Brunhes, *La géographie humaine*, 1917; the limits of the steppe regions are from E. Reyes Prósper, *Las estepas de España y su vegetación*, 1915. Each steppe district has a local name; *e.g.*, the one about Saragossa is called *Estepa ibérica*, the one about Granada *Estepa granadina*.

barbarian invasions, the accustomed routes of commerce were broken, and the invaded country dissolved into its component fragments.

In its fragmented condition the peninsula was weak and subject to foreign conquests; hence, when the Moslems came in 711, the country fell an easy prey to their armies. The success of the Moslems lay not in their political organization or military strength, but in the social and regional disorganization of the people of Spain. The northward progress of the Moors was almost unobstructed. In 718 they crossed the Pyrenees and invaded the country of the Franks, only to meet with defeat at the hands of Charles Martel at the battle of Tours in 732. Monasteries and cities, landowners and local rulers, paid tribute to the invader. Some of the people even accepted the Mohammedan religion.

The invaders had come from the desert. They were the last western

Weakness of the Spanish opposition to the Moors

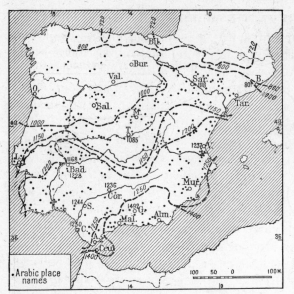

Fig. 77. The numbers represent the dates on which Spain and Portugal were reconquered from the Moors by Christian forces, in each case up to the limit shown by the broken line on which the date stands. It was only in 1492 that Granada, the last stronghold of the Moors, was retaken. The dots represent the locations of towns and geographical features that still have Moorish names. After Reclus, *L'homme et la terre*, Vol. III, p. 448; IV, p. 159.

extension of the great Arab wave that swept from east of the Red Sea over northern Africa. Their Mohammedanism was hardly orthodox; their blood was extremely mixed. The "Moors" were a sort of loose confederation of Arabs, Berbers, Syrians, and others, and they quarreled among themselves. The Berber revolted because he was assigned the barren central plateau. The various Arab tribes quarreled as a result of rivalries and disunion at the heart of the Arab world. Only by maintaining a mercenary army of African negroes were the Moors able to keep their Spanish possessions. At that they were never able completely to subjugate the peninsula; the Basques and other isolated groups in naturally strong positions on either side of the Pyrenees and in northwestern Spain maintained their independence throughout the long period of Moslem occupation.

Reconquest of the land We may summarize the greater part of the period of Moorish occupation by saying that it was thoroughly confused; and as order and organization developed in the Christian portions of Spain not occupied by the Moors, the long strife began which ended in the reconquest of the land. As military inefficiency and corruption increased among the Moors, the Christian kings advanced into the Moorish country with well-disciplined cavalry belonging to the great monastic military orders. Cordova was conquered in 1236, Seville in 1248, Valencia in 1237, and in 1340 at the battle of the Rio Salado the African invaders suffered a critical defeat, after which they were only occasionally a dangerous factor in Spanish life. Their last stronghold, Granada, fell in 1492.

From 1340 forward, Spanish history records a long and painful process of unification. It was not until the early years of the 18th century that a really ardent spirit of nationalism was displayed. Except for a common religion and a common throne, there would hardly have been any progress at all. For patriotism in Spain is a local thing that reflects the geographical division of the country; a man says he is a Galician, an Asturian, a Castilian, an Andalusian; he rarely thinks of himself as a Spaniard. While Castilian is the literary language of Spain, the people of each great region have a distinctive speech. In Aragon the people speak a dialect of Castilian; the people of Catalonia speak a dialect similar to that of southern France; the Basques have a distinct language of their own, and both Catalan and Castilian have several important dialects.

Locally, Spaniard is separated from Spaniard by mountain barriers, by tradition, by language, by social customs, by grades of society. Cities were long arrayed against cities, and villages against villages. There was unequal distribution of the taxes; there were special privileges to this and that city or monastery, and the nobles were exempted from taxation. With the increase of landed possessions by the nobles and monasteries, a heavier burden of taxation was thrown upon the towns. These difficulties have their effect even in our own time. The present contest between church and state reaches back to the time

Brown Bros.

FIG. 78. Granada, a stronghold of the Moors in Spain. After its capture in 1492 by Spanish troops the Moors were driven into Africa. The famous palace of the Alhambra stands on the height at the left.

Decline of Spanish character and the loss of empire

Fig. 79. The generalized language boundaries of Spain. From Agostini, *L'Europe ethnique et linguistique*, 1 : 10,000,000, 1917.

of the Christianization of Spain. In Spain as in France and Italy, and almost every other European country, the fortunes of the country are strongly affected by the complications of history. If society is steadied by age-old customs, it is also thwarted at times by the power of historical fact and precedent.

Though it had its glorious days, Spanish colonial history is remarkable not only for the great extent of its field, but also for its rapid decline after reaching a brilliant climax. The last stage of the process came in 1898, when, as a result of the Spanish-American War, Spain lost to the United States all but a few of her Pacific possessions, which few she later sold to Germany (page 202). Her West Indian possessions also were lost, and nothing now remains to her in the way of colonies except Rio de Oro, Spanish Guinea, a few small islands in the Gulf of Guinea, and small portions of Morocco — the northern and southern Spanish Zones (Fig. 80). The causes of Spanish colonial losses are many, and some of them are still embedded in the national life. Heavy emigration during the colonial period, the expulsion of Jews and Moors in the 15th and 16th centuries and also earlier, special exemptions from taxes, government interference in trade, a lack of industry among some classes, and an exceptional number of convents and monasteries, are among the chief causes. Government intervention in trade became a habit, and yet the government, until quite recent years, has never done anything constructive in modifying geographical conditions and increasing productivity. On the contrary, chiefly through the institution known as the Mesta, an organization of the pastoral interests, it long favored grazing at the expense of agriculture and forestry, and it did not adequately maintain the irrigation systems developed by the Moors in the south of Spain.

PRESENT POLITICAL AND ECONOMIC SITUATION

To break up along lines of race and local interest would be greatly to the disadvantage both of all Spain and of the smaller units, and one of the problems of the day is to accomplish a change toward democratic rule and yet hold the country together so that the different parts may have the benefit of free exchange of products in a fairly well-balanced state. The setting up of a number of independent states, with the resulting increase in boundary lines and the creation of boundary disputes, would complicate the social and commercial life of the Spanish peninsula and weaken the Spanish people.

Separation of Spain into small states inadvisable

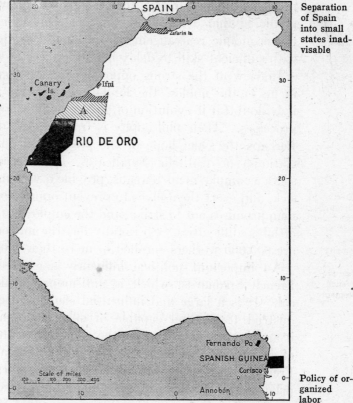

Fig. 80. Spanish possessions in Africa. It has been arranged with France that zone *A* may be occupied by Spain at her pleasure. The heavily shaded area north of zone *A* is the southern zone of Spanish Morocco; a similarly shaded zone south of Gibraltar is the northern zone. From Stieler's *Handatlas* and the *Geographical Journal*, June 1920.

The outstanding problems of Spanish government relate to the governmental attitude toward the policy of organized labor. The labor element is centered chiefly in three cities, — Barcelona, Bilbao, and Valencia. The demands of the labor party are for an autonomy so complete as practically to remove the laborers from the control of the non-industrial part of the population, but they would be clearly outnumbered at the present time by other political elements.

Policy of organized labor

The King of Spain is himself inclined toward larger and larger democratic rights, together with an increase in the constitutional powers of the law-making body. But more than once in the past few years it has been a question whether he would ally himself with the working population closely enough to maintain his throne. During the World War, though he was surrounded by pro-German influences, his sympathy for the Allied cause was repeatedly proved. By maintaining a neutral position, Spain was able to increase her trade, and the resulting

Attitude of the democratic king

prosperity helped to stay the oft-impending revolution. It was freely predicted that a revolution would occur directly after the war, but the economic rearrangement of the life of the country was effected with sufficient skill to delay it still longer.

In view of the strong opposition of the conservative Spanish elements — the nobles, the landed proprietors, and the capitalists — it is doubtful if evolution of government can come about by orderly processes. Their philosophy is frankly that of the privileged caste. Perhaps the chief hope of the present lies in the coöperative associations, or Catholic Syndicates, first organized in 1918. They serve as employment bureaus, provide a workman's bank, care for the sick, and exert themselves to prevent oppression; in return the workman promises not to strike, and the employer agrees to the arbitration of labor difficulties. So rapidly has the movement grown that there are 600,000 workers enrolled in more than 4000 local syndicates.

The pro-French element

An important political influence is exerted by a group of pro-French Spaniards, which is anti-monarchical as well as anti-clerical. It is a large and influential element, located chiefly in the industrial towns and capable of effective organization. Opposed to it are the aristocratic class, the church, and the peasantry. The line of separation between the two groups became sharper when the French government seized the church properties in France and expelled large numbers of priests and nuns, who took refuge in Spain (page 147). Opposition on this score cannot fail to diminish with the recent establishment of better relations between the French government and the Vatican (page 81).

Conflict with French interests

Spain continues to be suspicious of French expansion, in spite of the treaty of 1904, mutually recognizing Spanish and French rights in Morocco. In 1911 the two countries were close to a military clash. In 1912 their differences were harmonized by an agreement extending Spanish territory and giving to Tangier, with a district of nearly 150 square miles about it, an international status. Spain was to have 40 per cent and France 60 per cent of the stock of a railway to be constructed between Tangier and Fez.

Value of the Spanish Zone

Small as it is, the Spanish Zone of northern Morocco is a great drain upon Spanish resources. To keep the people of the region in order requires an army of occupation of 80,000 men, and the expense involved is not offset by products of equivalent value to Spain. The sole commercial advantage appears to be related to a railway tunnel which it is proposed to build under the Straits of Gibraltar as part of a line to extend southwestward to the coast of Africa at Rio del Oro,

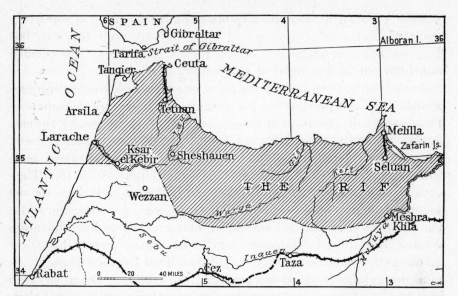

FIG. 81. The northern Spanish Zone in Morocco. The spelling oi "Zafarin Islands" follows the United States Hydrographic Office charts; on some maps the name is spelled "Chafarinas." After map in the *Geographical Journal*, May 1920.

where Spain holds additional African territory (Fig. 80). From that point and from Dakar in French West Africa there would be short steamer connection with South American ports. The project is one that could succeed only after agreement with France.

At the present time the rivalry between Spain and the United States is limited almost entirely to the field of Latin American trade. *America and Spain* Spain perhaps desires nothing else so much as to maintain commercial and spiritual bonds between Spanish America and herself. But her path in this direction is beset with many difficulties. In Mexico, for example, Spaniards are almost as much disliked as Americans. Spain depends upon the United States for cotton and in part for her coal, petroleum, lumber, and wheat, and this dependence has tended to keep alive commercial relations, which were developing rapidly between the countries just before the World War. Between 1912 and 1917 the general trade of Spain had increased but 25 per cent in value, while imports from the United States had increased 400 per cent.

As a neutral, Spain made large profits on war supplies. Gold flowed *Present prosperity* into the country in a steady stream. The output of coal of all grades increased from 4,400,000 long tons in 1914 to 7,200,000 in 1918. Water-power resources are being developed. The electrification of some of the railways has been begun. In spite of internal difficulties, the economic situation of the country is better than at any time since 1898.

CHAPTER SEVEN

PORTUGAL'S COLONIAL POLICIES

Anti-monarch-ist rising

PORTUGAL was in the midst of a period of national and colonial reconstruction when the war came in 1914 to add to her already complex problems. There had been grave dissatisfaction with the government, nominally a constitutional monarchy, but in reality a reactionary oligarchy headed by the king. In 1903 an insurrection of peasants took place at Fundão, and in the same year there were riots at Coimbra and a strike of weavers at Oporto. In 1908 King Carlos and the Crown Prince were assassinated and Prince Manoel succeeded to the throne, only to flee to England for safety in 1910. The corruption of the public service and the poverty of the over-taxed peasant and artisan classes had at last ended in revolution.

For many years the country had also suffered the difficulties of administering large and remote colonial possessions, which were so inefficiently managed as to require heavy annual subsidies for their maintenance. Portuguese administrators were weak; for the most part the colonies had an unhealthful climate; there was no capital for colonial development. The political and economic situation of Portugal was bad from every standpoint when the republic was proclaimed in 1910.

THE PROBLEMS OF THE NEW DEMOCRACY

Among the new policies of Portugal as framed by the present leaders, there are two items of special importance: (1) the separation of church and state, and (2) a larger degree of autonomy for the provinces and colonies of Portugal. But the country is far from unity in the matter of general policy, being broken up into nearly a dozen political parties, all struggling for the success of special and, on the whole, narrow programs of political and economic reconstruction.

Leader-ship with-out public opinion

The leaders of the political parties and their principal followers have very little in common with the mass of the people. Each party includes only a small minority of the electorate. With a population of 6,000,000, of whom 67 per cent live in the country, the questions of taxes and wages, of the price of crops and the improvement of transportation lines, appear to the people to be of far more importance than the political programs. The gulf between people and leaders is a matter of more importance by reason of a degree of illiteracy higher than anywhere else in western Europe. According to the census of 1911, the figures are 81 per cent for the women and 67 per cent for the men.

It has been said that Portugal's chief export is peasants. Emigration became a serious factor between 1890 and 1900, and even today adds 60,000 Portuguese annually to the population of Brazil. There is no money for the development of the land, and Portugal is chiefly agricultural. Capital cannot be made available for industries, of which the country has long felt the need and which would absorb the natural increase of population. *Portuguese emigration a grave problem*

Only a third of the land of Portugal is cultivated, since much of it on the east, along the common boundary with Spain, is too rugged for extensive cultivation, and elsewhere there are high moorlands too cold for agriculture and, in the south, regions too dry without irrigation. In all, 28 per cent is forest and 27 per cent pasture. *Portugal's domestic needs*

It was natural that Portugal should join with the western Allies in the World War, for she is traditionally friendly with England and she is dependent to a large degree upon imported coal and wheat and upon her relatively extensive fisheries. She was not placed, like Switzerland and Holland, where a lucrative trade with Germany could be carried on. Nor did she care to lose her colonies, which in the future may have more value to her than in the past, considering their supply of the raw materials needed by the industrial populations of the world. The pressure of Germany on the African colonies of Portugal had become embarrassing before the war, and it was feared that Germany was only waiting her time to absorb Portuguese East Africa. Indeed, Germany had already absorbed the so-called Kionga triangle (Fig. 263), about 400 square miles, south of the estuary of the Rovuma River. This danger is now removed; the Kionga triangle is restored to Portugal, and her ownership of her African colonies has been confirmed by the active part which she took in the fighting in Southwest Africa and in East Africa and by the help which she gave elsewhere through her army and fleet. *Portugal's interests in the war*

THE EXPANSION OF PORTUGAL

There is thus brought to an end the long decline in the extent of the Portuguese overseas territories, which, at the beginning of the 19th century, formed a larger colonial empire than that held by any other European power except Great Britain and Spain. These are now her possessions: *Extent of colonial possessions*

In Africa	*In India*	*In Melanesia*
Cape Verde Islands	Goa	Eastern Timor, with
St. Thomas (São Thomé) and	Daman	tributary island
Princes (Principe) Islands	(Damão)	and district
Portuguese Guinea	Diu	
Angola (Portuguese West Africa)		
Mozambique (Portuguese East	*In China*	
Africa)	Macao	

Historical view of Portuguese colonial policy

The earlier history of Portuguese colonization illuminates the whole modern period of Portuguese colonial development. The Portuguese were the leaders in pioneering the sea road along the western coast of Africa, even before the discovery of America. By twice defeating the Mohammedan fleets, Portugal confirmed her hold upon the trade of India, which she had developed after Vasco da Gama completed his voyage to India in 1498. She had broken the old route between Europe and India by way of the Persian Gulf and greatly obstructed the commerce of the Red Sea, and she stood at the Atlantic gateway of the Mediterranean. With Spain she had divided the New World by the treaty of Tordesillas (1494) and subsequent agreements, receiving the lands east of a north-south line 370 leagues west of the Cape Verde Islands; she thus acquired Brazil and confirmed her right to her possessions in Africa and India, including Ceylon and Persia. In 1500 King Emanuel assumed the title, two years later confirmed by the Pope, of "Lord of the Conquest, Navigation, and Commerce of India, Ethiopia, Arabia, and Persia."

Relations with Brazil

Close historical and commercial relations with Brazil

The relations of the Portuguese to their settlements in Brazil are of more importance today than the colonial possessions of Portugal in Africa, for here we have real intimacy between a new country of 25,-000,000 inhabitants and the home country with 6,000,000 inhabitants. Not only in the late colonial period but in all the years that have followed, down to the present, there has been in general heavy emigration from Portugal to Brazil. Moreover, there is in Brazil a sympathy for Portugal that has important commercial consequences.

The colony of Brazil was not only the most important one that Portugal possessed; it was also the best founded of the Hispanic colonies, owing to the fact that agricultural products of a tropical variety, chiefly sugar, were the early economic basis of the colony, and not gold and silver, as in the case of the Spanish possessions.

It was an accident that led to the Portuguese discovery of Brazil in 1500. Cabral, a Portuguese navigator, in laying his course for southern Africa and India, took advantage of the trade winds to go well to the westward, and thus came upon the Brazilian coast. Settlement was desultory and development neglected at first, and at one time Brazil was even thought worth so little that it might be abandoned. The colony was held in light esteem because the tide of development set toward India during the period of the discovery and early settlement of Brazil. It was only after India had been lost to the Portuguese that they turned their attention to the development of Brazil.

Early history of Portuguese settlement in Brazil

For three hundred years the efforts of the colonists were confined almost exclusively to sugar growing. Interest in the colony increased very rapidly after the discovery of gold in Minas Geraes during the early years of the 18th century and of diamonds in 1730. The immediate effect on agriculture was bad, because men were drawn away from the plantations and their interest in agriculture was diminished. The ultimate effect was to broaden their outlook and open up the interior. The colony also gained great impetus in Napoleon's time, when the Portuguese crown was transferred to Brazil. Rio de Janeiro became the real capital of the Portuguese Empire, and the royal family arrived there in 1808. But in 1822 the Brazilian democratic leaders proclaimed the independence of the country, recognized by the mother country in 1825. Thereafter Brazil had an imperial form of government until the revolution of 1889 and the proclamation of a republic.

Later history

But so closely connected were the peoples of Brazil and Portugal, and their differences of opinion had so much the character of a limited family quarrel, that there has been no real interruption of relations, either social or commercial. In fact, the relations would be far more close today if it were not for the fact that Portugal is economically weak and small, and cannot assist Brazil in the development of its resources. Such development has come from Great Britain, France, Germany, and the United States, all of which have made great demands upon Brazil's tropical and subtropical products in their industries. The result has been to diminish the effective participation of Portugal in the economic development of Brazil.

Limitation of Portuguese commercial influence

The African Colonies

In eastern Africa, Portugal found it necessary to overcome the Arabs, who by the 10th century had occupied the seacoast as far south as Sofala. After the conquest of the Arabs, Portugal had developed a trade between eastern Africa and Arabia, the Persian Gulf, and

Portugal in East Africa

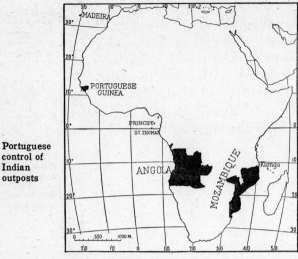

FIG. 82. Portuguese navigators were the first to explore the west coast of Africa and to conquer the Arabs of the east coast, particularly at Zanzibar. They were also the first to plant European settlements in distant India, where they still have Goa, Diu, and Damão. Brazil was lost in 1822. Colonial administration was so inefficient as late as 1914, that Portugal was in danger of losing even Angola and Mozambique. Reforms are now in progress.

Portuguese control of Indian outposts

Loss of Portuguese colonies

India. Like the Portuguese who came after them, the Arabs occupied the coastland rather than inland points. By 1510 the Portuguese were masters of all that portion of the eastern African coast formerly held by the Arab sultans.

The contest between the Portuguese and the Arabs in eastern Africa but continued the struggle that had lasted so long in the Iberian peninsula and in Africa against the infidel Mohammedans. The historic city of Goa, a Portuguese settlement in India, stood opposed to Aden, which was in Arab possession. In the contest between these two central posts of rival religions and political faiths we have a repetition in Albuquerque's time (the first part of the 16th century) of the early struggles of Portugal and Spain against the Mohammedans in the west. By establishing themselves in India the Portuguese made rich trade connections with farther India, China, and the Orient generally.

With the decline of Portuguese power at home and abroad, the Arabs won back, in the early years of the 18th century, all their African possessions north of Cape Delgado, and the Dutch, French, and British invaded Portuguese territory in the south. Between 1737 and 1740 Portuguese commerce was practically swept from the sea by Arab parties and rival European powers. A state of warfare among the inland tribes prevented effective Portuguese administration in the region lying behind the coastal strip; and with the explorations of Livingstone in the Zambesi basin (1850–1865) the British were led to establish settlements in the interior at the southern end of Lake Nyasa and in the Shiré highlands. Thereupon the pressure became continuously greater, and when the scramble for Africa was over Portugal held only a part of her former domain.

On the west coast of Africa, however, Portuguese Angola was held with little serious rivalry from neighboring colonial powers. For one thing, the Portuguese were the first claimants, having discovered and explored the coastal region from 1482 to 1485. The natives were in part reduced to submission (a process that ended only in 1907); Loanda was founded in 1576, Benguela in 1617. Prosperity was dependent upon the slave trade with Brazil. The frontiers were vague and brought boundary disputes with Great Britain, France, and Germany, until the period from 1885 to 1905, when successive agreements, treaties, and arbitral awards fixed the boundaries as shown in Figure 82.

THE COLONIAL POLICY OF PORTUGAL

Devoted to the maintenance of a powerful navy and an active commerce, Portugal's colonial activity was always governed by the principle that the seacoast should be held, rather than large territories that would require the sending of troops inland. Thus throughout the 16th century her settlements were confined to the coasts of Asia, Africa, and America, and the policy followed has had its effect down to the present time. There was no real development of the native and of the resources of the land.

Seacoast possessions

Contributing to the loss of the colonial possessions was the weakness of the whole Portuguese economic system. The merchants and bankers of Portugal sought to increase the amount of gold in the country rather than to increase the industrial output. This line of economic theory led to a decline of agriculture and the increased importation of raw materials which might have been produced at home, at least in part. Portugal soon became, commercially, a mere appanage of England.

Decline of colonial power

The home industries of Portugal have not grown at the same rate as those of other western European countries. Hence the colonies have been of less value to the people of Portugal itself than to other powers, particularly Germany, which had a large commercial fleet and well-established industries. Portuguese East Africa, for example, with its population of more than 3,000,000 and with the ports of Lourenzo Marquez, Mozambique, and Beira, has great capacities for the production and export of sugar cane, rice, coffee, rubber, and tobacco, as well as cotton and coconuts, and a part of it is high enough to produce wheat and cattle. There are also large deposits of coal and some of copper. The trade of the colony was artificially stimulated in 1909, when Portugal signed an agreement with the Transvaal government which gave Delagoa Bay more than half the import trade of the Transvaal; in return the Transvaal obtained the privi-

Portuguese East Africa, or Mozambique

lege of recruiting natives in Portuguese East Africa to work in the Rand mines.

Under the Portuguese the West African colony, Angola (Fig. 82), has developed hardly at all. It is of small present importance, yet it may ultimately develop into a rich and powerful colony. Its population is estimated at 2,000,000 and its area (485,000 square miles) is as great as that of Texas, California, and Washington combined. The coastal belt is in general dry; but with increasing altitude at the inner edge of the coastal plain, from thirty to a hundred miles from the sea, there is heavier rainfall and abundant vegetation. Then follows a relatively unproductive plateau with scattered vegetation and a more moderate water supply; this merges eastward into the forested basins of the Congo and the Zambesi, while in the south it runs into a barren sandy desert. The coastal region is rich in oil palms, and at the extreme north are dense forests of economic value. Some rubber is gathered from the wild rubber plants. Sugar, cotton, coffee, and tobacco, together with rubber, palm oil, cattle, hides, ivory, and gum, are the chief exports. The two most important commercial towns are Loanda and Cabinda, the latter the outlet for an enclave of Portuguese territory, surrounded by the French and the Belgian Congo.

While the colonies have required a subsidy, on the other hand there have been commercial compensations. By tariff and trade regulations much of the colonial produce was brought to Portugal, chiefly to Lisbon, and there reëxported. Two serious political and commercial difficulties were constantly feared:

(1) As the colonies wished to trade wherever they chose, and since Great Britain and Germany were the two powers by whom the products were carried, there was fear that the colonies might be taken over by one or the other of these two powers if they were to trade freely with them.

(2) If the colonies were given self-government, foreign capital would increasingly divert the colonial products and Lisbon would lose a large part of its trade.

German
penetra-
tion in
Portuguese
East
Africa

These dangers were the more real because the value of raw materials, such as the rubber, copra, cotton, and hides of the Portuguese African possessions, was increasing constantly with the rapid increase in the trade and industry of the world. Neglected for a time, Portuguese possessions have become an object of envy to stronger powers. Germany bought more Portuguese colonial produce than any other power, particularly cacao, coffee, and rubber (from São Thomé and Principe chiefly). And Germany still needs these things more than

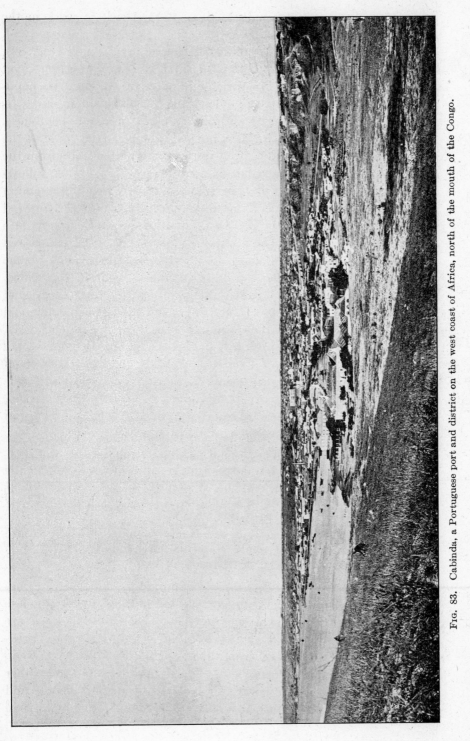

Fig. 83. Cabinda, a Portuguese port and district on the west coast of Africa, north of the mouth of the Congo.

any other power, and now has no colonies of her own on which to depend for a supply. German financial influence in Lisbon is likely to continue.

The government of the republic has made "colonial self-government" a part of its program. This it had to do, for a revolutionary spirit was active in the colonies, especially in Angola; the colonists felt that their backward condition was due to political and economic dependence upon the home country. In 1912 each colony was given a separate budget and a separate subsidy, where a subsidy was necessary.

Colonial
self-gov-
ernment

By a decree dated 10 May 1919, Portugal granted extensive autonomy to her colonies and promised administrative reform in continuation of her earlier declaration of 1914. State aid was promised to settlers, and expert agricultural and geological investigations were to be encouraged. These promises of reform and development were probably made to offset the desire of other states to benefit by Portuguese misgovernment. The Union of South Africa wishes to acquire Portuguese East Africa, or at least Lourenzo Marquez, and Belgium would like to secure northern Angola in order to lengthen the coast line of the Belgian Congo. Universal discontent in the colonies plays into the hands of outside powers.

Certainly improvements in colonial management are much needed. The colonies could furnish food needed by Portugal if transport by sea and land were available. About 30,000 natives annually leave Mozambique to work in the Transvaal gold fields. In 1916 the government deficit of Angola alone was $30,000,000.

More intensive agricultural cultivation of a modern type, the building up of home industries to absorb colonial products, the stabilization of her political processes, — these are vital needs for Portugal. By successfully meeting them she can keep her colonies and can become a powerful country again; if she loses her colonies, she will continue to rank as a declining power.

CHAPTER EIGHT

THE SCANDINAVIAN COUNTRIES AND HOLLAND

ONE of the most striking conditions of the World War was the persistent neutrality of four northern European states,—Holland and the three Scandinavian countries, Norway, Sweden, and Denmark. Each of them provided Germany with large quantities of foodstuffs and raw materials needed for the conduct of the war; yet each of them suffered the loss of lives and ships by German submarines, against whose use they frequently protested. However, because of their small size they felt unable to do more than protest. The Scandinavian countries carried their dependence upon each other to the significant point of making an agreement during the war to take no part on either side unless the three of them unanimously approved such action in advance. *The neutrality of Scandinavia*

In the future we shall find these four states playing an important part in international agreements affecting the North Sea and, more particularly, the Baltic. A possible Baltic Confederation would be of interest to all of them. For hundreds of years one nation after another owning a part of the Baltic coast has sought a dominating position on that sea. Four hundred years ago Denmark was the leading Baltic power. Later Sweden won preëminence, only to lose it to Russia. With the rise of her naval power in recent years, Germany held a superior position. The natural currents of trade in the Baltic basin require coöperation of the Baltic powers. Russia exports chiefly to Germany; Sweden exports to Russia and Germany; Denmark is a way station on the sea road eastward; Finland, like Norway, will have a large trade with England, but of more importance to her will be her trade with Esthonia, Sweden, and Germany. *A possible Baltic Confederation*

On 9 June 1920 there was held at Copenhagen a "Baltic and White Sea Conference" in which eleven nations participated. Germany was invited to the conference, and Russia was represented by non-Bolshevist agents. America was not represented at all. The conference took up questions of working hours, equality of trade in the Baltic and North Sea shipping, and the matter of rebates.

The virility of the Scandinavians is well known. Their men and women are physically strong and healthy. The northern climate, a high level of success in overcoming the natural difficulties of their environment, excellent maritime traditions — these have bred a wholesome race that has left its mark in history. Norwegian kings once ruled the northern Scottish islands. The Danes once held nearly *Scandinavian traditions of power*

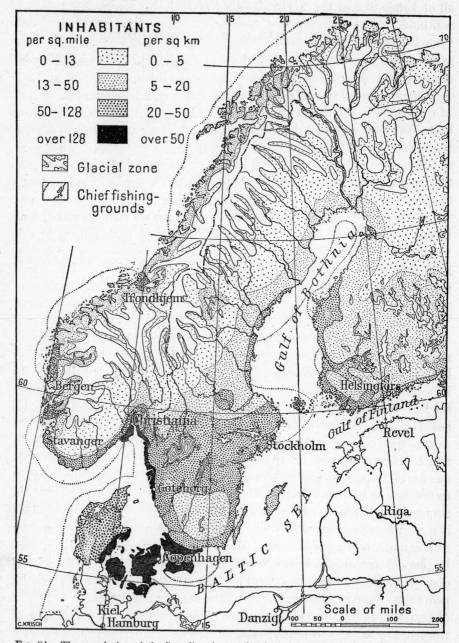

FIG. 84. The population of the Scandinavian peninsula is largely limited to a seacoast belt, except in the southern portion. The capital city of each of the three Scandinavian countries and of Finland is a salt-water port. Danzig will become Poland's maritime outlet. Riga is the capital of Latvia. Memel, between Danzig and Riga, may become Lithuania's sole port. Sea-borne trade is of interest to all, and Baltic agreements are likely to be made in the common interest.

all of England and the lowlands of Scotland. The English and the French prayer-books long contained an echo of those far times in the petition, "From the fury of the Northmen, good Lord, deliver us." The extent of the realm of Gustavus Adolphus, the greatest of the Scandinavian kings, is shown in Figure 85. The colonial enterprise of the Danes led to the establishment of colonies in Greenland, Africa, the Faroes, and the West Indies. It was only in 1917, by selling the Virgin Islands to the United States, that the Danes gave up the last of their possessions in the West Indies.

FIG. 85.   The Swedish state at the time of its greatest extent.   The first date in each case represents the year in which the district was won; the date in parenthesis, the year in which it was lost.   After Putzger, *Historische Schul-Atlas*, 1906, Pl. 25.

THE SCANDINAVIAN PENINSULA

If we turn to the commercial power of Scandinavia, we shall find some noteworthy facts. In proportion to her population, Sweden has a greater railway mileage than any other country in Europe. Norway possessed more than 4 per cent of the world's shipping in 1914, though her population numbered only 2,600,000, or less than 0.2 per cent of the world's total. Norwegian sailors are known the world over. Norway has forests of great extent, and fisheries upon which millions outside her own frontiers depend for sea-food. Sweden has a vast supply of timber (Fig. 87), and the development of her iron mines in recent years has made her one of the great iron-exporting countries of Europe. Though both countries extend far to the north, it is in the southern section that their chief populations dwell (Fig. 84). *Commercial importance of Scandinavia*

The main topographic axis of the Scandinavian peninsula lies close to the western side. Between the cold, rocky highlands and the sea is a very narrow fringe of country where more than 80 per cent of the people of Norway live (Fig. 84). Norway has but 4400 square miles of territory under cultivation. Rivers and lakes cover 4 per cent of the total area, as compared with an average of 0.5 per cent for Europe. Three fourths of the land is unproductive, and a fifth is forest-covered. Essentially a maritime nation, Norway has from the first been dependent upon open sea routes. *Geographical position of Scandinavia and its effects*

On the other hand, Sweden dwells on the eastern or long back slope

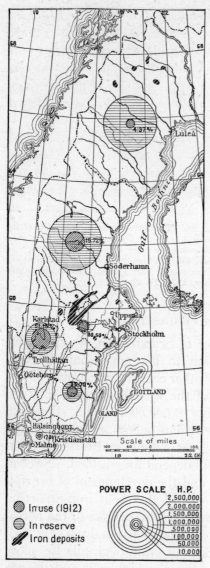

FIG. 86. Water power and iron ore. The iron ore of northern Sweden, in the famous Gellivare district, has opened up a remote and thinly populated region. Coal is lacking, except in small quantities, and water-power development is therefore well advanced.

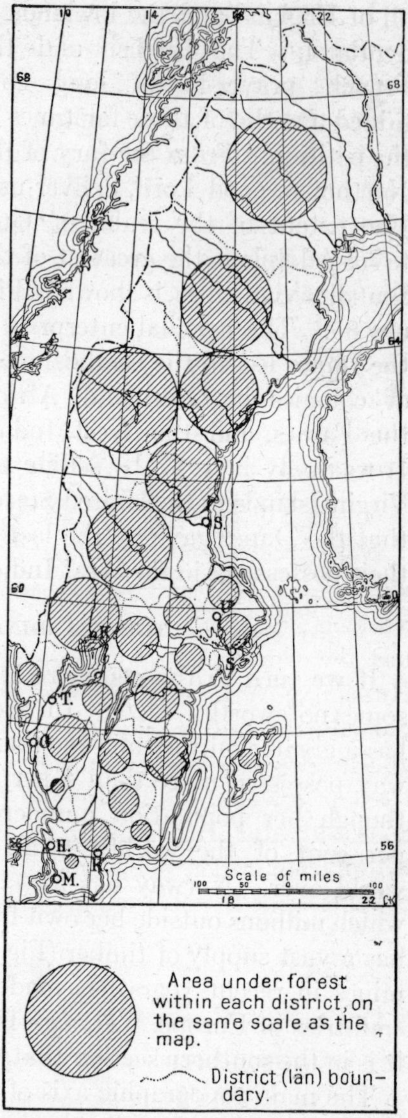

FIG. 87. Lying near highly industrial and larger nations in need of raw material, Sweden finds her forests a powerful asset. From *Sweden: Historical and Statistical Handbook*, 2d ed., 1914, Vol. II: forests, p. 169; iron, p. 243; water power, p. 325.

of the Scandinavian peninsula, and has a greater extent of fertile land. Norway and Sweden are also different as to climate. Eastern Sweden has the dry continental type of climate, while western Norway has the mild and moist climate of England.

In 1814 Norway was taken from Denmark, to which it had been joined since 1397, and given to Sweden as compensation for the latter's services in joining the European powers against Napoleon, with whom Denmark had become allied. The union of Sweden and Norway lasted until 1905, when a dispute arose over Norway's right to maintain her own consular service. The union was then dissolved without resort to arms, in spite of the high feeling aroused.

These historic estrangements are of far less present importance to the people concerned than are the common benefits which they have enjoyed by standing together during the past few years. Like the rest of the world, the Scandinavian countries have undergone a marked change in their political attitude since 1914; the old problems seem small and remote, and new problems are pressing upon them from every side.

PRESENT PROBLEMS

Norway is now less concerned over her relations with Sweden than with practical international guarantees for the freedom of shipping. Sweden no longer fears conquest by an imperial Russia, but she still has the vexed question of the future form and conditions of a new Russian government. Denmark long lived in fear of German encroachment, and would now welcome an international order in which guarantees would be given for existing boundaries and for equality of trade privileges. Only Holland stands on an independent basis. She is as watchful of the British as of the Germans; she will take no dictation from either, nor will she yield to Belgium on the question of the Scheldt or of Dutch Limburg (page 123).

MARITIME INTERESTS OF NORWAY

During the World War, Norway lost nearly 2000 sailors; she lost also torpedoed ships to the number of more than 800, with a capacity exceeding 1,000,000 tons. The commercial life of the country was deranged. Norway dropped from fourth to sixth place in mercantile tonnage, being replaced by Japan.

Opposite Norway, across the North Sea, is another maritime nation, Great Britain. Their interests are common in many respects. Norway, though neutral in the war period, was friendly to the British, for she has everything to gain by that extension of the power of Anglo-Saxon navies which is implied in the League of Nations covenant. She has joined the League of Nations. Under the League, the freedom of the seas is guaranteed by the large nations, and the over-

Brown Bros.

FIG. 88. Adde and the Sufjord on the Norwegian coast. Note the presence of flat land in the foreground (head of fjord) and the absence of it along the foot of the fjord wall in the distance.

seas commerce of the small trading nations, like Greece, Norway, and Holland, may be expected to grow rapidly as soon as the world has become more orderly, when industry is revived and capital is made available for the purchase or building of ships.

Since the trade of Norway will be chiefly between ports in foreign lands rather than between Norway and the world, security for goods and ships is Norway's principal need. She is not a manufacturing nation, except in a very limited way, and she has no vital need for colonies. She is satisfied if shipping is free to all flags.

Norway's claim to Spitsbergen In the security and ownership of fishing stations near home, however, Norway is much interested. Hence she pressed her claim to Spitsbergen, a group of islands in the Arctic Sea north of the Scandinavian

Brown Bros.

Fig. 89. - Buga, one of the oldest towns in Norway. Note the crowding of houses on the narrow fringe of flat land near the coast.

peninsula, in which claim her interest is heightened by the rich coal seams that outcrop on the main island, Norway herself having to import all her coal from overseas, chiefly from England. Ever since 1261 Norway has periodically asserted her claims to Spitsbergen, as in 1608, when the British began whaling off the islands, in 1666, when France did likewise, and in 1679, Sweden. The archipelago has been explored chiefly by Norwegian navigators.

The Norwegians already have wireless and meteorological stations at Green Harbor and a meteorological station on Bear Island. They have established fur stations; they have maintained regular navigation between Spitsbergen and Norway (since 1911); and they own the two largest of the four coal companies in the islands, with a production in

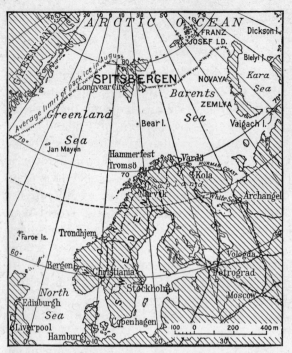

FIG. 90. Spitsbergen in relation to Norway. The group is now under Norwegian sovereignty, after an indefinite status and the expression of political or economic interest by both Great Britain and Russia.

1918 of more than 50,000 tons. Norway has otherwise no fuel except wood and no native source of power save the "white coal" of her waterfalls.

In recent years there have also been developed in Spitsbergen a whale-oil industry and general fisheries of importance. Though far north, — halfway between Norway and the North Pole, — the islands benefit by the warm Atlantic waters that drift right up to the Arctic Ocean, past the northern end of Norway, and create open winter ports even as far east as the Murman coast of Russia (Fig. 90).

In order to put an end to the status of non-ownership, the Allied and Associated Powers have put Spitsbergen under the Norwegian flag, but Norway does not receive the islands in unlimited sovereignty.

Guarantees secured from Norway

The Allied and Associated Powers have laid down certain specific guarantees. These affect only nations having actual vested interests in Spitsbergen at the present time, and direct the manner in which new commercial interests may be acquired. There is to be no naval base in the islands, and no use of Spitsbergen in time of war. The Danish government is to represent Russia's interests in the islands until that country gets on its feet again. The ships of all signatories to the Spitsbergen treaty are to enjoy fishing and hunting privileges in territorial waters. All ships are to be enabled to touch at some point in Norway on the way to or from Spitsbergen. Wireless stations are to be at the service of all, and an international meteorological station may be established. A Danish commissioner will examine all claims now outstanding, and final settlement is to be made by a

[1] By Spitsbergen are meant also Bear Island and all other islands between 10° and 35° longitude east of Greenwich and 74° and 81° north latitude.

tribunal of the interested powers, with the commissioner as president.

SWEDEN'S FOREIGN PROBLEMS

Sweden's foreign problems have arisen largely from her long-standing fear of Russia. In 1809 Russia took from her the country of Finland, thus removing a barrier between Sweden and the growing power of the Russian state. The reëstablishment of Finland as an independent state (page 370) will free Sweden from dread of Russia. {Sweden and Russia}

The evidence of Russian power took its most menacing form in possession of the Åland Islands, which are only seventy-five miles from Stockholm, and if fortified by an enemy power would prove a real menace to Sweden. Fortified by Russia early in the World War, they were temporarily occupied late in the war by the German fleet. Because Russia had broken up into a number of separate states, among which was Finland, and because of Allied recognition of Finnish independence, it was thought possible to settle the Åland question by direct negotiation between Finland and Sweden (1919). This plan failing, the matter was referred to the League of Nations, with the result that the case was studied by an Interallied commission for report and eventual settlement by the League. The Soviet government on its part also protested against any agreement regarding the islands to which Russia was not a party. {The Åland Islands}

DENMARK

Denmark's position gives it special importance in relation to the commerce of the Baltic, for its chief city, Copenhagen, is located on the island of Zealand, which borders the gateway to that sea. At one point the water passage is but three miles wide. Down to 1857 Denmark actually collected dues on cargoes passing through the "Sound," as the strait is called. Denmark's right to levy dues was always protested by other countries — in the 17th century by the Netherlands and Sweden and in the 19th century by the United States. For relinquishing the privilege Denmark was paid $20,000,000, of which sum more than a fourth was supplied by Great Britain.

The commercial welfare of Denmark depends largely upon the growing export of dairy products and the facilities offered by the free port and bonded warehouses of Copenhagen.[1] Denmark's geograph-

---

[1] Recently the free port of Copenhagen has been doubled in size, larger warehouses have been constructed, and every effort has been made to take advantage of its position as a port of call for steamers in the Baltic trade. These efforts were largely offset by a succession of strikes during 1920 and the ensuing diversion of trade.

ical position fosters close relations between its merchants and those of Germany and the United Kingdom. Its agricultural products (three fourths of the land is in farms) find a ready market in the industrial centers of its large neighbors.

Present colonial possessions of Denmark

Denmark's colonies were never commercially important. The Virgin Islands, its only West Indian possession, were sold to the United States in 1917 for $25,000,000 (Fig. 272). By virtue of explorations in Greenland, chiefly by Peary and Greely, the United States had certain vague rights there, all of which were given up as part of the general agreement whereby the Virgin Islands were acquired. Greenland, Denmark's sole remaining colony, has little commerce at present, its exports being fish, skins, seal oil, feathers, and small amounts of copper ore; but it is capable of some development and may ultimately have wireless telegraph stations of importance in commerce and war. On 1 December 1918 Iceland, a Danish possession, became nominally a sovereign state, though Denmark represents it in foreign affairs and is united to it in the person of the Danish king.

Scandinavian interest in German reconstruction

Norway and Sweden, like Denmark, are now most anxious to favor a policy that will re-create the industrial life of Germany, start ships moving in her ports, and renew her industries. They are Germany's neighbors, and their trade with that state has been an important part of their total commerce. Whatever they may have thought or done with respect to the issues of the war, the Scandinavian states cannot be expected to look with ill favor upon a more active merchant fleet in the Baltic and the renewal of the commerce and industry of the whole tributary region.

TERRITORIAL GAINS IN SLESVIG

Denmark's Alsace-Lorraine

The principal Danish-speaking portions of Slesvig have been returned to Denmark. The case grew out of former German ambitions. Until 1864 the duchies of Slesvig and Holstein were joined in a personal union under their duke, although Holstein was also a member of the German Confederation (from which in part the German Empire was formed in 1871). The two duchies were predominantly German, except for the northern part of Slesvig, which contained about 150,000 Danes and a few Frisians (Fig. 91). The Germans saw that it would be possible to dig a canal from Kiel to the mouth of the Elbe which would give German ships a direct passage between the North Sea and the Baltic. With the Kiel Canal in German hands, the German fleet could not be bottled up in the Baltic so readily, should war eventually come.

Consequently, in 1863, when the Duke of Slesvig and Holstein came to the throne of Denmark as Christian IX and attempted to unite both provinces to his kingdom, Denmark was invaded by Prussia and Austria, the two principal members of the German Confederation. After a short campaign, Christian was forced to surrender Slesvig and Holstein (1864). Two years later, however, Prussia and Austria came to blows about the disposition of the region. Prussia was victorious. She forthwith annexed the duchies and began a campaign of Germanization that continued without cessation until the beginning of the war in 1914.

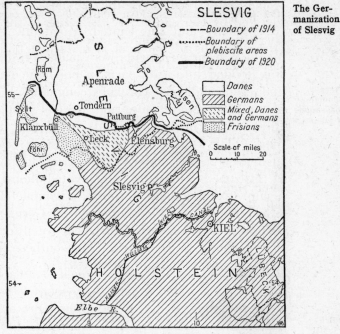

FIG. 91. Language boundaries in Slesvig according to Danish authority (Clausens, 1912). The northern plebiscite zone voted to join Denmark; the southern zone (between the dotted line and the solid one, except where the latter is bordered by dots) voted to remain German. The final boundary is shown by the heavy solid line. It differs from the plebiscite boundary only in detail, as at Pattburg and south of Alsen Island — adjustments designed to avoid disturbing the industrial relations of the people.

Between 1867 and 1895, there emigrated from the small territory of north Slesvig 57,000 persons. In 1898 about 1000 persons were expelled from the country. The Prussians made homeless those who had declared their intention to settle in Denmark, an act of oppression which contravened a privilege granted by the treaty of Vienna in 1864. All the children of those parents who declared their intention of returning to Denmark were forbidden to marry, and as soon as they married were expelled from the country. The Germans also obliged many purely Danish parishes to adopt German church services and forcibly colonized much of the land, giving state aid and more favorable terms of payment to Germans.

In the treaty of peace which defeated Austria signed with Prussia in 1866, it was stipulated that the inhabitants of northern Slesvig should have the right to decide by a free vote whether or not they would unite themselves to Denmark. This plebiscite was always deferred by Germany. By the terms of the treaty of peace between the Allied and Associated Powers and Germany at the close of the World War, arrangements were made for the plebiscite. The region was divided into two parts, a northern district voting as a whole, and a central district voting by communes. The northern district has about 1500 square miles and 165,000 people, and in February 1920 three fourths of its inhabitants voted that the region return to Denmark. The vote in the southern district, taken March 1920, resulted in an even greater majority in favor of Germany. The principal town of this zone is Flensburg, which voted almost solidly for German ownership. Neither side, of course, is completely satisfied. The Danes would like to have Flensburg, and the Germans want Tondern, a small district in the northern zone which voted for Germany, but which is now assigned to Denmark. The southern boundary of Denmark as finally drawn is shown in Figure 91.

HOLLAND

Dutch colonial power

Holland, with 12,582 square miles of territory, is a mere spot on the map in comparison with her colonial possessions, whose total area is 783,000 square miles. Of this area, 737,000 is in the Malay Archipelago of the East Indies (Fig. 254). The Dutch West Indian possessions, including Dutch Guiana on the mainland of South America, have an area of 46,000 square miles and a population of 90,000. Holland has a population but little in excess of 6,700,000, while her East Indian colonies have 47,000,000. The island of Java, a Dutch colony, is the most densely populated land mass in the world. It is noteworthy that all of Holland's colonies are in the tropics. They thus supplement the products of Holland and have long formed the basis for an important trade with Germany and Great Britain. Through their use of cheap Malay labor and their development of the plantation system, the Dutch laid the foundations of colonial success.

Colonial policy

Coffee and sugar culture in the Dutch East Indies have long had a vital relation to Dutch prosperity. More recently the production of plantation rubber has brought huge amounts of foreign capital and a fresh hold upon international trade. As far as treatment of natives goes, the Dutch "culture" system was at first absolutely ruthless and native exploitation became a highly developed art. Famine and pestilence resulted, and at last the system, which was virtually slavery, was abolished for one that provided for at least theoretically free labor. To make labor really free in the Dutch East Indies will be one

Fig. 92. Flensburg, a town near the border of Denmark and Germany and thirty-two miles north of the Kiel Canal. This was a center of rivalry between Danes and Germans during the plebiscite period. Consult Figure 91.

FIG. 93. The struggle for land in Holland. After R. Schuiling, *Nederland: Handboek der Aardrijkskunde*, 5th ed., 1915, p. 6.

of the problems to which the signatories of the Labor Convention will be compelled to address themselves in the near future.

The results of Dutch activity in the East have been excellent in other fields. The topographic surveys are of high grade and, along with scientific expeditions to little-known interior regions, have opened up valuable lands to future development. Telegraph lines, cables, lighthouses, and free harbors have promoted trade. Piracy has been all but suppressed, and the benefits of orderly government have been extended to peoples once lawless.

Holland's foreign policy

The conditions of life in Holland have created an intense interest in the principle of the freedom of the seas and the security of distant colonies held by the smaller powers. Threatened by the growth of Germany's submarine fleet, Holland could scarcely hope for German success. At the same time, she could not forget her historic naval defeat at the hands of the British, the colonies in South Africa that she had lost to Great Britain, or the kinship of the Boers who had fought in vain against British domination. As long as she was not directly threatened, she did not wish to disturb her profitable trade as a neutral with needy Germany. With Allied victory safeguarding her colonial titles, Holland had only to hold fast to all her European territory to come out of the war with relatively small losses. Her shipping and commerce had suffered by submarine sinkings and by American and British internment, but she had escaped the huge debts of the belligerents and their loss of man power.

Territorial disputes with Belgium

We have already reviewed her disputes with Belgium respecting Dutch Limburg and the left bank of the Scheldt (page 123). However desirable these additions might be for Belgium, their loss was not to be thought of by the Dutch. Limburg contains coal deposits, and Holland is poor in mineral resources of every sort. The Dutch have a remarkable maritime and commercial history, and they could hardly be expected to advantage a neighbor at direct loss to themselves.

Fig. 94.   Rotterdam, the chief Dutch rival of the Belgian port of Antwerp on the Scheldt.
See Figure 63.

Antwerp may need the lower Scheldt, but its growth would check the development of Rotterdam and other Dutch ports. That Holland's course might lead to Belgian enmity was a difficulty hardly to be avoided in any case, seeing that Belgium had revolted from Holland in 1830 and that Belgium's foreign policy favored France while Holland was commercially and politically more closely allied to Germany.

To secure sufficient soil for her people, Holland reclaims the shallow sea floor and marshes of the coast. The Dutch have a saying: "God made the sea, but man made the land." Vast sums have been expended on reclamation projects and more will follow if the plan of reclaiming part of the Zuider Zee is continued (Fig. 93). These efforts have induced an appreciation of land that makes the loss of it, in whatever form, appear to be a calamity.

The lower Scheldt is also vitally related to the whole matter of Holland's frontiers. On every side she seeks to develop the strategic value of water. A belt of marshes forms the northern third of her eastern frontier. The long and indented coast is fringed with shallow water easy to defend. Much of the reclaimed land is pasture and could be flooded, if the national defense required it, without destroying the principal towns. Like Belgium, the country occupies a highly strategic position between larger powers intent on maintaining the integrity of a small state which no one of them would like to see absorbed by another.

A third of Holland is pasture land in a high state of development. She can never rival Belgium's industrial production, but she has the navy, the colonial sources of raw material, and the thrift to develop her natural resources and her maritime trade to a high degree. In the past half century her industries have grown rapidly in response to her desire to be more nearly independent industrially, a desire that she could the more easily satisfy because of her colonial supply of raw materials — sugar, hemp, vegetable oil, and rubber.

CHAPTER NINE

RAILWAY AND TERRITORIAL PROBLEMS OF SWITZERLAND

At the end of the World War, Switzerland, though a neutral, was left with at least three possible sources of trouble:

(1) International traffic passes through Switzerland on a great scale (Fig. 95), and this fact affects the economic and political freedom of the country. The navigation of the Rhine has never been controlled to Switzerland's satisfaction; and she is also interested in the new Allied purpose of internationalizing by treaty certain ports, rivers, and canals. *International problems of Switzerland*

(2) The eastern part of the country is German-speaking, the western part French, and national opinion is strongly divided on questions that affect relations with neighboring states.

(3) The isolated mountain communities of western Austria, like the Vorarlberg, for example, wish to escape the heavy tax burdens imposed on Austria by the treaty of St. Germain-en-Laye, and to this end plead for admission to the Swiss Confederation as a separate canton or district.

Because of limited resources and heavy emigration, Switzerland has grown very slowly by comparison with other central European countries. As much as 28 per cent of the land is unproductive, though we must count as an asset the scenery, which attracts a heavy and profitable tourist travel. There are only 4,000,000 people, and while this number represents an increase over earlier years, more than 40 out of 187 of the political districts have had an actual decrease of population. The foreign element has increased despite the heavy emigration of the Swiss. Between 1880 and 1910, Italian citizens resident in Switzerland increased from 41,000 to 203,000, the greatest influx being due to the employment of Italians on railway and tunnel construction. They congregate in the cities and live in insanitary surroundings, thus increasing the social problems of the government. *Switzerland a land of very limited resources*

POSITION WITH RELATION TO OTHER COUNTRIES

An interior, landlocked state, without a seaport, without colonies, a buffer between powerful nations, Switzerland has maintained her independence in spite of aggressive and ambitious neighbors. But the independence or sovereignty of Switzerland is in actual practice limited. For example, take the convention of 1909 between Germany and Italy on the one hand and Switzerland on the other, made when the *Pressure upon the Swiss government by Italy and Germany*

181

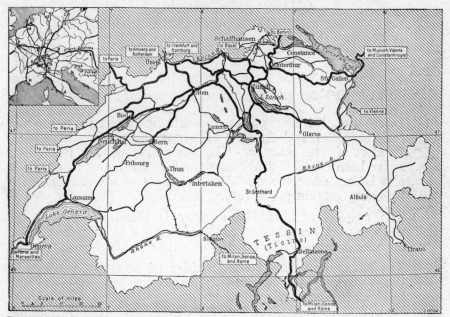

FIG. 95.   The place of Switzerland in the railway net of Europe.   Railways with more than ten freight trains daily are shown by heavy lines.   Railroads from *Atlas géographique et statistique de la Suisse*, 1915, Pl. 48, and *Documents cartographiques de géographie économique*, No. 1913.

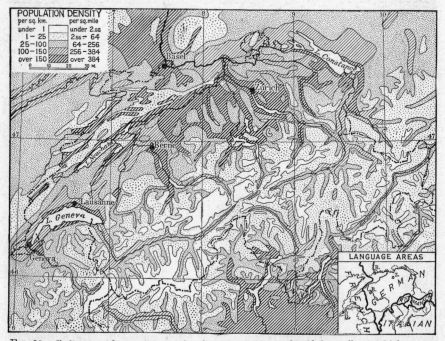

FIG. 96.   Switzerland has population bands (conforming to the Alpine valleys) which represent in many cases the extremities of similar though broader bands of population in adjacent countries.   With such a distribution of population, railways are peculiarly important (Fig. 95). From *Schweizischer Schulatlas*.

Publishers' Photo Service

FIG. 97.   Andermatt, in southern Switzerland near the St. Gotthard Pass, where a railway tunnel pierces the southern mountain wall.

Swiss government proposed to buy from its private owners the St. Gotthard railway system, which is a part of the through rail route between Germany and Italy, under the famous St. Gotthard pass in the Swiss Alps.   Germany and Italy objected to the purchase, unless Switzerland would promise to allow traffic at the same rates as over other parts of the system in Germany and Italy.

Switzerland protested, but her protests were of no avail until the treaty of Versailles was ratified.   In the articles governing Rhine traffic freedom of access to the sea for Swiss commerce was guaranteed and pressure heretofore brought to bear on Switzerland was removed. In return, however, it was stipulated that there was to be freedom of transit across Switzerland for goods and persons of neighboring states. *Swiss commerce now guaranteed free access to the sea*

Late in 1919 railway conferences between German, Swiss, and Italian interests were held at Heidelberg, Germany, and as a result the German-Swiss-Italian traffic was in part renewed in the summer of 1920. *Agreements with neighbors*

FIG. 98.   Interlaken, with the Jungfrau in the background — a typical Swiss landscape.

Switzer-
land the
interna-
tional
country

The peculiar position of Switzerland among the countries of the world is further emphasized by the fact that she has long been the refuge of exiled scholars and scientists from the less liberal countries of Europe.   She has been a center of advanced education and, at times, of political plots aimed by exiles at their enemies at home.   She has consistently preserved the rights of asylum, and during the war, as well as after it, she permitted numbers of political agents, exiles, ex-kings, and the like, to take refuge within her frontiers.

Switzerland is the home of a number of international organizations like the Postal Union and the International Red Cross Society; and Geneva has been selected as the seat of the League of Nations.

POLITICAL TENDENCIES OF SWITZERLAND

Swiss
political
tendencies
toward
socialism

State socialism has gone very far in Switzerland, and it has not yet reached its climax there.   For nearly thirty years the state has had a high revenue from customs duties, with which it has bought five great railways, guaranteed work to every able-bodied man, and enforced compulsory sickness insurance.

FRONTIER QUESTIONS

Switzerland has had no change in boundaries as a result of the war. Nevertheless, she faces a territorial problem on her eastern frontier, in relation to the Vorarlberg region (Fig. 99). Here, in a number of high Alpine valleys in the extreme western part of Austria,

Swiss opposition to incorporation of the Vorarlberg

FIG. 99.   Switzerland and the western provinces of Austria. L. stands for Liechtenstein (enclave of German territory) and V. for Vorarlberg (Austrian). The latter sought unsuccessfully to secure union with Switzerland that she might escape the fate of Austria under the treaty of St. Germain-en-Laye.

lives a group of people unwilling to remain a part of the Austrian Republic. Shortly after the armistice between the Allies and Austria-Hungary in 1918, delegations of Vorarlberg citizens, chiefly workmen and innkeepers, sought to secure incorporation of the district into Switzerland. This would add about 15,000 German-speaking people to the already heavy German majority in Switzerland, besides greatly increasing the present Catholic majority.

Switzerland long opposed the union, though there are the closest ties between her eastern districts and western Austria. It would increase her debts, for these former citizens of Austria-Hungary could not be allowed to escape their part of the heavy Austro-Hungarian debt by becoming Swiss citizens. They should pay a share of the pre-war debts, the war debts, and the so-called Rhine dues formerly paid by Austria. The people of Vorarlberg have sought union with Germany also.

Happily, the long-standing claim of Italy to the Ticino, a part of Swiss territory, will probably never be raised again. Italy has received such ample satisfaction in the Tyrol (page 134) that her irredentist claims on her Alpine frontier should be now fully satisfied.

The Swiss Federal Council has agreed to assume the diplomatic and consular representation of the principality of Liechtenstein. If the negotiations succeed, Switzerland will take over the postal, telegraphic, telephonic, and customs service. Liechtenstein, a detached part of Germany, also is seeking recognition as an independent state on account of her peculiar geographical position (Fig. 99).

Liechtenstein now the ward of Switzerland

CHAPTER TEN

PROBLEMS OF THE GERMAN PEOPLE

Former
German
commercial
power

Before the war of 1914–1918, the problems of the German people covered political and economic fields nearly as broad as those of Great Britain. German wares had been carried into every trading realm of the world, and the trader meant political as well as commercial penetration; colonies had been acquired in Africa and the Pacific, and concessions in China. The products of German industry were of high grade, and they were cheap. In central Europe, the Balkans, and Turkey, Germany's political influence was dominant and her trade was rapidly increasing. Supporting these advances in trade and colonies was an intelligent and industrious people, trained in the arts, and possessing enviable sources of mineral wealth, especially iron and coal.

Germany's
new orien-
tation

As we shall see from a list of her losses on a later page, Germany has been stripped of her overseas possessions, her merchant fleet has been surrendered, her good-will is gone, and the goods of other countries — former rivals in trade — have displaced German goods almost everywhere. Her problems are now of a new order. Domestic issues, chiefly social and economic, have attained first rank. In place of colonies to be developed, there are debts to be paid. Instead of continued territorial gains, there are territorial losses. Once she could threaten her rivals, in a diplomatic struggle for land or trade resources, with a powerful navy and army; now her navy is gone and she is required by treaty to reduce her army to 100,000 men. Once she looked out upon the world as a growing state; she must now turn her attention inward, for domestic resources and political arrangements must first be developed, in the reconstitution of the national life.

TERRITORIAL DISTRIBUTION OF THE GERMANS

Distribu-
tion of
German-
speaking
people

In rebuilding the German state, there is one factor of immediate concern — the distribution of German-speaking people on the map of Europe (Fig. 100). Formerly Germany and Austria contained the principal block, with an extension of 2,600,000 German-speaking people in eastern and central Switzerland, another much smaller group in Slesvig-Holstein, and scattered "islands" in Hungary, southern Russia, and the Baltic provinces, besides important "colonies" in southern Brazil, Chile, Colombia, and China.

Upon this geographical distribution there depend political relations

186

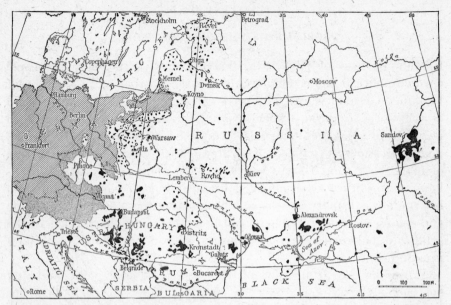

Fig. 100. The dotted area represents German-speaking people in former Austria-Hungary continuous with the main body in Germany. The black spots represent centers of German speech elsewhere in central and eastern Europe. They are due to many causes — religious differences, crusades in the Baltic region, settlements of frontier guards against Turkey in Transylvania, artisan groups invited into southern Russia. After Debes, *Handatlas*. See also the map on page 72 of *Kartographische und Schul-geographische Zeitschrift*, Vol. 8, 1919, for recent German opinion on the subject.

and influences of the first order. Some of the relations of the past throw light upon current problems.

FORMER GERMAN INFLUENCE IN NEIGHBORING STATES

In Austria-Hungary the Germans were so numerous — about 11,000,000 — that what with their compact distribution and the German origin of the Hapsburgs, they exercised a dominating influence on the political life of the empire, and at the same time served in part as a basis for the political views and ambitions of the Pan-Germans. The policies of Berlin were to a large degree reflected in the policies of Vienna. Moreover, the rulers of both empires had a cynical view of those people of non-German race and speech whom they had forcibly included within their imperial frontiers as minorities. For example, there was as little excuse for the Germans to withhold from the Danes of Slesvig a plebiscite promised by the treaty of Prague (1866) as for Austria to seize Bosnia and Herzegovina (1908).

German and Austrian co-operation

Among the other groups of Germans outside the German Empire, the two most important were those in southern Russia and in the Baltic Provinces. In southern Russia they comprised in large part

German centers in eastern Europe

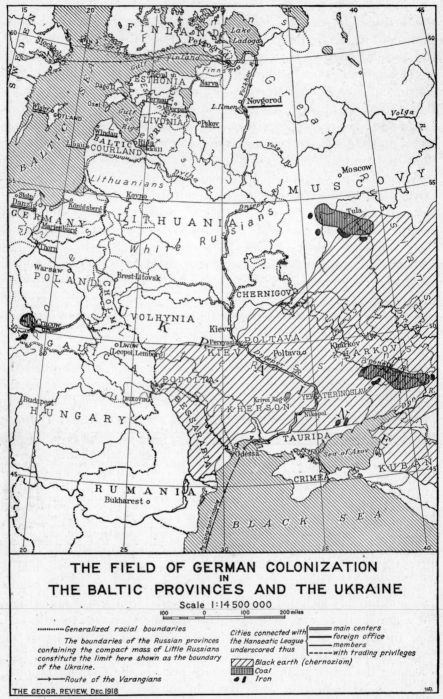

THE FIELD OF GERMAN COLONIZATION
IN
THE BALTIC PROVINCES AND THE UKRAINE

Scale 1:14 500 000

100   0   100   200 miles

••••••••••*Generalized racial boundaries*

*The boundaries of the Russian provinces
containing the compact mass of Little Russians
constitute the limit here shown as the boundary
of the Ukraine.*

——→—*Route of the Varangians*

*Cities connected with
the Hanseatic League
underscored thus*

▨ *Black earth (chernoziom)*
▥ *Coal*
● ▮ *Iron*

══ *main centers*
── *foreign office*
━━ *members*
---- *with trading privileges*

THE GEOGR. REVIEW, DEC. 1918

FIG. 101. Historical and economic aspects of the German penetration of Russia. National
boundaries as in 1914. "Racial," here as elsewhere in this book, is employed in the popular
rather than the scientific sense.

the artisan classes, the merchants, and engineers with technical skill; and in the Baltic Provinces they formed the land-owning class, the so-called German barons, or Balts, who formed a small percentage of the population but held about three fourths of the land. In both districts the German element was politically powerful, that of the Baltic Provinces being especially influential at the court of Petrograd. Libau and Memel are peopled chiefly by Germans, not Slavs. Riga had a powerful German commercial community with business connections that penetrated far into Russia.

Wherever the Germans have gone in eastern Europe they have carried the German tongue, German culture and political ideas, and German industrial power. They are scattered over the whole central and eastern European region as far as the middle Volga, and their influence has been felt everywhere. They have their own schools and trading associations; many maintain their citizenship in Germany. German colonists west of Kiev, in northern Ukrainia, owned the steel mills and many of the large landed estates; many entered the army and became celebrated officers. The Saxons of Transylvania, in the midst of a Rumanian peasantry, were given a privileged position by Hungary. *Germanization of eastern Europe*

If the Germans had been able to enforce their will through the treaty of Brest-Litovsk (repudiated as one of the conditions of the armistice of 11 November 1918), they would have ruled once more over the eastern Baltic coastlands as in the days of the Teutonic Knights (13th and 14th centuries). A German prince had been selected as king of a greater Lithuania; Esthonia and Latvia were to be mere political dependencies. Vast colonization plans were developed which were to include many principles long successfully employed by the Prussians against the Poles in the Polish Corridor and elsewhere. Had they succeeded, the number of German settlers would have rapidly increased; German commerce and political control would have been developed hand in hand; the new Baltic republics would have exchanged masters without gaining freedom.

Indeed, the process would not have stopped with the Baltic Provinces. The Bolshevists were at first subsidized by Germany and were favored by the German higher military command. But for the defeat of Germany by the Allies and the re-creation of the Polish buffer state, we should have seen in time a strong welding of Russian commerce with that of Germany and the development of the closest political relations.

FIG. 102.   The contest between German and Slav at the beginning of
the 15th century.   Based on Putzger, *Historischer Schul-Atlas*, and
Droysen, *Hand-Atlas*.

In Germany today there is a strong tendency to pivot future political and economic influences in eastern Europe, particularly in
Russia, upon these German colonies.   And if this policy is followed,
Germany will in the future have an eastern, as opposed to a former
western, orientation.   A practical exhibition of this tendency was
given in 1920 when thousands of Germans entered Lithuania to fight
on her side against Polish control of Vilna.

GERMAN MINORITIES IN THE NEW STATES

With the fall of German rulers in 1918, the democratic era, fore- Rise of German democracy and liberation of subject peoples shadowed by the Revolution of 1848 and by the steady increase of the Social Democrats in the Reichstag, at last began. There came also the final liberation of peoples who, by gaining independence, took away substantial portions of Germany, as well as the greater part of Austria and Hungary. Additional losses of population were incurred through the treaty of Versailles, which included many Germans in the new states, on the ground that the colonization methods of Germany and the forced ethnic penetrations of Austria and Hungary had put the former minority populations of these countries under a handicap. They had been driven out of districts in which they had a right to live on equal terms with the German-speaking newcomers. However, this political principle should not diminish appreciation of the service rendered by many German settlers on the eastern frontier of the German lands. While each one of the three great eastward-reaching prongs of German population, shown in Figure 100, is often described as the result of a war of conquest against Turks and Slavs, these wars were in the main a part of the general process of expansion of the higher civilization of western Europe eastward against the lower oriental civilization that long threatened to overwhelm it.

The historic boundary of Bohemia has become, for a part of its course, the new boundary of Czecho-Slovakia, although more than 2,500,000 Germans are thereby included; and the strip of land between Schneidemühl and Bromberg (part of the Polish Corridor) becomes a part of the new Polish state, in spite of the present predominance of Germans (Fig. 171).

The exclusion of large numbers of Germans from Germany raises Germans outside of Germany in neighboring states a group of problems which every thoughtful person should examine very closely. There is no more effective cry in the world than the cry of oppression, and Americans in particular have always had a sympathetic ear for a people in distress and struggling to be free, because as a self-governing, democratic, and free people they know what freedom costs to get and to keep. What if these excluded Germans in a few years raise the same cry as the peoples once held in their grasp? In general the world was not sympathetic toward France in 1870–1871; but by 1914 it had become educated to the wrongs done by the German overlords in Alsace-Lorraine. The Poles and Czechs, who, if they cared to, could now turn the tables on the Germans run grave risks if they choose the way of the vengeful oppressor.

Will Aus-
tria join
Germany?

The largest group of Germans outside the German Empire is that in Austria. To join this country to Germany would give the latter a total population larger and much more homogeneous than that which she had before the war. It would also throw the frontiers of Germany eighty miles nearer the head of the Adriatic. While the Baltic and the North Sea coasts would be left practically unchanged, except for the short strip at Danzig and Memel, there would be consolidated a solid block of German territory that might lead to the revival of the former Pan-German plan by which central Europe would again pass under Teutonic domination. The treaty of Versailles has forbidden this union, which will not be permitted until it is reasonably certain that German democracy is real and has come to stay.

The Ger-
mans of
the new
Poland

The limits of the German Empire as drawn in 1914 show that the largest linguistic or " racial " minority within it was the Poles. These have now joined with the Poles of Austria (Galicia) and of Russia (Congress Poland [1] and a strip of territory adjoining it on the east) to form the new Polish state. In the Polish state about 2,000,000 Germans will be included, but they form almost everywhere the minority of the population. Figure 170 shows that they were, in large numbers, officials of the Prussian state, officers in the German army, German teachers, colonists, foresters, and the like. They have the privilege of becoming Polish citizens before the end of 1921 or of moving into Germany if they wish to escape the handicap of German speech or birth.

It would be a great calamity for Poland if the whole body of Germans should choose to remain and to have representation in the Polish Diet, because they would form a minority party with an obstructionist policy, a party devoted to the harassing advertisement of wrongs real or alleged. The presence of such parties within the state was a standing difficulty with both Germany and Austria-Hungary. It embittered almost every debate and caused the neglect of purely national business to a deplorable extent.

The Ger-
mans of
Czecho-
Slovakia
and Tyrol

The same observation applies to those Germans, about 3,500,000 in number, that have been assigned to Czecho-Slovakia. Many citizens of that country regret their inclusion as a minority group without interest in national affairs. The Germans of the Tyrol are in the same situation with respect to Italy. Only the most careful treatment by these three nations — Poland, Czecho-Slovakia, and Italy — of

[1] Name given to a political division of Russia (created a kingdom under the Czar by the Congress of Vienna) which includes chiefly Polish populations. Its boundaries on the west and south were the former German and Austrian international boundaries. Its limits are shown in Figure 169.

the minority Germans within their frontiers will relieve the anxiety of statesmen lest they turn on their former oppressors and create in the future a new crop of troubles for themselves and the world.

The protection of minority rights is indeed one of the great prob- *The rights of minorities often difficult to guarantee* lems of the time. It cannot be solved by splitting up the world indefinitely. Not every tiny group can have its own flag and place in the family of nations. For the weakest peoples there is only one practicable alleviation — that minorities shall have a court of appeal and certain broad guarantees of personal rights of speech and religion.

CONSEQUENCES OF THE WAR

Instead of advancing her program of expansion toward Russia and *What Germany has lost in Europe by the treaty of Versailles* in Africa, the Pacific, and the Near East, Germany has lost territory, trade, and privileges. The following are to her the most important European consequences of the World War:

(1) German coal in the Saar valley has been given to France to offset the losses caused by the destruction of the French coal mines, chiefly at Lens and Valenciennes, during the war. A plebiscite at the end of fifteen years will determine final ownership of the Saar district; but the region may vote for France in spite of the restriction of the privilege of voting to persons living in the Saar on 10 January 1920. Before the war (1913), the Saar coal mines yielded 17,400,000 tons of coal, or about 9 per cent of Germany's total.

(2) Eupen, Malmédy, and Moresnet, ceded to Belgium, have mineral resources of value, but their total little affects the totals for all Germany before the war.

(3) The loss of a part of the Silesian coal fields of southeastern Germany is inevitable, and with that part will go some of the strength of the city of Breslau and the other towns near by. The area of the plebiscite zone is about 4000 square miles, and the population is 2,000,000. The coal production of the district was 43,000,000 tons in 1913, or more than one fifth of the total production of the German Empire (which exceeded 190,000,000 tons in 1913). It also produced 57 per cent of the lead ore of Germany and 72 per cent of the zinc. Though 65 per cent of the population of all German Silesia is Polish, the great economic loss to Germany which the cession to Poland would cause resulted in the decision to hold a plebiscite. The vote was taken in March 1921, and was on the whole favorable to Germany; but the final boundary, which will be determined by the Supreme Council, may not accurately reflect the results of the vote.

(4) The transfer of former German territory in the northeastern part of East Prussia beyond the Niemen River is justified by the presence of the Lithuanian population that has lived there for centuries (Fig. 184). With the recognition of a Lithuanian government will go, of course, the effort to join into one group the whole Lithuanian population, as far as this is possible. With the trans-Niemen country will probably go the former German port of Memel, the outlet of the Niemen basin and the terminus of a Russian railway. Pending a settlement of the Russian question, with which Lithuanian independence is intimately related, Memel is held by warships of the Allied powers.

(5) Exclusive of Danzig and Silesia, Germany has lost 2,800,000 people and 16,000 square miles to Poland; this territory includes the rich industrial province of Posen, besides valuable forest and agricultural lands, coal and other mines, and about one tenth the total German production of grain and one sixth the German production of potatoes.

(6) The separation of East Prussia from the main body of German territory doubtless will disturb the economic life of the region. But it is important to furnish a nation of 25,000,000 people (Poland) with a port (Danzig) and the means of a secure access to the sea (the Polish Corridor, or strip of land west of the Vistula that joins Poland with the Baltic). The middle of the Polish Corridor is only thirty miles wide, too narrow to be the base of great military operations; and the city of Danzig itself is to be governed by the League of Nations through a High Commissioner. The provisions for the management of the port of Danzig and for a treaty between Danzig and Poland respecting the use of the port guarantee freedom of transit to the Poles at Danzig and also to the Germans of East Prussia over the railroad from Königsberg to Schneidemühl and Berlin. Besides this there is free navigation of the Baltic for goods that may go by sea, and the common use by both East Prussia and Poland of the navigable (and internationalized) Vistula that separates their territory.

(7) The plebiscite held in southern East Prussia (Allenstein), resulted in favor of union with Germany. The people are Poles in race and speech, but they are Lutheran in religion, unlike the main body of Poles, who are Catholics. The total population is about 716,000. The neighboring plebiscite area of Marienwerder (Fig. 171) is almost wholly German and also voted to remain in Germany.

(8) The area which Germany has lost in Slesvig contains about 1500 square miles; the population is 300,000. This

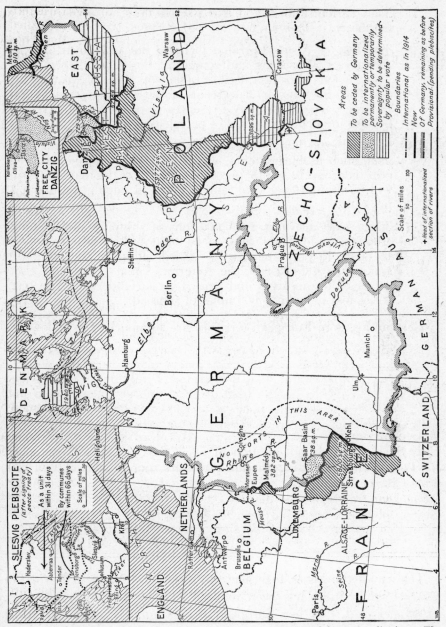

Fig. 103. Generalized view of the conditions of German territorial losses by districts. The figure under Malmédy represents the total for the districts of Eupen and Malmédy. The Allenstein and Marienwerder districts east of the Vistula have voted to remain German; only the northern of the two Slesvig districts voted to join Denmark. For details of final Slesvig boundary see Figure 91. Originally set apart as plebiscite areas, the Teschen, Orawa, and Spits districts have been settled by the Conference of Ambassadors (Fig. 179), though the Polish Diet has yet to ratify the agreement. Czecho-Slovakia eventually gains a small district northwest of Teschen. If Austria should join Germany (page 214), German losses of population and territory would be more than counterbalanced.

is an agricultural region and its loss does not seriously affect Germany.

(9) The loss of Alsace-Lorraine includes not only territory, but the city of Strasbourg and control of the Rhine River traffic. The region also produced 21,000,000 tons of iron yearly and 350,000 tons, or 3 per cent, of the world's potash supply. A large part of Germany's reserves of potash were in Alsace, besides important reserves of petroleum.

(10) All told, the loss in Germany's principal agricultural products, such as barley, oats, wheat, rye, potatoes, sugar beets, etc., is from 12 to 15 per cent. Her loss in manufacturing will be about 10 per cent, and her loss in population about 12 per cent.

(11) There were also lost 2,550,000 tons of shipping, not including 1,000,000 additional tons to be built in the next five years to offset in part the loss of Allied shipping by submarine sinkings. A fourth of the country's canal boats and thousands of locomotives and cars were surrendered. The territories lost include 35,000 miles of railroad.

German losses in European territory are summarized as follows:

AREA OF PARTS OF GERMANY AFFECTED BY THE TREATY OF VERSAILLES

	Sq. Miles
Neutral Moresnet	2
Kreis Eupen	68
Kreis Malmédy	314
Alsace-Lorraine	5,600
Saar Basin (possibly not permanent)	730
To Poland (not including Silesian plebiscite zone)	16,000
Free City of Danzig	729
Memel, or trans-Niemen, district	910
Slesvig plebiscite area (northern zone)	1,550
Total	25,903

Taking all the losses together, the former Germany in Europe of 203,834 square miles has been reduced by over 25,000 square miles, or 13 per cent. Of her European population, Germany has ceded 8,000,000, or about 12 per cent of her pre-war total. Owing to the losses of the war by disease and in battle, there has been a further reduction of the population by more than 5,000,000, including 2,000,000 young men.

Among the losses incurred in China by Germany are these:

Fig. 104. Distribution of industrial and agricultural population of Germany in 1895. The
map represents Germany in a period of transition.   In the decade from 1880 to 1890, German pig-
iron production increased 100 per cent. The same rate of increase was maintained during the
two succeeding decades. Note the belt of industrial population along the French and Belgian
frontiers. Compare this map with the map of population density (Fig. 60). The territorial
losses on the east involve chiefly agricultural population. From maps in *Statistische Jahrbuch
des Deutsches Reich*, 1898.

(1) The privilege of maintaining a postal service.   (All the powers
     enjoyed this privilege, which was gained before China had
     a postal service.)

(2) Concessions at Tientsin, Hankow, and Kiaochow (Fig. 244).

(3) The privilege of maintaining legation guards at Pekin.

(4) The Shantung railway, mines, and port rights now turned over
     to the Japanese government.

In addition to her losses in Europe and Asia, Germany loses all
her overseas colonies, amounting to an area of about 1,000,000 square
miles and a population estimated at 12,000,000. The colonies supplied a fourth of the total German demand for rubber, besides valuable oils and fibers.[1]

---

[1] For the value of these possessions see the chapters on Africa, Australia and the Pacific,
and the Far East.

The colonial losses not specified on page 197 are as follows:

Africa	*Pacific*
(1) Togoland	(1) Marshall, Marianne, and Caroline Islands
(2) Cameroons	
(3) German Southwest Africa	(2) Kaiser Wilhelm's Land and Bismarck Archipelago
(4) German East Africa	
	(3) German Samoa and Solomons
	(4) Nauru Island

FORMER COLONIAL INTERESTS OF THE GERMAN EMPIRE

Difficulties in the way of colonial expansion

Germany entered the field of colonial activity late in her national career. She made her first essay in colonial expansion in the Pacific as late as 1884; and it was only after much vacillation that she finally established herself in Africa in the same year. Her leaders had been opposed to colonial expansion; their sense of economy was shocked by the large expenditures that were necessary to keep distant and undeveloped territories under control. As a consequence, Great Britain and France had a full half century and more of advantage in time and experience. Between 1876 and 1884 these powers had laid claim to some of the choicest areas in Africa. The field of colonial expansion had been greatly narrowed.

Reasons for entering the colonial field

When Germany awoke to a full realization of the value of colonial raw materials to her magically expanding industries, she found that she could gain important advantages only by pursuing an exceedingly active policy. What she had lacked in initiative she now made up by aggression and skill Wherever her colonies touched the territory of other powers, she made the fullest possible use of any differences of opinion regarding the location of boundary lines or the extent of her concessions or the terms of her treaties with native chiefs. Her merchants had established trading stations on both the east and the west coasts of Africa. In 1859 Hamburg, Bremen, and Lübeck made a commercial treaty with the Sultan of Zanzibar. By 1884 about sixty German trading posts and a hundred or more of missionary stations were located on the west coast. To consolidate her interests, impose her own tariffs, and have strategic commercial and military bases for further gains now became accepted aims of Germany's African policy. The field of her activity was limited to central Africa, where vague boundaries enabled her to gain control without resort to war.

Struggle at Walvis Bay

German Southwest Africa was the scene of the first struggle. Fearing the results of the activities of German traders and missionaries in the Walvis Bay region, and yet momentarily timid in extending its own frontiers, the British government in 1878 declared the bay and fifteen miles round it British territory. The Germans responded by taking possession of Angra Pequeña, proclaiming it as German territory, and with it that part of the west coast between Portuguese Angola and the Orange River, save the small tract at Walvis Bay. In the same year (1884) Togoland was declared a German protectorate, on the ground that eight German trading stations had been established and that definite claims to the region had not been made by either France or Great Britain. Also in the same year, German political agents concluded treaties with some of the native chiefs of the Cameroons and the German flag was hoisted over the third of the newly won African colonies.

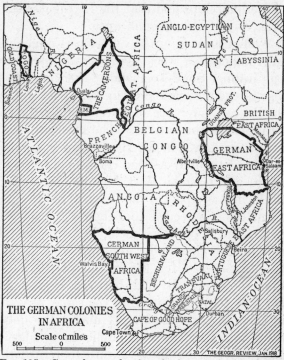

Fig. 105. General map showing the location of the former German colonies in Africa. For their disposition see Figures 15 and 49.

In the following year Great Britain acknowledged German commercial claims over East Africa. By 1888 some thirty coffee and tobacco plantations were in operation. Arab slave traders fomented a rebellion which was speedily put down, and in 1889 the German East Africa Society bought out the claims of the Sultan of Zanzibar to the coast strip, then under German control. Subsequent agreements with Great Britain in 1886 and 1890 fixed the boundaries of German East Africa and closed the first chapter of German colonization there.

Germany's ambitions looked not only toward the development of the African colonies, but also to the acquisition of other colonies near those already established. Her political moves in East Africa led the statesmen of rival nations to believe that she wished to acquire Portuguese East Africa as well as portions of French and Belgian territory. That the trade of the African colonies of Portugal was carried largely

German ambitions in Africa

by German ships and that the Portuguese colonial administration was weak, were facts of significance.

Africa the chief theatre of German colonial enterprise
While Germany's African colonies might ultimately prove to be of large importance, they were a drain upon her national resources (except in the case of Togoland). Neither was her control to the advantage of the regions she occupied. One of the reasons which impelled the Peace Conference of Paris to take the colonies from her was her treatment of the natives. The most striking case of the violation of native rights was in the Herero war in German Southwest Africa.

Two of the four African colonies of Germany — German Southwest Africa and German East Africa — fall under British administration, the former as a part of the Union of South Africa, the latter, except for a small portion ceded to Belgium (page 126), as a separate colonial possession. Neither is held, however, in full sovereignty, but as a mandated region under the authority of the League of Nations, to be administered for the benefit of the natives. Togoland and the Cameroons are divided between France and Great Britain (Figs. 267 and 268) for control in the same way. This is a new departure in colonial government. It makes the details of administration in these areas matters of public knowledge and approval. It also makes it possible in the future to return the colonies to Germany, though such a step is most unlikely in view of the flow of capital from the mandatory powers into the colonies and the strong objection of business to the unsettling effect of changes in political status.

FORMER GERMAN INTERESTS IN THE PACIFIC

Four stages may be recognized in the development of German ambitions in the Pacific. The first was purely commercial; the second was annexation — to extend the German Empire; in the next stage the islands of the Pacific were regarded not merely as additions to empire or as commercial assets, but as naval bases from which the power of the German government could be extended to rich and populous countries; the fourth, or present, stage is one of complete loss of former territories.

International Rivalries in Samoa

Beginnings of German expansion in the Pacific
Germany's first colonial activity in the Pacific was due to the effort of a Hamburg merchant prince — Godeffroy — who sent agents to Fiji and Samoa to establish cotton plantations. This was just after the American Civil War, when the European cotton famine turned the minds of merchants and statesmen to the necessity of producing

at least a part of their raw cotton within their own empires. Later the schemes of Godeffroy's company won a subvention from the German Reichstag.

But the field was not entirely open in Samoa, for the United States had had since 1839 the exclusive right to establish a naval base in the harbor of Pago Pago at Samoa, and the British colonies of Australia and New Zealand had developed an important trade in Samoa. In order to adjust the conflicting claims, the three powers — the United States, Great Britain, and Germany — sent representatives to a conference in Berlin which resulted in the Berlin General Act of 1880, providing a government for the kingdom of Samoa, the condominium, which existed down to 1899. In that year the three powers signatory to the Berlin General Act jointly agreed to annul the act and distribute Samoa. Tutuila was allotted to the United States, Upolu to Germany, and Savai'i to Great Britain. No sooner was this done than Great Britain gave Savai'i to Germany in return for concessions made by Germany to Great Britain in the Tonga and Solomon Islands. *The condominium in Samoa*

In German Samoa the native population is about 35,000, and the annual trade has a value of $2,500,000. These islands are now turned over to New Zealand to administer as a mandatory power of the League of Nations.

New Guinea

In 1884 Germany annexed the northern shore of New Guinea, from the Dutch boundary eastward to Dampier Strait, and inland as far as the supposed crest of the central range of mountains. Almost immediately thereafter she annexed the whole of the New Britain Archipelago (renamed Bismarck) and the northern Solomon Islands. Before these acts were committed, in 1883, Queensland had annexed the eastern half of the continental island of New Guinea, but the British government disavowed the act on the ground that it gave sovereign rights to a colony. It was in the face of this disavowal that the German annexation of the northeastern part of New Guinea (Kaiser Wilhelm's Land) took place. But the British government, yielding to popular sentiment, then annexed the southern shore of New Guinea and turned it over to Australia for administration, at the same time establishing a protectorate over the southern Solomons and Santa Cruz (Fig. 253). *German occupation of New Guinea, on the threshold of Australia*

The area of these territories, now assigned to Australia, is nearly 90,000 square miles, and the population numbers about 700,000.

Only two years after the acquisition of northeastern New Guinea, Germany hoisted her flag over the Marshall Islands, in protection of the commercial rights of a German company, and in 1899, the year after America had acquired the Philippines and the island of Guam from Spain, Germany bought from Spain the rest of her holdings in the Pacific — the Carolines, the Mariannes, and the Pelew Islands. These territories have an area of less than 1000 square miles and a native population of 70,000. All of them go to Japan except Nauru, which is south of the equator and goes to Great Britain (page 523).

Difficulties of colonial trade revival

With all the colonial possessions lost, German merchants are limited in their efforts at reviving overseas trade to general trading conditions like those that affect, say, the foreign merchants of Sweden or Switzerland. Since the commercial advantages and resources of every mandated region are open to the traders of all nations on terms of equality, German trade in her former colonies will revive, at least to some extent. And that it would revive quickly is certain, were it not for the lack of shipping. As a result of her unrestricted submarine campaign Germany was required, by treaty, in part to restore Allied shipping by surrendering her commercial fleet and allocating a large part of the tonnage to be built in the next few years.

In the colonies of other powers Germany's trade can be recovered only so far as tariff arrangements and good-will permit. France, Great Britain, and the United States have preferential rates; Italy, though her colonies have small interest to Germany, has restrictive shipping laws in force in Libya; Portugal puts all foreign traders under a handicap in her African colonies. Tropical raw materials will be less easy for Germany to obtain, and her trade with the nations of the temperate zone will be distinctly revived only when a stable government is formed, shipping built, currency deflated, and credit provided for new mercantile enterprises.

THE BURDENS OF THE NEW GERMAN STATE

The Spartacists or Bolshevists of Germany

The chief problem of Germany today is one of reconstruction to fit to her desperate needs the resources left in her hands and to stabilize the social and economic conditions created by the revolution (November 1918). The social and political conditions of Germany were becoming more and more critical even before the World War. Through the revolution that accompanied the armistice, they have become the vital problems of the day. The disorderly elements among the laboring classes in the industrial centers have taken advantage of the general turmoil to demand sovereign rights for themselves, which means merely that the tyranny of the militarists and imperialists has been exchanged for the tyranny of a small organized industrial class — the so-called proletariat.

It also remains to be seen whether Germany will become a great confederation or a collection of quarreling and self-seeking states, such as existed before the German Empire was formed in 1871. For the strength of the former empire is not a measure of the political resourcefulness of the people in the present democratic régime. The German people had never been able by peaceful processes to join together into a German union the various small Germanic states that had arisen during the two hundred years before Napoleon's time. *Possible revival of the German Confederation*

The growth of Prussia and the absorption of the smaller states of the German union was almost uniformly effected by military means, and when in 1870 France was conquered in a brief and spectacular campaign, military autocracy was confidently crowned with glory by the German people. Thereafter the government was supreme and molded public opinion to its will, instead of drawing its inspiration from public opinion. The growth of the empire had indeed been marvelous, but the principle of growth had been one of dependence upon military autocracy; and the spread of German culture implied the control, by that autocracy, of peoples who cherished liberty far more dearly than any benefits which German culture might bring. *Basis of former German unity*

No one should minimize the feat of the German people in holding together in one fashion or another through the days of the Spartacist[1] uprisings and the final realization of Allied victory. The terrible defeat of the German armies practically destroyed the dreams and ambitions of all but a desperate and limited group. Though the people tried to delude themselves into thinking that they had not met a military defeat, they all knew that such a defeat was a reality. All thought of a greater Germany was destroyed. Every one had been fighting in the hope of victory, and when defeat came, people had no alternative purposes or new sources of enthusiasm. They had neither hope nor a common plan of action. As with the Russian people, life had lost its old meaning. It will take time to develop constructive schemes. *The broken spirit of Germany*

Tending still further to disorganize German life was the length of the period of the armistice and of the blockade. The Germans had no raw materials, work would not buy clothes and food, and even the habit of work itself had been destroyed by the war, at *The long preliminaries of the new era*

---

[1] The name given to radical groups, organized almost wholly in the towns, who established local governments on the communistic principle (1918–1919).

least among tne returned soldiers. The effect was heightened by the stories of what the treaty of peace would do to Germany. The whole Silesian district, it was reported, would be given to Poland; and for a time the belief was current that the whole Left Bank of the Rhine would be given to France. For a short time a "Republic of the Left Bank of the Rhine" was in nominal existence.

Means of commerce destroyed

In addition, German merchants had been driven out of all the Allied countries and from Africa, the Far East, Turkey, and South America. There was no basis for foreign trade. The colonies were lost and the shipping had been surrendered. Transport facilities had to be rebuilt. Raw material was doled out to the Germans. There was not sufficient work even for those who wanted to work.

With the actual signing of the treaty of Versailles accomplished, Germany had her first hopes established, and immediately the radical movement received a severe check. Up to that time no German leader had a material basis for his program; he could build only on prophecy and hope. It was therefore natural that the radical and disorderly elements of the towns should have split the empire into a score of fragments. While there was a central government with headquarters at Weimar, later in Berlin, yet its authority was long recognized in only a small part of Germany.

The new constitution of Germany

The new constitution of Germany, framed by a constitutional assembly sitting at Weimar in 1919 and adopted by the Reichstag early in 1920, has many excellent features, but it remains to be seen if the people really intend to obey its conditions. There is liberty of speech and of the press as well as of association. There is complete religious freedom. The whole structure of the government is democratic — at least theoretically. The seed planted by the German thinkers and dreamers of 1848 is now bearing fruit. Though these men were exiled and imprisoned, they laid the foundations of the new Germany. The whole world was so shocked by the conduct of the war in the occupied territories and by the disclosure of sinister imperial designs in the treaties of Brest-Litovsk and Bucarest (which had put Russia and Rumania respectively in a state of economic slavery), that only actual and prolonged experience with the spirit of the new Germany will convince it that the change is sincere and lasting.

Amount of the German indemnity

Working against Germany in her economic struggle are the ill-will of much of the world and the headway other European nations have made during the war in seizing foreign markets. She will find it hard to get raw materials: her competitors control nearly all the sources.

Also, German goods will not be so readily purchased by persons who remember her evil course in 1914. Her people can overcome these handicaps only by work. According to the treaty of Versailles, for five years beginning in 1921, Germany must pay $250,000,000 a year, and thereafter $600,000,000 a year. This is arranged as interest on gold bonds amounting to $10,000,000,000, which Germany is to deliver to the Allies. A second issue of $10,000,000,000 at 5 per cent interest is to be made when Germany is thought by the Permanent Reparations Commission to be capable of paying the interest.

To avoid the business checks that grow out of the indefiniteness of the reparation total it was planned to fix that total while at the same time securing Germany's assent to it. The amount proposed was $55,000,000,000, to be paid in about forty years, and an export tax in addition; but Germany's representatives attempted to reduce this sum on the ground that it is economically impossible to pay it. When Germany finally rejected Allied proposals, French, British, and Belgian armies advanced still farther into western Germany, occupying places of strategic and industrial importance. They are to be withdrawn when Germany gives evidence of good faith in carrying out the terms of the treaty of Versailles and in meeting the first of her reparation payments.

The Allies had it in their power to impose much more severe conditions. In the matter of trade (which involves both access to raw materials and a market for her manufactures) Germany has come off well. Practically the only limitation is the reasonable one that her tariffs and other trade arrangements shall be uniform and shall be as favorable, at least, to her late enemies as those accorded to the trade of any other state. Even this arrangement is to be in force for five years only. Out of it may grow much simpler tariffs for all Europe.

Limitations on German trade

CHAPTER ELEVEN

THE NATIONAL EXISTENCE OF AUSTRIA

WHEN the Austro-Hungarian Empire fell apart in 1918, there was formed, out of the chief German-speaking element, the Republic of Austria, with Vienna as its capital and with a provisional democratic government. The frontiers remained to be defined by treaty with the Allied and Associated Powers. Ex-Emperor Charles took refuge, early in 1919, in Switzerland, where he still resides. The northern and southern Slavs set up new states; the Magyars, always loosely joined to Austria, adopted a separate national program; the Rumanians of Transylvania (Fig. 143) became a part of Greater Rumania; Galicia was included within the frontiers of Poland. These changes brought about a reduction of population from 51,000,000 for the whole Austro-Hungarian Empire (or from 28,500,000 if we exclude Hungary) before 1914 to 6,000,000 at the present time.

FIG. 106. Division and allotment of territory of the Austro-Hungarian Empire. The plebiscite areas are indicated by K for Klagenfurt (now Austrian), T for Teschen, O for Orawa, and S for Spits. For solution of the three last-named plebiscite areas, as recommended by the Conference of the Ambassadors, see Figure 179; for boundary between Italy and Jugo-Slavia see Figure 138.

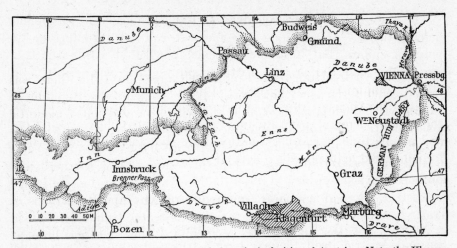

Fig. 107. The new Austrian boundary and the principal cities of Austria. Note the Klagen-furt plebiscite area, the southern border of which now becomes a part of the Austrian-Jugo-Slav boundary. Note also the addition to Austria of western, or German, Hungary. L is for Liechtenstein.

By the terms of the treaty of St. Germain-en-Laye, the area of Austria is reduced from 116,000 square miles to 32,000 square miles. Before the World War she had an outlet on the Adriatic at Trieste and Pola, and she also owned Dalmatia. With Hungary she controlled Bosnia and Herzegovina and thus held that long stretch of the eastern Adriatic coast that extends from the southern border of Montenegro northwestward for nearly 400 miles. With Hungary she controlled more than 700 miles of the course of the Danube. Her frontier ran for more than 1000 miles coterminous with that of Germany. She held the strategic passes in the mountains lying near the Italian frontier. East and west she had a maximum breadth of 750 miles in a straight line. North and south she extended 625 miles, thus spanning a section of country that extended from the plains of northern Europe to the Mediterranean lands on the shores of the southern Adriatic, and from the heart of the Alps on the borders of Switzerland in Vorarlberg to the plain of the Vistula on the farther side of the Carpathian Mountains.

The northern and southern Slavs (Czecho-Slovaks and Jugo-Slavs respectively) were chiefly in her domain. The Hungarians were allied with her in the empire. Her territory contained a large block of Rumanians, a smaller block of Italians, many Poles in Western Galicia, and 4,000,000 Ruthenians in Eastern Galicia and on the southern side of the Carpathians; it even included a large number of Mohammedans of Slavic race in the provinces of Bosnia and Herzegovina.

Extent of the Austro-Hungarian Empire

Racial complexities of the empire

The empire was geographically compact; ethnically it was highly heterogeneous. It was long customary to call Austria-Hungary the polyglot empire, but it should be remembered that within the Russian realm and the present British Empire there are many more ethnic complexities than Austria-Hungary had. The ethnic complexities of Austria-Hungary appeared the more prominent because the various elements were far more self-conscious politically and had had at one time or another a national life that formed a strong basis for continued agitation for independence.

THE PRESENT TERRITORY OF AUSTRIA

Extraordinary layout of the national domain of Austria

Viewing the Austro-Hungarian Empire with Hungary excluded, we find Austria itself to have been a fringe of country semicircular in form, reaching from near Cattaro on the eastern Adriatic northward to Fiume, Trieste, Vienna, and Prague; eastward to Cracow and Lemburg; and southward to Czernowitz and Kimpolung in Bukovina (Fig. 108). The length of this fringe exceeds 2000 miles and its average width is about 100 miles, reaching over 200 miles in Bohemia and Moravia, 250 miles in the Tyrol-Salzburg-Styria region, and narrowing to a strip of islands in the northeastern Adriatic and to a belt of mainland only 10 miles wide in southern Dalmatia.

Fragmentation of Austria

Within this area there is great diversity of relief, of ethnography, of density of population, of products, and of means of access to the sea. Neither the courses of the rivers nor the trends of the mountains justified so extraordinary a layout of the national domain. The various fragments of larger physical and commercial regions that formed Austria were held together by no natural bonds. The southern Tyrol is now politically united to Italy, by the treaty of St. Germain. Portions of Istria also were Italian, and they too are added to Italy by the treaty of Rapallo, which fixed the boundary between Italy and Jugo-Slavia. Except for Zara, the Dalmatian mainland goes to Jugo-Slavia. Bohemia and Moravia, populated chiefly by branches of the northern Slavs, become a part of the Czecho-Slovak republic. Poland has obtained all of Galicia. There is added to Rumania the former Crownland of Bukovina, except for a small salient on the northern frontier, which Poland has gained.

The fragments that have thus gone to a new or a rival power are in general in more natural relationship today than under the former system. The Bohemian plateau and its adjacent valleys have marked geographical unity. Galicia has a natural southern border — the

Carpathians—and a southeastward-trending valley lowland that contains a belt of dense population, a lowland which is continuous with the plains of the Vistula drainage basin.

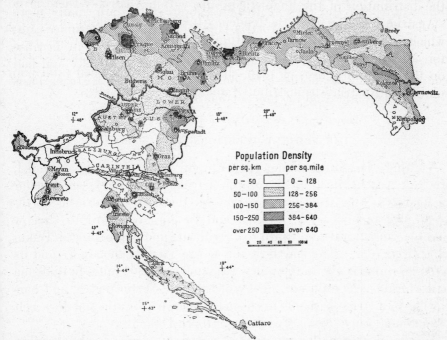

FIG. 108. The shape and population density of Austria according to the official census of 1910. For the break-up of Austria-Hungary and the relation of its parts to the denser nuclei of population shown above, see Figure 106. Note the denser population centers of Bohemia, the band of population in Galicia, the great contrast between the Viennese district and the western part of Austria proper, and the losses on the south to Italy and Jugo-Slavia. After Wallis, in the *Geographical Review*, July 1918.

Only a small portion of the Austrian frontier was left to a decision by plebiscite — the Klagenfurt area (Fig. 109). In trying to separate Jugo-Slavs (Slovenes at this point) from Austrians, there was one feature of the physical geography that gave much trouble. The Klagenfurt basin is enclosed by high land. It would seem wise to treat as a unit a region so well-marked by nature and by commercial relations. But the southern side of the basin is peopled by Slovenes, the northern side by Austrians. The city of Klagenfurt, with a population of 29,000, has a German majority, though this condition is of recent development. The matter was settled by a plebiscite in October 1920. It was arranged to take the vote in two zones, a northern and a southern. The people of the southern zone voted first and decided to join Austria. This made it unnecessary to take a vote in the northern district, which automatically remains Austrian territory.

Klagenfurt plebiscite and its results

RACIAL ELEMENTS

Ethnic differences

In sympathy with the main outlines of the physical system was the distribution of the linguistic groups within Austria — there is no "Austrian" race. Thus the tendency toward the break-up of Austria which is indicated by the unnatural physical relationship was reënforced by the strong ethnic differences. The following table, based on the Austrian census of 1910, shows how the 28,500,000 total population of Austria was distributed among the 17 provinces:

POPULATION, NATIONALITY, AND RELIGIONS OF AUSTRIA [1]

PROVINCE	POPULATION IN THOUSANDS	PERCENTAGES			
		RELIGION		NATIONALITY	
Lower Austria .	3,532	96% Roman Catholic		96% German	....
Upper Austria .	853	97 " "		100 "	....
Salzburg . . .	215	98 " "		100 "	....
Styria	1,444	98 " "		71 "	29% Slovene
Carniola . . .	396	94 " "		79 "	21 "
Carniola . . .	526	100 " "		94 Slovene	....
Trieste . . .	230	95 " "		62 Italian	30 Slovene
Goritzia . . .	261	99 " "		62 Slovene	36 Italian
Istria	404	99 " "		44 Serbo-Croat	38 "
Tyrol	947	99 " "		57 German	42 "
Vorarlberg . .	145	98 " "		95 "	....
Bohemia . . .	6,770	96 " "		63 Czech	37 German
Moravia . . .	2,622	95 " "		72 "	28 "
Silesia	757	84 " "		44 German	32 Pole
Galicia . . .	8,026	47 " "		59 Pole	40 Ruthenian
Bukovina . .	800	68 Greek Orthodox		38 Ruthenian	34 Rumanian
Dalmatia . . .	646	83 Roman Catholic		96 Serbo-Croat	....
Total . . .	28,574				

Present distribution of population

The new state has a population exceeding 6,000,000, distributed approximately as follows:

Lower Austria	3,500,000	Tyrol and Vorarlberg	450,000
Upper Austria	850,000	Styria	750,000
Salzburg	200,000	Carinthia	300,000

In the case of Tyrol, Styria, and Carinthia, only the German districts that are left to Austria are counted.

Emigration from Austria

Owing partly to the conditions of life under an autocratic government and partly to the general economic tendencies of the time, including growing industrialization, emigration from Austria rose to

[1] Up to this point we have been dealing chiefly with western European peoples. We now have to deal with new national and linguistic elements. Here we face the problem of the Magyar and the Slav. The reader should turn to Figures 111, 120, and 121 and to related pages for a general view of the population elements listed in this table.

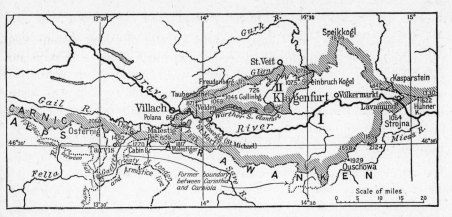

FIG. 109. The Klagenfurt plebiscite area. District I voted in October 1920 to remain with Austria on the north rather than be transferred to Jugo-Slavia on the south. As a result of this action, district II avoided a vote and automatically remained with Austria.

higher and higher figures in the years before the World War. From 1910 to 1913, the total net emigration from Austria to the United States averaged more than 80,000 a year, of which 36 per cent were Poles, 24 per cent Ruthenians, 10 per cent Czechs, and 7 per cent Germans. For many years 75 per cent of the overseas emigration from Austria has been to the United States, with 12 per cent to Canada and 4 per cent to South America, chiefly Argentina and Brazil.

Within Austria itself there was a tendency toward migration of the people from the country to Vienna and other large towns. In the period from 1880 to 1910, twelve towns had an increase of between 60 and 120 per cent, including such places as Vienna, Czernowitz, and Innsbruck among German towns, Lemberg and Cracow among Polish towns, Pilsen and Budweis among Czech towns, and Trieste among Italian towns, to mention the best-known places on the list. *Disproportion between city and country populations*

Among these Vienna had the most unnatural growth, partly because, as the capital of an empire of 51,000,000 people, it attracted thousands of officials, soldiers, and tradesmen and had a number of imperial institutions, and partly because of the forced growth of industries and its reputation as a center of culture. It now contains 2,000,000 people out of a total Austrian population of 6,000,000, a disproportion in population between capital and country greater than that of any other state in central Europe. Merely to exist requires of Vienna an economic and industrial reorganization of the most extreme kind. Already the suffering has been terrible; it remains to be seen if violence and anarchy can be averted. *Special problem of Vienna*

The hard conditions of life in Austria after the World War and the hopelessness of the future led to a separatist movement in western Austria among the people of the Tyrol and Vorarlberg. For a further discussion of the matter see page 185.

THE ECONOMIC PLIGHT OF THE COUNTRY

Economic
weakness
of Austria

If we now turn to the distribution of the crops and other resources as a basis for understanding the present condition of Austria with its non-German elements excluded, we shall find the country left in a strikingly helpless condition. Unnatural as the population distributions appear in Figure 108, the region had one great advantage over its present condition — it was economically strong. If it did not produce all that it needed, at least it had the means to import and pay for what it lacked. Railway systems were laid out with regard to the trend of trade, and the fact that they are now crossed by international boundaries results in great inconvenience. In principle, the relocation of a boundary always seriously disturbs custom, a powerful force in economic life.

A deficiency of
food

Let us see what Austria has lost by the setting up of the new nations formed in part from the several fragments of former Austria. The Czechs were the chief producers of sugar beets. Moravia was the most successful farming province, standing ahead of Bohemia in this respect. Maize and wine were produced in the Slovene region of Alpine forelands; barley was produced chiefly in Bohemia and Galicia. Istria was famous for its maize and wine; Goritzia yielded wheat and maize.

If we now exclude Hungary in addition to the subtractions already made, the situation of present-day Austria from the standpoint of food will be still clearer. The total wheat crop of Austria was about one quarter of the Hungarian crop. She must import corn, barley, wheat, rye, and other supplies from Hungary, Bohemia, Russia, and Rumania, by way of poor railroads and along the Danube and connecting canals.

The prime
need for
fuel

Since Austria has been set up as a separate state, her difficulties have been especially increased by lack of fuel. She has to import practically all her coal, and she needs a million tons merely for the elementary purposes of heat, light, and street railways. About half a million tons was promised from Poland and Czecho-Slovakia in 1919 soon after the close of the war, but only half the promised quantity was delivered in that year and 1920. Nor can Austria start her industries again without help from outside, for she has no rubber,

Fig. 110. Innsbruck in the Tyrol. The town lies in western Austria, where there has been a strong separatist tendency since 1918.

chemicals, fats, oil, or wool with which to supply her mills. She needs also copper and petroleum. There is very little iron. These conditions appear the more serious when we consider that Austria was formerly an industrial country, and 40 per cent of the total industrial population of the empire lived in Austria.

To create a trade balance, Austria must manufacture and export, and if she is to become a strong nation, she will have to do this more efficiently than in the past. Working to her advantage is her position in central Europe. There are already in operation the canals, waterways, and short hauls for the products of her factories. On the other hand, her sea outlets are no longer open to unrestricted use and development; they are in the hands of other powers. Only the Danube is left as a water connection with the commercial highways of the sea. It is difficult to see how Austria can create a commercial fleet under these conditions.

Tendency to unite with Germany

It is natural that, confronted by these difficulties, the Austrian leaders should have turned more and more to the possibilities of a union with Germany. In March 1919, the National Assembly framed a constitution which declared that German-Austria was part of the German Republic. It went on to say that the union was dependent upon arrangements yet to be made. But the Allied and Associated Powers required Austria to remain a separate country, at least until some future time. Again on 1 October 1920 the project was revived by the Austrian National Assembly, which directed the government to carry out within six weeks a plebiscite on the union of Austria with Germany, but it was never held. Such action would have the special support of the Pan-Germans. France would always oppose the project because of her fear of increasing the strength of her traditional enemy. For the same reason the project will be opposed by the small central European states just created, who are naturally suspicious of any augmentation of German power. With Austria joined to her, Germany would have a population of 65,000,000, as compared with the 64,000,000 she had before the war.

THE TREATY BETWEEN THE ALLIED POWERS AND AUSTRIA

Principal terms of the treaty

According to the treaty of St. Germain-en-Laye, Austria agrees to the following conditions, among others:

(1) Austria renounces all rights to territory formerly held by the Austro-Hungarian Empire outside the boundaries shown on Figure 107. This includes both the territory formerly held by the empire but now assigned to Jugo-Slavia, Italy, Czecho-

Slovakia, Poland, and Rumania, and also all her former rights and privileged positions in Morocco, Egypt, Siam, and China (concessions at Tientsin).

(2) She agrees to abolish universal military service, promises not to maintain an army of more than 30,000 men (under conditions laid down by the Allies), surrenders all her war vessels and aircraft, and submits to limitations respecting the manufacture of war material or trade in it.

(3) She promises to deliver for trial all persons accused of acts in violation of the rules of war. (As in the case of Germany, this clause was modified so as to limit the delivery of accused persons to a small number of the worst cases, which would serve as an example.)

(4) She acknowledges her indebtedness for the costs of the war and engages to pay an amount of reparation to be determined by the Permanent Reparations Commission, payments to extend through a period of thirty years and to begin 1 May 1921. (As an immediate advance she agreed to deliver live stock to Italy, Jugo-Slavia, and Rumania, during a period of three months after the coming into force of the treaty.)

(5) She grants freedom of transit through her realm for goods and persons passing to or from the territories of the Allied and Associated Powers, who are to enjoy most-favored-nation treatment. The Danube from Ulm (Fig. 103) is declared an international river, together with all navigable parts of its system. The courses of the Morava and the Tisza, in so far as they form the frontier between Jugo-Slavia and Austria, are also declared international.

(6) She is assured free access to the Adriatic, and freedom of transit for postal, telegraphic, and telephonic services.

In view of the clearly defined ethnic frontier between the German Austrians and the Hungarians in western Hungary, this frontier, with slight rectifications, was taken as the international boundary between the two states as recognized in the treaty of St. Germain-en-Laye. The change in boundary in western Hungary transfers 25,000 German-speaking people to Austria. This is the only case in Europe where an enemy power was given additional territory, though it is to be noted that the gift was made at the expense of another enemy power — Hungary — and that Austria lost elsewhere much more than she gained here.

Rectification of boundary between Hungary and Austria

CHAPTER TWELVE

THE NEW HUNGARY

Difficulties
following
upon the
division
of Hungary

HUNGARY has existed for a thousand years. Since 1867 it has been joined with Austria to form the Austro-Hungarian (or "Dual") Empire. The chief bond of union was the Crown. Each country had a separate parliament, and while there was a unified tariff system and joint consent was required to commercial treaties with foreign countries, in almost every matter of common interest there was the most violent difference of opinion between the two kingdoms. Only the clear recognition of their economic interdependence prevented the rupture of the empire and the complete political independence of Hungary. They agreed only as late as 1907, and after a bitter contest, to improve railway transportation conditions, each for the other's benefit.

Suddenly the aims of the Hungarian nationalists were achieved with the collapse of the Austro-Hungarian armies in October 1918. Hungary became an independent state. But she was not to be constituted of the large block of territory which she had acquired by her centuries-old struggle. The thousand years of Hungary's existence had also been in large part years of oppression for most non-Magyar peoples — Rumanians in Transylvania, Slovenes in Slavonia, Serbs in the Banat and elsewhere. The break-up of the empire offered these peoples an opportunity for political independence within roughly ethnic frontiers, and whatever the economic cost, they were determined to shake off Magyar rule. What they did not foresee was the inconvenience and disorganization that actual separation from Hungary would bring to the machinery of life — for themselves as well as their Magyar overlords. Cherished political freedom was won, but at a cost equal to that of a year of war.

It was the chief argument of the Magyar leaders during the period of the peace treaties of Paris (1919–1920) that a people accustomed to living together within long-established frontiers should not be torn apart, lest the organized life it had taken so long to develop should be destroyed. A new international boundary would cut across railways, watercourses, roads, and recognized administrative districts, requiring the creation of scores of new customs houses and railway stations; shipments would long be confused and delayed; food and fuel could not be distributed promptly and evenly; a fairly well-balanced production of live stock, cereals, forage, minerals, and manufactured goods would be impossible.

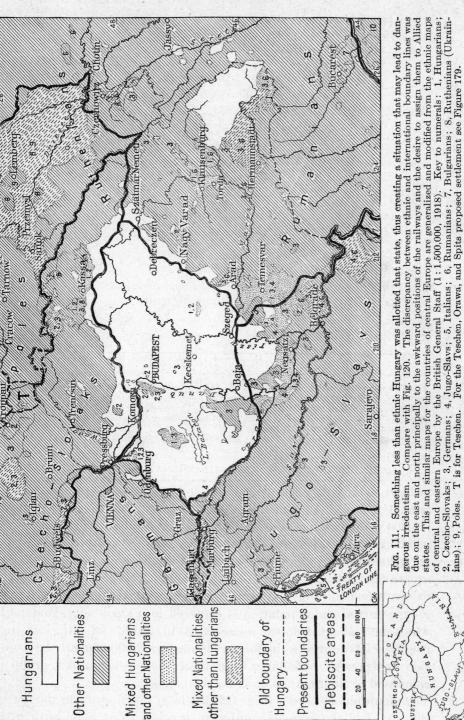

FIG. 111. Something less than ethnic Hungary was allotted that state, thus creating a situation that may lead to dangerous irredentism. Compare with Fig. 120. The discrepancy between ethnic and international boundary lines was due on the east and north principally to the awkward positions of the railways and the desire to assign them to Allied states. This and similar maps for the countries of central Europe are generalized and modified from the ethnic maps of central and eastern Europe by the British General Staff (1:1,500,000, 1918). Key to numerals: 1, Hungarians; 2, Czecho-Slovaks; 3, Germans; 4, Jugo-Slavs; 5, Italians; 6, Rumanians; 7, Bulgarians; 8, Ruthenians (Ukrainians); 9, Poles. T is for Teschen. For the Teschen, Orawa, and Spits proposed settlement see Figure 179.

Hungarians

Other Nationalities

Mixed Hungarians and other Nationalities

Mixed Nationalities other than Hungarians

Old boundary of Hungary

Present boundaries

Plebiscite areas

0 20 40 60 80 100 M.

Key to Fig. 111.

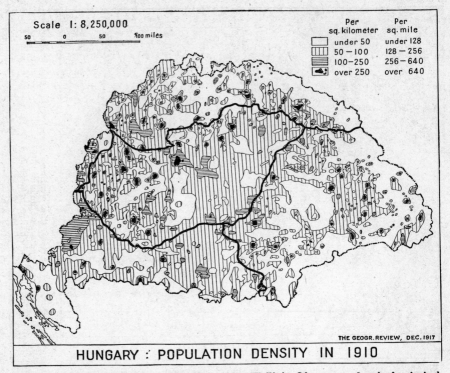

Scale 1: 8,250,000

	Per sq. kilometer	Per sq. mile
	under 50	under 128
	50 — 100	128 — 256
	100 — 250	256 — 640
	over 250	over 640

THE GEOGR. REVIEW, DEC. 1917

HUNGARY : POPULATION DENSITY IN 1910

Fig. 112. Population densities in Hungary. (After Wallis.) Of over one hundred principal centers of population (solid black) in Hungary as formerly constituted, about 12 are now transferred to Jugo-Slavia, 25 to Rumania, over 30 to Czecho-Slovakia, and about 35 remain in Hungary. New boundaries are shown by solid heavy lines; the outermost line (broken) represents the former boundary of Hungary.

THE DIFFICULTY OF MAINTAINING NATIONAL EXISTENCE

The new state a small and weak fragment of former Hungary

The new Hungary is indeed a problem. Within its present boundaries it is one of the smallest states of central Europe in both area (35,000 square miles — South Carolina has 30,500 square miles) and population (7,500,000, or 210 per square mile — Connecticut has 230 per square mile). Comparison with the pre-war area of 125,600 square miles and population of 20,900,000 (in 1910) shows a reduction to about one third of its former greatness. As in the case of Austria, a large part of the population is centered in a single city, Budapest, which had about 900,000 inhabitants in 1914. Of Magyars and closely related groups in former Hungary, 2,000,000 are left outside her present boundaries. Of these the most compact group is composed of the Szeklers of Transylvania.

A mountainous border (Fig. 113) has been taken away on the north, the east, and the extreme southwest, leaving a flat plain with little

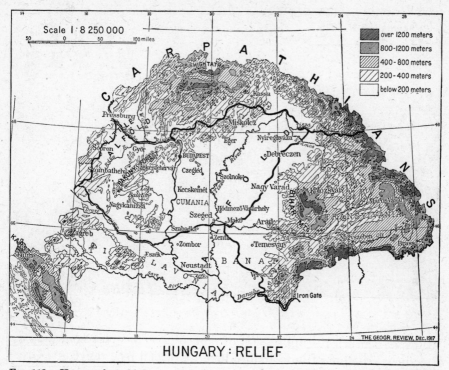

FIG. 113.   Hungary lost chiefly mountain country as a result of the war, but she also lost the richest plains country, the Banat (Fig. 142), which went to Rumania and Jugo-Slavia.

wood and practically no water power.   The country has neither sufficient fuel nor the raw materials with which to produce an adequate supply of manufactured goods.   Even before the war it imported a third of its coal supply.   Its frontiers everywhere lie upon an open plain.

Can such a state survive?   Certainly it cannot grow unless treaty arrangements permit the old currents of trade to resume their flow, perhaps in modified form; for a reasonable degree of economic prosperity is the first essential to successful government.   No political party can retain the confidence of the national parliament and manage public affairs steadily unless its program rests upon a hopeful economic basis.   This is true in Hungary as well as in Italy, or Russia, or Great Britain.   Even with a loan with which to start her industries and import raw materials, it would be difficult for Hungary to avoid anarchy.   *Can Hungary survive?*

It is customary to lay the blame for Hungary's plexus of evils upon the treaty-making powers at the Peace Conference of Paris; but it should be remembered that the prime causes of evil are the accumu-   *Causes of Hungary's distress*

Fig. 114.   The city of Budapest, capital of Hungary.

lations of centuries — oppression of non-Magyar peoples by Magyars, a medieval system of land tenure long discarded by France and Great Britain, a strangle hold upon the peasant (Magyar as well as non-Magyar) of the commercial system of the town, managed by powerful merchants, mainly Jews.   Add to these causes the four anxious and devastating years of war and the crushing disappointments of defeat, and it is clear that the people of Hungary would naturally strike out blindly against every proposal of restraint.   For a time there was downright Bolshevism, and then a wave of reaction toward a monarchical form of government.

MAGYAR RELATIONS WITH THE SUBJECT RACES

The Magyars

The Hungarians, or Magyars, a steppe people

For hundreds of years the ruling class in Hungary has been the Magyars.   Who are they?   Whence did they come?   They are a steppe people, originally a race of nomadic horsemen, who conquered the grasslands of the middle Danube basin about 895 A.D.   They have always been a plains people and have left to others the bordering highlands.   In the period of their early development in the grasslands of Hungary, they repeatedly ravaged Europe from mid-Russia to westward of the Rhine.   With a language totally different from

Brown Bros.

Buda on the left, Pest on the right, looking upstream.

that of their neighbors and a territory bordered for long distances by high wooded mountains, holding the heart of the land, they have stood together socially and politically, alien alike in speech and custom from the peoples whom they conquered, — the Rumans of Transylvania, the Ruthenians of the central Carpathian foothills, the Serbs north of the Danube, and the Slovaks of Slovakia. Out of a total Hungarian population of 20,900,000 in 1910, the Magyars claimed 48 per cent, but this number is excessive.

The Magyars' present claim to the gratitude of western European powers rests on their long struggle with the Turk. From 1363 on, when Turkish and Hungarian armies first met near Adrianople, the conflict was almost continuous. In 1529 and again in 1683 Vienna was besieged; but the second siege was lifted by the help of the Polish leader Sobieski, and in 1699 the Sultan acknowledged the rule of the Hapsburgs over all Hungary and Transylvania except the Banat. *The Magyar as the outpost of Europe against the Turk*

The subject races of Hungary were separated from each other on the rim of the central Hungarian plain. This separation and their unlikeness in speech and race prevented them in times past from uniting to fight the Magyar. Hungarian rulers gave them neither freedom of the press nor the right of association. In some notable instances, persons who made even trivial exhibitions of non-Magyar sentiment were cruelly persecuted; almost all officials were Magyars;

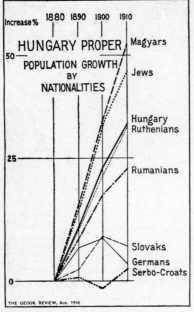

Fig. 115. Diagram showing, by nationalities, the population growth in Hungary proper (exclusive of Croatia-Slavonia) from 1880 to 1910. Logarithmic scale. After Wallis.

Magyar oppression of subject races

Hungary surrounded by enemies

elections were a farce; subject peoples were practically unrepresented in the national parliament.

With a passion for landholding, the Magyar, like the landlord of feudal times, has occupied huge estates, and this system of land tenure has pressed most heavily upon the subject border peoples. In the towns the Jewish Magyar as merchant and banker has eventually dominated the peasantry as well as the artisan classes. The new boundaries have recast ethnic percentages in such a way as to raise the proportion of Jews from 5 to 7 per cent.

Hungary is ringed about by enemies. Hatred of the Magyar is traditional with the people who are now her neighbors. Even in Magyaria itself the autocratic ruling class has been hated by the Magyar peasantry, whose economic condition has been only a shade better than that of the subject races. The latter were also denied equality of educational privileges, especially in districts where they were numerically greater.

The Rumanian and German Elements

Of all the subject peoples of Hungary the Rumanians were the most numerous, 3,000,000 in all. Behind them stood the people of the Rumanian nation, to whom they appealed constantly for liberation. Magyar persecution inevitably pressed hardest upon them, for their chances of liberation were best. If they were lost, so also would be lost to Hungary a million Szeklers and German-speaking subjects inhabiting the Carpathian foothill region east of Maros-Vasarhely and about Kronstadt (Fig. 143). Persecution was justified by the central Hungarian government on the ground that the Rumanians formed an illiterate peasantry incapable of ruling themselves.[1]

In late years the German element in Hungary has been declining in both influence and number. The scattered settlements of the German

[1] For further discussion of Transylvania see Chapter Fifteen, page 283.

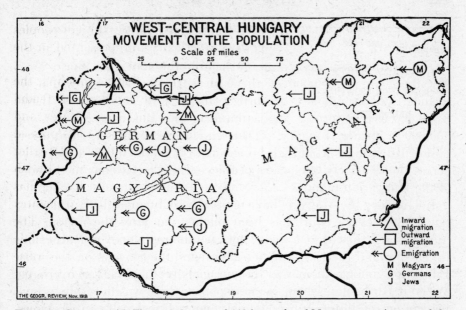

Fig. 116. Compare with Figures 123, 128, and 146 for results of Magyar oppression as a whole. Inward and outward migration refer to movements of population in and out of the region here shown in relation to the rest of Austria-Hungary, while emigration refers to movement to other countriss. The heavy solid lines denote present boundaries. After Wallis.

have not tended to make him politically strong. Emigration has been chiefly to America. In all there were about 2,000,000 Germans scattered here and there throughout Hungary. Their ancestors had been brought in principally during the 16th and 17th centuries in the process of beating back the Turk, first as frontier guards, to which fact witness still the German fortress-churches and the habit of storing grain near the churches as a safeguard in case of attack. Later, as colonists, they received grants of lands, freedom from taxation, and financial assistance in house building and the stocking of their farms. German settlements in Hungary

Many German place names dot the map of eastern Hungary. Wherever the Germans have gone, they have kept their ancestral customs and maintained separate German schools. For the most part they have lived in groups of villages. Their conservative and alien ways have kept racial antagonisms alive, but it is difficult to see how this could have been avoided; for on the whole they have represented a far more advanced type of living and could hardly have been expected to lower their standards to fit those of the people about them. Their scattered settlements form a speech mosaic very hard to reconcile with any principle of boundary making. The German colonist's disdain of his neighbors

The Ruthenians of Northeastern Hungary, Eastern Galicia, and Bukovina

Ruthenians in Hungary an overflow from Eastern Galicia

The Ruthenians were scarcely heard of before the World War. Yet there are 35,000,000 of them in central-eastern Europe, if we include the Ukrainians.[1] In former Russia were 30,000,000 of them; 3,500,000 live in former Austria (Galicia and Bukovina chiefly), and 500,000 in former Hungary. Those in Hungary represented an overflow of Ruthenians from their homeland in Eastern Galicia and Russia, across the relatively low passes of the central Carpathians to the edge of the Hungarian plain.

Treatment by the Magyars

In Hungary the Magyars have pressed heavily upon the Ruthenians. Since 1880, every effort has been made to occupy the region with Magyars and thus drive a wedge between the main body of Ruthenians (in Galicia and the Carpathian valleys) and the Slovaks on the west. Education among them was discouraged by the Magyar overlords. Without Ruthenian schools or newspapers there was naturally a high percentage of illiteracy and almost no political self-consciousness. Though incorporated with Czecho-Slovakia to the number of 475,000, they occupy a privileged autonomous position.

Reasons for assigning Galicia to Poland

In order to unite Poland and Rumania and combine their strength against Bolshevist Russia, and also to join to their kinsmen the Poles who dwell in the towns of Eastern Galicia, the whole of that province is desired by Poland. This would place about 3,000,000 Ruthenians (a clear majority in Eastern Galicia) under Polish rule. In the province of Bukovina, 300,000 of them are assigned to Rumania. The main body of Ruthenians in Russia formed a part of Ukrainia (page 400), which for a time vanished from the map with Bolshevist control of Russia, but which may return eventually.[2]

DISORDERS FOLLOWING THE END OF THE WORLD WAR

Rise of Bolshevism

In the land situation we have part explanation of the revolution of 1919 in Hungary and the quick growth of Bolshevism. In the face of approaching famine and with the collapse of the government that followed the abdication of the Emperor after the armistice of November 1918, the peasants seized the land and killed numbers of the landlords. Many of the larger estates were placed in the hands of coöperative production societies. Step by step with the disorders

[1] The word "Ruthenian" is now generally assigned only to the Ukrainians of Galicia, Bukovina, and former Hungary.

[2] For a discussion of the Slovaks, Jugo-Slavs, and Rumanians formerly under Hungarian rule see the several chapters on these nationalities.

of the countryside went the disorders of the towns, where the food situation was even worse. Completely freed from restraint, the evil elements of the population took advantage of the times to commit excesses. What was started in the form of a civil war, to win political and economic freedom, became wild disorder and crime. Karolyi began a sane and democratic program of reform (October 1918 to March 1919) ; he was succeeded by the "Reds," or Bolshevists, under Bela Kun (March to August 1919), who were in turn succeeded by a provisional government that represents little more than a succession of self-appointed public committees. The general tendency has been toward control by representatives of the old monarchical régime, and both Admiral Horthy and ex-Emperor Charles are thought possible candidates for the throne in a constitutional monarchy.

Bolshevism in Hungary was marked by downright theft from the public treasury of millions of dollars. The money was distributed on the order of no central authority and without obtaining receipts. It is a melancholy thought that here, as in Russia, there should have been started a liberal movement which at once degenerated into robbery. Hope turned to disgust when the people saw that in the name of liberty a new and terrible burden of loss had been laid upon them.

OCCUPATIONS BY RIVAL BORDER STATES

The portions of Hungary that were lost to her by the terms of the treaty of peace were occupied during 1919 and 1920 by rival bordering states. No one of these states waited until the peace treaty with Hungary was signed, but against the orders of the Peace Conference of Paris they rushed in to occupy the land they expected to receive. While Rumania was the most extreme and the one which seized and carried away the greatest amount of property, all followed the same general policy.

Rumania first went beyond the demarcation line set for her armies by the Allied and Associated Powers, then passed the line of the proposed new boundary, invaded central Hungary itself, and early in August 1919 occupied the capital, Budapest. In the two following months she defied the Peace Conference, and seized and sent to Rumania vast quantities of supplies. Her excuse was that much more had been requisitioned in Rumania by the Austro-Hungarian army authorities in the period of military occupation before the close of the war.

Rumanian occupation of Hungary

In addition to the Rumanian advance, Hungary suffered aggression at the hands of two other neighbors. At Pécs the Jugo-Slavs occu-

Similar
occupa-
tions else-
where

pied certain coal mines of Hungary without authorization. Lack of restraint was shown also in the acts of violence committed in the plebiscite area of Klagenfurt and in the occupation of Montenegro with several military contingents and persecution of members of the anti-Serbian party. Czecho-Slovakia likewise surpassed her demarcation line, before being authorized by the Peace Conference of Paris; and, like the Serbians and Rumanians, she began at once to persecute and drive out of the newly won lands the people who had formerly persecuted her. The military occupation of portions of Hungary by Czecho-Slovakia, Rumania, and Jugo-Slavia was not discontinued until the summer of 1920, after the peace treaty with Hungary had been signed, and then only under pressure of the Allied powers.

AGRICULTURE AND INDUSTRY IN THE NEW HUNGARY

Hungary
not well-
balanced
economically

The new state of Hungary is chiefly a plains country. It will have an excess of agricultural products for export, and it will have to import nearly all its manufactured goods, both now and in the future. The Tisza, next to the Danube the principal stream, has a fall of only a hundred feet in the two hundred miles from the Carpathian foothills to its junction with the Danube. The sources of the tributary streams that drain the Hungarian plain are all in foreign hands. Water power is therefore unavailable.

Hungary's
coal de-
posits

There is no precious metal in Hungary. There are, however, several important deposits of coal. The reserves of the Pécs field are said to amount to 110,000,000 tons, and the coal is of excellent quality. The Jugo-Slavs wish to exploit the Pécs mines (Fig. 131) for five years, as compensation for the destruction of their mines by the Austro-German armies. The losses of coal which Hungary suffers as a result of the new boundary arrangements affect chiefly her reserve supplies, and she loses but a comparatively small part of the coal beds in which production is practicable. Of her former iron-ore deposits those left to her represent but a fifth of her former production (more than a million tons in 1913). All the salt resources are in the ceded lands.

The cen-
tral plain,
the Alföld

The central plain of Hungary is called the Alföld (Fig. 113). It is a western outpost of the vast Eurasian steppe, and was formed by the gradual silting up of a great Alpine sea, remnants of which survive in shallow lagoons. The climate is of an extreme continental type, and the Alföld, a true grass steppe, is naturally treeless, in parts even semi-desert. Flooding is characteristic of the streams. This is especially true of the Tisza, and hence few towns have arisen on its

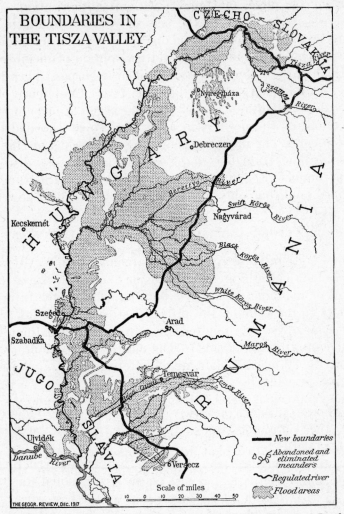

Fig. 117. The Alföld is the large and fertile central plain of former Hungary. Its chief river is the Tisza. The correction and control of the Tisza permits the use of most of the lands formerly flooded. The map shows the location of the new boundaries in the Tisza valley where Jugo-Slavia, Hungary, and Rumania meet. To reach the Danube a barge at Nagyvárad must pass through a corner of Hungary. Note the manner in which the boundary between Jugo-Slavia and Rumania in the Banat (west of Temesvár) crosses the streams. These inconveniences were considered less important than railroad questions (see Figure 135). Modified from map in the *Geographical Review*, December 1917.

banks. Szeged, the chief town on the river, was practically destroyed by flood in 1879. Between the Danube and the Tisza are patches of lagoon and some rather extensive arid, sandy tracts.

The influence of the drainage network on the life of the low-lying plain is shown in a number of striking ways. The people live mainly on the intermediate levels. East of the Tisza, floods are frequent

Where the people of the Alföld live

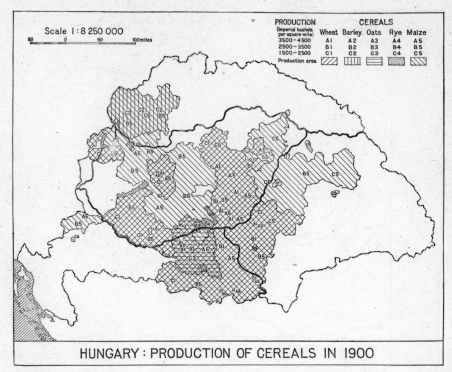

FIG. 118.   A comparison of former (broken) and present (solid) boundary lines shows what Hungary has lost.

and dry house sites are not easy to find.   Long stretches of the Danube, the Tisza, the Maros, the Drave, and the Save serve as county boundaries.

The rich agricultural region

Nearly three fourths of the people of Hungary derived their living from the land.   In the region east of the Tisza, noted for its wheat and maize, the yield of wheat equals that on the best wheat lands of England and northeastern France.   Sugar beets, potatoes, and oats also are grown extensively, both east and west of the Danube.   Cattle are raised everywhere.   The boundary line of greatest productivity tends to follow the limit of Magyar speech at the edge of the Transylvanian Mountains.

What Hungary can produce

Reduced to the limits of the new boundaries Hungary becomes a still   ore exclusively agricultural state.   Though she loses the maize and wheat lands of the Bačka and the Banat and the barley and sugar beet fields and rich pastures of the Little Alföld north of the Danube, the area of good agricultural land is higher in proportion to the population.   The population is reduced approximately to 35 per cent.   Wheat and rye are 40 per cent and 62 per cent respectively

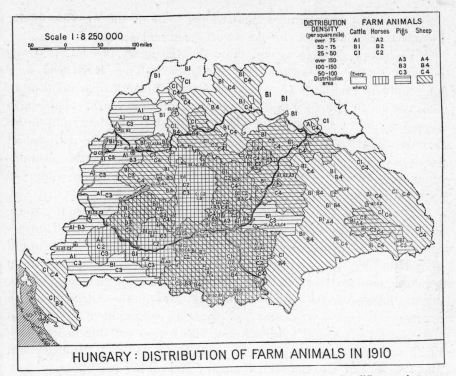

Scale 1:8 250 000

DISTRIBUTION DENSITY (per square mile)

	FARM ANIMALS			
	Cattle	Horses	Pigs	Sheep
over 75	A1	A2		
50 – 75	B1	B2		
25 – 50	C1	C2		
over 150			A3	A4
100 – 150			B3	B4
50 – 100			C3	C4

HUNGARY : DISTRIBUTION OF FARM ANIMALS IN 1910

FIG. 119. Losses due to the creation of new states are suggested by the difference between the present (solid) and the former (broken) boundaries of Hungary.

of former yields, barley 47 per cent, maize 27 per cent, and sugar beets 37 per cent. Such a proportion of crop yield to population might seem to indicate a very favorable situation, but it should be remembered that agricultural products are almost the only source of exports to pay for imported goods.

With the loss of the Carpathian and Transylvanian country Hungary loses not only mineral resources and sources of water power, but the great proportion of her valuable forests. Instead of exporting timber, she will have to import it.

Other losses in raw materials

Before the World War Hungary had 3750 large manufacturing establishments, of which she retains 2155; but many of these, being deprived of their sources of raw materials, are now idle.

Situation with respect to manufactures

Hungary has only a quarter of the former capacity to support sheep, and wool production will fall off accordingly; and at least half the required woolens must be imported. Cattle production falls to 31 per cent, horses to 40 per cent, and pigs to 44 per cent. Of hemp, with the pre-war figure cut to 15 per cent, not enough to supply the spindles is left. Two thirds of the flax lands have gone,

42 per cent of the spindles, and 84 per cent of the weaving looms. Nearly three fourths of the glass works will be lost.

A review of these facts will show that Hungary presents a strong contrast to the new states that border her. They have won their long fight for liberty. They have thus solved one of their main problems, which to Hungary is still a riddle, a question mark. They have almost no debt: Hungary has a pre-war debt, a war debt, and an indemnity bill. The Magyar nobleman points proudly to a thousand years of history; but he suffers from the reaction to the accumulated woes of that long time and at the hands of those whom he systematically oppressed.

Hungary's effort to form an alliance with Jugo-Slavia

One result of the Rumanian invasion of Hungary was to arouse such bitterness in that state that the government attempted unsuccessfully to form an alliance with Jugo-Slavia. This alliance would give Hungary the privilege of exchanging agricultural products on a complementary basis and would give her a better chance to secure adequate commercial outlets at Saloniki and on the Adriatic. Such a project is bound to be revived, for the geographical layout and the natural economic tendencies of the region call for coöperative tariff and transportation agreements not only between Hungary and Jugo-Slavia but also between Hungary and all her neighbors.

CHAPTER THIRTEEN

THE DOMAIN OF THE CZECHO-SLOVAKS

THE country of the Czecho-Slovaks runs in an east-west direction The national domain athwart a network of railroads that carry most of the commerce of central Europe. It is bordered by five nations, of which three (Rumania, Poland, and Germany) touch the sea, and of which two (Austria and Hungary) are, like itself, landlocked states bordering the Danube River. Of its 14,000,000 inhabitants 35 per cent are of different race or language: about 4,000,000 Germans, of whom 1,700,000 are in western Bohemia and other powerful groups in Silesia, Moravia, and the larger cities; 750,000 Magyars in Slovakia; 400,000 Ruthenians in the eastern districts bordering the Carpathians.

The state is a peninsula of Slavdom thrust westward into the heart A Slavic peninsula of Europe, a long and very narrow strip impossible to defend in its entirety against aggressive and more powerful neighbors, should it ever come to blows with them. Two long pincers of German population press upon it, the Germans of Silesia and the German-Austrians northeast of Vienna. Five nations, all at one time or another hostile, stand about its borders. It has no seaport, and its people own no railroad to the sea, from which it is distant more than 200 miles (Bohemia to Trieste or Stettin). Its central part is only from 50 to 125 miles across from north to south, yet from east to west the country extends 600 miles. Its area is 55,000 square miles, or slightly more than that of the state of New York. Its population density is also not far from that of New York.

From whatever angle we view the foregoing facts, we are forced Importance of international relationships to the new state to conclude that the welfare of Czecho-Slovakia is to an extraordinary degree dependent upon its international relationships. From the first, the statesmen of this new nation must face political questions of the gravest and most complex character. Almost before the new government was organized it had two serious quarrels on its hands: one with Poland over the coal lands of Teschen, and one with Hungary over the conditions of the military demarcation line east of Pressburg.

Between Czecho-Slovakia and its neighbors there must needs de- Possible forms of coöperation velop a bond of union in one form or another. This bond may take the form of commercial treaties respecting tariffs, transportation rates, and exchange of products, such as are now under discussion; indeed, two have already been ratified, those with Poland and Jugo-Slavia.

It may take the form of a treaty based on a military alliance with Poland and Jugo-Slavia, two other Slav states (page 241). It may take the form of a waterways convention with the other Danubian states — Austria, Hungary, Rumania, Jugo-Slavia, and Bulgaria. Or it may be that a treaty will be arranged affecting the use of railways, canals, maritime ports, and other instruments of trade, with all the other central European states. If these results should be achieved on a friendly basis, the economic welfare of the country would be assured; for, like several other new states of Europe, Czecho-Slovakia enters upon its national career with a relatively small debt (about a half billion dollars).

Problem of the minorities
The question of the treatment of peoples of different race and speech within the new state is likewise fraught with danger. That too may be settled upon the basis of justice or it may become the source of bitter and disastrous irredentism. The German-speaking populations will offer the greatest difficulties (Fig. 120). They will resist the overlordship of the Czechs if Czech rule is accompanied by unjust discrimination against them. (A harmonizing factor is the long-standing economic interdependence of Czechs and Germans in the principal towns of Bohemia and in just those districts where the Germans are most numerous, as in western Bohemia.) The Magyars of Slovakia will fight before yielding to Czech or Slovak exploitation. These are fundamental facts; in them may lie the seeds of failure and of future war. By forming a voting coalition in the national parliament, the non-Czech parties could leave the Czechs with so narrow a margin of control that vital measures for national security and development would frequently be endangered.

The welding of the parts of Czecho-Slovakia into a strong state is difficult also on account of the diversity of languages. Although Slovak and Czech are much alike, there is in reality no such thing at the present time as a "Czecho-Slovak" language. Czech is the official language for meetings, conferences, and oral and written official communications. Where racial minorities number 20 per cent of the population, however, they may use their own language before judicial and administrative bodies, provided they are citizens of Czecho-Slovakia.

THE HISTORICAL STRUGGLE

Beginnings of government
The independence of Czecho-Slovakia was formally proclaimed during the World War, on 18 October 1918, though earlier informal announcements were made in 1917. Even before the Austro-Hungarian

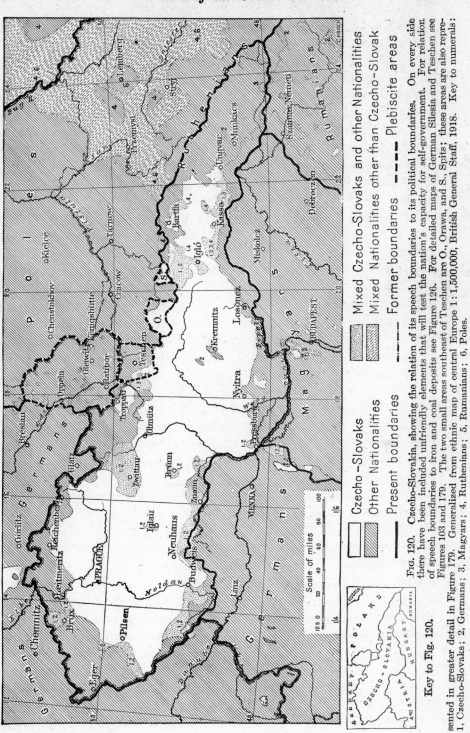

Fig. 120. Czecho-Slovakia, showing the relation of its speech boundaries to its political boundaries. On every side there have been included unfriendly elements that will test the nation's capacity for self-government. For relation of speech boundaries to iron and coal deposits see Figure 126. For detailed maps of German Silesia and Teschen see Figures 103 and 179. The two small areas southeast of Teschen are O., Orawa, and S. Spits; these areas are also represented in greater detail in Figure 179. Generalized from ethnic map of central Europe 1:1,500,000, British General Staff, 1918. Key to numerals: 1, Czecho-Slovaks; 2, Germans; 3, Magyars; 4, Ruthenians; 5, Rumanians; 6, Poles.

Key to Fig. 120.

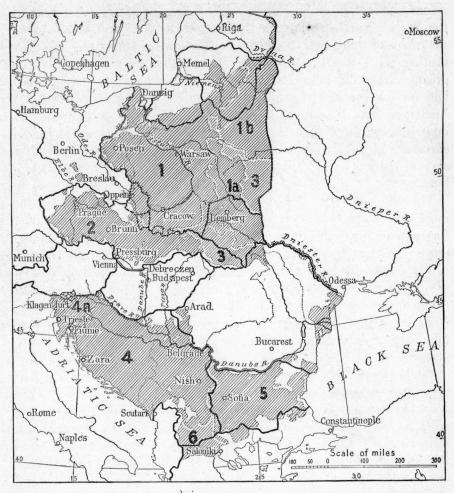

FIG. 121. Slavs in Europe outside Russia. The common boundary of Poland and Russia was tentatively laid down at the Riga peace conference in October 1920. The key to the numbers is as follows: 1, Poles; 1*a*, mixed Poles and Ruthenians; 1*b*, White Russians; 2, Czechs, Moravians, Slovaks; 3, Ruthenians; 4, Serbo-Croats; 4*a*, Slovenes; 5, Bulgarians (originally Finno-Ugrian but now principally Slavic); 6, Macedonians.

armistice of 4 November 1918 was signed, the new state had formed a provisional democratic government and had been recognized by the Allies. The returning soldiers formed an army to protect the still undefined frontiers from disorder. Money was borrowed to begin the operations of government. The United States, Great Britain, France, and Italy gave the new country credit and supplies. Masaryk became prime minister and minister of finance, and later the first president.

The new state has the benefit of stirring traditions and also of the recent heroic exploits in Russia, which form one of the great epics of the World War.   During the fighting on the Russian front in 1916–1917, tens of thousands of Czecho-Slovak soldiers surrendered to their brother Slavs, the Russians.   They were organized into armies in the prison camps, but before they could be brought into the field Russia had become Bolshevist, and the Czecho-Slovak corps opposed not Austrians, but Russians.   For many months they fought unceasingly against the Bolshevist armies, all the way from central Russia eastward along the Siberian railroad to Vladivostok.   Only after several years of exile were they returned, late in 1919, to their native land.

The achievements of the new Czecho-Slovak nation appear the more remarkable when we consider that the people have been under foreign rule for nearly four hundred years and that the present generation has had very little experience in government.   From the 10th century Bohemia was under the influence of Germany, and several of its kings became emperors of Germany.   Doubtless the Czechs could have been won to either people — the German or the Austrian — by benevolent measures; but the general policy of severity toward minorities of different race never permitted the ruling castes in the two states to tolerate political liberty, even in the form of local autonomy.

While primarily a Roman Catholic country, Bohemia was the seat of a bitter religious war in the early part of the 15th century, when John Huss, who had led the popular demand for clerical reform, was tried by an ecclesiastical council and burned (1415).   A civil war broke out which was to divide Bohemia for many years and cause the loss of a large part of her people.   When the struggle began, one third of the soil of Bohemia belonged to the clergy, and the taxes levied by church and state were intolerable.   It was therefore easy for the religious question to become joined with the question of land tenure.   Since the land question affected the peasants (chiefly Czechs), the movement of John Huss and his followers became also a peasant movement; and since the welfare of all the peasants was involved, it soon became a national movement.   It is interesting to note that Germans held almost all the ecclesiastical offices, and the problem of race was thus added to the problems of religion and land tenure.

Ranged against the Bohemians were the Catholic princes of the neighboring countries, who argued that if religious liberty were tolerated in Bohemia it would surely assume dangerous forms elsewhere.   Coupled with this view was the fear of the Hapsburg kings

(margin notes:) Epic of the Czecho-Slovaks in Russia

Long oppression by Austria

Religious wars

that their claim, made in 1526, to the Bohemian crown would be denied as soon as the principle of nationalism began to grow in the soil of religious liberty.

The question of the Bohemian language and literature was closely tied up with that of religious differences. It was in the Bohemian language that some of the severest denunciations of the clergy were written, and some of the most violent attacks upon the tyranny of nobles and kings. German officials secured control of the University of Prague and thereby sought to denationalize Bohemia, and to impose the German language and secure its dominance.

At just this period there was a division of the Papacy between Rome and Avignon which caused a division of authority and opinion, both political and religious, in many centers of the Christian world. In the Bohemian church the division was seized upon by the one party to impress German authority, and by the other to hasten the day of the national independence of Bohemia.

Battle of the White Mountain

The Catholic countries of Spain, Poland, and Bavaria aided Austria, and in the invasion of Bohemia the nationalist Bohemian forces were defeated at the battle of the White Mountain in 1620. Following the defeat the Protestant clergy of Prague were obliged to sell their goods and go into Saxony. Censorship of the press was established, statues of Huss were destroyed or altered, Protestants could not secure good titles to their land; in short, the movement to Catholicize Bohemia was really a movement to destroy its national aspirations. Towns that resisted were deprived of their charters. Thereafter Bohemian nationality was promoted very largely outside of Bohemia.

The tradition of hate

The battle of the White Mountain and its tragic religious and political associations are mentioned here because they assist our understanding of the present spirit of the Czechs as well as of other central European nationalities to whom the facts of history have a poignant significance. As a certain Czech statesman put it after the Czech forces had advanced into Magyar territory in northern Hungary: "We have now revenged the pain and grief of the great numbers of emigrants who fled after the battle of the White Mountain." But this battle was fought three hundred years ago! If all the wrongs of the past must become bitter traditions to be revenged sometime in the future, then Hungary may choose to remember alleged wrongs of the present and revenge herself three hundred years hence — or sooner. This is one of the terrible problems of the moment: Where is the process of hating to stop?

FIG. 122. Aussig, northwestern Bohemia, a town composed of German-speaking people who have been incorporated in the new Czecho-Slovak state. At the left are the lower ridges of the Böhmer-Wald Mountains on the southern boundary of Germany.

The suppression of the liberal movement of 1848, and the wars of 1866 and 1870, were steps in the progress of that Austro-German dominion of Bohemia which continued until 1918. The hope of freedom might have been altogether lost but for the stimulation of national consciousness and sentiment in the 19th century, when a few Czech patriots revived the almost-forgotten literature. Jan Kollar (1793–1852) inspired his people by a collection of poems called *Slavy Dcera,* or *Daughter of Slavia;* Šafařik (1795–1861) wrote *Slavic Antiquities* and *Slavic Ethnography;* Palacký (1798–1876) was the author of *A History of the Bohemian People.*

The struggle for independence in later years was often focused upon the question of the Bohemian language. On the one hand the insistence upon German speech was a constant attempt to deny equality of race as expressed in the national language; on the other it represented a repression of religious liberty which carried with it the persistent denial of civil liberty. Though Bohemia is largely a Catholic country today, most Bohemians have resented for centuries the measures taken by foreign princes to weed out Protestants by expelling them from the country (as in 1627). Only in this way did the rulers think it possible to kill the feeling of independence, which would inevitably lead to a separate national life. Instead of equalizing the German and Bohemian languages, the Hapsburg overlords prejudiced the latter by appointing only German-speaking officials and encouraging the growth of a German aristocracy. So fierce was the struggle between Czechs and Germans that the Provincial Diet of Bohemia was practically closed for some years before the World War.

The more numerous the repressive measures, the fiercer raged the struggle on the part of Bohemian students to prove a long-established nationalist sentiment. Archæological facts were brought to light proving that Bohemian culture had an independent or autochthonous origin; manuscripts were discovered which revealed a literary culture unmarked by German influence; every distinctive social and political phase of the past was set in high relief by the intense patriotism of Bohemian scholars.

INITIAL DANGERS TO THE NEW STATE

The Czechs have shown remarkable strength of purpose and a reasonable temper. Like all Slavs, they have extremely volatile elements in the population, so much so that it was for a short time a question whether they would be able to resist the Bolshevism they

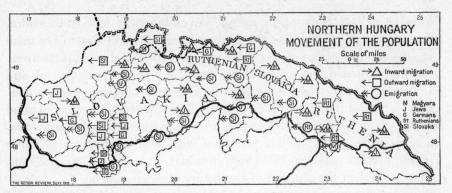

FIG. 123. The process of Magyarization in Slovakia. Out of 20 districts, 12 had incoming streams of Magyars, and 17 had outgoing streams of Slovaks of which 13 were emigrants and 4 migrants to other parts of Austria-Hungary. Education in Slovakia is on a very low level, and while the outgoing streams of Slovaks consisted chiefly of peasants the incoming educated Magyars comprised officials, large landowners, and capitalists. From Wallis, the *Geographical Review*, September 1918, with new boundaries added.

had so heroically fought in Russia and thus keep the friendship of the western powers. The protection which these powers can give Czecho-Slovakia is yet to be measured. Up to the present the Czechs have had chiefly to depend upon themselves. When their dispute with the Poles over the coal mines of Teschen brought them to the verge of war, the Allies sent an Interallied commission which demarcated a line of division for the armed forces, regulated coal production and shipment, and kept the peace.

On the south, also, the Czechs had the support of the Allies during 1919, through operations which kept Hungary's attention focused on her southwestern borders. Detachments of the French Army of the Orient under General Franchet d'Esperey were sent into Bulgaria and Transylvania; the Rumanians occupied a part of the demarcation line on the western border of Transylvania, where Hungarian troops sought to retain a hold over Rumanian districts and towns; a British admiral held the gateways of the Danube and operated a fleet of river monitors and coal barges. Held in the grip of the Allies on the south, Hungary could exert only feeble effort on the north. The new Czecho-Slovak armies maintained a frontier along the line established by the Allies after the armistice. Austria could offer no resistance at all. Thus the new state has come up to the present without invasion or Bolshevism or discredit. It appears to have real political and social vitality. *Allied help to new nations in central Europe*

An important source of anxiety to the Allies is the degree to which Czecho-Slovakia may form political or economic relations with Russia. "Race" may be a powerful factor in political affairs, and is still more *Relations and sympathies with Russia* powerful in the field of economic development. A Czech leader, Kramer, stated (1920) that the war could not be said to be over until the Russian question had been settled, that the Czechs should remember that they also were Slavs, and that they should remain faithful to Russia so that Russia might not have to seek alliance with Germany. He added that future relations with Russia would depend largely upon general European conditions. Beneš, the Czech premier, likewise favors closer relations with Russia, but never on a visionary basis. He says, "The individual states . . . are not self-sufficing, and in the Europe of the future they cannot be."

The Czechs were for some time ambitious to have direct territorial connection with Russia. It is for this reason that they have opposed the Polish ownership of Eastern Galicia. In the summer of 1919 there was organized in Prague, the capital of Czecho-Slovakia, a Ruthenian society which has for its object the promotion of the interests of the Ruthenians of eastern Czecho-Slovakia and of Eastern Galicia. Thus the state of Czecho-Slovakia is in a position to make trouble for Poland in the government of several millions of unfriendly Ruthenians northeast of the Carpathians.

Differences between the Poles and the Czechs

Yet Czecho-Slovakia and Poland, in spite of differences, are likely to become good neighbors, because they are similar in "race" at least, and they are both opposed to Germany. Moreover, their frontiers are exposed to German attack, and neither is strong enough to stand alone against the possible German armies of the future. The Czechs are more materialistic and less imaginative and romantic than the Poles. Poland's history is largely the history of her landed nobility; Bohemia has been historically a land of peasant farmers, like Austria.

Dangers of militarism

Like all the other new states of Europe, Czecho-Slovakia will run the risk of becoming militaristic. It would be possible for an ambitious military man to throw the Czechs into a state of nervous disorder and feed the spirit of war; he could point to long and exposed frontiers; he could dwell upon the greed and ill-will of unscrupulous neighbors. It was the "exposed" position of Germany that was the theme of her Junkers for a generation; the idea of the menace of the slow-encroaching Slav became fixed in the minds of the German people. Following this line of reasoning, every people in the world should have a powerful and aggressive army and navy and be prepared for war at any minute, even though the cost of such preparation be staggering.

The problem is not one for the Czecho-Slovak state to solve alone. If relief is not found in the plan of a League of Nations which will compel reduction of armaments and keep the peace of the world, it will have to be found in regional alliances designed for the same purpose. To some political students this would seem a feasible plan for the states on the Danube, which have a common bond of economic and military interest. A "Danubian Confederation" might thus be created in place of the old Austro-Hungarian Empire, to include also Jugo-Slavia, Rumania, and Bulgaria. Significant in this relation is the "Little Entente" formed by an accord between Czecho-Slovakia, Jugo-Slavia, and Rumania. It was designed for protection against Hungarian aggression directed toward Rumania and Jugo-Slavia, to promote trade on the Danube, and as a defense against Bolshevism should the Soviet armies pass Russia's western frontier. Treaties pending between Austria and Czecho-Slovakia, Bulgaria and Greece, Rumania and Hungary, Jugo-Slavia and Austria, Poland, Rumania, and Hungary, though involving complex and even contradictory political relations, carry at least the promise of a general accord in promoting peace and reviving trade through regional agreements of broad character which would still leave each national group independent.

A Danubian Confederation

POLITICAL PROBLEMS DEPENDING ON RACIAL ELEMENTS

The chief economic and social difficulties of Czecho-Slovakia are:

(1) The making of loans to build new roads, railroads, and canals, and to run the machinery of government.

(2) The execution of a program of social reform.

(3) The reform of the land-tenure system, to break up the huge feudal estates that still exist.

New roads and the division of the land

As seen by its leaders, the first and principal task of the new state is in the field of social reform. This is conceived not as a revolutionary but rather as an evolutionary process, not a radical break but a gradual development. In this view the efficiency, the enterprise, and the brains of capitalism are to be continued (not destroyed or discouraged, as in Russia), that there may be wholesale production of goods for consumption and export. In the Czecho-Slovak view, socialization does not mean a radical change whereby the state expropriates private property in order to set up state capitalism. With Russia's example before them, the Russophile Czechs might have been thought capable of uncritical acceptance of the Russian program. Even with so radical a difference of political and social views between the Russian and Czech leaders, the relations might

Czecho-Slovakia's program of social reform evolutionary, not revolutionary have been far closer — to the detriment of the latter — had there been better means of communication.

The mixed composition of the Czecho-Slovak people provides elements of almost certain political difficulty. The Czechs and Slovaks together form 65 per cent of the population, while the other nationalities number 35 per cent. In the spring of 1920 the first election was held for representatives in the National Assembly. Out of the total of 300 deputies, the Czechs command 147 votes and the other groups 153 votes, of which 41 are Slovak and 70 are German, described by the prime minister of Czecho-Slovakia as "resentful and powerful."

In the Czecho-Slovak state it is not thought possible to grant autonomy to Slovakia, owing to the mixed character of the population. Only 60 per cent of the people of this district are Slovaks; a quarter are Magyars; 8 per cent are Germans, and 7 per cent are Ruthenians. The total population is about 3,000,000. Therefore in any local Slovak parliament there would be a bare majority of Slovak members. In a crisis involving the Czechs, Slovakia might lean toward Hungary in a way that would imperil the existence of Czecho-Slovakia. Thus there is added still another to the many weaknesses that affect the destiny of the new state.

REGIONAL DIVISIONS

The long, narrow shape of the land of Czecho-Slovakia leads to serious difficulties as regards government, transportation, and even security, the more serious in that the Slovak peasant, who as a rule is ignorant and lives primitively, has little in common with the Czech, who has a high level of general culture, is democratic, and yet does not know how to govern tactfully. In Bohemia literacy is extremely high; in Slovakia it is as low as in Russia. The two peoples have a common literary language and the differences in vernacular are so slight that each can understand the other without difficulty. Politically they have nearly always been separate, and since 1031 they have not enjoyed political union. They are held together now, not so much by a desire for union as from the sympathies of a common struggle — the Czechs against the Slavs and the Slovaks against the Magyars. The Slovaks speak of the Czechs as "the Prussians of the Slavs." A Slovak revolt against the Czechs is not impossible, and should it succeed it would probably be followed by an attempt on the part of the Slovaks to form an independent state.

Bohemia, the land of the Czechs, is a basin-plain, bordered by

FIG. 124. Regional divisions of Czecho-Slovakia (light broken lines), international boundaries (heavy solid lines), and plebiscite areas (heavy broken lines). For a proposed disposition of Teschen and the two enclosed areas southeast of it, see Figure 179.

fertile mountain valleys and underlain in part by deposits of coal, lignite, and iron, as well as nickel, cobalt, and copper. More than 90 per cent of its land is agriculturally productive. It not only is rich by natural endowment, but also has highly developed metal industries, clothing mills, paper mills, etc. Its glass is famous the world over. Its silver and leather work have a long history. With the addition to the state of the coking coal of Teschen, which provides half the total fuel supply, it is industrially independent—perhaps as well balanced in this respect as any state in Europe. *The Bohemian basin*

The difference between Czechs and Moravians (Fig. 124) is very slight. Their physical features are not greatly different; the Moravian dialects vary but little from the speech of the Czechs of Bohemia. This is the more surprising when we recall the isolation of their mountain environment and the differences that such an environment commonly produces. It is the closely similar speech of the three Slav groups composing Czecho-Slovakia, as well as their common oppression by the Hapsburgs, that has helped to weld them into one nation. *Close resemblance of the " Northern Slavs "*

The Moravians are mostly farmers. They number about 1,800,000, and scattered among them are 735,000 Germans whose ancestors, coming by way of the valley of the March, which drains the heart of the country, settled on the border heights and in the towns, many of which they fortified (600 to 700 years ago). The German element is better educated and is the stronger industrially, because it has capital and technical education. The Germans are a class apart. Antagonisms between them and the Moravians have grown, not *The people of the Moravian country* lessened, with time. Religious differences also have had a share in keeping the races in a hostile attitude, for while the Moravians themselves are largely Protestant, most of the Germans in Moravia are Roman Catholic.

Land of the Slovaks

Slovakia, in the east, is a rough and more thinly populated country. The forested mountain land was, in earlier years, a natural refuge of the Slovaks. The people live in valleys separated by ridges that run southward to the edge of the Hungarian plain. The streams flow southward into the Danube. We may say that physically the country faces south, but politically it faces west. There are but two railway lines connecting it with Moravia and Bohemia. It is a land of small towns, farmers, shepherds, and lumbermen, rather than a land of mills, shops, cities, and railroads.

Oppression of the Slovaks

The Slovaks are the least important and the least capable of the three Slav groups that compose Czecho-Slovakia — the Czechs, Moravians, and Slovaks. None of the subject races of Hungary has been so much oppressed as they. There was for years a steady flow of Magyars into the lands of the Slovaks, where they took the places of Slavs who emigrated in large numbers to foreign countries.

ADVANTAGES AND DISADVANTAGES OF AN INTERIOR STATE

The Danube outlet

Like Switzerland and Hungary, Czecho-Slovakia is a landlocked state. It borders the Danube for less than a hundred miles, and this river, as we have seen, flows past so many other states that it is not a Czech stream as the Seine is French or as the Volga is Russian. To improve the facilities for water transportation, the Moldau and other tributaries of the Elbe have been canalized, although a great commerce cannot be developed on the Elbe until a deeper channel is provided in Saxony and Bohemia. With these and other improvements, the cheap export of goods would be favored. Further assistance is given by provisions in the treaty of Versailles for the export of Czech goods over German rivers (chiefly the Elbe) and from German ports, where it is stipulated Czecho-Slovakia shall have the privilege of making installations and shall enjoy rights of a special character. The importance of this is seen in the fact that before 1914 three times as much Austro-Hungarian commerce flowed through Hamburg as through Trieste, though special customs arrangements were responsible for part of this result.

If the Allies can enforce the international agreements they have signed respecting freedom of transit from one state across the territory of a neighboring state, the interior nations will not suffer because they do not themselves own ports and railways to them. It is provided that "goods and persons and means of transport" shall have free passage to the natural outlets of each country. This means in a sense a limitation of sovereignty of the state that owns such an outlet port; but the alternative would be

Right of access to the sea

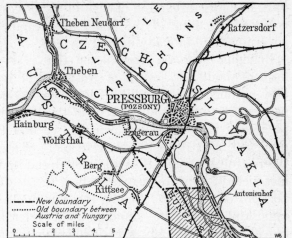

Fig. 125. Details of boundary arrangements in the region of Pressburg, Czecho-Slovakia's port on the Danube. For general relations see Figure 126. Germans constitute 42 per cent of the population of Pressburg, and Magyars 40 per cent.

annoying servitudes imposed upon interior states by stronger neighbors holding the coastal outlets, such for example as the servitudes formerly imposed upon Switzerland by Italy and Germany (page 183).

Should the arrangement with regard to transport of goods become effective, Czecho-Slovakia would have full rights of transit on the Danube, on the canals joining its streams to the Elbe, and on the Elbe itself, and the reasonable use of the ports of Danzig, Trieste, and Fiume, as well as Hamburg and Stettin. It is likely that the trade of the country will be chiefly with (1) agricultural Rumania and Hungary, whence must come much of Czecho-Slovakia's deficit in cereals and meat, (2) industrial Germany, and (3) agricultural and pastoral Jugo-Slavia.

The position of Czecho-Slovakia as well as her industrial power will make her one of the most important of the states of central Europe. She is near agricultural nations like Hungary and Russia; she can supply many of the needs of the Balkans for manufactured wares; she was not ravaged by the World War like Poland, Belgium, and Serbia. She has from 85 to 90 per cent of the soft coal and 60 per cent of the iron ore of former Austria. She made three fourths of all the shoes manufactured in the whole of Austria-Hungary, exporting largely to the Balkans and Russia. Moravia is a great producer of wool; Slovakia is rich in agricultural and forest resources; the Teschen mines supply an excellent coking coal. Prague and Pilsen are among the great industrial centers of Europe. Banks

Future power of the new state

have been organized and opened in the largest towns; unemployment is already a thing of the past; the people have accepted the new government and loyally uphold its laws.

Percentages of agricultural products

Bohemia, Moravia, and Silesia (that is, Austrian Silesia) together formed about one fourth of Austria, not including Hungary. Yet they produced 35 per cent of the wheat, 59 per cent of the barley, 48 per cent of the rye, 90 per cent of the sugar beets, 32 per cent of the potatoes. If we consider acreage, we find that these three regions produced from 10 to 100 per cent more of a given crop per acre than the rest of Austria. Bohemia alone produced 80 per cent of the former yield of hops in Austria, half of the flax and textile fiber, and 75 per cent of the fruit. Among these products sugar is one of the most important from the standpoint of international trade. Czecho-Slovakia was the only sugar-exporting country of Europe in 1919. In 1912–1913 (a normal year) Bohemia and Moravia had the one 5 and the other 7 per cent of its cultivated soil in sugar beets, and together they produced 8 per cent of the world's total.

The addition of Slovakia to the Czecho-Slovak republic greatly increases the national wealth. Of the whole Czecho-Slovak production, Slovakia provides 39 per cent of the wheat, 35 per cent of the barley, 87 per cent of the maize, 32 per cent of the potatoes, 86 per cent of the sheep, and 26 per cent of the cattle, in addition to important crops of tobacco, flax, and wine. Considering area, however, Slovakia has a lower per acre production than Bohemia; hence the inclusion of Slovakia within the new state brings down the average production per acre. Slovakia includes some of the most important oats and barley lands of former Hungary.

Czecho-Slovakia and the railway map of Europe

Several of the chief railways of Europe cross Czecho-Slovakia. The lines from Berlin to Vienna, from Warsaw to Trieste, from Switzerland to Poland, all pass through her larger towns. She can reach both the Elbe and the Danube by canals. Prague will become one of the greatest of the cities of central Europe. But as a whole, and especially in its eastern part, the country is still in need of railways to develop its varied natural resources.

The external economic arrangements of the state are in process of rapid adjustment. New commercial treaties with Bulgaria and Rumania are under discussion. By treaty with Poland the regular delivery of petroleum is assured, and commercial arrangements have also been made with Hungary. With Germany a treaty has been concluded which provides for the exchange of potash salts, delivered to Czecho-Slovakia, and coal, delivered to Germany.

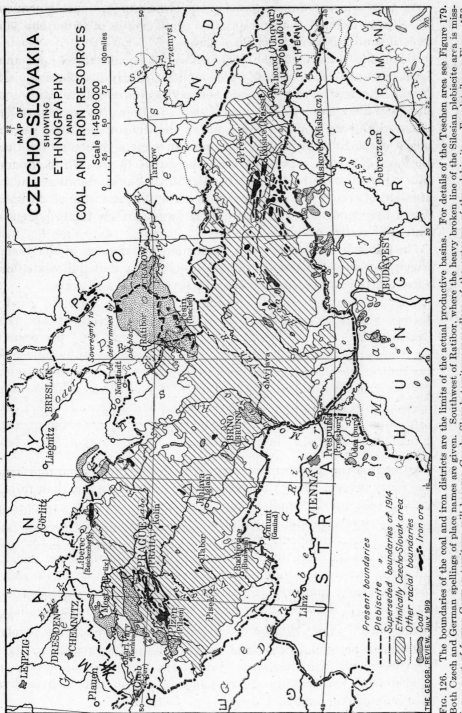

FIG. 126. The boundaries of the coal and iron districts are the limits of the actual productive basins. For details of the Teschen area see Figure 179. Both Czech and German spellings of place names are given. Southwest of Ratibor, where the heavy broken line of the Silesian plebiscite area is missing, a part of former German territory will become Czecho-Slovak territory regardless of the outcome of the plebiscite. For details see Figure 176. The term "racial" in the legend is employed in the popular sense to denote linguistic or ethnic differences. Strictly speaking, there are no well-defined racial boundaries, owing to the mixing process that has everywhere modified original types. True racial differences exist, but they are demonstrable only between widely separated centers of dispersal.

As a step in the direction of land reforms, the National Assembly has already ordered the expropriation of all estates of more than 475 acres if under cultivation and of 350 acres if uncultivated. Under this law the state will take 3,250,000 acres of cultivated land and 7,500,000 acres of woodland, or enough for nearly 500,000 families. It will be a severe test of social and political strength to carry the process of land division to its logical end. In Bohemia, and especially in the southwestern part thereof and in the Bohemian portion of the valley of the Elbe, are many huge estates, some of which go back to the days of Czech expulsions after the battle of the White Mountain. The effect is to diminish the size of the farms elsewhere. The situation is even worse in Slovakia as a result of the Magyar régime. It was this condition that accounted in large part for the heavy emigration of earlier years.

The following table gives the proportion of holdings in the three principal political divisions of Czecho-Slovakia that fall above or below a given size — three hectares or seven and a half acres :

COUNTRIES	FARMS OF 3 HECTARES (7½ ACRES) OR LESS		FARMS OF MORE THAN 3 HECTARES (7½ ACRES)		TOTAL NUMBER OF FARMS
	Number	Percentage of Arable Land	Number	Percentage of Arable Land	
Bohemia . .	580,073	23.5	1,890,405	76.5	2,470,478
Moravia . .	340,585	29.6	810,774	70.4	1,151,359
Silesia . . .	42,805	25.2	126,979	74.8	169,784
Total . .	963,463	25.4	2,828,158	74.6	3,791,621

A third of the peasant holdings of Bohemia range from fourteen to seventy acres. Many thousands of the farms have less than three acres. Some are as small as one acre apiece. In the expropriation of large estates small landholders, disabled soldiers, and legionaries[1] and their dependents, will be given preference and will receive farms that range from fifteen to twenty-five to thirty-seven and a half acres, the size depending upon the value and quality of the soil. The best arable land will go to actual farmers ; municipalities, corporations, and scientific institutions may acquire non-arable allotments, such as forest lands, pasture lands, and ponds.

[1] The Czecho-Slovak troops who fought their way across Russia and Siberia in 1918–1919 (page 235).

CHAPTER FOURTEEN

JUGO–SLAVIA[1] AND THE ADRIATIC

The Balkan countries — Serbia, Greece, Bulgaria, Rumania, Montenegro, and Albania — were long under the control of the Turkish Empire. By a series of wars against Turkey, in which at one time or another all of them participated, the Balkan countries gained first partial and at length complete independence. The next act in the historic drama of the freedom of the Balkans was played in the Balkan wars of 1912 and 1913. As a result of the two Balkan wars and the World War, the Balkan states now have an independent status,[2] unfettered by either Turkish rule or the protection of the greater European powers, save as to control of racial minorities (page 287) and freedom of transit across their territories.

For our immediate purpose it is not necessary to trace the historical sequences of each country in detail, but only to point to those recent events and conditions that affect the present national life. A view of their so-called racial characters is especially helpful in understanding the new frontiers.

The people of Serbia are Slavs, with slight linguistic differences between their language and that of the Bulgars. However, the latter were originally Finno-Ugrians of a later period of migration as contrasted with the early invasions of the Slavs farther west. Mixture with the Slavs already established in the region and with those who came later has quite changed the original Bulgar stock. Slavic populations also extend through Croatia and the eastern Adriatic region to the gates of Trieste. Northward, Slavic communities live beyond the Danube and the Save (Fig. 131). A broad belt of population of Slavic speech thus extends across the Balkans and includes the farthest outposts of the Slavic world in Europe. *Ethnic composition*

In Rumania there is a distinct population neither Slav nor Ruman, but a mixture of the two, in which the Slav element predominates. In Greece there is a distinctive racial contrast to the Slavic belt of the middle Balkans; but here also strong Slavic infusions have been introduced.

Throughout the Balkans the Greek Orthodox Church represents the prevailing religion, with a belt of Roman Catholic population in northern Albania and in the centers of Italian culture on the Dal- *The factor of religion*

---

[1] The official title of the new state is " Kingdom of the Serbs, Croats, and Slovenes."
[2] Except Montenegro, which is now included in Jugo-Slavia.

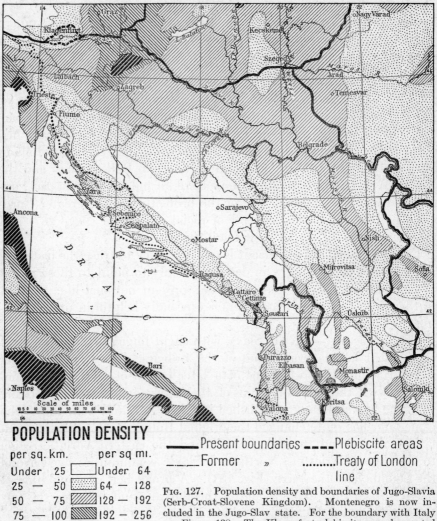

POPULATION DENSITY

per sq. km.		per sq mi.
Under	25	Under 64
25 —	50	64 — 128
50 —	75	128 — 192
75 —	100	192 — 256
over	100	over 256

———— Present boundaries ▬▬▬▬ Plebiscite areas
—·—·— Former " ·········· Treaty of London line

FIG. 127. Population density and boundaries of Jugo-Slavia (Serb-Croat-Slovene Kingdom). Montenegro is now included in the Jugo-Slav state. For the boundary with Italy see Figure 138. The Klagenfurt plebiscite area has voted to go to Austria. From *Schweizerischer Schul-atlas*, supplemented by *Petermanns Mitteilungen*, 1913.

matian coast. Other exceptions to the predominance of the Greek Orthodox Church are: the central block of Moslem Albanians; the Moslems (Croats chiefly) of Bosnia and Herzegovina; the Moslems of Thrace; the Pomaks (Moslemized Bulgars and Turks) of Bulgaria; and the Protestant and Catholic Saxons and Szeklers of Transylvania.

First Balkan War

The Balkan states threw off the last forms of Turkish control in 1912. They were encouraged to make their military effort of that year because the war between Italy and Turkey (1911–1912) had greatly weakened Turkey, who had exhibited herself as a power wholly incapable of holding in check the rising tide of nationalism in the Balkans. Montenegro declared war against Turkey, and was supported by Bulgaria and Serbia, who had agreed before the war to a secret treaty establishing new frontiers should Turkey be defeated. Shortly after, Greece joined them and the four conducted an intensive campaign that drove Turkish forces out of the Balkans, except for a mere patch of territory near Constantinople and extending from that city to the Chatalja line of defenses (Fig. 207). Greek troops besieged and finally took Saloniki. The Serbian army defeated the Turkish army in Albania, and the Bulgarians captured Kirk Kilisse, Lule Burgas, and Adrianople. With these three regions in their hands, the Balkan allies made peace with Turkey at Adrianople in 1913, and then proceeded to divide amongst themselves the territory that they had liberated.

In the process of establishing their mutual boundaries, the states fell to quarreling. The outcome was the Second Balkan War, in which Greece and Serbia, joined by Rumania, defeated Bulgaria. By the treaty of Bucarest (1913), Rumania obtained from Bulgaria a part of the Dobrudja containing 250,000 Bulgarians; Greece received Saloniki and a part of western Thrace; and Serbia extended her southern boundary to meet the boundary of Greece, thus dividing Macedonia. By a subsequent treaty with Turkey, Bulgaria returned Kirk Kilisse, Lule Burgas, and Adrianople to Turkey.

Results of the Second Balkan War

The general attack of the other Balkan countries upon Bulgaria in the Second Balkan War was responsible in part for the alliance of Bulgaria with the Central Powers in the war of 1914–1918. Defeated for a second time in the World War, Bulgaria underwent still further reduction of territory, as shown in Figures 151 and 153.

To drive out the Turk was for years the common ambition of the Balkan states, but Serbia had a special aim, that of uniting to herself the Slavic groups outside her limits, to form a Jugo-Slav state; for Serbia included within her frontiers only a third of the total Jugo-Slav population. "Only ten years ago the Jugo-Slavs were living under six different governments; and their deputies sat in fourteen different parliaments, national or provincial. To attain their unity they have had to disrupt two such empires as Austria-Hungary and Turkey."

Union of Jugo-Slavs, or Southern Slavs

In her struggle to effect the union of the Jugo-Slav groups, Serbia was opposed by Austria-Hungary, a far stronger power than Turkey. This opposition was due not merely to the fact that hundreds of thousands of Jugo-Slavs lived north of the Danube in old Austro-

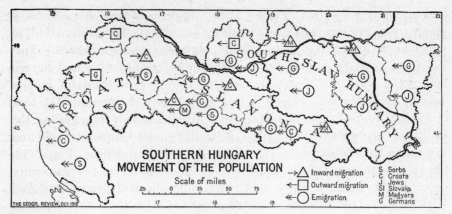

Fɪɢ. 128. Compare with Figures 115, 123, and 146 to show effects of Magyar discrimination against subject minority peoples.

Hungarian territory, but chiefly to the fact that the main mass of Jugo-Slavs lived in the provinces where Austria-Hungary had her only direct and unrestricted outlets to the sea; that is, in Bosnia and Herzegovina (occupied by Austria-Hungary in 1878 and annexed to the Austro-Hungarian Empire in 1908), in the Adriatic provinces, and about Trieste and Fiume.

Conflict of Balkan and Germano-Austrian interests

Behind Austria-Hungary stood a still stronger power, the German Empire. These two great empires, together comprising 115,000,000 people, were not willing to foster Balkan nationalism at the expense of their own political scheme of creating a Central Europe under German domination. Their aim was not merely to invade and seize the Balkan lands or limit the sovereignty of the Balkan peoples, for the Balkan lands are in general poor. Their object was more far-reaching: it was to use the Balkans as a passageway to the Turkish Empire; to build the Bagdad road to the head of the Persian Gulf; to win the subtropical products (chiefly raw materials) of Mesopotamia; and, from the Persian Gulf, to invade the great trading marts of the Orient, principally those of India and China.

We have referred to the low commercial rank of the Balkan countries. The point will be clearer if we look at the outstanding economic features of the Balkan peninsula.

Resources and commerce of Balkan countries

The four largest Balkan countries in 1914 had a total trade (combining imports and exports) of $400,000,000, or less than 1 per cent of the world's total. Together they had a commercial importance that outranked that of Portugal or Norway and was less than that of Sweden, or Spain, or even Denmark. Of the total Balkan trade Rumania supplied half.

Agricultural products are of chief importance in the export and import trade of the Balkans, forming three fourths of the whole. The industrially undeveloped state of the region is shown by the fact that products of the forest, the mine, and the factory form only from one fifth to one tenth of the total trade. They are composed chiefly of the lumber and petroleum of Rumania and the mineral ores of Greece.

In more highly developed industrial countries with exports like those of the Balkans, the imports would include raw materials for manufacture. Not so in the Balkan countries. For example, the imports of raw cotton form only one third of one per cent of the total value of imports. Greece alone among the Balkan countries has a deficit of cereals and must import grain. Even sugar and coffee are imported in very small quantities; the consumption of coffee is less than one pound per person a year and of sugar eight pounds, or about one tenth the per capita amounts used in the United States.

The exports of the Balkans went chiefly to the industrial districts and cities of central and northern Europe. Of Germany's total commerce with the principal Balkan states, 50 per cent by value was with Rumania. One half of the total imports of the Balkans came from Germany and Austria-Hungary. Measured by tonnage, 75 per cent of Germany's total Balkan trade was sea-borne, while 72 per cent of the trade with Austria was carried by rail. Of Germany's total commerce 8 per cent was river-borne, which indicates that Germany has as much interest in the physical improvement of the Danube and the commercial regulation of its trade as if she were a Balkan state.

BOUNDARY DIFFICULTIES

The new state of Jugo-Slavia consists of the former kingdom of Serbia, to which are joined the former kingdom of Montenegro and the districts of Bosnia, Herzegovina, Croatia, Dalmatia, Slavonia, a part of western Bulgaria, and part of the Banat of Temesvár. The total number of inhabitants is about 12,000,000, divided as follows: Serbs, 6,000,000; Croats, 2,500,000; Slovenes, 1,000,000; Macedonian Slavs, 550,000; Magyars, 450,000; Albanians, 250,000; Moslem Serbs, 625,000; Rumanians, 150,000; Germans, 450,000; others, 175,000.

Division of population

One of the most difficult problems of southeastern Europe — and the most likely to lead to future war — is the boundary problem confronting the new state of Jugo-Slavia. Practically every mile of her frontier, excepting only a portion bordering Greece, faces an unfriendly state. The danger springs from a number of complex causes, but is

Difficult situation of Jugo-Slavia

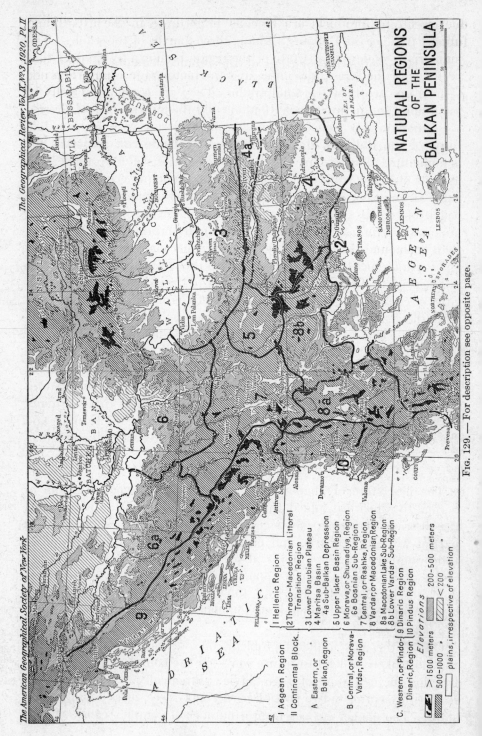

NATURAL REGIONS
OF THE
BALKAN PENINSULA

I Aegean Region

II Continental Block.

A Eastern, or
Balkan, Region

B Central, or Morava-
Vardar, Region

C. Western, or Pindo-
Dinaric, Region

1 Hellenic Region

(2 Thraco-Macedonian Littoral
Transition Region

3 Lower Danubian Plateau

4 Maritsa Basin
4a Sub-Balkan Depression

5 Upper Isker Basin Region

6 Morava, or Shumadiya, Region
6a Bosnian Sub-Region

7 Central, or Rashka, Region

8 Vardar, or Macedonian, Region
8a Macedonian Lake Sub-Region
8b Lower Vardar Sub-Region

9 Dinaric Region

10 Pindus Region

Elevations

> 1500 meters   200–500 meters

500–1000   < 200

plains, irrespective of elevation

The Geographical Review, Vol. IX, No. 3, 1920, Pl. II

The American Geographical Society of New York

Fig. 129. — For description see opposite page.

For description see opposite page.

due chiefly to four, whose effects must be closely watched in the future :

(1) The peculiar distribution of the ethnic elements of the Slav state, whereby peninsulas of Slav population interlock with those of other nationalities in a way that makes it impossible to divide the territory without leaving both sides resentful.

(2) The inclusion within Jugo-Slavia of blocks of territory inhabited almost exclusively by people who will constitute centers of irredentism in a politically weak state.

(3) The occupation of Montenegro by Serbian troops.

(4) The rivalry with Italy at Fiume and at Zara in Dalmatia, and with Italy and Albania at Lake Scutari, where a struggle may ensue for possession of the Drin outlet.

The basis of each cause is worth thoughtful attention.

(1) The northeastern boundary of Jugo-Slavia has been extended so far north of the Danube, especially in the region of the Banat of Temesvár (Fig. 142), that it includes numbers of Magyars and Saxons who are unwilling to be associated with the Jugo-Slav family and who will long favor a return of their land to Hungary, to which state they have belonged for a thousand years.

Bases of
difficulties

(2) Equally serious is the annexation to Jugo-Slavia of the Tsaribrod, Bosilegrad, and Strumitsa districts (Fig. 153) inhabited by Bulgars and taken from Bulgaria for strategic reasons. The three districts

---

Fig. 129. This map (on the opposite page) should be freely consulted in the reading of the chapters relating to the different Balkan countries. The characteristics of the regions shown are briefly summarized as follows :

1. Mediterranean climate and vegetation; population restricted to small cultivable areas and pastures; trading cities with maritime traditions.
2. Some rain in summer, in contrast to 1; better access to interior; a transition zone with respect to vegetation, climate, and population.
3. Continental extremes of climate; fertile loess soil, but wheat harvests apt to be affected by summer drought; Balkan mountains on south, though easily crossed, a cultural boundary.
4 and 4a. Mingling of Mediterranean and steppe characteristics; diversified relief, climate, and agricultural resources.
5. Elevated deforested country with small resources.
6 and 6a. Terraced plateau with abundant rain; modified central European type of climate; large maize and prune crops; home of main body of Serbian population.
7. Series of tectonic basins with fertile soil, graded river outlets, fine bordering pastures; center of ancient Serbian state.
8a and 8b. Cultivated basin floors; winter pastures supporting herds of migratory shepherds; climate and products reflecting Ægean influences.
9. No unifying centers of life and culture, yet markedly uniform linguistic and ethnic characters; absence of deep transverse valleys; upland pastures separated by barren broken zone from low littoral belt with Mediterranean climate and products.
10. Deep transverse valleys and high mountains bordered on seaward side by marshy coastal plain; difficult relief reflected in tribal life and general backwardness of people, though the region is well endowed with natural resources.

Fig. 130. The Rieka Valley, a typical landscape view in Montenegro.

approach rather closely to the main railway line leading from Belgrade and Nish southward through the Vardar-Morava trench to Saloniki, which is destined to be in time a great seaport and commercial outlet for Serbia.

Differences with Montenegro

(3) In addition to the difficulties on the east, due to the violation of the ethnic principle for reasons of strategy, there is added the Montenegrin problem on the west. Montenegro joined Serbia in the war against the Central Powers; but owing to a lack of public confidence in the king and his court (they left the country in 1916), a strong public sentiment developed in favor of union with Serbia, Croatia, and Slavonia to form a Jugo-Slav kingdom. It is natural that the officers of the old régime should wish to regain power, and that a separat st party should exist which will be a source of dissension and weakness for the newly created and experimental Jugo-Slav state. While Serbia has occupied Montenegro, the occupation was not ac-

complished without violence and disorder, and this unfortunate circumstance has diminished the faith of many of the Montenegrin people in the plan of union itself. There will long be a troublesome group of Montenegrins intriguing with the Albanians against the Jugo-Slav government.

A similar state of animosity exists on the Albanian frontier, where Serbs and Albanians are traditional enemies, the first being Greek Orthodox, the latter — in part, at least — Moslem. A large number of Albanians live in the region of Prizren and Üsküb and desire union with Albania. On the other hand, Jugo-Slavia wishes to retain them and to absorb all of northern Albania, at least as far south as the Drin, in order to get a railway outlet by way of the Drin valley and at the same time protect her naval defenses at Cattaro and the Lake of Scutari.

Troubles with the Albanians

(4) Formerly Serbia was struggling for a "window on the sea." At first she sought an outlet at Saloniki, but when this was lost to her by the Greek capture of that city in the First Balkan War, she sought an outlet on the Adriatic. The federation of all the southern Slavs offered her a long-delayed opportunity. Not merely a window, but the whole Dalmatian coast now became a chief territorial object, involving a prolonged diplomatic struggle with Italy which ended in 1920 with the treaty of Rapallo (page 269).

POLITICAL UNITY OF THE STATE

Overshadowing all the difficulties enumerated above is the inherent weakness of the entire plan of a Jugo-Slav state, viewed from the standpoint of national unity. The strength of the idea behind a Jugo-Slav kingdom has yet to be proved. Croatia long and steadfastly opposed the idea of Slav union, and thus played into the hands of Italy and Austria. Reconciliation of Serbs and Croats was achieved only as late as 1903. Though an actual government was organized at Agram only after November 1918, the political foundations of the present Jugo-Slav state were laid in the pact of Corfu (July 1917). Representatives of Serbia and of the Jugo-Slav Committee of London met at Corfu and adopted, among others, the following resolution: "The territory of the Serbs, Croats, and Slovenes will comprise all the territory where our nation lives in compact masses and without discontinuity, and where it could not be mutilated without injuring the vital interests of the community. It desires to free itself and establish its unity."

Pact of Corfu

The principal items of the pact of Corfu are as follows:

(1) The Kingdom of the Serbs, Croats, and Slovenes shall be a democratic, constitutional, and parliamentary monarchy under the Karageorgevichs, whose three co-national parts shall have a single allegiance.

(2) The equality of the three chief religions within the new state — Orthodox, Roman Catholic, and Mohammedan — shall be guaranteed.

(3) The Latin and Cyrillic alphabets shall both be used.

(4) The territory of the new state shall be extended over all areas where Jugo-Slavs live in compact masses — which involves the union of Montenegro and Serbia.

(5) The Adriatic Sea shall be kept free and open to all.

(6) Elections shall be by universal, equal, direct, and secret vote.

(7) A constitution shall be framed by a constituent assembly which shall serve as a basis for the life of the state.

Separatist tendencies In spite of the pact of Corfu, the different parts of the state have not yet become amalgamated. Croatia has been in a separatist mood, due to the uncertainties arising from the Fiume situation and to the failure of the Jugo-Slav government to oust the Italians, settle the foreign policy of the country, start railroad trains, supply coal, and defend the frontier against Italian aggression. The tendency toward disunion at one time (July 1919) reached a dangerous climax when an independent but short-lived Croatian republic was proclaimed, and conflict followed. If the separatist tendency should develop, the effects would be deplorable. The interests of all the peoples making up Jugo-Slavia are so closely related and their neighbors are so formidable in size and strength that a strong confederated union, economic as well as political, is required if the state is to survive.

Regional differences Though all three main ethnic groups of Jugo-Slavia are Slavs in race, there are strong provincial differences of custom and speech between the Slovenes, Croats, and Serbs. Some of the Slovenes and Croats — and their number is considerable — do not wish to have their capital at Belgrade, where, they feel sure, Serbian influences are bound to dominate the councils of the new nation. Finding themselves placed athwart the highways leading out of the densely populated hinterland of central Europe, the two northern elements (Slovenes and Croats) see many advantages in independence. As the boundaries now stand, Serbia would be practically compelled to find her outlet to the Adriatic through the northern provinces.

Related to the separatist problem is uncertainty as to the outcome of the long struggle which Jugo-Slavia has made, and through which it has not yet passed, to decide whether its government shall be strongly centralized or whether there shall be a high degree of local autonomy. In the pact of Corfu, as we have seen, a strongly centralized government was proclaimed, and this was reaffirmed by the Act of Union (1918), when the Prince Regent proclaimed the "Kingdom of the Serbs, Croats, and Slovenes." At that time the Croatian national assembly voted for the union. Later, in 1919, there was a sharp struggle, owing to the inability of the various political parties to agree on a cabinet which the national assembly could support. *(Struggle over centralization)*

The new country has had to depend for a long time upon a provisional government, and until a convention is held and the final form of government determined, it is not desirable that the provisional government should go too far in either direction; that is, either toward centralization or toward local autonomy of the people of the different regions. All parties in Jugo-Slavia outside of old Serbia are opposed to the dominance of Serbia in Jugo-Slav affairs. To add to the difficulties, schools and newspapers are few, illiteracy is high, and the people have for the most part a warlike disposition.

Having passed in review some of the outstanding current problems of Jugo-Slavia, we shall now return to each principal item and discuss it in greater detail in connection with the maps, Figures 131 to 142, before passing to the study of the economic strength of the new state and the character of its people. *(Difficulties of political organization)*

RIVAL TERRITORIAL CLAIMS

The Eastern Adriatic — Jugo-Slav or Italian

The most serious zone of friction is the Istrian peninsula, Dalmatia, and the uplands of Carniola bordering Italy. It is of prime importance to establish the facts, not merely in relation to a problem that was long prominent, but for the understanding of future boundary disputes that any present settlement will be unable to prevent. *(The Istrian problem area)*

Let us begin with an examination of the map which shows the ethnic distribution of Jugo-Slavs and Italians (Fig. 131). The Slavs are indisputably predominant up to and beyond the Isonzo. Trieste is, so to speak, an Italian island in a Jugo-Slav sea, and by far the greater part of the population of Istria itself is Jugo-Slav (Fig. 132).

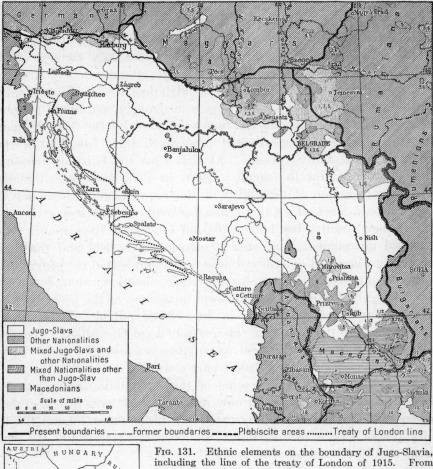

Key to Fig. 131.

Fig. 131. Ethnic elements on the boundary of Jugo-Slavia, including the line of the treaty of London of 1915. From British General Staff ethnic map, 1 : 1,500,000, 1918. Key to numerals: 1, Jugo-Slavs; 2, Italians; 3, Germans; 4, Czecho-Slovaks; 5, Magyars; 6, Rumanians; 7, Bulgarians; 8, Albanians; 9, Macedonians; 10, Greeks; 11, Vlachs; 12, Turks.

But the term "Jugo-Slav" includes Croats and Slovenes as well as Serbs, and while Serbia fought most gallantly in the World War on the side of the Allies, many Croats and practically all the Slovenes fought with equal tenacity on the side of the Central Powers. Italian armies faced Slovene and Croat divisions for more than three years. Yet when the Austro-Hungarian Empire fell apart and a Jugo-Slav kingdom was created, Slovenes and Croats who had been fighting against the Allies were suddenly thrown by a mere political phrase — "the Kingdom of the Serbs, Croats, and Slovenes" — into the ranks of the Allies.

By way of further explanation of Italy's attitude, it may be stated that Italian armies proved a big factor in the winning of the war, during which Italy suffered heavy loss, including at least 475,000 men killed — many of them at the hands of Slovene soldiers. Her northeastern provinces were devastated. Italian losses in the war not compensated by material gains

It would be easy to make out an equally good case for Serbia, which suffered even more cruelly from the war; but the argument cannot be applied to the whole of Jugo-Slavia. And, as we have seen, this is but one of the differences between the parts of the Jugo-Slav state, all of which make its continued existence uncertain, its boundaries, therefore, to a certain extent hypothetical. The integrity of the state depends upon its internal unity as well as upon external agreements with neighboring states. The forces of disunion in Jugo-Slavia are stronger than in any other newly created state of central Europe.

When we contrast these two sets of considerations, — the service of Italy to the Allies and the weakness of the Jugo-Slav state, — we see that the principle of drawing boundary lines on an ethnic basis is one that at times must be modified in favor of other factors.

Italy is a narrow peninsula with an extremely long and vulnerable seacoast. Added to dread of the overwhelming strength of a historic enemy on the northeast — the old empire of Austria-Hungary — was the fear of possible attack from the eastern Adriatic shore.

Faced by these historic conditions and the relative strength and importance of the Italian and Jugo-Slav states, the Jugo-Slavs themselves did not deny the right of the Italians to enjoy naval supremacy on the Adriatic. That Trieste should be in Italian possession and that Pola should be a great Italian naval base, were points conceded by every student of the problem.

Up to this point we have been dealing with matters about which there has been little, if any, serious dispute. We now enter the realm of controversial facts and conclusions.

The Italians claimed the Dalmatian coast on the ground that the culture of the whole eastern fringe of the Adriatic is Italian. It is true that Italians predominate: The fringe of Italian culture

(1) In the narrow western fringe of Istria.

(2) In the towns of Fiume (not including Sušak) and Zara.

(3) In the islands of Lussin and Unie.

But it is true also that the Italians scattered along the eastern Adriatic littoral are city and not country dwellers, traders and not farmers. They cannot be said to occupy the region. A like criticism may

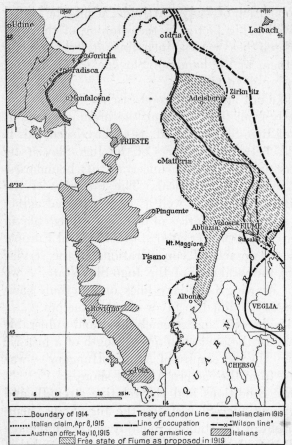

Boundary of 1914 — Treaty of London Line — Italian claim 1919
Italian claim, Apr 8,1915 — Line of occupation — Wilson line
Austrian offer, May 10,1915 — after armistice — Italians
Free state of Fiume as proposed in 1919

FIG. 132. Ethnographic and boundary map of Istria. Ethnography after the Austrian census of 1910. For detailed map
of Fiume see Figures 133 and 139. There are valuable mercury mines at Idria, now acquired by Italy.

be made of the cultural argument. The evidences of Italian culture in the towns belong to past importations and give no basis for true regional development.

The extent of Italian cultural influence is greater than the area in which Italians live. Italy was historically and culturally far advanced when, behind the coastal fringe, the uplands of Jugo-Slavia were a primeval wilderness.

Cultural considerations here form a peculiarly weak basis for national claims, because the ties of race, language, and political faith are stronger than the ties of culture, even though that culture be long established. The people are Jugo-Slavs and wished to remain Jugo-Slavs, and they did not wish to accept Italian sovereignty merely because from early times the coast of the region, formerly known as Illyria, had attracted Roman warriors and ship builders, traders, travelers, and priests. The Jugo-Slavs asked: "How many thousands of Jugo-Slavs are you going to claim because the architecture is Italian, and because the Romans hundreds of years ago cut timber on our coast, sent missionaries, raised large buildings, and traded with our people?"

The difficulties of the dispute between Italy and Jugo-Slavia arose in large part because the ethnic, cultural, and military lines do not coincide. It is hard to select a line that gives equal attention to these three considerations. If the best military line be selected, the ethnic principle is violated; if a cultural line be followed, military and naval considerations are set aside.

The geographic argument was often invoked for the union of eastern Adriatic lands with Italy. The climate and vegetation are "Mediterranean," like those of the Italian eastern coast, but so also like the coast of Greece. The physiography, wholly unlike that of eastern Italy, is a unit with that of western Serbia. The commercial relations have been Italian, and the people have always had a seafaring element, and so much at least depends upon geographical situation. As for similarity of geographical factors supporting the idea of political unity, this argument is at best a broken reed upon which to lean, wherever it is applied. The stage of civilization counts for much. What is geographically feasible and even advantageous in a modern state may have been impracticable in the period of Venetian power. The measure of obstruction which the Dinaric Alps and the Karst offer to the people east of them is not to be taken in hundreds of feet of elevation. The burden of transportation costs over the coastal mountains falls upon a vastly greater population today than in the days when the Italian frontier followed an interior line; and the per capita share is proportionately smaller. Finally, geographical unity involves the matter of scale and relationship. The unity of Venetian lands is a smaller and a more localized matter than the unity of Jugo-Slavia. The Appalachians were once a serious barrier, and their influence is still felt; but they hardly impair the unity of the United States. *{The two sides of the Adriatic geographically unlike}*

A situation so complicated as this is could hardly have been settled to the satisfaction of both sides under the most favorable conditions. But confusion, misunderstanding, and the causes of endless disputes and ill feeling were increased by the secret treaty of London, signed in 1915, between Great Britain, France, Russia, and Italy, under the terms of which Italy agreed to enter the war. By this treaty Italy was to receive: *{Secret treaty of London, 1915}*

(1) The Austrian Tyrol, to the Brenner Pass (Fig. 70).

(2) All of Goritzia, Gradisca, and Istria, and the city of Trieste (but not Fiume).

(3) Dalmatia to Capa Blanca, with practically all the Dalmatian islands (Fig. 138).

(4) Valona,[1] in Albania, with the surrounding region (Fig. 155).

(5) The Dodecanese and a zone on the Turkish mainland, to be defined later (see Fig. 158).

[1] Known also as Avlona and Vlore.

(6) The right to claim compensation in Africa, in case France and
    Great Britain should secure increases of territory on that
    continent.

According to the treaty of London, Italy was to get not only Trieste,
but Istria, Goritzia, and Dalmatia as well, and in all those districts
the proportion of Italians was less than of Jugo-Slavs, save along the
western margin of Istria.   On the other hand, in Dalmatia, out of a
total population of 635,000 there were only 18,000 Italians as opposed
to 611 000 Slavs   Of the 18,000 Italians, 11,768 were in the district
of Zara and 2357 in the district of Spalato, every other Dalmatian
town having less — generally much less — than 1000 Italians.

It would have been easy for everybody to accept the terms of the
treaty of London had the Austro-Hungarian Empire hung together.
Instead it broke up into its ethnic divisions, one of which was Carniola,
the country of the Slovenes.   This district was joined (by decision of
the Peace Conference of Paris) to Serbia and Croatia to form Jugo-
Slavia.   As a result, when Italy sought to annex the territory, she
found herself dealing not with an enemy (Austria-Hungary), but
with an ally (Serbia).

The city of Fiume is the chief focus of difficulty.   Counting the
suburb of Sušak, the city has a Slav majority (26,600 Jugo-Slavs to

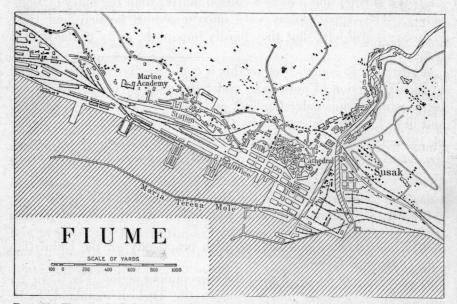

Fig. 133. The organized character of the port is in contrast to the backward state of ports on
the Dalmatian coast. Note that Sušak, a suburb on the east side of a small stream, is an integral
part of the city of Fiume.   From United States Hydrographic Office chart, No. 4072 (1915).

25,800 Italians); but the Italians are in a slight majority if this suburb is not included. Many persons talk loosely of Sušak as if it were another city separated from Fiume by a river. As a matter of fact, only a shallow brook separates the two; Sušak is as much a part of Fiume as Brooklyn is a part of New York. The country around Fiume is solidly Jugo-Slav.

In the hands of the Jugo-Slavs the trade of Fiume would grow, and the town would become a rival of the port of Trieste. The argu-

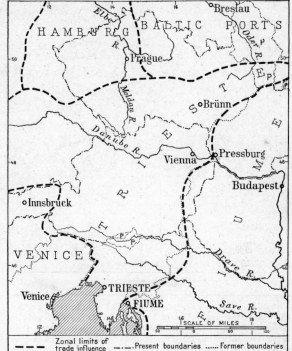

FIG. 134. The field of trade rivalry between Trieste and Fiume. From *Meereskunde*, Vol. 5, 1911.

ment advanced by the Jugo-Slavs is that if both ports are in the hands of the Italians, Trieste will be highly developed by them and Fiume left to stagnate. Fiume and Trieste are the natural outlets for a large commerce that is bound to be far more important in the future. Figures 134 and 135 show the relation of these two towns to the trade of the hinterland. As shown by the railroad map (Fig. 135), to take Fiume from Jugo-Slavia is to take away the focus of her northern railways, the one Adriatic port easily accessible to Jugo-Slavia and capable of high development, the natural center of a Jugo-Slav region, a possible commercial capital.

Figures 127, 129, and 135 together exhibit the relation of the distribution of people and railroads to the outlines of the country and to the seaboard. Most of the people of the new state live in interior valleys shut off from the sea by a broad belt of mountain ridges parallel to the coast. These ridges are difficult to cross; only two tortuous narrow-gauge railways traverse them.

It might be supposed from Figure 129 that the five hundred miles of deeply indented and island-bordered coastline of the eastern Adriatic

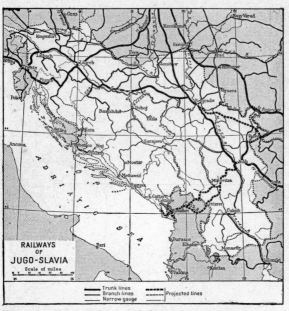

RAILWAYS
OF
JUGO-SLAVIA
Scale of miles

Trunk lines
Branch lines   Projected lines
Narrow gauge

Fig. 135. Fiume, Trieste, and Saloniki are the chief ports of the Jugo-Slav region as of 1914. The Dalmatian coast is difficult of access, and the completion of the projected Drin-Scutari outlet would involve Jugo-Slavia in international quarrels with Albania and possibly with Italy. From *Railways of Jugo-Slav countries*, 1: 2,300,000, Paris (1919?).

would furnish the new state with adequate harbors, even with Fiume lost to it. But this is not the case. The harbors are small and they are not capable of economical improvement. The mountains stand knee-deep in the sea, with so little flat land along the shore for the development of towns, and such steep descents from the uplands behind the towns, that port works on a large scale are almost prohibitive. Another disadvantage of the coast is the "bora," a cold and treacherous north wind that descends swiftly from the uplands and is exceedingly dangerous for ships in narrow passages and in deep water where anchorage is difficult.

Buccari is surrounded by steep cliffs and has a dangerous entrance; Porto Re is too small; Zengg is at the base of lofty cliffs and is noted for the fury of the bora from October to March; Spalato and Sebenico have good harborage, but they are separated from the interior by lofty mountains, and their narrow-guage railway is closed by snow nearly every winter for two or three weeks; Cattaro and Zara have no railroad; Metković, Gravosa, Ragusa, and Castelnuovo have a narrow-gauge railway connection with the interior, but the service is costly and uncertain.

The whole Dalmatian coast is almost exclusively Jugo-Slav. Within the treaty of London line as drawn for Dalmatia, there are more than 600,000 Jugo-Slavs and only 18,000 Italians. In two coast ports, Zara and Sebenico, the Italian element rises to higher proportions than elsewhere, and Zara, like Fiume, has been made a free port as a compromise.

The Jugo-Slavs assert that the justice of their claim to Dalmatia is

Fig. 136. A part of the water front at the port of Fiume. For a map of the port see Figure 133.

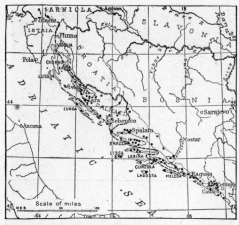

FIG. 137. Centers of Italian culture in Dalmatia. The broken line represents the line of the treaty of London, 1915. However, Spalato and Zara are the only cities which have an Italian population in excess of 1000. From Giotto Dainelli, *La Dalmazia*, 1918, Map 11.

further supported by the results of the plebiscite taken (1919) in all the communes occupied by Italian troops. More than three hundred and fifty towns participated in the elections, and the result was a vote of 96 per cent in favor of union with Jugo-Slavia. The nine islands all gave majorities above 95 per cent for union. Except for Zara, there is no town with an Italian majority in Dalmatia, and none other with more than 10 per cent of Italian population.

Some of the islands, notably Lagosta, depend entirely upon their trade with the Jugo-Slav coast. Fishing and grape culture are their two principal industries, and their products are abundant in Italy and needed in Jugo-Slavia. In some instances the people of the islands asserted that to give them to Italy would be to destroy their economic life.

Fiume and the Italian program

The agreement embodied in the treaty of London, to give Italy large territorial grants, handicapped France and Great Britain at the Peace Conference of Paris. Fiume, especially, had been excluded from the treaty of London agreement; this new desire was in response to the demands of political opponents of the Italian government, who forced Orlando a^d Sonnino, the chief Italian representatives, to adopt the most extreme imperialistic claims.

To make matters worse, when the armistice was signed in November 1918, between the Allies and Austria-Hungary, Italy was assigned the military occupation of the country between the London line and the sea; and she therefore came to the peace conference with the expressed hope that the terms of her secret treaty with France and Great Britain would be the basis on which her eastern frontier would be fixed.

France and Great Britain were willing to put into effect the treaty of London, since they regarded it as a solemn engagement. They could not concede anything more. Then came D'Annunzio to thrust himself into an already over-complicated situation. With several contingents of Italian troops he occupied Fiume in violation of the solemn pledge of Italy, in the armistice of 4 November 1918, whereby she was to keep only a handful of troops in Fiume as part of her obligation to maintain order in the former Austro-Hungarian Empire as far as the treaty of London line.

The Italian government felt that it could not send Italians to kill Italians, and therefore made no serious attempt to dislodge D'Annunzio. Before his ultimate surrender late in 1920 he was able to defy the Italian and Jugo-Slav governments, to raid Zara, to establish a postal service, to print money, and to attempt to organize an independent city state.

The boundary between Italy and Jugo-Slavia was settled in November 1920 by the treaty of Rapallo (Figs. 138 and 139).

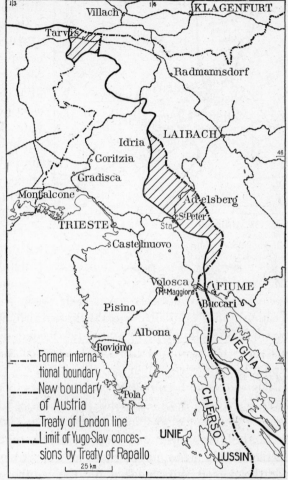

Fig. 138. Final settlement of the territorial dispute in the region at the head of the Adriatic. The shaded portion of the map represents the territory gained by Italy in excess of that pledged to her by the secret treaty of London, 1915. See Figure 139 for details in the Fiume region.

By the terms of the treaty Italy secured the important railway junction of Tarvis, a part of Carniola, and all of Istria **Treaty of Rapallo** as well as the adjacent islands of Cherso, Lussin, and Unie, and obtained for Fiume the status of a free city with direct territorial connection with Italy. She obtained also the Pelagosa Islands in the mid-Adriatic and the island of Lagosta at the southern end of the Dalmatian chain. Zara (Fig. 131), including part of the hinterland, was made a free city. Jugo-Slavia secured all the remaining islands along the eastern Adriatic.

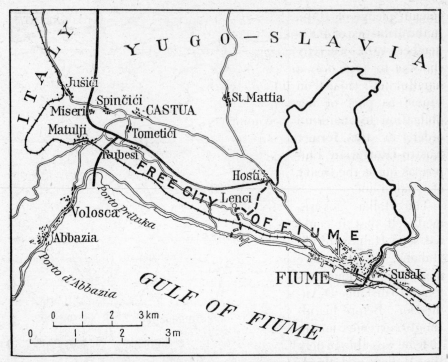

Fig. 139. New boundaries in the Fiume region according to the treaty of Rapallo, between Italy and Jugo-Slavia. The broken line at Lenci is part of the boundary of the "corpus separatum," and the remaining part is the solid line northward and eastward terminating on the coast between Fiume and its suburb, Sušak. From Lenci westward to Rubesi is the "strip" added to the Free State of Fiume to provide direct territorial connection between Fiume and Italy. The area of the Free State of Fiume is 11 square miles, and its population is 53,000. Spellings follow the 1 : 75,000 Austrian General Staff sheet.

Italian naval predominance in the Adriatic

Jugo-Slavia's fleet will long be small, and her hold upon the sea feeble. Only a few naval bases are available to serve as rendezvous for the armed ships needed for the control of the fishing industry, the supervision of the customs arrangements, and the protection of the ports. It had been the policy of the Allies to make Italy not merely strong, but in every respect predominant in the Adriatic; for her position on a slender peninsula, with a coastline mpossibly long to defend by land, puts the burden of national security upon the Italian fleet To have two equally strong navies on opposite sides of the narrow Adriatic Sea was deemed unwise. Italy's long-deferred hope to secure complete control of the Adriatic is now realized.

The Scutari Region

While there are scores of problem areas in the world and scores of points of friction between neighboring states, a few of them are of quite special importance because of the unsettled nature of the questions they present, and also because they lie in situations that offer every inducement for a quarrel. Among such the Scutari region is one of the most outstanding. It will be difficult to prevent Italy and Jugo-Slavia or Albania and Jugo-Slavia from becoming involved in actual war because of the complicated geographic and economic conditions that have their focus:

Rival claims of Jugo-Slavia and Albania about Lake Scutari

(1) On the lake and in the town of Scutari.

(2) In the Drin valley, which crosses northern Albania.

(3) At the Boyana River, which is the outlet of the Drin-Scutari basin.

Fig. 140. The broken line shows the position of the new international boundary between Italy and Jugo-Slavia at the southern end of the Dalmatian Islands, according to the treaty of Rapallo, November 1920. Lagosta and the adjacent islets as well as Pelagosa are added to Italy. The land mass at the upper right-hand corner is a part of Dalmatia; that in the lower left-hand corner is a part of Italy. The width of the Adriatic is here only about 60 miles.

(4) At the large port of Cattaro, which is the only port that by present arrangements can become a Jugo-Slav naval base.

It is worth one's while to make a close study of Figure 141, which shows the critical relations of the region. The Serbs would like to have actual possession of the Drin valley, for it is the natural main outlet of all that portion of Serbia from Nish to the Greek frontier in Macedonia. They would like also to have the Boyana River, which is the outlet of all the country centering on Lake Scutari, a country with rich trade possibilities and of great importance to Jugo-Slavia in the protection of her mountainous southwestern frontier.

Jugo-Slavia is eager to lose no trade advantage, and the northern Albanian tribes have

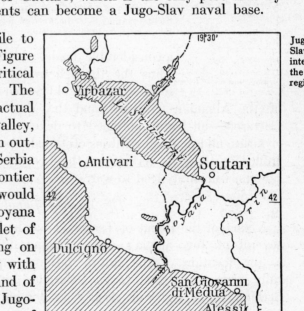

Jugo-Slavia's interest in the Scutari region

Fig. 141. Drainage relations in the Scutari region. The broken line is the boundary between Albania and Montenegro, now part of Jugo-Slavia. Both Albania and Jugo-Slavia wish to control the Drin Valley and Lake Scutari. Note the two outlets of the Drin and the connection of the Boyana with Lake Scutari.

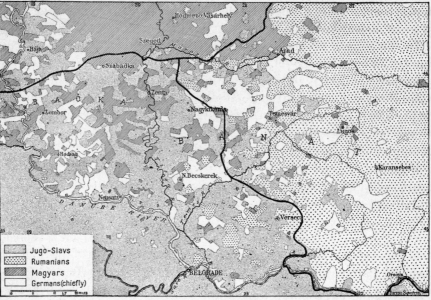

FIG. 142. The complex ethnography of the Banat and the Bačka districts, according to Cvijič, *Carteeth nographique des régions septentrionales Yougoslaves*, 1 : 1,000,000, 1919.

Key to Fig. 142.

a considerable trade, which Italy wishes to control. Thus the through trade of Jugo-Slavia, from the southern part of old Serbia to the sea, the local trade of the Albanian tribesmen and the Montenegrins, the defenses of Cattaro, — all have combined to develop trade rivalries, territorial rivalries, and political rivalries of the sharpest kind, which, if uncontrolled by the good services of the League of Nations or the larger powers, will surely lead to war.

The Western Banat

Dominance of Serbian interests in the new state

A part of the Banat of Temesvár has had a close connection with several of Jugo-Slavia's most pressing difficulties. One of these is the location of the future national capital. The Serbs naturally wish the capital to be Belgrade; but if that city is chosen, Serbian influences will greatly predominate in the government. Moreover, Belgrade lies near the margin of the country and with the Danube as a boundary would be open to attack from the north, where there is no effective military barrier. That is one reason (as well as deficiency of cereals in Serbia) why the Serbs carried on a diplomatic fight for the rich farming country of the Banat. They secured, not the whole district, but the western third, and this with a part of the Bačka, north of the Danube, gives them a bridgehead of great defensive value.

In the Banat, Serbia has a serious difference of opinion with Rumania. The peasants of Temesvár wished to join the Serbs; the landowners wished to join Rumania. This disagreement was a natural consequence of the general policy of the Rumanian government, which has long favored the large landowners, although division of the large landed estates has been compelled at times by revolting peasants or by special political conditions.

Both Jugo-Slavia and Rumania regard the Banat as vital to their future, not only from the standpoint of defense, but also from the standpoint of agricultural production. Jugo-Slavia lacks cereals; she does not produce enough food for her own people and must therefore import grain. The rich grain fields of the Banat would be a boon to her. The shepherds of the hill country (which is of large extent), the dwellers in the towns, the workers in the mines and factories, the fishermen on the coast, — all have need of other foodstuffs than those they produce, and the Banat, with the Bačka, is one of the most important sources of surplus food for the supply of the Balkans.

Serbian claim to the Banat of Temesvár

Unfortunately, it is hard to make a fair decision in a region whose population is so thoroughly mixed as that of the Banat (Fig. 142). In any case there would have been serious difficulties; but the difficulties were greatly increased by the heavy requisitions made by the Serbs in the Banat, especially during the latter part of the period of their military occupation (1919).

Since the drainage of the Banat in general runs across the boundary line between Jugo-Slavia and Rumania, some agreement will have to be made whereby the two states shall coöperate in the maintenance and development of the canals, waterways, and railways, for the mutual benefit of their people (page 290).

INTERNAL COMMERCIAL AND INDUSTRIAL PROBLEMS

We turn now to the domestic and internal problems of the new state. The resources of Jugo-Slavia are poorly balanced. Like Italy, she will have to depend upon northern Europe for coal. Her northern half, like Hungary, will have an excess of food supply over consumption. Like Albania, her southern half will be difficult to govern; for here live turbulent mountain elements, including Albanians, Greeks, and Mohammedans. The Danube offers a means for local commerce; but for export other than to Bulgaria and Rumania the Danube outlet is too roundabout. It strengthens the capital to

Jugo-Slavia not economically self-supporting

have all the drainage run toward it; but the economic life of the whole country would be better served if the streams ran toward the Adriatic instead of away from it.

Lack of
coal

Jugo-Slavia is poor in coal; the only mines of commercial importance are in Serbia and Bosnia. She formerly used about 300,000 tons a month, of which she produced about 270,000 tons, making up the deficit from Great Britain, Austria, and Germany. In the retreat of the enemy armies in 1918, the Serbian coal mines were largely dynamited and flooded, and production was all but stopped. Austria has to import most of her coal; Germany must export to France and Italy by the terms of the treaty of Versailles; Great Britain's export coal will be sent to her own colonies, to South America, to France, and to Italy. Serbia's neighbors have no coal to send her. Moreover, Jugo-Slavia is a region cold in winter. Its prevailing winter winds are from the north, and much of its surface consists of mountain upland, where coal or wood is a necessity. To complicate the situation, few of the railroads can deliver fuel; they cannot properly take care of even the products of the farms.

The new Serb-Croat-Slovene state (Jugo-Slavia) will not be able to mine 3,000,000 tons of coal a year. Of other commercial minerals, Jugo-Slavia has important deposits of manganese and iron. Slavonia has lead mines capable of further development. Within the new frontiers there are extensive forests and water-power resources; but neither of these can be utilized effectively without an extension of the present railway network.

Com-
mercial
treaties
with her
neighbors

In starting her commercial life, Jugo-Slavia has found it necessary to make commercial treaties with her neighbors, each party to the treaty improving its condition by marketing abroad its surplus and importing the complementary products of its neighbor. Commercial relations are already developing between Jugo-Slavia and Poland. The former sends meat, fat, tobacco, prunes, and distilled liquor to Poland, and Poland sends in return petroleum, salt, sugar, and manufactured goods. Jugo-Slavia also benefits from the conditions of a treaty with Austria which favors her transit traffic, and from a treaty with Czecho-Slovakia by which Jugo-Slavia receives large quantities of sugar in exchange for grain and cattle. Jugo-Slavia is attempting to exchange merchandise with Russia through the Pan-Russian Central Union of Coöperative Societies.

Land laws
in Bosnia
and Herze-
govina

Like all the other new states of central Europe, Jugo-Slavia has its share of land problems, owing to the dissatisfaction and poverty of the peasantry, who suffered terribly in the war. In Herzegovina the farm holdings as a rule are uniformly small, while in Bosnia a large part of the land is held in common by villages or is in the hands of landowners of moderate means who own several farms apiece. The new land laws of Jugo-Slavia have thrown this system into confusion by distributing the lands among many landless peasants, thereby creating a great deal of discontent among former owners as well as among dissatisfied peasants who want still larger holdings. As a result of general discontent, the farmers of Bosnia and Herzegovina have sought to form a separate political party for the protection of their rights, and opinion is tending in the same direction in Serbia. A first conference of farmer-peasants was held at Velika Plana in October 1919.

In that portion of former Austria-Hungary now included in Jugo-Slavia, about 35,000 acres of land have been divided among the peasants.

Every new state first organizes a government, and directly there- *Loan of* after seeks to borrow money abroad with which to pay expenses and *money to* start imports of food and raw materials. When industrial life has *states often* begun, commerce revives, and government "machinery" is provided, *a political* then taxes can be collected. But at first loans are vital to national *matter* existence. Confronted by this necessity, Jugo-Slavia finds that, like a number of other weak states, she can borrow money only under conditions that make the loans a factor in international politics. There seems to be no easy way to avoid this curtailment of freedom of action; for if a nation is unable to obtain its funds among its own people, it must appeal to its neighbors for help, and it is to be expected that help will be given only with undesirable stipulations.

THE TREATMENT OF MINORITY POPULATIONS

Like the other Balkan states, and also Poland and Czecho-Slovakia, *Minorities* Jugo-Slavia was required by the Peace Conference of Paris to sign a *treaties* separate minorities treaty with the Allies which guarantees certain rights to alien peoples living within the boundaries of the state. It was the thought of the Allied powers that the signing of these treaties would help to establish full liberty of speech, press, and religion, and that one of the causes of war would thus be removed.

The minorities treaties are alike in all essentials. They differ from *Char-* state to state only in that special provisions are made for special *acteristics* cases. Since Poland has many Jews and the others a relatively *of these* small number, special provisions were made for the Jews in Poland. *treaties*

In Jugo-Slavia special provisions were made for the Moslems (who may have a head of the church within the state), and for the special protection of cemeteries and religious establishments.

The minorities treaties remove all restrictions upon the use of languages, upon the exercise of any religion not injurious to public morals, and upon the press, public meetings, etc. All languages are to be given adequate facilities before the courts. All racial, linguistic, and religious minorities shall have the right to establish, manage, and control at their own expense charitable, religious, and social institutions, schools, etc. The national government may make the official language obligatory in all the schools, if it provides adequate facilities for other languages used by the people within its frontiers.

Clauses in favor of the Allied and Associated Powers

The minorities treaties also provide for the equitable treatment of the commerce of the Allied and Associated Powers within the states signing the treaties; and the central European states who have signed the treaties must give to the commerce of the Allied and Associated Powers, during the succeeding five years, at least as favorable treatment as they may accord to the commerce of those states with whom the Allied and Associated Powers have recently been at war. Vessels of commerce are to have equality of treatment, except for special provisions affecting coasting traffic, as on the Adriatic coast of Jugo-Slavia, the Baltic coast of Poland, and the Black Sea coast of Rumania.

The treaties also provide for the freedom of transit of persons, goods, carriages, wagons, and mails over the territory of the signatory powers, and for the freedom of transit of postal, telegraphic, and telephonic messages.

THE SPECIAL CASE OF SERBIA

Partly because Serbia is the largest of the political units of Jugo-Slavia and partly because it formed the nucleus of the new state, special mention must be made of its particular problems.

Winter retreat of the Serbian army across the mountains of Albania

The Serbian army was one of the first to feel the shock of war in 1914. After a brave defense of Belgrade it was overcome, and thereupon began its famous retreat across Albania, in the winter of 1915. The casualties were enormous, not only among the army but also among the half-million civilians who attempted to follow the same route. It is estimated that 10 per cent of the men died of famine and fatigue.

From the end of 1915 until the armistice of 1918, Serbia was occupied by Austrian and Bulgarian armies, which had as their declared object the extermination of the Serbian people. They stopped import of food to the starving population, drafted the young men into their armies, assassinated priests and teachers, abolished Serbian customs, closed schools and churches, and in some districts destroyed the entire population or drove it into the forests and mountains.

Attempted extermination of the Serbian people

The total population of 4,500,000 was reduced by these means by more than 1,300,000. In the army the killed and missing numbered 690,000; the civilian dead numbered 640,000. Of the total population, 30 per cent had been killed by the end of 1918.

To restore such a country to national life and happiness is a task of incalculable difficulty. The sources of revenue have been dried up, the country is devastated, the herds and flocks are largely destroyed. Seed is wanting, trade is stopped, industries are ruined. As a start in the direction of reconstruction, the All es have given Serbia, to be shared with Greece and Rumania, 6 per cent of the total indemnity exacted from Germany. Yet this is not enough to re-create her industries and to revive her industrial and commercial life, even if it could be obtained at once; and there is no certainty that it can be collected at all. As we have emphasized in an earlier chapter, the Central Powers destroyed far more than they can be made to repay (page 78). Serbia, like Belgium and northern France, will long retain the scars of war.

CHAPTER FIFTEEN

RUMANIA WITHIN ITS NEW FRONTIERS

People of
the Ru-
manian
homeland

THE life and history of the Rumanians is closely associated with the Carpathian valleys and bordering plains. Their settlements extend from within the edge of the Hungarian plain eastward to the Black Sea, and throughout the valleys of the southern Carpathians as far south as the Iron Gate of the Danube. Farther north they have long occupied the Bessarabian foothill region of the Carpathians. In the Timok valley in Serbia south of the Danube, there is a Rumanian area which has been made the basis for a claim to extend the Rumanian frontier toward Belgrade. In Transylvania, deep notched by rivers, the people live in farms and villages on the narrow valley floors and on flat-topped ridges and spurs where pasture abounds. The greater part of the Rumanians live on the Moldavian-Wallachian plain between the Carpathians and the Danube.

More than 80 per cent of the population live on farms, and they are not easily won to an industrial life. In the whole Rumanian region (Fig. 143) there is a population of 16,000,000, and so completely do Rumanians occupy the land that there are only about 3,750,000 non-Rumanian peoples included within the present boundaries: 1,500,000 Magyars, 400,000 Germans, 1,100,000 Ukrainians, and 750,000 Jews. It is a compact and virile nation, ranking (roughly) with Czecho-Slovakia in present economic power.

THE ORIGINS OF THE RUMANIAN STATE

Turkish
invasion

The rise of the Rumanian nation is an event of recent times. When the Turk occupied southeastern Europe and annexed Hungary in the 15th century, he turned his attention to the Rumanians, who fought valiantly under Stephen the Great, only to be defeated under the leadership of his son. Thereafter the Turk received the homage of the Rumanian and Transylvanian princes, though he never overran their country completely. This nominal overlordship continued until 1829, when, by the treaty of Adrianople, Czar Nicholas of Russia obliged the Turkish government to grant practically complete autonomy to Moldavia and Wallachia, the two chief provinces of modern Rumania.

Carpathian
gateways
and the
Danubian
moat

That the country of the Rumanians was never overrun by the Turk was due to the defensive wall of the Carpathians, rugged and forested, with few defiles, which kept the Turk invader from entering Rumania by the Carpathian passes from the west after his conquest of Hun-

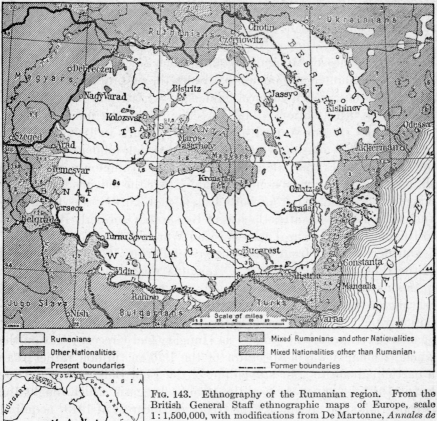

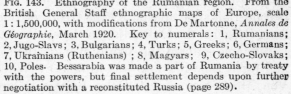

Fig. 143. Ethnography of the Rumanian region. From the British General Staff ethnographic maps of Europe, scale 1 : 1,500,000, with modifications from De Martonne, *Annales de Géographie*, March 1920. Key to numerals: 1, Rumanians; 2, Jugo-Slavs; 3, Bulgarians; 4, Turks; 5, Greeks; 6, Germans; 7, Ukrainians (Ruthenians); 8, Magyars; 9, Czecho-Slovaks; 10, Poles. Bessarabia was made a part of Rumania by treaty with the powers, but final settlement depends upon further negotiation with a reconstituted Russia (page 289).

Key to Fig. 143.

gary. And the broad and then unbridged Danube, its lower course bordered by wide, impassable reed swamps, was a protective moat at the edge of the fertile plains. After years of effort the Turk gained access to the Rumanian plains, only to find the population fleeing before him to the mountains. Thus the infusion of Tatar blood in Rumania is very small. Thus likewise the Rumanian was spared those religious and national antagonisms between the various Christian populations which the Turk always stirred up in order to strengthen his own hold on the subject races. The Rumans therefore have had a greater national and cultural solidarity than any other Balkan people except the Greeks.

Russian political influence in Rumania became marked with the revival, beginning about 1850, of efforts to defeat the Turk and reach the Dardanelles. Under Napoleon III, France began to work for the independence of Rumania, not so much to encourage the formation of a Rumanian nation as to thwart the ambitions of the Czar; and to this day French cultural influence is stronger in Bucarest than that of any other nation. The Russians ended the military operations of the Crimean War with the treaty of Paris in 1856, by which Moldavia and Wallachia were freed from Russian influence. In 1861 the two provinces were at last united under a common ministry and with a common national assembly, and by 1878 the independence of the Kingdom of Rumania from both Russia and Turkey was finally acknowledged, but only after the loss of Bessarabia (formerly Rumanian) to Russia, following the Turko-Russian War of 1877–1878.

During the years from the Congress of Berlin (1878) to the period of the Balkan wars (1912–1913), Rumania was occupied chiefly with questions of internal administration, and especially with difficulties relating to land tenure. There was also fear that Russian domination would become overwhelming, and there were flurries of feeling against several other neighbors, as Hungary and Greece. But on the whole, Rumania was a spectator of the Balkan turmoil rather than a participant in it. She stayed out of the First Balkan War (1912); but in 1913 she joined the coalition against Bulgaria which fought the Second Balkan War, and by the treaty of Bucarest of 1913[1] acquired from Bulgaria the Dobrudja, on the southeastern border.

Rumania entered the World War on the side of the Allies in 1916, and for a time her fate was in doubt. When German troops under Von Mackensen defeated the Rumanian army in Transylvania in December of 1916, German armies streamed through the Carpathian passes and held a line athwart the Rumanian plain. By the terms of the treaty of Bucarest of 1918, Rumania was to lose a strip of territory averaging five miles in width along the Carpathian frontier, including all the passes, observation posts, and valley heads that looked down upon the fertile plains and the capital city; and also valuable oil concessions (Fig. 144). Her losses included the Iron Gate of the Danube. This would have made her defenseless in any future war with the Central Powers. The treaty was never promulgated. It was drawn up in July 1918, but King Ferdinand saw to it that his prime minis-

---

[1] Two recent treaties are named after the Rumanian capital: (*a*) the treaty of Bucarest of 1913, which ended the Second Balkan War; and (*b*) the treaty of Bucarest of 1918, between the Central Powers and Rumania, which was to terminate the war with Rumania.

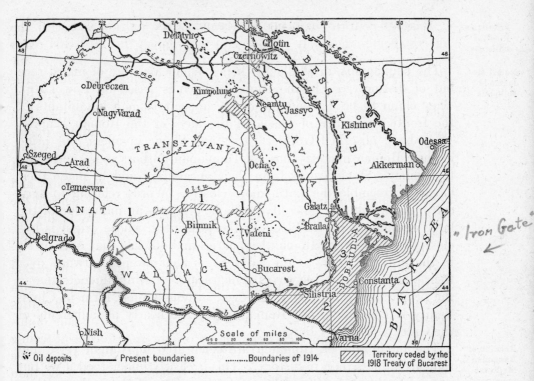

"Iron Gate"

FIG. 144. The eastern boundary of Rumania is the Dniester. The shaded areas were never legally transferred to Austria-Hungary or Bulgaria; the Rumanian king had not signed the treaty of Bucarest when the Austrian armistice of 4 November and the German armistice of 11 November 1918 required both these powers to abrogate the treaty. The shaded areas are: 1, territory to be ceded to Austria-Hungary according to treaty of Bucarest; 2, to Bulgaria; 3, to the Central Powers. Carpathian boundary of treaty of Bucarest of 1918 according to 1918 edition of Stieler's *Hand-Atlas*. Oil localities after Draghicenu, *Geologische Übersichtskarte des Königreiches rumänien*, 1891; Redwood, *Treatise on Petroleum*, Vol. I, 1913; *Deutsche Rundschau für Geographie*, Vol. 24, 1901–02, p. 418.

ter was never able to find him. He traveled through mountains and forests, and before his signature could be obtained, Marshal Foch had begun to strike the western German front from Château Thierry to the North Sea. By the armistice of 11 November 1918, Germany was forced to denounce the treaty of Bucarest. Thus Rumania had restored to her the Dobrudja up to the boundary of 1913, and the way was opened for broad extensions of territory on both her eastern and her western frontiers.

In the 1918 edition of Stieler's famous *Hand-Atlas*, it is interesting to find the new boundary of Rumania in the Carpathians shown by a red over-printed line—probably the only case in which these thorough German cartographers have placed on a map as an international boundary a line that was never established.

THE PEOPLE OF RUMANIA

The Rumanians, or Wallachians

Racial elements in Rumania

The Rumanians, or Wallachs (hence Wallachia), are of mixed race but of distinct speech, the Ruman, which is based on Low Latin. They claim to be descendants of the ancient Roman inhabitants of the frontier province of Dacia in the days of the Roman Empire. They have absorbed Gothic, Tatar, and Slavic invaders, but pride in their Roman ancestry has led Rumanian authors more and more to eliminate Slavic words from their vocabulary and to make their language resemble the Latin more closely. Words relating to agricultural pursuits are generally of Slavic origin — an indication of the large amount of Slavic blood in the peasantry, whose origin is less closely related to the Roman legionaries and officials that once dwelt in the province than to the early Slavs that swept eastward over their plains in successive waves of migration. Latin influences among the people are still marked, however, although their form of Christianity is Byzantine, not Roman; they are nearly all adherents of the Greek Orthodox Church.

Relation of Rumanian life to the mountains

The mountains of Rumania are celebrated in Ruman verse and romance no less than in history. This is clearly understood if we but remember that for a time they were the refuge of Rumanian nationality, when Slav and Tatar successively held the plain. The Rumanian came to know the passes, the mountain pastures, the secluded valleys, and the defensible gateways to the plain. When the people were able at last to reoccupy the plain and resume their agricultural life, they kept up their spiritual as well as their material connection with the mountains. Every summer the cattle still are driven to the high, rich mountain pastures. Every winter many of them are driven down again to the shelter of the deeper valleys and the plain. Many Rumanians have a plains residence and a mountain residence, to fit their twin occupations of farmer and shepherd. It is a distinctive form of seasonal migration, or nomadism.

The Vlachs

Home places of the nomadic Vlachs

Rumanian nomadism is seen in its purest form among the detached bands of people of Rumanian speech that inhabit parts of Macedonia, Albania, and Thrace — the Vlachs, or Kutzo-Vlachs. Many of their villages are inhabited only in winter; in summer they roam the mountain pastures with their herds and flocks. Colonies of them, each with its own dialect, live in the Olympus ranges, in the upper

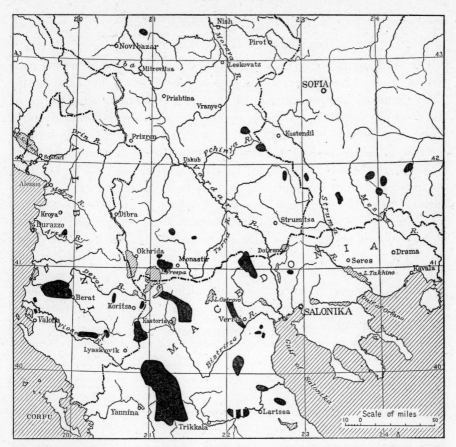

FIG. 145.   The Vlachs, or pastoral nomads of Rumanian affiliation, in the central Balkan lands.
From British General Staff ethnic map, 1 : 1,500,000, 1918.

Semeni and Devol valleys and at Frasheri in Albania, at Okhrida and
Krushevo and Monastir, in the Vardar valley in Macedonia, and along
the Greco-Bulgarian frontier.   Several times in the first decade of this
century they were the cause of disputes between Rumania and Greece,
disputes arising from the vigorous campaign of Pan-Hellenism which
the Greeks were carrying on in the Macedonian region.

Rumanians and Magyars in Transylvania

Their close historical association with the mountains has welded
together the Transylvanian peoples and those of Wallachia and
Moldavia.   In later years it fostered the irredentist movement which
arose from the cruelties of the Magyar oppressor.   Two and a half
million Rumanians of Transylvania wished to join their kinsmen on
the eastern side of the mountains and form an independent state.

Irreden-
tist move-
ments of
late years

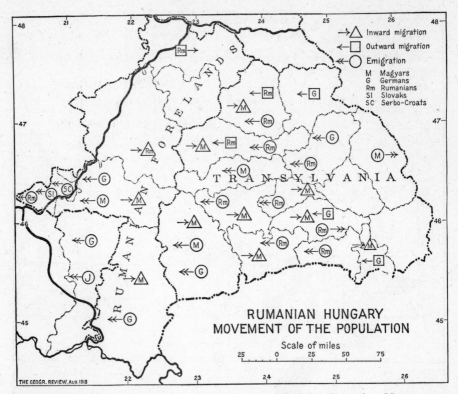

Fig. 146.　The territory east of the heavy line has been awarded to Rumania.　Magyar persecution before 1914 is suggested by a study of Rumanian emigration.　After Wallis, in the *Geographical Review*, August 1918.

They constitute half of the population of Transylvania and are the largest single ethnic element there.　The others are Magyars, Jews, Ruthenians, Slovaks, and Germans.　Kolozvár, the capital of Transylvania, is said to be an important center of intellectual and public life in Hungary.

The difficult terrain of Transylvania

Transylvania has a population of 2,700,000, for the most part agricultural and pastoral, with a relatively small city element.　The Rumanians of Transylvania are chiefly illiterate peasants, hillmen, and herdsmen whose permanent homes and villages are scattered along the narrow valley floors or in a belt of plains population just west of the mountains, at the eastern edge of the plain of the Tisza.　Their western limit is marked by a number of important towns — Arad, Nagy Várad and Temesvár in the Banat.　It also corresponds closely to a belt of dense population (dense in contrast to the light population of the rest of Transylvania) which has increased the difficulty of separating these Rumanians from the Magyars of the plains.　Travel

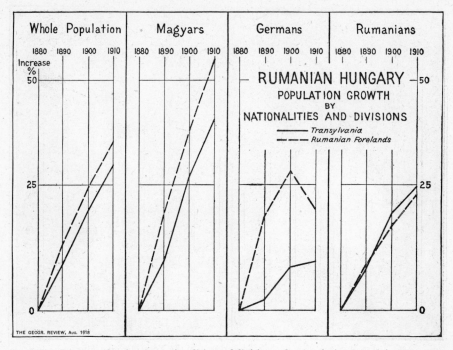

Fig. 147. Diagram showing, by nationalities and divisions, the population growth in Rumanian Hungary from 1880 to 1910 and the privileged position of the Magyar. Logarithmic scale. After Wallis, in the *Geographical Review*, 1918.

and transportation from one valley to another proceeds, not over the intervening forested ridge, but down the valley to the plain and back again to a neighboring valley. The new boundary, established by the treaty of peace with Hungary, includes in Transylvania — that is, in Rumania — the railroads and towns at the edge of the plain. To have left them out would have completely deranged the commercial life of the region. It should be noted, however, tha this arrangement to an equal or greater degree deranges the commercial life of Hungary, and it is hard to believe that the boundary will permanently remain in its present position Highly intelligent Magyars are here placed in great numbers under the rule of a people of lower culture. In some districts, especially in the towns they are locally in the majority. Irredentism will almost surely follow, unless more good comes from the application of the questionable minorities treaties (page 275) than can now be foreseen.

The antagonism between Magyars and Rumanians has been increased by religious differences, which always tend to reënforce differences of "race" and speech. The Magyars are Roman Catholics

Religious differences

Fig. 148.   A view in the timbered zone of the Transylvanian Alps.

chiefly; the Germans are Roman Catholics or Lutherans; while the Rumanians belong to the Greek Orthodox Church.

THE QUESTION OF MINORITIES

Problem of the Rumanian Jew   There are more than 750,000 Jews in Rumania, and there would be many more but for anti-Jewish laws that have led to a steady stream of emigration.   In the past hundred years these laws, to the number of several score, have denied equality to the Jew in the trades and handicrafts and in landholding, education, the professions, etc.   To the Rumanian the problem looked much as the Japanese problem appears to a Californian.   One of the considerations was the fear that all the land would be owned by the Jews unless restrictive measures were enforced.

The expulsion of Jews from Rumania before 1878, and their persecution, induced the makers of the treaty of Berlin of that year to demand of Rumania full citizenship for the Jew.   Less than a thousand Jews were then naturalized, but in a few years the treaty provisions were abandoned altogether.   One restriction after another diminished Jewish rights until all Jews were practically without standing under the law.

The Jews of Rumania offer a problem that has taken on an international character, now that Rumania has signed the minorities treaty with the Allied and Associated Powers, a compact which pledges her to give equality of privilege to all minority peoples (page 275). Rumania, mindful of the servitudes of the treaty of Berlin, long refused to sign the treaty, and the utmost diplomatic pressure was necessary to secure the signatures of her representatives at Paris in 1919. But for Allied assistance Rumania would have been destroyed in the World War, and this fact gave the Allied powers a strong argument in imposing the minorities clauses. It should be noted, however, that Allied assistance was pledged as a condition of Rumanian entry into the war.

It is doubtful if Rumania means to keep the terms of the treaty, for its significance pertains chiefly to the Jew. Czecho-Slovakia, Jugo-Slavia, Poland, and others were obliged to sign similar treaties, by which the Jews, the most widely distributed and generally persecuted minority element of the population, are enabled to combine in a powerful central European organization to force the League of Nations to take account of future persecutions or restrictions.

Equality of treatment to the degree specified in the treaties places restrictions upon the action of a people in making laws or modifying their constitution that may prove unendurable. Such restrictions are really a limitation of national sovereignty respecting internal affairs. They are justifiable only if the League of Nations will see that the minorities do not become a privileged class and do not carry on ceaseless and unjustifiable agitation. In the United States there is solidarity, in part through a common language. In central Europe the languages of the minorities are retained, and the state is compelled to countenance and even to develop them. Linguistic differences will be perpetuated and even increased. Irredentism will continue. Many of the wisest men of Europe and America deprecate these treaties; they regard them as a standing invitation to quarrel.

Minorities treaties a source of irredentism

THE BORDER REGIONS [1]

There remain to consider certain other areas where people mainly of Rumanian speech have now come under one national flag — Bukovina, Bessarabia, and the eastern Banat. There is also to be considered the Dóbrudja region, in Rumanian possession since the end of the Second Balkan War (1913).

---

[1] In addition to the territorial gains mentioned in this section, Rumania receives by treaty the island of Ada-Kalessi in the Danube. It is made a condition of the grant of this island that it is to be demilitarized.

Bukovina

People of
Bukovina

Bukovina, with an area of 4000 square miles, was a crown province of Austria at the opening of the World War. Though Austria has held it since 1777, its people are chiefly Rumans, Ruthenians, and Germans. The Rumans settled here by spreading northward from their plains country, which is continuous with that of Bukovina. They number at present a full third of the population, or about 275,000 out of a total of 800,000. The Ruthenians spread southward from Galicia and constitute more than a third of the total, or about 300,000. The Germans, about 170,000 in number, came as artisans and traders from Transylvania and Galicia.

Bukovina
divided be-
tween Ru-
mania and
Poland

The treaty of St. Germain (Austria) allots to Rumania all of Bukovina except the territory crossed by the railroad running from Laleszcyki to Kolomea; but it is interesting to note that the allotment is made on condition that Rumania keeps faith with the Allies. The small portion of Bukovina left out of Rumania is given to Poland, to include an important railroad junction on the Polish frontier.

The land is densely populated — 198 to the square mile — but the cultural level of the people is very low. Illiteracy was higher here than anywhere else in Austria-Hungary, except in Dalmatia. A third of the land is arable; half of it is forest covered. It is a country rich in agricultural resources and pasture lands.

Bessarabia

People of
Bessarabia

Bessarabia is the region between the Pruth and the Dniester. Its population of 2,700,000 is composed of over 1,000,000 Rumanians, 900,000 Ukrainians, scattered German colonists (Fig. 100), and 300,000 Jews. The Rumanians live in northern Bessarabia, on the broad hilly spurs of eastern offshoots of the Carpathians between the Dniester and the Pruth. The flat, marshy, treeless tracts along the Pruth and at the mouths of the Danube are occupied by Cossacks and Tatars. The mixture of races and the historical changes of ownership record the repeated migrations that passed over Bessarabia; Turk and Slav both made this region a corridor of conquest.

Doubtful
whether
Bessara-
bians wish
to become
a part of
Rumania

While more than half the people of Bessarabia are of Rumanian blood, there is not a clearly defined ethnic division, as in Poland or Czecho-Slovakia or Greece. Moreover, their culture is closely connected with that to the east of them. The Bessarabian people use the Cyrillic, not the Latin, alphabet; and the peasants all use the Russian language.

Bessarabia was a part of Russia from 1812 to 1856; a strip along the Black Sea was then restored to Rumania, but was returned to Russia by the Berlin Congress of 1878. With the fall of the autocratic Russian government, early in 1917, Bessarabian peasants took over all the land; but it was not until May 1917 that a "National Committee" was set up. In the autumn of that year there was a congress of Moldavian soldiers and officers which proclaimed the autonomy of Bessarabia. This congress elected a "Council of the Land," which in December 1917 formally proclaimed the country a republic. The Council maintained an orderly government, and when anarchy broke loose in Russia and overwhelmed the Ukraine (including Odessa), the Bessarabians held the frontier along the Dniester. Since January 1919, Rumanian military forces have occupied the country on the plea of maintaining a defense against Bolshevism, thus creating a complex political problem.

Beginnings of Bessarabian independence

The National Council formed during the Rumanian military occupation to supplant the Council of the Land was a Rumanian invention. It was what may be called a "rump" assembly, with no mandate from the people, and it was this Council that twice in 1918 asked for annexation to Rumania. Those who opposed its decrees were deported or imprisoned; democratic local governments were dissolved; Bessarabian judges were dismissed and courts abolished; all but pro-Rumanian newspapers were suppressed. Rumanians have also expropriated the estates of the large landowners.

In October 1920 there was signed a treaty between Rumania on the one hand and Great Britain, France, Italy, and Japan on the other, whereby Rumania is to receive Bessarabia. Minority rights are safeguarded by the usual clauses (page 276). Boundary questions are to be settled by a commission of the League of Nations, which likewise determines the proportional part of the Russian national debt that Rumania must assume with the addition of Bessarabia. Provision is made for consideration by the Council of the League of Nations of future objections and changes proposed by Russia, though pledges are given that such consideration will not affect Rumanian sovereignty as established by the present treaty. This clause, however, will almost certainly undergo revision if Russia emerges as a powerful state within the next few years. The United States is not a party to the treaty, having held that whether or not it joins the League of Nations it cannot approve the dismemberment of Russia without the consent of the Russian people and while that country is controlled by an unrepresentative government.

The Eastern Banat

Border
region of
the Banat

In the territorial settlements of Europe, the disposition of the Banat was a question in which Rumania and Jugo-Slavia had an equal interest with Hungary (page 272). It seemed impracticable to assign the whole region to any one of the three claimants; yet to separate the Rumanians of the eastern Banat from the Serbs, Magyars, and Germans, who live in the western half of the district, in a measure disorganizes the commercial life of the region.

The Banat is a very rich farming country with many railways and towns. It is just such a region as a rough hill country, like Serbia, would wish to obtain to supplement her deficient food supply. The language distributions are shown in Figure 142. They indicate clearly that Rumanian speech is dominant in the two eastern counties of Krassó-Szörény and Temes, while Torontál on the west is chiefly Serb.

It should be noted that the new north-south boundary in the Banat cuts across all the westward-flowing streams and also the railways and canals. It will take years to readjust the commercial life to the new arrangements. In the division of the region it was stipulated that agreements between Rumania and Serbia should be made at an early date to maintain and develop the irrigation canals for the benefit of both countries.

The Dobrudja

Possi-
bility of
trouble
in the
Dobrudja

In the present Rumanian occupation of the Dobrudja, the southern part of which is almost exclusively Bulgarian in population, there is a real cause for future trouble. After 1878, the year when, by the treaty of Berlin, Rumania got control of a large part of the Dobrudja region, the Rumanian government expropriated the lands of the inhabitants on a large scale, and even made the peasants pay for what was left to them. The expropriated lands were then sold to Rumanian colonists. Many property owners were reduced to poverty; others emigrated to America, Bulgaria, Russia, and Turkey, and a country theretofore prosperous was thrown into disorder.

The same methods have been followed since 1913, when, by the treaty of Bucarest which closed the Second Balkan War, Rumania won another slice of Bulgarian territory in the Dobrudja. It remains to be seen whether Rumania has profited by the lessons of the World War, or whether she will continue to exploit an alien people unfairly in the attempt to Rumanize it or expel it. If she follows a selfish course, trouble with Bulgaria is bound to come.

RUMANIAN INVASION OF HUNGARY

As an example of the difficulties which the larger powers meet in dealing with new states, we may cite the case of Rumania, which from a state of 8,000,000 has been raised by the action of the Allies to a state of nearly 16,000,000. It might be supposed that a state which owed its continued existence and the enlargement of its territory chiefly to the Allied armies would be willing to heed the directions of its protectors. Let us glance at Rumania's record during the invasion of Hungary in the summer of 1919.

Rumanian troops crossed the Allied demarcation line in Hungarian Transylvania in late July and took Budapest, the Hungarian capital, in August. They drained the city and the country of resources — food, rolling stock, live stock, war materials, etc. Only the sharpest notes by the Allied powers brought their withdrawal in October 1919.

Rumanian occupation of Budapest

The Rumanians say that the Hungarians broke the armistice terms by reënforcing their army, mobilizing the young men, and attacking the Rumanian troops. Rumanian leaders say, further, that the armistice of 4 November 1918 with Austria, and that of 11 November with Germany, gave the Allied powers vast quantities of cars, locomotives, money, implements, and coal. Rumania received nothing. She had steadfastly and gallantly fought on the side of the Allies, losing more than 332,000 in dead alone from the army, and as many more from the civilian population. She fought the Bolshevists in Bessarabia. Her land was devastated almost from end to end. Enemy troops stripped the country, taking food, telegraph and telephone wires, ammunition, live stock, grain, and other supplies. The Rumanians point out that in contrast to Rumania, Czecho-Slovakia was never invaded; that Jugo-Slavia obtained a great deal of material in Hungary and Slavonia; that Rumania repeatedly asked for economic help and could not obtain it; and that it was a choice between (1) helping herself to the things that had been taken from her by Hungary and (2) facing internal disorder and outside pressure brought to bear upon her by the Bolshevists.

It will not soon be forgotten in European political circles how readily the oppressed can become the oppressor, and how quickly a weak nation, as soon as it gathers strength itself, can adopt the outrageous methods of which it so loudly complained in the past. The new states of central Europe have yet to demonstrate that they possess moral strength equal to their new-found opportunities.

The oppressed become oppressors

THE RUMANIA OF TODAY

Rumania free of Bolshevism

It is noteworthy that the disease of Bolshevism is virtually unknown in Rumania, — a disease due chiefly to the break-up of the feudal system that long persisted in Russia and Hungary, where but a few landlords held a farming peasantry in virtual slavery. Rumania once had the same system; its destruction began in 1864, when the large estates owned by the monasteries were confiscated and each peasant family was given a farm between seven and a half and fifteen acres in extent. Over 400,000 peasants shared in the distribution of 4,000,000 acres.[1]

Land problems and peasant revolts in recent years

But the farms were still too small, in general, for the needs of peasant families, and in 1889 the government divided all the state domains — about one third of the total area of the country — into small parcels which were sold to peasant families. In 1907 the peasants still felt themselves so poor that they broke into revolt, and at the beginning of the World War the disorders were again repeated, each time ending in new action by the government to divide the remaining large estates and better the lot of the farmer. In 1912 there were 3755 large estates, while the peasant holdings, numbering more than 1,000,000, were still too small for the needs of the population. Nevertheless, the process of land division had gone so far that the Rumanian rulers were justifiably confident of an orderly people when Bolshevism overran the countries on either side.

Today, 40 per cent of the Rumanian land in old Rumania is in the hands of the large landowners. In Transylvania the big proprietors hold only 8 per cent. Under the new Rumanian land act, one half of the remainder of the big estates in Rumania is to be divided, so that only 20 per cent of the arable land will remain in the form of large estates. In Transylvania the Rumanians, under the guise of a reform in agriculture, are dispossessing and expelling the big Magyar landowners, thus leaving the Magyar peasants without leaders. Such is the Rumanian law that the state may take away land from the estates of all persons not of Rumanian citizenship. The minorities treaty will affect this law, but its provisions have yet to be tried by the fires of experience. Unless changed, the law means that forest

---

[1] An exception to the general rule of land distribution in Rumania is found in the area inhabited by the Szeklers, where small landholdings are the rule, and have been so for hundreds of years. In the 12th century the free Saxons colonized the region. There came a first liberation of serfs in the same region in 1848, a process that was completed in 1861. Altogether, about 1,200,000 acres, or one half the arable land in the possession of big landowners in the region, was divided among the peasants.

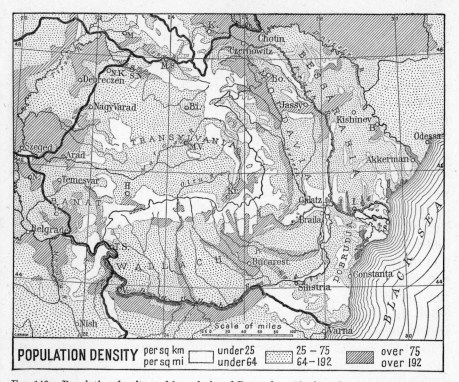

POPULATION DENSITY
per sq km | under 25 | 25 – 75 | over 75
per sq mi | under 64 | 64 – 192 | over 192

Fig. 149. Population density and boundaries of Rumania. The boundary of 1914 was on the Pruth River, but Rumania now holds Bessarabia, a former province of Russia. Her position there has been confirmed by treaty with Great Britain, France, Italy, and Japan, but not with either the United States or Russia. Adapted from De Martonne, *Annales de Géographie*, March 1920, supplemented by *Petermanns Mitteilungen*, 1913, Vol. I, Pl. 2. Key to place names not spelled in full on the map:

T. S.	Turnu Severin	Bo.	Botosani	N.	Nagy Kikinda
V.	Versecz (Banat)	M. V.	Maros Vásárhely	H.	Hátszeg
N. K.	Nagy Károly	Kr.	Kronstadt	Bi.	Bistritz
M.	Munkács	S.	Sulina	M. S.	Mármaros Sziget
S. N.	Szátmar Németi	B.	Bender	I.	Ismail
K.	Kolomea	V.	Vidin (Danube)		

lands and oil fields owned by foreigners, such as the British, French, and Italians, can be expropriated by the Rumanian government.

The wealth of Rumania is very great. The agricultural lands have long been famous for bountiful crops of wheat, maize, barley, oats, rye, and millet. Hemp, flax, wine, sugar beets, tobacco, and cotton are other important products. In the foothills of the Carpathians are large petroleum deposits in process of development by foreign capitalists (heretofore chiefly Germans), who hold 8 per cent of the invested capital. The production is about 13,500,000 barrels a year, or 3.5 per cent of the world's supply. The chief localities of production are shown in Figure 144.

Economic assets of the new state

Deposits of coal, iron, copper, and lead also have been discovered in the mountain country. All these resources are very little developed, and the vast forest wealth is almost untouched.

An agricultural country, with mining and forest wealth little developed, Rumania has few large cities today. There are only the beginnings of industries. The most important trade centers are Braila and Galatz on the Danube, and Constanza on the Black Sea, all of them grain-exporting towns of rapidly growing importance.

Rumania and Poland as a barrier against Bolshevism

Rumania stands in the world's family of nations, not as a weaker member, but as a vigorous state of growing power. National feeling was never so intense. Her financial system, based on the gold standard, is sound; her resources, though largely undeveloped, are vast; her leaders are intellectually alert and capable. She has been orderly in the midst of disorder, and now that her territory extends into Bukovina and that of Poland extends eastward to include all of Galicia, these two nations occupy a belt from the Baltic to the Black Sea, and are thus more likely to have a common policy with respect to Russia. Thus the government signed a treaty, early in 1921, with Poland and Hungary which sought to solidify the opposition of these two states to a possible attack by the Bolshevist army.

CHAPTER SIXTEEN

BULGARIA UNDER THE TREATY OF NEUILLY

In spite of a deficiency of mineral wealth, the Bulgarian nation had risen notably in the twenty-five years before the First Balkan War. At least some coal and iron mines had been opened, a few industries had developed, railways had been extended, the commerce of the state had increased 500 per cent. A population of more than 3,000,000 in 1888 had grown to 4,300,000 by 1910. To this number as a result of the Balkan wars of 1912 and 1913, Bulgaria added a net gain of 130,000 people.

From the time when the Turk overran Bulgaria, even before the capture of Constantinople in 1453, down to 1885, the northern Bulgars in the principality of Bulgaria, beyond the Balkan range, were separated from those in the southern province of Rumelia. The Bulgarians of northern Bulgaria obtained their autonomy in 1878 by the treaty of Berlin, which ended the Turko-Russian War; but their national history in modern times may be said to date from 1885, when, by the revolution of Philippopolis, they were joined to eastern Rumelia; and from that time onward, though the Bulgars were still under the suzerainty of the Turkish sultan, the growth of national feeling was rapid. Finally, in 1908, taking advantage of the Young Turk Revolution in Constantinople, the Bulgarian prince proclaimed himself Czar of the Bulgarians, and the country became completely independent of Turkey. *Growth of independence and national sentiment*

BULGARIAN AMBITIONS AND THEIR OUTCOME

When Bulgaria became independent, she was in an excellent position for growth into a modern state. The problem of the great land-owner had never vexed either the peasant or the government; small farmers had always been in possession of the soil. There had consequently grown up a spirit of independence that in turn developed intense patriotism and willingness to sacrifice for the national security and power. All would have been well but for the growth of an excessive nationalistic ambition. Bulgaria wanted to control the whole Balkan peninsula. Had her expansion been only at the expense of the Turk, the world would have applauded; but it was to be also at the expense of neighboring powers as worthy as herself. It was inevitable that such a course should end in disaster. *Beginnings of imperial ambition*

The First Balkan War

The next step in the Bulgarian drama was taken in 1912, when Bulgaria made a secret treaty with Serbia, which was soon followed by similar treaties with Greece and Montenegro. The object of the four states was to drive the Turk out of the Balkans and if possible into Asia, and thus not only liberate the persecuted Christian populations of Macedonia but also end the Turkish menace at their own doors. Each state agreed to put into the field a given number of troops and faithfully to play its part in the final act.

These arrangements were made when Turkey was embarrassed by the war with Italy (1911–1912). That war ended with Turkey enfeebled and discouraged. Disorders broke out again in Macedonia and Albania. In October 1912, hostilities were begun by the Balkan states. The armies of Turkey, poorly equipped and disease-stricken, numbered less than 500,000; those of the Balkan allies were nearly 800,000, of which number Bulgaria alone had 350,000 and Serbia 250,000.

The first contest came at Adrianople and Kirk Kilisse. The latter was captured, the former besieged. Farther south, on the line from Lule Burgas to Bunar Hissar, came the decisive battle of the war, a fierce four-day contest on a front of more than twenty miles, with losses of 50,000. The power of the Turk was broken. He retreated to Chatalja, twenty-five miles from Constantinople, and there fought out the winter, while the Montenegrins captured Scutari in northern Albania, the Greeks captured Yannina, and the Serbo-Bulgar armies took Adrianople. Earlier in the war, the Greeks had captured Saloniki and the Serbs had overrun Macedonia. The Turk retained only a toe-hold in Europe.

Turkey agreed to make peace, and by the treaty of London, May 1913, ceded all territory west and north of a straight line from Enos on the Ægean to Midia on the Black Sea (Fig. 150). She also gave up Crete to Greece and permitted the great powers to determine the final disposition of the Ægean islands and of Albania.

The whole world had recognized the heroic work and brilliant success of the Balkan armies. There was therefore general dismay when the Balkan states fell to quarreling, and at last to fighting, over former Turkish territory. The situation may be summarized thus:

(1) Bulgaria wanted and had been promised most of the captured territory.

(2) Serbia, blocked in Albania by the action of the great powers (they set up an independent Albania in 1913), had there lost a

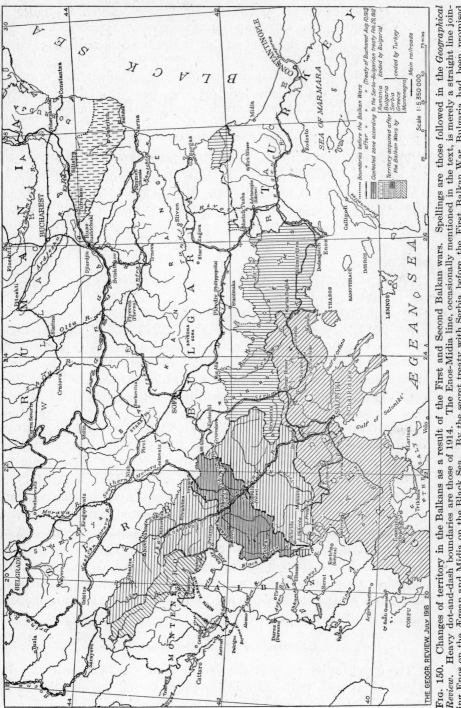

FIG. 150. Changes of territory in the Balkans as a result of the First and Second Balkan wars. Spellings are those followed in the text. The Enos-Midia line, occasionally mentioned in the text, is merely a straight line joining Enos on the Ægean and Midia on the Black Sea. By the secret treaty with Serbia before the First Balkan War, Bulgaria had been promised Macedonia south of the contested zone shown on the map, which zone was reserved for eventual arbitration by the Czar of Russia.

chance of access to the sea, and now wanted an outlet at Saloniki. She therefore claimed a part of Macedonia.

(3) But Greek armies had captured the town of Saloniki; Greece also wished a part of the Macedonian coast.

(4) Montenegro felt that she had received no substantial reward.

(5) Seeing Bulgaria gain territory elsewhere, Rumania urged that she be given the southern Dobrudja at Bulgaria's expense.

The Second Balkan War

Second Balkan War — causes and effects

Thereupon followed the Second Balkan War, in which Turkey joined Greece, Serbia, Rumania, and Montenegro against Bulgaria. The Turks retook Adrianople; the Rumanians seized the Dobrudja and advanced to within twenty miles of Sofia, and Greeks and Serbs closed in on the west. After a two months' war (June–July 1913), Bulgaria was obliged to make peace, signing the treaty of Bucarest of 1913, whereby:

(1) Bulgaria gave up northern Macedonia to Serbia, including Üsküb and Okhrida.

(2) Saloniki and southern Macedonia were given to Greece.

(3) Bulgaria retained the town of Strumitsa in eastern Macedonia and about seventy miles of the Ægean seacoast west of the Maritsa River, but not including the port of Kavala.

(4) Montenegro got the western half of Novi Bazar.

(5) The southern Dobrudja was ceded to Rumania.

Bulgaria made a separate treaty with Turkey, and the line between them was drawn as shown in Figure 150, thus shutting off Bulgaria from direct rail connection (along the west bank of the Maritsa) with the Ægean coast, except through Greek or Turkish territory.

The spirit of revenge

But the losses and gains in territory were a small matter compared with the bitter hatreds that the war had caused. Each of the Balkan states was even more jealous of the others than before, and the Bulgar felt himself humiliated and outraged. The nation had lost the flower of its manhood to win Adrianople and Lule Burgas in 1912, and now these strongholds were again under Turkish sovereignty. The hands of the clock could not be turned back; Bulgaria sullenly waited her chance to retaliate.

Bulgaria's Part in the World War

Bulgaria an ally of Germany in 1915

The opportunity came in the World War. In October 1915, after negotiations with both sides in an effort to sell her alliance to the highest bidder, Bulgaria joined Turkey and the Central Powers.

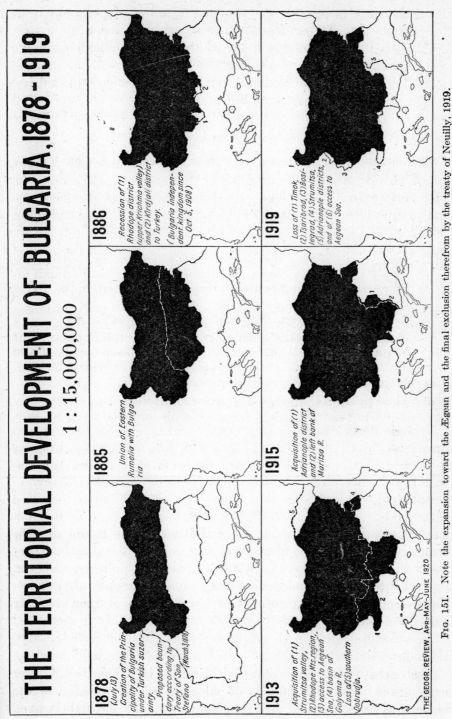

THE TERRITORIAL DEVELOPMENT OF BULGARIA, 1878-1919

1 : 15,000,000

1878
(July 13)
Creation of the Principality of Bulgaria under Turkish suzerainty.

Proposed boundary according to Treaty of San Stefano (March 3,1878)

1885
Union of Eastern Rumelia with Bulgaria

1886
Recession of (1) Rhodope district (upper Krichma valley) and (2) Kirdjali district to Turkey.

(Bulgaria independent kingdom since Oct 5, 1908)

1913
Acquisition of (1) Strumitsa valley, (2) Rhodope Mts.region,; (3) access to Aegean Sea, (4) basin of Golyema R. Loss of (5) southern Dobrudja.

1915
Acquisition of (1) Adrianople district and (2) left bank of Maritsa R.

1919
Loss of (1) Timok, (2) Tsaribrod, (3) Bosilegrad, (4) Strumitsa, (5) Adrianople districts, 2, and of (6) access to Aegean Sea.

THE GEOGR. REVIEW, APR-MAY-JUNE 1920

FIG. 151. Note the expansion toward the Ægean and the final exclusion therefrom by the treaty of Neuilly, 1919.

Her active part in the war was confined to military operations near the Serbian and Greek frontiers. She became also a thoroughfare between the Danube and the Bosporus for German artillery, ammunition, and reënforcements for the Turks. German officers controlled her armies on the Saloniki front. When the final Balkan drive of 1918 came, the Bulgar troops fled in disorder.

According to the terms of the treaty of Neuilly between Bulgaria and the Allied and Associated Powers (1919), Bulgaria:

(1) Renounces all rights to territory formerly held by her outside the boundaries shown on Figure 153.

(2) Agrees to protect alien minorities within her realm under terms laid down by the Allied and Associated Powers, and is assured like protection of Bulgarian minorities in neighboring states.

(3) Promises to reduce her army to 25,000 men, to destroy her vessels of war, to maintain no air forces, and to submit to the restrictions laid down with respect to war materials.

(4) Agrees to pay 2,250,000,000 francs gold ($450,000,000); promises to restore the equivalent of requisitioned live stock; and acknowledges her obligation to contribute to the liquidation of the pre-war external Ottoman debt. She will also supply 50,000 tons of coal annually to Jugo-Slavia for five years, in compensation for the destruction of Serbian mines.

(5) Allots to Greece, Rumania, and Serbia live stock to the number of 70,000 head by way of restitution for animals taken by Bulgaria during the war

(6) Gives the Allied and Associated Powers most-favored-nation treatment and freedom of transit for goods and persons. She is guaranteed like freedom of transit to the Ægean.

WHAT BULGARIA NOW FACES

Problem of the future

Like Germany and Austria, Bulgaria has now the enormous task of meeting the conditions of peace after a military defeat and the surrender of a great quantity of war material in compliance with the terms of the armistice, and in the face of economic disorder that everywhere, even in the Allied countries, has followed hard upon the long and terrible strain of war. Her people are profoundly discouraged.

Hereafter, Bulgaria's path will be beset by grave difficulties. Hers is a country agriculturally well-favored, a land of farms, with no great mineral deposits, no large manufacturing towns. The largest city, Sofia, has a population of only about 100,000. The chief seaport, Varna, has about 40,000. The greater part of the population lives

Brown Bros.

FIG. 152. The port of Kavala, on the Ægean, east of Saloniki between the valleys of the Struma and the Mesta. The port is the natural commercial outlet of western Bulgaria, but it has been in Greek hands since the Second Balkan War (1913).

in a strip a hundred miles wide, south of the Danube. Aside from the fertility of the soil, coal is the chief natural resource, and the amount of this is very small. The yield during 1911 was only about 325,000 tons. There are also small amounts of iron, copper, and zinc, but the mines have been but little developed.

Naturally poor in resources, Bulgaria has been losing man power rapidly for the past eight years. The Balkan wars took tens of thousands of her best men. These wars and the World War piled up a huge Bulgarian debt, which is now equivalent to the entire wealth of the country. It is impossible to calculate and impose revenues that will pay off this sum. Bulgaria is essentially bankrupt. Only the industry of her people and the fertility of the soil are left to her out of which to make a nation. The cost of her aggression at the end of the First Balkan War, and of her union with Germany from 1915 to 1918, is the complete failure of her unwise plans to dominate the Balkans, a terrible loss of life and property, and a heightened reputation for cruelty to non-Bulgarian people in territory occupied by her troops.

Bulgarians assigned to neighboring states

Bulgaria's neighbors have been given important groups of Bulgarian people. Greece in Thrace, Serbia in the Tsaribrod, Strumitsa, and Bosilegrad districts, and Rumania in the Dobrudja have acquired thousands of Bulgarians. The case of the southern Dobrudja is especially important. It became Bulgarian in 1878, is inhabited by Bulgarians and Turks to the number of 273,000, and was lost in 1913 owing to Rumanian aggression, against which weakened Bulgaria could not offer resistance. Rumania wished to obtain the port of Baltchik on the Black Sea.

On the other hand, we must remember:

(1) That in September 1915 Bulgaria agreed to join Austria-Hungary against Serbia, and in return was to receive a certain share of Serbian land and people.

(2) That Bulgarian authorities at one time declared that Serbia no longer existed, that it had become Bulgarian; closed schools and churches and even burned them; compelled the people to speak Bulgarian; and, like the Germans in Belgium and northeastern France, levied fines and contributions, took away food, and ruined the country.

(3) That out of tens of thousands of Serbians interned in Bulgarian camps, at least half died.

(4) That Bulgarian outrages upon Greeks and Serbs—men, women, and children — were among the most hideous of the war.

An unexpected difficulty for Bulgaria comes from the large numbers of refugee Bulgarians from Thrace, Macedonia, and the Dobrudja

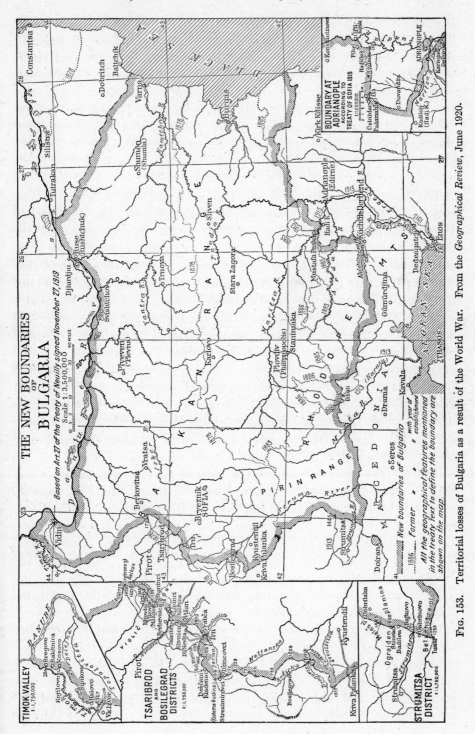

FIG. 153. Territorial losses of Bulgaria as a result of the World War. From the *Geographical Review*, June 1920.

Problem
of the
refugees

that fled when those regions were occupied by Allied troops. They
feared heavy reprisals. And some of them well deserved punishment. They have not yet established themselves in Bulgaria, and their
unsettled life, their restless mood, may affect their political and social
views; some of them have already become social agitators, preach-
ing disorder and disloyalty to the government. They form one of
the gravest of the internal problems of Bulgaria and may even affect
the carrying out of the provisions of the peace treaty.

THE NEW BOUNDARY LINES

Freedom
of transit
to Greek
ports

The treaty of Neuilly between Bulgaria and the Allied and Associated Powers has given the whole of the Ægean coast to Greece.
Restriction to the three Bulgarian ports on the Black Sea would require the roundabout routeing of goods; for this reason Bulgaria is
permitted to make use of the line to Dedeagatch at the mouth of the
Maritsa River and Kavala and Saloniki farther west. The "freedom
of transit" clauses in the treaty compel Greece to furnish adequate
facilities and security of transport for the commerce of western Bulgaria and southern Serbia; and the Maritsa will be declared an international river on the request of either Bulgaria or Greece.

Areas ceded
on the
western
frontier

Bulgaria has also lost four areas on her western frontier: the Tsaribrod district, with 21,000 Bulgarians and practically no Serbs, the
Bosilegrad district with 22,000 Bulgarians and no Serbs, the Strumitsa
district, which is occupied by 25,000 inhabitants predominantly Bulgarian, mixed with Macedonians and a small number of Serbs, and
the small area in the Timok valley on the northwest (Fig. 153).

These areas were cut off on the ground that their possession by
Bulgaria would threaten the railroad from Nish to Saloniki in time of
war. It was by way of Tsaribrod that the Bulgarians invaded Serbia,
cut the railroad line, and captured Nish, in the first few days after
Bulgaria began operations in 1915. The cession of these areas brings
the new boundary within thirty-five miles of Sofia, the capital of
Bulgaria, and puts the frontier just west of the Dragoman Pass.

Difficulties
created by
new fron-
tiers

In several instances the new boundaries of Bulgaria illustrate
the local difficulties that may be caused by the passing of territory
from one nation to another. For example, in western Thrace the
Greek boundary runs along a line of hills north of Xanthi and Gü-
mürdjina, including the Karluk Mountains. It seems the best frontier if we start with the assumption that Greece must have the
coastal strip; the region being mountainous and partly forested, it
would appear to separate the people in the valleys on either side of

the mountains. But it happens that the mountains are valuable as summer pasture grounds for the herds and flocks of the plains dwellers to the south. Every autumn several hundred thousand head, chiefly sheep, are driven from the mountains to the plains. The new boundary breaks up this movement.

There will probably be a marked shifting of population when the new boundaries in the Balkans are finally established by detailed surveys. The hatreds which divide Balkan peoples are long-standing, and to these there has now been added the feeling aroused by the atrocities (of which all the Balkan nations were guilty) during the Second Balkan War and the World War. The Macedonians flee from the Greeks in western Thrace, while the Jews and Armenians remain in order to profit by the new trade that Greek immigration into the area will create. The Turks, who form the largest element of the population, may wish to go into the new state of Constantinople or even into Asia, where they may come under French or British tutelage. *Internal migration and lessening of hatreds*

If the political boundaries have been drawn reasonably close to the ethnic boundaries, such a movement of population will have a wholesome effect. It will put people of the same race and religion under a common flag; it will prevent the starting of the irredentist movements that arise in islands and peninsulas of people separated from their kinsmen across an international boundary. The extraordinary hatred of one people for another throughout central Europe will be lessened only if the processes of migration are added to a strong economic revival. Hatreds are difficult to maintain in the face of profitable trade. Unless tendencies mitigating hatred are cultivated, the minorities treaties will be worthless; if natural tendencies towards friendship can be created, the minorities treaties will become obsolete.

There promises to be carried out in the Balkans an experiment in the transfer of peoples which will be of great practical interest as a means of reducing the problems of irredentism. By a treaty between Greece and Bulgaria (1919), provision is made for the reciprocal and voluntary migration of ethnic, religious, and linguistic minorities. This will enable Greeks living in Bulgaria, who desire to move into Greece, to do so under favorable conditions; and the same opportunity will be given to Bulgarians living in Greece, who desire to return to Bulgaria. It has frequently been suggested that such an expedient would greatly diminish persecutions and promote harmony by allowing people to leave a state whose laws and customs were irksome or whose treatment of them seemed hard. *Treaty for the transfer of peoples*

CHAPTER SEVENTEEN

THE ALBANIAN MOUNTAINEERS

The unruly mountaineers of Albania

OF all the unruly elements in the Turkish Empire there were few that gave so much trouble as the Albanians. One military expedition after another had to be sent out to punish disorderly bands. Though Albania is only a little larger than the state of Vermont and has hardly a million people, it is a Balkan storm center from which grave issues may arise. The Lake Scutari region on the northern frontier is a problem area where conflicting interests cannot be reconciled save by a long process of negotiation and adjustment.

Italy's long-standing desire to annex Albania

It will be seen from Figure 131 that Albania is just opposite the heel of the Italian boot. If the Adriatic is to be in truth an Italian lake, Italy will be vitally interested in Albania; in a similar case the United States declared in 1898, and has since maintained, that the affairs of Cuba are of vital concern to her, Cuba being a small and relatively weak country only a hundred miles from Florida. Albania is about half this distance, or forty-five miles, from Italy.

THE CHARACTER OF THE COUNTRY

Distribution of people in Albania

Albania is a country of mountains, deep-cut by streams that flow out to the Adriatic. There are settled populations in the valleys and about the ports. The narrow seacoast plains and deltas, while fertile, are unhealthful and thinly inhabited. The greater part of the country is occupied by shepherds who are in general of unsettled habits, migrating from place to place and preserving the traditions and customs of the past.

Custom of the feud between clans

Albania has few roads and almost no railroads. Her people, on account of the broken character of the relief, live in isolated groups; and the unit of organized life is the clan, which exhibits a spirit of local independence. Like some other mountain peoples, the Albanians have perpetuated the ancient custom of the feud. The processes of law are too slow and impersonal for the impatient habit of thought and freedom of spirit of men who enjoy the unrestrained life and open ways of the mountains. In their view, guilt is personal and punishment must be equally so, and it must be swift and hot. The trouble with the feud, here as elsewhere, lies in the never-ending chain of murders to which members of opposing tribes are committed by a system that has no place for the deliberate work of a jury. One can but admire the type of bravery which these mountain people exhibit. They have never stopped to soliloquize about honor. Whether it

306

was a wrong done by a
man from a neighbor-
ing clan or whether it
was the exactions of
the taxgatherer, they
went to the extremity
of physical danger to
defend their rights as
they saw them.

Ruling men such as
these, the Turk made
poor progress in his
nearly five hundred
years of control; for, in
spite of the fact that
the Albanians are com-
posed of Mohamme-
dans chiefly, their alle-
giance to the Turkish
rule was no stronger
than that of the Kurds
in eastern Turkey (Fig.
216), another lawless
element inhabiting a
mountainous country.
It is only a nominal ad-
herence that they have
given to the Moslem
faith. And many strong
tribes and influential
modern leaders are
Christians and have op-

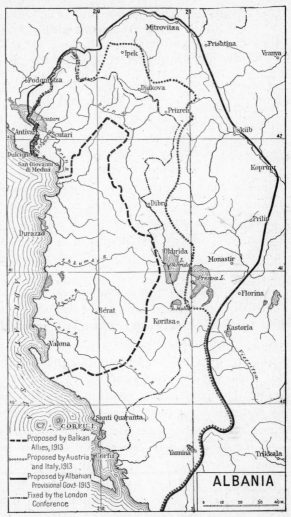

FIG. 154. Various proposed boundaries of Albania. After
a map in the *Geographical Review*, April 1918.

posed Turkish rule and promoted interest in a national Albanian
program. Let us see what progress in settling the Albanian question
the other powers have made since 1913.

INTERNATIONAL ASPECTS OF THE ALBANIAN QUESTION

At the close of the First Balkan War, the Turkish possessions in
Europe were divided and taken over by the Balkan states, except
for two areas (treaty of London, May 1913[1]):

Dictum of
the great
powers in
1913

[1] To be distinguished from the secret treaty of London of 1915 (page 263).

(1) From the Enos-Midia line (Fig. 150) to the Straits, Turkey was still to have sovereign rights.

(2) The ill-defined region known as Albania was to have its boundaries and status determined by the great powers.

Serbian and
Austrian
rivalry in
Albania
The second of these two decisions was taken at the insistence of the great powers, who were influenced by Austria's demand that she be freed from the menace of Russian intrigue on the Adriatic. This she feared if Serbia (a Slav state backed by Russia) were to gain access to the Adriatic by absorbing Albania. Now the possibility of acquiring at least a part of Albania was precisely one of the considerations that had tempted Serbia to join Bulgaria and Greece in the First Balkan War for the overthrow of Turkish power in Europe. She was landlocked, and she wanted a window on the Adriatic or on the Ægean (Saloniki). The dream of a Jugo-Slav state, with Dalmatia and Montenegro to furnish the desired outlet, had not then attained the shape of reality.

Austrian
fear of a
Serb ris-
ing north
of the
Danube
Austria-Hungary was the more anxious to keep Serbia small and weak because she had millions of Jugo-Slavs within her frontiers, and their restlessness had time and again given the Austrian rulers grave anxiety. Should they develop the war spirit of their victorious countrymen in Serbia, they might menace the integrity of the polyglot Austro-Hungarian Empire. The other great powers confirmed Austria-Hungary in her position and kept Serbia out of Albania and the Dalmatian region. Thus they furnished Serbia with an additional reason for embarking on the Second Balkan War.

Proposed
boundaries
of Albania
in 1913
As for Albania, her vague frontiers were never defined by the successive powers that dealt with her. Various proposals are shown in Figure 154. The line fixed by the London Conference of 1913 was accepted by all, except the Albanians themselves, as marking the limits of national sovereignty. The limits were highly artificial, cutting not only lines of economic intercourse but also tribal ties, the strongest bond in the primitive society of Albania.

William of
Wied for a
short time
ruler of
Albania
William of Wied, a German prince, was placed on the newly established throne of Albania (1913). When the war began in 1914, both throne and monarch disappeared, and Albania reverted to a condition of local government. Northern and central Albania were overrun by the Austrian armies, which for four years held a military line a little north of Valona. In 1918 the Allied armies in the Balkans advanced, and Albania was re-won.

By a secret treaty made between France, Great Britain, and Italy just before Italy entered the World War, the great powers planned

First plan — to divide Albania

to divide Albania, giving the northern part to Montenegro or to Jugo-Slavia (treaty of London, 1915). The central section was to become a self-governing Mohammedan state. The southern section, with Valona, was to become Italian territory. In June 1917 Italy declared a protectorate over Albania, and assumed that the Allies approved her remaining there.

Albania not well organized to oppose foreign control

The Albanian national leaders charged that directly after the armistice of 1918, Italy sought by forcible colonization and the introduction of Italian schools to Italianize southern Albania. It is difficult for Albania to contest the acts of her neighbors, because she is not united. Her political institutions are elementary and weak; she has no railroads to knit the country into a unit; there is no really strong national feeling on the part of the majority of the people; her position tempts stronger neighbors to covet her land and ports.

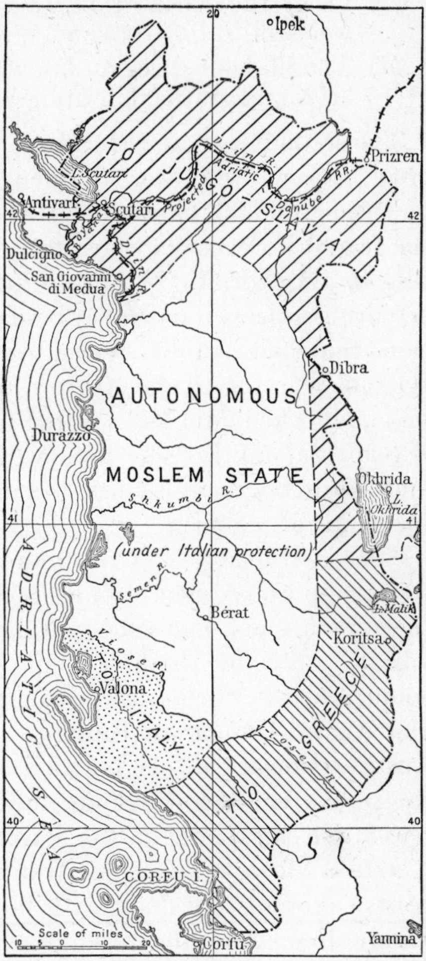

FIG. 155. Schematic representation of proposed division of Albania according to the secret treaty of London, 1915, between Italy, Great Britain, France, and Russia.

Italian desire for mandate over Albania

For a long time Italy insisted that in any case she must have a naval base at the port of Valona and a sufficiently large protecting zone for land operations in case of attack. This would assure her naval supremacy in the Adriatic and protect her entire eastern coast, a highly important matter when we realize that she is singularly exposed to attack by sea and has the densest population of any Mediterranean state (Fig. 67). In the face of a strong land attack by Albanian forces, Italy withdrew from Valona in the summer of 1920. The Albanians were stirred to action by the belief that Italy had agreed to approve the cession of southern Albania to Greece and was on the verge of securing an Albanian mandate from the great powers.

Distribution of Albanian people

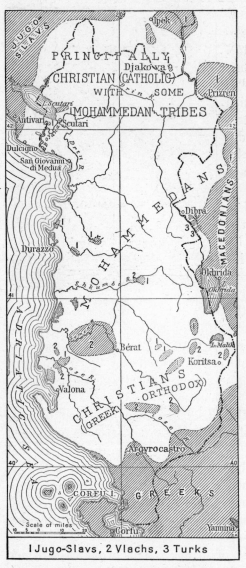

PRINCIPALLY CHRISTIAN (CATHOLIC) WITH SOME MOHAMMEDAN TRIBES

MOHAMMEDANS

MACEDONIANS

ADRIATIC SEA

CHRISTIANS GREEK (ORTHODOX)

GREEKS

JUGO-SLAVS

1 Jugo-Slavs, 2 Vlachs, 3 Turks

FIG. 156. Albanian ethnography, religions, and boundaries. For a key to the numbers, see the panel at the bottom of the map. The region north of the Shkumbi River is the more typically Albanian. Greek sentiment prevails at Argyrocastro and Albanian sentiment at Koritsa and Valona. Note that all the principal towns, of which Scutari is the largest, lie near the border of the country and have been occupied one after another by foreign powers most of the time since the First Balkan War (1912), despite the fact that Albania won its independence from Turkey in 1912. The effect has been to prevent the people from taking united action on national questions. See Figure 129 for a relief map of the Balkans.

Centers of Albanian interest and opposition

THE PEOPLE OF ALBANIA

The northern Albanians are distributed along the valley floors tributary to Lake Scutari, and about the lake border itself. South and east of these groups are the true mountaineers, the most primitive of all, a pastoral people of rude life and custom. Still farther south are bands of population along the valleys, separated from each other by high and steep mountain chains with few passes. At the southern end of the country are good agricultural districts with larger towns, like Koritsa. Along the eastern margin of the main Albanian mountain mass are broad, rich valleys where outliers of Albanian population live in large numbers, as for example, Üsküb, Prizren, and Okhrida.

The people of southern Albania have many resemblances to the Greeks. In the neighborhood of Argyrocastro there is a strong pro-Greek feeling, on account of Greek schools; but north of this region again the Albanian national spirit is strong and hatred of the Greeks intense. The town of Koritsa is Albanian, and so is the territory around it.

In northern Albania the mountain people depend upon the market towns for a great many of their life needs, and

FIG. 157. Part of the town of Koritsa, southern Albania.

these market towns, with the exception of Scutari, are in Serbian or Montenegrin territory. The result is that in mountain communities, far from Scutari, there is almost general scarcity of the products of the towns. Everywhere the frontiers are practically closed, and there is almost complete stagnation of economic life.

The life of the Albanian mountaineer has been unsettled by long military occupation. Patrols of Albanians and Serbs were obliged to guard almost all the roads in 1919–1920, after the Italian and French forces of occupation had gone. No one could travel in Albania without an armed guard, and bands of mountaineers committed atrocities in many sections. The general unrest was fostered by Serbian conscription in areas of Albanian population included within the Jugo-Slav frontiers. *Prevalence of unrest and brigandage*

THE PROSPECT FOR UNITED ALBANIA

In the meantime Albanian leaders are working for the union of the Albanian people into one state, and their efforts have resulted in admission to the League of Nations and a recognition of independence. A provisional government has made a preliminary agreement with Italy which leaves the latter in possession of the peninsulas on either side of the harbor of Valona and of the islands that guard the approaches, but releases the town and port to Albania. Italy also *Present plan of union* obtains recognition of her paramount political interest in Albanian affairs ss part of her general program of Adriatic defense. It will be important to have the final boundaries of Albania carefully drawn, so as to bring about union, as far as possible, of all Albanians directly connected with the main body, and ensure economic prosperity, which forms one of the bases of enduring peace. However, the process of making a unified state will be doubly difficult in a land with almost no railroads, few newspapers, and a high degree of illiteracy. Also opposed to the unifying processes are the rivalries of bordering states — Greece, Jugo-Slavia, and Italy. If in furthering their commercial interests these states employ the traditional forms of political propaganda, there may ensue disorder, if not disaster.

CHAPTER EIGHTEEN

THE REUNITED GREEK LANDS

THERE are three salient periods of development in Greek history to which attention may be directed for an understanding of the modern Greek program and the new boundaries of Greece :

(1) The early period of Greek settlement on the shores of the Mediterranean.

(2) The revival of Greek national feeling that led to the war of independence in 1829.

(3) The territorial growth of the immediate past (1912 to 1920) that has culminated in the Greece of today.

The first period spanned a space of many centuries, until Greek colonies were established along the thousands of miles of coast from the Pillars of Hercules (Gibraltar) to the eastern end of the Black Sea. By the 8th century B.C. the Greek people occupied an area far greater than Greece itself, and some of the larger and earlier settlements, particularly on the Ægean, "were ready to send out colonies in competition with those of the parent land."

The motive for emigration was at first the pressure of population in Greece. Later the Greeks invaded the Phœnician trading areas, their pirates preying upon the commerce of the Phœnicians. A spirit of adventure, travel, and foreign settlement marked the rise of Greek power upon the sea. It was natural that conquest should go hand in hand with the development of this power, and at length in Alexander's time (331 B.C.) effective Greek control was extended as far as the Euphrates, which for many centuries was to mark the line between the enterprising, virile peoples of the west and the more static oriental culture of Asia. *Rise of Greek commercial and political power*

The maritime traditions of the Greeks, their skill as traders, their occupation of the entire Ægean realm, their distribution throughout the Mediterranean and Black Sea basins as merchants and carriers, their hold upon the commercial outlets of the lands tributary to these basins, their settlement in patches and fringes of population on the seacoasts of lands inhabited by non-Greek peoples — all these factors converge upon the problems of the moment and render the tracing of Greek boundaries exceedingly difficult if justice is to be done to the nations that border Greece in the Near East.

Fig. 158. The map embraces the whole field of Greek territorial claims. For detailed boundaries in the Smyrna and Constantinople districts see Figures 161 and 207. The Armenian boundary southwest of Trebizond is subject to modifications in detail. The cession of the Dodecanese to Greece by Italy (excepting Rhodes, which Italy retains) was by treaty between Italy and Greece, but with general Allied sanction. With "Boundaries granted by the Peace Conference" in the legend are grouped present *de facto* boundaries such as the Albano-Greek and Serbo-Greek boundaries.

Rise of the city-state

Hand in hand with the rise of Greek power there went the development of the city-state, the first great milestone in the progress of liberal government. Attica became the symbol of democracy, and though it was but a seed that was planted there, the fruit eventually borne contributed to the political life and institutions of democratic governments everywhere throughout the world.

Change in ethnic character of Greeks

We shall not attempt to trace in detail the fortunes of the Greek people in the period of their long eclipse. In modified (Byzantine) form Greek civilization survived during the interval between the conquest of Greece by the Romans in 146 B.C. and the ultimate winning of Greek independence in 1829 (the treaty of Adrianople). At least in name, Constantinople was a Greek city for a thousand years. Here the Greek Orthodox Church took its rise, and from this and other centers of Greek life and culture there radiated the power of Greek ideals in literature, art, and government that for centuries profoundly affected the Roman world; some of its impulses are felt even in the life and institutions of our own time. Yet in the long centuries of eclipse, profound changes were to affect the Greek people. The racial character itself was ethnically altered. Strong Slavic infusions took place. The genius of the people declined. Many of the modern Greeks, including even those who live within sight of the Acropolis, are ignorant of the noblest traditions of Greek life. In place of the

odysseys of ancient Greece, we have in modern times the sordid tale
of petty trading and bartering in the ports of the Near Eastern world.

In spite of the Greek decline, there are two qualities that stand out
with striking prominence. The first is the capacity of the Greek to
absorb the people who invade his lands. The invader, whether it was
Albanian or Slav, who penetrated the Greek peninsula, came to have
something more than a veneer of Hellenic culture; for it is difficult
to resist assimilation into a mode of life, a regional spirit, as distinctive as that of the Hellenic lands. Something of this regional spirit
may be at the bottom of the second quality — the tenacity shown in
never-fading desire for independence and the reunion of Greek lands,
at least about the borders of the Ægean. Doubtless there could more
than once have been a realization of this aim if the Greeks had not
lacked that vital thing necessary to national power and welfare—the
unity of its people. Just as the city-states fell to quarreling with each
other (for example, in the Peloponnesian War of 431–404 B.C.) and
finally almost extinguished their national inheritance, so in the later
history of Greece rival chieftains and the leaders of opposing factions
have harmed Greece as much as has the outsider.

Independence a persistent aim

Finally, through the bitter lessons of Turkish rule, from 1456 down
to 1829, Greek leaders were taught the necessity of working for a common purpose, and in the Greek war of independence at last achieved
freedom from the Turk. The history of Greece from that time forward is marked by almost incessant internal disorder and by the
practical overlordship of the great powers of western Europe. To
mention only one episode in her foreign relations, the war with Turkey
in 1897 brought upon Greece a heavy indemnity of $20,000,000; and
in addition she was forced to submit to a loss of territory on her
northern frontier.

Greek war of independence

At the outbreak of war in 1914, the pro-German sympathies of
King Constantine, who had married a sister of Emperor William of
Germany, led to a long internal struggle, ending in 1917 with the
flight of the king and the elevation to leadership of Venizelos, one of
the most remarkable men of modern Europe. Thereafter Greece
fought on the side of the Allies, and though her total war effort in
1917–1918 amounted to but little, she had participated heartily in the
Balkan War of 1912 by which Turkey was all but ousted from Europe.
She had still further extended her territory, at the expense of Bulgaria, in the Second Balkan War, and in 1914 her frontier stood as
represented in Figure 150. Late in 1920, as the result of popular vote,
the government of Venizelos fell. Constantine returned to the Greek

throne, but it cannot yet be said whether this means a repudiation of the Venizelos program.

In the new settlement of the Balkans and the Near East it was the Greek plan to lay claim to the most important Greek lands in the Near Eastern realm. These we shall now discuss in detail in the following order: Macedonia, Thrace, the Dodecanese, Smyrna, Epirus, Trebizond, Cyprus.

THE DIVISION OF MACEDONIA

Macedonia under Alexander became the heart of a great empire, and some measure of its greatness was retained by the country until the Turkish invasion of the 14th century, when, in common with other Balkan lands, it became a part of the Turkish Empire. With the revival of nationalities in the Balkans, particularly in the 19th century, the Macedonian question in its modern aspect took form.

Macedonia
a transition
region

The region has always had indefinite boundaries. It reaches the sea at Saloniki on the south, extends westward to Lake Okhrida and the Albanian frontier, merges almost insensibly on the east into Bulgarian territory in the Strumitsa region, and on the north reaches as far as Üsküb. Within these limits the population may be estimated around 2,000,000, of whom more than half are Christians and the rest chiefly Mohammedans, with some Jews in the towns, notably at Saloniki. In population as in position the region is a transition land. The language has qualities that resemble both Bulgarian and Serbian. Church membership in many cases classifies a man "racially." From Figure 159 it will be seen that Macedonia lies at the meeting place of three Balkan states, Serbia, Bulgaria, and Greece, and it was natural that each of these states should make an effort to impose its culture upon the people and develop a nationalist sentiment among them. Bulgarian claims rested upon one-time possession of the region and the racial character of the people. But the Serbs also held the country for a time and left a deep impress there, for example, in architecture and literature.

A theater
of political
propaganda

The chief media of propaganda were the school and the church. Until her wars for independence early in the 19th century, Greece led in influence because of the strength of her church organization and her superior culture. Her hold was all the stronger because she operated chiefly in the towns, where powerful Greek merchants lived, and the towns in turn greatly influenced the country districts tributary to them. Even Rumania joined in the effort to penetrate Macedonia and win adherence to her program of national expansion. This she

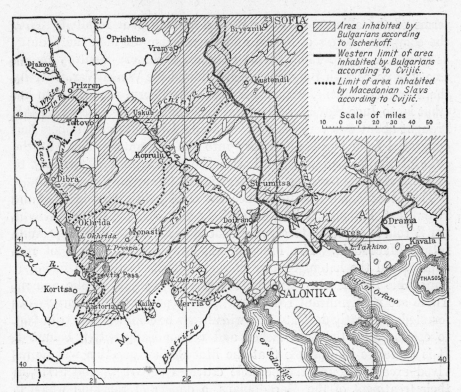

Fig. 159. Conflicting views on ethnography of the Macedonian region by a Bulgarian, Ischerkoff (*Petermanns Mitteilungen*, 1915, Pl. 44), and a Serbian, Cvijić (*Report of the International Commission to Inquire into the Causes and Conduct of the Balkan Wars*, Carnegie Endowment for International Peace, 1915). Existing international boundaries are shown by heavy dash-and-dot lines.

was able to do because of the presence of Vlachs in large numbers — probably between 75,000 and 100,000 in all in the Macedonian country (Fig. 145). In the struggle for supremacy Bulgaria was favored by the establishment of the Exarchist, or Bulgarian, church in 1870 by Turkish authority. The Exarch was head of the church and was able to further Bulgarian interests by impressing upon all members of his church the national, or Bulgarian, character of their religion.

By the secret alliance between Serbia and Bulgaria before the First Balkan War a detailed line was agreed upon, beyond which Serbia was "to formulate no territorial claim," and a contested zone which extended westward far enough to include Üsküb and Dibra was reserved for arbitration by the Czar of Russia (Fig. 150). But Bulgaria made unexpected gains in eastern Thrace, and the powers decided to form an independent Albania in the regions where Serbia had hoped to increase her territory. Wherefore Serbia denounced the territorial

Macedonia in relation to the Second Balkan War

terms of the alliance, and the Second Balkan War resulted. With the complete success of Serbia and Greece they divided the country as shown in Figure 150. Serbia obtained still more territory by the treaty of peace with Bulgaria which followed the World War, whereby the Strumitsa salient, with other bits of territory, was ceded to her (that is, to Jugo-Slavia). The local disarrangement of life which this brought about was very serious. Macedonians in large numbers had emigrated from Serbian territory into the Strumitsa salient at the close of the Balkan wars, and with the cession of this territory to Jugo-Slavia they have again been required to move.

Present state of the Macedonian question The Macedonian question, once the chief political problem of the Near East, has passed into an entirely new phase. Neither Greece nor Serbia is expected to give up Macedonian territory for a possible future Macedonia. The Macedonians are without leaders of real ability, and the heterogeneous character of the population makes it impossible for them to have or to express a common public opinon. There are no significant resources. It is a poor country, largely de-forested and partly desolate, and will always be commercially tributary to communities that are richer and economically better balanced. It is therefore improbable that the Macedonian question will be re-vived except through the possible cruelties of Greeks and Serbs in their treatment of the Macedonians, a danger of the kind which it was the chief purpose of the minorities treaties to avoid.

THE QUESTION OF THRACE

Distribu-tion of Greeks in Thrace An extension of her eastern frontier in Thrace as far as the Black Sea gives Greece control of the entire southern littoral of the Balkan peninsula, and with this acquisition go commercial advantages of peculiar interest to a seafaring and trading population like the Greeks. In support of her claim to this important strip of territory Greece pointed to the thousand years of control of Constantinople by the Greek or Byzantine Empire, and to the large number of Greek people in eastern and western Thrace, who would have numbered still more had it not been for the massacres by Turks and Bulgarians in the Balkan wars and in the recent World War itself. An ethnic map of the region is difficult to construct because of the unequal character of the statistics and the lack of any statistics at all for important places. This much is surely known, that the two principal towns, Adrianople and Kirk Kilisse, are chiefly Greek and that in the region as a whole Greeks outnumber Turks. Bulgarians form the third of the three principal ethnic groups. The mixture of populations is

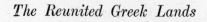

FIG. 160.   The village of Kalambaka at the head of the Thessalian plain.   A typical landscape in northern Greece.

due to the historical character of Thrace as a transition region between Turkish and Balkan peoples. The problem was further confused by the effect of the two Balkan wars and the World War, which displaced or destroyed whole sections of the population. Before 1912 the Greeks in eastern Thrace (east of the Maritsa) numbered 400,000 as against 250,000 Turks and 50,000 Bulgarians. According to Greek estimates western Thrace had a population of 400,000, of whom 70,000 only were Greeks, 59,000 Bulgarians, and 285,000 Turks. Bulgarian figures ascribe 185,000 Bulgarians to the region and only 32,000 Greeks.

Greek acquisition of Thrace

In laying claim to the whole of Thrace, Greece had the powerful argument that if any portion of the coast bordering the Ægean were left in the hands of Bulgaria or Turkey, the harbors of that coast would furnish bases for submarine attacks upon the long coast line of Greece. By the terms of the Turkish and Bulgarian treaties she wins all the territory of eastern and western Thrace except a small area at Constantinople, though a coastal strip on the sea of Marmara is to be under Allied control (Fig. 158).

Restrictions and obligations

By acquiring Thrace, Greece has achieved the principal part of her program of the reunion of Greek lands. She is restricted, however, in three important matters:

(1) She must guarantee Bulgaria freedom of transit to the Ægean through Thrace.

(2) The Maritsa is to be constituted an international river upon application to the League of Nations of the states bordering that river, — that is, of Bulgaria and Greece.

(3) She undertakes to protect minority populations, especially at Adrianople, where the racial elements are to have representation in the local government according to a scheme prepared by Greece.

It is further provided, on account of the large number of Turks in Thrace and the large number of Greeks on the southern shore of the Black Sea and elsewhere under Turkish sovereignty, that Greece and Turkey may negotiate for the reciprocal exchange of their nationals.

THE DODECANESE AND OTHER ISLANDS OF THE ÆGEAN

Italian occupation in 1911

When she secured liberation from Turkish rule in 1829, Greece acquired only a portion of her national territory. An important part of her population is located in a group of islands off the coast of Anatolia and south of Smyrna, known as the Dodecanese. The population comprises 100,000 Greeks as compared with 12,000 persons of other nationalities. By the terms of the treaty of Lausanne, which closed the Italo-Turkish War, the islands were to be occupied by Italy until Turkey had withdrawn officers, troops, and officials from Libya. Before these agreements had been completed the World War broke out, and in the peace settlement of 1920 with Turkey the Dodecanese were ceded to Italy; but at the same time Italy and Greece signed a separate treaty transferring the islands to Greece. Rhodes alone was retained by Italy, though a qualified plebiscite is provided for at the end of five years (page 326).

Commercially the islands are not important. They have little arable ground, no industries of importance, and no maritime activity except some sponge fishing. Conditions of life are distinctly hard. But the islands do form an important base for the commercial penetration of Anatolia. *Possible cession to Greece*

As a result of the Balkan wars, Greece had already received Lemnos, Samothrace, Mytilene, Samos, Nikaria, and Chios, in addition to other smaller islands in the Ægean. She now receives Imbros and Tenedos. The total area of these islands is somewhat less than 2000 square miles, and they have a population of about 325,000, of whom 90 per cent are Greek. The islands are of moderate commercial importance. *Greek gains in the Ægean islands*

THE SMYRNA REGION

Among outlying territories it is the Smyrna region that is of chief interest to Greece, for here live about 500,000 Greeks in an area but little larger than the state of Connecticut. The city of Smyrna has 375,000 people and is now the largest city in the Greek world, Athens having but 168,000. Ever since the coming of the Turk (early 15th century), these Greeks have been under the government of an alien conquering race. During the World War they were badly treated, and during the period of peace-making they were alleged to be in serious danger of massacre by Turkish troops. *The Greeks of Smyrna*

To save the Greek population from possible attacks by the Turks, the Allies permitted Greece to land troops at Smyrna and occupy the adjacent district. Allied warships were present to take part in the operations if necessary, an action that was complicated by the presence of the Italians immediately to the south. Unauthorized by the Peace Conference at Paris — in fact, in the face of its direct protests — the Italians landed troops in the Adalia region on the pretext of protecting their interests. As a matter of fact, they have no inter- *Greek occupation of Smyrna; complications with the Italians to the South*

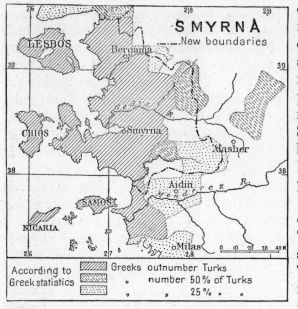

Fig. 161.   Map of the Smyrna region, showing the ethnic basis
of Greek claims according to Greek statistics.

ests there worthy of mention.   Clashes occurred between Greek and Italian troops, and finally (July 1919) the peace conference sent a military mission to Smyrna to establish the limits of the Greek and Italian military occupations.

The Greeks are a coast and island people. The Ægean is their sea historically.   The Trojan War was primarily an issue of the Greek need — a need still existing — for free access to the grain lands of the Black Sea.   In the Smyrna region Greeks have been settled for thousands of years.   With the city and the region adjacent to it is associated a great deal of Greek history and tradition, and it has long been a trade focus.   Greek traders here met the laden caravans that every year journeyed out of Inner Asia across the wastes of Persia and the Syrian desert with the rich spices, teas, silks, and jewelry of the East.   Camel caravans may still be seen, but now a railway connects Smyrna with inland towns that may grow to be important cities under a reorganized Turkish government.

As the outlet for a large part of western Anatolia, Smyrna is a commercial prize.   In 1914 the chief exports were:

Tobacco	$1,380,000	Valonia	$208,000
Opium	1,365,000	Olive oil	148,000
Figs	700,000	Raisins	80,000
Licorice root	460,000	Wool	20,000
Carpets and rugs	400,000	Walnuts	17,000
Emery stone	280,000	Peas	17,000
Skins	233,000	Preserves	14,000

The table shows that Smyrna is the port not only for the district immediately around it, but for the far interior as well.   The products of the desert, where a certain amount of grazing is possible, the prod-

FIG. 162. Smyrna, western Anatolia, seen from Mt. Pagos. This was the second port of Turkey in total trade, Constantinople being first, and the first port in export trade. The city and district (Fig. 161) are now in Greek hands.

ucts of the irrigated oases at the borders of the desert, as well as the products of the farms and orchards in the mountain valleys that face the sea behind Smyrna — all find their outlet through this, the greatest of Turkish ports except Constantinople.

Terms of
Greek
control of
Smyrna
Some statesmen think that Greek control of Smyrna would have the advantage of combining the principal Greek element in the eastern Mediterranean with the home country, and of strengthening the Greek nation. Others contend that it would be unfair, as it would so weaken Turkey as practically to destroy her economic life.

According to the terms of the Turkish treaty (still unsatisfied), the management by Greece of the Smyrna region (Fig. 161) is to follow the lines indicated in the following summary :

(1) Turkey keeps her sovereignty over the region, but transfers her "rights of sovereignty" to Greece, who may maintain the military force necessary to keep order, though compulsory military service is forbidden.

(2) The ports, railways, and waterways of the region are included within the régime for European waterways provided by the earlier treaties of 1919–1920 between the Allies and the Central Powers.

(3) Greek customs are to be collected on the frontiers of the region.

(4) Greece is to provide diplomatic and consular protection for Turkish nationals from the Smyrna region abroad.

(5) A local parliament is constituted, including representatives of all races. The principles of the Greek constitution are to govern the relations of this parliament to the Greek administration.

(6) The final status of the region is not determined. In 1925 the local parliament may ask the League of Nations to permit the union of the region to Greece, in which case the Council of the League may require a plebiscite.

(7) Turkey is to have a customs zone at Smyrna, in which she is to enjoy full freedom of commerce without paying customs dues.

NORTHERN EPIRUS

Northern Epirus (southern Albania) has a population estimated to number between 250,000 and 300,000. It is equally divided between members of the Greek Orthodox Church and Mohammedans, the former speaking Albanian, but presumably having Greek sympathies.

FIG. 163. A laden camel caravan marching toward Smyrna from the interior of Anatolia.

For a time just before the war, the Albanian Greek Orthodox people of Epirus proclaimed themselves an autonomous state, and established a provisional government at Argyrocastro. In 1914 "sacred battalions," said to have been composed in part of Greek citizens, ravaged the country of the Albanian Moslems and massacred or drove out a great many people, at the same time destroying their villages. Twenty thousand people fled into the Valona region. At the Conference of Corfu in May 1914, the Albanian government and the great powers agreed upon a separate government for northern Epirus.

Albanians violently oppose the Greek claims to northern Epirus. Their arguments are similar to those advanced in so many other disputed regions of Europe. The people of the region speak Albanian, and nearly half are Mohammedan in religion. Koritsa, the most important town in the disputed zone, is a center of Albanian nationalist influence. The schools are almost exclusively Greek, and Greek culture and economic influence are dominant. The sentiment of the Albanian population here, as elsewhere, is very difficult to estimate. It has had no practice in free voting and has always been distracted by the propagandist agents of neighboring powers.

Albanian view of Greek control

The disposition of the northern Epirus region long awaited the settlement of the Albanian question. Now that Jugo-Slavia and Italy have come to an agreement that does not include Greece, Greek claims in southern Albania have little importance. The return of Constantine to the Greek throne has also diminished Allied support of

Greece. Moreover, Albania has won recognition as an independent state from the League of Nations, and as such she is now probably secure from selfish territorial encroachment.

TREBIZOND

The strip of Greek population along the southern shore of the Black Sea that includes the city of Trebizond numbers 350,000, but it is far from the central portion of the Greek world. For these reasons the Greek desire to have a zone of influence there met with no support from the treaty makers at Paris in 1919. The only advantage that has been won for these people is their protection as a minority population, partly within the new Turkish state and partly within the new Armenia.

CYPRUS

Great Britain "occupied" Cyprus from 1878 on, according to an agreement of that year whereby she should remain in Cyprus as long as Russia occupied the Transcaucasian provinces of Kars, Batum, and Ardahan, which she had taken from Turkey. Though Cyprus is Greek in population, it forms a link in the British strategic chain. On 5 November 1914 the British government annexed the island, and this action was confirmed by all the interested powers in the Turkish treaty of 1920. Finally, Article 3 of the Franco-British agreement of 23 December 1920 provides that Great Britain shall not cede or alienate the island without the previous consent of France.

Connected with the question of Cyprus is that of Rhodes, held by Italy since the Italo-Turkish war of 1911–1912. By treaty with Greece (1920) provision is made for a plebiscite in five years. If the inhabitants vote for Greece Italy will withdraw, provided Great Britain will withdraw from Cyprus.

THE OUTLOOK FOR GREECE

As a result of the treaties which closed the two Balkan wars and of the terms of the Turkish and Bulgarian treaties and other arrangements with the Allied powers in 1919 and 1920, Greece has won so much territory that her area is now twice what it was in 1911. Before the Balkan wars she had a population of 2,700,000. With the addition of 1,400,000 in Macedonia, Epirus, and Thrace, some hundreds of thousands inhabiting islands now ceded to Greece, and about 1,000,000 at Smyrna, her population is about 5,000,000, and of the population gained since 1912 about 2,250,000 are Greek.

With inspiring sea traditions, Greece is now on the way to becoming one of the strongest minor powers of Europe. At the beginning of the World War the tonnage of Greek merchant ships was about 820,000; that is, in proportion to the population, Greek merchant tonnage compared favorably with that of all but four countries. Greece has acquired new harbors of great importance to her. Saloniki was added in 1912, Dedeagatch and Smyrna in 1920, not to include such important inland stations as Adrianople, Kirk Kilisse, etc. This advantage is offset in part by shipping losses during the war, which have brought her total down to 291,000 tons.

There is promise of increasing strength in the internal economic situation of Greece. In order to stimulate commerce and industry, as well as agriculture and the merchant marine ministries of agriculture and shipping have been created in the cabinet of the government. Fortunately, there is no troublesome land-tenure question; in late years the proportion of small estates has increased rapidly, and production has been stimulated by the formation of coöperative agricultural societies.

It is too early to estimate the political and economic effects of the return of Constantine to the Greek throne. Certainly it will be more difficult for Greece to secure loans from the Allied powers; and Greek participation in the Turkish treaty may be far less favorable to her. The Allies have it in their power to embarrass Greece, if they wish to do so, by refusing military and moral support when clashes occur, as they are bound to, between Greek civil officials and troops of occupation on the one hand and minority groups in the newly won territories on the other. Whether Allied help will be withdrawn is a matter of vital importance to Greece, whose present territorial status is almost wholly an Allied creation.

CHAPTER NINETEEN

POLAND AND ITS DISPUTED BORDERLANDS

AMONG the reconstituted nations of the world there is none other that has had so great a past as Poland. The Polish realm long included Lithuania, and as late as 1740 it extended from the Baltic almost to the Black Sea (Fig. 165). At that time it nearly reached the Oder on the west; it passed the main stream of the Dnieper on the east. Warsaw was then one of the great capitals of Europe. The trade of the Ottoman Empire in part flowed northwestward from the Black Sea and the Bosporus through Polish towns.

During the 12th and 13th centuries Poland was the scene of costly civil war, owing to the quarrels of the rival Polish princes. Military pressure by Mongols and Prussians further diverted the strength of the Polish government. By attaching Lithuania to itself in 1386, Poland had increased its territory so greatly that for several centuries thereafter it was one of the two or three largest nations of continental Europe. But its internal and external difficulties were at last to prove fatal. As Prussia advanced on the west, Poland sought to advance eastward. It was a great and historic mistake, and one which Poland appears determined to repeat. Poland does not seem to be able to absorb large Russian elements successfully. Within thirty-two years of the climax of its power and one hundred and twenty-four years after the time of its greatest expansion, Poland suffered the first of the divisions known in history as the three partitions of Poland (1772, 1793, 1795).

The three partitions of Poland, in which its territory was divided by Russia, Prussia, and Austria, left it paralyzed. National pride was humiliated. The robber states set up new boundaries that completely disregarded the natural relations of the region. The social and economic life of the people was shaken to its foundation. Rivers that once pulsated with life became merely "dead border lines." Though revolutionary movements were started in 1831 and 1863, the latter being suppressed by outrageous cruelties, until 1918 Polish nationality was hopelessly enchained.

A review of Poland's problems will show that its situation and international relations are matters of vital importance to the future stability of Europe. The elements of danger are as great as in the Balkans, and most of the available leaders are untried in administration and government. It will strain Poland's intellectual resources

FIG. 164. Based on Droysen, *Allgemeiner Historischer Handatlas*, Pl. 40. From the *Geographical Review*, Vol. 4, 1917.

to provide officials of the right kind to manage her complex problems of state. Among the historical and geographical elements to which attention is here given are the following:

(1) The geographical position of the country is in the midst of a vast plain without natural frontiers eastward toward Russia or westward toward Germany.

(2) Though Slavs, the Poles are Roman Catholic, whereas the Russians are Greek Orthodox and the Germans chiefly Protestant.

(3) Though Slavs, the Poles represent western, as opposed to eastern, culture.

(4) Once a great nation, there would be a natural tendency for Poland to wish to include within the present frontiers all of its former territory, even if acquired at the expense of neighboring states.

(5) The Poles were once divided among three rival powers — Russia, Germany, and Austria — and this fact, in part, makes them the enemies of their two strongest neighbors, Germany and Russia.

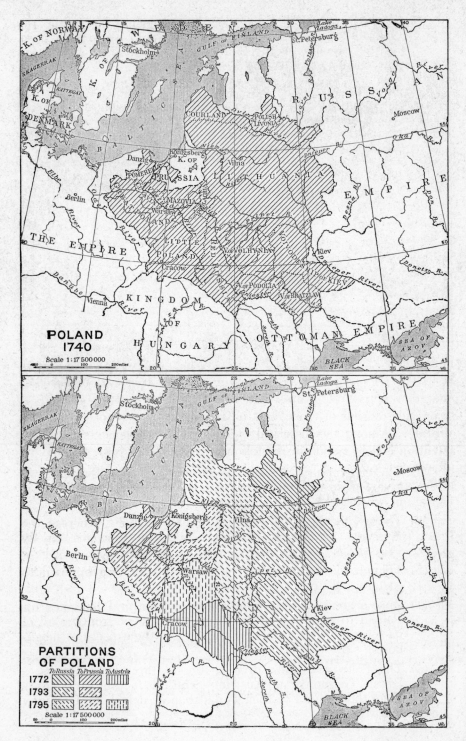

POLAND
1740

Scale 1:17 500 000

PARTITIONS
OF POLAND

	To Russia	To Prussia	To Austria
1772			
1793			
1795			

Scale 1:17 500 000

(6) Though a strip of Polish population reaches the Baltic, this strip is very narrow; if widened it would be at the expense of the Germans, who already have protested at even so narrow a strip as that shown in Figure 171.

(7) The eastern border of ethnic Poland is ill-defined, and the recent growth of Polish population in this region is more rapid than anywhere else on the borders of Poland. It follows that Polish statesmen desire a new frontier to be established as far east as possible.

ORGANIZATION OF THE NEW REPUBLIC

There is a saying that when the white eagle of Poland flies in the sky, the red eagle of Prussia must come down. But the red eagle was in the sky for a hundred and forty years. Had the Polish people not had great tenacity and a long national history, they might this day be divided among neighbors of different race and speech. But throughout the long period of oppression by Russians, Prussians, and Austrians they kept alive their national consciousness and pride, and despite enormous difficulties organized a central government in 1918.

The white eagle of Poland and the red eagle of Prussia

Pilsudski became the military leader and provisional president, and Paderewski was later appointed president of the council of ministers, or premier. The latter's knowledge of American and English character made him a most powerful exponent of Polish affairs at the Peace Conference of Paris. The steadying effect of his work was of vast benefit to his people. He was threatened by Bolshevism outside of Poland and by doubters within; he was confronted by almost general want, the lack of money and troops, the absence of rolling stock, a threatening horde of Germans on the west, and the Ukrainian army in Galicia on the southeast.

Two great leaders: Pilsudski and Paderewski

These difficulties were increased by the extraordinary nature of the Polish program. Almost every Polish leader wanted to see the greatest possible Poland created, no matter at what expense to the neighboring states. Many wished to see even East Prussia included. It was taken for granted that Danzig would become a Polish port. All of Eastern Galicia was assumed to be naturally Polish territory, though inhabited chiefly by Ruthenians. No leader could have won on such a program before a general congress of European leaders striving to adjust rival claims. The best that Poland could do was

---

Fig. 165 (upper). Based on Shepherd, *Historical Atlas*, Pl. 130–131, and Droysen, *Allgemeiner Historischer Handatlas*, Pl. 44.

Fig. 166 (lower). Based on Putzger, *Historischer Schul-Atlas zur alten, mittleren und neuen Geschichte*, Pl. 25. Both figures are from the *Geographical Review*, 1917.

FIG. 167. Ethnography of Poland and its border zones. Eastern Galicia is occupied, but without treaty confirmation. Poland did not accept the eastern boundary as proposed by the Peace Conference of Paris. For the boundary with Soviet Russia see Figure 169. The Allenstein and Marienwerder plebiscites have been held, and the vote was almost unanimously for Germany; but the powers have yet to delimit a boundary. The division of Silesia will be based on a plebiscite held on 20 March 1921. Teschen, Orawa, and Spits have been recommended for division between Czecho-Slovakia and Poland by the Council of Ambassadors (Fig. 179). Ethnography based on British General Staff ethnic map, 1:1,500,000, 1918. Key to numerals: 1, Poles; 2, Germans; 3, Czecho-Slovaks; 4, Magyars; 5, Rumanians; 6, Ruthenians (Ukrainians); 7, White Russians; 8, Lithuanians.

far short of her hopes, and the leader of the hour was destined to enjoy only a short period of authority.

Breach between Pilsudski and Paderewski

Gradually Pilsudski and Paderewski became the heads of opposing factions. Paderewski led a party which desired to see a liberal government developed, and one which should have the good-will of the Allies. Pilsudski, a socialist before the war, had now become a sort of military dictator who wished to arrange an understanding with either Germany or Russia and to free himself from Allied control.

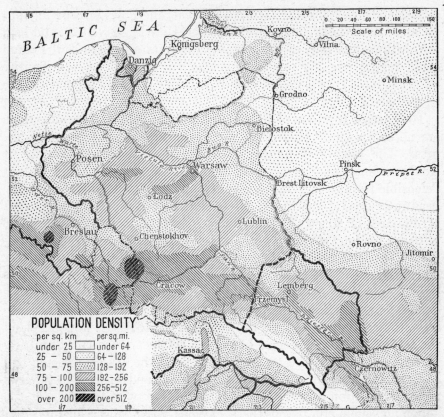

Fig. 168. The Cracow-Czernowitz region of dense population is the eastern end of a belt that extends northwestward into Belgium. Notice the lighter grades of density in the region of Brest-Litovsk and Grodno, just where the absolute number of Poles is increasing. See inset of Figure 182. Based on Romer, *Atlas géographique et statistique de la Pologne*, 1916, Pl. 7, supplemented by Andree, *Handatlas*, Pl. 30, and *Petermanns Mitteilungen*, 1913, I, Pl. 2. For later boundary details see Figures 179 and 180.

In the ensuing political contest the advantage was all with Pilsudski, who held the reins of power, had the army and the police with him, and was supported by prominent groups with imperialistic and militaristic aims. He gradually won to his favor the political leaders, and Paderewski was forced to resign early in 1920, after which he became Poland's representative at Paris until his retirement in January 1921.

Success of Pilsudski

POLAND AND RUSSIA

The policies of Pilsudski were not continued in the direction of closer relations with Russia. Early in 1920 the Soviet government had defeated Denikin, the Cossack leader who organized the anti-Bolshevist forces of southern Russia and the Kuban. Anticipating a Soviet attack following Denikin's defeat, the Poles pressed forward for more than three hundred miles, took Kiev in May 1920, and held the northwestern part of the Ukraine. It now appeared as if Poland could realize her aspiration to settle her difficult eastern frontier question in her own way. Let us examine the background of the situation.

Indefinite frontiers of eastern Poland

The eastern frontiers of Poland are difficult to define because there are no sharp lines, whether of race, religion, or national consciousness. The historic boundary of 1772 is out of the question; it would include more non-Polish than Polish populations. The best defensible frontier is a line drawn through the Pripet marshes, in the headwater area of the Pripet River, but this also is far beyond (east of) the area of strictly Polish speech. And the world can never be at peace for long if every nation struggles for the best strategic frontier. No sooner is one strategic advantage gained than another farther on is desired to protect it. The process is endless.

The eastern boundary of Poland as recommended by the Peace Conference at Paris is shown in Figure 169, and it was planned to leave to negotiation between the governments of Russia and of Poland the settlement of the precise boundary between these two countries. It was not thought wise to go further until the Russian people had a chance to reorganize their political affairs and express their views as to the position of the Polish frontier.

Poland could not forget those glorious pages of her history that recounted the heroic deeds of her leaders in eastern fields of war and commerce. Polish military power and intellectual force had made themselves felt from Vilna to Kiev. Polish colonies are scattered throughout this broad region. To be confined to ethnographic Poland was to accept the historic injustice from which she had so long suffered.

Attack of Soviet armies on Poland

The Russian Soviet government now took up the offensive with a concentration of forces along the Polish eastern frontier, and a vigorous attack swept the Polish army back to the gates of Warsaw (August 1920). With its armies in a favorable position it was the turn of the Soviet government to make extreme demands upon the Poles. The acceptance of these demands would have made Poland a vassal of Russia and guaranteed the extension of Bolshevism into western Europe. Russia was to have a large army on Poland's frontier, and Poland was to have scarcely any army at all. Radical groups in Poland were to have government sanction, and there were to be no restrictions upon the spread of Soviet propaganda. Only in the matter of eastern territorial limits was there an apparent liberality;

but the other terms made this condition of no consequence. Faced by these conditions, Poland had no choice but to fight.

With French leadership, munitions from the Allies, and fresh recruits from every rank of Polish society, the Polish army now took the offensive. In a few weeks it had reached a line corresponding roughly to the line of German occupation in 1918 and the treaty of Brest-Litovsk. Here it remained while a treaty on new lines was framed by Russian and Polish representatives at Riga, the capital and chief seaport of Latvia (October 1920). The treaty was preliminary in nature, involving an armistice or truce of uncertain duration. Nor can it wear really serious aspects until a stable all-Russian government is formed in place of the present class government of the Soviets.

The treaty of Riga fixed the eastern limits of Poland beyond the line recommended by the Peace Conference of Paris (Figs. 169 and 180). It required the payment of an indemnity to Poland. It was framed on the principle of no victory for either side and, most significant of all, it was signed by representatives of the Ukraine. Though the Ukrainian representatives were Bolshevist and not from Petlura's Republic of the Western Ukraine that had been fighting against the Poles during 1919 and with them in 1920, yet the fact that the rights of the Ukraine as a national or semi-national unit were recognized would make it appear easier, if the Allies, including Poland, later desire it, to establish a line of cleavage between White Russia (Fig. 191) and the Ukraine. It is often argued that Russia should be united because all the parts are needed to make a well-balanced state; but this is hardly true of the Ukraine, the most nearly self-sufficing unit. In general it would be to the advantage of Poland, Rumania, and the western powers to divide Russia. Her reserves of man power are enormous, and if focused upon a weak border state like Poland or Finland might prove to be overwhelming.

The treaty between Poland and Soviet Russia has one feature that will intensify the long-standing and bitter differences between Poland and Lithuania. It provides for an eastern Polish frontier that embraces the entire hinterland of Lithuania. It was precisely here that Lithuania herself expected to expand at Russia's expense. Moreover, the signing of the treaty was followed immediately by the Polish occupation of Vilna, in the heart of the country in dispute. The occupation was carried out by army leaders acting on their own initiative and under formal government censure, yet the sympathy of the Polish government for the acts of the irregular forces was unquestioned. The matter was considered especially unfortunate because

The Vilna storm center

a truce had just been arranged between Lithuania and Poland, through the good offices of the League of Nations, that appeared to promise a settlement of their acute difficulties in the Suwalki region southwest of Vilna, where fighting had been going on for months. The action of the Poles at Vilna nullifies this decision and makes the disputed zone a possible source of the gravest trouble.

Anti-Russian feeling in Poland

The hatred of the Pole for the Russian is based on differences of culture and mode of thought, on marked differences of religion, and on the terrible persecutions of the past hundred and fifty years. Poland is a nation of western ideas; Russia is almost oriental by contrast. The strength of the hostility is suggested in the romantic poetry of Poland, which is full of anti-Russian allusions.

Basis for a pro-Russian policy

Nevertheless, so fiercely concentrated is the feeling against Germany that there has grown up a very strong pro-Russian policy. It is not that this new party hates Russia less, but that it hates Germany more. It foresees failure and a new division of land and people if Poland does not become rather closely attached to one or the other of her two powerful neighbors. This was preëminently the theory of Pilsudski. Yet the settlement of almost every detail of the Polish frontiers has raised up an enemy. Russia will take nearly as lively an interest in the fate of Eastern Galicia as Germany takes in Upper Silesia or Czecho-Slovakia in Teschen. Another reason for a working agreement between Poland and Russia lies in the fact that before the World War the Polish textile mills depended upon Russia for a market. Most of the manufactured products were sent east, not west. If this normal pre-war stream of trade is to be revived, permanent peace with Russia is the first essential.

POLAND'S OUTLET TO THE SEA: DANZIG AND THE POLISH CORRIDOR

The Polish Corridor west of the Vistula

Poland is ill favored in the matter of its "corridor" to the sea, a narrow band of Polish population that extends along the western side of the Vistula to the Baltic (Fig. 167). It was the dream of all Poles that the peace settlement should give them a broader stretch than that occupied by "indisputably Polish population"; the more so since the Vistula has been regarded from the earliest periods of Polish nationality as a Polish river in its entirety. From the Carpathians almost to the sea the banks of the Vistula have always been bordered by Polish populations.

It was this ethnic corridor to the sea that the Germans for many years had been trying to Germanize. While the corridor was the scene of most intense penetration, the process was general throughout eastern Germany. German officials in great numbers were established everywhere. The Prussian government, working chiefly through the Imperial Colonization Commission, had sent more than 100,000 colonists into German Poland, giving them such substantial preference that the Polish farmer was gradually forced out. Large tracts were bought up by the government as forest reserves. Danzig, at the coastal end of the corridor, had its Polish population gradually reduced until Poles numbered but 10 per cent of the total of 170,000. Thus was fought out the last of the many struggles that were waged here between German and Slav for the possession of a strategic zone which each considered vital to its national security.

The corridor upon which Poland depended for its "secure access to the sea," as promised by the Allied powers, had been so narrowed by artificial German settlement for many years before the World War that a strip but fifty miles across could be assigned to Poland on ethnic grounds. Danzig, the outlet port for the corridor and for Poland, was

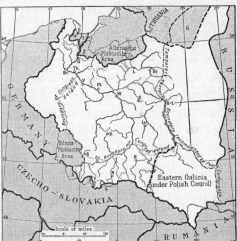

turned into a Free State, or Free City, though with Interallied guarantees to the Poles that will assure them full and regulated use of the port for goods and transport of Polish origin or destination (page 343).

Danzig thus returns to somewhat the same status that it enjoyed for more than three hundred years — 1454 to 1793. It was then practically a free republic, though joined voluntarily to Poland and living under its sovereignty. During this period there was attached to the free city an area about half that of the present district. It managed its own internal government, yet was Polish in sentiment and had common economic interests with the Polish state. The Polish government could pro-

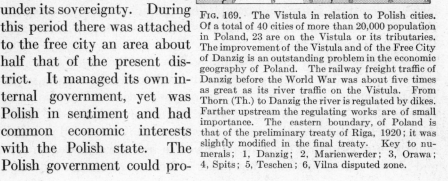

FIG. 169. The Vistula in relation to Polish cities. Of a total of 40 cities of more than 20,000 population in Poland, 23 are on the Vistula or its tributaries. The improvement of the Vistula and of the Free City of Danzig is an outstanding problem in the economic geography of Poland. The railway freight traffic of Danzig before the World War was about five times as great as its river traffic on the Vistula. From Thorn (Th.) to Danzig the river is regulated by dikes. Farther upstream the regulating works are of small importance. The eastern boundary of Poland is that of the preliminary treaty of Riga, 1920; it was slightly modified in the final treaty. Key to numerals; 1, Danzig; 2, Marienwerder; 3, Orawa; 4, Spits; 5, Teschen; 6, Vilna disputed zone.

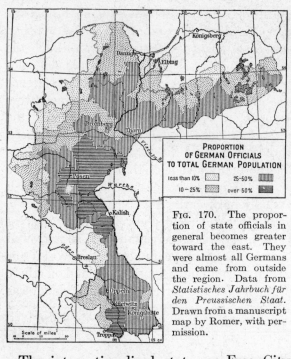

PROPORTION
OF GERMAN OFFICIALS
TO TOTAL GERMAN POPULATION

less than 10%   25–50%

10 – 25%   over 50%

Fig. 170. The proportion of state officials in general becomes greater toward the east. They were almost all Germans and came from outside the region. Data from *Statistisches Jahrbuch für den Preussischen Staat.* Drawn from a manuscript map by Romer, with permission.

tect itself from foreign attack at Danzig, close and reopen the port in case of danger, maintain a state official there to look out for national interests, and share to a moderate degree in the revenues, chiefly those derived from shipping. On the other hand, the free city could be represented in the Polish Diet on great occasions; and it enjoyed full religious freedom, coined money, and controlled the navigation of the natural waterways of the city.

Government of the new Free City of Danzig

The internationalized state, or Free City, of today has a High Commissioner appointed by the Council of the League of Nations. The boundaries of the Free City (which include both the city and the district about it) correspond roughly with the limits of German population, so that there will be the least possible cause for friction between two antagonistic racial elements. This, of course, gives the Poles not quite the entire length of the river, but at the same time it does give them a chance to get it in the future; for if Danzig is in truth to be the commercial focus of the new Poland, as it has become the only large seaport, its population will inevitably change from German to Polish, and new provisions will be made for giving Poland a still larger interest in its management. The population of the Danzig Free City zone is about 300,000, of which more than half resides in Danzig and Neufahrwasser.

The future port of Danzig

The port of Danzig without doubt will be rapidly improved by the nations responsible for its government. While Neufahrwasser is the port for Danzig (inset, Fig. 173), ocean-going steamers can also go to Danzig direct. Through Danzig will come cotton and wool for Polish mills, machine tools for the manufacture of machinery needed in Polish industries, agricultural implements, Swedish iron ore, Norwegian fish, and all the varied products, not made in Poland, of foreign mills and

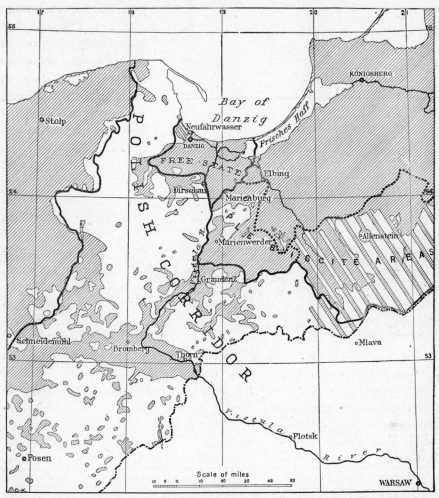

Fig. 171. Ethnography in the Polish Corridor, focus of conflict between Poland and Germany. The shaded areas represent German-speaking majorities; the blank areas, Polish majorities. Solid heavy lines, present boundaries; dotted line, plebiscite boundary; dot-and-dash line, Russo-German boundary of 1914. The Marienwerder and Allenstein plebiscite areas have voted for union with Germany.

factories. Down to the port will go, by way of the Vistula and the bordering railways, timber, salt, cement, hay, sugar from the beet sugar farms in which Poland has excelled, grain, and distinctive wares of Polish manufacture. It is noteworthy that though its rail connections never have been particularly favorable, the city's rail traffic tonnage before the war was about five times its river traffic, if we exclude the lumber rafts and floats on the Vistula. The improvement of the Vistula and a reorganization of the facilities of transport are required to make Danzig a great Polish port.

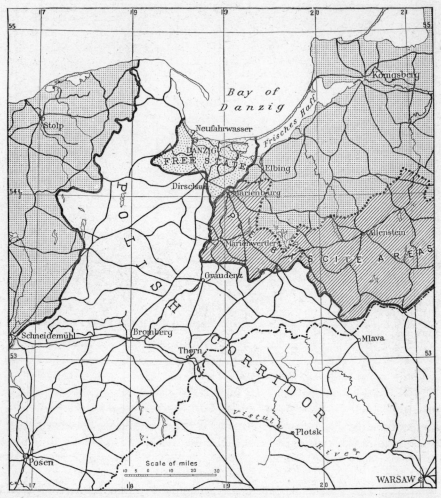

Fig. 172. Railways in the Polish Corridor, suggesting the difficulties of separating East Prussia from the rest of Germany and the equally great difficulties involved in depriving Poland of a maritime outlet by way of the Vistula.

In the second half of 1919 a large number of new firms established themselves in Danzig in anticipation of the future importance of the free city as Poland's outlet to the sea.   Most of the new firms were of German origin, many of them being branches of houses that had had no representatives at Danzig.   Others came from Poland, from Scandinavia, and from the Netherlands.   Only one American firm, one French, and two British shipping firms were reported, besides a branch of the British Trade Corporation with a general banking and insurance business.   There are at least eight steamship lines established between Danzig and English ports, the trade with England

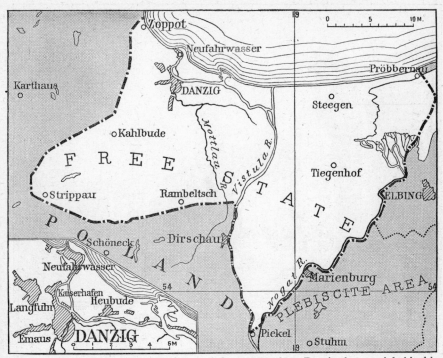

FIG. 173. By the treaty of Versailles most of the country about Danzig that was inhabited by Germans was united to Danzig to form a Free City, named Free State in the map above. It is not a "city" in the ordinary sense of the word. The inset shows details of the port and suburbs of Danzig.

consisting chiefly in the export of timber and sugar and the import of coal and herring. The imported coal is used mainly in Danzig itself, since it cannot compete farther inland with the coal of southern Poland.

ON THE WESTERN BOUNDARY

South of the Free City, or State, of Danzig under Allied control, Poles and Germans face each other on the Vistula, where the historic struggle between the two races is bound to continue. Their common boundary is twenty-five miles long, and some sort of international supervision seemed necessary if both were to use the river. While the Poles own both banks, German access is assured, for Article 18 of the minorities treaty between Poland and the Allied and Associated Powers provides for the application to the Vistula, including the Bug and the Narew (Fig. 168), a branch of the Bug entering it near Warsaw, of the international waterways régime as established in the treaty of peace with Germany.

Commerce on the Vistula has not yet been developed on a large scale. For commercial, political, and sentimental reasons, however,

Poles and Germans again facing each other across the Vistula

International Film Service

FIG. 174.   Part of the water front at Danzig.

the Poles will quickly begin the improvement of the river, since it is their main stream.   Poland embraces nearly the whole watershed of the Vistula (Fig. 169).

The Vistula in need of many improvements

Large sums of money will be needed for dredging and diking.   The course of the stream is "braided" in places; that is, it is broken up into separate currents or channels by shifting sand bars, notably near Thorn.   Ice rafts lodge upon the bars in winter and block the channel. From Thorn to the Baltic the river never has less than three feet of water; but the difference in level between high and low water is here from twenty to twenty-five feet.   Dredging and partial canalization are needed to deepen the main channel and thus permit the use of large river and canal boats, as on the Rhine, the Rhone, and the Seine. Improvements are now projected which would enable vessels of a thousand tons' capacity to reach Warsaw.

Canals to connect with other hydrographic systems

The improvement of the Vistula would also permit the construction of branch canals.   The Mazurian lakes lie near some of the eastern tributaries of the Vistula, and have several hundred miles of navigable waterways that could be utilized.   In a similar way the Russian rivers have been brought within reach of the Vistula system (Fig. 168).   The Netze and the Vistula on the western Polish frontier are already connected by the Bromberg canal, as shown in the same figure.

A preliminary economic agreement has been signed between Poland and the Free City of Danzig. Among its main provisions are the following:

(1) Danzig and Poland form a single customs territory so that customs are not levied on goods passing from one to the other.

(2) Danzig will collect and pay over to Poland duties on goods for Poland originating outside of Danzig and passing through that port.

(3) Coöperation is assured in the use of railways, since Danzig is in part dependent on Polish lines and, until a new line is built, Poland can reach parts of its Baltic territory northwest of Danzig only by crossing the Free City territory.

(4) Danzig guarantees Poland all necessary shipping facilities and permits importation of war material destined for Poland.

(5) There is ample provision for the free and early development of adequate postal, telegraphic, and telephonic service between Warsaw and other Polish towns and Danzig.

POLISH AUTHORITY IN EASTERN GALICIA

On Poland's southeastern frontier lies the former Austrian province of Galicia, and there Poland faces one of her major problems. The western half is Polish, the eastern half Ruthenian. To differences of race are added differences of religion: the Poles are Roman Catholic; the Ruthenians are Greek Orthodox Uniate. The culture of Eastern Galicia is Polish, and Poles form the chief population of the towns; no other section of the Polish people is more ardently Polish in nationality. It is the seat of a large university (Lemberg). Hardly any other part of Polish territory has published so high a percentage of Polish books and newspapers. *Polish traditions in Eastern Galicia*

The Ruthenians, who form the majority (59 per cent) of the population of Eastern Galicia, are closely allied to the Ukrainians or Russians rather than to the Poles. Lemberg and other similar districts are Polish islands set in a Ruthenian sea. The Ukrainians and Russians wish to unite with them all people classed as Ruthenian: the Poles ask to have recognized their predominant culture and former ownership, and especially to have their territory extended southward so as to join with Rumania (Fig. 2). The territorial junction with Rumania would give these two countries better defense against a Bolshevist penetration of central Europe; it would provide what is *Contest between the Poles and Ukrainians in Eastern Galicia* called a military "barrage," or "sanitary cordon," all the way from the Baltic to the Black Sea, for a time one of the main objects in the Polish and even the Allied program.

The Ruthenians of Eastern Galicia unquestionably desire union with a democratic Russia. On account of Polish persecutions, they do not wish to unite with Poland. But Eastern Galicia has been unable to keep order within its own house, and so far as an intelligent class exists, it is composed almost wholly of Poles, who form 27 per cent of the population.

Foreign capitalists are especially interested in the oil fields of Eastern Galicia (Fig. 175), and political interest in this district is correspondingly keen. Of $65,000,000 invested in oil land and refineries there, $50,000,000 is British, $10,000,000 French, and $5,000,000 Belgian. According as they are friends of Poland or of Russia will these nations be likely to favor one or the other in deciding the ultimate fate of this valuable territory.

The most important oil pools lie in the foothills of the Carpathians. The wells are operated by trained Polish workmen. Now every new state is vitally interested in its future fuel supply, because with this goes the growth of manufacturing and commerce and, in general, better material existence for its industrial population. Junction with Rumania would give Poland control over the headwaters of the Dniester and permit the shipment of oil and other goods to ports on the Black Sea.

The problem of Eastern Galicia is further complicated by the historical division that existed between Eastern and Western Galicia as early as the 10th and 11th centuries. We shall not here trace this division in detail. The matter entered its modern phase in 1848, when a Ukrainian movement began in Austria that had for its object the creation of the eastern part of Galicia as a separate province. For several years there was much controversy with the Poles over the question; but in 1867 Austria made the whole of Galicia a single province with a common assembly, or Diet.

Since that time the Poles have become dominant in Galician affairs. They live chiefly in the towns, while the Ruthenian population is for the most part agricultural. Of the Ruthenians more than 60 per cent are illiterate, of the Poles 23 per cent only. The Poles naturally lead in the professions and in commerce. They have controlled administration, courts, and education, and have obtained much of the land. Their methods have not always been above reproach. The struggle was one of those minor contests of nationality that were overshadowed

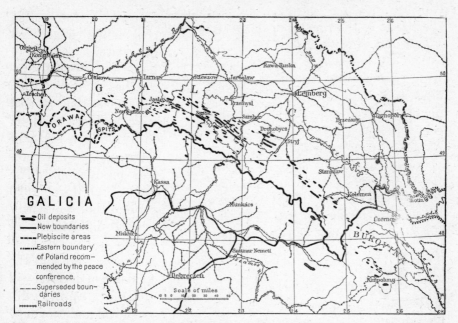

Fig. 175. Distribution of known oil deposits in Galicia, with railroad lines related thereto. The recommended eastern boundary of Poland was designed to be temporary. For further details respecting the boundaries of Poland and its neighbors, see Figure 169. Oil deposits after Redwood, *A Treatise on Petroleum*, 3d ed., 1913, Vol. I.

in the past by the common antagonism of all subject races to the central government of Austria-Hungary.

According to the terms of a proposed treaty between Poland and the Allied and Associated Powers, Eastern Galicia was to have an autonomous government within the Polish state, freedom of speech, press, and assembly, and a single-chamber Diet, elected every five years by universal suffrage. The final status of the district has yet to be determined. In view of Poland's recent treaty with Russia (Riga, 1920) there seems little doubt that Eastern Galicia will be incorporated eventually as an integral part of the Polish state.

Treaty with Poland concerning Eastern Galicia

THE PLEBISCITE AREAS

The ownership of a large part of the Polish borderland was determined by plebiscite in three districts: (1) Mazuria, which comprises the whole of the District of Allenstein, and which voted overwhelmingly to remain German; (2) the part of West Prussia that lies east of the Vistula, which also voted to remain German; and (3) a part of Silesia, which, except in a few districts, voted to remain German. The case of Silesia is peculiarly important, for the

Plebiscites determining part of the boundary of Poland

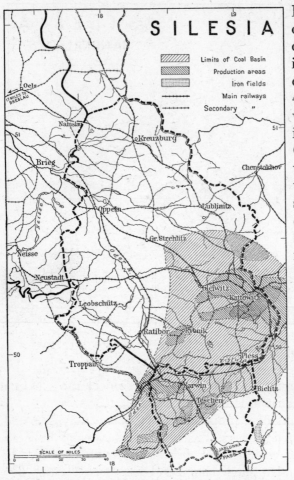

SILESIA

Limits of Coal Basin
Production areas
Iron fields
Main railways
Secondary　　"

17 MILES TO
BRESLAU

Oels

Namslau

Kreuzburg

Brieg

Chenstokhov

Oppeln

Lublinitz

Gr. Strehlitz

Neisse

Neustadt

Gleiwitz

Kattowitz

Leobschütz

Ratibor

Rybnik

Troppau

Pless

Karwin

Bielitz

Teschen

JABLUNKA
PASS

SCALE OF MILES
0　10　20　30　40

Contest for the coking coal of Teschen

FIG. 176. Coal and iron deposits and railways of the disputed areas of Teschen and Silesia. In the mineral districts both main and secondary railways are shown, elsewhere only main railways. The Silesian plebiscite was held on 20 March 1921. The Teschen dispute was transferred from the plebiscite commission to the Council of Ambassaders (footnote, page 347). If their recommendations are confirmed, Poland will retain the town of Teschen and all territory east of the principal north-south railway; Czecho-Slovakia will obtain the railway and all territory west of it (Fig. 179). Coal from various maps accompanying *Handbuch des oberschlesischen Industriebezirks*, XII, *Allgemeiner deutscher Bergmannstag, Festschrift*, Band II. Iron from F. Bamburg, *Schulkarte zur Kultur-Wirtschafts und Handels-Geographie von Deutschland*, 1 : 750,000, 1913.

Prussian state-owned coal mines might become the center of important Polish industries. More than 45,000,000 tons of coal were produced in Silesia in 1913, or a sixth of Germany's total pre-war production. The vote of 20 March 1920 showed that a majority of the inhabitants of Silesia preferred German ownership, but the final line of division will depend upon geographical and economic conditions as well as the plebiscite. In Mazuria, Poland lost a large element which is Polish in speech and race, but Protestant-Lutheran rather than Catholic like the majority of Poles.

Teschen

The former Duchy of Teschen (Fig. 178) has had a singularly important part to play in Polish affairs. Here is the source of supply of coking coal for both Poland and Czecho-Slovakia. But Poland has large deposits of higher-grade bituminous coal, while Czecho-Slovakia has lower-grade bituminous coal and deposits of inferior brown lignite. In addition, the coal mines of Teschen lie in the western third of that district, just where the Czech population lives.

It was decided to attempt agreement between Poland and Czecho-Slovakia, through the Council of Ambassadors, established by the Allies. By the terms of the preliminary agreement the larger western part of Teschen would go to Czecho-Slovakia and the rest to Poland; the Polish part includes the headwaters of the Vistula, where these take their rise in the Tatra, the lofty northern summits of the Carpathians. If the agreement is confirmed, Czecho-Slovakia will own the coal mines but will deliver a part of the output to Poland. The central railway would go to Czecho-Slovakia, while Poland would secure the town of Teschen.

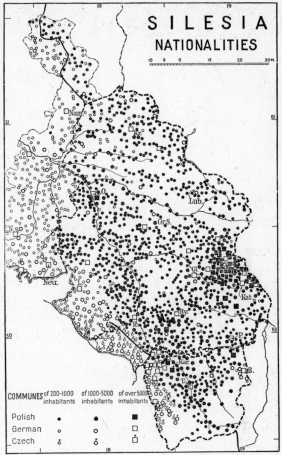

FIG. 177. Ethnic distributions in Silesia and Teschen. The boundary of the Silesian plebiscite area (heavy broken line) takes in only a part of German Silesia. For general comparison and key to names see Figure 176. After Romer, *Travaux géographiques*, Vol. IV, 1919.

Associated with the Teschen settlement were the two districts of Orawa and Spits, which have small groups of Polish people that Poland wished to include. By a decision of the Council of Ambassadors [1] the territorial limits were recommended as shown in Figure 179. In Orawa the new boundary is located southward of the main Carpathian divide; in Spits it is located north of the divide. As in the Teschen dispute, the matter awaits final decision, the Polish Diet, or Parliament, having so far (April 1921) withheld its approval in the hope of securing a larger share of the Teschen coal.

---

[1] The Council of Ambassadors, composed of Allied ambassadors, was organized after the Peace Conference of Paris early in 1920. Its chief function is to execute the treaties of peace. In addition there have been various conferences of Allied premiers at San Remo, Hythe, Boulogne, etc.

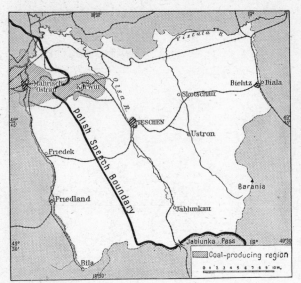

FIG. 178.   The Teschen region, ownership of which is in dispute between Poland and Czecho-Slovakia.   For preliminary boundary see Figure 179; for general relations see Figure 167.

MILITARISM AND THE FRONTIER PROBLEMS

Dangers of militarism

Everywhere the frontiers of Poland are on the open plain except in the south, where the high Carpathians form a natural common frontier between Poland and Czecho-Slovakia. Nothing therefore could be clearer than that Poland should strive to win the friendship of her neighbors. She has to choose between two courses of action. If she becomes militaristic, like the Prussians, she, like them, may be strong for a time, only to fall a victim to her own strength. To be sure, a limited army is necessary to prevent her from being helpless in case of wanton attack.

Fear as a basic cause of war

The old argument that "we are hemmed about by enemies" and that open plains everywhere invite attack was the stock in trade of the war party of Berlin. If leaders can get their people to believe it and to become sufficiently "jumpy" about it, they can impose heavy taxes for large armies that are meant, not for the defense of the country, but for aggrandizement and the satisfaction of greed, until at last, having dug a pit for others, they fall into it themselves. The Polish army now numbers nearly 800,000, which, in the ratio of the two population totals, would correspond to an army of 3,500,000 or 4,000,000 for the United States. Beginning her new national life without a debt of great consequence, Poland has a chance to be free. If her army continues big, her debt will rise; her neck will be placed in a yoke from which centuries of effort may not free her.

Poland potentially a wealthy nation

If she chooses the road of reason, Poland may become a great state. She starts with a population of 25,000,000, or more than that of Spain and about as large as that of Brazil. Her territory is drained chiefly by a single large stream capable of improvement from the Baltic to Warsaw and far beyond. Her forests have an extent of about 300,000 square miles. Her soil has long been famous for its fertility. There

F𝐈𝐆. 179. Division of disputed territory in the three districts of Teschen, Orawa, and Spits. The Teschen settlement is now awaiting the approval of the Polish Diet (page 347). For details of the Teschen area, see Figures 176 and 178.

is abundant water power in the glaciated northern regions and in the Carpathians on the south, where large, swift streams flow through dense forests before reaching the agricultural plain.

INTERNAL PROBLEMS

Industrial Recovery

Poland's immediate problem is to secure sufficient credit to start her mills, factories, and mines. Warsaw, a city of 900,000 people, had its machinery largely destroyed or stolen by the Germans. The same fate was suffered by Lodz, one of the great textile cities of the world and often called the "Manchester" of Poland. Germany set out to cripple Polish industry. It will take money and credit to revive it. Lodz alone requires $10,000,000 merely to purchase the necessary machinery.

Need for credit to start industries

The Lodz factories have a higher production than any others. A quarter of the Polish cotton and woolen mills had resumed operation by the summer of 1920. Every month Poland must import 4000 tons of cotton, 2000 tons of wool, and 13,000 tons of jute, to supply her textile factories. Credit for raw materials is the largest present need of Poland.

There are rich deposits of salt, potash, zinc, lead, and oil, all likewise dependent for their development upon credits and railways,

Fig. 180. Boundary complications of Poland's borderlands. The approximate limits of the Ukraine are shown by a heavy broken line. Note that Poland's eastern frontier as established at the Riga peace conference with Soviet Russia extends northward to the Dvina and cuts off Lithuania from contact with Russia. For the settlement of the three small areas of Teschen, Orawa, and Spits in southwestern Poland (numbered 2, 3, and 4) see Figure 179. The area numbered 1 is the Silesian plebiscite area. The Polish-Ukrainian agreement referred to in the legend is that of April 1920.

security of life and property, and stability of government. Poland's natural resources can be developed only when the agencies of commerce are organized, and especially when the railroads are put into sound condition and coal production has risen to correspond with the manufacturing needs of the country.

Displacement of Population

Devastated region of Eastern Poland

During the World War the territory of Poland was overrun first by the Russians and then by the Germans and Austrians. The effect was wholly to depopulate large tracts. Still farther east the country was in part denuded by the Bolshevists of everything necessary for living. What was once the seat of a dense farming population became a desert. People flocked to the cities and there increased the number of idle, restless, and desperate elements, already large because of unemployment, for the Germans had taken away all the spindles and gear from the mills and in many cases burned or blown up the factory buildings.

If we use the ordinary terms for Polish suffering, it is difficult to describe the broad zone at and beyond the eastern borders of the Famine zone east of ethnic Poland country, inhabited by Lithuanians, White Russians, Ukrainians, and Jews, which almost down to the present has remained a sparsely populated desert, following its devastation by Grand Duke Nicholas during the Russian retreat, in the autumn of 1915. The famine zone begins at Brest-Litovsk. Factories are idle, streets deserted, shops closed, because there is nothing to sell. People live principally on the cheapest vegetables. Fuel is hardly to be had at all. The death rate rose from 15 per 1000 in 1914 to 29 per 1000 in 1919 in the town of Pinsk.

The wave of agricultural population now spreading eastward from Changing ethnography of eastern Poland the cities to occupy the land is of different ethnic character from the old population. Although many of the former residents are returning to their old firesides, many others have been killed, and some have emigrated, with the result that for many years, or until a new census is taken, all maps of eastern Poland showing density of population and ethnic distributions will be mere guesses based on local statistics and the reports of travelers.

Three Unlike Sections

One of the difficulties of the new government of Poland is to weld Problem of welding three un- like sec- tions together three unlike sections. There were really three Polands — German Poland centering at Posen, Russian Poland centering at War- saw, and Austrian, or Galician, Poland centering at Cracow and Przemysl.[1] Under normal conditions these three could supplement each other; but at the end of the war they were administratively and commercially unorganized, and the railroads and rolling stock were in bad condition, so that one part was enduring famine whilst another had an abundance of foodstuffs. Industrial disorganiza- tion and unemployment were the two chief troubles. The three sec- tions are also unlike socially and politically. German Poland is the most progressive and prosperous section, Congress (Russian) Poland has a population less alert, and Austrian Poland has, in part, a large low-grade population of Ruthenians.

Proportional to its industries and the density of its population, that part of Poland that was included in Russia had few railroads,

---

[1] At the time of the outbreak of the World War in 1914, the territory and population of ethnographic Poland were divided about as follows: Russia, 45,000 square miles, 12,000,000 inhabitants; Germany, 22,500 square miles, 4,000,000 inhabitants; Austria, 11,000 square miles, 5,000,000 inhabitants.

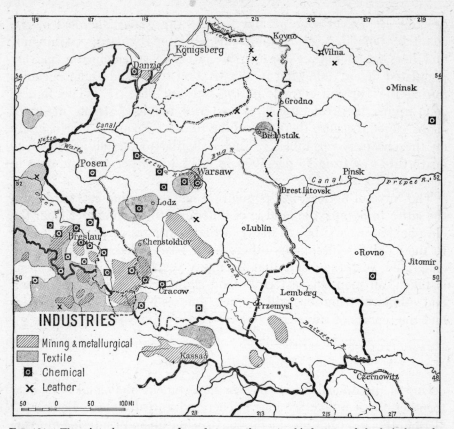

FIG. 181. There is a close correspondence between the seats of industry and the foci of population as shown in Figure 168. Based on Romer, *Atlas géographique et statistique de la Pologne*, 1916, Pl. 30, supplemented by Andree, *Handatlas*, Pl. 40.

Production and emigration in former Russian Poland

and the cart roads were little better than tracks. Agriculture was backward and crop production low. The Polish peasant in many districts lived more primitively than any other class of people in central Europe. In some regions where production was highest there were no foodstuffs for export, farms being small and families large. From the standpoint of its actual industrial development, Russian Poland was overpopulated, and the mass of the population survived only because of the relief afforded by a continuous stream of emigration. In 1913 there came to the United States 174,000 Russian Poles (excluding Jews), and there was heavy seasonal migration, more than 350,000 Poles going to Germany to work on German farms in the summer months during the year just before the World War, and about 50,000 to other countries. A similar migration of Poles took place to and from the Westphalian coal fields of Germany.

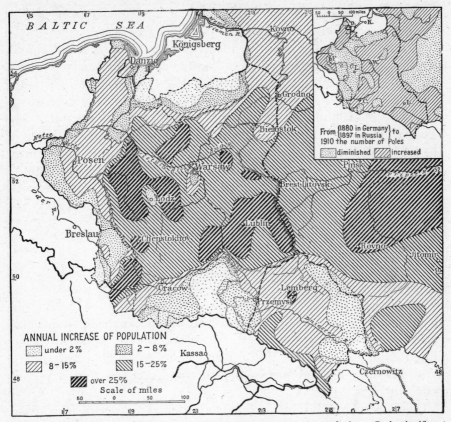

Fig. 182. Note that Russian Poland had the greatest increase of population. It is significant in relation to Polish claims and ambitions on the east that Poles have increased in Eastern Galicia and in general in the belt of country just east of the line recommended by the Peace Conference at Paris (heavy broken line). Such a tendency might ultimately change the ethnic situation. Based on Romer, *Atlas géographique et statistique de la Pologne*, 1916, Pls. 7 and 11.

Having rich mineral resources, Galicia, or Austrian Poland, is well supplied with railways. The same is true of German Poland, where industrial development had been carried far, especially in the Posen district. In the latter the number of textile factories had increased between 1901 and 1910 by 87 per cent and the output by 65 per cent.

The Land Situation

Most of Poland is a land of farms. The agricultural population is greater in numbers to the square mile (190 for Congress Poland) than in any of the other countries of Europe save Italy, Belgium, and Holland (Fig. 168). It is a compact and, to this extent, a powerful nation. The area of ethnographic Poland is about 80,000 square miles, or 40 per cent as great as Spain, or twice the state of Ohio.

Poland a compact nation

Like their neighbors, the Poles have a land question of serious aspect. Among large landholders, 18,000 own 40 per cent of the total area of Poland and leave much of their holdings uncultivated, with resultant overcrowding of adjacent agricultural communities. To better the conditions of life, the Polish Diet in July 1920 voted drastic land partition laws. But even this action will not give everybody a piece of land, nor will it necessarily increase production. The new law permits the Polish General Land Office to take the lands of the former Prussian Colonization Commission and other government owned land, as well as large privately held estates, and sell them to actual farmers, with preference to soldiers wounded in the war. Depending upon location, the maximum size of farms may not exceed 150, 450, and 600 acres.

The Jewish Population

How Poland became a refuge for the Jews

The most serious racial problem in Poland concerns the Jew. He is more numerous there than in any other country in the world except Russia. During the 14th and 15th centuries the Jews came to Poland in great numbers, partly because of expulsion from many other European countries, partly to escape almost universal persecution elsewhere. In the 18th century many came from Austria and West Prussia. Poland was one of the few countries that never expelled the Jew.

Jewish rights and restrictions

Then the Jews became so numerous and powerful that they secured a general assembly in 1600 to apportion taxes among Jewish citizens and protect the rights of the race, and this continued until 1764. Jews competed with Christians in commerce and in the crafts with such success that eventually they were restricted by law. For example: in Galicia they were forbidden to be grain dealers; they could not export salt or deal in alcohol; their artisans could not be employed by Christians. By 1895, while only 14 per cent of the total population of Russian Poland were Jewish, 84 per cent of the merchants were Jews, 20 per cent of the literary men, 51 per cent of the educators, and 24 per cent of the physicians. Only 2 per cent of the farmers, factory workers, and miners were Jews. (From Russian census reports of 1897.)

Jewish desire for a state within a state

The main difficulty of the problem springs from the lack of national feeling among Jews. Throughout Poland's history they have worked rather for racial rights than for national revolutionary aims. In 1907 they opposed the Polish national parties and contributed to a Socialist victory.

In 1919 the problem entered a new phase with the disorders at Recent disorders involving the Jew Vilna and elsewhere. The Polish Jew had not thrown himself wholeheartedly into the development of the new state. It was natural that the patriotic Pole should view his new-found freedom with ardent feeling and should have little toleration for any race that resisted the strong tides of nationalism. Better relations have now been established, and there need be no further political importance in the Jewish problem if religious liberty is guaranteed and the Jew attempts to seek no special political rights.

In common with the states of Rumania, Greece, Jugo-Slavia, The minorities treaties Czecho-Slovakia, Austria, and Hungary, Poland signed a minorities treaty with the Allied and Associated Powers.[1] The matter is especially important for Poland in relation to the Jews. Article 10 provides that educational committees shall be appointed locally by the Jewish communities of Poland and shall be subject to the general control of the state; it provides for the distribution of the proportional share of the public funds allotted to Jewish schools, and for the Special provisions in the Polish treaty organization and management of these schools. Article 11 requires that Jews shall not be compelled to perform any act which constitutes a violation of their Sabbath, the only exceptions being in case of military service or the preservation of public order. Poland will refrain from holding elections, either general or ocal, on Saturday.

POLAND'S RELATIONS WITH FRANCE AND GREAT BRITAIN

France has taken a keener interest in the new Poland than has France deeply interested in Poland's welfare any other nation. The French wish Poland to be both free and strong, and thus provide a powerful ally in case of future trouble with Germany, one favorably placed to strike with France on either side. This explains the encouragement given in France (1916–1919) to the organization and equipment of the Polish Legion, the use of French instructors in Haller's army, which was trained in France and entered Poland in 1919, and French diplomatic aid to Poland. It will explain much in the international arrangements of Europe in the future. Trade agreements with Poland will reflect French interest, for French goods have not been sold widely in the former Russian Empire. Moreover, there is a historic cultural basis for the friendship of the two peoples. French and Polish artists and men of letters have long

---

[1] In common with the other states that signed the minorities treaties, Poland must give equality of trade conditions to the Allied and Associated Powers, and, in addition, she agrees to the application to the Vistula, the Bug, and the Narew rivers of the international waterways régime as set forth in the treaty of Versailles.

had a marked community of sentiment and interest. Henry of Valois, Duke of Anjou, was invited to become King of Poland, and reigned at Warsaw for a few years before he became Henry III, King of France. Napoleon revived Polish nationality for a brief period (Duchy of Warsaw, 1807–1815). One of the four best collections of Polish books outside Poland was established in Paris by the poet Mickiewicz and is still directed by his son. (The three others are at Petrograd in Russia, at Rapperswil in Switzerland, and in the British Museum at London.)

British naval and commercial interests in Danzig and Poland

British economic interest in Poland is expressed in three ways:

(1) Desire to have a British High Commissioner at Danzig.

(2) Heavy British investments at Danzig and in the Galician oil fields.

(3) British-held stock in the factories and mills of Lodz and in the coal companies of the south and southwest.

With Danzig an active commercial center and eventually a large city, and with British naval strength capable of controlling the city's government in time of war, Great Britain may be said to have won a commercial victory by securing a free-city régime for Danzig. She followed steadfastly the policy of not allowing it to return to Germany, nor would she consent to Polish sovereignty.

The French and British policies, opposed as they are with reference to all things Polish, were thrown into sharper contrast when, beginning in March 1921, the Silesian disorders became a matter of international concern because of their relation to the reparation payments. The German government sought to delay beyond May 1921 an agreement on reparations required by the treaty of Versailles, saying that the fate of the mineral wealth of Silesia was related to the amount of the payments Germany could make. An ultimatum from the Allies brought Germany to terms and the Silesian problem will have an independent settlement. But the problems of both Silesia and Danzig cannot be settled by fiat. In the years ahead French and British policies may be expected to clash again and again in these key situations, and full advantage will doubtless be taken by Germany of the political possibilities of impending disagreements.

CHAPTER TWENTY

LITHUANIAN DEVELOPMENT AND RELATIONS

THE Lithuanians are a weak people politically, though numbering more than 2,000,000, and including up to 4,000,000 of population in their territorial claims. Historically they have had close relations with Poland; yet they now fiercely hate the Poles. Ethnically they grade into Russians on the east; yet they desire nothing else so little as a return to Russian domination. Commercially they are disorganized, undeveloped, dependent; yet they wish independence and a hold upon the trade of Russia that normally flows in large volume through the Lithuanian port of Memel. A brief review of their historical struggle and their geographical environment is needed to understand their present anomalous political situation.

Present weakness of Lithuania

EXPANSION OF LITHUANIA

For centuries the Lithuanian pagan tribes occupied a part of the Baltic fringe of eastern Europe, and their settlements extended inland only to Kovno on the Niemen (Fig. 183). They were shut off from the people about them by the heavy forests of the region and by the innumerable lakes and marshes. When the forests were partly cleared away and a commerce had developed, strong covetous neighbors invaded the land, for there are no mountain barriers — it is a plains country throughout — and the coast is easily accessible to other Baltic states. In the 13th century came the first invaders, the Teutonic Knights (page 362). Hard pressed by the newcomers, the Lithuanians withdrew from the coast and rapidly extended their eastern limits.

Coming of the Teutonic Knights

The power of the nation seemed to grow in proportion to its difficulties. From a small state of 30,000 square miles in 1263, it became a large nation of 250,000 square miles in 1385 (Fig. 183). In little more than a hundred years, Lithuania pushed its southern frontier to the Black Sea. It controlled the entire Dnieper and the Niemen, one of the great historical highways across Europe during the centuries before. This brought it to the Polish frontiers, and eventually it joined the Polish state.

Former greatness and extent

THE UNION WITH POLAND

The union of Lithuania and Poland in 1386 was a personal union through the king, who was as much the king of Lithuania as of Poland. This lasted until 1569, when there was effected a closer union

357

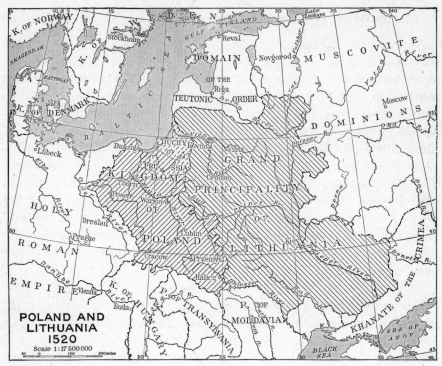

FIG. 183. Based on Droysen, *Allgemeiner Historische Handatlas*, Pl. 37.   From the *Geographical Review*, Vol. 4, 1917.

through a common Diet, with Lithuania still keeping a separate army and treasury and having its own administration.   In 1691 the former distinction between the Grand Duchy of Lithuania and the Polish state was abolished.   Thereafter there was to be a common administration, one army, and one treasury.

Thus Lithuania was assured the support of Poland, at first against the Teutonic Knights and later against the growing Muscovite power, and was able to preserve its western civilization against the rising tide of oriental influence.   Had Poland remained independent, the fusion of Polish and Lithuanian peoples would probably have been uninterrupted and the present antagonism between them would not exist.   Nationalism has been carried so far that most groups, however small, seek separate existence.

Revival of national sentiment in the 18th and 19th centuries   In the 18th century a great educational movement began, which resulted in the printing of grammars, dictionaries, poems, stories, etc.   In the 19th century came a further revival of national sentiment, and the publication of newspapers, folklore, ballads, and fables.   All these publications were greatly stimulated by the religious spirit of the times.

FATE OF LITHUANIA IN THE PARTITIONS OF POLAND

At the time of the partitions of Poland (1772–1795), the greater part of Lithuania came into the hands of Russia, which organized it as a province and put a governor in charge. The land-owning nobles were left in local control. In 1831 and 1863 the Lithuanian and Polish higher classes revolted against Russia, whereupon the Russian government confiscated many of the large estates of the nobles and divided the land among the peasants, exiling the revolutionists. After 1864 the printing of Lithuanian books in Latin script was prohibited. The Russian language was made obligatory in the schools and in official reports and documents. The government seized Lithuanian books printed in Germany or Austria and imported into Lithuania. In 1905 a Lithuanian congress met at Vilna and protested against the acts of the Russian government, demanding Lithuanian autonomy and the use of the Lithuanian language. *Russian rule in Lithuania*

In that portion of Lithuanian territory which lay north of the Niemen and which was included in East Prussia, the Germans have carried on the usual Germanizing process (Frederic William I, in the 18th century, sent several thousand colonists into the country), but the region has remained strongly Lithuanian despite their efforts. In 1844 the Lithuanian language was forbidden, but later it was permitted in the schools for instruction. In 1896 it was decreed that German was the official language. *The Lithuanians of East Prussia*

THE ECONOMIC BASIS

Lithuania is without mineral deposits of commercial importance and must depend primarily upon its forests and crops for means of livelihood and commerce. The chief occupation is a primitive type of agriculture, with cereals, flax, and potatoes as the principal products. Not more than half the tillable land was formerly owned by the peasants. The population consists mostly of small farmers. Since the organization of the provisional government of Lithuania, most of the landed estates have been seized and divided among the peasants.

One of the great difficulties of a state of this character is to develop products which industrial nations want and which create a trade balance, for this makes possible the purchase of foreign wares like machinery, shoes, cloth, and special articles of food. The only way in which Lithuania can obtain such a trade balance is to sell its raw products, of which the most important in value are flax, rye, and flaxseed, in the order named. Its transportation conditions are still poor. *Need of a favorable trade balance*

The part nearest East Prussia has almost no good roads, though its soil is more fertile than that of any other part of the country.

The commercial organizations are almost wholly in the hands of foreigners — Jews especially, and Germans. Lithuania was a part of the Jewish Pale (Fig. 192), and the towns are more Jewish than those of Poland. Vilna is often called the Jerusalem of Lithuania.

PRESENT TERRITORIAL AND POLITICAL PROBLEMS

The Niemen, an old Lithuanian frontier

While a good many Lithuanians live south of the Niemen (or Memel), they form a large majority north of that river at the tip of East Prussia, and it was this section, including the port of Memel, that, by the treaty of Versailles, Germany ceded to the Allied and Associated Powers, by them presumably to be turned over to Lithuania. The Niemen is to the Lithuanians what the Danube is to the Rumanians and the Rhine to the French.

> The Niemen separates the Lithuanians from their foes:
> .   .   .   .
> On this side throngs of Lithuanian youths,
> .   .   .   .
> On the other, in helmet and armor,
> The Germans on horseback stand immovable.
> Each party watches the crossing.
> So the Niemen, once famed for hospitality,
> That linked the realms of fraternal nations,
> Now for them has become the threshold of eternity
> For none without loss of life or liberty
> Could cross the forbidden waters.
>
> ADAM MICKIEWICZ, *Konrad Wallenrod*

Disputed boundaries of Lithuania

The territorial and political problems include the settlement of the disputed boundary between Poland and Lithuania in the Suwalki region and in the provinces of Vilna and Kovno. A disputed boundary also exists on the east, where Lithuanians and White Russians merge into each other without strong ethnic distinctions. Here is a region fertile in political disputes. No one can say with certainty what are the distinctions between Lithuanians, Poles, and Russians. A demarcation line had to be established in 1919, as shown on Figure 180, to prevent fighting between Poles and Lithuanians, and no arrangement has yet been made between Lithuania and Russia. It is just here that the Poles wish to extend their territory according to their eastern program and the preliminary treaty with Soviet Russia, signed at Riga in October 1920. If confirmed by a later treaty with a permanent or an All-Russian government, the present treaty will interpose a belt of Polish territory along Lithuania's hinterland and put Poland in a favorable strategic position with respect to Russia's Baltic trade. Territorial and commercial restriction of this sort has been Lithuania's apprehension, and she may be expected to oppose it with all her strength.

The population of the disputed zone has little political self-consciousness. Its outlook has been admirably summarized by Golder: *Hopes of the people*

This brings us to the question of the common people. How about them? What do they think and how do they feel on these matters? On the border districts many of the inhabitants do not know and do not care to what nationality they belong. For generations Polish, Lithuanian, and Russian peasants have lived side by side, have intermarried, have laughed over the same joys, and have wept over the same sorrows. They have even a 'common speech' which is different from any one of the three national languages. For generations they have been exploited by Lithuanian, Polish, and Russian landlords, and they have not much love for any of them. The poor peasants are not interested either in cultural development or in national independence; many of them do not even understand the meaning of these words. What they want is steady work, good wages, and plenty to eat. They hate landlords of all nationalities, and they have no reason to think that a bishop of their own people would treat them with more consideration than one of another people. Ninety per cent of every nationality in Europe is more interested in social than national problems, in the question of food and wages than in culture and independence.

It might be to the interest of Lithuania to combine with either Esthonia or Latvia, or both, and form a confederation (page 368); for the Letts are closely related to the Lithuanians in language, race, and customs, and their economic and political problems are about the same. The danger of political exploitation by the German barons is always real. But it would probably be lessened by a confederation which would permit the ready flow of information and would probably increase the number and effectiveness of joint proposals to end foreign domination. *A possible Baltic Confederation*

The status of Lithuania itself has not yet been settled. While it seeks independence, no final recognition can be made until Russia, of which it once formed a part, is orderly again. The present provisional government is strongly anti-Polish, but there is no doubt that if Lithuania voluntarily joins Russia, it will be only on the basis of a large local autonomy. *Fate of Lithuania still undetermined*

CHAPTER TWENTY-ONE

LAND TENURE AND TRADE OUTLETS IN ESTHONIA AND LATVIA — THE FORMER BALTIC PROVINCES

AT the beginning of the World War, Esthonia, Livonia, and Courland, known as the Baltic Provinces, were parts of the Russian Empire. The people of the region have now formed two states: (1) Esthonia, which is composed of the old province of Esthonia and more than half of Livonia; and (2) Latvia, formed out of the rest of Livonia and the whole of Courland. The Esthonian National Council was provisionally recognized by Great Britain on 3 May 1918, and similar recognition of the Letts was made on 18 November 1918, after the formation of the Lettish National Council at Riga (late in 1917) and the organization of a provisional government. Final recognition of both states was effected January 1921.

DOMINATION BY OTHER PEOPLES

Exploitation of peasants by German and Russian overlords

These two new states do not base their claim to independence upon historical precedents, for they were always under the control of others — Germans, Swedes, or Russians. Their claim springs from the desire of the mass of the people to avoid that exploitation which has been their lot for centuries. No one can understand their present desire for self-government without examining the historic causes that have sharpened their opposition to the overlordship of Russians and Germans alike. The exploitation of the peasants, who form the bulk of the population, has been carried on through a system of land tenure that has its roots in the events of the 12th century, when German traders first visited the region to exchange wares with the natives.

Brothers of the Sword and Teutonic Knights

With the traders came missionaries, and finally crusaders. Thus in 1200 came Bishop Albert, with twenty-three shiploads of knights, organized into an order called "Brothers of the Sword," or Livonian Knights. They converted the heathen natives and subdued the land by force, making a place for the colonists, whose settlements have remained distinct to this day. This order of knights suffered severe defeat in 1236 and thereupon united with the Teutonic Knights, another order devoted to forcible Christianization. The struggle with the natives of the Baltic Provinces was then renewed. During the 14th century, and again in the 16th century, there was a series of religious wars; the religious orders were weakened, and their territory was overrun by Poles and Swedes. After 1561, Poland held southern Lettland, and Courland became a Polish duchy. Amid

362

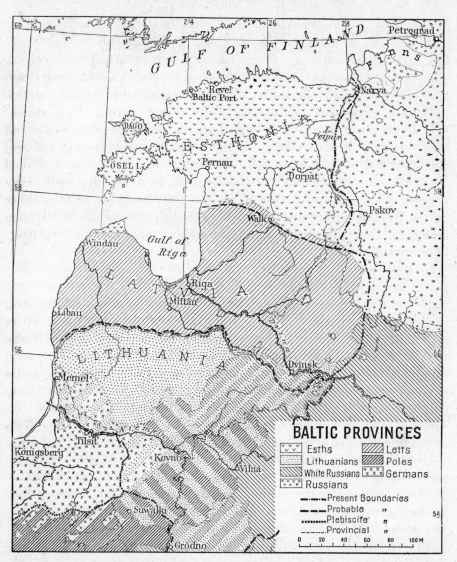

Fig. 184. Ethnography and boundaries in Lithuania and in the former Baltic Provinces of Russia. The eastern boundary of Lithuania as shown above represents the line established by treaty between Lithuania and the Soviet government (1920). It may be altered as a result of the occupation of Vilna by Polish irregular troops, which has led to a decision to hold a plebiscite to determine whether the Vilna region shall belong to Poland or to Lithuania.

all these and later changes the Prussian landlords kept their political hold upon the country, and with it their control of the land and the means of commerce.

In 1629 Sweden, under Gustavus Adolphus, got control of Lettland, to give way in turn to Russia in 1721, in the time of Peter the Great. Under the Swedish rule of almost a hundred years (1629–1721) many

Swedish
liberality
in con-
trast to
Russian
oppression
of the Prussian landlords had to give up their estates. The people
were able also to maintain schools. But under the Russian rule that
followed, all the privileges of government were returned to the German lords. Churches, schools, and police laws were under their control, and they made the fullest use of their opportunity. The peasants were made serfs, which practically meant slaves. They could
be sold or given away; the lords had the power of life and death
over them. Not until 1804 could the peasants own property or land.
But the granting of this right of ownership accomplished little.
The landlords obtained still more land until, by 1850, they owned 60
per cent of the whole. Between 1845 and 1863 laws were promulgated
by the Russian government which limited the rights of the landlords,
and since that time the peasants have been able to obtain a fresh
hold upon the soil.

Forcible
Russifica-
tion of the
people
In 1884, with the active coöperation of the German landlords, the
government of the Czar began a Russianizing policy which continued
until the revolution of 1905. The Russian language was prescribed
in the schools, in the University of Dorpat, and in the whole civil
administration. German support of these measures tended to increase
the differences between the peasants and the German barons; because the pastors were German, congregations refused to attend
church or were disorderly during services. At last there was a settled
determination to develop a nationalistic movement, which, should it
succeed, would rid the people of the German barons and of the autocratic rule of Russia.

Disorders
accompany-
ing the
revolution
of 1905
In 1905 socialism spread rapidly in the general effort to overthrow
the existing government, and many of the estates of the German
landlords were seized. The Russian government put down the
revolution with great vigor and brutality. From that time until the
formation of republican governments in 1919, the Germans on the one
hand and the Russians on the other were equally hated by the Esths
and Letts.

A great
coloniza-
tion
scheme
It was the presence of the German barons in the Baltic Provinces
that led Germany to hope for the conquest of this country early in
1918, when the German army completed its advance of the last months
of 1917 and established itself on a line which it held down to the end
of the war. By the treaty of Brest-Litovsk (between Germany and
Russia, in 1918), all the country west of the line shown on Figure 180
was to be made into states whose government and economic control
were to be in the hands of German princes. The German government
also organized a great colonization scheme, advertising large estates

that were made vacant by the flight of Lettish peasants. It was called the Hindenburg Colonization Plan. Every Courland landowner whose estate exceeded a certain figure had to sell one third of it to the land company, which itself fixed the purchase price, if necessary by compulsory auction.

GERMAN ATTEMPTS TO RETAIN CONTROL

For more than a year after the war closed, the fate of the region was in the balance. By an unfortunate article in the armistice of 11 November 1918, Germany was required to remove her troops from the Baltic Provinces only when ordered by the Allies to do so. A long delay ensued. This gave the army leaders and the powerful German land-owning barons, or Balts, who had controlled the country for centuries, an opportunity to interfere with the newly formed and weak governments of Esthonia, Latvia, and Lithuania. Von der Goltz, the German army commander, supported by soldiers of fortune from Germany and the local German nobility, tried to bring the whole Baltic region under German control, intending thus to hold the Baltic outlets of a vast hinterland and provide a base for German economic and political penetration of Russia.

German delay in evacuating the Baltic Provinces

Several times, as a result of Allied pressure, the German armies withdrew over limited areas and permitted the Bolshevists to come in and work their will on the defenseless inhabitants. They stripped the country of every useful object, as well as of food; agricultural machinery, factory equipment, beds, upholstery, etc., were carried away. By this action, Von der Goltz and the nobles created a still wider gulf between the native Lettish peasants and the German landowners; instead of increasing German influence, they put an end to it. The result was open conflict, destined to throw out finally and completely the remnants of German power and to free the region from a control that had lasted for eight centuries. Under the supervision of an Interallied military mission, the evacuation of the German armies was completed late in 1919, but the mission would probably not have succeeded at all if a strong Allied blockade had not been maintained for several months on the Baltic coast of Germany.

Country stripped by Germans and Bolshevists

THE BASIS OF THE NEW STATES

Political power in the three former provinces at last has passed into the hands of two national assemblies. These are inexperienced bodies, and it remains to be seen whether they can form strong governments. Tacit recognition of Esthonia and Latvia — and at the same time

Weakness of the national assemblies

Brown Bros.

Fig. 185. Part of the harbor of Riga.

of Lithuania (page 362) — was accorded in 1919 by the Peace Conference of Paris in dealing with the delegations from these states. Poland recognized Latvia in October 1919, and agreed to help her against the Bolshevists. A treaty was made at Riga late in 1919 between Esthonia and Latvia which provided for:

(1) The division of military forces on the frontier opposed to the Bolshevists, including agreements about military supplies.

(2) The demarcation of the Lettish-Esthonian boundary.

AGREEMENT WITH THE PRESENT GOVERNMENT OF RUSSIA

Treaty of Dorpat, between Esthonia and Russia

Having obtained recognition from the Allies, it was important for Esthonia to arrange peace with Soviet Russia, so that industries could be revived, order maintained, and an eastern administrative boundary established.

As a result of a conference at Dorpat an armistice was concluded on 3 January 1920 between the Esths and the government of Soviet Russia, the Esths obtaining practically the whole of the territory they claimed on ethnic grounds.

(1) Article I of the treaty announces the cessation of hostilities and the conclusion of peace between the two countries.

(2) The Russian government recognizes the right of a nationality within the former Russian Empire to separate from Russia

and to enjoy absolute independence, basing this action on the principle of self-determination; it therefore renounces voluntarily and forever all sovereign rights over Esthonian people and territory. The frontiers are defined as shown in Figure 184.

(3) It is further provided that no armed vessels shall be kept on Lakes Peipus and Pskov. Guarantees are given to disarm military and naval units of other powers that may be on the soil of Esthonia or of Russia. Direct telegraphic connection is established between Wesenberg in Esthonia on the one hand and Petrograd and Moscow on the other, as well as with Pskov, which is the headquarters of a mixed commission to carry out the military guarantees.

(4) Russia renounces all claims to former Russian property, money, etc., located in Esthonia, and agrees to pay to Esthonia 15,000,000 rubles in gold.

(5) Esthonia has no responsibility for Russian debts or other obligations created by the issue of paper money, etc., and the Russian government undertakes to restore to Esthonia valuables of all kinds that were taken away from the country.

(6) Of particular interest is the section of the treaty dealing with economic relations, providing for the equality of trade in commercial, industrial, and financial enterprises, ships and cargoes, farms and industries, agricultural products and exported goods. "No customs duties or tariffs shall be levied on goods transported across the territory of the other signatory of this treaty." Freight rates are to be no higher in one country than in the other country, for goods of the same nature over the same distance. Esthonia is to provide Russia with whatever port space is needed for commercial purposes, with a free port in Revel, or wherever a free port may be established.

(7) Special agreements must be made between Esthonia and Russia for any artificial diversion of the water from Lakes Peipus and Pskov which may lower the average level of the water of these lakes by more than one foot, and in a similar way fishing on the two lakes and the operation of commercial vessels are to be regulated.

(8) Russia is to have the right to obtain electric power from the waterfalls of the Narova River, and Esthonia is to have the right to construct and exploit a direct single- or double-track railway connection from Moscow to some point on the Esthonian frontier.

(9) Finally, Russia grants to Esthonia rights over 2,700,000 acres of forest land in the governments of Petrograd, Pskov, Tver, Novgorod, Olonetz, Vologda, and Archangel.

These provisions are, on the whole, surprisingly liberal to Esthonia, and, if carried out, will assure her a favorable basis for her economic life. If the Soviet government should be overthrown, the agreement is of interest as forming the probable basis of a new treaty, though the items mentioned in paragraphs 8 and 9, above, are likely to be modified in Russia's favor.

INTERNAL AFFAIRS

In both area and population the two new Baltic states are small:

	AREA	POPULATION
Esthonia	20,000 sq. mi.	1,750,000
Latvia	25,000 sq. mi.	2,400,000

The new states an agricultural region with little industry

Only a small part of the population is engaged in transportation and commerce, and another equally small part is engaged in industrial occupations. The chief basis of life is agriculture, which furnishes employment for more than half the population. While the holding of land in large estates enabled the German landowners to exploit the peasants, it is also true that these landowners formed the most intelligent part of the population and were responsible for the introduction of modern agricultural machinery and diversified farming. In Esthonia the Germans constituted 13 per cent of the total population and owned about 50 per cent of the land. The peasants have won freedom from the Balts, but they have lost an important part of the brains of the country. While both states have been repeatedly overrun by armies during the war, Latvia was almost destroyed. It is estimated that in the district of Courland the decrease in population from 1914 to 1917 was from 800,000 to 300,000.

Present political program

As for internal political and economic problems, they relate principally to the land question. All parties are agreed that the land should be divided among the people, that church and state should be separated, and that the form of government should be liberal. While opposed to Bolshevism, Latvia is a socialistic state. The economic condition of the region is not favorable. A large part of the country is forested, and there is not a closely organized commercial life. Transportation, except along the few railways, is still primitive and slow. As late as 1911 Esthonia had no paved roads at all.

Esthonia and Latvia would be strengthened commercially if they were to form an economic union and include Lithuania. The political obstacle to such a union is the lack of sympathy between the different elements. They have different languages and have no close historical or political associations, in spite of the similarity of their social and political problems in the past. Such a combination might also enable the German barons to regain political control; being more experienced in commercial and political affairs, they could play one nationality against the other to their own advantage.

INTERNATIONAL POSITION OF ESTHONIA AND LATVIA

The importance of the region in international affairs springs from the fact that the ports of the Baltic — Riga, Libau, Windau, and Baltic Port — are the rail outlets for a large part of interior Russia, and all have an important commercial rank; Riga, the largest, is sixth in importance among the ports of Russia. Also, the exports are raw materials — like flax and wood — and these are of importance to the industrialized nations of western Europe, whose own production of such materials is small and who must find additional stocks on or near a seaboard, where water transportation assures low freight rates.

The Baltic ports important outlets for the raw materials of a large region

The recognition of the two governments of Esthonia and Latvia by Great Britain has a commercial significance, not only in respect of the future of Russia, but with reference to general imperial policy and understandings with the French. It appears to be understood that the Baltic Sea is a British trade realm in which there will be important developments in the future. Thus it was the British navy that blockaded the coasts of Germany and Soviet Russia. A British High Commissioner sits at Danzig, and British naval units have patrolled the coast of the Baltic and guaranteed the safety of commercial exchange. All this is in line with the British traditional policy of establishing influence or control in ports and coastal belts serving as outlets for interior populations from which flow important currents of trade.

Great Britain's Baltic policy in harmony with her tradition of coastal control

CHAPTER TWENTY–TWO

FINNISH PROBLEMS IN THEIR GEOGRAPHICAL SETTING

Treaty of
Dorpat FINLAND's chief territorial problem lies on her eastern frontier, long in dispute with Soviet Russia. The main points in contention were the question of an outlet for Finland on the Arctic Ocean (Pechenga region) and the disposition of eastern Karelia, a province occupied by a people racially allied to the Finns. An agreement was finally reached in a treaty signed 14 October 1920 and ratified 29 December 1920. The boundary articles of the treaty of Dorpat assign to Finland a strip of the Arctic coast and connecting territory as shown in the inset of Figure 188; and other articles provide for the neutralization of the frontier. The treaty also guarantees autonomy to eastern Karelia and to the Karelian population of Archangel and Olonetz (northeast of Lake Ladoga), which is Greek Orthodox in religion and Russian in civilization and has no marked political preference. Transportation and rafting of timber on waters crossing the boundary line is to be permitted to both countries. Commercial freedom of wide scope is guaranteed in articles on the use of ports, railways, telegraph lines, freight and customs rates, on fishing rights, harbor fees, and the like.

Finland to
have an
Arctic
warm-water
port The Pechenga region which Finland gained is a small, barren strip on the Arctic shore. Its significance arises out of the tempering effect exercised by a branch of the warmer waters of the north Atlantic drift (usually called the Gulf Stream), whereby the ports of Pechenga and Alexandrovsk, 250 miles north of the Arctic Circle (Fig. 186), remain open throughout the winter months, when all the ports of the eastern Baltic and the White Sea are closed by ice. Archangel is icebound for nine months each year. It was to secure an open port that Russia built the Murman railway to Catherine Harbor (Alexandrovsk). The northern ports would be of far less importance if it were not that Russia has already lost all her Baltic ports except Petrograd and may lose others on the Black Sea and in eastern Siberia.

GEOGRAPHICAL CONDITIONS

Of all of the new nations of Europe, Finland is farthest north. What are its resources? What is the physical basis of its strength?

As outlined in Figure 186, Finland is a third as large as Ontario. While the extreme north grades into Arctic tundra, the country as a whole resembles the Lake Superior region in surface and climate. Everywhere the surface is rocky and lake-dotted, with an irregular drainage, a thin soil, and an extensive forest cover. In the milder south, where there is a deeper soil, there are farms producing hardy grains like rye, barley, and oats.

The population of Finland is 3,500,000. Helsingfors, the capital, has 187,000. The towns are small, and include only 15 per cent of the population (in the United States about half the population is urban). In the cold and remote north the density of population is less than 1 to the square mile; but in the warmer and more fertile south, on the edge of the Gulf of Finland, it reaches 93 to the square mile.

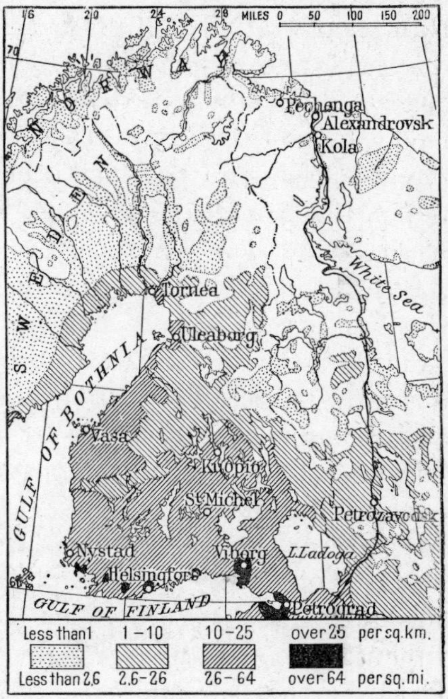

Distribution of the population

Half of the population lives by agriculture and cattle raising, but only 8.5 per cent of the land is cultivated or used for pasture. Nearly a third of the surface is covered with peat marsh and bog, and nearly half is forested. Barley is grown up to latitude 68° north and rye to 64°, or to 67° in favorable years. The farther north one goes the longer — and also the hotter — the summer days; and whereas barley takes 116 days to ripen in the Åland Islands, there are but 63 days between sowing and harvest in the higher latitudes, the limit of its range.

Fig. 186. Population densities for Finland. Note the coastal position of the highest density grades and compare with Figure 189, showing the field of Swedish colonization. Based on *Petermanns Mitteilungen*, 1913, I, Pl. 2, and Debes, *Handatlas*, 1913, Pl. 12 *c*.

No other civilized race lives so far north as the people of Finland. "The Finns have been bred in the school of adversity." As a whole the country is poor and famines are not rare. In 1867, for example, there was a fearful dearth, owing chiefly to the poor crop of rye, the principal food. Again in 1869 there was general want, due to the partial failure of the potato crop. The Finns have emigrated in large numbers, chiefly to North America, for Finland cannot support its people on its own produce.

Crop failures and famines

The chief wealth of Finland lies in its forests and its water power.

Of the 3,000,000 horse power available, only 100,000 are now in use. In 1913, wood and wood products formed 75 per cent of the exports of the country. Mineral resources are almost unknown. The total mileage of railways is 2500, which, in relation to the number of people, is a high figure and compares favorably with that of industrial countries like France and Belgium. In relation to area, the railway mileage is small. The long and indented seacoast, with innumerable havens and extensive fishing grounds, has naturally bred sailors. Before the World War, Finnish ships plied between Stockholm, Antwerp, London, Havre, and Bordeaux.

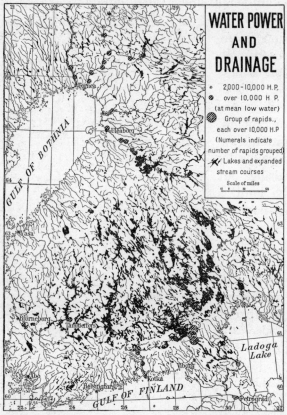

For the most part settlements in Finland follow the watercourses, just as they did in the Stone Age, because these are the natural ready-made means of communication. Finland has forty times as much inland water as France. Certain canals date from the Middle Ages. The Saima Canal connects lakes of the Saima system, which covers 2600 square miles of

FIG. 187. Water resources of Finland, a glaciated rocky country like Quebec. The Saima canal system, mentioned in the text, is shown just above Kotka on the Gulf of Finland. From *Atlas de Finlande*, 2d ed., 1911, Pl. 14.

water, the largest lake group in Europe, of which more than 2000 square miles are in Finland (Fig. 187). This system connects directly with the Gulf of Finland and is an outlet of incalculable benefit to the country.

THE PEOPLE OF FINLAND

The Finns are closely allied to the Esthonians and the Letts on the Baltic; that is, they belong to the Finno-Ugrian stock, which is quite distinct from the Slavic stock of eastern Europe and from the Teutonic (Nordic) stock of Scandinavia and Germany. Finnish is the language of 88 per cent of the population; more than 11 per cent speak Swedish. Though small numerically, the Swedish element is very important because it controls a large part of the wealth of the country and is active politically out of proportion to its numbers. The small remainder of the people comprises about 1300 Lapps in the north and about 2000 Germans and 6000 Russians in the southern portions.

Education in Finland is on a remarkably high level. Practically every Finlander can read. There are two universities, Helsingfors and Abö. Finland has one of the two geographical associations in the world that admit to membership only geographers who have done original work.

The discovery by Elias Lönnrot of the great epic of the Finns, the Kalevala, first published in 1835, gave a great impulse to the study of the Finnish language and culture. More than 300,000 legends, sagas, and proverbs have been collected.

All this intellectual activity, but especially

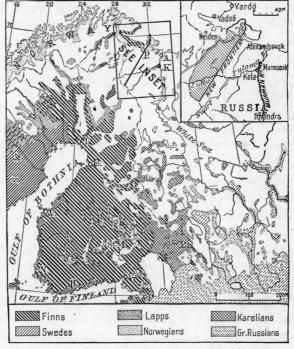

Literature and folk-lore of the Finns

Finns
Swedes
Lapps
Norwegians
Karelians
Gr.Russians

Fig. 188. The Karelians, though Finns, have many Russian characteristics. Were they added to Finland, that country's eastern boundary would be the White Sea. It is through the territory of the Karelians that the Russians have built the railway to Kola (*K* on the map) and Alexandrovsk (*A*). Based on *Atlas de Finlande*, 2d ed., 1911, Pl. 46, and Debes, *Handatlas*, 1913, Pl. 12 *c*. The inset shows the final boundary of Finland in the Pechenga district (page 370). Pechenga is shown by a small circle on the inset, and two fine parallel lines locate the road now running to that port, which will probably soon be served by a railway.

the publication of the Kalevala, has had a strongly stimulating effect on the nationalist movement and has brought the Finnish element of the population to the front. Despite the difficulties of her geographical environment and of ever-threatening trouble from the east, Finland has risen to the rank of a nation of great promise for the future — an outpost of western civilization.

RELATION TO NEIGHBORING STATES

Finland's present problems in the field of political geography follow for the most part from the country's position between more powerful peoples of different race and speech — the Swedes on the west and the Russians on the east.   Here, as elsewhere, the ruling political philosophy of the past has brought the heel of the conqueror on the neck of the small nation that stood in the path of empire.   In the 12th and 13th centuries the Swedes, after repeated crusades against the country, conquered it; and they kept it until 1809 — more than six hundred years.   During this time the history of Sweden is the history of Finland.   The whole country was impregnated with Swedish culture.   Then came Russia.

Through four centuries Russia has consistently extended her frontiers on all sides toward open water, that is, toward the Baltic and Black seas, the Pacific, the Mediterranean, and the Persian Gulf.   Her rulers have made this the main national political objective throughout the two centuries since the time of Peter the Great.   Finland stood in her path.   So Finland was conquered by the Russians during the Napoleonic wars and was held by them down to 1917, when the Czar was deposed and the Russian democratic government set up.

By the treaty of Fredrikshamn, in 1809, Russia, gaining control of Finland, agreed to respect its independence; but, as with all autocratic governments, the word of a treaty proved to be a thing easily broken when it suited the ruler's purpose to break it.   How artificial was the process of Russification may be seen by the fact that Russian culture, after a century of artificial stimulation, is practically nonexistent in Finland today.

Åland Islands a
source of
dispute
between
Sweden
and Finland

In the alternate ownership of Finland by Sweden and Russia, the Åland Islands have been a matter of dispute.   They lie only seventy-five miles from Stockholm and twenty miles from the Swedish coast, and if fortified by a neighboring power would be a grave menace. Their strategic value grows out of their good harbors as well as their geographical position.   They were ceded by Sweden to Russia in 1809, but their population of 19,000 is almost exclusively Swedish. They have been recommended for assignment to Finland by the commission of the League of Nations that was appointed to study the Åland question.

Fortunately for the Finns, the Allies maintained a military front in northern Russia through 1918 and 1919.   The Archangel sector protected Finland's flank, thus enabling the Finnish armies to hold in check the Bolshevist troops based on Petrograd. Thereby the country was enabled to right itself, after several brief internal struggles between the "Whites" and "Reds" which ended in qualified victory for the "Whites." This outcome put at least a temporary end to Bolshevism in Finland, won recognition and assistance from the Allies, and started the country on its national career.

The protection of the Allies

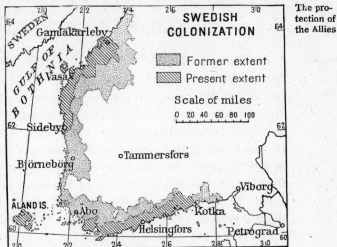

Fig. 189. Swedish colonists, former Swedish ownership of Finland, and the wide distribution of Swedish culture have combined to make the Swedes a powerful political group in Finland. From *Atlas de Finlande*, 2d ed., 1911, Vol. II, p. 20, text to map 46.

THE OUTLOOK FOR FINLAND

Communist agitation still continues among the soldiers of the regular army, and together with Bolshevist propaganda has undermined the morale of the army to some extent. The bitterness that arose in the civil war of 1919 has continued, and adds its problem to that of the contest between the working classes and the rest of the population, particularly the *bourgeoisie*. The conservative part of the population fears Red disturbances, and the Reds fear that the Whites will set up a reactionary government. The progress of the settlement and unification of the political life of the country is made more difficult by proximity to Soviet Russia.

Whites and Reds

The strong racial differences between Finns and Russians, the long political oppression of the Finns by the former Russian government, and lately the evil effects of Bolshevism, will limit the relations of the Finns and Russians for many years to come, even in commercial matters. Of political union or confederation there can be none at all. Finland and Sweden having had the friendly assistance of the League of Nations in the settlement of the Åland Islands dispute, the bond between these two states ought to become as strong as will be, in time, that with the Esths and Letts. In short, the external political problems of Finland are relatively simple; her chief danger lies in the radical elements within her borders and the difficulties that naturally attend development of a strong democratic government.

Finland's problems chiefly domestic, not international

CHAPTER TWENTY-THREE

THE POLITICAL GEOGRAPHY OF RUSSIA

Russia: an imperial advance

A DRAMATIC theme of statesmen and publicists for many years before the World War was the growing danger of absorption of neighboring lands and people by the huge Russian Empire. British statesmen were anxiously contemplating every Russian advance in Central Asia. By 1893, Russia's frontier almost touched British India at Kashmir in the Pamirs; and Russian political agents were scattered through the distant Chinese provinces of Eastern Turkestan, Mongolia, and Tibet, as well as in Persia, Turkey, and Afghanistan. It was the steady growth of Russian influence in Manchuria and elsewhere in northern China that led to the Russo-Japanese War in 1905. The Russification of Congress Poland continued from 1815 down to the opening of the World War, and German leaders never allowed their people to forget the menace of the Slav. In 1907 the constitutional guarantees of the Finns were set aside. Russian influence was aggressive in northern Turkey — on the borders of Transcaucasia — and in both Persia and Turkey toward the Persian Gulf, whither Russia sought a railway outlet to warm water. With a strongly centralized government, Russia had been able persistently to absorb or penetrate those border regions of chief strategic importance in commerce and war.

The break-up of the Russian Empire now seems a rather natural event, seeing how diverse were its various parts in customs, ideals, ethnography, history, and mode of life. The apparent harmony of the political map was merely the expression of centralized imperial power exercised upon an ignorant peasantry. Just as soon as industries developed trained men and educational facilities, the old system failed, not so much because it was ill-adapted to modern needs, as because it ceased to function, particularly in the World War. First came the democratic revolution of 1917, and second the general disintegration of political life as a consequence of the rise and spread of Bolshevist philosophy and power.

In its present fragmented condition and state of disorder, will Russia be able to gather itself together again and form a unified government? We shall be able to estimate the chance of such reorganization only if we know, first of all, what peoples composed the empire, what divergencies existed among them, and finally what geographical, political, social, economic, or religious bonds may now be made to serve as unifying principles. Consideration will first be given to ethnic character.

376

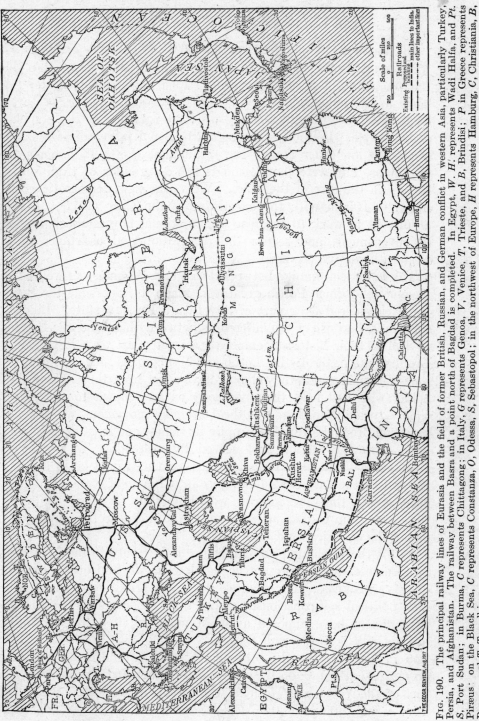

Fig. 190. The principal railway lines of Eurasia and the field of former British, Russian, and German conflict in western Asia, particularly Turkey, Persia, and Afghanistan. The railway between Basra and a point north of Bagdad is completed. In Egypt, *W. H.* represents Wadi Halfa, and *Pt. S.* Port Sudan; in Burma, *C* represents Chittagong; in Italy *G* represents Genoa, *V*, Venice, *T*, Trieste, and *B*, Brindisi; *P* in Greece represents Piræus; on the Black Sea, *C* represents Constanza, *O*, Odessa, *S*, Sebastopol; in the northwest of Europe, *H* represents Hamburg, *C*, Christiania, *B*, Bergen, and *T*, Trondhjem.

THE ETHNIC GROUPS OF THE RUSSIAN EMPIRE

Of the many ethnic groups comprised in the table on page 379, the ten that are starred represent peoples that were the chief internal cause of border insecurity. Each one wished to stand by itself as an independent or at least autonomous power, or to ally itself with a neighboring country which it regarded as the homeland of its people. Political self-consciousness and power of organization were of a low order among the Lithuanians, Letts, Esthonians, and Georgians, but were more strongly felt on grounds of tradition and history in the case of the Poles. When the new democratic régime began in Russia with the overthrow of the Czar (1917), all these groups set to work to organize their national life, establish agencies of government, and secure the recognition and assistance of the western European powers.

The historical enmity between Poles and Russians, as well as the memory of former Polish greatness, made it impossible for Poland to be considered as a part of any future Russian state. Likewise, the Finns, because of the differences between them and the Russians as well as their historical enmity, were set apart as a lost element. Gradually, too, the Esths, Letts, and Lithuanians sought to establish a new order in which they should have relief from the German land-holder, who had held them virtually as serfs down to the present time. In addition there was the Ukrainian movement, which sought to detach from the Russian Empire its richest and most densely populated part, the section best served by railroads. To permit the Ukraine to form an independent government would be to throw all the rest of the vast Russian Empire into a state of economic dependence, seeing that the interior would be shut off more completely than ever from the sea, whereas improved access to the sea has been one of the historical and vital aims of Russia.

As for the remaining non-Russian ethnic groups in the former empire, some of them represent negligible elements and others elements of grave weakness. For example, the more primitive Siberian tribes lack political self-consciousness, and their geographical position and environment have imposed a low standard of life. Their commercial activity is feeble, and they play no vital part in the reconstruction of Russia. On the other hand, some of the rather primitive groups in Turkestan, on the shores of the Black Sea, and in the region east of the Volga, are Moslems whose religious attachments are with Turkey and the rest of the Moslem world, and whose self-conscious-

ETHNIC COMPOSITION OF THE RUSSIAN EMPIRE ACCORDING TO THE CENSUS OF 1897,
AND WITHIN THE BOUNDARIES OF 1914

(Figures represent thousands. Names of loosely attached border peoples are starred.)

	RUSSIA IN EUROPE	POLAND	CAUCASIA	SIBERIA	CENTRAL ASIA	FINLAND	TOTALS
ARYANS							
SLAVS							
Great Russians . . .	48,559	267	1,830	4,424	588	6	55,674
Little Russians* . . .	20,415	335	1,305	223	102		22,380
White Russians . . .	5,823	29	20	12	1		5,885
Poles*.	1,110	6,756	25	29	12		7,932
Other Slavs	213	7	4				224
LITHUANIANS*.	1,345	305	5	2	1		1,658
LETTS*	1,422	5	2	7	1		1,437
IRANIANS	2		418		364		784
ARMENIANS*	77		1,096		5		1,178
RUMANIANS*	1,122	5	7				1,134
GERMANS	1,312	407	57	5	9	2	1,792
SWEDES	14					350	364
OTHER ARYANS	132	1	105	6	1		245
SEMITES	3,715	1,267	40	33	8		5,063
URALO–ALTAIANS							
FINNO-UGRIANS							
Finns*	143					2,353	2,496
Karelians	208						208
Lapps	2					1	3
Mordvinians	990			21	13		1,024
Other Finno-Ugrians . .	1,090			32			1,122
Esthonians*.	990	4	4	4			1,002
TURKO-TATARS*							
Kirghiz	264			33	3,989		4,286
Tatars	1,953	4	1,510	210	60		3,737
Bashkirs	1,488		1	1	3		1,493
Sarts					968		968
Chuvashes	838	1		4			843
Uzbegs					726		726
Turkomans	8		25		249		282
Osmanli Turks. . . .	69		139				208
Other Turko-Tatars . .			205	227	623		1,055
MONGOLS	171		14	289			474
OTHER URALO-ALTAIANS .	4			82			86
GEORGIANS*			1,352				1,352
OTHER CAUCASIANS .			1,092				1,092
HYPERBOREANS . . .				39			39
CHINESE, JAPANESE .				86			86
TOTALS	93,479	9,393	9,256	5,769	7,723	2,712	128,332

ness has been raised to the rank of a political force by the progress of
the Pan-Islamic and the Pan-Turanian movements. The Armenians
and Georgians are each seeking national independence; they will not
find it easy to associate themselves with any government formed far
north of the Caucasus.

Fig. 191. Generalized ethnographic map of Russia in relation to the boundaries of the larger natural regions. Ethnography after Debes and natural regions after map by Hanelik in Rudnyckyj, *Der Östliche Kriegesschauplatz*, 1915. For population density and explanation of cities see Figure 198. Smaller ethnographic elements, like the Lapps in the north and the Kirghiz about the eastern and northern Caspian, are not shown. "Caucasian" refers to locality, not race. Note the close approach of the bends of the Volga and Don near Tsaritsyn. The Cossacks of the Don, the partly nomadic Kirghiz east of them, and the Tatars of Azerbaijan about Baku constitute a broad belt of non-Russian population with separatist tendencies, encircling the Caspian.

The Jewish problem

Within the so-called Jewish Pale, shown on Figure 192, are more than 5,000,000 Jews. Though they were in general prohibited from living in Great Russia, this prohibition did not actually affect the wealthiest and best educated, who are scattered throughout the

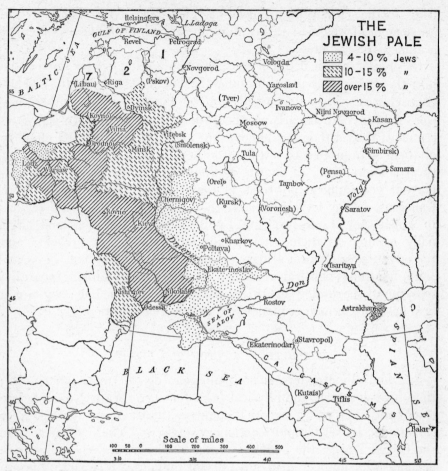

FIG. 192. The Pale of Settlement, western European Russia, according to the *Jewish Encyclopædia* (article on Russia). In none of the Russian governments without shading on the map do the Jews form as much as 1 per cent of the total population, except in the Baltic region, where percentages of Jews are given in figures (1, 2, 7).

country, while still being chiefly settled in Lithuania, Courland, the Ukraine, and Bessarabia. In Russian Poland, Jews constitute 14 per cent of the total population, and in Bessarabia about 12 per cent, though from 30 to 60 per cent of them are in the cities.

It is characteristic of the Jews that they have a community life distinct from that of the people about them, and they have grown so numerous as to become an object of persecution throughout Russia, under the new régime as well as the old. The antipathy toward them is not wholly because of their religion; it is aroused partly by their success in business, particularly in money-lending. Many of them take no interest whatever in political affairs, or limit their activities to the gaining of privileges as a distinct race. The Jews form an element of weakness rather than of strength in the development of a unified Russian state.

Scattered German colonies

Of greater political importance are the Germans who have come into the Baltic Provinces, forming the landlord, tradesman, and artisan classes. They live mainly in the larger towns, whither they were first invited as early as the 16th century by the Russian government, Russia then lacking artisans and traders. In 1762 numbers of them were invited to settle in southern Russia in separate agricultural colonies, and, as shown in Figure 100, they now occupy important geographical positions in the Don region and the northern Caucasus. They have increased the economic value of the regions in which they dwell, profiting by the allotment of rich land originally granted to them, their exemption from military service, and the advantages of local self-government. In the Ukraine they exercised a strong political influence during the Ukrainian separatist movement (beginning in 1918), and wherever located they are a firm basis of German economic and political penetration.

THE DEFECTS OF THE OLD SYSTEM

Character and high ideals lacking in the " old régime "

Soil and climate, forests and minerals, do not make an empire; they furnish merely the physical basis for one. While Russia before the World War was a big, rich country, the Czar was a weak ruler surrounded by selfish and reactionary advisers. The real rulers were the Grand Dukes, the high government officials, and the nobility in general, who numbered about 140,000 families. It was this group that put into motion schemes for robbing the people, for exiling to Siberia leaders who manifested any independence of political thought; and it was they who were responsible for the bad management of the war, when, through graft and inefficiency, millions of Russians were obliged to fight under every sort of handicap.

Religious and economic bonds of the Russian peasant

The hands of the rulers of Russia were in large part upheld by the religious sentiment of the people as expressed in their almost universal membership in the Greek Orthodox Church and the various sects within it. The national church was identified with the state, and it became an instrument of political power to serve the heads of the Russian government.

Nearly 90 per cent of the people belong to the peasant class, and the peasant was held in economic as well as spiritual bondage to the political forces that surrounded him. Though successive

Fig. 193.   The heart of Moscow, with the buildings of the Kremlin in the background.

efforts were made by his leaders and even, through the fitful adoption of liberal policies, by the government itself, to release him from serfdom and allot him land, these movements were so widely separated in time and so meager in results that the situation of the peasant improved scarcely at all.   He might possess land, but he was still in debt to a wealthy landowner.

In short, the Czar and his advisers and the thousands of the nobility learned that the strength of their system lay in the ignorance of the peasant; their wealth and privilege were gained at the expense of the misery of the peasant.   When the masses also learned this, they were not long in seeking a remedy, however drastic.   Of immediate importance to them was the fact that the old régime had to go; the only question was the manner of its going.

THE BACKGROUND OF RUSSIAN DISORDER

We have touched on the weaknesses of the former Russian Empire for the purpose of understanding the basis of that present disorder which is Russia's immediate anxiety. By far the most serious politico-economic problem of the present is the reconstruction of Russia. This would seem to be most soundly based upon the traditional and distinctive Russian institutions known as the zemstvos and the coöperative societies. Coupled with these semi-social institutions there will doubtless be a central government of a liberal order. Finally, the whole political and social structure, to succeed, must have a solid industrial and financial basis. That is, the processes of reconstruction must follow the lines of economic development already laid down in Russian life. These considerations impel us to look a little more closely at the economic tendencies of Russia just before the war.

Former serfs of Russia

One of the chief causes of the present troubles of Russia has been the ignorance of the masses. While many factors have contributed to this end, a principal one is the system of land tenure practiced in Russia. For generations the land has been held in large estates; a hundred years ago, and even later, nine tenths of it was so held. It was tilled by the millions of serfs that made up the bulk of the population. The serfs were not only ignorant; large numbers of them were indolent and of drunken habits. Their life was extremely wretched. The greatness and power of the empire meant nothing to them. For a long time, indeed, they were slaves in fact if not in name.

The serfs made "free"

Finally, in a series of edicts dating from 1859 to 1866, Alexander II abolished serfdom. At the same time he divided the land into two parts: one part was left to the landlords; the other was given to the serfs, on condition that they pay the landlords for it. To the peasant this arrangement looked like robbery. Instead of solving the land question, it made the difficulty only more acute.

Famines among the Russian peasants

During the next fifty years the population increased so rapidly and the need for land became so great that the Russian peasant was on the verge of starvation practically all the time. During 1890 and 1898 there were actual famines in which thousands died of starvation.

Revolution of 1905

Conditions such as these can be remedied only if the form and spirit of the government are altered by an intelligent people. Since in Russia the rulers were stupid and vicious and the people ignorant, matters became worse instead of better, and finally when the war with Japan (1904–1905) turned out badly, disturbances became general. The peasants burned many of the houses of the nobles; mutinies were of frequent occurrence in the army and the navy; the country was in a state of semi-anarchy.

After trying with ill success to suppress the wave of disorder, the Czar at last issued a manifesto (1905) which promised freedom of speech and of the press; it also created, through general elections, a representative assembly, or Duma, which was to have the right of giving final approval to all laws before they were promulgated. But by one means or another the powers of the Duma were taken away or modified, until it no longer represented the people at all. Once more the fight for liberty had failed. The Duma, or National Parliament

Imperial ambitions demanded complete political assimilation of included peoples, and the methods followed were harsh and provocative in the extreme. Between 1907 and 1914 the old policy of frightfulness continued. The Poles were treated worse than ever; from the Finns were taken the last vestiges of an autonomous and constitutional government. The serfs became even more discontented than before; the land question was growing more and more acute. There was also added a new political element, the most threatening toward the autocratic régime of all the forces in the empire, one that was to be in time a powerful element — the industrial classes. Return of the evil government of autocrats

Under Count Witte, a great statesman who became minister of communications in 1892, Russia had built railways. Before that time it was almost without a railway system; in fact, there were but six detached lines, serving only the principal towns. Witte argued that as the country was chiefly agricultural, it would be at the mercy of the big industrial nations of western Europe until it changed its ways; if it was ever to be free economically, it must use its own raw material and labor to create manufactured wares. Witte also urged state protection for infant industries, encouraged foreigners to invest capital, and started Russia on an industrial career. Witte's development of railways and mines

One of the immediate consequences of Witte's policies was the rapid growth of the industrial cities. In the sixteen years following 1897, Odessa, Kiev, and Kherson increased their population 55, 150, and 40 per cent respectively. These cities are the chief centers of steel and iron manufacture. The manganese ores of the Caucasus, the oil of Baku, the platinum of the Urals, and the forests of the north have all been developed at a tremendous rate — tremendous, at least, for Russia.

It was as natural as could be in an autocracy that the laborers, better organized than the peasants, more closely in touch with newspapers,

Fig. 194. The plain of the Dnieper at Kiev.

Industrial middle class

in general more intelligent, should have revolutionary theories and should spread them. They and the students of the universities were the leaders in every radical movement. Side by side with the laborers and as a result of the same process of industrialization, there grew up a middle class, which up to that time had been all but wanting in Russia. These were the capitalists and business proprietors. They were demanding, as time went on, a greater share in the government.

Low state of agricultural practice in relation to famines

In spite of its wealth of natural resources, in spite of the liberation of the serfs and the tendency toward more liberalized forms of local government, the management of the Russian commonwealth was deplorably bad. The agricultural problem had never been thoroughly studied, and no far-reaching and thoroughgoing schemes of agricultural reform had been worked out, to say nothing of their application. More than this, large portions of the agricultural population lived upon land beyond the border of the zone of dependable rains. In the Volga region the winters are longer and more severe than in the Ukraine and droughts are more common. The peasants are always in a state of misery. Here is the border zone where the settler is tempted to an agricultural way of life, though the physical environment is such that he must make intelligent and substantial modifications of usual farming practice in order to succeed; his problem is similar to that of the farmer in the semi-arid western states of Kansas, Nebraska, and Oklahoma, where by dry farming, with its special methods of water conservation, the disadvantage of repeated drought is partly offset.

The change from the old régime of the Czar, which ended in March 1917, to the present communistic, or Bolshevist, régime, was not immediate. The first step was the organization of a provisional government under Kerensky, who continued to fight with the Allies against Germany and Austria until his government was overthrown by the Bolshevists in November 1917. It was a failing venture from the first. The peasant did not hate Germany and was not interested in the war; he wanted land — the form of his government and its diplomatic and military policies interested him not at all. At first, he took up with the new and extreme policy of the Bolshevist leaders because they promised him land. The peasant would as readily have tolerated any other social or political theory. He has been as unwilling to fight for Bolshevists as for the Czar. In this respect he is to be sharply distinguished from the proletariat, the laboring classes of the towns, who sought to control the masses of peasant folk, reorganize the social life on a communistic basis, and by force impose social revolution and a theoric and alien form of government upon the peoples of the rest of the world. The war and its issues were left far behind. The Allies, no more willing to accept the dictatorship of the Russian Bolshevists than the military dictatorship and *Kultur* of Germany, parted company with Russia and stood thereafter in hostile, or at least neutral, relation to its unrepresentative government.

The peasant and the new régime

BOLSHEVISM [1]

Justifiable as the Revolution of 1917 proves to have been, Russia is in a most unfortunate condition today because, in changing from

The poison of Bolshevism

[1] The name of the present Russian government is " The Russian Socialist Federal Soviet Republic."

one autocracy, that of the Czar, she has fallen into the hands of another autocracy, that of the Bolshevists, whose leaders, like the three wise men of Gotham, have attempted to go to sea in a bowl:

" 'Whither in your bowl so free?'
'To rake the moon from out the sea.'"

Russia's losses

Bolshevism is the rule of society by a class, the "proletariat"; its methods destroy property — they do not create it. It has done more harm to Russia, materially and spiritually, than the World War did. Many of the most intelligent people, including teachers, doctors, and lawyers, have been killed. Thousands have fled to France, Great Britain, and the United States. Many others have been so long underfed and terrorized that they have no spirit left for a new time of peace and order, even if such a time should come soon. The actors, the writers, the investigators, are spiritually dead. For years to come these men will not produce a great play, a great novel, a great newspaper, a great university. Bolshevism has meant a step backward toward the barbarism of earlier times.

Soviet industrial régime

Many persons believe that nothing less than the slavery of the masses will result from the latest labor regulations of the Bolshevist leaders. An Industrial General Staff with vast powers is at the head of the whole industrial organization of the country. The liberty of labor is stated to be an impossibility in a communistic state. Military discipline has been adopted, and the managers of workshops, appointed by the government, are given military rank and almost unlimited powers. If they desire, authorities may transfer men from one industry to another; if a worker does not lay brick to suit them, or handle tools to their satisfaction, he may be sent into agriculture or the mines. The peasants are less free than they were under the Czar.

How the peasant looks at things

The Russian people may be sentimental and mystical, but they are also extremely practical. Lenin and Trotsky have used these qualities for their own ends; they could not succeed unless their new teachings were supported by very practical aims. Dividing the land was taken as a symbol of fraternity, but it also meant the gift of land, It was the sole proof that an era of good will had set in. Public debt. national honor, foreign relations — such terms are mere unintelligible words to most of the ignorant peasants. In their thought the world is divided between Russians and foreigners.

The American citizen speaks pretty directly through his congressman. The Russian citizen proceeds through his soviet to provincial and regional congresses, which in turn lead up to the All-Russian

Congress of 1500 members, a central committee of 250, and thence through 17 commissars to the leaders, such as Lenin and Trotsky. So tortuous a channel of approach to authority would try the spirit of an educated people; to the Russian masses it presents impossible conditions of political navigation.

MILITARY OPERATIONS SINCE 1917

Thrown into a state of general disorder, Russia found herself in 1919–1920 involved in not a single war, but a threefold war: **Russia's threefold war**

(1) A war between the Bolshevists and the non Bolshevist elements

    (a) Within former Russia

        The Bolshevists have fought Denikin (southeastern Russia and eastern Ukraine); Petlura (western Ukraine); the Poles; the Lithuanians; the Letts; the Esths; the army of Yudenitch; the Finns; Kolchak (Siberia); Wrangel (Crimea); etc.

    (b) External conflicts

        The Bolshevists have fought Allied armies on Russian soil in the Archangel region; in Siberia (Czechs, Americans, and Japanese); in southern Russia (Rumanians and French).

(2) A war between city and country

        The country is food-sufficient; the city is not. The city must supply the country with manufactured goods in exchange for food, and these materials of commerce the city could not get and deliver. With its function gone, it starved.

(3) A war against banditry

        The returning soldiers took arms home with them. Many of them lived in organized bands that increased in numbers and looted, burned, and devastated wherever they could. It will take a long time to get rid of them.

Without any cohesion among the forces fighting the Bolshevist forces, there was a general circle of opposing armies that grew to large size by the middle of the summer of 1919. It was felt by nearly all the Allied powers that the extremely bad economic condition of Russia would soon bring about a collapse of Bolshevist rule, provided that outside military pressure was maintained. France was especially eager to achieve this result because of the declared opposition of the Soviet government to any plan of payment of the pre-war debt, held **Fight against Bolshevism** chiefly by French bankers. Nothing stiffened general Allied resistance so much as that part of the Bolshevist program which demanded the overthrow of the existing social and economic systems everywhere in the world.

Bolshevist
Russia
blockaded
Hoping to bring the Bolshevists to terms, oblige them to renounce their program of world conquest, and make a peace fair to their neighbors as well as to Russia, the Allies, in August 1919, sought to establish a semi-blockade, the principal features of which were as follows:

(1) No clearance papers were to be issued from or to Bolshevist Russia; there was to be a land embargo of a similar nature; and no passports were to be given to travelers to or from Russia.

(2) No banking business was to be transacted with Russia; and as far as possible all telegraphic and mail communications were to be stopped.

Finding that this policy did not bring peace, the Allies, in the early months of 1920, adopted the principle of trade but not political recognition. Nothing practical came of this policy because the Soviet government insisted on combining trade agreements and political recognition. In the summer of 1920, after a rapid invasion of Russia as far as Kiev, the Polish armies were driven back and Poland itself was invaded by the Bolshevist armies. The terms which the Russian leaders sought to impose on Poland were so severe as practically to extinguish Poland, and the Allies supported the Poles with supplies and military leadership.

In the ensuing struggle the Russian Soviet forces were thrown back far east of the border of ethnographic Poland (Fig. 167). The Soviet government thereupon agreed to peace negotiations at Riga, in Latvia, with the result that a truce and preliminary peace were signed between Poland and Russia early in October 1920 (page 335). By midsummer of 1920 military opposition to the Bolshevists developed in the Crimea, where General Wrangel, with French recognition and assistance, had reorganized the remnants of Denikin's army. It was partly owing to Wrangel's success that the Soviet government hurried its peace parleys with Poland and agreed to acceptable terms. A promising aspect of Wrangel's work was his agreement of 13 April 1920 with the Cossacks of the Don, which provided for their complete independence in domestic affairs and at least some measure of power in foreign relations that affect Cossack territories or people. With the

Poles eliminated, the Soviet army was concentrated on Wrangel, and in November 1920 all his forces were either driven out of the Crimea or captured.

If the Allied and Associated Powers have repeatedly changed their policy toward Bolshevist Russia, it is also true that the Bolshevists likewise have changed their policies and views from time to time. Their present tendency appears to be toward a more moderate plan of government, though this change is interpreted by some students to mean only a respite in the war by which they expect ultimately to overwhelm the world. The dire calamities which Bolshevism has brought to Russia spring from deep-seated causes. It is important to understand these to see how artificial the system would be if transplanted to countries with an economic and social life wholly different from that of Russia.

ECONOMIC SITUATION

In spite of government neglect and the natural rigors of the country, the population of Russia is rapidly increasing. As in the case of Austria-Hungary, a political contest could have been avoided only by thorough reforms and the application of modern engineering skill. The reforms and the skill Russia's autocratic government could not supply, and one of the most serious questions confronting the country today is whether her government, with its tendency toward communism and the leveling of classes — and particularly the leveling of advantages — can ameliorate the conditions that formed the basis of the political troubles of the past.

Low state of industrial development

Russia has always been in a low state of industrial development. Household industries, in response to the long and otherwise idle winter, are still maintained on a large scale (Figs. 196, 197), and trade by barter is on a greater scale than in any other civilized country of the world. Trade is still centered in part in village and city fairs of great commercial importance. More than 16,000 of these fairs are held in Russia, 85 per cent of them in European Russia. They are trading centers for the sale and in part for the exchange of goods, and like those that have been maintained in Latin America ever since the colonial period, they have retained not a little of the medieval aspect of the fair.

In normal times more than 100,000 visitors attend the Nijni Novgorod fair from 28 July to 7 September. The principal products dealt in are tea, raw cotton, furs, hides, woolen goods, undressed fur, camel's hair, iron and other metals.

Fig. 195. View of Nijni Novgorod and the fair across the Oka River.

Imported raw materials

In the factories of the large cities, wages have hitherto been low, while the cost of production has been high on account of the numerous church holidays and the tendency of the Russian industrial worker to return to the land for the harvest season. A considerable quantity of the raw material for manufacture was imported, the rate of transportation was high, the industrial centers were far from the sea, capital and the higher grades of skilled labor had to come from abroad.

Disadvantages of the navigable streams

In the absence of first-class roads and with few railroads until recent years, the streams and canals were the basis of transportation in large districts for a considerable part of the year. They have, however, only limited advantages. The great change in rainfall from summer to winter renders the streams unnavigable for part of the year, and

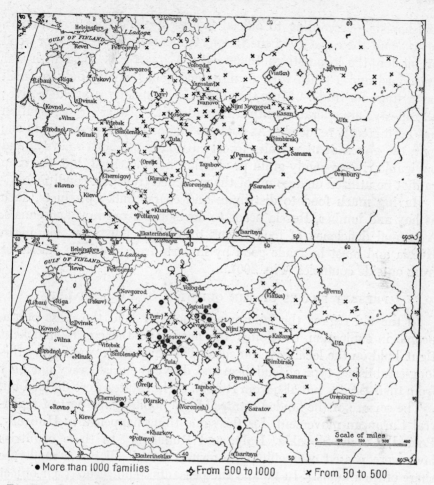

● More than 1000 families   ◇ From 500 to 1000   ✕ From 50 to 500

FIG. 196. Peasant industries: metals and minerals (upper panel). The rise of large industries in Russia is a recent and limited development. The long winters of the central and northern portions and the poor roads have impelled the peasants to engage in industry locally and on a household scale. Compare with Figures 198 and 199.

FIG. 197. Peasant industries: textiles (lower panel). Wood, leather, and other peasant industries show about the same distributions and form an interesting contrast in position and character with the mining and metal industries on a great scale that have developed in southern Russia, notably in the Donetz basin near the Black Sea.

all of them are frozen for a part of the year, — the Volga for nearly half the year in the north and for three months at Astrakhan on the Caspian Sea; the Don for more than 100 days on the average; the Dnieper for the same period; the Dvina for about 125 days; and the Vistula at Warsaw for more than two months.

Russia is still poorly served by railroads, and what is almost equally bad, her rolling stock (especially her locomotives) has been all but used up, first in the World War, and later in the civil war of the

Bolshevists. According to official figures of the Soviet government, nearly half the capacity of the freight trains is filled with coal or wood or oil for the locomotives themselves, a quarter is filled with war materials, and a tenth with confiscated goods, leaving only a small percentage for trade. More than half the locomotives are defective; all railways are operated with a huge deficit. River transportation has been greatly reduced. As coal production has dropped nearly one half, the government permits forest cutting along both railways and navigable rivers. Only grain production has increased, but the crop cannot be utilized on account of the wretched transport conditions.

Having much food to distribute and coarse bulky products, such as hay and lumber, Russia needs to develop her railways and canals. A normal deficiency of food occurs over three fourths of European Russia and must be made good by imports from southern Russia or from outside countries (Fig. 200).

PRESENT PHASES OF THE QUESTION OF LAND TENURE

In the old régime the land-owning nobility held the mass of the people in subjection, controlled the army and the courts, and kept tight hold on the local government. The revolution swept away this long-established type of feudalism and drove the aristocracy not only from their estates but also from Russia. The estates were divided up.

The seizure of the landed estates of the nobility was part of a general European movement, for the same thing happened in Hungary, Poland, Czecho-Slovakia, Italy, and Rumania. In these countries laws were passed compelling the owners to sell all but a moderate share of their lands. In Poland the peasants could secure their object only by joining the Socialists of the towns, but this alliance will not last long, for, in every respect except their attitude toward the land-owners, the radicals of the towns are the exact opposite of the conservative peasant class. In Italy, on the other hand, there were violent disorders in October and November of 1919, as a result of the peasants' forcible seizure of the land. In Germany the big landowners have until 1921 in which to sell their estates. The process of division of large estates is going on in the Ukraine also, in the Baltic Provinces, and in Rumania.. A great landholding nobility, long politically powerful, has lost its monopoly of the soil of eastern and central Europe. Thus both the democratic and the nationalist movements of central and eastern Europe have had a strong socialistic background.

In the peasant class we may find the steadiest force of the future commonwealths of Russia, Hungary, Poland, and Czecho-Slovakia.

Once they have the land that they have long desired, once they own property and require laws to protect it, once they have their own products to market, the peasants will desire a steady government and individual ownership of property instead of the communism of the Bolshevists.

THE SEPARATION OF THE BORDER PEOPLES

When Russia became Bolshevist the border peoples everywhere broke away from the central government, organized local governments, and sought to win recognition as independent sovereign states. The people of each region had long felt that their provincial problems were neglected by the former central government, and, infected by the general unrest and disorder of the World War, they sought a change of authority. The Bolshevist leaders were willing to sign with Germany the treaty of Brest-Litovsk in 1918, which withdrew Russian sovereignty from the Baltic Provinces, thus recognizing the measurably non-Russian character of the Esths and Letts as well as of the Finns, Lithuanians, and Poles. That treaty was denounced by Germany in the armistice of 11 November 1918, but the action of the Bolshevist government is significant in the history of later attempts of these border peoples to lead an independent national life. Of equal significance is the recognition by the Soviet government in May 1920 of the "Far-Eastern Democratic Republic" of Siberia, and its expressed desire to conclude commercial and political agreements.

The following table gives the area, population, and degree of ethnic purity of the groups (exclusive of Finland and Poland) that have broken away from Russia in Europe and Transcaucasia:

	AREA IN SQ. MI.	POPULATION	ETHNIC PURITY
Esthonia	20,000	1,750,000	93
Latvia	25,000	2,400,000	70
Lithuania[1]	20,000	2,500,000	66
Ukraine[2]	200,000	30,000,000	70
Kuban	33,000	3,500,000	—
North Caucasia	58,000	4,300,000	—
Azerbaijan	40,000	4,000,000	75
Georgia	35,000	2,000,000	75
Armenia (Russian Armenia only)	25,000	1,500,000	50

Russia may become stronger politically for the loss of her subject

[1] Figures for Lithuania exclude the Vilna area and adjacent country in dispute with Poland.

[2] Attempted separation repeatedly.

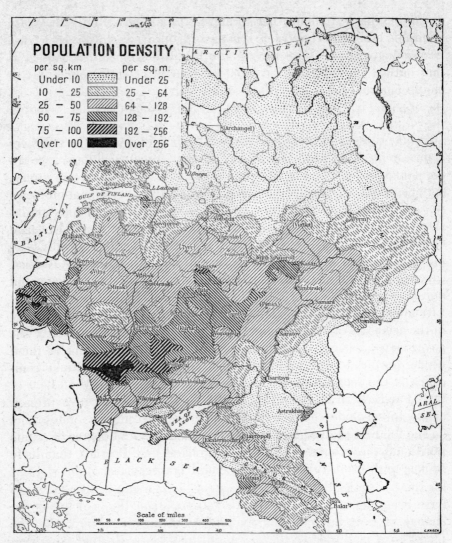

FIG. 198. The distribution of population densities in European Russia as in 1910 according to *Petermanns, Mitteilungen*, 1913, I, Pl. 2, and Romer, *Atlas géographique et statistique de la Pologne*, 1916. Note the effect of withdrawing Poland, the Baltic Provinces, Finland, the Ukraine, and Transcaucasia. The boundaries of the different governments of pre-war Russia are shown by fine dotted lines; the capitals are given in each case, without parentheses if the population exceeds 100,000, with parentheses if under 100,000.

races, the Poles, the Finns, the Georgians, the Letts, the Esths, and the Lithuanians; the struggle of these peoples for freedom threatened the unity and institutions of the Russian state. The freedom-seeking peoples within the borders of the former Russian Empire were more democratic than their rulers, the Russian nobility. When they became free they discarded the rule of a medieval caste for the ballot of a modern state, but their political strength and their ability to create favorable economic conditions remain to be proved.

Working against the union of the fragments of former Russia is the nature of the land itself. In Siberia, for instance, broad mountains and plateaus (the Yablanoi and Stanavoi ranges) cross the region in the neighborhood of Lake Irkutsk and separate the lower Amur provinces from western Siberia; the trans-Siberian railroad cuts across them, but one railroad is too slender a thread to unite governments and people so widely different in opportunity and in contact with the outside world. The chief rivers of Siberia flow northward to an ice-choked sea, accessible only from the west. Working towards separation is the desire of each section to profit by the special resources in its possession. Thus the Republic of Georgia produces 44 per cent of the world's manganese and wishes to profit by it, and a similar motive animates the Azerbaijan Tatars, who produce 13 per cent of the world's oil in the Baku region and do not wish to share the benefits with the rest of Russia. *Physical diversity of the Russian Empire*

If union can be effected at all, it will be only by forming the scattered parts into a loose confederation that will guarantee that the needs of the local groups, or county governments, shall be met, while protecting the larger interests to which every state is committed, especially in regard to foreign trade.

The growth of coöperative societies in Russia is an extraordinary expression of the community spirit for a country in which more than 80 per cent of the population are illiterate. In the last forty years the number of societies has increased from less than 400 to nearly 50,000, with a total enrollment of 20,000,000 heads of families. But for these societies the economic needs of the Russian people could not have been met at all. Their work is based upon the principle of exchange of raw materials for manufactured goods. They take the place, to a large degree, of the middleman class of other countries. Given peace and a restoration of foreign trade, Russia may quickly gain a place as a great trading nation through the development of her large coöperative unions.

The Transcaucasian peoples have broken away from the main mass of Russians and possess nominal independence (pp. 450–461). Theoretically, Georgia and Armenia are republics. The high snowy wall of the Caucasus separates them from the wheat-growing Cossacks of the Kuban, southeast of the Sea of Azov. The Caspian and Black seas are their natural frontiers east and west. In the valley lowland between the Caucasus and the Armenian plateau we have a thoroughfare for *Transcaucasian peoples* commerce for trans-Caspian or Russian Turkestan, an outlet for the manganese of Georgia and the rich oil fields of Baku. Inhabited by small nations the region would not be an outpost of Russian imperial designs on the Persian Gulf or on Alexandretta in the Mediterranean, where Anatolia and Syria meet.

Possibility of a Black Sea Confederation
Even if the whole of former Russia should not unite into a common empire, there is a real possibility of a Black Sea federation, because of the common interests of the Ukraine, the Don, and the Kuban. The three wish to have:

(1) Access to Black Sea ports.
(2) Free use of the Dardanelles.
(3) Strong defense against disorder.
(4) Technical help and loans from foreign powers.
(5) Free inter-regional trade.

The Kuban produces rice, wheat, wool, tobacco, and copper; the Ukraine sends to the Don and the Kuban corn, sugar, flour, and iron and steel products. Free interstate commerce is a real necessity, whatever political ties may be developed.

A Siberian and a Turkestan confederation are other possibilities, but of them nothing definite can be said at this time.

Russian extension into Asia a thing of the past
The future international problems of Russia cannot be forecast clearly, but if the government becomes in truth democratic, the long struggle with England in central Asia will probably not be revived. In Mongolia and Tibet, in Persia and Afghanistan, in Caucasia and at Constantinople, the Russian has been pressing forward for three hundred years, and no system of government can stand that denies him proper commercial outlets. His slogan has been "a warm-water port." That explains his reaching out in the Far East to Vladivostok, which proved not to be ice-free in winter; it explains his effort to reach the head of the Persian Gulf, where he was blocked by the British; it explains the development of the Murman coast, where a branch of the northern Atlantic warm-water drift keeps Alexandrovsk, north of the Arctic Circle, open even in winter; it explains the struggle with Turkey and the west-European powers for Constantinople.

Economic consequences of Ukrainian separation
The advantage of reorganizing the Russian realm on the lines of a great confederation instead of allowing it to break up indefinitely is most clearly seen when we consider the economic and geographical effects of withdrawing the southern region — a possibility involved in the Ukrainian movement. As originally delimited in 1918, the Republic of the Ukraine would have an area of 20,000 square miles and a population, chiefly Ukrainian, of about 30,000,000 (page 224), out of a total of

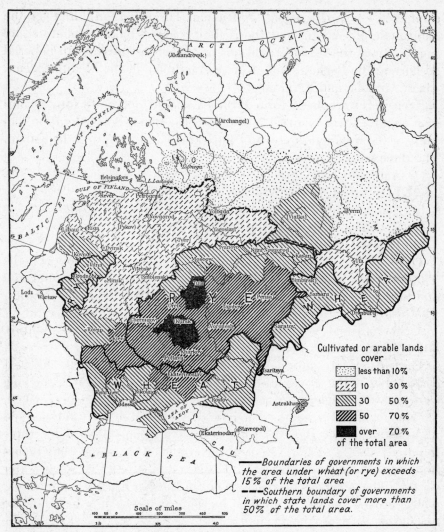

FIG. 199.   Wheat and rye, cultivated and arable lands of European Russia.   Compare with Figure 191.   Poland, Finland, the Caucasus region, and western Siberia are omitted.   From maps in *La Russie à la fin du 19ᵉ siècle*, Paris, 1900.

100,000,000 for all European Russia (Fig. 180).   This means that the Ukraine includes 15 per cent of the area of European Russia and 30 per cent of the population.   Its population density is 150 to the square mile, as compared with 70 per cent for European Russia.

In European Russia about 25 per cent of the land is arable and 40 per cent is woodland; but in the Ukraine the arable land constitutes 65 per cent and the woodland 10 per cent of the total area (forests, 3 per cent).   The Ukraine is the garden of Russia, a pleasant, warm

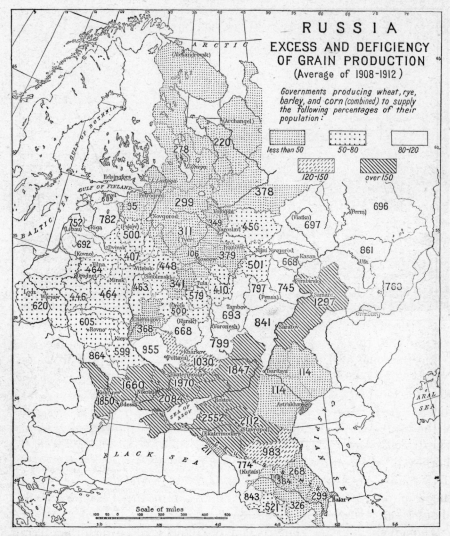

Fig. 200. The chief cereal supply of European Russia. A belt having neither marked excess nor deficiency trends northeastward from northern Rumania to the Urals and separates a huge northwestern cereal-deficient tract dependent upon the southern Ukraine, the Don region, and the Taurida northwest of the Caucasus. The map suggests one of the grave problems of the rest of Russia should the Ukraine become independent. The figures give the average annual per capita production for each government. The average annual consumption of the four grains mapped is about 800 pounds a person.

southland quite unlike the northern half of the country. It produces 40 per cent of the wheat of the whole empire, 50 per cent of the barley, and more than 80 per cent of the sugar. In addition it produces two thirds of the tobacco of European Russia. Its grain crop in 1919, in spite of disturbed conditions, was one third larger than in peace times,

Fig. 201. Part of the harbor of Odessa, the chief Russian port on the Black Sea.

The Ukraine also has very valuable deposits of coal and iron ore. Nearly 70 per cent of Ukrainian coal comes from the Donetz basin, which is located partly in Ekaterinoslav and partly in the Don territory. These two regions together (Donetz and Don) yield 90 per cent of the total coal production in European Russia, exclusive of Poland. The Ukraine exports coal to Austria by way of the Danube and to Turkey by way of the Black Sea ports. Of its exports 83 per cent (by weight) pass through Black Sea ports. About three fourths of the iron ore produced in Russia comes from the Ukraine, chiefly about Ekaterinoslav and the province of Kherson.

Though the Ukraine comprises about 10 per cent of the former territory of European Russia, it has 25 per cent of the railway mileage.

These figures for crops, coal and iron production, export, and railway mileage, show in a striking way the dependence of the central and northern parts of Russia upon the Ukraine for food, fuel, and access to the sea. The Ukraine is dependent, but not to an equal degree, upon the rest of Russia. It needs the oil of Baku, the timber of the northern forests, the dairy products of Siberia, the cotton of Transcaucasia and Turkestan. Russia would be a far stronger country if it held together instead of breaking up into fragments. While its economic conditions make the Ukraine a fairly self-dependent unit empha-

Interdependence of the Ukraine and the rest of Russia

sized by its geographical situation and character, it has never had political unity, and its people do not form a distinct and homogeneous nation. There is no distinctive social and cultural type. These facts were clearly seen when the Ukrainian government began to function after the fall of the first democratic government under Kerensky in 1917. Division and conflict began at once to sap the national strength. A western Ukrainian Republic under Petlura was organized and opposed Poles in the west, Bolshevists in the northeast, and the central Ukrainian government on the southeast. Later the central Ukrainian government disappeared and Petlura joined the Poles against the Bolshevists. In case of the complete defeat of Soviet authority, the policy of the Poles and the French would probably be to favor the creation of a separate Ukrainian state and thus reduce the strength and the chances of future Russian aggression.

THE COUNTRY OF THE DON COSSACKS

Still another group that favored a separatist movement and that is of great geographical and political interest is formed by the Don Cossacks, who live in southeastern Russia in a province divided by the Don River. The country is in general level. It is the transition region in climate and products between Asia and Europe. The soil east of the Don River is more suitable for grazing than for farming. The soil west of the Don is a deep, black, rich loam. The river itself is not navigable except for small craft. There are important deposits of coal, iron, and salt.

Tribal organization of the people

The people are of Tatar origin and originally lived by fishing, hunting, and plundering. It is only recently that they have become stock raisers and farmers. They own a higher percentage of live stock than any other group in the former Russian Empire. There are also 20,000 fishermen on the Sea of Azov and the lower Don.

Wherever the soil was tilled, the labor was done by serfs. The Cossacks themselves disdained agriculture. They had a loose tribal organization which involved an assembly that determined questions of war and peace, and elected officers, including a headman, or hetman.

Their enmity toward the Turks

In the 17th and 18th centuries the relations between the Cossacks and the Russians, which had been marked by mutual ill will, became closer because of their common interest in fighting the Turk on the northern coast of the Black Sea and in the Caucasus. There is an army of about 25,000 Cossacks in the Don Province in peace times, but five or six times this number may be called out. They are all good horsemen and fight admirably in the old-fashioned way, but not against modern artillery and in prolonged campaigns.

The total population of the country of the Don Cossacks is about 4,000,000, of which 67 per cent are Great Russian and 28 per cent Ukrainian. During the civil war of the Bolshevist régime they have formed an independent unit, fighting first under the leadership of Kolchak, then of Denikin, and later coöperating with Wrangel. Their local successes were due to the nature of the fighting, which was carried on in flat, open country where horsemen have an advantage over foot soldiers. *Denikin's army of Cossack soldiers*

THE SIBERIAN REALM

An important feature of the character of the Russian people is their ready adaptation to new conditions. This quality has exhibited itself throughout Russian history. Successive waves of population swept across European Russia in the 7th, 8th, and 9th centuries of our era, and one may say that the entire population consisted of pioneers experimenting under new conditions. There went on during this period a process of ethnic absorption and modification, until there was evolved the Slav type of the present day, fairly uniform in racial quality in later times. The Russian has always been able to become farmer, tradesman, hunter, fisherman, or cattle breeder, without losing the community organization that more than any other thing characterizes his life. This adaptability to circumstances has made him a successful explorer and colonist and has been one of the most powerful agencies of empire. *Russian power of adaptation*

In recent years the Russian colonizing movement has been most effective in Siberia. A narrow belt of European population has been thrown right across Siberia for 4000 miles from Omsk to Vladivostok (Fig. 203). With its 13,000,000 people, the region is so important to the future of Russia that its historical development as well as its economic and political problems deserve special consideration.

Up to the 16th century, Siberia was not safe for the settler or the traveler. Trade across it was from point to point through tribal territory, and continued thus until the subjugation of the southern region, first by the Turks and then by the Russians. By the early 17th century, after repeated efforts and failures by others, Yermak, a Russian Cossack explorer, had opened wide the door to the Orient and made possible the acquisition by Russia in later years of the vast Siberian realm, that includes a fourth of all Asia. For Russia the work of Yermak marks the beginning of a new epoch. By 1630 the *Early Russian conquests in Siberia*

Russians claimed to be masters of the Yenisei. In 1638 tea was first imported from China. By 1643 the Cossacks had reached Lake Baikal, and by 1656 they had reached the Bering Sea, every step accompanied by hardship. There followed a fierce contest with the Manchurians for the possession of the Amur country, which ended in 1688 with Russian colonists firmly planted on China's northern frontier.

Russia's period of scientific exploration

In 1658 Russia seized the Amur, and by the treaty of Aigun the Amur was made the boundary between the Russian and Chinese empires. In 1733 came the expedition of Bering and Chirikov, who discovered the mainland of North America, the Aleutian Islands, and the Kuriles north of Japan. There followed great activity in trade and trapping. Just before 1800 the Russian-American Company was organized, with enormous privileges.

With the Russians firmly planted in eastern Siberia, the power of the Mongol-Tatar hordes was forever broken. If western civilization held back the Slavic hordes, the latter in turn defended western Europe from further Mongol invasion. To Russia, the advance into Siberia was the opening of an epoch as important for her as the discovery of America and the opening of the water route to India were to the western powers.

Spread of colonists and exiles

Colonists and criminals were sent into Siberia to establish settlements around the fortresses, to work in the mines, and to guard the fur-trade routes. In the 16th and 17th centuries these movements of colonists and prisoners or exiles became an established custom. The first Siberian prisoners were sent out in 1593, and at about the same time state aid was given to a first group of farmer colonists.

The census of 1897 gave Siberia 300,000 prisoners out of a total population of 5,700,000. Of the present total of 13,000,000 population, 9,000,000 are Russians. In the past twenty-five years the population of Siberia has doubled. In the early 19th century, Russian state settlers began to go into the region in large numbers, and they are increasing faster than the total by about one fifth. The 6000-mile trans-Siberian railway was pushed to completion in 1904, not only for the purpose of defense but also in order to get colonists into Siberia.

Poor facilities for export of products

Figure 203 shows the distribution of Russian settlements in Siberia and their close connection with the trans-Siberian railroad and its branches. However, in spite of the railroad, the conditions of transportation are still exceedingly difficult. The freight rates are high, and the markets of the Far East and of Europe, which furnish the only

Fig. 202. Russian colonists emigrating to Siberia.

outlet for the grain, dairy products, etc., of Siberia, are far distant. As a result the development of the country is still slow, in spite of the fact that the quantity of grain produced is almost double the amount consumed.

Grain and dairy products are produced in huge quantities in the pastures and prairies of the northern section, just at the edge of the great *taigá*, or forest belt; cotton is the chief commercial crop of the southern section in Turkestan, where irrigation is developing to give life to the desert country beyond the Caspian. Just before the World War, great trading companies had started a regular fleet of nearly eighty steamers on the Siberian rivers and had brought out butter, furs, lumber, etc., in huge quantities; they had demonstrated the possibilities of the Arctic route to Siberia, a thing that Nansen, the Arctic explorer, had long advocated. *Arctic route to Siberia*

With the revolution of 1917 in Russia, Siberia broke up into groups. Soviet committees were formed in all the important centers and included all classes, even bankers and business men. At first the system worked well, because it was democratic and there was no violence; but soon opposition "soviets" appeared. Democratic republics were organized in many places. With the coming into power of the Bolshevists, eastern Siberia fell into disorder, until the military *Political break-up of Siberia* expedition of the Allies into eastern Siberia quieted the region and Admiral Kolchak on the west gained control of the border. With the defeat of Kolchak late in 1919 disorder again became general, and no coherent authority is now exercised.

A republic of Eastern Siberia has been organized, but its power will be feeble so long as it has no effective railway connection with Europe and so long as Japan holds Vladivostok, the eastern commercial outlet of Siberia.

Objects of revolutionary groups in Siberia

In European Russia the land question had been one of the bases of revolutionary agitation for many years, and with the passing of the old régime, the reform of the land tenure system became a part of the Soviet program. In contrast with this situation is the absence of a land question in Siberia. Hence the Soviet government was able to organize in Siberia local governments sympathetic towards it, not for the usual reasons, but for the reason that Siberia is composed of frontier peoples who had always striven for local self-government of the zemstvo type, as promised by the Czar in 1905.

This promise has now been repeated by the Soviet government, but there is no substance to the promise, since there is no unity among the Siberian people as to the practical form that local self-government shall take, and there is likewise as yet no uniformity or stability in the

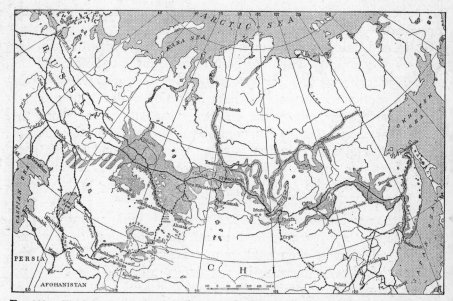

Fig. 203. The field of settlement of Russian colonists in Siberia according to the *Atlas of Asiatic Russia*, 1914. Note the scattered settlements in dry Turkestan and the continuity of settlements in the belt of heavier rainfall on the margin of forest and grassland farther north (Fig. 204).

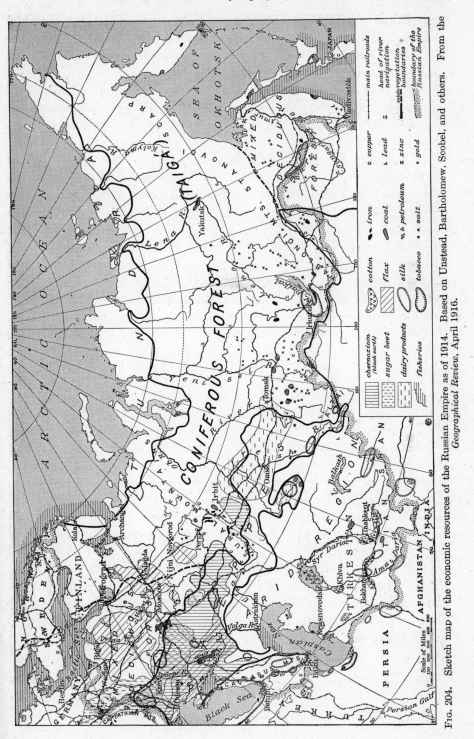

Fig. 204. Sketch map of the economic resources of the Russian Empire as of 1914. Based on Unstead, Bartholomew, Scobel, and others. From the *Geographical Review*, April 1916.

Fig. 205.   Samoyeds of the island of Nova Zembla, a Russian possession in the Arctic.   Russia's northern country for the most part is inhabited by primitive peoples of which this is one type.

Soviet government itself.   Siberia is without leaders.   Its people are interested in the discussion of theories of government, but only a few are sufficiently educated to work out practical measures, and there is also a large proportion of lawless people who make the organization of life and government still more difficult.

Great size of Siberia and great extent of its frontier

Siberia is a country difficult to control at best.   Its area is 4,832,000 square miles, excluding the Transcaspian, Turkestan, and steppe provinces, or 6,294,000 square miles if we include these provinces. Thus in size it is far greater than the United States, and it is more difficult of access than northern Canada.   The length of the Russian-Chinese boundary is 4700 miles; the northern coast line from Kara Bay to Bering Strait is about 10,000 miles long; the length of the eastern coast line on the Pacific is nearly 8400 miles.   To guard the excessively long and remote frontiers, partly in the north, partly in the mountains, is a problem of first importance, and but for the fact that long stretches of the frontier are yet uninhabited, effective government control could not be exercised.

CHAPTER TWENTY-FOUR

CONSTANTINOPLE AND ITS THOROUGHFARE

THERE are four cities, it is said, that belong to all men rather than to the people of one nation — Rome, Athens, Jerusalem, and Constantinople. All four are closely related to Mediterranean history. The capture of each one of them at one time or another has been a turning point in human affairs. Their temples have seen the growth of powerful religious influences. Their streets have echoed more than once to the tramp of armies bent on conquest far beyond "the rim of the known world." *Constantinople one of four world cities*

Constantinople is one of the most beautiful cities in the world and has a history full of color and tragedy and romantic adventure. Jason sailed past the site of it in his search for the Golden Fleece. From the days of Xerxes and of Alexander the Great down to its capture in 1453 by the Turks, it was a point of great military interest. For nearly a thousand years it was one of the chief centers of culture and the capital of the Byzantine, or Eastern, Empire. Its natural defenses are very strong. Napoleon believed that its possession was worth half an empire. Even under the handicaps of Turkish rule Constantinople remained a great port. Its position at the crossroads of Europe and Asia enabled it, down to recent times, to profit enormously from the trade of southern Russia, the Transcaucasus, Persia, and Mesopotamia, and also, in earlier years, from the overland trade of Inner Asia, India, and the Far East. Through it ran a part of the Berlin-Bagdad railway line, by which Germany expected to control the Near East and the road to India. *Historic setting of the city*

As a commercial thoroughfare for eastern products, the Constantinople region has now only a limited value. A large part of the commerce of the Straits — that is, both the Dardanelles and the Bosporus (Fig. 207) — passes the door of the city but does not enter it. While its historical position as a focus of sea and land roads is still maintained, the development of ocean commerce in modern times and the possibilities, supplied by the Suez Canal (opened in 1869), of an all-sea road from Persia and India to western Europe, have greatly diminished its importance in this respect. It has profited little from the rapid development of Black Sea lands during the past hundred and fifty years. Southwestern Russia, in that period, was transformed from a pastoral to an agricultural realm, rich in cereals. Cities grew marvelously; industries sprang up; oil and manganese *Only a small part of the trade of the Bosporus sent through Constantinople*

FIG. 206.   General view

were exported in large quantities.   From 70 to 90 per cent of the total exports of these products went by way of the Straits.

But in just the proportion that these lands became economically strong, Constantinople — the gateway of southern Russia — gained in political and military importance.   For centuries it was one of the settled aims of intelligent Russians, as well as of Russian rulers, to gain possession of the city; and religious motives were added to commercial reasons : Constantinople was the city from which Russia got her religion.

Russian desire for Constantinople

The pressure of the Russians was first exerted against the Greeks (for example, in the 10th century), and after 1453 against the Turks. In 1878 Russian soldiers were almost within sight of the minarets of Constantinople.   In 1914 it was promised to Russia by the Allies if they should win the war.   It is the only "warm" port and one of the three "open" ports that Russia could expect to have.   The others are Vladivostok in eastern Siberia (Fig. 244) and Alexandrovsk on the Murman coast of the Arctic (Fig. 90).[1]

[1] At Riga the period of ice blockade is reduced to one month by the use of ice-breakers. Vladivostok, though called an "open port," is closed for a short period in extreme winter weather; hence, in part, the struggle for Dairen (Port Dalny) during the Russo-Japanese War.

of Constantinople.

Brown Bros.

CONSTANTINOPLE'S PLACE IN THE PAN-GERMAN SCHEME

It was during the period of rapid growth of Black Sea commerce from 1880 to 1914 that there was developed in Germany a policy which went under the name of Pan-Germanism and which was fostered by the military party and the Hohenzollerns. It sought to achieve many imperial objects, among which was the control of the rich lands of the Near East as a source of raw material for the crowded industrial districts of Germany. In 1898 the German Emperor visited Damascus, Jerusalem, and Constantinople, making his visit the occasion for the furthering of Pan-German aims. From that time until the opening of the war in 1914, Germany pressed the construction of the Berlin-Bagdad railway as part of a general scheme for reaching into subtropical lands and controlling a larger share of the world's raw materials. She aimed to build the Bagdad railway to the head of the Persian Gulf, whence she could divert the commerce of India and the Far East. The Bagdad railway and its branches were her means of reaching the copper of the Taurus Mountains in southwestern Armenia, and of bringing out the tobacco, fruits, cotton, and wool of Mesopotamia and Kurdistan in return for manufactured articles from German mills.

Growth of German political and economic influence

German
goods in
competi-
tion with
those of
England
and France

German enterprise was highly successful, and German imports into the Turkish Empire rose from 6 per cent in 1887 to 21 per cent in 1910; those of Austria from 13 per cent to 21 per cent. During the same time the imports of English goods fell from 60 per cent to 35 per cent, and of French goods from 18 per cent to 11 per cent of the total. German business men from 1908 to 1911 obtained very important concessions for the port of Alexandretta and for the building of a line from Bagdad to Basra, in territory of great strategic importance to India and the Far East and in relation to the politics and commerce of the Mohammedan world (Fig. 23). In 1913 General Liman von Sanders headed a German military mission at Constantinople which thereafter practically controlled the Ottoman army.

The latest struggle for Constantinople began early in the World War. It led to the disastrous Gallipoli expedition of the Allies against the Turks in 1915–1916; and after the defeat of this expedition and the entry of Bulgaria into the war, direct railway connection was established from Berlin to Constantinople, thence across Anatolia and via the tunnel through the Taurus Mountains to the head of the Gulf of Alexandretta, and again through the tunnel that pierces the Amanus range to Aleppo and eastward to Nisibin. Germany did not relinquish her hold of the Bagdad line until the end of the war. She furnished supplies and ammunition for the Turkish armies operating in Palestine, which armies the Allied forces (chiefly British) could dislodge only by building another line from El Kantara in Egypt northeastward through the Sinai desert to Gaza, and thence to a connection with Jerusalem.

ELEMENTS AFFECTING THE SETTLEMENT OF THE CONSTANTINOPLE QUESTION

Free use
of the
Straits of
interest to
many
powers

It was natural that the people of the other three world-cities, mentioned on page 409, should be greatly concerned in the fate of Constantinople. Italy has a traditional friendship for Rumania, which she can reach directly only by passing Constantinople. The Jews of Palestine, and likewise the Syrians and Armenians, farther north, watched with intense interest the fate of Constantinople in the World War; the capture of the city by the Allies, it was believed, would free all the oppressed peoples of the Turkish Empire.

Greece has long hoped to restore to the protection of the homeland those Greeks who live in all the fair lands bordering the Black and Mediterranean seas (Fig. 158). She could never relinquish the

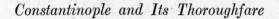

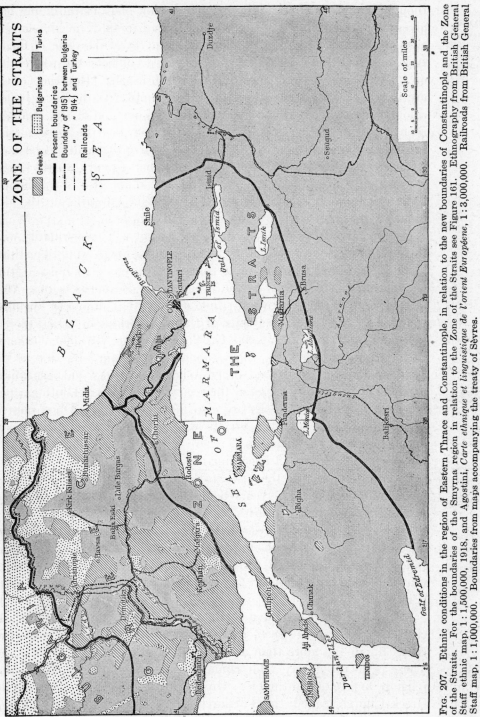

FIG. 207. Ethnic conditions in the region of Eastern Thrace and Constantinople, in relation to the new boundaries of Constantinople and the Zone of the Straits. - For the boundaries of the Smyrna region in relation to the Zone of the Straits see Figure 161. Ethnography from British General Staff ethnic map, 1 : 1,500,000, 1918, and Agostini, *Carte ethnique et linguistique de l'orient Européene*, 1 : 3,000,000. Railroads from British General Staff map, 1 : 1,000,000. Boundaries from maps accompanying the treaty of Sèvres.

Greek
wish to
have
ownership
of Con-
stantinople

thought that her thousand years' possession of Constantinople had
given her the strongest historical claim. Greeks form the largest
element in the Christian population of the city. The war of Greek
Independence (1821–1829) had for one of its objects the re-creation
of a Byzantine Empire, including Constantinople. But the Greeks
are not experienced governors of alien people. To be sure, in the
colonial period Greece had settlements from one end of the Mediterranean to the other; and like most other peoples the Greeks wish
to see their ancient glories restored. Of course that can not be done
without ignoring the ancient glories of other equally worthy states
whose claims overlap those of the Greeks. If the risk of war is ever
to be seriously diminished, rival nations will have to give up the idea
of a restoration of ancient glories by force of arms.

Constantinople is a rich city to hold; and it will grow rapidly with
the development of its tributary regions. Its growth would be stimulated by the construction of a tunnel or bridge — or both — from
one side of the Bosporus to the other. The Bosporus is only 2000
feet across at the narrowest point, or less than half the distance
spanned by the Brooklyn Bridge or the Eads Bridge at St. Louis.

Changes in
the popu-
lation of
the city

In addition to the 150,000 Greeks, there are 400,000 Turks in
Constantinople, and less than 150,000 Armenians, besides 50,000
Jews, as well as Kurds and other Asiatics. Greeks and Armenians
are almost certain to increase their city populations. Both peoples
are traders, and the Greeks are also famous sailors. Allied control
of Constantinople and the Straits will favor Greek influence there
and throughout the Near East, where within the next fifty years the
Greeks have a chance of becoming a powerful people.

Constantinople was the last stronghold in Europe of the Turks,
who had taken it forty years before Columbus sailed for America.
For four and a half centuries the Turk has been astride one of the
world's chief thoroughfares of commerce. The Mediterranean and
its eastern approaches in the region of Constantinople have been
called the moat between Christianity and Islam. It was a moat
that had been crossed at but two places, Constantinople and Gibraltar
(Fig. 23).

In modern times we have thought of Constantinople as a Turkish
city; but, as we have seen, it was the capital of the Eastern Christian Church for more than a thousand years, before the Turk came.
There is no absolutely vital connection between the Mohammedan
religion and Constantinople. On the other hand, the head of the
Greek Church, called the Patriarch, lives there and signs himself

Archbishop of Constantinople. To be sure, the Sultan declared himself to be the supreme head of the Mohammedan religion, but this assertion was not agreed to by all the Mohammedans themselves. Mecca has always been their religious capital. In actual practice the Sultan delegated his religious power to the Sheikh-Ul-Islam, and every Moslem law or decision was supposed to be confirmed by him; but the Arab chiefs of Mecca, Medina, Bagdad, Smyrna, Yemen, and Asir never acknowledged this ruling.

It was jealousy among the great powers that kept the Turk so long in Constantinople. No power wanted to see another in control of the strategic gateway of the Bosporus. This jealousy is in large part the basis of the present settlement. In many respects the policies of France and Great Britain are directly opposed to each other here, as well as elsewhere in the Near East. For example, the British would like to see the Greeks stay in Smyrna, because it would put not only the Smyrna region but its Turkish hinterland under the influence of the British fleet and British commercial interests. On the other hand, the French would like to see the Greeks driven out of Smyrna, where they would greatly foster British trade and become rivals of French trade. *[margin: Conflict of British and French policy in the Near East]*

In Constantinople we are likely to see this rivalry become acute. For the French have been active, ever since the Turkish armistice, at Constantinople and in the Balkans, where the Allied army was for a long time under the command of a French general. This general has assumed, and all his officers with him, that Greece, Rumania, Serbia, and Turkey are a French sphere of influence, a policy that has called forth a great deal of opposition among all the peoples affected. Rather than see French influence extended, the British prefer to let the Turks remain in Constantinople. If the French thought that putting the Turk out of Constantinople would bring the British into control of the region, they would prefer to have him stay. The French policy was materially helped by opposition within the Mohammedan world, chiefly in India, to a removal of the caliphate to Asia.[1] The result was a provision of the treaty of Sèvres (1920) between Turkey and the Allied powers that left Constantinople nominally in Turkish hands. *[margin: Acute conflict at Constantinople]*

The tables below show the trade of Smyrna, Trebizond, and Constantinople; they show also the overpowering strength of British shipping in that trade. They indicate how strong is the hold of

[1] For a further discussion of the caliphate see page 441.

the British upon the coastal regions and towns in areas of commercial and strategic importance in the Near East. Indeed, the organized commercial life of the whole world at the present time depends upon Great Britain to a surprising degree.

Not only is the through commerce of Constantinople large; the city is also the most important focus of Turkish trade. In 1910–1911 it had nearly a third of the total import trade of the Turkish Empire:

COMMERCE OF THE PRINCIPAL PORTS OF THE TURKISH EMPIRE (1910–11)

	IMPORTS	EXPORTS	
Constantinople	31.48%	9.00%	
Smyrna	10.87	20.60	
Saloniki	10.64	5.04	
Beirut	9.98	4.66	
Haidar Pasha			Total of 5.94%
Trebizond	2.24	1.28	
Dedeagatch	1.65	1.82	

Total value of exports in 1910–11 . . . . $80,000,000
Total value of imports in 1910–11 150,000,000

The primacy of British shipping in the Mediterranean region is shown by the following figures, which give for the Mediterranean and Black seas, Red Sea, and Persian Gulf in 1913–1914 totals of (approximately):

	TONS		TONS
British	14,000,000	Italian	4,000,000
Austro-Hungarian	6,500,000	French	4,000,000
Russian	5,500,000	German	2,750,000
Turkish	5,000,000	Greek	2,250,000

Dutch, Belgian, and Rumanian, less than 1,000,000 tons each

For Russian, German, Austro-Hungarian, Greek, and Italian shipping, the total is about 1,000,000 tons each for Constantinople, with British shipping at 6,500,000 tons.

THE NEW STATUS

Constantinople is left in Turkish hands by the terms of the treaty of Sèvres (1920), and with the city goes a tiny hinterland (Fig. 207). All the rest of Turkey's European possessions are definitely lost:

(1) To the Allies, at Suvla Bay, where an international cemetery (British, French, and Italian) is to be created for the soldiers who died in the ill-fated Gallipoli expedition.

(2) To Greece, which obtains both Western and Eastern Thrace.

The Straits are to be under Allied control; and the northern coast of Marmara, while under Greek sovereignty, is to be neutral more than nine miles inland. The new status of Constantinople excludes fortification. The definite intention of the great powers is to secure the freedom of the surrounding territory. It is thought that there is no need even for the fortification of any of the islands in the Ægean. Nearly all of these pass to Greece, whose navy is bound to remain too small to be a menace either to the great powers or to the security of the trade routes of the countries that border the eastern Mediterranean. Italy secures temporary possession of Rhodes, but as her navy can never rival that of Great Britain or of France, her position there is not a matter of great international importance. Statesmen are agreed that anything less than free passage of the Straits would be a source of irritation both to the people of southern Russia and to those of Georgia and Armenia, all of whom desire unrestricted passage for goods and ships, including war vessels.

Constantinople under the new Allied régime

The principal provisions for the regulation of the neutral zone of the Straits, as established by the treaty of Sèvres,[1] are the following:

(1) The Straits are to be under the control of a Commission of the Straits, composed of representatives of Great Britain, France, Italy, Japan, Russia (if and when it becomes a member of the League of Nations), the United States (if it is willing to participate), Bulgaria (if and when it becomes a member of the League), Turkey, and Greece. But nominal sovereignty of the zone is divided between the two last-named powers, Constantinople and the southern shore being Turkish, and the north shore west of Constantinople being Greek.

(2) The Commission is to have complete control of the navigation of the Straits, and shall maintain equality of all charges or dues, regardless of the port of origin, or destination, or departure, or flag, or ownership. Sanitation and the life-saving service also are to be under its control.

(3) Consular courts have supervision over infringements of the laws by their nationals, and in time the Turkish courts are to have jurisdiction over their own nationals.

(4) The Straits are to remain open in peace and in war for all craft, and are to be neutral in time of war. They are not to be subject to blockade or other hostile act.

(5) All fortifications within the neutral zone are to be demolished.

[1] At the London Conference of March 1921, various compromises favorable to Turkey were discussed. If these are adopted, the treaty of Sèvres as outlined in this chapter may be greatly modified in Thrace and Smyrna and also with respect to the capitulations and the Ottoman Debt.

CHAPTER TWENTY-FIVE

PALESTINE: A JEWISH HOMELAND UNDER A BRITISH MANDATARY

The Jews a minority in Palestine

THOUGH Palestine is the birthplace of both the Hebraic and the Christian religions, neither faith predominates there today. Of Christian sects there are a few, the members belonging for the most part to religious orders that are associated with the holy places. Jews form barely an eighth of the total population of 700,000. The rest are chiefly Moslem Arabs, Druses, and Turks. Since there are about 15,000,000 Jews in the world, it is seen that the 80,000 who live in Palestine are but a small fraction of the total number.

THE PROPOSED ZIONIST STATE

Religious differences likely to cause trouble to the new government

The widespread interest in the creation of a new Jewish state, one of the chief objects of the Zionist movement, springs from the fact that such a state would form a homeland for Jews outside as well as inside Palestine and would afford an opportunity to establish a nation in which Jews might become, in time, the majority race. The most serious problem that arises is political control. To turn the government of the new state over to either the Jews or the Arabs would sow discord at the start. The population has had no experience in government, and it would certainly carry into its first political contests a fanatical religious feeling that but for outside supervision would spell disaster.

In the light of these possibilities there appeared to be but one course for the great powers to take: to make a strong western power the mandatary. In the treaty of Sèvres (1920) it was provided that Palestine should be administered by a mandatary, and that this mandatary should carry out the terms of the British declaration of 2 November 1917, which guaranteed the establishment of a Jewish national home. At the same time it was specified that the rights of non-Jews were not to be prejudiced.

Great Britain appointed the mandatary of the League of Nations

It was natural to select Great Britain as the mandatary, because of her interest in the security of the Suez Canal near by and in the orderly behavior of the Arab tribes that adjoin Palestine on the east and south. Experienced in controlling unruly peoples of diverse race, speech, and religious faith, Great Britain, with a strong and mobile fleet, will be able to maintain order and thus supply an opportunity for the natives to learn the processes of self-government. Having been selected as the mandatary, Great Britain proceeded to

418

appoint a High Commissioner. The announced policy of this commissioner is : first, to provide for equality of treatment of the population elements ; and second, to provide a national home for the Jews, permitting them to return to Palestine only as the development of that country guarantees the normal absorption of immigrants for rising industries and reclaimed agricultural lands.

Jewish colonies began to be established in Palestine as early as the 16th century, but the principal efforts have been made within the last fifty or sixty years, partly because of the pogroms and other persecutions in Russia, and partly for reasons of sentiment. By 1914 there were in Palestine 46 agricultural colonies, of which 20 were in Judea, 7 in Samaria, 16 in Galilee, and 3 east of the Jordan. They vary in population from 20 to more than 3000. The total number of colonists is about 12,000. The area of land they cultivate is about 2 per cent of the whole of Palestine, or possibly 10 per cent of its cultivated area. Most of the colonies are agricultural. A few of them, like Telavio, are composed in large part of shopkeepers, teachers, and engineers. The colonists produce oranges, olives, grain, dairy products, vegetables, and poultry. An agricultural experiment station is maintained by Jews at Haifa. *Origin of Jewish colonies in Palestine*

RELATION OF PALESTINE TO THE WORLD

The decision which has placed Palestine under British control is but one step in a long historical sequence. Foreign influences have always surrounded and permeated Palestine. The seacoasts of Syria have called forth from the vast interior of Asia caravan and army. Up and down the Mediterranean coast, Turk and Egyptian have passed again and again. Doubtless the land would have no political individuality whatever, had it not been for the plateau of Judea, a region from 2500 to 3000 feet above the sea, to one side of and above the main historical currents of western Asiatic life. When the Israelites sought to hold the lower flat land, like the Negeb at the southern end of the plateau of Judea, they were driven out. The armies of conquest kept to the roads in the fertile coastal plains. The Jew still looks out, westward from his plateau, across a rich coastal plain held by unfriendly people whom he has never been able to conquer, except here and there for short periods. *Foreign influences in Palestine*

It was in Samaria, northern Palestine, that outside influences were strongest. Here the trade routes ran just south of the Sea of Galilee to the Plain of Esdraelon and the port of Haifa. Thus they avoided the mountains of Lebanon on the north and the rocky plateau of Judea *Samaria at one of the crossroads of western Asia* on the south. Foreign influences penetrated the life of Palestine at the north, but were largely shut out of the region of Judea.

Palestine is a tiny country. Set down in the United States, it would cover about the same area as Vermont, and it has about twice as many people. It has been called "the least of all lands." Yet so mighty a force has emanated from it — the Christian religion — that its spiritual influence has penetrated every part of the globe. The inspiration of the great Crusades of the Middle Ages was the freeing of its holy places, then held by the Moslem Turk. It has long been a place of pilgrimage for the devout. No other land in the world so well illustrates the political force and historical importance of ideas. Christ said, "My Kingdom is not of this world," but even the most ambitious and forceful rulers of history were unable to acquire empires whose extent equals that of the Christian realm at the present time.

THE PECULIAR POSITION OF THE JEWISH PEOPLE

The Jew has spread from his homeland in Palestine throughout the world, and he is everywhere marked by strong racial characteristics. All told, there are about 15,000,000 Jews in the world, of whom 4,000,000 live in Russia, about 2,500,000 in Poland, and about 1,000,000 in former Hungary. There are also large Jewish colonies in Constantinople, Saloniki, Barcelona, New York, and London, as well as in the larger German cities.

Wherever he has gone, the Jew has formed a race apart. This is due to his religion as well as to his social customs and his personal character, and also to the attitude toward him of the peoples among whom he has lived. He has been terribly persecuted in Russia, where repeated pogroms have had the aspect of wholesale massacres. The old Jewish Pale of Settlement in Russia (Fig. 192), east of which Jews could not settle, was designed to segregate him. The Russian policy resulted in a large concentration of Jews in western Russia, particularly in Poland; and it led also to heavy emigration to America. The American Jews are chiefly from Russia and Poland; very few are from Palestine. In Europe the Jew is found in every great trading center. In many cities either the local law or the instinct of the Jew has led him to congregate in a certain section, known as the Jewish Quarter, or Ghetto. Normally the Jew has maintained a certain aloofness toward the political and social life of the country in which he has lived.

It is a striking fact that in his own country the Jew was historically not a trader. The Jews of Palestine were a secluded people, devoted to agriculture, who went out from their own land across the sea to distant countries because their own country was small and poor and because of Roman policy during the first few centuries of the Christian era. Thus the race has undergone a complete transformation, for the Jew outside of Palestine is preëminently a trader. Indeed, a great deal of the general antagonism toward him, on the part of other races, is due to his exclusive devotion to trade and personal gain and his success therein. The Jew of Palestine a farmer, not a trader

POSSIBILITIES OF AGRICULTURAL DEVELOPMENT

The heart of Palestine is the plateau of Judea, flanked on either side by lowland. On the west is the fertile, well-watered coastal plain, a hundred miles long and about fifteen wide. The eastern margin is abrupt — a very steep scarp that leads down to the Ghor, the flat-bottomed depression in which are the Jordan and the Dead Sea, the latter more than 1200 feet below sea level. This scarp is the Wilderness of Judea, a rocky belt of land with steep valleys — a barren, waterless country, the home of the wandering Bedouin. Here early Christians took refuge in caves, and here a few Christian orders still maintain monasteries. Eastward, beyond the Ghor, is the Syrian desert, broken in three places by tracts of higher and better watered country. Form of the land

The plateau of Judea ordinarily has enough rainfall for a limited agriculture, though there are occasional droughts that turn the grain fields yellow before their time. On the east the aspect changes gradually. The rolling desert is grassy near the margin of the plateau, but parched farther east. In years of extreme drought the nomadic Arab comes up to the border of the desert, where the grain fields and the settled habitations are located and where fierce feuds arise between the settled farmer and the marauding shepherd. Only the center of the plateau of Judea has broad fields and fertile valleys; here also are the principal towns — Jerusalem, Bethlehem, and Hebron; and here the land is densely inhabited, though the total population is not large (Fig. 43). Isolated plateau of Judea

By contrast the Negeb south of the Judean plateau is a desert land, uninhabited except for a few small permanent villages supported by wells. It is a parched country in strong contrast to the grass-covered slopes of the adjacent highlands with their cereal fields, their flocks, and their historic cities.

The coastal region has a rainfall of more than 30 inches a year and is rich in verdure, except during the dry summer months. The great caravan routes of the region run along it. Here also are the populous cities and the ports. Four thousand years ago, in the days of Babylonia and Assyria, and again in the time of the Romans, the caravan trade was enormous. The whole region has been smitten by drought again and again, throughout its history, as in the terrible years of 1869 and 1870.

Palestine is capable of great agricultural development, a matter of extreme interest in the life of a new state that has practically no mineral deposits. Its climate and soil are so varied from place to place in short distances that many plants become adapted to a wide range of temperature and rainfall. The olive grows on land from 850 feet below sea level in the hot Jordan valley to 2500 feet above sea level in upper Galilee and 4000 to 5000 feet at Hermon and in the Lebanon, where there are freezing winter temperatures. The fig is grown abundantly in upper Galilee, where the population is dense and labor cheap, but export is on a small scale, owing to the lack of shipping facilities. The crop is sold chiefly to the Bedouins. Grapes are grown in large quantities. Besides having a local use, they are carried by donkey and camel to centers of trade for nomadic peoples on the desert's rim. Barley is a standard crop, even in some localities having but 10 to 12 inches of rain.

Water poverty is the great stumbling block to agricultural development. As a means of relieving it a Norwegian engineer has proposed the utilization of the difference in level between the Mediterranean Sea and the Dead Sea. The plan is to construct a tunnel some thirty-seven miles long which would carry water from the streams of the Mediterranean coastal belt to the lower end of the Jordan valley. A more immediately practical plan is to turn into the valley lands of northern Palestine a portion of the waters of the Litani River and of its tributaries. The necessity of securing additional water for irrigation in northern Palestine stimulated the Zionists to claim a northern boundary which should include most of the Litani watershed, but this claim was not allowed in the final settlement of the boundary by France and Great Britain (Fig. 209).

Outer
border of
land of
permanent
settle-
ments

East of the Dead Sea depression is a belt of transition country between Palestine proper and the Syrian desert. Its most important member is the Hauran, a plateau rising to 2000–3000 feet above the sea (Fig. 45). It has rich soil formed on volcanic rock; and though it has very few streams, it is sufficiently well watered to have wheat

Fig. 208. Nazareth, a town of lower Galilee.

fields and pastures of wide reputation throughout Syria and the Near East. The harvests are sent to Damascus and thence to the port of Haifa, formerly by camel caravan, since 1895 by railroad.

South of the Hauran is the region of Gilead. Its summits rise to 4000 feet and support evergreen oak and other trees. Portions of the valley floors and plains round about are watered by springs and streams and have orchards and vineyards, and occasionally fields of wheat and barley. Its chief wealth is in its herds. Like the Hauran, the Damascus region, and Moab in the south, Gilead is a land of countless ruins, witnesses of the denser population that once lived here.

Moab, to the south, completes the line of heights east of the Jordan and marks the outpost of the agricultural land at the borders of the Syrian desert. Sheep and cattle live in great droves on the upland pastures and find water on the canyon floors and at scattered springs. It is also a region of agricultural importance, though subject probably more than other lands nearby to raids from the desert Arabs, who look upon the farmers' fields as placed there by Providence for their enjoyment.

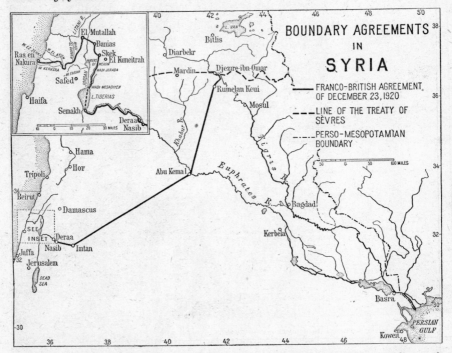

Fig. 209. Boundary between Syria and Mesopotamia, with related localities, according to the text of the Franco-British agreement of 23 December 1920. Only that section of railway is shown which is mentioned in the treaty.

CHAPTER TWENTY-SIX

ANATOLIA: LAST REMNANT OF THE TURKISH EMPIRE

FEW persons realize how far into Europe the Turk once penetrated Penetration of central Europe by Turkish power and how dangerously near he came to overwhelming our western civilization. For more than two hundred years he was the aggressor against European peoples, chiefly Germans and Magyars, who bore the brunt of his repeated assaults; but in 1683, at the second siege of Vienna, he was decisively defeated by forces under the Polish leader Sobieski, and since then the field of his power has slowly diminished. As late as 1908 the Sultan of Turkey was the nominal or technical ruler of the Adriatic provinces of Bosnia and Herzegovina, although the special position of Austria-Hungary made her emperor the actual ruler. The Mohammedans of Bosnia (chiefly Croats) number 30 per cent of the total population of the province; yet it is almost as far from Bosnia to Constantinople as from Bosnia to Paris.

Before the Balkan wars the Turkish Empire was as large as Russia in Europe; its population was nearly as large as that of France.

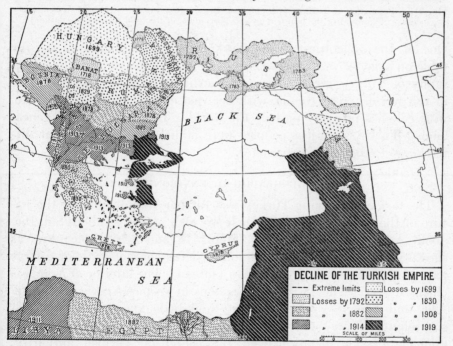

FIG. 210. Only the large white area (most of Anatolia) remains to Turkey in unrestricted sovereignty, though she enjoys limited sovereignty over the Constantinople region and on the southern side of the Sea of Marmara. A mere shadow of sovereignty also remains to her at Smyrna—the privilege of flying the Turkish flag over one of the outer forts. The western border of Armenia is represented in a diagrammatic way; for details see Figure 225.

425

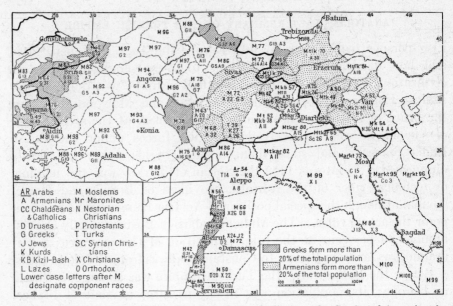

Fig. 211.   Population of Turkey, with emphasis (by shading) on the Greek and Armenian elements.   (Figures after the letters represent percentage of the total district population.)

Complexity of the Turkish population

One of the difficulties of the Turkish rulers is illustrated by the table on page 427, which reveals a degree of complexity in the ethnography of Turkey greater than that exhibited by any other empire in the world except Russia, with her vast extent, and Great Britain, with colonies in every part of the world.   To the ethnic differences among Turkey's subject peoples were added equally important differences of religion and character.

THE GEOGRAPHICAL ENVIRONMENT

Peoples of the Turkish Empire separated by relief and climate

The task of governing Turkey was further complicated by the nature of the country.   Locally there are rich plains, as about Smyrna, about Adana (Cilicia), and at Trebizond and Adrianople; but, as shown in Figure 213, a mountainous relief is characteristic of a large part of the border of the Anatolian plateau.   The interior of Arabia is chiefly desert.   The Turkish possessions in western Arabia — Hedjaz, Asir, and Yemen — were so remote and little known that Turkish sovereignty there was but a shadow.   We commonly fail to appreciate their distance from the center of Turkish authority. Arabia is about half as large as that part of the United States west of the Mississippi (Fig. 29).   It is as far from Constantinople to Mocha at the southwestern tip of Arabia as it is from New York to San Francisco.   Outside of the Balkans, Anatolia, and the Syrian

CLASSIFICATION OF THE PEOPLES OF ASIATIC TURKEY [1]

NAME	RACE	RELIGION	SPEECH	HOMELAND	ESTIMATED NUMBER
Alevis (see Tahtajis)					
Ansariyehs	Armenoid	Monotheistic	Arabic	Syrian Mts. and Cilician plains	175,000
Aptals	Armenoid	Sunni	Arabic	Syrian Mts.	uncertain
Arabs	Semitic	Mohammedan	Arabic	South of Tauric and Armenian Mts.	300,000 ?
Arameans	Semitic	Hebrew	Aramean	Mesopotamia	300
Armenians	Armenoid	Christian	Armenian (Aryan)	Armenian highland, Taurus and Anti-Taurus ranges	1,000,000 [2]
Asdias (see Yezidis)					
Avshars	Turki	Shia	Turkish	Anti-Taurus	uncertain
Balikis	Armenoid	Mixed Mohammedan and Christian	Mixed Arabic, Kurdish, and Armenian	Near Sasun	uncertain
Bejvans	Semitic	Mixed Mohammedan and Christian	Arabic	Near Mosul	uncertain
Chaldeans	Semitic	Roman Catholic	Syriac, Kurdish, and Arabic	Near Diarbekr and Jezireh; Sert and Khabur basin	50,000
Chepmis (see Tahtajis)					
Circassians	Mixed Turki and Indo-European	Mohammedan	Turkish	Anatolia, N. Syria, N. Mesopotamia	500,000
Druses	Armenoid	Mohammedan	Arabic	Lebanon; Anti-Lebanon, Hauran Mts., around Damascus	200,000
Greeks [3]	Mediterranean	Christian	Greek	Coast districts, mining districts, large cities	2,000,000
Ismailyehs	Armenoid	Mohammedan	Semitic	Northern Syria	22,000
Jacobites	Semitic	Christian (Monophysites)	Syriac	Syria, Mesopotamia	15,000
Jews	Mixed Semitic, Mediterranean, and Armenoid	Hebrew	Hebrew	Jerusalem; environs of Damascus	150,000
Karapapaks	Turki	Shia	Turkish	Tutakh-Patnoz	3,000
Kizilbash	Armenoid mixed with Turki	Shia, or mixture of Shiism, Paganism, Manichæism, and Christianity	Turkish	Angora and Sivas vilayets; Dersim	400,000
Kurds	Indo-European	Mohammedan	Aryan languages	West of the Sakaria River; Kurdistan	1,500,000
Lazis	Georgian branch of the Cacaso-Tibetan peoples	Mohammedan	Grusinian	Lazistan; north of Choruk Su, around Riza	uncertain
Maronites	Armenoid	Christian	Arabic	Mt. Lebanon, Anti-Lebanon	350,000
Metauilehs	Probably Armenoid	Shia	Arabic	Northern Lebanon	under 50,000
Nestorians	Armenoid	Christian	Syriac	Basin of the Great Zab; valleys of the Bohtan and Khabar	60,000
New Chaldeans	Semitic	Christian	Syriac	Alkosh	uncertain
Sabeans	Semitic	Christian	Syriac	Amarar and Muntefik sanjaks of the Basra vilayet	3,000
Samaritans	Semitic	Hebrew	Hebrew	Near Nablus	300
Syrians	Semitic	Christian and Mohammedan	Arabic	Syria and Mesopotamia	uncertain
Tahtajis	Armenoi l	Mohammedan	Turkish	Lycian Mts.	5,000
Tatars	Turki	Mohammedan	Turkish	Anatolia and Cilician plains	25,000
Terekimans (see Karapapaks)					
Turkomans	Turki	Mohammedan	Turkish	Angora, Adana, and Aleppo vilayets	uncertain
Turks	Turki mixed with Armenoid	Mohammedan	Turkish	Anatolia mainly	8,000,000
Yezidis or Asdais	Mixed Armenoid and Indo-European	Devil-worshipers, mixture of the old Babylonian religion; Zoroastrianism, Manichæism, and Christianity	Kermanji	Kurt Dagh on the W. to Zakho E. of the Tigris; Badi near Mosul; Sinjar range	40,000
Yuruks	Armenoid	Mohammedan	Turkish	Konia vilayet	200,000
Total.......					15,048,600

[1] From Leon Dominian, *The Frontiers of Language and Nationality in Europe,* 1917.
[2] The figures for Armenians and Greeks require revision in view of the systematic efforts of the Turks to extirpate these two peoples. The massacres of the entire Greek population of villages of the Ægean coasts and the atrocities perpetrated on the Armenians of inland communities have largely depleted these two Christian subject groups.
[3] Hellenes, or subjects of the King of Greece, number about 20,000.

region, there were almost no railroads in the Turkish Empire, and there has always been a central administration whose effects could hardly have been offset in any circumstances.

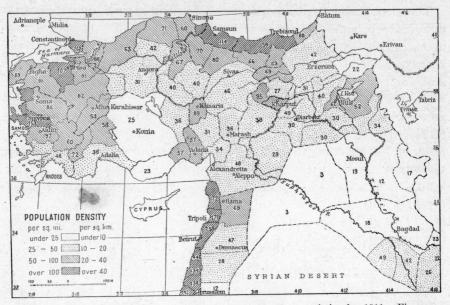

Fig. 212.   Population densities in Turkey by sanjaks, after statistics for 1911.   Figures on the map represent density per square mile.

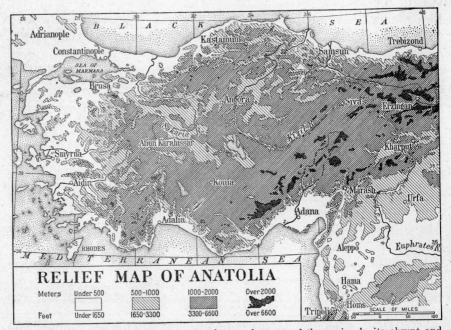

Fig. 213.   Relief of Anatolia.   Note the plateau character of the peninsula, its abrupt and indented border, and interior valleys and basins.   Of special interest is a comparison of new boundaries and of ethnic distributions in Figures 210 and 211 with the coastal valley lowlands as represented here.   Contours reduced from the sheets of the millionth map, British General Staff.

The strong and varied relief of the Turkish regions and the great differences of climate from place to place have had a marked effect upon the division and mode of life of the people. The Turks are largely confined to the mountain-rimmed and partly desert highlands of Anatolia; Judea is a relatively dry and inaccessible plateau where the Hebrew race had its early development; the Armenian race grew up in the high valley floors about Lake Van; the Syrians hold a fertile strip of land along the Mediterranean, shut off by the mountains of Lebanon on the south and the Syrian desert on the east; the semi-nomadic Kurds keep largely to the mountain pastures at the headwaters of the Tigris and Euphrates rivers; the Arabs live independently in the oases of the vast interior desert of Arabia or in locally fertile districts about the desert border. Each people has a distinctive homeland.[1]

HISTORICAL RELATIONS AND POLICIES

The complexities of race have also in part grown out of a long and changeful history. Military expeditions of the past, no less than commercial life, passed and repassed the sites of modern tribes. Hittite and Syrian, Persian and Greek, Egyptian and Assyrian and Babylonian, European crusader and Moslem, Arab, and Turk, sent their armies across this part and that to capture towns, take spoils, enslave peoples, or guard a highway of approach.

Military campaigns across Turkey

The great Eurasian trade and political movements have involved some part of the Turkish Empire — sometimes all of it — ever since its formation. Armenia was a meeting place of the inner trade routes; Syria was the maritime outlet of the hinterland trade; Mesopotamia and the Persian Gulf region were a focus of eastern commerce. Important towns grew up at critical places; Haifa is an historic port where caravans gathered; Mosul, or "Central Gates," is near a high pass leading up to Armenia; Konia, once the capital of Turkey, was at a desert meeting-place of north-south and east-west routes in Anatolia; Aleppo was a focus for traffic about the shores of the Gulf of Alexandretta.

Historic trade routes of Turkey

When the Turk captured Constantinople from the Byzantine rulers in 1453 and thus completed control of the gateways to Asia and the rich trade of India, European traders earnestly sought a new route to

Diversion of oriental trade

---

[1] This chapter deals only with the Turks and the region of Anatolia. For discussion of non-Turkish groups formerly included in the Turkish Empire see the chapters on Greece, Transcaucasia, Palestine, France (for Syria), and Great Britain (for Mesopotamia, Arabia, and Egypt).

FIG. 214. In the desert of Syria. A tribe of Anezeh Arabs moving from an exhausted pasture to a fresh one.

India, for with increasing risks of trade over the old route went higher costs. Finally Dias discovered the southern end of Africa (1488), and soon after a new and all-water route to India which avoided the Turk was found by Da Gama (1498). The Suez Canal in our own time (completed in 1869) diverted trade still further from the old caravan routes across Asia Minor.

Oppression of subject peoples

The troubles of Turkey in modern times have arisen in large part because of the uninterrupted government policy of oppression of subject races. The present partition of the Turkish Empire calls for a just disposition of these races, to the end that there may be a reasonable chance of future peace and liberty. Let us now examine the political basis of the problem.

Almost all the oppressed peoples of the world would have said that once the old autocratic political systems of Germany, Austria-Hungary, Russia, and Turkey were destroyed, everything would be set going again without delay in an era of democracy and happiness. They have found instead that they have merely shifted a great many of the most trying political and economic problems from their former rulers to themselves. Not everything that the past administration had done was wrong, and in any case it had kept the affairs of the country running in one way or another. Granted the old system had to be destroyed, it was equally necessary that a new one be created to take its place. A period of revolution must be followed by a period of building.

There are two regions in which the people have not yet begun the building process — Russia and Turkey. Their territories join in the Caucasus, and there is now a great block of unsettled country extending all the way from the Indian Ocean to the Arctic.

Disorganization of the huge empires of Turkey and Russia

The historic weakness of the Turkish Empire was due primarily to two causes:

(1) The country's central situation at one of the greatest crossroads of the world and its bridge-like character between central Asia and southeastern Europe.

(2) The inclusion of a large number of different peoples in a low stage of development.

It will help us to understand the present problems of the Turkish people and the difficulties of the European nations who now have assumed control of the former empire, to look for a moment at the rise and spread of Turkish power. A background of historical facts is in this case peculiarly important.

Historical development of the Turkish Empire

The Turks are made up of two chief branches:

(1) The Seljuk Turks, whose original home was in Mongolia; they conquered Anatolia from the Byzantines (8th century) and imposed the Turkish language and the Mohammedan religion on the inhabitants that remained after conquest.

(2) The Ottoman Turks, who migrated westward from the Altai Mountains and the plateaus of Inner Asia; they supplanted the Seljuk Turks, founding an empire in 1326, with the capital at Brusa. Later (1371) Adrianople became the Turkish capital.

In the eight years from 1512 to 1520, the Turks conquered Syria, Egypt, and the holy places of Mecca and Medina. By the latter action, Sultan Selim I of that time became the "Defender of the Moslem Faith," and made himself Caliph, or Head of the Church.

His successor, Suleiman, pushed the Mohammedan conquests far into Europe, besieging Vienna in 1529, though without success. In 1565 Malta likewise was besieged. Thereafter there was a decline in Turkish power, especially after the defeat of the Turkish navy at Lepanto in 1571 and the second siege of Vienna, which ended disastrously for the Turks in 1683.

Wherever they extended their conquests outside of Anatolia, the Turks forcibly Islamized the Christians, drafted their young men into the army, and placed many of the girls in the Turkish harems. This policy kept the Turkish stock in Asia Minor from being wasted in foreign battlefields and swelled the numbers of Moslems.

Territorial
losses

During the 18th century Hungary was lost to the Turks. Then followed the loss of the northern shore of the Black Sea. In the early part of the 19th century the Greeks and Serbs successfully rose against the Turk, and from that time down to recent years the pressure of the Christian against the Turk has been almost unremitting. But for the antagonism between the Russian and British empires, the struggle might have ended long ago in the expulsion of the Turk from Europe.

Contest
between
East and
West

Internal difficulties in the Turkish Empire, and even revolution against the Turkish authorities, continued until in 1876 the liberal elements were able to force the introduction of a constitution and a parliament. But conflicting racial and religious interests were so strong that the parliament no sooner set to work than it showed itself impotent; and in the long period from 1876 to 1909 Sultan Abdul Hamid II held the reins of power exclusively in his own hands. He fought western liberal ideas in his court and in the country, and tried to make Pan-Islamism a political force. Through it he hoped to continue his leadership of the Moslem world and to exercise strong political influence among the Moslem populations of:

(1) Great Britain, in India, Egypt, eastern Africa, etc.

(2) France, in northern Africa.

(3) Russia, on the northern Black Sea coast, in Transcaucasia, and in Russian Turkestan.

THE REVOLUTION OF 1908 AND THE NATIONALIST POLICY OF THE YOUNG TURKS

"Young
Turk"
revolution
of 1908

Only a few years before the World War the autocratic policy of the Sultan was most unexpectedly interrupted, with profound effects upon the subsequent history of Turkey, and indeed of the world. In July 1908 the Young Turks came into power, overthrowing the ruling party and forcing the reactionary Sultan to restore the constitution of 1876. It was thought that the period of liberty and freedom had at last set in; there was the greatest excitement and rejoicing all through Turkey. The Greeks of Smyrna, the Albanians in Europe, the Armenians, the Arabs, and even the Turks themselves said that the day of deliverance had come. The racial and religious hatreds seemed to disappear in a day; and in their place came the spirit of good will.   There was almost equal rejoicing abroad when it was recalled how badly governed Turkey had been, how many of her own citizens she had massacred, how rotten was her internal organization.

At first the troubles of the Young Turks were due to the efforts of the old régime to regain control.   After a mutiny in the army at Constantinople had been put down, the Young Turk party made the Sultan a prisoner at Saloniki and put his brother, Mohammed V, in his place. Abdication of the Sultan

Then began the rule of the Young Turks.   Their first thought was given to a great nationalizing movement known as "Pan-Islamism," by which the scattered units of the entire Mohammedan world were to become federated in a vast political system.   The power of Islam was to be consolidated.   Even Finland and Hungary were to be brought into the scheme.   United Turkey was to form the center of the Islamic world, though permitting distant peoples, like the Arabs of Egypt, Morocco, and Tunis, and the people of Persia and Afghanistan, to enjoy local autonomy. Proposed union of Mohammedan elements in Pan-Islamism

To further their objects and stimulate popular enthusiasm, the officials and teachers idealized such barbarian leaders as Attila and Genghis Khan and wrote in poetic style of the glories of these so-called heroic figures.   Scholars and writers formed clubs, published books, and held celebrations to revive Turkish hero worship.

One phase of the movement was attention to national economic problems.   The leaders asserted that as long as trade and industries were in foreign hands the Turk was not in power.   The Greek and Armenian traders and shopkeepers were persecuted, boycotted, and expelled, and national banks were started, as at Aidin and Konia.

But the Young Turks failed from the very beginning.   They began to oppress the subject races; made no effort to punish the men who had carried out the terrible Adana massacres of 1909, in which more than 30,000 Christians were killed; tried to suppress the liberties of the Greek Orthodox Church; started a commercial boycott of the Greeks; and sought forcibly to colonize Macedonia by bringing in Mohammedans from other parts of Turkey.   Instead of bringing together the diverse peoples of their empire, the Young Turks in the end only started into fiercer life the age-old racial and religious hatreds. Failure of the Young Turks

These events made men despair of a solution of the Turkish problem by the Turks.   All the old ambitions of race, religion, or nationality revived.   The Armenians wished to be free; the Balkan states banded together to throw the Turk out of Europe; Czar Fer-

Young
Turk revo-
lution the
first of a
long chain
of events

dinand of Bulgaria proclaimed his country entirely detached from Turkish rule; Austria formally annexed Bosnia; Italy seized Tripoli, and forced Turkey to conclude peace in 1912. Instead of good will and fraternity, there was redoubled hatred and war and the setting into motion of that long series of events that through the Balkan wars led finally to the World War of 1914–1918.

ZONES OF INFLUENCE OF THE GREAT POWERS

One of the most serious consequences of the lamentable events that occurred in Turkey at the end of the old and the beginning of the new régime was the renewed ambition of the great powers to gain larger spheres of influence in Turkey, so that if the empire vanished they should have richer spoils.

Russian,
Italian,
and Brit-
ish spheres

It will be seen by Figure 47 that Russia was to have the whole northern Armenian region, not as sovereign territory but as a sphere of commercial and political influence, which meant that if the Turkish Empire disintegrated, Russia would hope to own this part of it. Italy was to have special rights in Adalia and Dodecanesia. France was given a similar position in the Adana region, Syria, and southern Armenia; while England was to have a sort of protectorate over Palestine and Mesopotamia. These arrangements were made as late as 1916, during the war.

Rise of the
Trans-
caucasian
people

With the complete collapse of orderly government in Russia in 1917, the Russian sphere fades from the map of Turkey and in its place there appear three countries — Armenia, the Georgian Republic, and the country of the Azerbaijan Tatars (Fig. 220). Each one desired an independent existence, though repeatedly attempts have been made to unite the three in a Transcaucasian confederation.

Italian
occupation
of the
Dode-
canese

The Italian zone at Adalia represents a recent ambition. When the Turkish Empire was in a state of disorder in 1911, Italy sought to increase her territorial holdings in Africa by acts of aggression in Libya (Tripoli). Austria-Hungary had seized the provinces of Bosnia and Herzegovina, Bulgaria had declared her independence of Turkey — why should Italy not have Libya? War with Turkey followed. It was a hard campaign, and before it was won Italy seized the group of islands known as the Dodecanese, from which she was to withdraw as soon as Turkish troops were withdrawn from Libya. Italy also obtained railway concessions in the Adalia region from the weak Turkish government, and strengthened her hold upon the coal mines of Heraclea on the southern Black Sea coast east of Constantinople.

As the World War progressed, it became more and more important for the Allies to have the aid of Greece, on account of the progress
of German operations in the Balkans and the possibility of a submarine campaign with the Greek coast as a base.   Greek adherence
to the Allied cause could be won only if the Greeks felt that there
would be a chance, after the war, to unite the Greek populations of
the Ægean.   While there was no agreement to this effect, there was
a tacit understanding.   Now the islands known as the Dodecanese
(Fig. 158) are exclusively Greek in customs, language, and religion.
Neither the Turks through centuries of rule, nor the Italians in a
few years, could change the fundamental character of the people.
To this day the sailors of Dodecanesia maintain the Hellenic traditions of the past.   Moreover, the islands lie near that part of the
mainland of Asia Minor that is predominantly Greek, and that has
Smyrna for its capital.   By the treaty of Sèvres[1] between Turkey
and the Allied powers the islands were ceded to Italy and have since
been again transferred by treaty to Greece (except Rhodes).[2]

Greeks of the Dode- canese

THE POLICY OF CAPITULATIONS

Whatever their location and character, the Turks are poor, and
the standard of education is low.   As a result, almost all the business
of the country is in the hands of non-Turkish people — Armenians,
Greeks, Jews, Italians, French, Germans, and English.   Wherever
mines have been developed, railroads or irrigation works constructed,
foreign capital and foreign brains have been chiefly responsible.

Turkish business in foreign hands

At first thought it might be supposed that foreign assistance would
be nothing but a benefit to Turkey.   And so it would, if it were not
that foreigners occupy a privileged position in the country.   In fact,
citizens of Great Britain, Italy, France, Germany, and Austria-Hungary were in many respects in a separate class from Turkish citizens,
whether Turks, Greeks, Armenians, or Jews.   A citizen of any of the
great powers was practically exempt from the payment of income taxes
and several other kinds of taxes to which the Turk was subject.   He
was immune from search, could secure passports from his own consul,
and could be tried in courts of his own nationality.   All these special privileges together constituted a body of privileges known as
"capitulations."   One entire region, the Lebanon, was placed in

Privileges of the for- eigner

---

[1] The treaty of Sèvres is discussed here and elsewhere as if it had been ratified, but ratification by Turkey had not taken place as late as 1 June 1921.   See footnote on page 417.

[2] For a more detailed discussion of the Dodecanese and of foreign spheres of influence in
this region see the chapters on Greece and Constantinople.

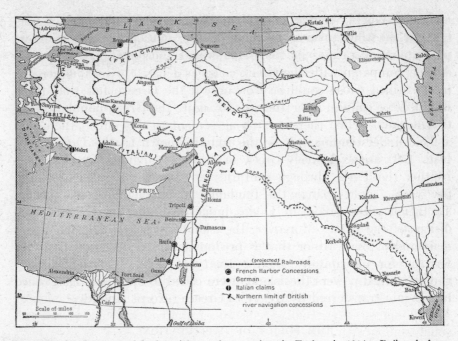

Fig. 215. Navigation and harbor rights and concessions in Turkey in 1914. Railroads from the *Geographical Journal*, April 1920; Dominian, *The Frontiers of Language and Nationality in Europe*, 1917; and British General Staff map, *Railways in Asiatic Turkey*, No. 2246, 1911. 1 : 7,500,000.

a privileged class and passed under foreign control in 1864. Upon declaring war in 1914, Turkey abolished the capitulations, but the powers refused to recognize her action.

It should not be thought, however, that the capitulations sprang from a purely selfish desire on the part of foreign powers to control Turkish affairs. It was found that foreigners were ill treated, given unfair trials in the courts, and unnecessarily delayed in their legitimate business by Turkish officials. The case was parallel to that of China (page 514).

Turkey as a field for political rivalry

Each nation which has in the past secured business concessions in Turkey wishes to retain and develop to its own advantage all the property that it formerly held, and these rights are now to be confirmed by treaty. It is difficult to see how this can be done and at the same time the natural growth of Turkey be assured. By the terms of the treaty of Sèvres (1920) consular courts would hereafter have supervision over all infringements of the laws by their nationals within the area of the neutral zone of Constantinople and the Straits. Furthermore, until such time as Turkish judicial procedure becomes better regulated, the Turkish courts will relegate jurisdiction over their own nationals in the neutralized area to courts of the Allied powers. Outside of Constantinople — that is, in Anatolia — there is to be put into effect a plan of judicial reform, to be drafted by the principal Allied powers with the help of technical experts of other powers formerly related to the scheme of capitulations. This plan is to replace the former capitulatory system as far as that system related to judicial matters.

Political life had never been anything but corrupt in the whole history of Turkey; but with the capitulations went increasing corruption. Officials sought bribes at every opportunity, withheld the proceeds of a vicious and discriminatory tax system, ruined every struggling industry by graft, and fought with massacre every show of independence on the part of Turkey's many subject peoples. *Political corruption*

To these difficulties were added pressure from without and revolution within. The Russians persistently sought access to the Mediterranean through the Bosporus and the Dardanelles; the Bulgarians and Serbs secured large autonomy and, later, complete independence; Macedonia was perpetually in disorder; the Greek people of Smyrna sought union with Greece.

THE OTTOMAN PUBLIC DEBT

The question of debt was politically important to Turkey even before the World War. Should the treaty of Sèvres be ratified, it will be fundamental and vital; for with the control of her public debt are related still larger schemes of political control, through which the commercial interests of the world will seek to gain advantages that may not be to Turkey's interest.

The total pre-war debt of Turkey originally amounted to $716,000,000. France, the chief creditor, had 60 per cent of the total, Germany came next with 20 per cent, and Great Britain next with 15 per cent. The debt was administered by a Council of Administration of the Ottoman Public Debt, which consisted of one representative each for France, Great Britain, Holland, Germany, Austria-Hungary, Italy, and Turkey, and one representative of the Imperial Ottoman Bank. The president of the Council was a Frenchman or a Britisher in alternate years. *Administration of Turkey's pre-war debt*

Now let us see how the debt affected the political and economic life of Turkey. In the first place, the Council controlled many of the important revenues of the empire. If there was a loan to be raised, it was the Council that administered the service of the loan. If money had to be found to pay the interest or the principal, the Council col- *Importance of foreign financial control* lected a certain amount of the ordinary revenues. The Council had reached into almost every corner of Turkish financial affairs. Its control even went so far as to affect the tax on live stock in certain districts. On the other hand, it introduced modern methods in certain industries, and was the principal influence in establishing the silk industry. Its staff of trained employees totaled nearly 9000 in 1912.

Need for abolition of special privileges

Students of the Turkish problem have long held that if Turkish affairs are to be improved, the exclusive privileges involved in the public debt and in the concessions must be modified or abolished. They assert further that it would be greatly to Turkey's interest if all the revenues of the state were controlled by a central treasury, instead of by many collecting and disbursing agencies, as in the past. So complicated are these financial affairs as they now stand, so poor is Turkey since the World War (she had already lost one tenth of her revenue and one sixth of her population in the Balkan wars of 1912–1913), so great is the rivalry of the powers, that it was impossible to make Turkey pay a war indemnity comparable to that which has been demanded of the other defeated powers. The principle of reparations was set aside by the Peace Conference of Paris, and in its place full validity was given to the pre-war Ottoman Public Debt.

French and British rivalry

Owing to the importance of the Ottoman debt in the political development and administration of the Turkish Empire, France and Great Britain naturally were jealous of each other in this field. French sentiment was opposed to a British mandate for Constantinople, and England objected to French occupation. Moreover, there will be an inevitable conflict between the obligations of the old debt, chiefly held by France, and the obligations of the new debt that must be incurred to provide a financial basis for government — for the engineering works that are required to provide sanitation in the cities, and railway facilities and irrigation works for potentially rich but undeveloped regions.

Present administration of the debt

Under the treaty of Sèvres signed between Turkey and the Allied powers, the Ottoman Public Debt is to be administered as before. It will be in charge of a council composed of British, French, and Italian representatives, and the Council is to levy all revenues intrusted to its management before 1 November 1914. In order to regulate the income of Turkey and provide for the interest and sinking fund necessary for the debt, there will be appointed a Director General of Customs. It is further arranged that all detached states — that is, Mesopotamia, Armenia, etc. — are to assume a share of the Ottoman Public Debt as it stood before 1 November

1914, the amount they assume being proportional to the amount of their average revenue and the ratio between the latter and the average revenue of the whole of Turkey.

The Council is to operate until the Ottoman Public Debt has been liquidated. When this result has been achieved, Turkey is to consult the Council of the League of Nations to decide whether further advice and administrative and financial assistance are necessary, and if so, in what form.

The administration of the Ottoman Public Debt will be facilitated by a financial commission, for which the Allies have arranged, to conserve and increase the resources of Turkey. When we consider that there will also be an Interallied commission of control and organization to supervise the execution of the military clauses of the treaty of Sèvres, it is clear that the new government of Turkey will be for all practical purposes in the hands of the principal Allied powers. Added to the control delegated to these organizations is the provision that all concessions prior to 1914 are conserved and confirmed; this also means that the influence of outside powers upon Turkish internal affairs is confirmed and increased. The control of outside powers is not limited to military and financial matters alone, but applies also to import and export duties, to the reorganization of the electoral system, and to the proportional representation of the races within Turkish frontiers.

The treaty practically an Allied receivership

OTHER TERMS OF THE TREATY OF SÈVRES

Allied control over Turkish financial matters extends even to the approval or supervision of the national budget, financial laws and regulations, and the improvement of the Turkish currency. Neither the tax system, nor the customs system, nor internal or external loans, nor new concessions, may be arranged without the consent of the financial commission of the Allied powers. To provide against the economic penetration of Turkish territory by Germany, Austria, Hungary, or Bulgaria, the Allies may liquidate the property of citizens of those countries in Turkish territories. If the liquidation affects government property, the proceeds are to be turned over to the Reparations Commission set up by the earlier treaties of peace with Germany, Austria, and Bulgaria. Turkish property rights in certain railway companies pass out of German control.

Financial details

Finally, Turkey is required to grant freedom of transit to persons, goods, vessels, etc., passing through her territory, and such goods in transit are to be free of all customs duties. Rates of transport

Freedom of transit

are to be reasonable, regardless of the ownership or nature of the means of transport. To insure the carrying out of these provisions in commercially strategic places, certain ports are declared to be of international interest. In these ports all states that are members of the League of Nations are to enjoy complete freedom and equality of treatment, particularly in the matter of charges and facilities. In all of them there are to be "free zones." The ports are: Constantinople from St. Stefano to Dolma Bagtchi, Haidar-Pasha, Smyrna, Alexandretta, Haifa, Basra, Trebizond, and Batum.

Outlets for Transcaucasia

Though Georgia, Azerbaijan, Persia, and Russian Armenia lie outside the Turkish frontier, the treaty provides for free access on the part of these four states to the Black Sea by the port of Batum. To Armenia are granted special facilities in the use of the port of Trebizond, where she obtains a lease of an area for her own use.

Indemnity but not full reparation

In view of the loss of territory which Turkey incurs as a result of the treaty of peace, she is not required to pay a general reparation bill; but she is required to pay indemnities due on account of the claims of the Allied powers for reparation for damages suffered by non-Turkish people. These claims are to cover losses or damages suffered by *civilian* nationals (as distinct from losses to *military* forces) of the Allied powers during the war and up to the time that the treaty of peace goes into effect. In addition, Turkey must pay the expenses of the military forces of occupation since 30 October 1918.

THE NEW NATIONALIST PARTY

Rise of a Turkish Nationalist movement

With the collapse of Turkish military power in 1918, the occupation of Constantinople and adjacent waters by an Allied army and fleet, and the threat of dismemberment, Turkish sentiment for the integrity of the Turkish Empire crystallized in the form of a Nationalist party. Organized in October 1919, the new party soon carried Adrianople and Brusa. It had the whole interior of Anatolia in which to develop, for only the coastal regions were held by the Allies. The French were attacked and defeated at Marash late in February 1920; and their retreat was accompanied by a fresh massacre of Armenians in the Cilician region. The British were harassed on the borders of Kurdistan by tribesmen who were instigated by Turkish officials. The Greek forces that held the demarcation line at Smyrna were hard pressed. The Allied armies had largely disbanded, and the greater part of the world was stricken with disorganization and laden with debt.

Seeing these influences at work, and seeing also their own country disintegrating, the Turkish leaders revived the national sentiment and spurred their people to new efforts to defeat the scattered battalions of the Allies and regain the empire. In the hope of arresting Nationalist ambitions, the suggestion was made in a number of quarters, particularly in France, that there should be Allied supervision of Turkish officials, without actual replacement.

It is of course a serious question whether Turkey will ratify in good faith the treaty of Sèvres with the Allied powers. If the Nationalist movement becomes stronger, and if at the same time there should be a growing reluctance on the part of the strong western powers to spend money in maintaining order in Turkey, few of the provisions of the treaty will have any force. If the provisions are accepted in good faith, the government of Turkey will be but a shadow. The Turkish army is limited to 50,000 men, of whom 35,000 are to be a gendarmerie organized and maintained for the purpose of keeping internal order. Turkey will have no fortresses left under her exclusive control. She merely flies a flag over one of the outer forts of Smyrna, while the forts in the Straits region are to be demolished within three months of the signing of the treaty.

Will Turkish ratification have any validity?

THE QUESTION OF THE CALIPHATE

A question of importance to Turkey is that of the caliphate, or headship of the Moslem church. The Turkish Caliph's claim of descent from the Prophet is not recognized as authentic by important elements both without and within the Turkish Empire. The Sultan of Morocco, the Mahdists of the Egyptian Sudan, the Senussi in the Libyan Desert, the Wahabis in central Arabia, have never made acknowledgment of the Turkish Caliph. Nor has such recognition been given by the Arabs of the Hedjaz, Palestine, and Syria, which contain the holy places of Mecca, Medina, and Jerusalem. Today, throughout the country from Mecca to Aleppo, the Sultan's name has been replaced in the Friday liturgy by that of Sherif Hussein, the hereditary guardian of the holy cities of the Hedjaz, who is referred to as "The Commander of the Faithful," though he has himself not assumed the title of Caliph. On the other hand the Moslems of India and of Anatolia have always supported the Turkish caliphate (page 415).

Division of opinion and of religious authority

In spite of these divergent views as to the caliphate, the fact remains that it is the Caliph at Constantinople who is the center of the Ottoman Empire and the concrete force that stands for the Islamic cause in the world, and it is a matter of import whether he shall retain his

Religious significance of Constantinople confirmed

residence in Constantinople, the seat of authority for many generations. The Turks feared that if this seat were transferred to inner
Anatolia, Moslem faith and Moslem political power would diminish
throughout the world and lose ground in the struggle with Christianity and other religions. It was the pressure of the Moslems of
India upon British leaders and French desire to prevent British commercial control of a possible free state at Constantinople that turned
the scale in favor of the Turk and left h m at least a shadow of authority in his capital. Moslem faith is still dominated from Constantinople, though as a military center its power has disappeared.

ETHNIC AND ECONOMIC BASIS OF THE NEW STATE

Natural limits of Anatolia

From a huge empire Turkey has shrunk to a small state. The
natural eastern boundary of Anatolia is formed by the Taurus and
Anti-Taurus mountains (Fig. 213). The Black and Mediterranean
seas limit it on the north and south. On the west it is terminated by
the Smyrna district (now occupied by Greece) and by the Sea of
Marmara. This gives Anatolia an area a little larger than that of
California and a population of more than 8,000,000, of which only
a small part is nomadic.

The population of the new Turkey is broken up into self-con-
tained, isolated groups, ignorant of the outside world, with primitive
carts and plows, very poor roads, no modern towns, houses built of
adobe (rarely of wood). There are large areas of unoccupied country
and extensive pasture lands. Brigandage is common.

Treaty agreements respecting lost prop-erty and protection of minori-ties re-maining in the new Turkey

In 1915 Turkey passed a law which practically confiscated the properties abandoned by people who had been exiled on account of her
severe persecutions, and this law Turkey is required to void by the
treaty of Sèvres. She is also to facilitate the search for lost people
(Armenians, Syrians, and others driven into the desert and mountain
districts during the war) and the restoration of their property, though
of course the internal administration of this measure will be exceedingly difficult, if not impossible.

Turkish minorities are to receive protection at the hands of the
Armenians, the Greeks, the British, etc., in the areas under their
respective control, and on her part Turkey is to protect minorities
within her new frontiers. The treaty requires Turkey to permit
minorities to participate in the use of charitable and educational funds.

Quite different from the Turkish peasantry of Anatolia are the Turkish rulers, who form an official caste. Also a class apart from the peasants are the Turkish nomads who have come into the Anatolian steppes

since the conquest. The differences between the three Turkish elements — officials, peasants, nomads — extend to the fields of thought and social custom, and it will take time and experiment to demonstrate the capacity of the three elements to become welded into a single nation.

The possession of Smyrna by Greece cuts off the Anatolian hinterland from its natural outlets on the Mediterranean. Its commerce will flow through alien hands — a distinct handicap. The new Turkey will consist essentially of a mountain-rimmed plateau with a desert interior, though well-watered near the border, where it is capable of high development. If the new government will turn its attention to internal improvements rather than to external conquest and the rule of non-Turkish peoples in remote regions, Turkey may in time become a strong state. Otherwise it must become a liability, an expensive dependency of the great powers.

Best ports of Anatolia now in foreign hands

Turkey was heavily laden with debt before 1914, and her system of taxation was notoriously bad. As a result, her productive and commercial power had steadily declined. An aspect of her commercial life suggestive in this connection is the purchasing power of the people; in 1912 the imports averaged only $9 per capita, as compared with $40 for France and $127 for Belgium.

Turkey a debt-ridden country

It is to trade that Turkey must look for her chief sources of revenue, and she is so poor that her commerce will long be required to sustain a very heavy burden of taxation. Her exports for a good many years to come must consist of special articles not produced in agricultural communities near by. Rumania and Russia can produce large quantities of grain much cheaper than Turkey, but Turkey is better suited for the production of dried fruits, tobacco, opium, and fine skins. Turkey's undeveloped wealth will gain in importance because of foreign need for new raw materials to feed the industries of the world. While half of Anatolia is desert, steppe, and mountain, there are locally fertile areas upon which silk, cotton, tobacco, fine wool, and subtropical fruits can be produced. Improved irrigation works will greatly increase the production and will make cotton growing possible even on the central plain of Konia, where now much of the land is desert, for lack of a proper application of the available water supply.

Necessity for commercial growth

Irrigation possibilities

CHAPTER TWENTY-SEVEN

THE MOUNTAIN HOME OF THE KURDS

In the organized world of today there are but few groups of people that may lead a wholly isolated and unruly life. If a quarrelsome folk raid neighboring settled peoples, or interfere with the security of railways — as do the robber bands of Manchuria, for instance — foreign interference is bound to come. To other reasons why the Kurds of eastern Turkey will not be allowed to pursue their disorderly way without restraint, there is added the powerful reason that they are near vital British interests in Mesopotamia; part of the completed Bagdad line passes close to Kurdish territory.

Are the Kurds a powerful people? Has the war left them in control of their former territory? What will be their disposition in the settlement of the territorial problems involved in the partition of Turkey?

SETTLED AND NOMADIC POPULATIONS

The mountain homeland of the semi-nomadic Kurds

There are about 2,500,000 Kurds in Turkey, of whom the greater part live in eastern Asia Minor in the mountain region called Kurdistan (Fig. 216). They are related to the Persians in race and language, but most of them belong to a different Mohammedan sect (the Sunni). Because a part of their territory lies in Persia there is created a problem somewhat similar to that in Armenia where, before the World War, the Armenian people were divided between two powers, Turkey and Russia.

The Kurds are a semi-nomadic people, going up into the high valley pastures in summer to return in winter to the warmer valleys and lowlands. This seasonal migration brings them into conflict with the settled Armenians of the high valleys round about Van, Mosul, Kirkuk, Bitlis, and Kharput, and with the Persian villages of Kermanshah, Isfahan, and Seistan. In some respects the Kurds are to the Mesopotamian and Armenian plains what the Afghans are to northern India or the nomadic Arabs to the oasis dwellers of Syria.

The Kurd a tool of the Turk

The fiercer spirit and wilder mode of life of the Kurds have been the cause of their forcible settlement in many of the Armenian valleys, where it was designed by the Turkish government that they should make a Mohammedan majority among the people. Downright lawlessness was practiced whenever it suited the Turkish government to make an occasion for it. The Kurd could always be counted upon

444

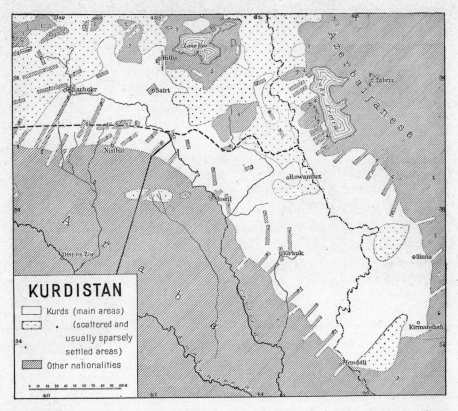

FIG. 216.   The home of the Kurds about the headwaters of the Tigris.   Key to numbers:
1, Turkish-speaking peoples;   2, Armenians;   3, Chaldeans;   4, Assyrians (Nestorians);
5, Jacobites; 6, Persians; 7, Lurs; 8, Arabs.   The heavy dot-and-dash line is the old Turko-
Persian boundary; the dashed line is part of the temporary southern boundary of Turkey and
Armenia; the heavy solid line divides Syria and Mesopotamia (page 103).   Note the difficulties
in establishing a state that embraces most of the Kurds.   It would require revision of parts of
two treaties (Sèvres and the Franco-British agreement of 23 December 1920), and difficult
negotiations with Armenia and Persia.   From British General Staff, *Map of Eastern Turkey in
Asia*, etc., No. 2901, 1 : 2,000,000, 1910.

to assist in the massacre of the non-Moslem populations, and in return he received partial autonomy, having only to pay moderate
taxes and to furnish auxiliary troops in time of war.

To hold the Armenians in subjection at the time when they threatened revolt, to follow the policy of persecuting the Christians, and at
the same time to content the Kurds, the Turks created a Kurdish
cavalry, supplied it with uniforms and arms, and permitted it to raid
Armenian and other Christian elements.

At the present time the Kurds are more numerous and better armed
than the Armenians and may create trouble for the new republic
of Armenia.   They have persecuted the Nestorian Christians of

FIG. 217.   Kurdish village in Upper Mesopotamia.

Urmia as systematically and plundered them as regularly as they
have the Armenians.

Nomad and sedentary Kurds   The semi-nomadic tribes of southern Kurdistan are the most
intelligent and industrious of the Kurds.   In winter they dwell in
villages on the plains east of the Tigris; in summer they migrate
with their flocks to the Persian border, where they make temporary
shelters or bowers of green wood.   The wilder tribes farther north
live principally in the rugged mountain districts near the Persian
frontier; some of them are settled on the land and have terraced
and irrigated farms, others are nomadic.   While the different Kurdish tribes vary in a minor way in their habits, all have two rather
distinct types of settlements — those in the upper zone of pasture
and those in the lower zone of valley farms.

The Kurds were known to Marco Polo and yet earlier travelers
as "an evil generation whose delight it is to murder merchants."
While the settled people tend to be hospitable, the treacherous
nomads rob passing caravans.   Some of the Kurd migrations from
the mountains to the plains carry the nomads through villages of their
own race, which they systematically plunder of everything that can

be carried away, since they hold their sedentary kinsmen in contempt. In return the farmers, when they are strong enough, demand a toll of the nomad Kurd who wishes to cross their cultivated land or ford a stream whose passage they control.

In addition the Kurds happen to live in mountain valleys which lie athwart both ancient and modern trade routes (Figs. 42 and 216). Yet travel among them is hardly safe. They control the mountain passes — the eastern Anatolian gateways — and exact heavy tolls from passing caravans. Indeed, this is one of their chief sources of revenue. *Traffic preyed on by the lawless Kurd*

The difficulties confronting the administration of Kurdistan lie partly in the fact that the Kurdish tribes claim rights in Christian villages, due to the survival of an old arrangement which allowed the nomadic tribes to winter in any Armenian village. Something will have to be done with the tribes that have raided the Armenians, Nestorians, and sedentary Kurds. Self-government among the Kurds seems out of the question, owing to their deterioration under the Turkish régime, their habit of plundering, and their general inability to read and write, as well as their tribal mode of life. With the Turk eliminated, at least some groups of Kurds may choose to settle down and become peaceful neighbors, as they have done in certain places in Mesopotamia and Persia. As a result of invasions by both Russians and Turks during the war, some of the settled communities within the range of the Kurds have been extinguished and others reduced to a state of such poverty that it is no longer profitable to *The impossibility of Kurdish self-government*

Fig. 218.   Kurds and Arabs in typical costume.

raid them. In spite of themselves, therefore, some of the Kurdish tribes already have had to give up their predatory habits and settle down to agricultural pursuits in order to live.

Tribal organization of the Kurds

Permanent settlement is also in line with their tendency during the past twenty years and with the policy of the Turkish government, which aimed to split up tribal organizations through fear that the Kurds might combine in large units to fight Turkish troops. But whether settled or nomadic, the Kurd has persisted in maintaining his tribal organization. Each tribe rules and owns the district in which it is settled, and is under the power of the tribal chief in case of war. The Kurds are devotedly attached to their sheikhs, who are responsible for occasional outbursts of fanaticism.

TREATY ARRANGEMENTS AFFECTING KURDISTAN

In the treaty of 1920 between Turkey and the Allied and Associated Powers, the provisions that apply to Kurdistan are as follows:

(1) A commission composed of French, British, and Italian representatives is to frame an autonomous government for predominantly Kurdish areas east of the Euphrates, south of the future boundary of Armenia and north of the Syria-Mesopotamia boundary, provided the Kurds shall some time in 1921 express to the League of Nations a desire to be independent of Turkey (Fig. 216).

(2) The Kurds of the Mosul vilayet may voluntarily join the independent Kurdish state.

(3) Safeguards are to be provided for the Assyro-Chaldeans and other non-Kurdish populations.

(4) A commission composed of British, French, Italian, Persian, and Kurdish representatives is to rectify the frontier between Kurdistan and Persia.

Present British control

By mid-October of 1919, the British had completed their pacification of a large section of Kurdistan. British troops visited many of the enemy villages as well as the valley frontiers delimited by the armistice of November 1918, overcoming all opposition and establishing temporary peace. British columns occupied the valleys of offending tribesmen and inflicted punishments for numerous hostile acts. British political officers with small detachments of troops occupied many of the widely scattered villages of Kurdistan, and were able to do this by arming local authorities and turning them into police to administer the country.

During 1920 there were risings among the Kurds as well as the Arabs of northern Mesopotamia and renewed fighting, with the result that the British forces were withdrawn over a wide area. Accused by opposition elements at home of extravagant plans for conquest, the British government was obliged to curtail its program of pacification. Having a mandatary for Mesopotamia, Great Britain naturally sought to control the headwater region of the Tigris and Euphrates upon which depends the water supply for the irrigation of Mesopotamia.

The question of ultimate control of Kurdistan remains unsettled, nor can it be settled until the Turkish treaty is ratified and Turkish affairs are entirely reorganized.

CHAPTER TWENTY–EIGHT

THE TRANSCAUCASIAN PEOPLES

Weakness of the new states

TRANSCAUCASIA is one of three narrow connections between East and West. The Suez Canal forms a second; the Bosporus and Dardanelles sever Europe and Asia at the third. It is a fair inference that much history is made or is in the way of making wherever an isthmus connects two great populated land masses or a strait connects two great seas whose shores are peopled by settled folk and traders. The Transcaucasian land bridge is broadly divided into three parts: Georgia, Armenia, and Azerbaijan (Fig. 220). It has been an historical battleground of rival interests. In its later phases, the struggle for possession has been between Russia and Turkey. At present the struggle is between three new republics, no one of which has sufficient vitality to stand alone. In any event the three will be the pawns of their neighbors unless protected by one of the western powers.

THE NEW GOVERNMENTS AND THE GREAT POWERS

Internal rivalries of Transcaucasia

Shortly after the Russian revolution of March 1917, an autonomous government was organized in Transcaucasia. It took the form of a federal republic, the members of which — Georgia, Armenia, and Azerbaijan or the country of the Tatars — were governed by separate national councils. But the Federal Republic of Transcaucasia failed to harmonize the discordant aims of its three constituent members; nor could it offer effective resistance to Turkish aggression in the spring of 1918. The Mohammedan Tatars could not be counted on to oppose the Turks and thus assist the Armenians; the Georgians were chiefly interested in their own national security, and even looked to Germany as a protector; the Armenians would not join their two neighbors, because elements among them favored an understanding with Soviet Russia. Consequently the federal arrangement was discarded and Transcaucasia as a political organization fell apart.

The former Turkish provinces of Kars, Ardahan, and Batum (Fig. 219), which had been taken by Russia in 1878, were renounced by the Soviet government under the Brest-Litovsk treaty of 3 March 1918 and occupied by Turkey. Under Turkish auspices a plebiscite was held, resulting in a forced decision in favor of annexation by Turkey. Turkey acquired an additional strip of territory in Transcaucasia by the separate treaties which she concluded with the three

Transcaucasian republics in May 1918. The extent of this second annexation was not precisely defined, and its validity disappeared with the final collapse of Turkish power in October 1918.

In January 1919, France and Great Britain appear to have agreed to divide southern Russia between them as spheres of influence.

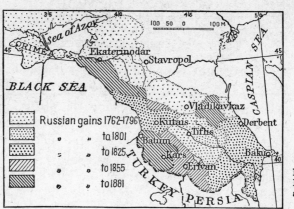

FIG. 219. Successive advances of Russia in Transcaucasia.

France was to have the western Ukraine, and Britain was to have the whole Caucasus and Kuban region. At the same time that the British occupied Transcaucasia, a French expedition was sent to Odessa to supervise Ukrainian affairs and direct military operations against the Bolshevists. But the expedition was withdrawn after the refusal of the Ukrainians to yield to the demands of the French leaders for complete military, economic, and political control. The failure of the French at Odessa dangerously weakened the British in Transcaucasia and ultimately led to a change of policy.

The almost exclusive control of the unsettled Transcaucasian region remained in the hands of the British only until July–August 1919, when their troops were withdrawn from Armenia and Georgia, except for a few officers at each of the main towns and especially at the city of Batum. The withdrawal was due in small part to the charge made against Great Britain that she was seeking to gain control over additional territory rich in oil, and in larger part to the expense of maintaining alone, in so remote a region, costly military forces and works — an expense that drew vigorous criticisms against the government in the House of Commons.

For a time it appeared probable that Italy would succeed Great Britain in the military occupation of the region, since a certain amount of Italian capital is invested there, especially near Batum, and Italy is extremely poor in fuel. Moreover, Italy theretofore had not been assigned any important rôle in maintaining order in the disturbed sections of the Near East.

The plan for Italian participation came to nothing, however, and after the British withdrawal (1919) almost no military men were

French and British agreements

Withdrawal of British troops

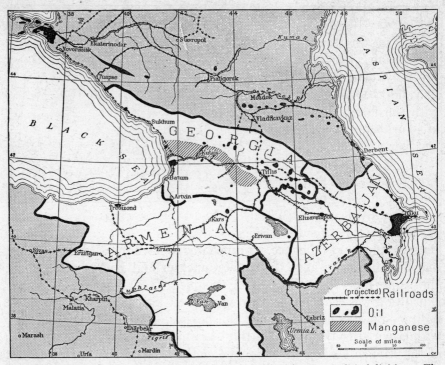

Fig. 220. Transcaucasia and the indeterminate boundaries of its three political divisions. The western boundary of Armenia is tentative; it was agreed to leave the final settlement to President Wilson. Many parts of the other boundaries represent merely paper agreements and have as yet no actuality in boundary posts and administrative control.

Relief work carried on after the withdrawal

left in the region. A small force of officers and women assistants attached to the Interallied relief organization went to Kars and Erivan. No relief work was undertaken on the Turkish border and towards Azerbaijan, because the Kurds and the Tatars had taken possession of the region in the belief that the Armenians had been deserted by the Allies.

RACIAL DIFFERENCES AND THEIR POLITICAL RESULTS

Intermixture of races

Transcaucasia has remnants of almost all the races which for ages past have crossed and recrossed its frontiers and sought refuge within its bounds. Five main groups are divided into forty odd subdivisions, of which from twenty to twenty-five are indigenous.

It results that in starting their national life the three Transcaucasian states are confronted by extremely difficult boundary questions, because no one race inhabits a given region exclusively, all being intermingled throughout a wide zone. This is especially the case on

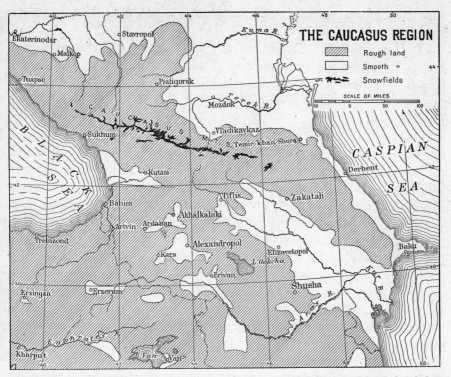

THE CAUCASUS REGION

Rough land
Smooth "
Snowfields

SCALE OF MILES

FIG. 221. Note the small extent of smooth land in Georgia and Armenia and the isolated character of the Armenian basins. The boundaries between rough and smooth lands are generalized from various relief maps. The outlines of the snowfields along the crest of the Caucasus Mountains follow Stieler's *Hand-Atlas*, 1916.

the eastern frontier of Russian Armenia, where Armenians and Tatars are hopelessly mixed. In the Turkish treaty of 1920 it is provided that Armenia, Azerbaijan, and Georgia are to agree mutually upon their frontiers. All of them are to have special privileges at the international port of Batum.

The Georgians number 1,600,000, the Armenians about 1,000,000 (not counting refugees from Turkey), the Azerbaijan Tatars about 3,000,000.

Number and character of the population

There is great diversity in the character of the people. In Georgia the inhabitants have a settled way of life, whereas the Tatars of the mountain region on the southeast live in a primitive fashion and depend chiefly upon herds and flocks, though they have control of the oil wells at Baku. In Georgia there is a small feudal aristocracy and a large farming peasantry. The northern mountain border of Georgia is inhabited by unruly mountaineers.

The Tatars are Mohammedans, disposed to be friendly to Turkey, while the Georgians and Armenians are Christians and seek release from Turkish control.

The Armenians of Transcaucasia, dwelling in a highland region broken by many valleys, are farmers and herdsmen. To their other causes of weakness are added their inland position and the penetration of their villages and pastures by Kurds on the south and Tatars on the east.

Differences and misunderstandings

If allowed to perpetuate their quarrels, these three unlike peoples cannot do otherwise, in the unsettled state of the world, than fall into complete financial and political ruin. The religious differences accentuate the racial differences. Men go armed almost everywhere. Murder is common. Robber bands make travel dangerous. The Tatars and Kurds hate the Armenians and massacre them at every opportunity, being massacred themselves in turn. Such a region is peculiarly adapted for international intrigue unless held in control by a strong European power.

Argument for federation under a single mandatary

It has been argued that though each Transcaucasian group might be kept distinct, the whole region should be placed under the League of Nations or a single mandatory power, because of the geographical position of the country at one of the crossroads of Eurasia. It is thought that if placed under separate mandataries, the three constituent peoples would intrigue against each other and quarrel endlessly over boundaries, customs, the migrations of nomadic villagers, water rights, irrigation privileges, mines, and all the other conditions and resources whose development is necessary if the lot of the people is to be bettered and orderly governments are to be maintained. Some sort of outside supervision seems absolutely essential to peace.

INTERNAL ECONOMIC CONDITION

Transcaucasia backward but rich in resources

The problems of Transcaucasia at the present time are chiefly:

(1) To maintain order.

(2) To develop the country's resources.

(3) To build wagon roads and railways.

(4) To develop an organized community life under the protection of one or more of the great powers.

The three nations occupying Transcaucasia are young, inexperienced, and in the main disorderly and poor. The leaders are corrupt and incompetent. The government of Georgia has nationalized the land without compensation to the original owners, and for a time flew the red flag of Bolshevism above the Georgian national flag. Only with the help of British troops of occupation was order established and railway and telegraph service improved, at least for a time. The people of Azerbaijan are ignorant, lazy, and superstitious, occupying a country shut off from the western world. But within its frontiers there are rich oil deposits, centering at Baku, and a pipe line conveys the crude petroleum to Batum on the Black Sea coast of Georgia. The life of Azerbaijan can be stabilized only if political and general education go hand in hand with economic development.

Russian Armenia (as distinct from Turkish Armenia) is in a worse condition than either Georgia or Azerbaijan. For several winters its people have been on the verge of starvation. Many have died of famine and of the diseases that come in its train. Such roads as it had are falling into ruin. There is stagnation of business, with rising freight rates, increased poverty, and community wars at every turn. Finally, the country has been invaded by Russian Soviet forces and a Bolshevist government set up. *Plight of Russian and Turkish Armenia*

The condition of Turkish Armenia is even worse. Only a remnant of the area formerly occupied by Armenians can be put under Armenian administration. Half the Armenians in Turkey were killed or died of disease or starvation. Less than a million are scattered through a district that once held two or three times that number. And few Armenians living abroad will care to return to a land where life offers primitive and even dangerous conditions.

LOCAL TREATIES

Pending the final settlement of the affairs of the three countries of Transcaucasia, provisional settlements were arranged; but the general insecurity of the region and the political and social instability of the world give little hope that these local settlements will bring peace. The Armenians of Karabagh made an agreement with the Republic of Azerbaijan whereby both Armenians and Tatars were to be represented in the civil administration of the district: this is because the populations are so thoroughly intermingled that it is impossible to draw a dividing line between them. *Agreement between the Armenians of Karabagh and the Tatars*

The Republic of Georgia and the Republic of Azerbaijan likewise concluded a treaty, whose main provisions are as follows: *Treaty between Georgia and Azerbaijan*

(1) Neither side can start a war with an outside government without previous agreement with the other.

(2) Each state agrees to join its neighbor in case a war is brought on by another state.

(3) The treaty is to last three years.

(4) The two states mutually agree to safeguard each other's independence.

The provisions of such treaties between politically unstable peoples have little significance beyond indicating the aspirations of the moment. Out of the wreck of successive agreements something is always salvaged that comes at last to be incorporated in the permanent treaties of stable governments.

SPECIAL FEATURES OF GEORGIA

The
Georgian
Republic

Georgia declared itself an independent republic in 1918. Government is by an elected national council, or assembly, with a responsible ministry. The new state at first accepted German protection and Germany sent troops to Tiflis and probably restrained the Turks from occupying Georgia. By the Russo-German treaty of 27 August 1918 (supplementary to the treaty of Brest-Litovsk), Russia acquiesced in Germany's right to recognize the independence of Georgia. In 1920 Georgia concluded a treaty with Soviet Russia in which the

FIG. 222.   Tiflis, capital and chief city of the Republic of Georgia.

Brown Bros.

FIG. 223. The harbor of Batum, principal port of Transcaucasia on the Black Sea.

independence of Georgia was recognized within the following territory: the provinces of Tiflis, Kutais, and Batum, the districts of Zakataly and Sukhum, and a part of the Black Sea government. But the military conditions imposed gave the Bolshevists practical control of the republic. The treaty has theoretical force only so long as the Soviet government exists, and no practical force whatever so long as organized military forces under anti-Bolshevist leaders control the Kuban and the Don country.

The Georgian Republic has an area of 35,000 square miles and a population of 2,000,000. The region is well located as a thoroughfare for the trade that flows westward from territory east of the Caspian Sea and from Persia, whence a railway runs north across Armenia to join the Georgian system. It has some oil fields and copper deposits. It has also the greatest manganese deposits in the world, which were the source of 44 per cent of the world's supply in 1913; in 1918 and 1919 production had dropped practically to nothing. It has fertile valley lands and an excellent climate for cereals and subtropical products, like tobacco, cotton, dried fruits, raw silk, etc. The borders of the Armenian highland on the south and the snow-capped Caucasus on the north form excellent natural frontiers. Within this territory the population is three fourths Georgian.

People of Armenia

FIG. 224. The broken lines represent Armenia's claim; the heavy solid line enclosing the stippled area, maximum limits of Armenia as now established by custom in Transcaucasia and by treaty (Sèvres, 1920) between the Allied powers and Turkey. It was arranged that the final boundary on the west should be based on the recommendation of President Wilson.

Armenia proclaimed its independence early in 1918 at Garine, a place located in the center of the high plateau of Armenia. The claims of the new republic are shown on Figure 224, but within these frontiers only a small part of the people are Armenian; the rest are principally Kurds, Turks, and Syrians. With these facts in mind, the leaders of the Allied powers required Turkey to relinquish sovereignty over but four vilayets — Van, Bitlis, Erzerum, and Trebizond (Fig. 225) — with an area of 75,000 square miles, 50 per cent more than that of the state of New York. The Armenian population has been so much reduced that probably only 300,000 at the most live in these four districts. Turkey, Armenia, and the Allied powers have mutually agreed to leave the exact location of the Armenian-Turkish frontier ·on the south and southwest to the recommendation[1] of President Wilson. While the decisions of the Turkish treaty of 1920 (treaty of Sèvres) cut Armenia off from access to the sea at the Gulf of Alexandretta, there is provided an outlet at Trebizond. In addition, Armenia will have an outlet at Batum, which may become a free international port with outlet facilities on terms of equality to all the Transcaucasian peoples. In Transcaucasia, Armenia claims about 25,000 square miles of territory; but the number of people in the region can hardly be estimated, even, owing to the losses by war and starvation and the flight thither of refugees from Turkish Armenia. Before the war it had a total population of all elements of about 2,000,000, of which half were Armenians. It is an agricultural country with a small urban population. The principal towns are Kars and Erivan. There are extensive alpine meadows, but no forests. A few rich irrigated valleys, a type of which is Aras, export fruit and wine. Erivan produces cotton and Karabagh exports raw silk.

The Armenian nation had an independent existence in the past, but lost this position when the Turk extended his rule over Asia

[1] Submitted near the close of the Wilson administration but not yet announced by the Allied powers, owing to chaotic political conditions.

Minor in the 13th and 14th centuries. Thereafter the Armenians were persistently persecuted. For example, in 1894–1895 the Moslem Turks attacked the Christian Armenians and put to death from 100,000 to 200,000 of them. These atrocities were repeated in 1909, in the Adana region especially.

Deportations and massacres of the Armenians and Syrians

Taking advantage of the World War, the Turks "deported" thousands of Armenians and Syrians, young and old; that is, the "exiles" were driven into the wilder parts of the mountains and the Syrian desert and left to die. Only to mention a directly calculable result, more than 800,000 Armenians were assassinated, burned alive, or starved by the Turks between 1914 and 1918. The Christian nations of the West, therefore, sought not only to end the rule of the Turk in Europe (except for nominal sovereignty over a mere patch of land northwest of Constantinople), but also to free his subject peoples at Smyrna and in Mesopotamia, Syria, Palestine, and the Armenian districts bordering Russia.

Americans have long had great interest in the missionary schools and colleges, the hospitals, and the social development of Turkey.

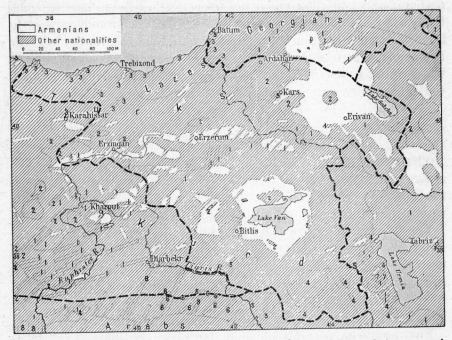

Fig. 225. Ethnography and boundaries in the Armenian country. All boundaries are provisional, including the one with Persia (page 448). The western boundary as shown here represents the units of the four Turkish vilayets renounced by Turkey. A more detailed boundary was recommended by President Wilson. Key to numerals: 1, Turkish-speaking peoples; 2, Kurds; 3, Greeks; 4, Assyrians (Nestorians); 5, Chaldeans; 6, Jacobites; 7, Persians; 8, Arabs.

There is a missionary college at Beirut in Syria, one at Kharput in Armenia, and one at Constantinople. On this account the European powers were unanimous in desiring America as the mandatary of Armenia; but it is unlikely that the United States will accept so remote and costly an obligation, in view of the acute problems nearer home, especially in the Caribbean and the Philippines.

Armenians a minority in the historically Armenian area

Though the massacres, historical and recent, have left but a fraction of the race, in modern times Armenians never have formed more than a minority in any large administrative district. There could not be established a new Armenia similar to the Armenia of a given period of the past, without putting into it populations of different race and speech, far more numerous than the Armenians themselves — a case similar to that of the Jews of Palestine.

Dependence upon Allied support

The Armenians could not police or develop the whole region that some of their leaders claim. At least, they could do so only with loans from the Allies and with the support of Allied officials and possibly Allied troops. These forms of assistance would be expensive and cannot be lent at this time. Moreover, such a plan would be a great encouragement to other minorities to seek Allied aid in holding country for the maintenance of which they have neither the moral nor the financial strength. Such a proceeding would create nations of artificial character without real stability. These are practical considerations which must be faced as squarely as the sentimental considerations that spring from a desire to achieve historical justice.

AZERBAIJAN — A TATAR BOLSHEVIST REPUBLIC

Tatars of Azerbaijan

The Azerbaijan Tatars are of totally different race and speech from either Armenians or Georgians. Part of them live just across the frontier of Persia (Fig. 220). They number about 3,000,000 in Russia, and live in an area of 40,000 square miles.

The Tatars of Transcaucasia, after establishing the Azerbaijan Tatar Republic, with a national assembly and council of ministers, altered the form of the government, which is now similar to that of Bolshevist Russia. The republic is reported to include the former governments of Baku and Elisavetpol, and to be aiming at union with Persian Azerbaijan and Daghestan, a province of Russia north of the Caucasus.

Successive British and Bolshevist occupation

Baku, with its valuable oil wells, fell under Bolshevist control at first; but subsequently a more moderate government, friendly to the Allies, seized power, and a British expeditionary force occupied the city late in 1918. When the British force was withdrawn, the city was captured by the Turko-Tatars and annexed to the Azerbaijan Tatar Republic.

In May and June 1920, Bolshevist forces invaded Azerbaijan, captured the British war vessels at Enzeli on the southern coast of the Caspian Sea, and invaded Persian territory. This campaign was carried out in spite of a prior agreement with Persia to abrogate the understandings of the Czar's government respecting concessions and a sphere of influence in Persia. Embarrassed in the west by Polish resistance and on the south by Ukrainian forces under Wrangel and others, the Bolshevist leaders curtailed their Transcaucasian program and withdrew from Persia.

CONCLUSION

The political situation in the Transcaucasian region is thoroughly confused and will remain so until the larger forces are resolved which affect these weak and poor communities. The Armenians sought peace with Turkey only to be presented with impossible terms. A Bolshevist invasion followed, and an unrepresentative Soviet-Armenian government was established. Georgia was next attacked and its capital, Tiflis, besieged, but it had neither the strength nor the unity and experience to withstand the Bolshevist forces without and within. Azerbaijan has offered no real resistance to Bolshevist control. Under these circumstances there can be no independence and reorganization until there has been established a definite policy toward the Bolshevist government of Russia by the western powers. Should no such policy be forthcoming, Russian Soviet control is designed to extend to its old frontiers in Transcaucasia; for it was not so much against the Transcaucasian governments themselves as against Turkey that the Bolshevist attack was aimed as an answer to the effort of the Turkish Nationalists to exterminate Armenia and expand to the Georgian frontier. It is a mark of the ever-changing character of the politics of the Near East that the Nationalists of Turkey and the Bolshevists of Russia should have followed this difference with a reconcilement and even a treaty. By May 1921 military supplies were shipped in some quantity from southern Russia to Turkey.

CHAPTER TWENTY-NINE

PERSIA IN RELATION TO BRITISH INTERESTS

Persia
once a
powerful
state

EACH of the ancient nations of Europe and Asia was in its time a center from which there radiated a host of civilizing influences. The Roman and Greek civilizations are the better known because of their military exploits and their high culture, with its profound influence on western civilization. A more remote but appreciable influence has been exerted by the civilizations of the "transit" lands of the Near East. Persia, the outpost on the east, has always been of interest to the western world. In the middle of the 6th century B. C., Cyrus created a powerful empire stretching from the Ægean to the Oxus and the Indus. The brilliant recrudescence under the Sassanian kings (3d to 7th centuries A. D.) shared the common fate of the transit lands, Arab conquest being followed by Turkish and Mongol invasions. The Iranian oases lie open to the steppes and deserts of Central Asia. As Omar Khayyam depicted the sophisticated civilization of the oasis, so the great epic poet Firdousi immortalized the struggle between the sedentary Iranian population and the nomad Turanians and Tatars. The situation has not lost its significance today; Persia remains a transit land on the road to the east, open on the north to the power that controls the steppe.

FIG. 226. One of the gates of Teheran, the capital of Persia.

462

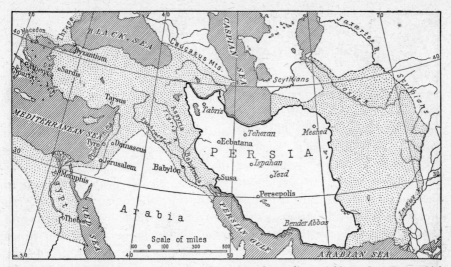

FIG. 227. Persia's present boundaries are shown by a heavy line. Additional territory which was part of the Persian Empire at the time of its greatest extent (500 B.C.) is shown by stippling; according to Shepherd, *Atlas of Ancient History*, 1913, Pl. 8.

LAND AND PEOPLE

Only in the central and eastern parts of Persia, between the Caspian Sea and the Persian Gulf and eastward to the Afghan frontier, does there survive a considerable block of population of rather pure Persian type, who still speak the Persian language. In the west (the provinces of Tabriz, Kermanshah, and Khuzistan) the population includes Kurds, Armenians, and Arabs, rebellious in temper, remote from authority, living in broken country difficult to conquer or to police. In the northeastern part of Persia the people are Turkish in origin and speech; for example, Turkomans from Russian Turkestan. Along the shores of the Persian Gulf there are Arab and negroid elements. These ethnic variations are due to Tatar, Arab, and Turkish conquests, which were carried out frequently between the 10th and 18th centuries.

Persia is one fifth as large as the United States, and consists of country about as extensive and twice as populous as that portion of the American West between the Rockies and the Pacific, south of Idaho and Oregon. All told, the population numbers less than 10,000,000 (Fig. 228). A large part of the country is mountainous and desert, difficult to cross, and almost without inhabitants. The population is distributed in widely scattered irrigated spots; each part tends to live to itself, and there is no national cohesion. To govern so large and varied a country under primitive conditions of travel, away from the few railways and automobile roads that run between

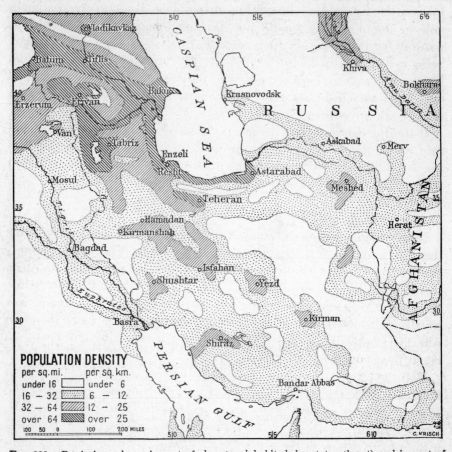

FIG. 228. Persia is made up in part of almost uninhabited desert (southeast) and in part of densely inhabited irrigated valley lands (northwest). In modern times it has not been able to develop its own resources, lacking capital and initiative; and its rich stores of petroleum have brought rival powers (Russia and Great Britain) into the field of domestic as well as international politics. Modified from Philips, *Comparative Wall Map of Asia*, 1:12,000,000, 1912.

the chief towns, would be a big task for a strong central government. The Mohammedan elements in the country do not want this kind of government; they thrive on graft and disorder. Even if left to itself, the decent element would find it exceedingly difficult to put down brigandage and make life, property, and travel safe.

PERSIAN AZERBAIJAN

We have seen that Persia's border people have always given trouble to the central government. One of these border elements is Persian Azerbaijan, a region peopled by Tatars related by ties of religion and language to the Tatars of Russian Transcaucasia, just across the international boundary line. The disposal of Russian Azerbaijan is still in doubt. If it should not become independent, it would be natural for Persia to get it, because part of it was formerly Persian, being ceded to Russia by treaties in 1813 and 1828. It should not be turned over to Persia unless the natives desire it, however, and even then only if Persia gives conspicuous evidence of a capacity for orderly self-government.

If the Persian and the Russian portions of Azerbaijan remain separate as before, Russian Azerbaijan will be a field of intrigue for Bolshevist influence within the Persian border so long as the present Russian government continues.

A FIELD OF FOREIGN RIVALRY

In addition to her internal difficulties, Persia has had to face the interference of three European powers, especially in the past twenty-five years. Russia and England have both tried to push their control of Persian affairs to the greatest lengths. Just before the World War and also during the early stages of it, Germany was courting the Persians and corrupting them, hoping to have their aid when German and Turkish armies should march through Persia to begin their conquest of India. *European interference in Persia*

Railways have been the focus of Russian and British rivalry. Russia has wished to secure a trans-Caucasus line to the head of the Persian Gulf (Fig. 230), as one of her possible warm water outlets. Great Britain, on the other hand, has been quite as eager to complete a railway to India across southern Persia and Baluchistan. In addition to this, British statesmen have always kept a very jealous eye on all incursions by foreign powers into the Near Eastern realm whereby Britain's road to India might be threatened in even the slightest degree. *Important railways that will some day cross Persia*

The chief differences between Russia and England were settled in 1907 by an agreement which gave Russia a sphere of influence in northern Persia that was more than 300,000 square miles in area. It extended from Afghanistan to Kurdistan and included the capital, Teheran. The British sphere included southern Persia on the borders of Baluchistan, an area scarcely half as large as that assigned to Russia. The British thus got control over the outlet of the Persian Gulf, which would enable their navy to prevent the landing or the embarkation of an enemy expeditionary force at the head of the gulf. It was intended to leave central Persia either independent or neutral ground; but it was inevitable that Russian and British *For Russia a huge northern and for Great Britain a southern sphere of influence*

Fig. 229. General landscape view in the vicinity of Teheran, Persia.

interests should extend their sway farther into the interior until they controlled the whole country.

Great Britain's interests both political and commercial

With Russia diverted by civil disorder, her influence is for the moment withdrawn from Persia, while that of Great Britain has become more powerful. The Bolshevists have denounced the 1907 Anglo-Russian agreement as being unjust to Persia. In addition, the present Russian government has informed Persia that it is ready to surrender all the concessions in Persia obtained under the régime of the Czar and to forego interference in Persian affairs, though the value of this promise by the Bolshevists can amount to little in view of their oft-expressed contempt for treaties, even those bearing their own signatures. On its side the British government steadily withstood the Persian request for recognition by the Peace Conference of Paris and for a status of independence and self-government, free from foreign control.

BRITISH OIL INTERESTS

Great Britain's desire to guide Persian affairs is due not only to one of the lessons of the war — that British India in time of general disturbance has some very rebellious elements (there are more than 66,000,000 Mohammedans in India) — but also to the British policy of securing as great a share as possible of the world's oil supply. That this is not the policy of British commercial interests alone is shown by the

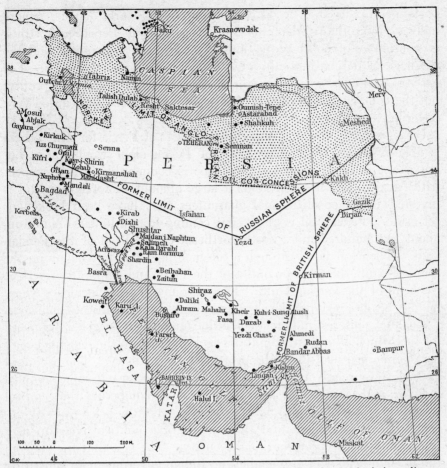

FIG. 230. British progress in Persia. The former Russian sphere has no basis in reality on account of the present disordered state of Russian political life; the former British sphere is for practical purposes replaced by the concession of the Anglo-Persian Oil Company, Ltd. (in which the British government owns a controlling interest), and by the terms of the Anglo-Persian treaty of 1919. Based on data in Redwood, *A Treatise on Petroleum*, Vol. I, 1913; Schweer, *Die türkischpersischen Erdölvorkommen*, 1919; Morgan, *Mission Scientifique en Persie*, 1895; Stahl, *Handbuch der regionalen Geologie*, 1907; *Geographische Zeitschrift*, Vol. XXI, 1915, pp. 483–499; *Geographical Journal*, Vol. IX, 1897, pp. 528–532; Stieler's *Hand-Atlas;* and other sources.

fact that the British government itself is the chief stockholder in one of the great Persian oil fields. One of the largest operators is the Anglo-Persian Oil Company, Ltd., which was formed in 1909 and in which the British government purchased control in 1914, increasing its holding in 1917 to $25,000,000, with enormous annual profits. British government investment in Persian oil cannot fail to influence British policy in Persia, quite apart from the position of that country as a buffer state. All British imports for development, as well as exports, are tax-free. The oil concession covers nearly 500,000 square miles, or more than three fourths of the area of all Persia, and with it go guarantees of police protection by the Persian government and the privilege of purchasing cultivated land belonging to the state. For her rights, Persia was to obtain 16 per cent of the annual net profits; but the company has withheld this profit and thereby has caused very bitter feeling in Persia.

Great oil resources of Persia

Oil is probably the chief undeveloped asset of Persia for which there is a keen demand. The oil fields of Persia alone would make her important in international affairs; she is comparable in this respect with Mexico, in whose oil lands a large amount of foreign capital is invested under constitutional guarantees that have been broken or set aside. Persian oil is at present coming from Maidan-i-Naphtun, about two hundred miles north-northeast of the head of the Persian Gulf. Thence it flows through a ten-inch pipe line to Abadan on the Shatt-el-Arab, the common outlet of the Tigris and Euphrates rivers at the head of the Persian Gulf. There are many other localities where oil may be obtained, but development awaits stable political conditions.

British dependence upon fuel oil

England's interest in Persian oil is due not only to the general concern for fuel which all industrial nations feel, but also to the dependence of her commercial fleet upon the protection of the navy. The use of oil as fuel is especially favored for battleships, because it is economical in space and labor. The growth of great oil companies that control the world's output of oil might some day make the price excessive to the British government and thus have grave political consequences that would threaten her national security. The fact that the oil from the Persian fields will also enable the Indian government to substitute oil for coal on the Western Indian Railways increases Great Britain's interest in maintaining her hold on Persia.

One of the problems of the future is to make the British administration in Persia square with Persian right to independence. If the oil merchant controls Persian affairs, the future state of the country will be no better than the past. And it goes without saying that the people of Persia must themselves benefit by the use of the oil. It is a part of their natural inheritance which should not be taken by either force or intrigue. They are entitled to a fair share of the profits, and this has been denied them in the past.

ANGLO-PERSIAN TREATY PROVISIONS

On 9 August 1919, Great Britain and Persia signed the Anglo-Persian treaty, which has as its chief provisions:

(1) Great Britain respects the independence of Persia. (This is, however, a purely nominal independence in view of the provisions that follow.)

(2) The British government will supply expert advisers to the Persian government at the latter's expense. (Naturally Persia will be pressed to follow their advice whether she wishes to or not.)

(3) The British government will supply the Persian government with officers, munitions, and modern military equipment for a military force designed to preserve order in the country and on its frontiers. (And thus secure order on the frontiers of British India.)

(4) The British government will make a loan to Persia which will be guaranteed by the revenues from customs or other sources.

(5) Great Britain will build railroads and other means of transport to extend trade and prevent famine. (With British capital and to the profit of British investors as well as for the benefit of Persia.)

(6) Persia and Great Britain agree to appoint a joint committee of experts to revise the existing customs tariff.

As one of the Allies who have been consulted in the matter, the United States will not give approval of the treaty of Great Britain with Persia until the people of Persia support it, for it was due to British influence that Persia was prevented from presenting her case at the Peace Conference of Paris. The influence of British interests is seen in the fact that the treaty itself was negotiated in secret.

United States opposed to a treaty not sanctioned by the people of Persia

ALTERNATIVE POLICY

If the government of Persia could be given complete freedom from outside or foreign interference, there would undoubtedly follow for a time a period of internal disorder. Were disorder confined to the neutral central area where it would interfere least with investments held by foreigners, it would do the world no immediate harm. It might even lead to the development of strong men who could at last set Persia free from reactionary and paralyzing Mohammedan influences, from her superstitions and indolences, and create an independent state, capable of managing its own affairs, of carrying out internal reforms in every branch of the government, and of restoring some of the glories of the past.

Need of a stronger government

CHAPTER THIRTY

INNER ASIA: THE UNSETTLED LAND OF THE NOMAD

IN the vast interior of Asia are small groups of peoples of importance to the whole circle of countries roundabout them. Thus Tibet, long nominally a province of China, has recently become independent (under British protection); former Russian penetration of Inner and Outer Mongolia involved China in constant difficulties; at intervals Afghanistan has threatened the peace of India and, more recently, of Persia: Turkestan has a variety of unstable Mohammedan peoples.

THE GEOGRAPHICAL ENVIRONMENT

An arid continental interior

Inner Asia is in general a land of interior drainage, with mountain streams descending to the desert borders, where at greater or less distances from the base of the mountains they are lost in salt lakes or desert sands. Much of the region is wholly uncultivable because of the aridity. Part of it is composed of sand and gravel desert, part is covered with heavy incrustations of salt, part consists of high, cold mountain country, and part of rich valley floors capable of irrigation.

Belted arrangement of soils and vegetation

The sand and gravel deserts have very little vegetation, and are covered in part with shifting sand dunes called *barkhans*, as for example in the desert of Takla-Makan (in Eastern Turkestan). The sand deserts with the accompanying salt deposits and brackish lakes occupy portions of the central desert floors. The border of each basin is composed of gravelly waste deposited in a broad belt at the foot of the mountains, and supports a thin vegetation useful to the nomads in their wanderings from summer pastures in the mountains to winter pastures on the borders of the oases. Large tracts of Inner Asia, especially Mongolia and the northern part of Russian Turkestan, are covered with loam formed upon heavy deposits of wind-blown loess. Upon the loamy soil grass grows in relative abundance during the rainy season of spring, and supplies pasture to the tent-dwelling nomads that inhabit the region.

While each desert basin has its belts of soil and corresponding belts of vegetation and of population, as in Eastern Turkestan, the whole of Inner Asia may be described as having its chief salt and sand districts in a broad belt extending from the Caspian Sea eastward through Eastern Turkestan, Tibet, and western Mongolia, and principally from the Aral Sea to Lop Nor (Fig. 232).

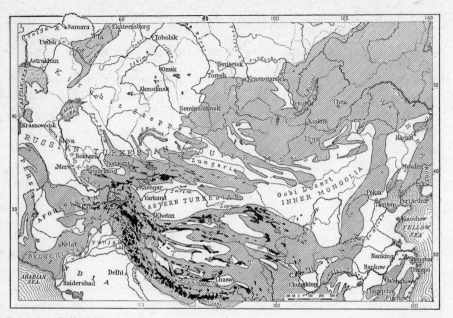

Fig. 231. Relief of Inner Asia. The cross-lined areas represent rough land, the unshaded areas smooth land, as generalized from the best atlases and other sources. The solid black areas represent snowfields whose outlines are reduced from the topographic sheets of the *India and Adjacent Countries Series*, 1 : 1,000,000, 1913–1916.

It is north of this sandy belt that the grassy steppes occur in an equally broad zone extending from the Volga near Samara, eastward past the northern end of the Caspian, all the way across Siberia to the Pacific. North of the steppe country is a vast belt of forest, which extends across Siberia from the Urals to the Bering Sea (Fig. 204).

The movements of the nomadic people are controlled by the belted arrangement of the vegetation and the differences in climate from place to place. Just as there is a movement from mountain to basin floor in each separate basin with the approach of winter, so there is a general movement of the nomads from the grassy belt of southern Siberia southward to warmer winter pastures on the borders of the desert. The wanderings of the people are a response to geographic conditions that are here seen to be a more powerful influence than in almost any other primitive society of the Old World. *Nomadic movements of the people*

In the earliest times, when civilization first arose and the cultivation of cereals began (long before 8000 B.C.), the inhabitants of Inner Asia were fixed upon the land as agricultural peoples, or as hunters who had their homes in the oases. It may be presumed that later the hunters, growing in numbers, turned shepherds as animals were domesticated, and extended their wanderings farther and farther afield *Region of sedentary peoples*

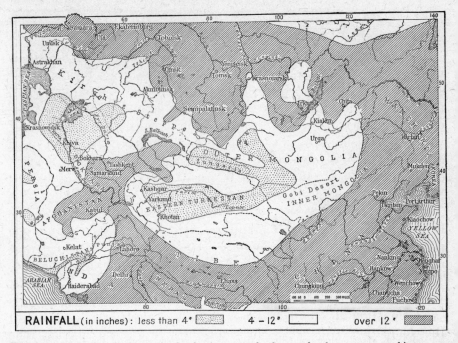

RAINFALL (in inches): less than 4" [ ]   4 – 12" [ ]   over 12" [ ]

FIG. 232. To bring out the grazing lands more strongly the map has been constructed in a somewhat unconventional way, the intermediate grade of rainfall being represented by the white, or unshaded, part of the map. Some of the land having over twelve inches of rainfall is grazing country, and some even of the driest territory has populous towns where irrigation is practiced, for example, Khiva. Based on *Atlas of Asiatic Russia*, 1914 (in Russian); *Atlas climatologique de l'empire de Russie*, 1900; and Bartholomew, *Atlas of Meteorology*, 1899.

in search of fresh pastures for their increasing herds. There was thus produced a tendency toward a division of the population, so that throughout the historical period the Iranian (that is, Persian) population of western central Asia and the Persian plateau remained settled in towns and tilled fields, while the Mongol stock of the region toward the east took to nomadism to a steadily increasing degree.

Basis of the Mongol conquests

The nomad is used to long journeys on swift and strong horses accustomed to desert climate and forage; and as his tribal organization developed he was capable of ranging widely to raid settled lands, escaping without punishment. Here we have the basis of the success of the Mongol conquerors, who found ready-made an instrument of empire superior to any that could be opposed against them. Even today the wanderings of the nomads carry them over a great reach of country. Some of the Kirghiz in the eastern part of Russian Turkestan winter in the region of the Aral Sea and drive their flocks to summer pastures in the steppes of Omsk, eight hundred miles or more away to the north.

THE WESTERN STEPPES OF THE KIRGHIZ REALM

The northern portion of the steppe region of western Siberia is marked by fertile black soil; the middle portion has a poorer brown soil; and the southern portion is desert, or at least semi-arid. From time immemorial this has been the grazing ground of nomadic tent-dwelling peoples, the Kirghiz, wild and unruly horsemen of the steppe, whose main sources of wealth are horses, sheep, cattle, goats, and camels. The total population of the region is more than 5,000,000, of which only about 10 per cent is urban. (Note the region marked "Khirghiz Steppe," in Figure 232.)

Since the middle of the 19th century this great steppe region has been settled by Russian agricultural colonists, who have in large part displaced the nomadic hordes. The first active settlement was in the early 18th century, when Cossack posts were established. There followed a slow infiltration of Russian settlers, — peasants, voluntary religious exiles, and additional Cossacks (Fig. 203). *Nomadic realm invaded by the Russian settler*

Colonization and immigration on a large scale began in 1894 with the completion of the trans-Siberian railway in western Siberia. The manufacture of butter has become a great industry with the new colonists, and, like agriculture, would have developed much further if it were not for a wholly inadequate transportation system and a generally primitive organization of commercial facilities. Trade is carried on by fairs chiefly, of which every town of consequence has one each year. There is still a considerable caravan trade with Inner Asia. Wheat, rye, oats, and millet are the chief field crops. Copper is normally exported from the mines of the southern Urals, and fish from the Ural River.

Politically the region is important because of the displacement of the Kirghiz by the Russian colonists, who have penetrated in the north chiefly, because here they find a rich soil and greater accessibility to the railroad. Thus the native nomads have been pushed farther south into the brown soil belt and the more arid steppe region, where life has become harder. The antagonism between the Russian settler and the nomad has been increased by an attempt made at the beginning of the World War, but later abandoned, to enforce compulsory military service among the steppe people. This was particularly obnoxious because the Kirghiz had by special royal charter long enjoyed freedom from such service. For refusing to give noncombatant service behind the military lines, thousands of them were killed by Russian troops in 1916. *Rivalry for the land between Russians and Kirghiz*

The Kirghiz are unwilling to become sedentary under Russian pressure. The habit of roving is in their blood. "He feels it to be the greatest misfortune and humiliation when he must take to the plough, somewhere by a water course on the edge of the desert; and so long as the loss of all his herds has not hopelessly crushed him, he does not resign himself to that terrible fate which Mahomet has proscribed with the words: 'Wherever this implement has penetrated, it has always brought with it servitude and shame.'"

There is a growing feeling of unity among the people that comes from the spread of Pan-Islamic ideas and the Pan-Turanian movement, the latter intended to organize politically the widely scattered peoples of Turanian stock. They are all Mohammedans of Turkish-Mongol blood and of Turkish speech.

RUSSIAN TURKESTAN

Russian advance into central Asia It was in 1734 that Russia received the surrender of all the Kirghiz hordes; but it was not until the military successes of General Peroffsky in 1848 had been achieved that the Khirghiz ceased to be an obstacle to Russian advance toward the east, particularly in Russian Turkestan. Then followed the fall of the khanates of Turkestan. By 1865 Tashkent had been captured; by 1868 Samarkand. In 1873 Khiva and the Amu Daria district were taken; in 1875 Ferghana, Kokand, and Bokhara fell into Russian hands. There were still the Turkoman

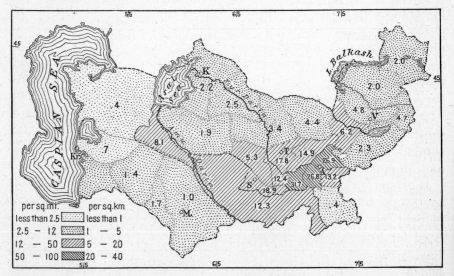

Fig. 233. Population densities of Russian Turkestan by districts. Figures refer to number of persons per square kilometer; for approximate transforming factor to derive population densities per square mile, see legend. From *Atlas of Asiatic Russia*, 1914 (in Russian).

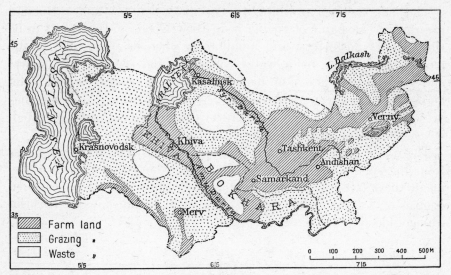

Fig. 234.   Land classification map of Russian Turkestan.   After *Atlas of Asiatic Russia*, 1914 (in Russian).

robbers and slave dealers to reckon with, and after repeated efforts these were definitely conquered in 1884, when Russia stood at the Persian and Afghan frontiers, and the whole Turkestan region was rounded out.

The territory of Russian Turkestan is an extension southward of the steppe region of the Kirghiz, and it also includes a desert tract 1200 miles from east to west which extends southward to the foot of the mountains that fringe the northern border of the great plateau of Iran.   The desert portion is marked by irrigated bands of country along the northward flowing streams and by towns of both historic and recent importance — Merv, Khiva, Samarkand, etc. — connected with the Caspian at Krasnovodsk by the trans-Caspian railway (Fig. 190). The region is hemmed in on the south and east by the mountains of central Asia, broken in two places by the Zungarian " gates" (Fig. 231), through which have passed practically all the ravaging hordes of Turks and Mongols that streamed into western Asia and eastern Europe.

Russian Turkestan is a great lobe of the Russian Empire thrust southward into Inner Asia, and it has brought Russia a large crop of political troubles.   The frontier of a great empire does not remain fixed for long; it is nearly always advancing.   Each fresh advance tempts the empire-builders to go a step farther.   As a result, Russia has pressed against China in Eastern Turkestan, has troubled and has been troubled by the British in Afghanistan and Persia, and has encroached on Turkey along the frontiers of Transcaucasia.

Physical features

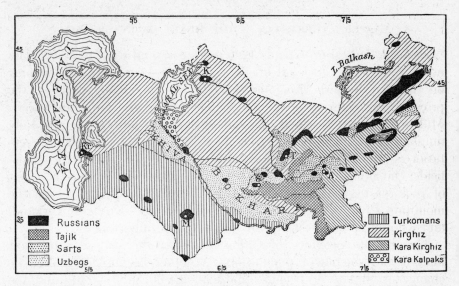

FIG. 235. Ethnography of Russian Turkestan. From *Atlas of Asiatic Russia*, 1914 (in Russian).

Peoples of Turkestan

The entire Turkestan region (Russian, or western, Turkestan; and also Eastern, or Chinese, Turkestan) is peopled in the main by folk of Turko-Mongol origin — Kirghiz, Uzbeg, Sart, Turkoman, etc. Among these the Kirghiz are represented everywhere, forming in some places as high as 80 per cent of the whole. All are clannish to a degree, owing to their present and former wandering habit of life; and though their religion is Islam, to which they were converted in the 16th century, their attachment to the Koran is relatively feeble. The Turkish effort, during the World War, to stir up a feeling of racial solidarity as part of the great Pan-Turanian scheme, was almost a complete failure among these peoples, in contrast to the favorable reception accorded the idea among the Kirghiz farther north and west.

The Uzbegs of Russian Turkestan number about 2,000,000. They form 60 per cent of the population of Khiva and Samarkand and constitute about a third of Bokhara. Formerly nomadic, this group is now almost entirely settled on farms. They are of Mongol origin chiefly, and nearly all are Mohammedans.

Nomad dislike for governmental control

The people of Turkestan might become independent if they were not so diverse in racial character and if it were not for their strong antipathy toward governmental control, a characteristic of the nomad. On the south, whoever controls the cities will control the mountain peoples, who live in part by trade with the cities. It seems impossible that the people of the region should be able to form an independent state without foreign assistance.

EASTERN TURKESTAN — THE HEART OF INNER ASIA

Eastern Turkestan extends 1200 miles east and west, and 600 miles north and south.   It is an uneven, mountain-bordered plain opening on the east toward Mongolia (Fig. 231).   The higher parts of the province are snow-covered (above 15,000 feet), the lower are desert. Midway between is a belt of rough canyoned country, also virtually uninhabitable.   The people live chiefly in two belts of grassy vegetation — the one on the mountain meadows just under the snow-fields, the other on the edge of the basin plain where there is a belt of rock waste, well supplied on its desert edge with water from the mountain streams.   The chief river is the Tarim.   Kashgar, Yarkand, and Khotan on the west are the only cities of importance.

This remote province of China has been the seat of important historic movements of population.   Whether because of a periodic change of climate or because of the nomadic habit of life and the constant shifting of population which this entails, the people of Eastern Turkestan were pressed westward, and some of them even moved across Afghanistan and then into India as part of the Indo-Scythian invasion (in the 2d and 1st centuries b.c.).

For almost twenty centuries, down to our own time, the control of the region shifted from Chinese to Turk, to Mongol, and back to Chinese.   By the 1st century b.c., all Eastern Turkestan had passed under Chinese "protection."   Thereupon there was developed an important trade, but only feeble political control, and by the end of the 1st century a.d., the Chinese had practically withdrawn behind their Great Wall.   Turkish control then came in, and lasted for more than five hundred years.

Farthest limits of Chinese control

Chinese control as well as cultural influence again extended into Eastern Turkestan as far as Kashgar by the middle of the 7th century.   Then Turk and Tibetan and Chinese struggled for ownership of these remote oasis peoples, until Genghiz Khan conquered the land in the 13th century; less than a century later came the conquest by another great Mongol leader, Tamerlane.   During the 15th and 16th centuries there was a long period of civil war which ended in 1758 with the re-conquest of the whole region by the Chinese.   Only for brief intervals was the province independent.   Civil war followed, and the repeated invasion of the whole region by large Chinese armies. In 1862 a Mohammedan rebellion broke out in China, and taking advantage of it, this remote province massacred thousands of Chinese and ended Chinese rule until 1876, when the whole region once more

Interruptions in Chinese rule

Fig. 236. Faizabad bazaar,

— and finally — fell into Chinese hands.   In thus driving a wedge into central Asia and colonizing a far distant province, the Chinese were responding partly to motives of empire-building and trade, for across the region ran the great caravan route to western Asia.   They were also in fear of the people who lived just beyond the Great Wall; it was in this debatable ground that from the earliest times there had been fierce and continual struggles between the civilized and sedentary population of China and the nomadic barbarian hordes of Inner Asia.

Conflict between Russia and China In the later development of her government in Eastern Turkestan in the past few decades, China has treated the region as a colony on the same footing with the eighteen provinces of China proper.   Most of her difficulties hitherto have been due to the disturbed state of the Kokand region, east of Tashkent.   Intrigues hatched in Kokand among a fanatical population constantly troubled the people of China on the western borders of Eastern Turkestan.   To placate the Khan of Kokand, China formerly paid a yearly subsidy of about $15,000. These troubles ended with the absorption of Kokand by Russia in 1876, and though there has been danger of Russian absorption of Kashgar since that time, there has been nominal peace for nearly fifty years.

The oasis life of the people of Eastern Turkestan is easy and isolated, and it is in the oases that the population (Turki) chiefly live. Only 10 per cent are nomadic shepherds (Kirghiz), and there is a small group of fisher-folk (Lopliks) who live in the lakes and reed swamps of Lop Nor.   Nearly all are Mohammedans.

Chinese Turkestan, east of Kashgar.

Brown Bros.

In spite of Mongol influences, the people of Eastern Turkestan **Widely scattered towns of the oases** show little kinship to the Mongols. Instead they are more closely related to the Iranian stock. Hence the anomaly of the weak Chinese holding a remote people of different culture and speech. A strong local government could not be formed, because the oases are widely scattered and are separated by difficult desert or mountain country. The towns and oases are from a hundred to two hundred miles apart. A population of only a little more than 1,000,000 is strung out over a belt of country two thousand miles long. It has been the prey of every invader.

The largest trade is with Russian Turkestan, and there is some **Commodities of trade** trade with India also, in spite of the hazards and difficulties of the long mountain roads and the cold high passes. Transport is by cart and caravan, the latter chiefly. Cotton, hemp, and tobacco are grown, besides grains and vegetables. Silk and cotton are among the chief exports and are produced in the warm oases at the lower elevations, but the list is headed by felts and rugs, products of the numerous flocks and herds of the pastures on the desert and mountain border. Jade and gold also are exported to China.

The Republic of Turkestan in Russian Turkestan was proclaimed early in 1918, but the proclamation had little effect in Eastern Turkestan. The Moslem Turks would like to get control of Eastern Turkestan as part of their Turanian realm. But the people take life so easily that they will never do much to help the Mohammedan or the Turkish cause. They will long remain as clay in the hands of the potter. Russia's interest in Eastern Turkestan has always been keen, since the rich western part of the province, which has all the large cities, lies on her frontier. Through trade and political agents, she has long sought control as part of her process of penetrating India on the one hand and the northern Chinese trade realm on the other. With the present disorganization of Russia, this pressure has ceased; but it may begin again if the Soviet government attempts to extend its rule and its teachings into the densely populated and turbulent Indian peninsula.

Possible Bolshevist control

The region is of interest to China chiefly as a thoroughfare for trans-Asiatic commerce. If China fails to form a stable government, she may find this province allying itself with the western Asiatic forces to which it is more closely related by ties of blood, language, and religion.

THE MONGOLIAN REALM

From the earliest times, the wild and nomadic Mongols raided the adjacent fertile Chinese provinces. Their military and political power was consolidated in the 12th century, with the establishment of the "Empire of the Great Moguls." Under Genghiz Khan, in the early years of the 13th century, a well-drilled army was organized which penetrated the Great Wall and again and again ravaged and plundered the Chinese provinces. When Genghiz Khan turned his attention westward, he conquered most of Inner Asia, captured Tabriz and Tiflis, and with his Mongol armies swept westward as far as the site of Odessa. Farther north, Moscow was captured, then Nijni Novgorod; Poland was ravaged as far as the Vistula, Hungary invaded, Budapest taken. Down to 1914 prayers were still said in some of the churches of Galicia for deliverance from the Mongols.

The plundering Mongols

No subsequent leader equalled the exploits of Genghiz Khan, and after periods of revival under Kublai Khan (late 13th century) and Tamerlane (14th century), the Mongol empire fell apart. The fragments are now divided among China, Russia, and Great Britain. The Mongols have fallen behind in the science of war. Their weapons were once the best in the world, their people had great endurance, and the nomadic life admirably suited them for wide conquests in the grass lands of eastern Europe and western and central Asia. Their arms are now obsolete, though if trained by the Chinese the Mongols might become once more an important military factor.

Decline of military power

Mongolia is today under Chinese rule. China has been compared to a sea into which all waters flowing become salted. Thus she has

FIG. 237. Hauling stores to Mongolia through Hannorbar, Chihli, fifteen miles north of Kalgan on the road to Urga. Typical mode of transport over large parts of Inner Asia. See also Figure 242.

absorbed into her population or modified by her culture one after the other of the dynasties of barbarian origin that sprang from the region of Mongolia north and west of the Great Wall.

Mongolia, as shown in Figure 252, is the largest region under Chinese sovereignty outside of the eighteen provinces of China. It has nearly half the extent of the United States. It contains the great Gobi Desert, with an area of nearly a half-million square miles, extending 1000 miles from east to west and from 450 to 600 miles from north to south. It has no permanent through-flowing streams, and is a region of great contrasts of temperature between summer and winter. *Extent of the Mongolian region*

The Gobi Desert is not everywhere a sandy waste. In the eastern part between Kweihwacheng, or Kalgan, and Urga the surface is flat and the ground is covered with thick, short grass that supplies excellent pasture. Though the region is capable of rapid and high development, there has been no marked advance in Chinese commerce for fifty years.

The Mongolian realm is divided into Inner Mongolia and Outer Mongolia (Fig. 231). Inner Mongolia is populated by two classes, the nomadic and the agricultural. In former times the Mongols invaded China, as noted above; but in later years the Chinese have penetrated the region of the Mongols, where they become not only *Chinese penetration* agricultural but pastoral people as well, and this with great success. Their penetration has been unusually active during the last twenty years.

Since freight is always from twenty to forty times more expensive by land than by water, the cost of cart and caravan transportation across the vast plains of Mongolia is readily appreciated. We may also judge thereby the benefits which the building of railways would bring to the widely scattered towns that form the chief centers of trade. Owing to the poverty of the land, the population numbers only 2,000,000. The limited resources, the scattered and thin pastures, and the traditions of the people make nomadism the rule. Large numbers of Chinese cart and pack animals come from Mongolia. It is estimated that 100,000 camels are used for the transport of tea from Kalgan in northern China to Siberia, and that the caravan trade employs 1,200,000 camels and 300,000 oxcarts.

Caravan routes in Mongolia

Mongolia is crossed by historic roads, important in both former and present commerce. Among the most important of the old roads is the one to Eastern Turkestan, the great Inner Asian trade route, the main communication between east and west. It has a total length from Peking to Kashgar of 3500 miles. For much of its distance the road, which passes through deep and narrow gullies, can be used by a single line of traffic only. For hundreds of miles it winds through depopulated and untilled country. It crosses mountain passes 10,000 feet high. Here and there are well-watered oases with an abundance of vegetation, and with prosperous but sleepy towns. The road is slippery in wet weather and deeply ravined.

Trade between Russia and Mongolia

While the old caravan trade of China dates back beyond the Christian era, the rich trade with China which Russia enjoyed is not more than two hundred years old. In 1689 a treaty was signed between China and Russia, granting to a limited number of Russian merchants the privilege of trading with China. Almost at once there was a lively traffic between the two countries. Silk and tea were carried across the Mongolian deserts and the Siberian steppes and mountains into European Russia. A small Russian settlement sprang up at Peking.

For a time there was an interruption of this trade, owing to political differences between the two countries, which grew out of the asylum that was given in Siberia to a large band of Mongol robbers; but in 1725 a new agreement was reached in the treaty of Kiakta. By the terms of the treaty the frontier cities of Kiakta in Siberia and Maimachen just across the line in Mongolia became the gateway to Chinese trade. Warehouses and caravansaries were built, and a

Fig. 238.   The Great Wall at Nankow Pass, China.   This was the great defensive work built by the Chinese to keep out the people of Inner Asia and specifically the Mongols.   From Clapp, the *Geographical Review*, 1920.

great trade once more developed.   All Russians had the right to trade with China.   Cloth and hardware were brought from Russia and were exchanged for the silks, porcelains, tobacco, cotton, and tea of China.   This trade continued until the building of the trans-Siberian railroad, whereupon the camel commerce of the overland road rapidly declined.   It is possible that a railroad will be built across the pass through Kiakta and the ancient trade revived in a new form.

The strength of former Russian influence may be judged by the fact that in 1911 Russian agents induced certain Mongol princes to ask the Czar to take Mongolia under his protection.   This was shortly after the outbreak of the Chinese Revolution, which threw China into a state of disorder that, with many changes, has continued down to the present (page 514).

THE UNRULY STATE OF AFGHANISTAN

In its later aspects Mohammedanism presents one of its most acute problems on the northwestern border of India, where, tucked

Afghanis-
tan as a
center of
Moham-
medan
fanaticism

away in the heart of Asia, is Afghanistan, a small country of unruly Mohammedans. Though weak, it has hitherto stood between the two slowly growing empires of the British on the south and the Russians on the north, and it has fought them both.

The Afghan wars of 1839 and 1842 were followed by better relations between England and Afghanistan, which culminated in the treaty of Peshawar in 1855. But even after this there was only a limited admission of British officers. Afghanistan wished to adhere to the policy of isolation.

British
policy in
Afghanis-
tan

Thereafter the British policy was one of inactivity or at the most of petty meddling in the affairs of Afghanistan, until Russian successes in Turkestan (1875) forced England to frame a new policy in which Afghanistan was regarded not merely as a border country to India but as a possible avenue of Russian advance. The British had either to control Afghanistan or to endure the Afghan raids of the warlike and independent tribes bordering the Punjab in northern India.

Afghan
raids on
the Indian
border

Afghanistan has been called "the land of rocks and stones and sanguinary feuds." Before the Afghan lies the region of northern India, which he has long coveted. He has frequently gone down and raided the plains and border valleys. He says in substance: "God in His goodness has placed these people nearby to be our lawful prey, that we may go down and reap their harvests when our own crops fail."

It was in 1914, under the influence of a fanatical preacher, that the independence movement broke out in its wildest form on the northwestern frontier of India. At one time the British had to employ 250,000 Anglo-Indian troops to subdue the country. But for the refusal of the ruler of Afghanistan to join in a Holy War, the whole of northern India would have been aflame. At best, he could not prevent the wildest of his border tribes from giving the British occasional trouble. The latest disturbances on the northern Indian frontier began about the first of October 1919, when a band of Afghans some three hundred strong ambushed a British column. Rather heavy fighting on the Baluchistan and Afghanistan frontiers, involving principally the Wazirs, has been reported a number of times since then.

Order, the
price that
Afghanis-
tan must
pay for
freedom

Afghanistan can keep its independence only if it becomes more orderly. The right of a people to be independent depends upon ability to police its own frontiers, to prevent its land from becoming a base of operations for raids on the people of a peaceful neighbor, and to observe treaty obligations.

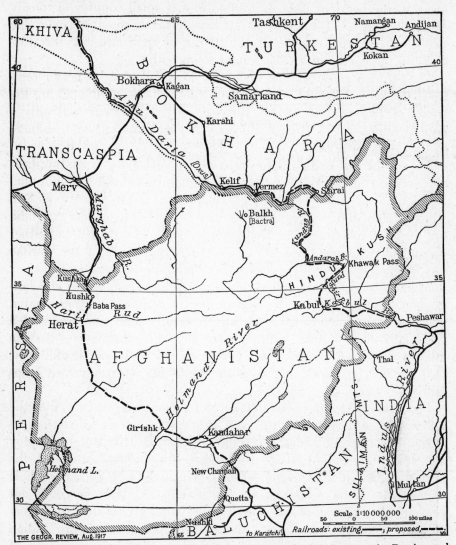

FIG. 239. Outline map showing in detail the proposed connections between the Russian and the Indian railway systems through Afghanistan.

The question of the independence of disorderly peoples deserves a moment's further consideration, for to a marked degree it affects international policy in critical places. For example, in 1862 France got by treaty the right to support the independence of the Sultan of Maskat. This has enabled unscrupulous merchants to raise the French flag on Arab and Indian sailing vessels, and thus to get guns and ammunition into Afghanistan, by way of Djibouti (in French Somaliland) to Maskat and thence to the coast of Persian Baluchistan, thereby furnishing the means of raising those perpetual border revolts against British rule that may some day lead to a Mohammedan rebellion in India.

It was in the same way that a great deal of trouble was given the United States by shipments of German arms into Mexico when the United States was in armed dispute with that country in 1916. In the past English merchants have carried arms to Morocco for the Moors to use against the French and Spanish, and to Madagascar for the use of the Hovas against the French. Some of the small turbulent states would probably have been taken over long ago by the great powers if it were not, as all the world knows, that the powers are jealous of each other and hitherto have expected to profit by disorder. A great deal of the turbulence is caused by merchants of these same big powers who find their trade in arms profitable in spite of all the risks of capture and confiscation.

THE TIBETAN HIGHLAND

The area of Tibet is a little less than 500,000 square miles, or nearly twice that of the state of Texas. It is a land of exceedingly lofty mountains and high desert tablelands and valleys. Some parts of

FIG. 240. Outer wall of Kabul, capital of Afghanistan.

FIG. 241.   Near the border between Afghanistan and Baluchistan.

the region were not known until recently, one great section, including a mountain range theretofore unknown, having been explored by Sven Hedin as late as 1906–1908.   Until recent years only Chinese representatives were permitted to enter Lhasa, the capital of the country.

In all there are about 2,000,000 Tibetans, living in semi-independent tribes, each with its religious leader, called a Lama.   The chief religious ruler, called the Dalai Lama, has hitherto lived at Lhasa in the royal monastery.

In recent years British interests in Tibet have become more important because of the British government's desire to protect its northern Indian frontier, to establish trade relations between the people of India and Tibet, and to gain access to southern China by way of the more populous eastern and southeastern sections of Tibet. The Tibetans have always opposed political and commercial penetration on the part of Great Britain and China.   Though agreeing in 1893 to the establishment of a trade market at Yatung, situated in Tibet just outside the Sikkim frontier in northern India, the Tibetan government later authorized the tearing down of the boundary pillars between these two provinces, and the building of a wall across the way. *British interests in Tibet*

Fearing that the continued hostility of the Tibetans was inspired by Russia, Great Britain sent a military expedition into Tibet in 1903–1904, under command of General McDonald and Colonel Younghusband.   The latter entered Lhasa on 7 August 1904.   The Dalai *British military expedition to Lhasa*

FIG. 242.   Camel transport in Inner Asia.   Tibetans carrying merchandise, Shansi, China.

Lama fled, but a treaty was signed with Tibetan representatives which opened three places in Tibet to Indian trade: Yatung, Gyangtse, and Gartok.   Trade was to be free.   This proposal was agreed to by China, Tibet then being nominally under her control, and in 1906 she signed a treaty approving the Tibetan treaty and promised not to let any other power interfere in the affairs of Tibet.   England, on her side, promised not to annex Tibet or interfere with her administration, and in 1907 confirmed this position by the Anglo-Russian treaty.

Activities of the Dalai Lama   When the Dalai Lama fled from Tibet in 1904, he first took refuge in Mongolia.   From there he went to Peking, where he was told by the Chinese government that his land was really Chinese territory and that he must subject himself to the Chinese authorities.   He was given an annual pension and sent back to Lhasa in 1909.   Disorders occurring in his country just before and directly after his return, the Chinese government sent a column of soldiers to Lhasa and the Dalai Lama fled to India in 1910.

Conflict of Chinese and British interests   Then came the Chinese revolution in 1911 and the establishment of the Chinese Republic.   In 1912, Mongolia and Tibet were declared to be integral parts of China.   These activities of the Chinese government called for a protest from the British government, because of the fact that England had independent treaty relations with Tibet in which she did not recognize Chinese sovereignty.   China stopped the advances of her troops and declared she had no intention of making Tibet a Chinese province.   In 1913 the Tibetan authorities declared the independence of Tibet, and Chinese officials withdrew from the country in October 1913.   Thereupon delegates from England, China, and Tibet met at Simla and in April 1914 arranged Tibetan affairs.   These representatives came to an agreement, but the Chinese government would not subsequently accept it.   It divided Tibetan territory into two parts:

(1) Outer Tibet was to be a separate province.   It was to include the province of Chiando and was to have an autonomous government, only nominally under Chinese authority.   Neither England nor China was to interfere with internal affairs, but their agents could visit Lhasa.

(2) Inner Tibet was to include Litang and Batang, and was to be under the direct control of China.

Outer Tibet has therefore become practically an independent state under the guarantee of Great Britain and as a dependency of hers, on the ground that the Chinese government, though it repeatedly sent military expeditions into the country, was unable to stop disorders that in turn created trouble on the Indian frontier, a source of danger to Great Britain.

Tibet now under British protection

To avoid those minor conflicts out of which larger issues grow, the frontiers of Tibet should be definitely established as soon as possible, with the assistance and agreement of the local native governors.   Neither those in the direction of India nor those that separate Outer from Inner Tibet have been fixed.

Need for definite frontiers in Tibet

CHAPTER THIRTY-ONE

THE FAR EAST

European
commercial
penetration

IN reaching for the commerce of the Far East, European powers found themselves confronted by two established nations, China and Japan, whom they could not reduce to the status of dependencies. Japan has maintained her sovereignty intact and has taken her place among the great powers; China, far stronger and richer potentially, but actually weak and now disorderly as to internal government, has not been able to ward off the repeated encroachments of the European powers.

In the islands of the Pacific, on the contrary, there was little difficulty in achieving complete ownership, for the primitive inhabitants were easily subdued or won over by the Europeans. Objects of rivalry at first for their raw materials, many of the islands came to be considered important for their strategic value also. They were regarded as an approach to the mainland of Asia, and their possession was thought to be essential to the control of the trade of eastern Asia. Thus, through trade, Europe was brought across the Pacific and Indian oceans to the doors of the Far East. Relations were at first sporadic, as at Macao, near Hongkong (Portuguese), Deshima, at Nagasaki (Dutch), and Formosa (both Portuguese and Dutch). Later they were persistent and even aggressive, as when the English got Hongkong (1842) and the French by successive steps (1863, 1864, 1867, 1884, 1896) established themselves in Indo-China. Each acquisition furnished local subtropical products and a market for European goods, and became also a base for trade conquests farther afield.

THE CONTROL OF RAW MATERIALS IN THE FAR EAST

Great
Britain's
interest in
the raw
materials
of the Far
East

When it is realized how large a part tropical and subtropical products play in modern industrial and commercial life, it seems natural that it should be the policy of Great Britain, the largest trading empire in the world, to get as great a share as possib'e of the raw materials and trade resources of the Far East, and she has pursued this policy with marked singleness of purpose ever since she acquired the Suez Canal. To take a single instance, — through her control of the free ports of Hongkong and Singapore she has made London one of the chief world markets for rubber, tea, spices, jute, gums, and hides. With her huge war debt, trade control and development are matters

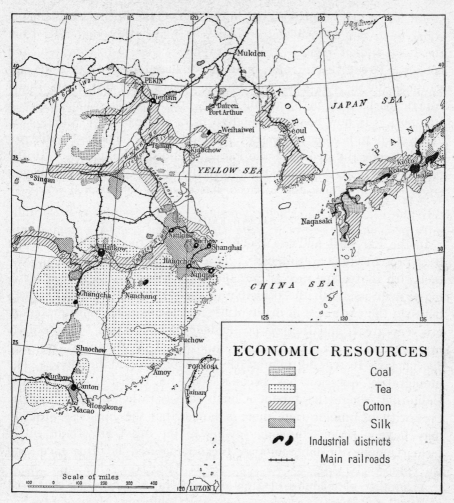

Fig. 243. Some of the economic elements in the political geography of the Far East.

of vital importance. She has the banking facilities and also the commercial experience of the past to increase production in new lands. In recent years the trade motive has also become a more active factor in Japan's foreign policy, especially in relation to eastern Asia. These two powers, as well as France, will seek to improve their financial and ocean transportation facilities in the Far East.

In the past the United States has bought the products of the Far East chiefly through Great Britain, Japan, and Germany. Her annual purchases of Oriental products just before the World War exceeded $200,000,000, and her exports were more than $100,000,000. The largest single source of American trade in the Orient is Japan

Manila as a center for American trade interests in the Orient (total of nearly $150,000,000 in 1913). The Straits Settlements come next, Singapore being a great port for the raw materials from the East Indian region — tin, hides, spices, rice, fish, tungsten, and rubber. Great Britain and Japan have maintained their trade advantages in the Far East, because they have their own ports there. Americans have been operating chiefly from Manila, which is not a free port. It now has large modern piers and extensive warehouses, and were it to become a free port, it would have an enormous influence in developing the wealth of the Far East and the Philippines. In the past twenty years American trade with the Philippines, chiefly in hemp, sugar, vegetable oils, and tobacco, has risen to $50,000,000 yearly.

RACIAL FACTORS

Racial questions in the Far East

In the Far East and the Pacific the world's racial problems reach their present climax of intensity; here the white race comes into contact with the yellow race, a part of which — the Japanese — is striving to win assent to the principle of race equality. The differences between the two races in mode of life and ideals, and even in religion, are very great, and there is no tendency among them toward intermarriage. In Canada, Australia, and the United States there are special laws restricting immigration of Chinese and Japanese. The immigration question has become acute in British Columbia and California, where the Japanese birth rate is rather high and where, even without immigration, there is danger that the Japanese problem may have a serious outcome, owing to the rapid growth of bitter feeling among the labor unions, the unorganized laboring men, and the landowners.

A number of colonies of Japanese rice farmers live on the coast of Brazil and there is a colony in Lower California, Mexico. In São Paulo, Brazil, where laborers on the coffee plantations grew scarce during the World War, there was increased Japanese immigration, encouraged by subsidies from Japan and the welcome of the Brazilian government. There are now 20,000 Japanese laborers in São Paulo alone, of whom 4000 own coffee plantations.

Tendency of Japanese emigrants to go to southern climates

In Europe, where comparatively crowded lands do not tempt immigration from the Far East, the problem of the yellow race scarcely exists. The harsh climate of northern Europe, as contrasted with the relatively mild climate of Japan, also has a deterrent effect. The tendency of the Japanese is to move into the warmer belts, like California, Hawaii, and the Philippines (Fig. 257). This tendency causes some of the people of Australia to be apprehensive lest large numbers of Japanese may settle in the East Indies and Polynesia and become their unwelcome neighbors (Fig. 257 and related text, page 526). It is argued that the Japanese multiply so rapidly and live so cheaply that they drive out the white workman wherever they compete with him on equal terms.

At the Peace Conference of Paris in 1919, the Japanese plenipotentiaries long insisted that restrictions of immigration based on race should be finally removed the world over, but to this proposition the other powers would not give their consent.

Failure of Japanese attempt to secure equality

(A) The Rise of Japan to the Rank of a World Power

When Japan was still a kind of hermit kingdom, both her foreign and her internal problems were simple. By centuries of experiment, life had become adjusted to resources. Her people lived apart from the rest of the world. For more than two centuries before Commodore Perry's visit to Japan, her sole point of contact with western nations was a single trading station on the island of Deshima opposite Nagasaki, where there was a limited commerce with the Dutch.

Japan until recently a hermit kingdom

EMERGENCE OF JAPAN

It was in 1853 that the United States government sent Commodore Perry with an American fleet, demanding Japanese protection for American sailors and property wrecked on the coast, and permission for American ships to use Japanese ports as a base for food or for trade. The Perry expedition forced Japan into the current of modern international life.

After 1868 Japan modified her political and social institutions in what is probably the most complete and radical change of its kind that has ever occurred in the world's history. The basis of Japanese social and military organization had been feudalism. In 1868 the system was abolished by revolution, and a national spirit sprang up that was to be used as a powerful instrument in empire-building. The first railroad was begun in 1870; today there are nearly eight thousand miles of rail. In 1872, military service became universal and obligatory. A constitution was granted in 1889, and Parliament met for the first time in 1890.

Radical changes in the social and political life of Japan

It was just in the midst of this process of modernization that Japan consolidated her island possessions. In 1875 she got from Russia the Kurile Islands, thus rounding out her domain on the north. In exchange she relinquished her claim to the island of Sakhalin, the southern half of which was again recovered in 1905; the northern

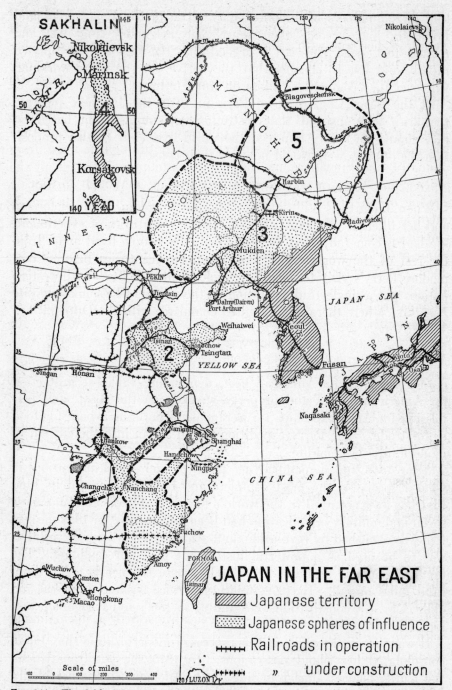

FIG. 244. The field of Japanese ownership and influence in eastern Asia. Key to numbers; 1, southern China; 2, Shantung; 3, Mongolia; 4, Sakhalin (inset); 5, Manchuria (military occupation following the war). A portion of the northern end of the island of Sakhalin appears in the upper right-hand corner of the main map.

half is occupied at the present time. In 1876 she seized the Liukiu Islands, which extend southward almost to Formosa. In 1895 as a result of her war with China she won Formosa, the richest of her island prizes, with a population of 3,650,000. Her island empire fringes the coast of Asia for 3000 miles and embraces an area of 261,000 square miles.

The merchants of Japan turned to overseas trade and her business men began to manufacture articles of commerce. At the present time the Japanese trader can be found everywhere through the East, from Sumatra and Singapore up through the Philippines and in all the open ports of the coast of China. Japanese banks and warehouses sprang up in India during the World War, and Japanese merchants went in numbers into the Malay States, buying up rich concessions. Japan's commerce with Siam doubled during the war, and in the same period she increased her trade with the Dutch East Indies fivefold. In New Zealand the Japanese have won over the former trade of Germany and have taken away much of British trade also. A fleet of Japanese steamers makes regular runs to Seattle and San Francisco and another fleet plies between Japan and the west coast of South America. Japanese trade expansion on a huge scale in southern Asia, the Far East, and the Pacific, is one of the really marvelous economic consequences of the World War.

Japanese overseas business

EXPANSION TOWARD THE MAINLAND OF ASIA

The rise of Japan to the rank of a world power was marked by two wars in which she won striking military victories: the war with China in 1894–1895 and the war with Russia in 1904–1905. But at the close of the first war Japan's military success was followed by diplomatic humiliation. She had driven the Chinese out of Korea, invaded Manchuria, and occupied the Liao-tung peninsula. China hurriedly agreed to make peace, and by the treaty of Shimonoseki, April 1895, she ceded Port Arthur (Fig. 244), the Liao-tung peninsula, Formosa, and the Pescadores Islands (west of Formosa) o Japan; she further agreed to pay a large indemnity and to recognize the complete independence of Korea.

Two modern wars won by Japan

It seemed that at last Japan stood firmly planted on the mainland with an outlet for her rapidly growing population. But Russia stepped in and combined with two other western nations — France and Germany — to compel the eastern nation to give up Port Arthur and the Liao-tung peninsula and withdraw from the mainland, on the ground that, near Peking, Japan would be a menace to the peace

Japan compelled to withdraw from the Asiatic mainland

of the Orient. All parties in Japan now began to look forward to the time when they could strike at Russia.

But the great powers were thinking much of themselves, their trade privileges and possible yellow hegemony, and very little of China, when they bade Japan leave the mainland of Asia. In 1897 Germany sent a fleet to China, ostensibly because two German missionaries had been murdered in the province of Shantung. As a result China was compelled to give Germany a ninety-nine year lease of the fine harbor of Kiaochow and a surrounding area of more than 250 square miles, besides large commercial privileges in the province of Shantung, which has a population of nearly 40,000,000 Chinese (Fig. 246).

Russia also seized the opportunity of robbing a weakened China. It seemed clear that she intended ultimately to annex the whole of the great province of Manchuria. For the time being she took a twenty-five year lease of Port Arthur, from which she had driven Japan by diplomatic weapons in 1895. England acquired Wei-hai-wei on much the same terms. China was forced to open a number of additional treaty ports and to permit foreign capitalists to build railroads and develop mines. Weak, pacifistic, rich, undeveloped, China appeared to be in the same class as Africa; the powers seemed to regard the country as so much booty to be divided among themselves.

Then in 1902, for the first time in modern history, an Asiatic power — Japan — made a defensive alliance with a European power — Great Britain — on terms of virtual equality. This meant that in the impending war with Russia, who was constantly adding to her armed forces in Manchuria and about Port Arthur, Japan would have the help of Great Britain if any other power came to the help of Russia.[1]

In February 1904 the Russo-Japanese War began, to last until September 1905. It was closed by the treaty of Portsmouth, named after Portsmouth, New Hampshire, where the peace delegates assembled on the invitation of President Roosevelt. Japan had gained wisdom as a result of her previous experience with the great powers, and pressed insistently for territorial advantages; Russia was made to recognize Japan's paramount interest in Korea, though that country was to be independent; Russia transferred to Japan her rights at Port Arthur and in the Liao-tung peninsula, and evacuated Manchuria and the southern half of the island of Sakhalin.

In July 1916 the Japanese and Russian governments signed a

---

[1] For the present status of the Anglo-Japanese treaty see page 26.

treaty which was practically an alliance. By this treaty Russia recognized Japan's rights over the bulk of China, while Japan recognized Russia's special interests in China's western territory, especially Mongolia and Turkestan. While this treaty has no present force owing to the political disorganization of Russia, it is important as one step in Japan's long and hard struggle to force recognition of her alleged special rights in China. By acts such as these Japan was to outdo the western powers in the penetration of China and the winning of special privileges.

Up to the time that Japan entered the Chinese field, other nations had won special privileges there without arousing acute anxiety in the United States government. But so comprehensive were the claims of the Japanese, so aggressive their methods, so favorable their geographical relations, and so marked their racial advantages, that the full import of a foreign penetration of China was quickly realized in America. China being weak and her officials corrupt, she could always be made to grant concessions, even though these interfered with her domestic life or threatened her territorial integrity. From this time forward, the United States indirectly played the rôle of the champion of China. The Japanese question thereafter was not solely a matter of restricting Japanese immigration, but also a matter of ending the period of unfair commercial rivalry in China so that territorial rivalry and war might not inevitably follow. Equality of commercial opportunity was called the principle of the "Open Door," a principle fraught with great importance to the world's peace. *[margin: Policy of the Open Door]*

Eventually, by the Lansing-Ishii agreement of 1914, the policy of the Open Door was modified to the extent of recognizing Japan's *special interest in China's future*, which some statesmen defend as parallel to the course of the United States in the West Indies and which others regard as a regrettable admission.

RESULTS OF THE WORLD WAR FOR JAPAN

In the World War of 1914–1918, Japan was obliged by the terms of her treaty with Great Britain to come to the aid of her ally. She took Kiaochow and the Marshall and Caroline Islands. German New Guinea was taken by Australian troops, German Samoa by New Zealanders. German power was thus swept from the Pacific and the Far East. What new alignment of forces would be made by the peace treaty? The war had made but little drain on Japan's resources. By contrast, the Russo-Japanese War cost her about $1,000-000,000 and 230,000 in killed and wounded. Under the bounties *[margin: Extension of Japanese gains during the World War of 1914–1918]* and subsidies granted to the Japanese mercantile marine, the gross tonnage increased from 255,000 tons in 1896 to 2,300,000 tons in 1919. Shipbuilding and iron and steel industries have grown enormously as a result of the war. Japanese merchants and shipowners have invaded every accessible market. The results of their enterprise are extraordinary.

Japanese trade gains in Far Eastern markets

Between 1914 and 1917 the total exports of Japan had increased 170 per cent in value; to Europe 143 per cent; to America 181 per cent. In the same period her imports from Asia increased 63 per cent; from America 252 per cent; from Europe they decreased 61 per cent. From India she received 38 per cent more goods in 1917 than in 1914, and she exported thither nearly 400 per cent more. In the Philippines, Japanese exports and imports more than doubled during the war. The Australian and New Zealand markets have been deluged with Japanese goods — clothing, hardware, chemicals, jewelry, toys, silk and cotton cloth, electrical machinery, porcelain ware, and even hats and buttons. Eastern Siberia and China are commercially dependent upon Japan. Korean trade is now almost exclusively in the hands of the Japanese.

Every Japanese resource of diplomacy, of industry, of financial power and technic, has been organized to penetrate the trade areas of the Orient. In the same period American trade in the Far East also has greatly increased — with Japan itself, with the Dutch East Indies, with the Philippines. Upon the relations of these two powers in the Pacific trade realm will depend in large part the future peace of the world.

Japanese control of Shantung

For the Far East the principal result of the World War and of the peace arrangements that followed it, has been to turn Shantung and Kiaochow over to the Japanese for an indefinite, or at least unstated, period of years: in other words, Japan takes over Germany's former possessions. Japan has sought to establish herself in control of the Chinese Eastern Railway, thus shutting off European access across the continent to the Pacific. She has set her heart on the commercial development of Shantung and of the tributaries to the Tsingtau-Chinan railway, as well as the railway itself. She is firmly established at Port Arthur. Peking lives under a Japanese shadow. All the northern gateways of China are sentineled by the Japanese fleet. Korea, though solemnly promised autonomy in 1905 by treaty between Japan and Russia, was annexed outright in 1910.

The position of Korea may have the gravest consequences for Japan and therefore deserves special consideration. For centuries the

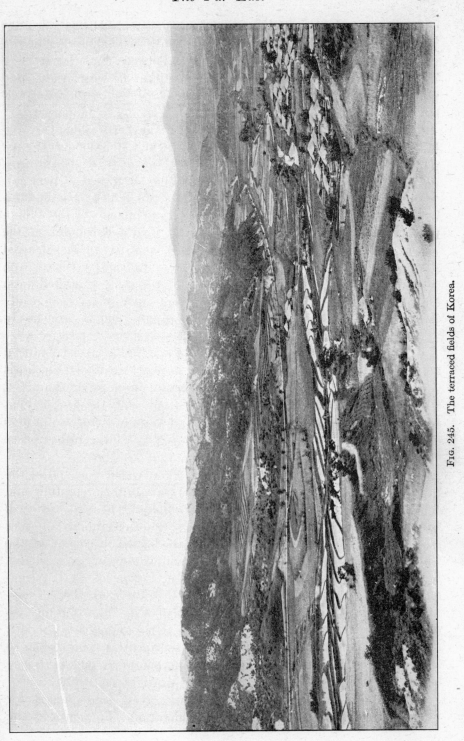

Fig. 245. The terraced fields of Korea.

country enjoyed only the shadow of sovereignty. It was long subject to either China or Japan, paying tribute and acknowledging its
subordinate position by treaty. The war between Japan and China
in 1894 was the direct result of competition between these two
powers for the control of Korea. The Japanese victory was followed by the proclamation of Korean independence in January 1895.

Korea
under
Japanese
control Meanwhile Russia was advancing into northern China. Korea
borders Manchuria for five hundred miles, and it lies between two
naval bases — Vladivostok and Port Arthur — which Russia then
owned. Agreements with Japan were made by Korea in 1896 and
1898, ostensibly to give equal opportunities ; but by taking advantage
of internal political dissensions, the Russians obtained a powerful hold
over the reigning king, who from 1896 to 1900 gave them valuable
concessions in timber, fisheries, and ports and let them construct
military roads. The result was war between Japan and Russia, and
Korea became a Japanese prize of war. Promised a civil administration in 1919, Korea is still in control of the military authorities.
One oppressive measure has followed another. Domination by an
alien government has bred resentment, then violence. Japan's every
act of sternness has been met by renewed hostility on the part of the
Koreans. Patriotic societies have been formed, vast public protests
arranged. Assassination of Japanese soldiers and officials has led to
wholesale retaliatory violence by the Japanese military forces. The
material improvement of the country — afforestation of bare hillsides,
the building of railways, the improvement of agricultural methods —
does not offset the sense of humiliation that arises from the daily
interference of Japanese officials in the life of the Korean people.

Corruption and weakness are the historic traits of the Koreans.
They have never been able to stand alone. The price of their
weakness is foreign domination, never a welcome thing, and here
especially distasteful because of militaristic methods of control that
have followed outright annexation of Korea by Japan.

CONFLICT OF CHINESE AND JAPANESE INTERESTS AT SHANTUNG

Chinese
opposition
to Japanese
control of
Shantung By the settlement of 1919 (the treaty of Versailles) nothing was
restored to China of all those privileges which the powers had taken
away. The disposition of Shantung (Figs. 244 and 246) aroused a
feeling of national disaster among the Chinese. Forty million Chinese
became, to all intents and purposes, Japanese subjects, though Shantung is one of the richest provinces of China and is sentimentally
and historically dear to the Chinese. They speak of it as "the cradle

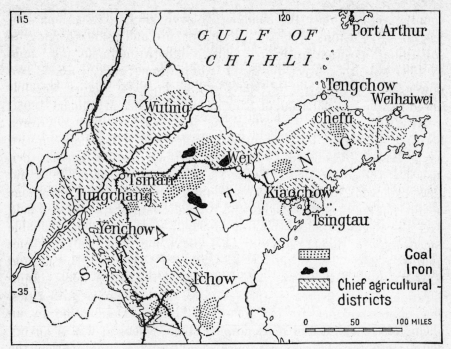

FIG. 246. The province of Shantung, home of 40,000,000 Chinese, recently placed under Japanese sovereignty for an indefinite period. Until 1914 Germany held the territory inclosed by the broken line about Kiaochow in lease from the Chinese government.

of Chinese civilization," "the Holy Land of the Chinese people." So great was the feeling aroused in China by the award of Shantung to Japan that a popular boycott against Japanese goods rapidly spread. It is estimated that at one time Japan's trade with China was reduced 80 per cent. Japan in Shantung holds the economic key to the country — the railways. At Tsingtau she has possession of an economic gateway. In holding both she stands in the very midst of the Chinese commercial realm, and is feared the more because she has an organized and powerful government and a highly developed industrial system. Strategically her position is no less important.

Japan has agreed to exercise no political rights in the peninsula and to retire from it at the end of an unspecified term. The great powers have the opportunity of proving their sincerity in seeking to win China's assent to the treaty of Versailles (which put Japan into Shantung) by making no further invasions of China's sovereign rights, by developing her resources on terms that will give the Chinese a share of their own natural riches, and by demanding for the foreigner no unwarranted special privileges. *Japan's promises*

Japan has further agreed neither to make exclusive economic use of

Japan's
important
economic
" rights "
in China

the port of Tsingtau, nor to give herself or her nationals the benefit of lower rates or other special privileges over the railways. Japan secures, however, the right of maintaining a Japanese settlement at Tsingtau; the ownership of the Tsingtau-Chinan railway is to be a joint Sino-Japanese enterprise, and Japan is to own the coal mines tributary to the railway and to have rights in several other railways which may be built: this much is legally hers, on the basis that these are economic rights once held by Germany and now forfeited by her to Japan.

Prospect
that Japan
will fulfill
her obli-
gations

Doubt has been expressed as to whether Japan can successfully withstand the very grave temptation to make her economic rights the basis of a quarrel with China from which she would issue with increased political rights in Shantung. The famous "twenty-one demands" of May 1915, made upon China by Japan under the threat of war, have not been forgotten.[1] But for the misgivings aroused by them, faith in Japanese policy in the Far East would be stronger.

THE PRESSURE OF POPULATION

Unequal
population
densities
one of the
ultimate
causes of
war

One of the oldest and most powerful basic causes of war is an unequal birth rate on opposite sides of a boundary line. From the great migrations of history down to the recent World War, men have always looked across their international line-fences and envied the wealth of their neighbors. Germany, for instance, before 1914 had more than 65,000,000 people and France had less than 40,000,000, and their areas were but little different.

Japan's
needs for
colonial
outlets

Japan is today in the situation of a country that must overflow its boundaries. Only about one sixth of her total area of 176,000 square miles (including Formosa, but not Korea) is under cultivation, because so much of it at the north is cold — too cold, that is, for typical Japanese agriculture — and a large part of the rest is mountainous. Her poets sing the praises of Fujiyama, but the mountain cannot grow rice. Sixty-one million people are crowded together on an area only a little larger than that of California. The average size of a farm is two and a half acres.

---

[1] As originally presented to China on 18 January 1915, the Japanese demands were twenty-one in number. By them Japan was to acquire former German rights in China, and China was not to lease any part of the province of Shantung to a third power. Japan obtained also valuable railroad concessions, the opening of important cities and towns in Shantung as commercial ports, a lease of the southern Manchurian and other railways, special trading privileges in eastern Mongolia, and mining rights in southern Manchuria and eastern Inner Mongolia, as well as other valuable concessions in mines, railways, and harbor works. China agreed to employ influential Japanese advisers in political, financial, military, and police departments. The demands involved the virtual surrender of China to Japan.

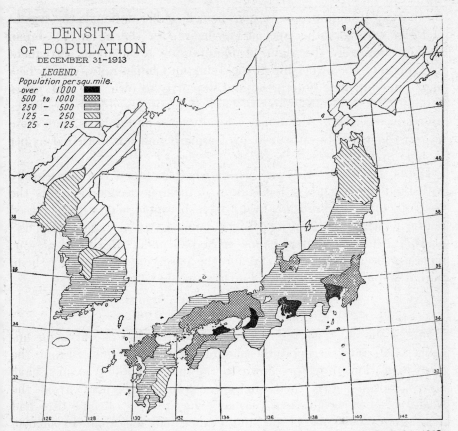

Fig. 247. Sketch map of the population density of Japan and Korea on 31 December 1913, according to data supplied by N. Yamasaki of the Geographical Institute of the University of Tokyo. Scale, 1 : 16,000,000. From Jefferson, the *Geographical Review*, Vol. 2, 1916.

Before Japan was opened to European trade her people had by long experience learned to be self-sustaining. They cultivated every available spot and lived frugally. When a whole people has practiced thrift and industry for many generations, it acquires a stability that gives it relatively great commercial power. With the growth of foreign trade the Japanese were able to export some of their products and import food, with an immediate improvement in standards of living. To extend these advantages requires still more trade, and this invites both territorial expansion and the stimulation of industry.

Social and economic experimentation are the natural consequences of these conditions among the Japanese people, responsive as they are to the progressive thought of advanced western nations. In the past few years there has been a marked drift of the rural population to the cities, where it becomes part of a restless industrial class. This

FIG. 248. Japanese village and adjacent farms — a typical scene.

creates a lack of tenants for the landed proprietors. Where rural population declines one may see, side by side with the untilled fields of the well-to-do, the tiny garden of the poor farmer. The inevitable result is rural discontent, such as in Europe has led to the division of the large landed estates (page 394). Some farmers have emigrated to Hokkaido, one of the large and relatively cold northern islands of the Japanese archipelago, where they have adopted modern agricultural practice. Wishing to become self-supporting in the matter of wool, Japan grants annual subsidies to farmers who keep sheep. The eastern Siberian realm and adjoining parts of Manchuria and Mongolia are the natural fields of expansion for stock farming. With these virgin empires in her hands, Japan will let go of strategic points in Siberia only with great reluctance. She is still in possession of them, though at one time (1919) she had agreed to evacuate her troops.

Like Germany, Japan has seen her colonists go out and swell the populations of other lands. She desires to keep them together under her own flag, and she can do this only if she provides the land and the business opportunities. Therefore she has looked westward across the sea, where she beholds fair lands thinly populated. Manchuria and Mongolia are empires in geographical extent, far larger than Japan, and in parts of them are fertile plains that could support a dense population. There are vast pastures for the production of meat and wool, two products that in the past fifteen years have become increasingly and alarmingly scarcer in the world. There are oil and coal and iron, and her supply of these things Japan, with rapidly growing industries, desires to augment.

To aid production and industry, Japan has recently created a Department of Agriculture and Commerce, which plans to assist manufacturers in the solution of industrial problems and problems of the export trade. The department is authorized to grant liberal subsidies. Japanese shipping subsidies are among the largest in the world. Great shipyards have been built recently. On raw materials imported into Japan there are rebates, and these enable the Japanese manufacturers to compete successfully with European countries and with America in many lines of trade in China. In some cases the government actually guarantees a certain percentage of profit on home manufactures.

FUTURE POLICY OF JAPAN

In forecasting their future relations with Japan, the great powers (particularly the United States) find themselves confronted by these questions:

(1) Will Japan push her assertion of race equality to the point of demanding equal treatment of Japanese and Americans in California, and of Japanese and British in Australia, New Zealand, and British Columbia; and if she does demand this, will she be able and willing to go to war for it?

(2) Is her "mainland" policy in eastern Asia designed to carry the Japanese frontier far into that continent, and especially into China, with the object of gaining special privileges for Japanese trade to the exclusion of white traders?

(3) Will she abandon Shantung at the end of an indefinite period, as she has agreed to do? And, if she does abandon it, will her merchants not have so strong a hold on the political

life of the province that they will inevitably be brought into conflict with the Chinese government when it resumes the exercise of its sovereign rights? (Germany promised in 1864 to hold a plebiscite in Slesvig-Holstein, and Chile promised to hold a plebiscite in Tacna-Arica after the war with Peru in 1879–1884; both failed to keep these solemn promises.)

(4) Will she exercise her mandatary in the Marshall and Caroline Islands in such a way that she will win the approval of the other great powers, or will she make every effort to remain there without supervision or even under the criticism or disapproval of the other interested powers?

(5) Will she develop local self-government in Korea or will she continue her present policy of repression and persecution?

The test of Japanese idealism to come in the near future

It is easy to reply that criticisms similar to those made of Japan might be made of the other great powers and that nowhere else in the world have these powers themselves given exhibitions of more selfish ambitions than in the Far East, at Japan's very door. But on the other hand it must be remembered that all of Japan's modernization dates from the past fifty years. She has the forms of western civilization, but has she also its idealism? For side by side with the old selfish deplorable policies of the great powers there grew up in the modern western states another set of ideas. Thoughtful men saw special trade privileges and imperialistic national policies and the oppression of weak peoples give rise to war, and they have said: "War is a fine and a noble thing when men fight to kill ignoble ambitions and to defeat selfish and cruel oppressors; but is it a fine thing when men kill each other for dollars and the pride of kings and the sport of persecuting a 'racial' minority?" We are not sure that Japan is of this mood. There is a powerful militaristic element in high places but little affected by the lesson of Germany's defeat; there is a sense of pride and ambition characteristic of the young rather than the mature nation. Furthermore, there is a racial ambition mixed with that pride and tinged by a sense of the humiliations of the past, when the great powers gained privileges in the Far East which they denied to Japan. Finally, the Peace Conference of Paris, to Japan's chagrin, decided not to adopt the principle of race equality.

The convergence of European and American political and economic interests upon the Far East will probably bring Japan's political program and the ideals of her people into great prominence. The real test of her diplomatic power and her idealism is yet to come.

(B) China's Immediate Problems

China would not sign the treaty of Versailles, feeling that her rights had been ignored in the Shantung settlement. She therefore confronts five major problems : [1]

(1) She has yet to make peace with Germany and to complete international or diplomatic arrangements with the Allied and Associated Powers. (However, she became a member of the League of Nations by signing the Austrian and other peace treaties which have incorporated in them the League of Nations Covenant.)

(2) She has Japan as a neighbor on the mainland, a thing she has dreaded ever since 1894 because of the economic stranglehold which she fears that progressive and ambitious Japan may secure, in pursuance of her "mainland" policy in eastern Asia.

(3) She has not yet ceased to fear aggression by the western powers, who have taken treaty ports, concessions, and territory in the past. (For example, Great Britain was ceded the island of Hongkong in 1842 after the Opium War; Germany took Kiaochow in 1897; Russia took Port Arthur in 1898.)

(4) She must make with foreign capitalists financial arrangements that will enable her to develop her resources in a manner favorable to her own interests.

(5) She is in the midst of an internal political and military struggle, the end of which is still in doubt.

How came China to her present unfortunate pass? The Chinese were a highly civilized nation when the Europeans were still in the Bronze Age. With her external commerce dependent upon sailing vessels, cut off by high mountains and deserts from western civilization, China developed a culture much higher than that of surrounding countries. She was a civilized nation in contrast to the barbarians on her frontiers. Japan borrowed much from her. But the Chinese were isolated and, following Confucius, their greatest philosopher, extremely pacifistic. The Chinese despised the "foreign devils"; they desired to be left alone. All of this might be sound philosophy if the rest of the world would leave them alone in return.

China's five major unsettled problems

How China became weak

[1] Besides these five, China still has her opium problem. By the treaty which closed the Opium War with England (1842) the opium trade was restricted and later abolished, but the illicit introduction of opium and morphia continues, to the great harm of the people. For example, at Macao the Portuguese permit trade in opium and the use of opium. By the Opium Convention of 1912 the powers were to put further and more stringent restrictions upon the opium trade, and the Third International Opium Conference of 1914 sought means of putting the Convention in operation. The war interrupted the termination of effective arrangements, but the treaty of Versailles, if signed by China, provides promising guarantees.

ECONOMIC PENETRATION OF CHINA BY FOREIGN POWERS

1 Montreal
2 Pittsburgh
3 Columbus
4 Savannah
5 Duluth
6 Topeka
7 Tucson
8 San Francisco

FIG. 249. The area of China compared with the United States. Note the length of the Great Wall. The key in the lower left-hand corner will serve to locate a few American cities for comparison.

The economic advances of outside nations have penetrated the whole economic life of China. With strong navies and a determined policy these nations demand and get "rights," concessions, exemptions, franchises, almost innumerable. They have established open ports (page 511), supervised the use of borrowed money, sought administrative control of territory adjacent to the railways over which they have practically sovereign control, secured exclusive exploitation privileges, exempted themselves from Chinese taxes on imported material, and even maintained separate post offices.

China's potential resources and commercial power

It is the great wealth of China that attracts foreign countries to her. She is the world's largest producer of antimony; she has large lead, tin, and oil deposits. She has the largest undeveloped iron and coal deposits of all the nations in the world. The anthracite coal deposits of Shansi and the regions adjacent are equal to those of Pennsylvania; and the quantity of bituminous coal is at least as great as that in the United States. The iron deposits of the Hankow district are in control of the Japanese. Those of Manchuria will almost certainly fall into the same hands, for the Japanese are specially anxious to increase their iron and steel production. Of value to Japanese plans is the opposition of the Chinese government to granting further concessions to foreign capitalists. The Chinese buy the concessions; then the Japanese buy out the Chinese owners. In 1915 Japan obtained exclusive mining rights in eastern Mongolia and in Shantung, to mention two of the most important acquisitions.

Between 1894 and 1898 the struggle for concessions reached its climax and each one of the big European powers got its sphere of influence in China.

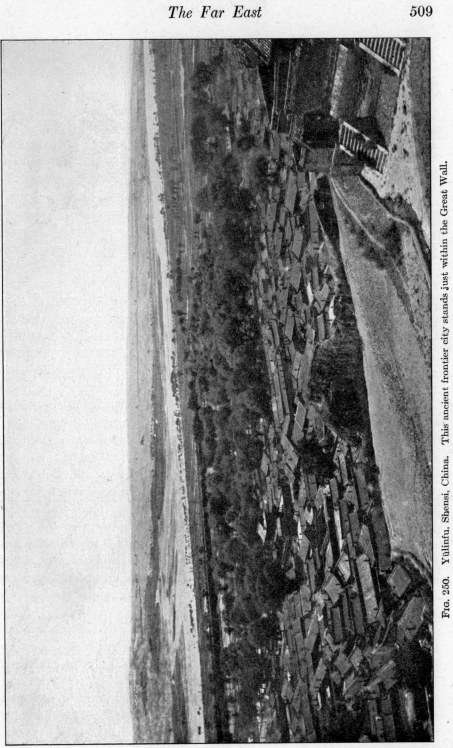

Fig. 250. Yülinfu, Shensi, China. This ancient frontier city stands just within the Great Wall.

It was as if the Russians and the English had just seized rival reservations on Long Island and the Jersey coast, commanding New York City; as if the English had wrenched away Charleston; the Germans, Philadelphia; the French, New Orleans; and Cossacks were garrisoned in strategic points throughout New England. It was as if the New York, New Haven and Hartford Railway were manned and guarded by Slavs, the New York Central by Belgians, the Pennsylvania by Prussians; as if the Pittsburg mines were handed over *en bloc* to an English corporation, and the Russians had exclusive mining rights to the gold of Alaska's Yukon region. BATES.

By 1899 the process had gone so far that it looked as if the principle of the equality of commercial advantage in weak and powerless China would be entirely set aside, and therefore the United States attempted to establish the principle of the Open Door (page 497).

The Treaty Ports

Chinese seclusion and the opening of treaty ports

At the opening of the 19th century Canton was the only port open to European trade. By the treaty of Nanking, which closed the Opium War (1840–1842), the Chinese opened five treaty ports to European powers, Japan, and the United States, for foreign residence and trade, and ceded Hongkong to the British. Since then China has opened, or has been compelled to open, a large number of other ports. In Manchuria, since 1900, she has opened a number of treaty ports under pressure from Japan; since 1898 she has voluntarily opened a number of desirable ports, with a view to keeping them under Chinese control. Of this class are the towns of Chinwangtao, the winter port of Tientsin, and Tsingtau, the capital of Shantung. There are no foreign concessions in the voluntarily opened ports; in them the international settlement, or "trade quarter" where foreigners reside, is under Chinese administration.

Status of the treaty ports

At present China has 56 regular treaty ports and 8 voluntarily opened ports, 25 ports of call, and 16 frontier caravan stations, or marts. In agreement with the twenty-one demands presented by Japan to China in 1915, China promised to open additional ports in Shantung and in eastern Inner Mongolia (Fig. 251).

Great Britain has concessions at a number of places; for example, Amoy, Canton, Hankow, Tientsin, and Shanghai (Fig. 251). Japan has concessions at Amoy, Foochow, Hangchow, Hankow, Newchwang, and Tientsin. Russia had concessions at Hankow, Newchwang and Tientsin; France at Canton, Hankow, Shanghai, and Tientsin. The United States has given up practically all its concessions. Belgium and Italy have concessions at Tientsin; and Germany and Austria-

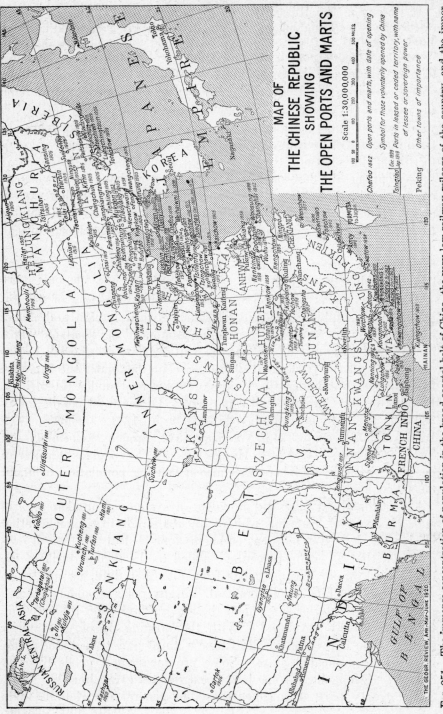

Fig. 251. The immense concentration of population in the broad coastal belt of China, the very low railway mileage of the country, and the importance of river transportation, all furnish a background for an understanding of the significant hold which European nations have on Chinese trade as a result of their control of 2000 miles of Chinese coast.

Hungary also had concessions there which were surrendered by the terms of the treaties of Versailles (Germany) and St. Germain-en-Laye (Austria).

Foreign privileges

At each treaty port is a tract called a "concession," where foreigners reside and manage their own affairs. They levy taxes and special charges, build churches, and own warehouses, paying a land tax to the government. Foreigners enjoy equal rights, no matter what nation operates a given treaty port. Foreigners can also be tried in courts of their own at the treaty ports; that is, there is extraterritorial jurisdiction. Cases between foreigners and Chinese are judged under the law of the defendant, who has freedom as to counsel and supervision. In Manchuria the foreigners live in so-called New Towns, built around the railway stations and subject to either Japanese or Russian administration. The ports of call differ from treaty ports in that foreigners cannot reside there or have business there, and all goods to and from ports of call must pass through a treaty port.

Foreigners in the treaty ports

The treaty ports present interesting features in respect of the distribution of shipping and the relation between foreign and native population. We take for illustration the port of Tientsin, which ranks third among Chinese custom stations and is growing in importance. Of the trade in 1916, 39 per cent was under the Japanese flag, 33 per cent under the Chinese, 26 per cent under the British. Before the war Germany had 9 per cent. Of the total population of 800,000, the Chinese numbered 750,000 in 1914, Japanese 1772, British 1530, Germans 753, Americans 542, French 294, Italians 93, Swiss 85, Danes 74, Austro-Hungarians 54, Norwegians 15, Portuguese 6, Spanish 4. There was also a floating population of about 60,000 coolies.

Chinese tariffs and transit dues

Unfortunately, China had in vogue a system of municipal tariff and other transit exactions which subjected trade in China, whether foreign or domestic, to great embarrassment. But in 1842 it was arranged that a certain percentage added to the regular tariff of the treaty port would exempt goods from all other dues, no matter to what place in China they were sent. Many ports should be opened up if the vast interior spaces and the mineral and other resources are to be effectively developed. With the opening up of the interior should come a revision of the Chinese tariff and transit dues, now in a very complicated state. Some provinces allow goods to enter duty free (Mongolia); some have local rebates (Manchuria).

The treaty port arrangements are, in general, restrictions upon

Chinese sovereignty, and there has been a growing desire on the part of the Chinese to discontinue these concessions or to modify them. Unless the Chinese carry through the reform projects already begun and give honest and reasonable administration, they will long continue to suffer from the servitudes that are now imposed upon them in the use by foreigners of Chinese ports and other trading centers.

China's objection to the invasion of her sovereignty

The seizure of ports by rival powers was accompanied by the acquisition of tributary spheres of influence which in practice became commercial zones parceled out among British, German, French, Belgian, and Japanese merchants. Not having free ports or a sphere of influence, the United States carried on its Chinese trade under every form of handicap. This condition, coupled with the rivalries of the powers already established, was dangerous for all; but the vested interests had grown so enormous that for some years American insistence upon the Open Door policy had little effect.

A promising measure is the New Consortium, organized in 1919. It is composed of a group of banks and bankers from the United States, Great Britain, France, and Japan, formed as an international partnership and at the request of their governments. Its object is to finance the development of transportation systems, highways, and other basic enterprises by loans to the Chinese government. By these means, it is hoped to preserve the independence and territorial integrity of China and diminish international commercial rivalries in the Far East. Future concessions by China and concessions already given upon which substantial progress has not yet been made, are to be pooled with the consortium so that the four banking groups already named may have an equal chance of participation. Japan sought to reserve parts of Manchuria and Mongolia from the scope of the consortium, but was finally induced to relinquish these demands except with respect to certain branch-line railway projects in southern Manchuria, the political significance of which cannot be overestimated. The full importance of the consortium can only be realized if and when a sound constitutional government is formed in China. Such a thing does not at present exist. The northern and southern factions are still at war. The military governments of the provinces prefer disorder, and this calls for heavy financial outlays.

Plan for equality of financial privileges

INTERNAL ADMINISTRATION

In 1912 China became a republic, with a president instead of an emperor, but she is not yet in a settled state. Her interior regions, like Yünnan and Mongolia, always unruly because more remote

Civil war in China

from the central government and composed of far more independent people, have not yet accepted the new order of things; and between the democratic south and the more monarchically inclined north there has been taking place a struggle fateful to the welfare of China. It is nominally a civil war, but really a contest between four factions for control of the Chinese people, their tax system, and their foreign policy. The group in control of Peking is recognized abroad as the de facto government. The present state of disorder recalls an earlier period of revolution: the Taiping Rebellion of 1852–1864, in which most of eastern China was devastated, with the loss by war and famine of twenty millions of people. Though China abolished the feudal system several hundred years before the Christian era and concentrated her government at Peking, it was not an effective concentration. Local self-government continued, and on the whole has been beneficial. But it has led also to local, not national, patriotism, owing to the ignorance of the mass of the people and the lack of modern means of communication. Such conditions favor the separatist policies of local leaders in periods of general disorder. Until a network of railways, wagon roads, and telegraph lines is built in China, there will not be developed that public spirit upon which national solidarity depends.

Courts of foreign or extra-territorial jurisdiction

In view of the bad state of the government of China, it is not surprising that its judicial system is both antiquated and corrupt, two qualities which have marked Chinese administration for hundreds of years. Therefore the powers, as soon as they had secured vested interests in China, obtained extraterritorial jurisdiction which enabled them to try criminal charges against their own citizens in special courts of their own appointment. To restore China to full sovereignty requires the abolition of these rights; but the special courts can be dispensed with only if the Chinese codes of law and judicial procedure are revised and simplified and honest judges are appointed.

By the terms of the commercial treaty between the United States and China (1903) the United States undertook to assist China in revision of the legal code and agreed to relinquish extraterritorial rights when satisfied that a real change for the better had been made. China thereupon began such revision in 1904. Cruel and unjust punishments were abolished in 1905. Trained judges were appointed.

In the past decade bureaus have been created in the fields of agriculture and commerce, postal service and education, police and constabulary, in an effort to centralize the authority of the government and improve its civil service. The army has been drilled

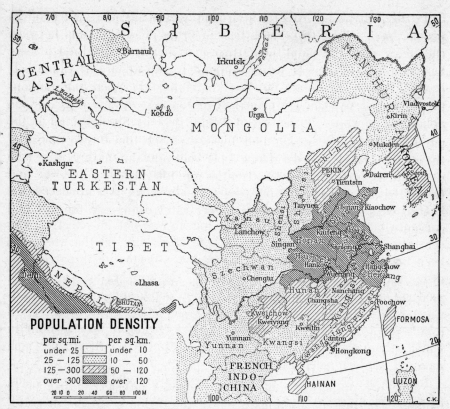

Fig. 252. The density of population in China, by provinces. Note the position of Shantung and Korea and compare with Figure 244. Based, for China, on statistics in the *Statesman's Year-Book.*

by foreign instructors, and the government has bought back some of the foreign railroad and mining concessions.

In proportion to her supply of important raw materials, China has the smallest railway system and the largest labor supply of all the nations   Should she ever become industrialized, her industrial and commercial power would be incalculable.   Like the United States, she has lands spread from the subtropical south to the temperate north, and in spite of her great population, in places dense, China has undeveloped territories capable of settlement, as in Mongolia and Manchuria.   At least two thirds of her population of 400,000,000 live in a narrow belt relatively near the sea.   Great rivers, valuable alike for irrigation and for commerce, cross her fertile plains.   She has ample natural harborage.

Possible commercial power

The rivalry of the European powers in the field of Chinese trade is likely to continue unless it is arranged that all the commercial agreements between China and other countries shall be discussed openly

Revision of tariff laws needed

and agreed to by all. In the past each power has pressed China for special customs privileges, as in the tariff on overland trade between China on the one hand and Russia, Great Britain, France, and Japan on the other. It is the judgment of leading statesmen that China's tariff should be revised, and that its regulation should be in Chinese hands and under the supervision, not of one power, but of all the powers. There was held in 1918 at Shanghai an international conference which had for its object the standardizing of the customs rates, in order that a 5 per cent ad valorem duty might be charged, as provided by the treaties of 1902 between China and Great Britain and of 1903 between China and Japan and the United States, with the possibility of a higher rate to increase the national revenues.

THE STRUGGLE FOR MANCHURIA

Russia for a time unable to defend her own interests

In eastern Asia the disposition of the former rights and privileges of Russia raises questions of large importance. She had gained railway privileges in Manchuria, and was fast developing her Amur province. In the struggle with Japan for possession of the indefinite zone between China and Russia, her people invested capital and made settlements. Until Russia finds herself again, the Allies are unwilling that her property should be turned over either to Japan or to China. The present administration of the region is divided between Japan and the Republic of Eastern Siberia (page 406).

Railways as instruments of penetration

A problem fraught with danger to the peace of the Far East is the disposal and control of the railways of Manchuria, which have been powerful political as well as economic instruments. They serve a region of great extent which has some of the best agricultural land in eastern Asia, besides iron mines and timbered tracts. The Chinese Eastern Railway, more than a thousand miles long, was under Russian police authority until 1917, and Russia also had the right to exploit certain resources — for example, coal — along the line of railroad and in some districts outside the railroad strip as well. Russia's claim to the exercise of police authority was based on the fact that the region is infested with armed robbers, and that her line and equipment could not be safeguarded by Chinese police.

Russia also built part of her trans-Siberian line across Manchuria, linking it with the Chinese Eastern Railway; she thus extended her influence throughout northern Manchuria. She had planned to build southward, to Port Arthur and Dairen (formerly Dalny); thus Dairen would become the real ice-free port of eastern Siberia and

Vladivostok would become a naval base. By 1903, just before the outbreak of the Russo-Japanese War, Manchuria was practically under Russian control. Then came the war with Japan, and the Japanese entered southern Manchuria to the exclusion of the Russians, at the same time adding Korea to their sphere of influence. This forced Russia to build her all-Russian line north of the Amur.

During the period of active Russian expansion in northern Manchuria, the Chinese Eastern Railway was nominally a private Russo-Japanese corporation, although in reality it was a political instrument of Russia. Russia made Harbin the administrative center for the railroad. Harbin is naturally the economic center of northern Manchuria, and lies in the midst of the great wheat and soya bean region. Russian railroad officials have ruled Harbin and the railroad strip as sovereigns, and the Japanese have copied every Russian invasion of Chinese rights in southern Manchuria on the South Manchuria Railway, over which Japan has control. *The Chinese Eastern Railway the most important*

Through her agreement with China, Japan has been able to exclude other foreigners from railway enterprise in southern Manchuria. She has secured control of blocks of territory along the line and also of the naval base at Port Arthur and the commercial port of Dairen. The railway officials refuse cars to Chinese shippers and supply them to Japanese; carry Japanese mail and refuse Chinese mail; and give Japanese shippers rebates to guarantee successful competition. As the railway is policed by the Japanese, the Chinese cannot prevent trade privileges. Finally, the Japanese have used physical force in getting control of valuable properties, especially coal and timber land. They have increased their financial and political power in Manchuria by depreciating the value of Chinese copper money and by demoralizing the silver and paper currency market (Chinese currency is still on the silver basis). Japan has also obtained railway concessions elsewhere in China in regions of great economic value. In all this, Japan has been allowed by western powers to have a free hand. *How Japan controls Manchuria*

In 1910 Russia and China signed an agreement, ostensibly to restore the sovereignty of northern Manchuria to China. But the agreement really left the railroad administration sovereign, at least in the cities and on the railroad line itself. The open door in Manchuria is therefore non-existent. Japan is growing stronger commercially throughout both the northern and the southern districts by the exercise of privileges wrested from China. The matter is the more serious because the region is an agricultural one capable of rapid and high development; it is needed by China as an outlet for her dense population, and she has repeatedly but ineffectually tried to safeguard her rights.

Problems of navigable rivers

The Manchurian question is further complicated by the drainage lines. The middle Amur and Ussuri are boundary rivers, and the lower Amur is exclusively in Russian territory, while the Sungari is in Manchurian territory (Fig. 251). In 1910 China agreed to give Russia a privileged position on the Sungari for traffic between that river and ports on the Amur within the free zone of the boundary (50 versts, or 33.15 miles). Thus Chinese and Russian vessels have in actual practice exclusive trading privileges on the Sungari.

GERMANY IN SHANTUNG

The German sphere

Like the other European powers, Germany sought a share in the land and trade of China. We have seen how she got a foothold (page 496). Her control of the leased territory of Kiaochow was complete. The railway was protected by German guards and a German postal service was established. It appeared that Germany was bent upon a policy similar to that which Russia was pursuing in Manchuria or the French in Yünnan. Germans also undertook a system of afforestation, controlled floods, and built macadamized roads, forts, modern harbor works, and a scientifically planned city. Schools were established. German officials cultivated the Chinese and, on the whole, maintained agreeable relations with them; nor were any attempts made to colonize Shantung by German immigrants.

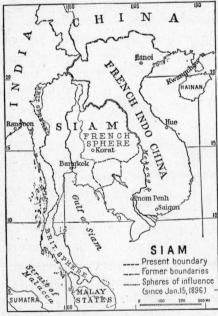

French sphere of influence in the south

FIG. 253. French and British spheres of influence in Siam, a buffer state.

THE FRENCH IN CHINA

French interests, apart from treaty ports and mineral and railway concessions, are centered in southern China. In 1885 France forced China to give up entirely her sovereignty over Annam, and agreements were made with China for the regulation of the trade between Chinese southern provinces and Tonkin, whereby goods from

Tonkin enjoyed a reduction in tariff rates. By the convention of 1895, France also obtained special privileges for railways in southern Chinese territory. There was thus in southern China a railway penetration under French guidance comparable in its objects, although not in its methods, to that of Russia in Manchuria. The policy of the French in the management of their principal railway in Yünnan (completed in 1910) was to secure a monopoly of the trade of the region and to close the door to other European and to American trade.

CHAPTER THIRTY-TWO

THE PACIFIC REALM AND AUSTRALIA

Significance of the sea route to India

THE wealth of India, the Far East, and the East Indies was known to Europeans several centuries before the all-sea route thither had been pioneered by Vasco da Gama from the west and by Magellan from the east. But its control could not pass into European hands until the sea route was discovered; for the land routes were too long and difficult from the physiographic standpoint and they were beset by incurable disorders. Illuminating in this respect is the early abandonment of the Red Sea route (which was taken by Covilham in 1487 on his way to India), though it involved the crossing of so small a strip of land as the Isthmus of Suez. The physical geography of Asia helped its native peoples to exclude the rest of the world until time had worked a mighty change and the European became indomitable upon the sea.

Trade focus in southeastern Asia

Once the key to Asiatic trade conquest had been discovered, western merchants were swift to extend their range of power. Covilham and Vasco da Gama were soon followed by other Portuguese explorers, who pushed eastward and northward as far as Japan (Pinto, 1543). The Dutch were close behind them. Spain, with the Philippines as her chief center of trade, maintained a galleon service with Mexico. Japan and China were closed empires. The focus of activity was southeastern Asia. Long after their discovery Australia and New Zealand were counted as of no value, and the mazes of islands and archipelagos of the vast outer Pacific were on the whole regarded as mere stations for supplying food and water to the mariner.

Changes in political geography

As in our day, the subsequent chapters in the political geography of the Pacific are closely related to the general European conditions of diplomacy and war, and for our present purpose need not be detailed. The vast Portuguese possessions shrank to mere footholds, as at Macao in southern China, and at Goa and elsewhere in India. The Dutch, though ejected from South Africa, held a large part of the East Indies. Spain's sphere in the Pacific was static. Russia, as a result chiefly of Bering's expedition, broke over the northern edge of the Pacific and planted her flag in Alaska; but Siberia was too distant and extensive and Russian commercial organization too primitive to permit effective penetration of the field of eastern trade until the modern period of overland rail exploitation in northern China.

It was the English who won supremacy in naval power in the early

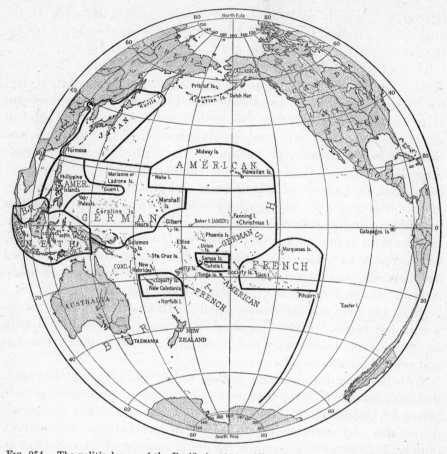

FIG. 254. The political map of the Pacific in 1914. All of Germany's possessions north of the equator have now been assigned to Japan as the mandatory power of the League of Nations; and those south of the equator were similarly assigned to Great Britain, to Australia, or to New Zealand, including the island of Nauru immediately south of the equator. On account of its nearness to the Philippines and its value as a cable station, the island of Yap has been of particular interest to the United States, though Japan claims it by virtue of the treaty of 1916 with Great Britain (page 522).

colonial period and, with shrewd foresight, backed up their great chartered trading companies that were for long thereafter the pioneers of empire. India is Great Britain's chief prize, but the power of her merchants is felt in every port of the vast trade realm of the Far East and the Pacific. France came into the region hesitatingly and won only fragments here and there until the second half of the 19th century, when she seized Indo-China. Germany came later and got less, being restricted in the Pacific to relatively poor and widely spaced island possessions; and she had no hold at all in densely populated Malaysia. The United States, though winning rights in Samoa

Unequal European penetration

(Pagopago) as early as 1839, did not obtain tangible authority there until 1889. Hawaii in 1898 and the Philippines and Guam later in the same year were the succeeding steps in a belated advance.

Throughout the first half of the 19th century the large European nations, in the full tide of industrial organization, sought eagerly for overseas markets, in the Pacific and the Far East as elsewhere. It is significant that during this period neither the United States nor Japan, the two strongest powers bordering the Pacific, participated in the division of territory. The United States, so lately expanded westward, had cheap land and a multitude of domestic enterprises that absorbed her energies and capital; and she sought extension of power on the sea only when foreign trade was needed to supplement domestic resources. Japan, who kept her ports closed to European trade until 1854, pursued a strictly provincial policy with respect to additional territory. Her interest in the Pacific, once aroused, was long restricted to the consolidation of island holdings off the eastern Asiatic mainland, until the whole archipelago between Formosa and the Kurile islands, with an extent of 3000 miles, was in her hands. Thereafter she looked toward the mainland and its readily exploitable people and wealth rather than toward the outer and poorer Pacific islands.

With the spread of Japanese settlers to the Philippines and Hawaii and the phenomenally rapid growth of her overseas commerce, particularly during the World War, Japan sought every possible territorial advantage. By agreement with Great Britain in 1916 she was to obtain all of Germany's islands north of the equator, and Great Britain all of those south of the equator, in the event of Germany's defeat. This agreement, confirmed subsequently to the treaty of Versailles, places Japan in a wholly new relation to the western powers.

EXTENSION OF JAPANESE POWER IN THE PACIFIC

Japan's position in the middle of the Pacific, where her capture of the Marshall and Caroline Islands (1914) has placed her, is of great concern to the naval strategists of the United States. In earlier years the defense of American territory in the Pacific was related to the idea of the so-called American quadrilateral. As Figure 255 shows, this consists of four possessions, widely spaced: Dutch Harbor in the Aleutian Islands, Alaska; Guam, 1520 miles east of the Philippines; Hawaii, 2100 miles southwest of San Francisco; and Samoa, 1600 miles northeast of New Zealand. American concern for the means of naval protection in the Pacific first manifested itself about

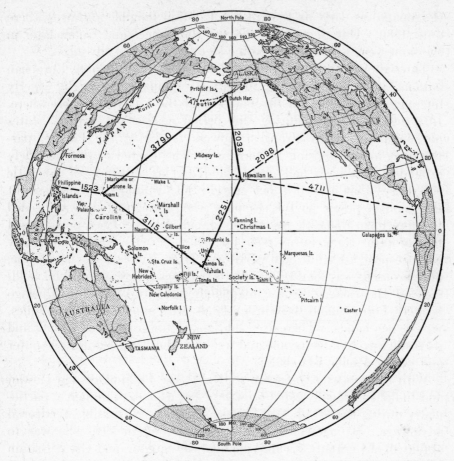

Fig. 255. Distances and positions of critical interest in the American scheme of naval defense in the Pacific.

fifty years ago, when part of Samoa became an American responsibility. There were added the Philippines and Guam in 1898, and the Panama Canal Zone in 1903. These possessions cannot be protected adequately save by holding forward bases in the Pacific.

From San Juan, Porto Rico, to Manila, in the Philippines, is almost halfway around the world. To defend these widely separated areas will require a great fleet of warships, powerful squadrons of seaplanes, abundant coaling and cable facilities, and large and powerful radio stations at strategic points.

Into the midst of this area Japan has now thrust a long finger, and no sooner did she capture the Marshall and Caroline Islands and turn out the German authorities than she set to work to Japanize the towns and local industries and increase the defensive strength of the strategic points.   As the mandatory power under the League of Nations, Japan will be expected to observe certain conditions : the islands should remain unfortified, their people should have some measure of autonomous government, the rights of other nations should be protected, and there should be a reasonable approach to equality of trade opportunity.

Were the control of the Pacific a matter of strategy only, the Japanese intrusion might arouse little concern.   But, unlike the European powers who hold their possessions for trade or native development of agriculture, the Japanese are themselves tropica colonizers.   They form half the population of Hawaii and are spreading into the Philippines. But for exclusion aws they would figure more largely in the population of northern Australia.   Their ethnic penetration of the lands of other powers is favored by their manner of living and the prime necessity of the white planter in the tropics of securing acclimated labor.   Such penetration will inevitably be followed sympathetically by the home government and made the basis for claims of equality of treatment and, in case of successful war, for territorial control.

Figure 254, with text, shows the status of the Pacific islands.   As commercial assets, the islands outside of the East Indies and the Philippines have only moderate value.   The total trade of the principal groups in 1913 amounted to $40,000,000.   The islands assigned to Japan, by agreement with Great Britain, have a total population of 70,000 ; their foreign trade amounts to $2,500,000 and consists chiefly of the export of copra and phosphates.   They are of great strategical importance.

As coaling and cable stations, islands are important if placed near or on the direct steamship routes.   The United States, for example, is interested in its small scattered holdings as they assist communication between Hawaii and the Philippines.   The Pacific cable of the Commercial Cable Company runs from Hawaii to a relay station at Midway, and to Yap in the Palau group.   From Yap an American-British line extends northward to the Bonin Islands, where it connects with the Japanese line to Tokio.   There is also a connection at Yap with British lines to the Chinese coast, and the American cable extending to Manila has connections with New Guinea and with Menado in the northern Celebes.

Islands have also gained in importance because of the use of airplanes and hydroplanes in modern warfare.   The innumerable islets and protected inland waterways that abound in the Pacific furnish

ideal hiding places for submarines, and it is unthinkable that the use
of submarines should be permitted on the long highways of commerce
that criss-cross the Pacific.

If these considerations affect American opinion, how much more
seriously will they be taken by the small nation of Australia with
one twentieth the population! The Australian leaders have not always
found British statesmen in sympathy with them, and they claim
that breadth of view regarding the Japanese question is possible only
in proportion as one is geographically removed from the menace of
immigration. Let us see what special aspects the problem wears in
the white man's lands of the southern Pacific.

THE COMMONWEALTH OF AUSTRALIA

There are two British possessions — Australia and the Union
of South Africa — in which the political problems of the time depend not so much upon the physical setting of the race as upon
public opinion with respect to the exclusion of other races. In South
Africa, the problem is to keep the black within the limits of the broad
coastal zone where the climatic conditions are more favorable to him
than to the whites; in Australia, the problem is to keep out the
Malays, the natives of India, the Chinese, and the Japanese. In

Racial problems of Australia

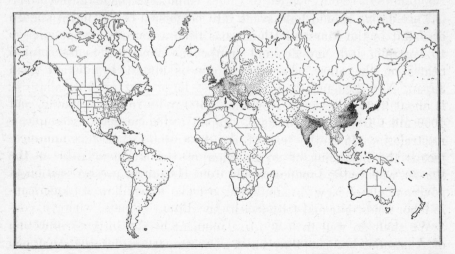

Fig. 256. Population map of the world. Each dot represents 500,000 persons. In Australia
the white man found a habitable and an almost empty continent. Distance is measured in time
as well as in miles, and modern transportation has shortened the time of ocean journeys. Once
two months apart, Australia and India are now ten days apart, and the same is true of Australia
and China or Japan. The migration of colored labor from temperate and subtropical India,
China, and Japan to temperate and subtropical Australia has raised the question of race exclusion
to the rank of an international problem. From Finch and Baker, *Atlas of American Agriculture*,
1917.

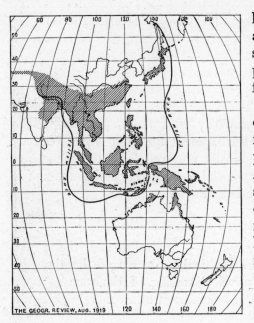

Fig. 257. The heavy line encloses the area peopled by the yellow race in the tropics. It has settled exclusively in regions receiving over 50 inches of rain per annum (shaded area). A similar climate prevails in only the northern part of Australia.

both cases there is a very frank avowal of the desire of the white settlers of European stock to possess the land as a heritage for their children.

Up to the present the people of Australia have consistently followed out their restrictive policy. About 98 per cent of Australia is occupied by persons of British stock or their descendants born in the commonwealth. There is no problem of foreigners entrenched in the country, as in the French Canadian district of Quebec and in the Boer colonies of South Africa. The number of full-blooded Asiatics is very small, probably not more than 35,000 to 40,000, with the Chinese in the majority.

Australian view of Japanese expansion toward the south

That Japan should have come into possession of the naval station at Jaluit in the Marshall Islands has been a source of great anxiety to Australia and New Zealand on the one hand and to the United States on the other. For the station is almost equidistant from Japan, New Zealand, and the nearest large port of Australia. It is about 2100 miles from Honolulu, 3500 miles from Hongkong, and 4000 miles from San Francisco. Japan has come 2000 miles nearer Australasia. It is the fear of the Australians that this approach means the beginning of an invasion of the warmer lands of the Pacific, whence the Japanese would exert a stronger pressure upon the governments of New Zealand and Australia to be allowed to compete in labor fields on equal terms with the whites.

Effect of geographical conditions in Australia

We shall do well to look for a moment at the internal problems of Australia, because they have some important international implications. This leads us first to consider the extraordinary physical setting of the continent. The eastern portion is mountainous and receives rainfall from the southeastern trade winds. All the rest of the country is desert, save for a small district in the southwestern corner which has winter rains sufficient to give it better resources,

FIG. 258. Sugar plantation in North Queensland. For a contrast
to this tropical scene see Figure 259.

FIG. 259. Wheat harvest in southeastern Australia.

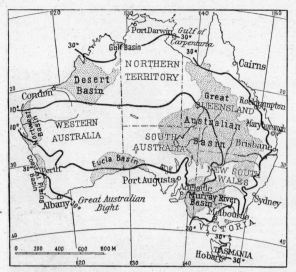

FIG. 260.   The probable and known artesian areas in Australia are shaded.   The heavy solid lines represent grades of rainfall in inches.   Where there is less than ten inches annually and no artesian water, grazing is limited and there are no towns, except where mines have been developed, as at Coolgardie and Kalgoorlie, 350 miles east of Perth.   From official *Australian Year-Book*, 1919.

and a strip on the north coast which falls within the limits of the equatorial rains during the southern summer.

In fact, the land of Australia would be far less valuable than it is if it were not for the great artesian belt, which permits the pasturage of stock far from the region of perpetual streams (Fig. 260). Dry farming has also helped to carry the inner border of the productive belt far inland.

The population is disposed in a manner to correspond with the

Distribution of population
rain belts (Fig. 262).   Nearly half of Australia is uninhabited.   Only 1 per cent of the total area is under cultivation.   Fewer than 5000 people live in an interior area larger than all of the United States west of the longitude of Denver.   Though Australia is as large as continental United States without Alaska, the population numbers only 5,000,000, and the average density is less than 2 to the square mile, if we include the whole area.   In the more densely settled portions in the southeast and southwest the density is from 8 to 16 or more inhabitants to the square mile.   In a belt of country 100 miles wide along the eastern, southern, and southwestern coast live 80 per cent of the people.   The population tends to become urban to an increasing degree, 40 per cent of the total living in the six principal cities.

Attitude of the commonwealth toward Asiatic immigration
In 1901 the Australian Commonwealth came into existence.   The separate states have much larger rights as contrasted with the central government than is the case in the United States.   While the central or commonwealth government controls immigration, each state can confront the immigrant with prohibitive regulations that greatly hamper him, if they do not exclude him.   The different states have different tests of eligibility for the enjoyment of the ordinary rights of a citizen to hold whatever property or engage in what-

Fig. 261. View of the harbor of Port Jackson, Sydney, Australia. This is one of the chief points of naval defense in the Pacific and one of the finest natural harbors in the world.

ever occupation he chooses. The Labor Party is in practical control of the government of the Commonwealth, a circumstance which has aggravated immigration difficulties, by reason of the fact that the labor unions steadily oppose the introduction of Chinese, Japanese, and Indian labor.

Two island groups that lie relatively close to her northeastern coast— the New Hebrides and New Caledonia — are of special interest to Australia. Following the Anglo-French convention of 1906, France and Great Britain exercise control of the New Hebrides through a condominium and a joint court. This procedure has not proved to be a success; it invites delay and does not give the native justice, though it has regulated the recruitment of the native population by labor contractors. Two thirds of the area of the New Hebrides, and the best islands, are in French possession. **The New Hebrides**

Related to the problem of the New Hebrides is that of New Caledonia, which is an isolated possession of France, long used as a convict colony. Strategically it is important because it lies near Australia — in fact, too near for comfort. The commercial value of the group, which supplies nickel, cobalt, and chrome to French industry, depends in less degree upon the immediate products than upon the relation to the trade of Australia and the East Indies, and France is keenly aware of this relation. **New Caledonia**

NEW ZEALAND AND THE SAMOAN MANDATE

Western Samoa to be administered by New Zealand

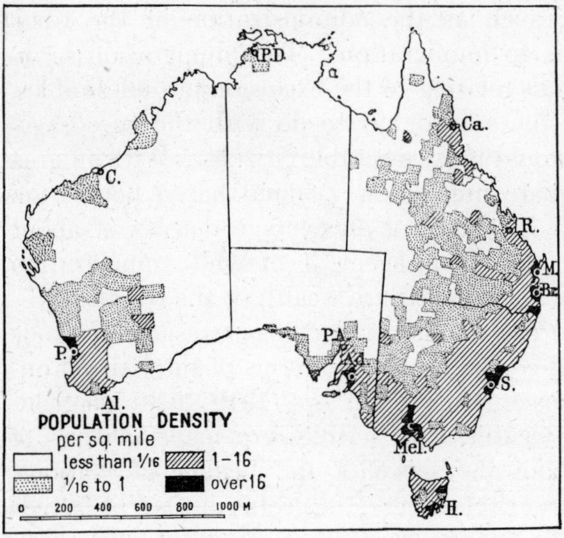

FIG. 262. Australia extends almost from 10° S. to 40° S. To develop the northern (hot) region a low-grade labor supply is needed. But the Australian people wish to keep the continent as an inheritance of the white race. Japanese, Indian, and Malay exclusion has brought into being grave international questions. The northern part is tropical, the southern temperate. All the foci of population are on the coast. The initials represent cities which are spelled in full in Figure 260. From official *Australian Year-Book*, 1919.

POPULATION DENSITY
per sq. mile
less than 1/16   1–16
1/16 to 1   over 16
0   200   400   600   800   1000 M

Western Samoa, which before the World War belonged to Germany, consists of the islands of Savaii and Upolu, and these have been assigned to New Zealand for administration under a mandate of the League of Nations (1919). For a period of a year this mandate was to be temporary in character, and it will probably be made permanent in 1921. There are undertakings on the part of New Zealand to prohibit the slave trade and forced labor, except as the latter is necessary for public works and services. Traffic in arms and ammunition is to be controlled, and the importation or manufacture of intoxicating spirits for natives of the territory is prohibited. No military or naval works are to be constructed. In Samoa, New Zealand faces at once the problem of imported labor hitherto derived from China and the Solomon Islands.

Apportionment of the phosphate of Nauru

New Zealand also laid claim to the island of Nauru, just south of the equator in longitude 167°, on the ground that its rich phosphate deposits were essential to the agriculture of New Zealand. The Australian government also having requested possession of the island or a mandate for it, the mandate was finally given to the British government, and a subsequent agreement was made by which the United Kingdom, Australia, and New Zealand divide the output of the phosphate works. The United Kingdom and Australia are each to receive 42 per cent of the output, and New Zealand the remaining 16 per cent. The island is estimated to contain a phosphate reserve of 42,000,000 tons, enough to last for 200 years at the present rate of production.

New Zealand has created a department of external affairs to take over the responsibility for the Samoan mandate and to handle other external questions, such as the administration of the Cook Islands and regulations as to immigration. The immigration problem has two phases, the first relating to the exclusion of undesirables, especially Asiatics, while the second has to do with the encouragement of immigrants who would make desirable citizens. With an area of more than 100,000 square miles New Zealand has a population of only a little more than 1,000,000, or an average density of about 10 to the square mile. The encouragement of white immigration would therefore greatly increase the future wealth of the country.

Immigration question in New Zealand

New Zealand has a labor problem in her Pacific possessions that bids fair to be of international concern. By the terms of the Labor Convention included in the peace treaties of Paris (1919–1920), the conditions of labor and the treatment of natives are made matters of international interest within the scope of the League of Nations.

Like many of the local groups elsewhere, the people of the Fiji Islands (a Crown Colony) have talked of the equality of races until they have worked themselves into a belligerent mood that has resulted in serious disorder, and even in loss of life. The trouble arose because of a strike of East Indians, and almost all the people of this race in Fiji (about 60,000 in number, estimated at 37 per cent of the population) were concerned. The Indians demanded equal rights with the whites, declaring themselves to be as good as the whites. Matters reached a climax in February 1920, when it was necessary to put down the disturbance by the use of military forces. The men were chiefly employed in the sugar fields of the Rewa River. At one time there were 30,000 striking coolies outside the capital, Suva.

Labor problem in Fiji

CHAPTER THIRTY-THREE

AFRICAN COLONIES OF THE EUROPEAN POWERS

Colonial expansion in Africa a struggle for raw materials

IN Africa the colonial rivalries of European powers had developed their most intense phases. Every statesman and economist sees in the wealth of labor supply that the continent affords and in its enormous and still rapidly expanding volume of raw mater als — fibers, oils, hides, minerals, rubber — sources of industrial and political power of great importance to enterprising nations of the north temperate zone. Indeed, some students find in this struggle for raw materials, rather than in rivalries in the Balkans and Asia Minor, the basic cause of the World War. The two latter regions, it is thought, are of immediate interest only as transit lands that must be crossed to reach the markets of more distant places — India and the Far East.

Colored peoples called to fight a white man's war

As far as serious politico-geographical questions arose respecting Africa, they were between European nations up to 1914, for Liberia and Abyssinia are the only independent divisions of African territory. But the World War has added a new aspect. Fearful of losing that civilization which it had taken centuries to create, each of the western powers, in the stress of war, called to its aid every nation tributary to it, even though small and weak. To assure loyalty, the tributary peoples were given exceptional privileges, which they later translated into terms of independence. Having paid in blood and treasure for the realization of democratic principles, they themselves sought to win the full measure of democratic liberty.

Growing "self-consciousness" of the African races

Finally, the idea of "self-determination" was added to the problem. Every group, however small, worked out an independent program. Nationalism was intensified; where it had not hitherto existed it was created. The effect in Africa has been to call into question everywhere the right of the European to rule. Revolts have occurred in Portuguese East Africa, in Libya (Italian), and in Egypt (British), and an already dangerous feeling has been intensified among 5,000,000 South African blacks.

Portions of the African world still loyal to European powers

Fortunately for the peace of the world, large portions of Africa have remained loyal in spite of the desire of their peoples for a larger measure of independence. Morocco sent thousands of soldiers to help France. Algeria and Tunis were quiet during the war at least. The 10,000,000 natives within the Belgian Congo were loyal to Belgium and assisted her with a powerful colonial army which took part in the conquest of German East Africa (now Tanganyika Territory). Uganda and British East Africa (now Kenya Colony), Nyasaland, Northern Rhodesia, Gambia, Sierra Leone, the Gold Coast, and Nigeria remained loyal members of the British Empire, and contributed decisively to the conquest of German East Africa, Togoland, and the Cameroons.

THE PROBLEMS OF RACE AND RELIGION

The relations of African peoples to Europeans are governed in large part by certain outstanding racial, social, and religious tendencies. Let us look for a moment at the ethnographic background of the problem. Africa was invaded from Asia, by way of Egypt and the Arabian coast, at a time when an indigenous African culture could scarcely be said to exist. Successive waves of population spread west and south into every part of the land many thousands of years before the last period of intense white exploration in the middle of the 19th century. Distinct racial, linguistic, and cultural traits were developed, in some respects adapted to the geographical environment, in other respects a reflection of earlier racial history. The low culture of the agricultural negro in the hot, moist, forested realm of the central part of the continent contrasted with the high civilization developed by the Nilotic peoples on the northeast. The Berber, and later the Arab, spread over the northern desert (Sahara) and had a type of life unlike that of either the forest negro or the Nile farmer. In part sedentary oasis dwellers, both Berber and Arab were also in part nomadic — men of desert trails, watering places, and temporary pastures, and given to a free life.

Races and cultures of Africa

Under Mohammedan influence, the Arab, fiercely fanatical and seeking the conquest of Christian peoples, came into Egypt; thence he spread across northern Africa, and into the Sudan. This was in the 7th and 8th centuries and represents one of the most important migrations of history. It was followed, centuries later, by the invasion of Spain and prolonged Moorish control, not completely broken until the fall of Granada in 1492. An earlier stream of Arab migration had flowed down the eastern coast of Africa, to Zanzibar and Mozambique. With the rise of Mohammedanism these Arab outposts in eastern Africa accepted the new religion, but they never became fanatical, owing probably to their political independence and to the remote and isolated positions they held. Though conquered locally, the Arab has been at all times a restless element.

The negroes form the most numerous race in Africa. They number (with the Bantus) about 120,000,000 persons, or four fifths of the

The black populations

total black population of the globe, the remaining 30,000,000 living for the most part in Australasia and in America. Though occupying the least desirable parts of Africa, where insects, malaria, and heavy forests made white conquest long impossible (it is still extremely difficult), the negro has multiplied and has developed great resistance to endemic diseases and the effects of tropical sunlight. His tribal organization is in some places extremely primitive, in other places well systematized; but group development has been nowhere carried to the point where it broke through the barriers of geographical position and environment to make the black a conqueror. In fact, the pure-blooded negro never exercised any self-originating political influence over other races. His is a plastic and imitative temperament. As one writer has put it: he has never founded a stone city, or built a ship, or produced a literature, or suggested a creed.

Moslem influence among the blacks

The white and the brown peoples have long competed for political and religious control of the blacks of Africa. Arab penetration was centuries ahead of the white conquests that followed the Age of Discovery (15th and 16th centuries). Had that age been long delayed, the growth of Mohammedanism would have put the combined Arab and Turkish worlds in possession of a vast and exceedingly dangerous reservoir of man power. For "Islamism brought with it, almost without fail, political organization, a certain amount of civilization, commercial activity, and the establishment of slavery as an institution." The defeat of the Moor (Moslem Arab and Berber) in Spain late in the 15th century and of the Turk in southwestern Europe in the 17th century, and thereafter the steady waning of the Turkish Empire, was succeeded in Africa during the 18th century by gradual possession, on the part of western nations, of strategic coastal localities There followed in the 19th century trade development, the rapid increase of missionary activity, and the partition of Africa.

The Zambesi the southern limit of Islam

The growth of Islam is far more rapid than that of Christianity among the negroes and will tend to increase their warlike tendencies. It may eventually bring the negro into conflict with the white man for possession of the continent. It has spread chiefly among the blacks of the Sudan, where there is intimate contact with the desert centers of religious influence, particularly the fanatical Moslem sects like the Senussi (page 57). Islam is still virtually unknown among the natives south of the Zambesi. The white man there dreads its appearance, fearing its effect upon the entire social and political organization.

The contest in Africa between white-skinned Christian and brown

Moslem populations reaches its climax in the northern zone of the continent — the Sahara and, more important, the northern coastal belt.   The Moors, when expelled from Spain late in the 15th century, retired to Morocco, where they more firmly established the principle of Moslem opposition to Christian advance.   Under the ardent teaching of Turkish agents from Constantinople and elsewhere, the Egyptian nationalist movement, with strong religious aspects, has combined with other forces to threaten perpetual disorder.   The scattered oases of the Sahara are the homes of unruly people.   Great Britain has had to send yearly military expeditions against some of the tribesmen of the Anglo-Egyptian Sudan.   France is faced by local but nearly continuous disorder in Morocco, Tunis, and Algeria, and on the desert edge of French Equatorial Africa.   Only as a result of costly military expeditions was it possible, a generation ago, to break up the Arab military organizations of the Belgian Congo and of the Lake Nyasa region.

The rivalries of unlike peoples and cultures (not religions) are equally acute and even more dangerous in South Africa, where the white man is greatly outnumbered.   The blacks have given incessant trouble, which has been augmented in later years by the growing ambitions of the Indian population, first introduced to work on the eastern coastal plantations.   But for the segregation of blacks largely on the eastern margin of South Africa and the fairly rapid spread of the whites to the mines and pastures of the central and southwestern portions, where a cooler climate prevails, South Africa would never have been won as a white man's country, or if won would have been quickly lost, as far as effective settlement is concerned.

One of the effects of the political occupation of Africa by European nations has been a more rapid increase of native population, already so large as to threaten white supremacy.   It is asserted that the population of the Anglo-Egyptian Sudan dropped from 8,000,000 to 1,800,000 through massacre and famine during the period (1870–1896) of disorder immediately before British conquest and occupation. The creation of great irrigation works and of a famine relief service has greatly increased the population of India.   The same effect of white control is witnessed in Jamaica and Barbados.   The stopping of tribal wars has of course greatly diminished the death rate in both India and Africa.   In some of the native reservatoins in South Africa tribes have increased several hundred per cent in fifty or sixty years.

The effect of European penetration in Africa, no less than in other regions where primitive races have been brought under the control of the white man, is marked by an almost complete derangement of indigenous social and political structures. With their strongly developed tendency to introduce changes, with their incessant political activity and its rapid imposition of new forms of government and society on native races, the Europeans brought what amounted to a revolution in the way of life of every people with whom they came in contact. Native society in many instances has disintegrated before the European advance, and the problem of local self-government is in many cases one of adapting native forms to modern conditions without destroying the native sense of organization and responsibility.

THE WHITE MAN'S LANDS IN TROPICAL AFRICA

Though white settlements are scattered about the margins of the continent and in strategic trade centers in the interior, they are at present grouped in an effective way in only two belts of limited extent— a northern and a southern. Along the sea border in Egypt, Libya, Morocco, Algeria, and Tunis, nearly 1,000,000 whites have settled; and there are 1,500,000 whites of Dutch and British blood in South Africa. These two extremities of the continent were long thought to be the only lands capable of white colonization.

Cool grassy uplands of central Africa

What are the possibilities of white settlement elsewhere? The striking feature of the topography of central Africa is the extent of large uplands where the white man can live and work, as shown on Figure 263. These are now in process of being tied to the ocean by trade routes and railroads that penetrate from Egypt, from former German East Africa, and from the Union of South Africa. Long removed from the political control of the whites, the interior highland mass now invites people of white blood not only through its climate but by its products, and from the fact that it borders the densely populated districts which produce valuable raw materials.

It should not be thought that the shaded portions of Figure 263 represent the limits of white occupation in the area within the scope of the map. Many lower tracts have nuclei of white settlement here and there. Some of the elevated tracts cannot be effectively occupied until bordering regions through which they are reached are supplied with roads and railways and cleared of tropical diseases. Not all uplands are free of malaria, and the effects of such climatic characteristics as the great diurnal and slight seasonal variations of temperature remain to be seen before white colonization can be proved truly successful. Finally, there is toward the south a progressively cooler climate, so that not merely the most elevated districts but the whole

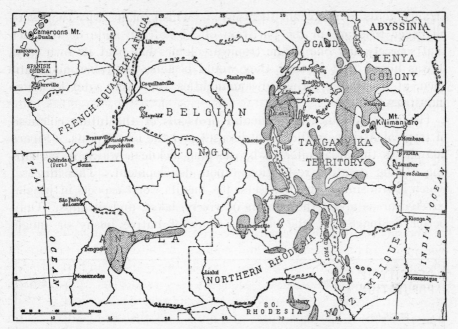

Fig. 263. The shaded areas represent districts with an elevation above or near 5000 feet and with relatively cool climate. They are the "white man's lands" of central Africa. However, white settlement on the uplands will depend not only upon altitude but also upon accessibility to railroads and the sea, the nervous effects of living at abnormally high elevations, the amount and seasonal distribution of rainfall, and the quality and amount of native labor. From 3000 to 5000 feet elevation the country is still possible for whites for prolonged periods. Below 3000 feet white men cannot long retain normal vigor and are subject to serious tropical ailments. Toward the south increasing latitude makes the upland country of Rhodesia habitable for whites at lower elevations. Compiled from the British General Staff sheets, scale 1 : 2,000,000, 1919.

upland becomes available for white occupation, as in most of Rhodesia, where Salisbury is located — a modern town, the center of an extensive grazing and mining region.

It is not, however, the region of cooler climate but rather the tropical lowland portions of Africa that furnish the kinds of goods that the countries of the temperate zone most require for their industries, particularly the European countries which lie much farther north than the United States. It was in Afr'ca that Germany wished to secure large areas suitable for the production of coffee, cotton, cacao, rubber, palm oil, cane sugar, bananas, tobacco, besides minerals of which she had little, such as petroleum, tin, gold, and copper. The United States grows cotton at home, in the southern states and many other subtropical products she gets close by — in the West Indies, Central America, and northern South America. European countries must get these materials from abroad, and of course they would prefer to get them from their own colonies, where they can make trade

Valuable products of tropical Africa

arrangements favorable to themselves. This explains why they were all eager to share in the partition of Africa. In spite of the fact that scarcely any one of the tropical colonies has paid its own way, it was hoped that in time they would become profitable, and until then, at least they furnished commodities that were vital to many industries.

Control of germ diseases and insect pests

The most serious environmental problems of the future colonists of tropical Africa are the germ diseases and the insect pests. Figure 265 shows the areas affected by sleeping sickness, which is perhaps one of the greatest restrictions upon development. This disease, which is transmitted by the tsetse fly, has its worst aspects in jungle-covered areas about the borders of rivers, lakes, and swamps. Only better drainage and the clearing away of native bushy or jungle

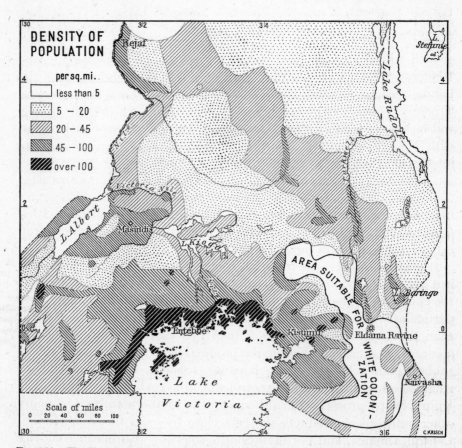

DENSITY OF POPULATION

per sq. mi.
— less than 5
— 5 – 20
— 20 – 45
— 45 – 100
— over 100

Scale of miles
0 20 40 60 80 100

FIG. 264. The Uganda region of central Africa. Note the importance of a dense native population near a large lake and a belt of "white man's lands" still undeveloped. Based on Sir Harry Johnston, *The Uganda Protectorate*, Vol. II, 1904, 2d ed.

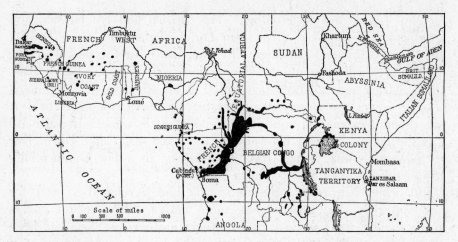

Fig. 265. Distribution of known sleeping sickness districts and localities in Central Africa. Compare with map of belts of vegetation, Figure 270.   After map from Sleeping Sickness Bureau, London, 1909.

growth will enable the white man to live safely or to keep cattle. Rinderpest further limits the grazing industry. Cholera and the bubonic plague recur in the low, hot, dirty, and humid coast ports. Tropical Africa is rich, and it can be won by the white man; but it will be won only after a long struggle by white settlers in coöperation with physicians trained in tropical medicine, and by governments intelligent enough to help the pioneer.

THE PENETRATION OF AFRICA

In its modern aspects the problem of land division in Africa, and particularly in the cooler uplands, involves European nations in many complex questions that cannot be really understood unless they are placed in their historical setting.   This setting we shall now attempt to supply.

The first period of European control of Africa was in the second half of the 15th century, when traders, chiefly Portuguese, sailed along the west coast.   Before America was discovered they had reached the southwestern extremity of the continent.   Another Portuguese expedition at this time explored the Red Sea and reached India; in 1498 Vasco da Gama sailed up the east coast and also reached India; the Far East was next brought within the field of European trade, and a Portuguese settlement, still in existence, was founded at Macao, in China.   The English and Dutch followed quickly.   Africa itself was then of less commercial interest than the Orient.   The rival nations were content with mere footholds that served as way stations

Early period of white expansion

for ship repair and revictualing. The British had St. Helena, and later a part of the Gold Coast; the Dutch, Table Bay (Cape Town); and the Portuguese, Zanzibar. In fact, down to the period of the exploring expeditions and missionary journeys of Livingstone (1840–1873), Africa had not been penetrated at all effectively, as the maps of sixty years ago clearly demonstrate; and as a colonizing field it was thought expensive, unhealthful, and of little value. In a general way the native brought his wares to the coast (*e.g.* Cape Town, Dar es Salaam, Sofala, Table Bay, Loanda) or to a few commercially strategic inland centers (*e.g.* Lake Ngami).

Beginnings of colonial rivalry

But when European industrialization had developed a need for raw materials that yearly grew more active, when vacant spaces in the Pacific, the Far East, and southern and western Asia had been allocated, with South America a politically closed world on account of the Monroe Doctrine, Africa was the only large free realm in which political power and colonial trade could yet be won together. France annexed Algeria between 1830 and 1847; the English occupied a few places at the southern end of the continent, from which they had crowded the Boers, who thereupon established their settlements inland beyond the Orange River; Morocco was independent; the Turkish Empire nominally extended along the whole northern coast, but effectively was limited to Egypt and Libya. For the rest only scattered settlements and trading posts on the coast had been established by the European nations, including Holland (until 1871), Spain, Denmark (until 1850), and Portugal — but not Germany; the beginning of German colonial policy was a thing of much later growth.

Exploration of central Africa

The memorable explorations of Stanley at last effectively awoke Africa. He crossed the continent from 1874 to 1878, explored the great Congo River system, and untangled some of the long-discussed complexities of the equatorial lakes. By 1880 the whole civilized world was interested in the exploration story of Africa. The more enlightened nations of Europe were determined to stamp out slave trading, which was still carried on extensively in the interior, though the exportation of slaves from Africa had practically ceased by 1850.

No other continent had such large unappropriated spaces, so many unattached peoples. There followed a general European rush for territory desirable chiefly because of its commercial value rather than as a home for colonists. The period of exploration of the interior therefore became the period of partition and of appropriation by big trading companies and concessionaires. France assumed a protectorate over Tunis in 1881; England occupied Egypt in 1882;

Portugal put forth claims to much of the Congo, as well as the hinterland of Mozambique, where English traders and missionaries had penetrated. Belgium called a conference of the powers in 1876 whose outcome was an International African Association, and in 1885 Leopold II, King of the Belgians, declared himself sovereign of the Congo Free State. In less than half a century the interior of Africa had been transformed from an unknown wilderness to the colonial frontier of Europe.

From that time to this, there has never been a moment when the colonial policies of the European nations have not been profoundly affected by the African situation. Germany was at first more interested in her African colonies than she was in her Pacific possessions or the Near East. Only as late as 1904 were the long-standing differences between France and Great Britain that had once threatened war (the Fashoda incident, page 558) at last composed by a division of spheres of influence. In 1911 the Agadir crisis (page 107) almost precipitated war between Germany and France. *Africa a threat to the peace of the world*

FORMER GERMAN COLONIES IN AFRICA

The chief effect of the war upon the political geography of Africa was the transfer of the four German colonies of Togoland, the Cameroons, German Southwest Africa, and German East Africa to France, Great Britain, Belgium, and Portugal. By skillful diplomatic work at Berlin and by remarkable activity in the field, Germany had won these four territories in the face of active British, French, and Portuguese opposition, laid claim to a part of the Sudan bordering Lake Tchad, elbowed France down to the Congo, pushed the northeastern corner of German Southwest Africa over to the Zambesi River (the Caprivi salient, Fig. 14), and as a result was in position to plan still broader African conquests. The addresses of her statesmen leave no room for doubt that had she won the World War a Central African realm under German control would have been created out of Portuguese and Belgian territory and German domination would have been assured in the African politics of the future.

Every year Germany was losing nearly 250,000 of her population, who went to foreign lands, and it was her hope that parts of these African colonies might provide homes for some of her numerous emigrants, though her chief interest lay in the development of the plantation system and use of native labor for the production of tropical raw materials, supplies of which she also hoped to command. Great Britain and America control 90 per cent of the world's cotton *Colonial homes for emigrants and a source of raw material for German mills* supply, and for about three fourths of her cotton Germany had to rely on the United States, for about one fourth on Egypt and India. Of special value to German industry was the production in her African possessions of oils, particularly palm oil. While production was not high, it was in the way of rapid development. Germany's increasing importation of food had also turned her attention to the possibilities of food production in her African colonies.

The territories and resources that Germany lost and that France, Belgium, and Great Britain gained will be briefly described in the succeeding sections.

Tanganyika Territory (former German East Africa)

The large native population

More was heard about German East Africa, now Tanganyika Territory, than any other German colony because it is relatively more thickly populated and was the most valuable of all Germany's African possessions. It has a total area of 384,000 square miles, or nearly twice that of the whole former German Empire. The native population numbers nearly 8,000,000 and is of excellent stock, trained to agriculture. In addition there are about 15,000 people from India and Arabia, and a population of 5300 whites.

The cool interior tableland, capable of development by white men

The least favorable portion of Tanganyika Territory is the coastal strip from 10 to 30 miles wide in the north and broader in the south. This is a fever-infested region of heavy rainfall and poor drainage. Farther west is the interior tableland, marked at its eastern margin by broken country with steep streams. There is a well-marked dry season, and the natural vegetation of the interior is savana, grass steppe, or scrub. Variation of relief gives opportunity for great variety in cultivated products. At present the most important plantation crops are sisal hemp or rubber (Ceará). There are considerable possibilities for coffee and cotton production and for cattle raising in districts free from tsetse fly. On the slopes of Kilimanjaro and the Usambara Highlands products of more temperate latitudes can be grown. Though limited in area, these districts should be valuable as a "white man's country."

Two railways now connect the upland with the coast, one south of Kilimanjaro Mountain, near the frontier of Kenya Colony (British East Africa), and another from the port of Dar es Salaam.

Ruanda constitutes the densely populated, northwestern part of German East Africa. It has now been detached from former German East Africa, which (as Kenya Colony) passed under British mandate and has been added to the Belgian Congo (Figs. 5 and 66).

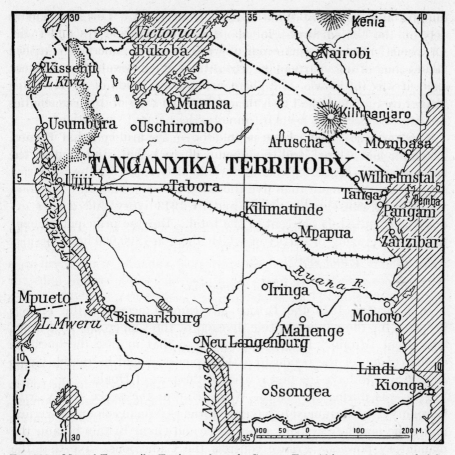

Fig. 266. Map of Tanganyika Territory, formerly German East Africa; at present adminis-tered by Great Britain as the mandatary of the League of Nations, except for the northwest-ern corner, ceded to Belgium.

German Southwest Africa

German Southwest Africa is important, not because of the number of inhabitants, but for its extent and its relation to the protection of the Union of South Africa, with which it is continuous. It is a huge desert region with an area of 325,000 square miles, a native population of 250,000, and a white population that numbered 15,000 in 1914. It has been turned over to the Union of South Africa, with which it has connection by rail and by sea. *A desert country thinly in-habited*

The coastal desert is from fifteen to eighty-five miles wide. It is marked by great sand ridges p led up by the southwesterly winds to heights that in places reach several hundred feet. The rainfall is, for the most part, less than one inch a year. Fogs are characteristic, due to the cold longshore current from the south. There are guano deposits on the offshore islands. The whole region resembles the Atacama-Tarapacá desert coast of western South America. Farther inland the rainfall increases on account of higher elevation and better exposure to the winds, and there are grazing lands of value. Still farther east is the Desert of Kalahari, with an interior drainage ending in salt pans, and with belts of dunes and scattered vegetation.

There will never be a large population — the aridity is too intense. The grass is scattered, and the amount of stock that can be supported is small. It is estimated that the whole of German Southwest Africa cannot maintain more than five thousand farms. There are diamond washings of considerable value, and in 1913 ivory and copper exports constituted 95 per cent of the total. But the principal occupation is the grazing of cattle, of which there are 200,000 head, besides 1,000 000 sheep and goats.

The Cameroons

In February 1916 the British government accepted the French proposal for the administrative division of the Cameroons by France and Great Britain. It was arranged also that in case the question of the cession of the region to a third power should be raised, Great Britain was to have the first refusal of the port of Duala.

This was during the World War. But in the peace treaty with Germany it was arranged to have the former German colonies governed under the mandate system, and France and Great Britain became the mandatory powers. France controls the Cameroons, save that the small portion west of the main mountain range but including Cameroon Mountain (Fig. 267) is now joined to British Nigeria. The boundary between Nigeria and the Cameroons was an arbitrary one and therefore disturbing to native life. In the final settlement of the affairs of the colony there was made a rectification of this frontier, and the new boundary runs in such a way as least to disturb local tribal arrangements.

The products of the Cameroons are mahogany, rubber, palm oil, cacao, and small quantities of tobacco and cotton. It has valuable grasslands in the interior, though these are difficult of access. The rubber resources might have led to the great development of the colony, had it not been for the competition of East India rubber, which began to be produced on a great scale in 1913, and which so reduced the price that the gathering of rubber from wild sources by primitive methods was no longer profitable.

The colony has an area of less than 200,000 square miles and a total population of more than 2,500,000. Besides unhealthfulness in the lowlands, the chief physical difficulty in its development is the large number of falls which break the courses of the streams and thus prevent transportation of the interior products by cheap methods. Commerce would be almost at a standstill were it not for two small railroads which have been extended inland beyond the belt of falls.

Togoland

By agreement made between France and Great Britain in 1919, the latter assumed the administration of the western strip of Togoland (Fig. 268); the former took over the higher and cooler eastern districts.

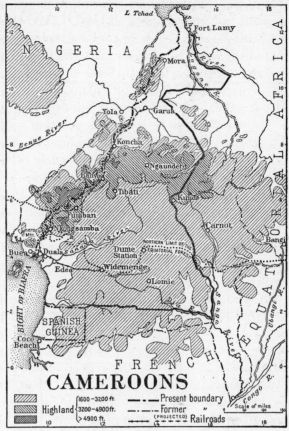

FIG. 267. French Equatorial Africa now includes the whole of the large region called the Cameroons, except for a narrow strip on the northwest which has been added to British Nigeria. That part north and west of the heavy solid line is mandated territory; that part south and east of this line is ceded to France unconditionally according to Article 125 of the treaty of Versailles, thereby restoring the boundary of 1911, modified in Germany's favor at the time of the Agadir incident (footnote, page 107). Note the northern limit of the equatorial forest, which suggests the grazing lands that lie between the forest and the desert Sahara beyond Lake Tchad. The *Geographical Review*, Vol. 5, 1918.

British and French division of the country

Future of Togoland

France and Great Britain have agreed to make a joint recommendation to the League of Nations regarding the fate of Togoland. It was the smallest of Germany's African colonies, and the most densely inhabited, with at least 1,000,000 native population. The country is unhealthful near the coast, but the highlands are capable of great agricultural development (Fig. 268). This is one of the colonies from which Germany hoped to get an increasing quantity of cotton for her home

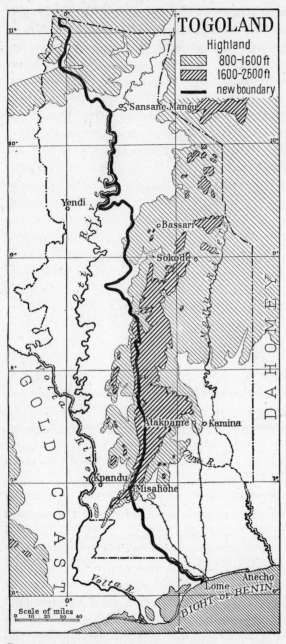

FIG. 268. Old and new boundaries in Togoland, one of Germany's four African colonies before 1914. The western portion is now a British mandatary, the eastern a French mandatary.

manufactures. There are also valuable cacao and tobacco plantations, but they are small in extent. As a source of palm oil the region, like the rest of West Africa, is of constantly increasing importance. The colony has no good port.

The most serious condition to be overcome is the spread of sleeping sickness by the tsetse fly, which infests the underbrush near the coast and along the rivers. From Figure 265, it will be seen that Togoland is particularly affected by this disease.

THE PRINCIPLE OF THE MANDATE

The new arrangements of the Peace Conference of Paris regarding Africa have grown out of the old problems. The Allies have disciplined Germany, it is true; but they have also made rules for themselves. The purpose was not merely to take away from Germany some colonial possessions, but to provide against the kind of evils that she had practiced as well as the evils that the European nations saw in each other's policies and plans.

In estimating the probable success of the new scheme for the control The mandatory system yet untried of former German territory in Africa under the mandate system of the League of Nations, we should not lose sight of the hitherto universal failure of schemes for joint control.   The condominium was a failure in Samoa and led to the division of the island group between Great Britain, Germany, and the United States.   Joint control has been sadly deficient in the New Hebrides.   In Tangier, it has been a disgrace to Europe.   France and Great Britain gave up joint control of Egypt after a short trial.   The Berlin Conference of 1884–1885 was designed to establish international rules for the expansion of European national claims to African territory, and although the effect as to the trade in arms, liquors, and slaves was beneficial, it increased rather than diminished the intensity of the scramble for territory.   The new plan, however, has two promising features: (1) it takes control out of the hands of one power and places it in the hands of the several powers associated in the League of Nations, thus inviting review and correction of official acts; (2) it leaves actual administration to a single power, thus providing against the delays and abuses of joint responsibility.

TRADE POLICIES AND NATIVE CONTROL

In spite of eagerness for territory in Africa, none of the European African colonies a financial burden powers were able to make their tropical colonies a commercial success, except Germany in Togoland and Great Britain in Nigeria.   All had preferential trade agreements which favored their own commerce. The colonies were reserved for the benefit of the traders of the home country.   This was the policy of the French, for instance, in northern Africa, in Senegal, French Guinea, and Madagascar.   For example, French preferential trade in the colonies of French West Africa there is a 7 per cent ad valorem surtax upon all goods coming from countries other than France, and there are restrictions upon the export of vegetable oil products to all countries except France.   The natural result of French policy was the virtual extinction of British and German trade in the French Congo and Madagascar.   There is scarcely such a thing as free commerce in Tunis.   Privileges of great value, known as concessions, are also part of the plan of aiding French commerce.   The only exceptions, in fact, were Dahomey, the Ivory Coast, and French Somaliland.   To foster her wine business France has permitted and even pushed the sale of brandy and absinthe throughout Tunis, Algeria, and French West Africa, just as England permits a profitable gin trade with southern Nigeria.

Welfare of
the native

These things are secondary, however, to the question of relations
with the natives, whose welfare must be the chief thought of the
European powers if the risks of bitterness and racial war are to be
reduced. In the ill-treatment of the African native, Germany was
easily first; though at one time or another every European power,
and especially Portugal, had treated the native cruelly. In 1904
Germany pushed her punishment of the Herero tribes of German
Southwest Africa to the point where these people were reduced in
number from 60,000 to 18,000. Millions of Moslem Berbers and
Arabs in French North Africa dislike the French (because they are
Christian, not because they are French) as much as the Moslem
Egyptians dislike the English.

Native rule
not always
possible

The peace treaties of 1919 provide relief for some of the causes of
dissatisfaction on the part of the native, short of granting him political control. The European nations cannot leave large sections
of the world's low-grade populations to their fate. Zeal for the
happiness and welfare of the native cannot always be carried to the
point of permitting him to do as he wishes; had the United States
left the Filipinos to themselves, their islands would soon have
been in a state of anarchy and probably would thereafter have belonged to Japan. Firmly as this principle has become embedded in
foreign-office policies and justifiable as it seems from the general point
of view, it must not be forgotten that it is, except in a few instances,
outside the thought of the people to whom it is applied. Some of
them would indeed prefer anarchy to foreign rule.

If France were to withdraw from northern Africa, it would be a disaster to civilization there as great as that which followed the fall
of the Roman Empire, when the Roman settlements of the same land
one dy one were abandoned and fields long cultivated reverted to the
desert. Equally dark would be the prospect if England withdrew
unconditionally from Egypt.

INTERNATIONAL AGREEMENTS RESPECTING LIQUOR TRAFFIC, LAVE TRADE, AND PROTECTION OF WILD ANIMALS

Slave and
liquor
traffic

After Stanley's return from the exploration of the Congo, the
European rivalry for territorial gains in Africa became still more
intense. This led to a number of international projects and agreements, to which at least brief reference must be made. These were
foreshadowed by the Brussels Conference of 1876, called by the King
of the Belgians while Stanley was yet in Africa. Its object was the
opening up of the continent through an International African As-

sociation. At first international in character, this soon became an almost purely Belgian organization, and by various steps, too detailed to record here, led to the acquisition of the Congo by King Leopold of Belgium. The Berlin Conference of 1884–1885 established the Congo Free State, provided for traffic regulation of the Congo River, laid down a free-trade zone in central Africa, and fixed the conditions of ownership by rival European powers. A second Brussels Conference, in 1890, delimited a slave-trade zone and a zone in which trade in arms and spirituous liquors was to be regulated.

The slave trade is an old question in African administration. Early in the 19th century slave trading was prohibited by the more enlightened European powers. Slavery itself was abolished by nearly all the powers by about the middle of the 19th century. But slave trading continued to be active in the interior of Africa. For years before the defeat of the Mahdist forces at Omdurman in 1898, slave-raiding Arabs under Mahdist control terrorized the natives of the Sudan. Even now slave trading has not been wholly discontinued. Until the Italian occupation of Tripoli in 1912 the Senussi (page 57) sent slaves through Benghazi and, with the help of the Turks, received arms and ammunitions. Today the traffic is under the ban of law, and international coöperation is chiefly responsible for its lessening practice. *Suppression of slave traffic*

The regulation of the liquor traffic was of peculiar importance to the development of the African native. It is bad morality as well as bad business to debauch the native. His temper is more ardent, his impulses less subject to control, than in the case of the white.

Unless the civilized world is prepared to back up by force, if necessary, and especially by strict police regulation, the control of the sale of liquor to the natives of Africa, they might better be left to run their own affairs. The world was shocked by the extent and cruelty of the slave trade; in the 19th century it was one of the chief pretexts of the European colonizing nations that they were bent on controlling territory so as to control the slave trade; it gave a pious turn to their acts which peculiarly fitted the spirit of the age. But it were far better to continue the slave trade under purely native responsibility than to substitute for it the unlicensed use of liquor. *Police regulation for control of liquor traffic*

Between the heavy lines of Figure 269 there was defined by the Brussels Conference of 1890 a zone for the preservation of wild animals, and this was confirmed by the Convention of London, May 1900. It is a matter of very great importance to the continent of *Protection of wild game*

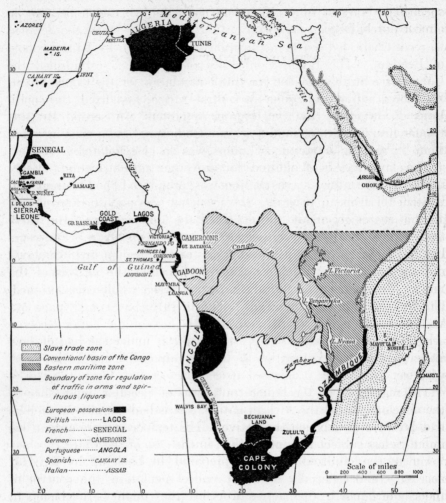

Fig. 269. The black areas represent European possessions in 1884 before the Berlin Conference of that year. The upper half of the legend represents international regulations adopted at the Berlin Conference and the Brussels Conference of 1890. After Keltie, *The Partition of Africa*, 1895. There was added by the London Convention of 1900 a zone of protection of wild animals extending from the Zambesi and the northern limit of German Southwest Africa up to the twentieth parallel of north latitude.

Africa, which has the largest and most varied assortment of big game animals in the world. On the grasslands bordering the central tropical forest area, on the south and east, there are still many zebras, gazelles, hippos, rhinos, and waterbuck. They are in localities where they do not interfere with present settlements and should be protected on huge reserves regulated by law. They have been exterminated in some places in order to prevent destruction of the crops of settlers; but the process of extermination serves no useful purpose elsewhere, especially when carried on by irresponsible hunters intent on making a record of killings.

BENEFITS OF COLONIAL DEVELOPMENT

We gain some idea of the possible benefits of colonial development by looking at what France has already accomplished in northern Africa. The farms that the Romans had made with such care the French found a desert, and they immediately set to work to reclaim them by making hundreds of artesian wells, by damming up the streams that had been allowed to waste their precious waters in the sand, by fighting the swarms of locusts. Lion, hyena, and leopard had ravaged the flocks and herds; the French set to work to exterminate them in the neighborhood of settlements. They built several thousands of miles of roads and constructed hundreds of miles of railways. The fine cedars of the Atlas Mountains were in the way of extinction, and the French forest service came just in time to save them. By many different means France has placed under cultivation at least 100,000 square miles of land (or about twice the area of Colorado or Alabama) that was formerly desert waste. *Work of the French in northern Africa*

In 1894 Timbuktu was captured and the indigenous population released from the tyranny of its Tuareg masters. Since then eastward penetration has progressed apace. Before and during the World War, Tilho explored a vast area northeast and east of Lake Tchad, including the fastnesses of Tibesti. With small detachments, chiefly of native troops, he sought out and dispersed those tribesmen who, under Senussi influence (page 57), sought to consolidate Moslem power in one of the least accessible places in the French Sahara. The isolated territories on the southern edge of the Sahara thus brought under the French peace are susceptible of economic development, provided they can be made more accessible. Plans for a trans-Saharan railroad to this end include a line across the Sahara, connecting the coast of Algiers with the Niger and Lake Tchad, which shall eventually connect with the British system that reaches north from Cape Town (Figs. 15 and 49).

Best of all, France has done these things with little disturbance to native political and social organization; she has taken no land away from native holders; she has put money and effort into the improvement of the life of the people. Her work has extended into Madagascar, where the Hovas, a tyrannical Malayo-Polynesian people who settled in the island in the 16th century, had long practiced slavery, thus depopulating large tracts in the south and southwest. *French respect for native rights*

MINOR COLONIAL PROBLEMS AND TRADE INTERESTS IN AFRICA [1]

Portuguese policies in Africa

The possessions of the smaller powers in Africa are bound to give trouble in the future. The Portuguese, for example, have carried the policy of differential duties on colonial commerce to such an extreme as practically to shut out all trade except with Portugal. If they had money and men with which to develop their own country, matters might not be so bad. But Portugal itself is poor and feeble, with a population under 6,000,000. It has lower railway mileage than any other country of its size in Europe. Its colonial governors follow no fixed policy except one of weakness and immoral toleration of the sale of liquor to the native. The home government has been so unstable during the past ten years that it has completely demoralized colonial administration. In southern Angola there has been fairly rapid development, with the help of British capital and enterprise. Spanish Guinea belongs to the same class of feebly developed colonies; Spain has long ceased to be a capable colonizing nation.

Heligoland and Zanzibar

Perhaps no other part of the British Empire seems to us as remote as Zanzibar, yet were any other power to try to get possession of it, a political storm would be aroused in England. The Zanzibar Arabs have favored the British in trade and politics; British strategy in relation to India and South Africa requires possession of the region; cables have been laid to it. It is a British protectorate with Zanzibar Town as a free port. England's position there, long contested by Germany, was finally confirmed and strengthened by the Anglo-German treaty of 1890, when she ceded Heligoland to Germany in exchange for additional rights in Zanzibar and Pemba. The cession of Heligoland was felt at the time to be of doubtful advantage, and it became a matter of great regret to Great Britain in the World War, when that island became a base of operations for the German High Seas Fleet.

British Uganda Protectorate

It was in 1890 also that, by the terms of an agreement with Germany, Great Britain assumed a protectorate over Uganda. Egypt, the Anglo-Egyptian Sudan, Uganda, and British East Africa, thus connected, form a broad strip, of imperial extent, that looks out upon the Mediterranean at one end and upon the Indian Ocean at the other. It flanks the route to India. Possession of it put the Cape-to-Cairo project a step nearer realization.

---

[1] The major colonial interests of the great powers are described in the separate chapters on these powers; e.g., Egypt and South Africa, in Chapter Two, *Imperial Problems of Great Britain.*

Germany was well satisfied with these changes, because with them went substantial advantages for herself. Besides Heligoland she obtained the Caprivi salient, a long arm of territory extending from German Southwest Africa eastward to the Zambesi (Fig. 15); she extended the northern boundary of Cameroons to Lake Tchad; she became established in the Victoria Nyanza region inland as far as the Belgian Congo. Increased German power in Africa

France was equally fortunate. By the Anglo-French agreement of 1890 she established a protectorate over Madagascar (it became a French colony in 1896) and became the recognized power of the western Sahara. In 1904 she had her favored position in Morocco recognized by Great Britain. Recognition by Germany came only in 1911 after the Agadir incident, as explained previously (page 107). France then bought German recognition of her Moroccan position by ceding to Germany a large section of French Equatorial Africa (strip to the Congo, Fig. 267). French protection of Morocco

There remained a dispute between France and Spain which explains the odd disposition of territory south of the Straits of Gibraltar. Naturally, Spain has always been interested in the African coast opposite her. In 1912 she confirmed France's special position in Morocco and herself obtained a narrow strip along the coast, now called the Spanish Zone, and in addition an enclave on the southwestern coast of Morocco at Ifni. Two hundred and fifty square miles at Tangier became an "international zone" (Figs. 80 and 81).

WEST AFRICA

West Africa includes a belt of territory nearly 3000 miles long, extending from Mauretania at the western end of the Sahara south and east as far as the Portuguese possessions in the Congo region (Fig. 82). It comprises a score of organized states belonging to Great Britain, France, Belgium, Spain, and Portugal. Including the Belgian Congo (pages 125 to 128), the region has nearly a half-billion dollars' worth of trade, carried on at more than forty ports. Great Britain has most of the trade; Germany ranked second before 1914. West Africa includes Togoland and the Cameroons, former German possessions now divided between Great Britain and France as mandatory powers of the League of Nations (Figs. 267 and 268). Great Britain owns the richest territory and the largest number of trade agencies. Her position and interests, to which we now turn, illustrate the value of West Africa in the commercial world.

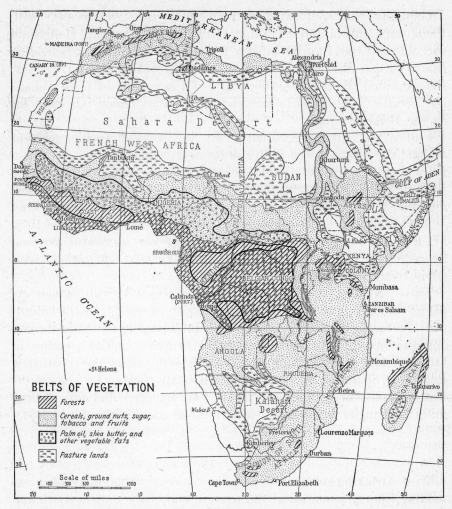

Fig. 270. West Africa, from the Congo to Senegal, has been the field of keenest commercial rivalry in respect of raw materials.   Note the variety and concentration of vegetation belts there. A small white population controls the commercial system of a large native population in West Africa.   The map is diagrammatic in part, as in the Nile Valley and in the interior of the Sahara and of Arabia.   After Sir Harry Johnston, the *Geographical Journal*, Vol. 45, 1915.

Commercial rivalry in West Africa

Among Great Britain's possessions, British West Africa, next to India, is the most important from the standpoint of raw materials. It includes (without the recent British portions of the mandated areas of Togoland and Cameroons) Sierra Leone, the Gold Coast, Nigeria, and Gambia, and contains 20,000,000 native people in an area of 450,000 square miles.   Ocean transportation being the cheapest there is in the world, and the distance from West Africa to the English Channel being but three thousand miles, the rich resources of the region became the object of strong commercial rivalry between Germany and Great Britain. As a result of the World War and the peace settlement, Germany is now out of this market; her agencies are gone, she has lost her former prestige among the natives, she has no ships for the carrying trade.

West Africa is rich in cacao and palm oil particularly, although it has important tin, coal, and gold deposits, as well as an increasing production of timber, nuts, rubber, fiber, and cotton. Among these the richest in immediate possibilities is palm oil. With the rapid development of machine industry, lubricating oil is in great demand; the world's consumption of soap is also steadily growing; substitutes for butter are now in favor. All these things and more the palm tree will supply. From the seed an oil is obtained that has the greatest variety of uses. From Nigeria alone, in 1917, there were $20,000,000 of palm oil exports, or almost one half the total in value. Southern Nigeria has the further advantage of having a dense population of more than 100 to the square mile, and here there is the greatest degree of prosperity, owing to large quantities of raw material that may be gathered or produced upon the hot and wet coastal lowlands and to geographical position, or accessibility.

Valuable resources to feed industry

Before the war Germany took most of the palm-nut exports, employing even the meal of the nut for cattle feed. This trade has now been diverted entirely to British firms, who are about to open additional motor roads and railways in order to tap several thousand square miles of palm territory, native transportation methods being primitive. Hand in hand with such development will go the stimulation of other lines of production, especially cotton and cacao. In 1916 the cacao produced on the Gold Coast alone was valued at $18,000,000.

Diversion of trade to Great Britain an effect of the war

ADEN

In connection with the minor European colonies in the horn of Africa mention must be made of the adjacent Arabian territory pertaining to the port of Aden. Though the British territory at Aden has only 50,000 people, who live on very poor land totaling about 80 square miles, the British protectorate covers some 9000 square miles. The place is important because of its strategic value in the defense of India and the Suez Canal, and because it is the focus of the Red Sea trade as well as that of Abyssinia and all that eastern portion of Africa known as French, British, and Italian Somaliland. All told, the population of the region of which Aden is the commercial focus is above

Aden as the commercial focus of a large region

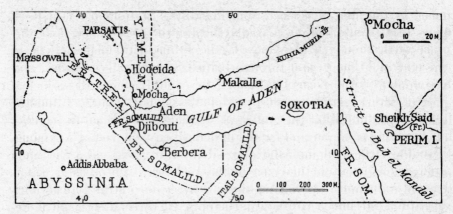

Fig. 271. The Aden region and the Strait of Bab el Mandeb, a focal point of eastern trade with Europe. The British own Perim Island, between which and the French possession of Sheikh Said lies the principal ship channel. Each power is therefore anxious to get control of the other's position.

12,000,000, and the region includes 850,000 square miles of territory, in places capable of early development.

THE THREE SOMALILANDS AND ERITREA

Nomadic peoples of Somaliland

British, French, and Italian Somaliland are alike in possessing an arid or semi-arid lowland that rises in the interior to hills and table-lands with a somewhat moister climate, particularly in British Somaliland. The people are everywhere nomadic, moving from one water hole to another with their flocks and herds according to the seasons. They are all Moslems, practically without education, and all are in a measure difficult to govern. Except for the seaports there are no towns and hardly any permanent villages. No newspapers or other periodicals are published in Somaliland.

AREA AND POPULATION OF SOMALILAND BY POLITICAL DIVISIONS

	AREA IN SQ. MI.	POPULA- TION	PRODUCTS EXPORTED
British Somaliland	68,000	300,000	Hides and skins, gum arabic, cattle, ghee butter
French Somaliland	5,800	208,000	Hides and skins, coffee, ivory, beeswax
Italian Somaliland	139,000	400,000	Hides and skins, butter, durra (a kind of millet)

Statistics of area and population for the three Somalilands vary greatly according to the point of view. For example, the most recent French figures, in the Annuaire Statistique, 1917, give 46,000 square miles as the area of French Somaliland, the Statesman's Year-Book gives 5800, and the Encyclopædia Britannica gives 12,000.

Through French Somaliland via the Franco-Ethiopian railway to the port of Djibouti and through British Somaliland via camel caravan routes to the port of Berbera (the capital) comes the principal part of the overland transit trade of Abyssinia. This fact and the grazing possibilities of the grasslands of the region explain the conflict of claims in the hinterland for the ill-defined eastern part of Abyssinia.

Besides Italian Somaliland and Libya, Italy holds also the small colony of Eritrea on the coast of the Red Sea. The coastal belt is barren and sandy, but inland there is a fertile central plateau with a cool climate and a better water supply. There has been little development of the region up to the present time. Its 45,800 square miles are inhabited by 330,000 people, divided between settled villagers on the plateau and pastoral tribes in the lowlands. Life is so primitive that there is very little commerce, and the colony has no real commercial importance at the present time, except as a transit land for Abyssinian trade and as a focus (at the port of Massowah) for a part of the Red Sea coast of Arabia. The colony stands out in industrial development principally by reason of the low grade of development of the regions adjacent. Besides stock raising there is pearl fishing and potash mining and, in recent years, even meat packing. An Italian government mission has just surveyed the resources of the colony, in view of Italy's acute need for additional raw materials. *Italian colony of Eritrea*

THE INDEPENDENT STATES OF ABYSSINIA AND LIBERIA

Abyssinia is one of two independent states in Africa. It has an area estimated at 400,000 square miles and is largely isolated from surrounding lands by its mountainous character and the deep canyons that nick the outer borders of its plateaus. There is a limited amount of barren lowland, especially on the east and south, but the plateau and mountain sections have a cool and moist climate. The population numbers between 8,000,000 and 10,000,000. While the state of development of these people is low and their standard of living simple, they are so numerous as to furnish the basis for a considerable trade. Ivory, beeswax, and gums have been the standard exports, and recently potash has been worked on a commercial scale. There are also undeveloped coal and oil resources. *Unique position of Abyssinia and its international relations*

The eastern frontier of Abyssinia has never been accurately defined, and here there has been rivalry between France, Great Britain and Italy for possession of the land. The Fashoda incident of 1898 brought Great Britain and France to the verge of armed conflict.[1]

Origin and character of Liberia

The negro republic of Liberia is situated on the west African coast between Sierra Leone (British) and the Ivory Coast (French). Its total area is about 40,000 square miles (a little less than that of Pennsylvania) and the population has been variously estimated, the figures ranging from 700,000 to about 2,000,000, of whom all but about 50,000 on the coast are quite uncivilized. Liberians of American origin number some 12,000.

The foundation of the republic was the result of efforts made by the American Colonization Society, founded in 1816 to settle free American negroes on African soil. In 1820 actual settlement began, and in 1847 the colonists promulgated a declaration of independence and drew up a constitution. Even today the government does not effectively control the interior regions, and this has led to the progressive diminution of Liberia's territory by French encroachment. Should this or similar absorption by Europeans threaten Liberia with real danger of extinction, the United States would doubtless play a guardian's part.

Interests of the United States in Liberia

The political influence of the United States has been carried directly into Africa by treaty with Liberia, so that the United States has now assumed obligations that cover a stretch of 15,000 miles, or three fifths of the circumference of the earth, from Liberia to the Philippines. The United States loaned Liberia $5,000,000 in 1918 for the construction of roads, etc., and has assumed the position of chief financial adviser to the republic, a position which was previously held by a joint commission of representatives of Great Britain, the United States, and Germany.

The development of the resources of the region is hindered somewhat by the constitutional provision that none but Liberian citizens may hold real estate, except for colonization, missionary, educational, or other benevolent purposes. The present head of the government of Liberia holds broader views of the country's future than his predecessors held and is seeking to provide better commercial opportunities for whites, upon whom the economic progress of the country must depend.

---

[1] With the intention of linking her possessions in east and west Africa across the territory of the Upper Nile, France penetrated to Fashoda, a fortress on the Upper Nile, in 1898, at just the time that Kitchener, after defeating the Dervishes at Omdurman, was proceeding up river to complete the conquest of the Sudan. Extreme diplomatic tension was created by the meeting of the rival military forces, and actual hostilities were averted only with great difficulty. The outcome was the withdrawal of the French and hence a British victory.

CHAPTER THIRTY-FOUR

LATIN-AMERICAN TRADE AND BOUNDARY DISPUTES: RELATIONS TO THE UNITED STATES

THE great problems of our time are not confined to European fields. They occur in almost every occupied part of the world from Spitsbergen to South Georgia. With the use of airplane and submarine for commercial and strategic purposes, even remote islets have a new importance. The natural pastures of the moss-covered tundras of Siberia, Lapland, and northern North America are now thinly inhabited and of low value, but they may some day be the scene of strong rivalry as a source of meat supply. At some future time even the sea may be marked out politically in zones of economic development, if the food value of its hordes of now unused but useful marine organisms should ever be developed. The Amazon valley, hot, forested, unhealthful, and thinly inhabited, seems now of small importance; but it may yet be a source of incalculable energy when medical science conquers the tropical germ diseases and when the resources of the temperate zones are taxed to capacity by rapidly growing populations. *World-wide distribution of problem areas*

Therefore in a realm so vast as that stretching from the Rio Grande to Tierra del Fuego, the home of 20,000,000 people of white blood, of nearly 20,000,000 Indians and negroes, and of 35,000,000 more of mixed blood, it should not surprise us to find problems of practical interest to the whole world and of paramount interest to the United States.

THE UNITED STATES AND LATIN AMERICA

To every thoughtful person in the United States, Latin-American relations and problems appear the more important because of past diplomatic and commercial neglect. Though the people of the northern republic call their Latin neighbors "Americans," make much of the protective value of the Monroe Doctrine, and lay particular stress on the good effects of closer commercial ties, the United States must face the cold fact, whether agreeable or not, that satisfactory relations have not yet been established. The ties appear to be artificial. There is lacking the bond that is in general the strongest in the world — a common language. Then there are differences of race which are even more nearly fundamental. They manifest themselves in manners and dress, in literature and ethics, in sports, and in social and political ideals. *Need for a basis of good understanding*

559

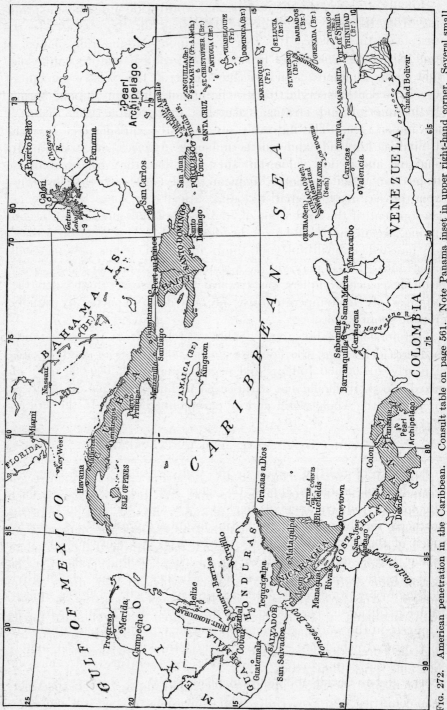

Fig. 272. American penetration in the Caribbean. Consult table on page 561. Note Panama inset in upper right-hand corner. Several small islands of the Virgin group are in British possession.

Finally, there is the instinctive and world-wide antagonism springing from the fear and dislike of the weak for the strong. In the case of Latin America this fear rests upon a foundation of fact as well as upon a measure of instinctive antagonism due to unlike race and lesser commercial and military power. The steady growth of the United States in territory and influence, mainly among former Latin-American possessions, naturally arouses anxiety as to future advances. The following table reveals the surprising fact that the United States has extended its influence and control more rapidly since its annexation of Hawaii (not to mention the earlier acquisition of territory originally Latin-American in the southwest) than any other great power, even imperialist Russia.

Name	Date	Relationship	Area in Sq. Mi.	Population
Hawaii	1898	Annexed	6,450	250,000
Cuba	1898	Virtual protectorate	44,150	2,900,000
Porto Rico	1898	Annexed after war with Spain	3,600	1,250,000
Philippine Islands . . .	1898	Annexed after war with Spain	115,025	8,500,000
Guam	1898	Annexed after war with Spain	210	14,500
Tutuila (Samoa) . . .	1899	Annexed by treaty with Great Britain and Germany	77	7,250
Panama	1903	General supervision	32,400	450,000
Santo Domingo	1907	Supervision of finances	18,500	955,000
	1916	Military administration		
Haiti	1915	Supervision of finances	11,000	2,500,000
Nicaragua	1913	Virtual protectorate	49,500	746,000
	1916	Grant of canal rights and naval bases to U. S.		
Virgin Islands	1917	Ownership by purchase	132	26,000
		Totals	281,044	17,598,750

The United States is classified as a democracy, and it has in recent years disavowed imperialist designs and even protested against such designs on the part of European powers; yet the fact is that the tendency to expansion has been shown in an emphatic manner from the beginnings of settlement in colonial days, through the period of the Louisiana Purchase and the annexation of Florida, during the period immediately before and after the Mexican War, down to the present. The protectorate over Haiti assumed in 1915, the treaty with Nicaragua in 1916, whereby the United States obtained for 99 years the right to construct a canal through Nicaraguan territory, and the purchase of the Virgin Islands in 1917, are merely the latest in a long series of advances. *American expansion in practice*

The events referred to above are facts that impress the Latin-American countries more powerfully than expressions of good will and devo- *Basis of expansion* tion to democratic ideals. In part the expansion of the United States is a manifestation of the almost universal land-hunger of the peoples of the world; in part it is an expression of that pioneering instinct which has ever driven the people of the United States beyond their territorial frontiers; in part it is a conviction of the superiority of American institutions over those they displace in some Latin-American countries that are too weak and backward to manage themselves; and in part it is a recognition of the commercial advantages that are naturally associated with a higher degree of political control.

Opposition to expansion a new experience for the United States

Whatever European nations might have preferred to do, they have in practice — at times under direct compulsion — recognized the Monroe Doctrine and left the United States free to pursue its southward advance; but such expansion has in recent years evoked a certain hostility among the Latin-American states, a hostility based on the assumption that their economic and political liberties were at stake; and the United States is therefore confronted with direct and powerful political opposition for the first time since it embarked upon its policy of expansion overseas. Here we have a problem of the first rank. For the people of the United States are as unknown to themselves as they are to the rest of the world. They do not know how they will take interference with their policy of expansion, for in that expansion they have not had, so far, a single misadventure. While such an experience has left them in an amiable attitude toward others and has given them a generous appreciation of the point of view of others, there is danger in that they do not know what fires of passion may be lighted by active opposition.

Coöperation an aspiration rather than a reality

The eagerness of the United States to coöperate with Latin-American republics has shown itself in the organization of the Pan American Union, in friendly interest in the once active Central American Court of Justice, and in acceptance of the offers of the A B C powers — Argentina, Brazil, and Chile — in the Mexican trouble of 1916; but it is not certain that coöperation is equally acceptable to the Latin Americans, who have a quite different character and a markedly different social order, and whose governments, though patterned after that of the United States, are actually run in a quite different way. Moreover, they cannot help seeing that the history of the last twenty-five years shows the United States as an expansionist power of rapidly growing strength, with a population that now numbers 105,000,000, or more than the population of the entire group of twenty Latin-American nations. They realize that in any coöperative enterprise the United States would play the dominant part.

Fig. 273.   The city and harbor of Charlotte Amelie, Virgin Islands, now an American possession.

Then, too, there are marked differences of opinion between the people of the United States and those of Latin-American countries as to the social and political problems of the day.   To take a single instance, there are great differences with respect to colored populations.   The tendency to intermarry with the native races is a marked characteristic of the Latin Americans.   In Chile whole sections of the former Indian population have become mixed with the whites, and though the Indian element is strongly marked, there is no longer any recognition of the existence of the Indian in those particular sections, the population calling itself Chilean.   Similarly, a large mixed class exists in Peru and Bolivia, to cite two more illustrations out of many.   In short, the barriers of race are far less marked in Latin America than in the United States. *[Differences with respect to the color line]*

There can be recognized in parts of Latin America a considerable decline in the quality of the population.   Our common thought is that the world is improving; but as a matter of fact portions of it have actually lost ground.   This is particularly true in Haiti and Santo Domingo, in parts of Central America, in Venezuela, and in Mexico.   In actual practice democratic principles have been left far *[Decline of population and political ideals]* behind. There are a few countries in which military dictators are in actual control, instead of truly representative governments. Professing the same general political principles, they show the utmost divergence of political practice.

Anxiety
respecting
encroach-
ments of
rival
powers

Should there be increasing weakness on the part of small and politically disintegrating states, the possibilities of encroachment by powers with imperialist designs would require consideration. It is feared by the neighbors of the United States that the impulse to dominate the Caribbean and the Pacific will grow stronger, and may lead eventually to sovereign control. One argument always stands ready for effective use: that only in growth can guarantees be found that colonies and naval stations of other powers will not be established near the shores of the United States to threaten its security as well as its peace. This consideration explains the purchase of the Danish West Indies during the World War, the protectorate over Haiti, the special arrangements with Cuba (the Platt Amendment), with Santo Domingo (a receivership amounting to a protectorate), with Panama (direct ownership of the Canal Zone and special treaty arrangements with the Republic of Panama), and with Nicaragua (the purchase of canal rights and the regulation of her financial affairs). If the United States allows financial operations to be carried on and obligations to be incurred in Latin America by its commercial rivals, protectorates and naval stations of its own will be the natural outcome; for these rivals look to the United States to guarantee the integrity of Latin-American states included under the general protection of the Monroe Doctrine.

Develop-
ment in
tropical
lands a
task for
progressive
peoples

The United States is also impelled to expand commercially in the part of Latin America nearest to it by the necessities of modern civilization, which require tropical products in increasing quantities. Were tropical America occupied by more progressive peoples than those which race, history, and climate have conspired to develop there, economic relations might be built upon a basis of ordinary exchange, as between France and America. Instead there is a population locally incapable of protecting itself or of managing its affairs, and in a few places in a state of political and economic decline. Only under the stimulus of necessity and through the influx of the agents and capital of temperate lands are the tropical products of weak countries made available. With the importation of aggressive men and capital into the tropics goes the importation first of economic and then of political systems.

The only serious fear connected with such an importation is that it may lead to the exploitation of unwilling peoples by unfair means.

Political discontent and even war have sprung again and again from this imposition of ideas and power upon other peoples. Such imposition is not restricted to tropical America, but is world-wide; it is associated with the extraordinary expansion of the political and economic systems of the densely populated industrial nations of the north temperate zone into the tropical lands of America, Africa, and the East and West Indies. <small>*Dangers of imposing alien ideas upon tropical peoples*</small>

COMPETITION FOR SOUTH AMERICAN TRADE

Though serious efforts have been made to turn the tide of Latin American students and travelers toward the United States, it must be said that it still flows far more strongly toward Europe, and particularly to France. For the Latin Americans find that the older cultures of Europe more nearly meet their taste in manners and accord better with their point of view, their philosophy, and their ideals. This congeniality of mind and the keener needs of the European merchants for raw materials (as compared with the United States) have conspired with the extensive type of South American production to put the commerce of Latin America very much into the hands of the commercial and financial interests of western Europe. To this end also has contributed powerfully the better shipping service to South America from England and France. <small>*Tides of travel and business toward Europe*</small>

A prominent Briton wrote in 1913 that one of the eleven main probable causes of future wars in which Great Britain might take part would be <small>*British and American competition for Latin-American trade*</small>

" . . . any attempt of the United States to exercise peculiar political or commercial privileges in South America, east of the Panama Canal Zone, and in general any attempt on the part of an outside power to interfere with the independence of the South American republics; or a disposition on the part of any South American state to confer peculiar privileges in commerce on the subjects of any foreign power to the detriment of the free-trade principle."

It is important to note that the writer does not include Central America and Mexico in his list, and it is equally important to note that he speaks as a representative of a free-trade nation. He has given us, therefore, both a broad political statement related to the independence of the South American states and a narrower statement relating to trade arrangements that shall give the British merchant the same chance as the American.

Great Britain is by far the largest investor in South American

British commercial interests in South America

enterprises: her citizens own large concessions in the Mexican oil fields and in Colombia; her railway financiers built the Argentine railways; and for a time she was the largest owner among foreign nitrate companies in northern Chile. The Peruvian Corporation (British), which has almost sovereign rights in Peru, temporarily holds the rich guano concessions of the Chinchas Islands and owns the Southern Railway, from Mollendo and Arequipa to Lake Titicaca and Cuzco.

American business interests in Latin America

The chief advances made in the trade of South America have not yet brought the United States into acute conflict with British interests, but they are likely to do so in the near future unless there is agreement with Great Britain on a common policy. American capitalists have very largely increased their railway holdings and will tend in the future to have a stronger hold upon land transport, which will greatly stimulate American industrial enterprises. Large American export houses have established themselves in the main coast ports. A chain of banking houses has been founded to offer banking facilities to the American merchant and investor. At Chuquicamata, in northern Chile, American interests have acquired the largest deposit of commercial copper known in South America. An American firm owns the rich copper and silver mines of Cerro de Pasco in Peru, and those of Braden in Chile. During the World War many manufactured goods formerly obtained from Europe were imported from the United States, and some of that war-time trade the United States has held, owing to improved knowledge of the needs of South American people and their peculiar desires and to the better freight rates that the new cargo carriers in the South American trade were able to offer for a time.

Business combinations for foreign trade

Of great influence in future world trade, and especially in United States trade with Latin America, is the Webb Law, passed by Congress on 10 April 1918, which permits a combination of business firms engaged in export trade. Formerly such combination was forbidden by the Sherman and other anti-trust laws. Under the Webb law it may be expected that American export trade will be promoted. Already some of the large manufacturing, banking, and exporting firms have laid plans for the pooling of their business and the development of American export trade on a great scale, in order that through coöperation rather than competition they may hold and develop a larger share of the world's trade.

The growth of Spanish interests in Latin America was very rapid from 1914 to 1919, partly for sentimental and political reasons and partly for business reasons, seeing that Spain, by engaging in trade as a neutral country during the war period, greatly increased her bank reserves. After the war she appointed a committee of engineers at Madrid to investigate the possibilities of commercial expansion with the Spanish-speaking republics of Latin America, with the object of promoting closer business and political relations. There is to be a permanent exhibit of Latin-American products at Madrid. Spanish interests in Latin America

But in spite of the growth of Spanish, Italian, and French trade in Latin America, the interests of the United States clash with those of no European power save Great Britain. Let us follow this fact into Central America and see some of its consequences there.

In 1850 the United States signed a treaty with Great Britain, called the Clayton-Bulwer treaty, by which the United States agreed not to construct an isthmian canal save as a joint enterprise with Great Britain. But the growth of Caribbean interests led to the abrogation of that treaty in 1901 (by the terms of the Hay-Pauncefote treaty) and left the United States free to construct a canal by itself, provided that the canal be open to the ships of all nations on the same terms. In fact, European countries have looked to the government of the United States to maintain order and guarantee the security of their loans in Central American states, and this the United States cannot do unless it occupies a privileged position and holds the main strategic points. During the past fifteen years the United States has frequently landed and even maintained marines in Honduras and Nicaragua, and has taken over indefinitely the functions of the defaulting government in Santo Domingo. In September 1915 an agreement with Haiti provided that the United States may take such steps as may be necessary to maintain an adequate government. The United States also undertook to supervise the financial and military affairs of Haiti. Pershing's military expedition into Mexico in 1916 was in line with the American custom of maintaining order, or at least taking the lead in quelling disorder, in the parts of Latin America that lie nearby. American influence in Central American affairs

Opposed to this supervisory policy of the United States are large and influential sections of South America, and these sections have followed their big neighbor's behavior with the closest attention. Chile has been watchful and suspicious, because the United States befriended her rival, Peru, in the bitter war of 1879–1883. The manner in which the Panama Canal Zone was acquired offended Colombia deeply, and it will be long before that country is in truth the friend of the United States. Though belated, American action in recognizing Attitude of Latin-American nations toward the United States not always friendly the neglect of Colombia's interests in 1903 by the agreement of 1921 to pay her $25,000,000 and grant special transportation privileges in the Canal Zone is at least a necessary first step in the direction of better relations. The United States and Colombia are naturally closely allied through the large trade, and especially the large fruit business, which is conducted in the Caribbean coast region.

THE MEXICAN PROBLEM

Results of disorder in Mexico

The unsettled state of Mexico offers the problem of most direct and keen interest to the United States today. Border populations must not be in constant danger of raids by bandits from the southern side of the Rio Grande. Investments in mines, oil fields, and cattle ranches, if these have been honestly acquired and administered, should have security. In Mexico thousands of people have been killed by revolution and banditry, thousands of others impoverished, political opponents imprisoned, and foreign debts neglected. The total number of Americans killed on the border or in Mexico in recent years runs into the hundreds. The number of Americans in Mexico was reduced, chiefly by emigration to escape death or avoid the confiscation of property, from 75,000 in 1910 or 1911 to 12,000 by September 1919. American losses in Mexico of all kinds during the past few years have a total value of nearly half a billion of dollars.

It remains to be seen whether Mexican elements can restore Mexico to the honorable position that she so long held. To employ force would be a painful alternative for the United States and would produce a fresh crop of suspicions among those Latin Americans who heretofore have not relinquished the hope that America desires to avoid the absorption of small and weak states even when they are dishonest and provocative in international conduct.

These are problems which cannot be solved by saying that capitalists, large landowners, and corrupt government officials once held the mass of the Mexican people in economic bondage. Unless the whole structure of the organized world is to be destroyed and the worship of chaos to begin, with such suffering as mankind has not yet known, a change of government cannot be made the excuse for repudiating debts and disclaiming all moral obligations.

THE WEST INDIES

At the entrance to the Gulf of Mexico, there begins a chain of islands that runs to the east until it makes a sharp turn and curves southward to the coast of Venezuela. The larger islands in this are

— Cuba, Jamaica, Haiti, and Porto Rico — lie nearest Mexico and the United States. On the outer side of the arc, and near Florida, lie the Bahama Islands, almost parallel with Cuba and Haiti. Next to the Bahama Islands come the Leeward Islands, which are on the turn of the curve downward toward South America. Next, running almost directly south, comes the chain of small islands, the Windward Islands, that ends with Trinidad near the mouth of the Orinoco.

The largest and most valuable islands of the entire group of the West Indies were in Spanish possession from the Age of Discovery. Some of the smaller islands, particularly those farthest east, were transferred from power to power in the days of the struggle, first between Dutch and English, later between English and French, for colonial and naval supremacy. Up to 1898 possession of the islands had remained settled for some time: Cuba and Porto Rico were Spanish; the Bahamas and Jamaica were English; on the island of Haiti two republics had been established, Haiti and the Dominican Republic; of the Leeward Islands one small group — the Virgin Islands — was Danish, and the others were divided about equally between France and Great Britain, while the Windward Islands were entirely English. The Dutch also held a smaller group, one of which is Curaçao, to the west of the Windward Islands near the Gulf of Venezuela. *Foreign control of the West Indian Islands*

Since 1898 there have been several changes in the ownership of these islands. Cuba is now a republic practically under United States protection, as are also the republics of Haiti and Santo Domingo. Porto Rico has become a part of United States territory. The latest change is the purchase from Denmark in 1917 of the Virgin Islands, the group immediately to the east of Porto Rico, by the United States.

The purchase of the Virgin Islands from Denmark, like the Panama Canal transaction in 1903, notified the world that America regarded herself as having special and rightful interests in the Caribbean and along its shores. In a similar case, the general recognition of the British protectorate in Egypt in 1919 acknowledged Great Britain's special and rightful interest in the route to India and especially the Suez Canal. Experience with Spain in Cuba before 1898 justified the United States in undertaking to maintain order since that time in the whole of the American Mediterranean. *Special interests of the United States*

In the days of sailing vessels the presence of European powers in the island groups to the southeast, while sometimes noted as a disadvantage, was not felt by the United States to be a source of great danger. Swifter means of communication increased the fear that a foreign power might use the islands as a base of attack on the United *The Caribbean a region of special interest to Americans*

States. With the acquisition of the Panama Canal, the presence of other powers in the chain of islands separating the Atlantic Ocean from the Caribbean Sea became troublesome, a possible menace to the safety of the canal.

The use that was made of the submarine by Germany during the late war and the powerful strides in aerial navigation and radio communication have greatly increased the width of those border protective zones that all commercial nations seek to control.

FRONTIER ZONES OF FRICTION IN LATIN AMERICA

Boundary
disputes
due to
ignorance
as well as
to ambition

Every boundary dispute is a possible cause of war, and boundary disputes grow out of ignorance as well as ambition. "Frontiers are indeed the razor's edge on which hang suspended the modern issues of war or peace, of life or death for nations." The unsettled boundaries of the Latin-American nations are therefore matters of general concern. If the frontiers of the Latin-American states were well-known through exploratory surveys, and if their history were carefully worked out, an impartial tribunal could very soon make a decision that would commend itself to the world, if not to the nations in the dispute. One of the prime functions of an international court of justice will be the settlement of boundary disputes by peaceful means, making use of the resources of geographical research and exploration.

Chile-
Argentina
dispute of
1900

The proof of this argument is found in the settlement of Latin-American boundary disputes in the past. In 1900 Chile and Argentina were on the verge of war over the interpretation of the treaty of 1881, which defined the boundary in Patagonia as "the crest and watershed" of the high cordillera, though the divide between the Atlantic and Pacific drainages in places lies not on the crest of the Andes but east of them. As neither side knew the country thoroughly, they agreed to send a party of surveyors under Colonel Sir Thomas Holdich, and within a year an award was made, on the basis of topographic surveys, that has satisfied both sides.

Bolivian
disputes
with Peru
and Brazil

The Peruvian-Bolivian boundary north of Lake Titicaca has had a similar history. In 1910 the newspapers of La Paz and Lima were full of war talk. In 1911 a party of English surveyors was in the field to establish a line that has since proved satisfactory. The boundary between Bolivia and Brazil in the heavily wooded country of the southwestern Amazon plains was settled and surveyed after armed forces had faced each other across the Acre River for months.

What unsettled boundaries remain to be surveyed? Where are the frontier zones of friction? What are the chief differences of

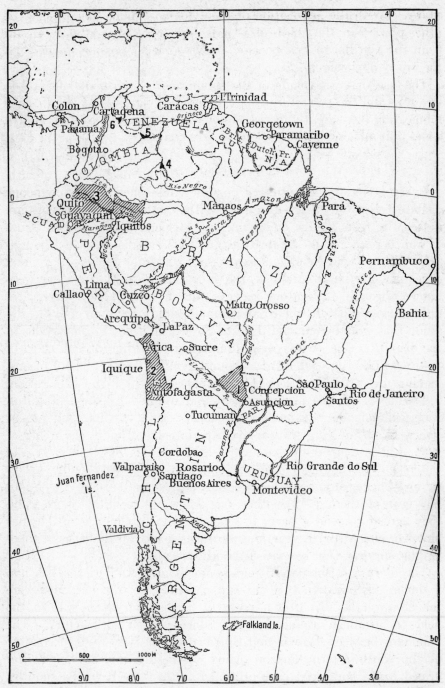

FIG. 274.   The zones of friction in South America: 1, the Gran Chaco; 2, Tacna-Arica, Tara-pacá, and Antofagasta; 3, the junction of Ecuador, Colombia, and Peru; 4, 5, 6, minor disputed areas in the Colombia-Venezuela frontier.   There is also the dispute over the boundary in the La Plata estuary (Fig. 280).

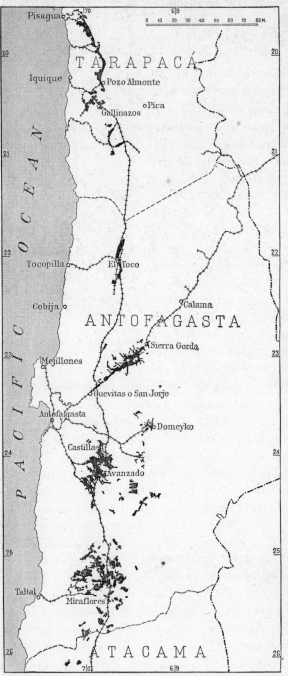

Value of
the almost
uninhabited
desert of
northern
Chile

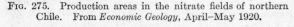

Fig. 275. Production areas in the nitrate fields of northern Chile. From *Economic Geology*, April–May 1920.

opinion as to land titles and resources? In the succeeding pages are discussed those boundary disputes that have seriously threatened or at this moment are threatening the peace of Latin America. Some of them involve vast wealth; others affect few people and small tracts of territory.

The Tacna-Arica Boundary Dispute

The greatest territorial dispute pending in Latin America, the one most interesting in its history and its economic bearings, and most likely to lead to war, is that between Chile and Peru in the Tacna-Arica district. Before 1879 the southern frontier of Peru included the province of Tarapacá, and Bolivia held the province of Antofagasta on the south. Within Tarapacá lay much of the exceedingly rich nitrate deposit that, until the discovery of the process for the recovery of nitrogen from the air a few years ago, produced 99 per cent of the world's supply.

For three hundred years the frontiers of Peru, Bolivia, and Chile remained ill-defined because almost no people lived in the region; indeed, most of it is utterly desert. It is partly owing to the extreme aridity that nitrate salts have accumulated there. By 1850 these salts had become commercially useful and, with the marked advances of industrial chemistry (1860–1880), they had become so valuable that they formed a great natural endowment to the country owning them. Naturally this state of affairs led to dispute, and, in 1879, to war. Chile had a powerful fleet, Peru had inferior ships of war, and the sea is the great highway along the west coast of South America, where a stretch of desert sixteen hundred miles long makes land travel arduous and costly. Within a year the Chilean army had captured Lima, all the coast ports of Peru were destroyed or in Chilean hands, and the Chilean government was in possession of the nitrate fields, which Chile has held ever since. Bolivia offered very little resistance and until recently accepted exclusion from the sea with only nominal protest.

War of the Pacific, 1879–1883

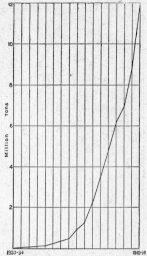

Fig. 276. The production of nitrate in Chile by five-year periods. Figures for 1830–1839 are from Paz Soldán, *Geografía del Perú;* for 1840–1894 from Ortúzar, *Chile of To-day;* for 1895–1914 from F. López Loayza, *La Provincia de Tarapacá,* and from current numbers of the *South American Journal.*

By the treaty of Ancon, signed in 1883, Chile agreed to hold a plebiscite and thus let the inhabitants of Tacna-Arica — the part of the captured territory that is unquestionably Peruvian — decide whether Chile or Peru should own the region. Once in possession, however, Chile could not let go her hold. The plebiscite, for one reason after another, has never been held. In the meantime diplomatic relations between the two countries have been suspended again and again, there have been frequent local mobilizations and strategic disposals of naval units, and, worst of all, serious persecutions of Peruvians. Thousands of persons have been mobbed and robbed and driven into Peru. In 1910 Chile expelled all Peruvian priests and closed their churches. The latest of these persecutions took place in 1919, when Chilean mobs closed Peruvian stores in the towns of Arica and Tacna and Chilean authorities expelled influential Peruvian residents. By way of retaliation, Peruvian workmen go on strike frequently, refusing to unload Chilean steamers. The two countries have remained in a warlike state, and but for the

Promised plebiscite not held by Chile

Fig. 277. Location and railway connections of the Tacna-Arica, Tarapacá, and Antofagasta districts. The focus of the present difficulty is Tacna-Arica, where Bolivia seeks a territorial outlet, or "window on the sea," and where Peru insists on complete ownership in view of Chile's broken promise to hold a plebiscite according to the treaty of Ancon, 1883. Before the war of 1879 between Chile on the one hand and Peru and Bolivia on the other, Antofagasta was a Bolivian province and Tarapacá and Tacna-Arica were Peruvian territory.

terrible expense of war and the influence of business men and foreign diplomats they would long since have reopened the struggle.

Into the conflict between Chile and Peru for the possession of the Tacna-Arica territory there has been introduced a third element — landlocked Bolivia's claim for a commercial outlet at the port of Arica. Bolivia (with Chilean coöperation) has built a railroad from La Paz direct to the sea, across lofty mountains and barren desert to Arica, and now claims the right to have an outlet to the sea and to a strip of land on either side, so as to take control of the railroad out of foreign hands. That much seems to be needed to give this landlocked state, the only interior country of South America, except Paraguay, undisputed access to the sea roads of the Pacific. If the land north of the protecting strip were returned to Peru and Peruvian citizens were once more repatriated, the matter would be finally settled. This solution would give Chile sovereignty over the greater part of the territory captured in 1879–1880 and would establish her frontier 200 miles south of its present position. The population of Tacna-Arica is about 38,000, of whom two thirds live in Tacna and one third lives in Arica.

The rumor that Bolivia had agreed with Chile to give up Bolivian claims to Antofagasta in return for Chilean assistance in gaining Arica aroused Peru to vehement protest that culminated in an exchange of sharp notes in March 1920, in which both reviewed their claims. Bolivia insists that her right to Arica goes back to colonial days and also to the early years of her independence, specifically 1826. Peru also asserts an historical claim and declares she will not have peace until the dispute is settled by arbitration or through the instrumentality of the international court of justice of the League of Nations.

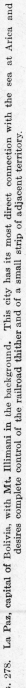

Fig. 278. La Paz, capital of Bolivia, with Mt. Illimani in the background. This city has its most direct connection with the sea at Arica and desires complete control of the railroad thither and of a small strip of adjacent territory.

FIG. 279. The Morro de Arica, on the summit of which in 1880 was fought one of the decisive battles of the war between Chile and Peru.

The La Plata Estuary

A dispute still unsettled between Argentina and Uruguay involves an artificial channel 120 miles long and extending from a point northeast of Buenos Aires to English Bank at the mouth of the La Plata estuary. This is the main outlet of Argentine commerce. In 1828 Argentina and Uruguay agreed that the natural channel of the Uruguay and the northeastern bank of the Rio de la Plata should be the frontier of Uruguay. Uruguay now claims the median line of the estuary, which would give her control of the channel built, lighted, and buoyed by Argentina and maintained at Argentina's expense. The estuary is so shallow, with a depth varying from 8 to 18 feet, and the shoals are so extensive, that navigation is limited to an artificial channel. Paraguay, Bolivia, and Brazil also are interested in the matter, because an increasing portion of their interior commerce must pass by this route. Questions of law and of international policy as to problems of this class remain to be determined before the dispute can be settled. Particularly important in the settlement is the question of the proper present-day limits of so-called territorial waters, in past practice a three-mile zone.

The Bolivia-Paraguay Boundary

Bolivia and Paraguay have a dispute in the Gran Chaco region, which lies between the Pilcomayo River on the south and the Paraguay

River on the east. The disputed zone is virgin grassland in part and will have high commercial value in a short time. Bolivia has occupied the right bank of the Paraguay River in the Gran Chaco, establishing a fort and telegraph station and maintaining troops there. She has effectively occupied the country for many years, one of her main streams of commerce passing across the Gran Chaco to the Paraguay River. On the other hand, Paraguay claims territory west of the Paraguay River to the limits of her old colonial boundaries. She has also granted or sold foreign concessions on the west side of the Paraguay River for the establishment of sawmills (for quebracho wood) and cattle ranches. At a few places she has penetrated at least a hundred miles west of the river.

In 1913 the two nations agreed to annul all former arrangements and to try to settle affairs directly between themselves; if they failed, they were to submit the matter to arbitration. The boundary is still in dispute.

The Peru-Bolivia Boundary

The boundary dispute between Peru and Bolivia appears now to be happily disposed of. It concerned the region north of Lake Titicaca, over the eastern Andes and into the lowland forests at the edge of the Amazon basin, the cordilleran section including the valuable alpaca pastures of Apolobamba. In 1910 the trouble was so serious that both governments mobilized forces at the frontier.

The boundary survey was begun in 1911 and concluded in 1913 by English surveyors. The two countries agreed that any dispute between the commissions of their respective governments should be submitted, without the right of an appeal, to the President of the Royal Geographical Society of London. The reports were published in 1918.

The Colombia-Venezuela Boundary

The dispute between Colombia and Venezuela concerns an almost uninhabited country near the headwaters of the Orinoco. It has arisen because of the indefinite texts of the various treaties, the changing fortunes of the frontier towns, and the overlapping jurisdiction of the local or district governments. In the course of the attempts made by the national governments concerned to settle their disputes, technical commissions have studied and partly demarcated the position of the line in the field. The dispute has been reduced to three small areas in which the population is so limited and the resources at present are so unimportant, that there would be little

FIG. 280. The disputed entrance to Buenos Aires. Uruguay wishes to establish the median line of the La Plata as a boundary with Argentina. This would give her possession of the ship channel near Montevideo and above Colonia. The channel was dredged and buoyed and is maintained by Argentina at great expense, owing to the large amount of river silt constantly being deposited in the estuary. Hitherto the boundary has run close to the northeastern bank of La Plata. The broken lines represent ship channels.

difficulty in settling the matter were it not for the fact that in one or two places a good deal of traffic crosses the boundary. There are no foreign concessions guaranteed by either government in the disputed territory.

The Colombia-Ecuador-Peru Boundary

The area in dispute between Peru and Colombia is shown in Figure 274. If one or the other party should secure its full claim, or if a compromise should be arranged on a common line of division, Ecuador would be reduced to a mere coastal strip. A large part of the disputed region, while densely forested country with a scant Indian population, has become important recently because of its rubber resources. At one time or another Peruvian, Ecuadorian, or Colombian officials have nominally controlled the same region.

In 1900 a Peruvian navigation office was established on the Napo, and from that time Peru took active steps to extend her authority over this river, as well as over the Putumayo and Caqueta rivers, establishing custom houses and military posts, and offering armed resistance to the Colombians who attempted to navigate them. In 1910 there was a quarrel amounting practically to a battle between the armed forces of the two republics. In 1911 the two agreed to make no further attacks upon their respective settlements, since which time neither country could enforce the law without armed opposition from the citizens of the other.

In 1916 (Treaty of Bogotá) Ecuador and Colombia came to an agreement on their common boundary, and this agreement has subsequently been confirmed (1920) and the boundary demarcated. The eastern extremity of the line, however, cannot be regarded as settled until confirmed by Peru, since her claims overlap those of both Colombia and Ecuador.

The Guatemala-Honduras Boundary

The boundary between Guatemala and Honduras was never determined by surveyors except over a short distance, and the administration of the frontier zone was left to chance or tradition. Some towns had been under Guatemaltecan, others under Honduranean governors for many years. The ecclesiastical districts did not always conform to these arrangements, nor was the political boundary always a line separating citizens of Honduras and Guatemala. Some of the frontier land was mountainous, with swift encanyoned streams; some of it was low, hot, swampy, and unhealthful. Government by tradition might have gone on for many years if the low country had not become valuable to banana-growers. The United Fruit Company, an American corporation with property at various points between northern Colombia and Guatemala, has established a line of steamers to many ports that are the outlet for the banana lands of the Caribbean. The company desired concessions, that is, the right to own and cultivate plantations and erect port works. Suddenly the lowlands on the frontier became valuable. Each government was eager to draw the boundary to its own advantage. *Government by tradition leading to the threat of war*

In earlier times war would surely have ensued, and it seemed indeed very difficult to avoid. Both governments were persuaded a few years ago to submit their claims to the Secretary oi State of the United States for recommendation. The first necessity was a survey to clear away ignorance and establish the facts of history and of actual administration during past years as well as the nature and value of the economic resources involved. The work was placed in the hands of a scientific party administered by the American Geographical Society of New York. A definitive settlement is yet to be made. *Arbitration of the Guatemala-Honduras boundary*

The Panama-Costa Rica Boundary

The governments of Colombia and Costa Rica, wishing to settle an old frontier dispute, agreed to submit their rival claims to President Loubet of France for arbitration (1900). The application of President Loubet's decision proved difficult, owing to lack of detailed knowledge of the wooded and partly swampy terrain and the different interpretations that might be placed upon the language of the award. After Panama gained its independence (1903) by secession from Colombia, the old boundary dispute became an issue between itself and Costa Rica. In 1905 there was concluded a treaty between Costa Rica and Panama which sought to amend, in the interest of both parties, the award of 1900; but unexpected difficulties arose, and it was agreed that the question should be submitted to Chief Justice White of the United States Supreme Court for arbitration. The disputed points related to that part of the boundary between the central watershed and the Atlantic coast, and of that part little was known. Once again a territorial dispute depended in large part upon ignorance of local geography. Unfortunately the contestants could not more readily agree to accept the decision of Chief Justice White in 1913 than that of President Loubet in 1900, or their own partial agreement respecting the southwestern end of the boundary in 1910. Long negotiation having failed to compose the differences, resort was made in late February 1921 to threats and warlike

preparations, in spite of the fact that both countries are members of the League of Nations, whose covenant provides the means of peaceful settlement in such cases.

The problem is complicated by the responsibilities of the United States to maintain order in Panama and *to guarantee its independence* in accordance with the Canal Zone purchase agreement of 1904. At that time the government of Panama, needing protection in view of its obvious weakness and its recent secession from Colombia, was willing to assent to restrictions which it was later to repent. Repeated attempts have been made to secure freedom from full American control, but without success. The United States is therefore confronted with the possibility of direct interference not only with Panama, but also with Costa Rica should the latter attempt aggressive acts against Panama. On the other hand, to resist such acts is to invite the criticism of Latin-American countries. After hostilities between Panama and Costa Rica had actually begun, though on a very small scale, the American government pressed the issue of peace March (1921) and the trouble subsided at least temporarily. The problem illustrates anew the delicate position of the United States as a consequence of its advance into the Caribbean and the grave issues that are linked with the ownership and protection of the Panama Canal, in every way vital to its commerce and defense.

The quarrel of these two states illustrates the difficulties in the way of confederating the Central-American countries, as proposed in 1907 and again in 1920. Interstate trade between the small countries of Central America is greatly hampered by frontier regulations, especially irksome on account of rapidly changing national policies and governments and the inexperienced character of the officials. The first attempt was made on the initiative of Mexico and the United States; the second attempt was in response to a circular telegram from Salvador to the other republics of Central America, suggesting a conference for the purpose of unifying their constitutions, of equalizing customs and moneys, and of adopting one national shield and flag. While the idea of the conference was accepted in principle, disagreements as to the precise nature and limits of the program of the conference and the repeated disturbances growing out of boundary disputes have prevented the consummation of the plan, though the tendency appears to be steadily in favor of confederation.

Attempts at confederation of Central-American states

BIBLIOGRAPHY

(*Acknowledgments and references*)

CHAPTER I. GENERAL

H. R. MILL, *The International Geography* (New York, 1909), and the articles on the various countries in the *Encyclopædia Britannica*, 12th ed. (1911), present the primary geographic facts with respect to all parts of the world.   E. A. FREEMAN, *Historical Geography of Europe*, 2 vols., incl. atlas, 3d ed. (London, 1903) ; a classic on the history of political boundaries.   W. Z. RIPLEY, *The Races of Europe* (New York, 1900) ; a standard reference on the anthropology of European peoples, illustrated with many photographs of ethnic types and a series of clear and valuable distributional maps.   SIR H. J. MACKINDER, *Democratic Ideals and Reality* (New York, 1919), is a striking philosophical essay by a distinguished English geographer ; it puts into high relief two contrasting aspects of world conquest — routes and methods of warfare upon the land and upon the sea — and thus supplies a broad geographic and political basis for understanding the World War and the probable tendencies of the future.   H. J. FLEURE, *Human Geography in Western Europe*, 2d ed. (London, 1919), and JEAN BRUNHES, *Human Geography*, Engl. ed. (Chicago, 1920), will be found especially valuable in supplying a geographic framework for European studies. SIR THOMAS H. HOLDICH, *Boundaries in Europe and the Near East* (London, 1918), with the same author's *Political Frontiers and Boundary Making* (London, 1916), upholds the idea of the value of barriers as boundaries.   A. P. BRIGHAM, "Principles in the Determination of Boundaries," *Geogr. Rev.*, Vol. 7, 1919, pp. 201–219, discusses the rôle of boundaries as zones of assimilation.   L. W. LYDE, *Some Frontiers of Tomorrow: An Aspiration for Europe* (London, 1915), presents the argument for assimilative rather than defensive frontiers. LEON DOMINIAN, *The Frontiers of Language and Nationality in Europe* (New York, 1917), and A. J. TOYNBEE, *Nationality and the War* (London, 1915), deal with ethnic and political problems ; but they were written before the present boundaries were established. The *Cambridge Modern History*, 14 vols., incl. atlas (1902–1912), is a large standard work of importance to the student of history and political geography ; it contains especially useful bibliographies, but its articles vary greatly in value.   SIR EDWARD HERTSLET, *The Map of Europe by Treaty*, 4 vols., with maps (London, 1875 and 1891), contains the basic treaties and agreements for the period 1814 to 1891.   CARLTON J. H. HAYES, *A Political and Social History of Modern Europe*, 2 vols. (New York, 1917), is a readable work that supplies a good historical basis for the study of current political problems ; the second volume covers the period between 1815 and 1914.   C. D. HAZEN, *Europe since 1815* (New York, 1910), is also useful for this period.   J. H. ROSE, *The Development of Modern Europe*, 5th ed., 2 vols. in one (New York, 1916), deals with the period from 1870 to 1914 in considerable detail.   CHARLES SEYMOUR, *The Diplomatic Background of the War* (New Haven, 1916), has become a standard work in its field.   See also F. M. ANDERSON and A. S. HERSHEY, *Handbook for the Diplomatic History of Europe, Asia, and Africa, 1870–1914* (Washington, 1918), and the bibliographical notes therein contained.   (For further reference to this work see the introductory note to the Appendix).   SIR HARRY JOHNSTON, *Common Sense in Foreign Policy* (New York, 1913), is an able statement of many of the leading international problems as they stood just before the opening of the World War.

C. H. HASKINS and R. H. LORD, *Some Problems of the Peace Conference* (Cambridge, 1920), is the best available treatise on the historical bases of European territorial disputes that were affected by the peace treaties of 1919–1920.   H. V. TEMPERLEY, editor, *A History of the Peace Conference of Paris* (London, 1920), to be published in 5 volumes, 3 of which have appeared, under the auspices of the Institute of International Affairs, contains much documentary material bearing on the peace conference, together with interpretive chapters.   The British Foreign Office is publishing as Peace Handbooks the material prepared

583

for the British delegation at the Peace Conference of Paris. The geographical commission of the French Service Géographique de l'Armée publishes a valuable series of military handbooks on various parts of the world; they are illustrated with maps, and describe in some detail the regions with which they deal. KARL ANDREE, *Geographie des Welthandels*, 3 vols. (Frankfort, 1910–1913), is a very satisfactory general treatment of its subject. F. LANGE, *Landwirtschaftlich Statistischer Atlas* (Berlin, 1917), contains a valuable series of production maps. FINCH and BAKER, *Geography of the World's Agriculture* (Washington, 1917), is a useful study of the sources of the world's supply of food and other agricultural products. E. GRUNER and G. BOUSQUET, *Atlas Général des Houillères* (Paris, 1909), consists of an atlas with accompanying text, and contains large-scale maps of the various European coal areas. *World Atlas of Commercial Geology, Part I, Distribution of Mineral Production*, by the United States Geological Survey (Washington, 1921), is one of the most useful government publications ever printed; it is a world survey (text and maps) of the chief commercial minerals and will be followed in time by a second atlas on mineral reserves. The International Institute of Agriculture, which has its central office at Rome, publishes a valuable annual that contains statistics respecting the production, consumption, and international exchange of the principal foodstuffs. SIR BOVERTON REDWOOD, *A Treatise on Petroleum*, 3 vols., 3d ed. (London, 1913), is both comprehensive and conveniently arranged for reference; it contains a number of maps and diagrams. W. M. FULLERTON, *Problems of Power* (London, 1913), discusses pointedly some of the critical disputes that ultimately led to the World War. ALBERT DEMANGEON, *Le Declin de l'Europe* (Paris, 1920), pictures the changes in world trade that the war has caused; Engl. ed. (New York, 1921) entitled *America and the Race for World Dominion*. G. G. CHISHOLM, *Handbook of Commercial Geography* (London, 1908), is still the best single reference in its field. M. DUBOIS, J. G. KERGOMARD, and I. LAFITTE, *Précis de Géographie Economique*, 2d ed. (Paris, 1903), and J. G. BARTHOLOMEW, *Atlas of the World's Commerce* (London, 1906), are important general references. ABRAHAM BERGLUND, "The War and the World's Mercantile Marine," *Amer. Econ. Rev.*, Vol. 10, 1920, pp. 227–258, contains an authoritative statement of the after-war shipping situation and of the probable commercial policy of the various nations.

The publications of the Institut Colonial International include eleven series of monographs (Brussels, 1894–1914) on subjects relating to colonies and colonial life. The following books are especially recommended for the subjects indicated in their titles: P. M. OGILVIE, *International Waterways* (New York, 1920); G. KAECKENBEECK, *International Rivers*, Publications of the Grotius Society, No. 1 (London, 1918); SARAH WAMBAUGH, *Monograph on Plebiscites* (New York, 1920); A. G. KELLER, *Colonization* (Boston, 1908).

The following volumes appear annually, and will frequently be found useful: *The Annual Register*, a summary of political happenings devoted chiefly, but not entirely, to the British Empire; *The Statesman's Year-Book*, especially valuable for its statistical material and its bibliographies; *The New International Year Book*, an annual supplement to the *New International Encyclopedia*.

Among geographical periodicals the following publish many valuable articles in the field of political geography, and are indispensable to the scholar: *The Geographical Review*, the American Geographical Society of New York; *The Geographial Journal*, the Royal Geographical Society of London; *La Géographie*, la Société de Géographie de Paris; *Annales de Géographie*, published by Armand Colin, Paris; *Petermanns Mitteilungen*, published by Justus Perthes, Gotha. The following periodicals contain a certain amount of material of exceptional value in the fields of economic and political geography: *The American Economic Review; The American Historical Review; The American Journal of International Law; The American Political Science Review; Political Science Quarterly* (issues an annual record of political events); *The Economic Review* review of the foreign press); *L'Afrique Française; L'Asie Française; The Near East; The New Europe* (discontinued in 1920); *The Round Table* (devoted chiefly to the British Empire and its problems);

Current History Magazine (published by the New York Times). Valuable material will sometimes be found in the *United States Commerce Reports*, in the *British Diplomatic and Consular Reports*, and the annual *Colonial Reports* of the various British colonies.

CHAPTER II. BRITISH EMPIRE

The Oxford Survey of the British Empire, edited by A. J. HERBERTSON and O. J. R. HOWARTH, 6 vols. (Oxford, 1914), is the best general survey of the empire and its parts. In addition there may be noted a series of volumes edited by SIR CHARLES LUCAS under the title, *A Historical Geography of the British Colonies* (Oxford, 1887–   ). Among shorter treatments of the same subject are the following: LIONEL CURTIS, *The Commonwealth of Nations* (London, 1918); its subtitle, "an inquiry into the nature of citizenship in the British Empire, and into the mutual relations of the several communities thereof," explains its purpose; admirable in treatment are its maps and diagrams (some in color), which attempt a critical display of the facts of distribution and area by comparative values; ED- WARD JENKS, *The Government of the British Empire* (Boston, 1918); SIR CHARLES LUCAS, *The British Empire* (London, 1915); A. F. POLLARD, *The British Empire: Its Past, Its Present, and Its Future* (London, 1909); W. H. WOODWARD, *The Expansion of the British Empire, 1500–1911* (Cambridge, 1911). On the government of England, see the standard work on that subject, *The Government of England*, 2 vols. (New York, 1912), by A. LAW- RENCE LOWELL. W. A. DUNNING, *The British Empire and the United States* (New York, 1914), surveys Anglo-American relations in the century from 1814 to 1914. A. B. KEITH, *Responsible Government in the Dominions*, 3 vols. (Oxford, 1912), has a detailed and well-documented account of dominion government. SIR H. J. MACKINDER, *Britain and the Brit- ish Seas* (Oxford, 1906), is a geographical treatment of the British Isles. A. J. SARGENT, *Seaways of the Empire* (London, 1918), gives a clear picture of the geography of transport between the various parts of the great British trade realm; it contains good semi-diagram-matic maps and recent statistics. MARK JEFFERSON, "The Distribution of British Cities, and the Empire," *Geogr. Rev.*, Vol. 4, 1917, pp. 387–394. For an authoritative survey of the natural resources, trade, and food and raw material requirements of the British dominions, see the *Final Report of the Dominions Royal Commission* (London, 1918). H. STANLEY JEVONS' monograph on *The British Coal Trade* (London, 1915) is excellent; it contains a chapter on the world's coal resources. A. W. KIRKALDY, *British Shipping: Its History, Organization, and Importance* (London, 1914), may be mentioned.

Official yearbooks are issued by most of the British colonies and dominions, and they form most valuable reference works. *The Colonial Office List*, issued yearly by the Crown, is informative; it contains short descriptions and historical sketches of each of the British colonies, and a list of the Crown officers. H. J. ROBINSON, *Colonial Chronology* (London, 1892), will still be found useful. On the history of Canada see SIR JOHN G. BOURINOT, *Canada under British Rule, 1760–1905*, in Cambridge Historical Series (1909), or A. G. BRADLEY, *Canada*, in the Home University Library (London and New York, 1912). A. E. ASPINALL, *The British West Indies* (Boston, 1912), and *Pocket Guide to the West Indies* (Chicago, 1914). For South Africa, in addition to the official yearbook, reference should be made to LAITE's *Commercial Blue Book for South Africa* (Cape Town), *The South African Year-Book* (London), and *The Guide to South and East Africa*, published annually by the Union-Castle Steamship Company, the latter covering the region from the Cape to Tan-ganyika Territory. ERNEST BARKER, *Ireland in the Last Fifty Years* (1866–1918), 2d ed. (Oxford, 1919), is a short but illuminating and rational survey of the Irish problem. SIR HORACE PLUNKETT, *Ireland in the New Century* (London, 1904), is an indispensable ref-erence written by a scholar with practical experience in Irish affairs. W. O'C. MORRIS, *Ireland: 1494–1905*, in Cambridge Historical Series, 2d ed. (1909), is a review of the entire Irish question.

On the Moslem confraternities see G. F. ANDREWS, "Islam and the Confraternities in

French North Africa," *Geogr. Journ.*, Vol. 47, 1916, pp. 116–130, and the titles listed in the accompanying bibliography. For the present condition of agriculture in Egypt and an outline of the controversy between the Anglo-Egyptian Sudan and the Egyptian administration respecting the control of the Nile waters, see the two principal papers in the controversy : (1) Sir William Willcocks, *The Nile Projects* (Cairo, 1919) ; (2) Sir Murdock MacDonald, *Nile Control Works* (Cairo, 1919). Sir William Willcocks and J. I. Craig, *Egyptian Irrigation*, 2 vols. (New York, 1913), is both technical and general. Lord Cromer, *Modern Egypt*, 2 vols. (London, 1908), is a masterly survey of British rule in Egypt.

The *Imperial Gazetteer of India*, 3d ed., 26 vols. (Oxford, 1907–1909), includes a complete survey of India, as a whole and by parts, together with an excellent atlas. For a concise historical account consult Vincent A. Smith, *The Oxford Student's History of India*, 3d ed. (Oxford, 1911). Sir Thomas H. Holdich, *India* (London, 1904), presents the country from the geographical standpoint. B. H. Baden-Powell, *The Land Systems of British India*, 3 vols. (Oxford, 1892), and *The Indian Village Community* (London, 1896), are standard works on the subject. The student should also consult John Matthai, *Village Government in British India* (London, 1915). Lajpat Rai, *England's Debt to India* (New York, 1917) presents an Indian view of the English occupation of India. A. Loveday, *The History and Economics of Indian Famines* (London, 1914), is a convenient study ; it contains a history and tabulation of Indian famines from early times to the present, with a discussion of relief organization and protective measures. For accounts of India's problems on her northwestern frontier see Sir James Douie, *The Panjab, North-west Frontier Province, and Kashmir* (Cambridge, 1916), and Sir Thomas H. Holdich, *The Gates of India* (London, 1910). J. C. Jack, *The Economic Life of a Bengal District* (Oxford, 1916), is an interesting study of the income and expenditure of persons living in Faridpur district, Bengal. C. W. Harrison, editor, *An Illustrated Guide to the Federated Malay States* (London, 1919?), has valuable material, including maps, not easily found elsewhere. W. E. Gibbs, "British Malaya : A Story of Empire," *Journ. Manchester Geogr. Soc.*, Vol. 35, 1919, pp. 8–18, is a short historical, social, and economic survey of the Malay States. Sir J. S. Scott, *Burma : A Handbook of Practical Information* (London, 1911), is useful and excellently illustrated. Miss G. L. Bell has prepared a British official report entitled *Review of the Civil Administration of Mesopotamia* (London, 1920), which presents the views of the chief Arab sheikhs of Mesopotamia toward British administration of the region.

CHAPTER III. FRANCE

G. Hanotaux, editor, *Histoire de la Nation Française*, to be completed in 15 volumes, has been announced, and the first of two volumes by Jean Brunhes on the human geography of France has appeared (Paris, 1920) ; it will cover all phases of French history. Vidal Lablanche, *La France* (Paris, 1908), is the standard work on the regional geography of France ; it is exceptionally well illustrated. Onésime Reclus, *Atlas de la Plus Grande France* (Paris, 1913–1915), contains maps of the various French departments and colonies, together with descriptive and interpretive text. For a useful graphic presentation of the results of the census of 1901, see *Album Graphique de la Statistique Générale de la France* (Paris, 1907). Raymond Poincaré, *How France Is Governed* (New York, 1914), and E. A. Vizetelly, *Republican France, 1870–1912* (Boston, 1913), contain respectively a description of French political institutions and a history of France since the Franco-Prussian War. W. M. Davis, *A Handbook of Northern France* (Cambridge, 1918), will be found especially valuable for its sketches and block diagrams of the region covered and for its compact physiographic descriptions. A. H. Brooks and Morris F. La Croix, *The Iron and Associated Industries of Lorraine, the Sarre District, Luxemburg and Belgium*, Bull. 703, U. S. Geol. Surv. (Washington, 1920), is a thoroughly scientific piece of work of great present interest in view of the close interweaving, in the Franco-German frontier zone, of political and economic forces. The authoritative presentation of the French position with respect to Alsace-Lorraine, the Saar valley, Luxemburg, and the Rhineland is to be found in *L'Alsace-Lorraine, et la Frontière du Nord-est* (Paris, 1918); it constitutes Vol. 1 of the *Travaux du Comité d'Études*, a series of handbooks and monographs for the work of the Peace Conference of Paris, 1919. P. VIDAL LABLACHE, "Évolution de la population en Alsace-Lorraine et dans les départements limitrophes," *Ann. de Géogr.*, Vol. 25, 1916, pp. 97–115, 161–180, has maps showing density and movement of population. The following works contain presentations of the problem of Alsace-Lorraine from various points of view: BARRY CERF, *Alsace-Lorraine since 1870* (New York, 1919); C. D. HAZEN, *Alsace-Lorraine under German Rule* (New York, 1917); COLEMAN PHILLIPSON, *Alsace-Lorraine: Past, Present, and Future* (London, 1918), advocates a plebiscite and contains an extensive bibliography; LUCIEN GALLOIS, "Alsace-Lorraine and Europe," *Geogr. Rev.*, Vol. 6, 1918, pp. 89–115, is chiefly concerned with the economic resources in relation to the political geography. For three valuable articles on the Saar basin, presenting respectively its historic, economic, and demographic characteristics, see *Ann. de Géogr.*, Vol. 28, 1919, pp. 249–292. For an abstract of the third of these articles and a reproduction of the map showing density of population in the Saar basin on the scale of 1 : 1,430,000, see *Geogr. Rev.*, Vol. 10, 1920, pp. 42–43. RUTH PUTNAM, *Luxemburg and Her Neighbors* (New York, 1918), recounts the history of the grand duchy and outlines its international position before the war.

Useful yearbooks are issued by most of the French colonies. In addition the following bibliographies will be found of value in the further study of France's African colonies: GEORGES BRUEL, *Bibliographie de l'Afrique Equatoriale Française* (Paris, 1914); EDMOND JOUCLA, *Bibliographie de l'Afrique Occidentale Française* (Paris, 1912). E. ROUARD DE CARD, *Traités de Délimitation concernant l'Afrique Française* (Paris, 1910), contains texts of treaties and illustrative maps for the period up to date of publication. R. GODFERNAUX, *Les Chemins de Fer Coloniaux Français* (Paris, 1911), is quite detailed and complete (to date of publication). The following works on Morocco should be consulted by the student desiring further information: J. GOULVEN, *Le Maroc: Les Ressources de ses Régions; Sa Mise en Valeur* (Paris, 1919); E. D. MOREL, *Morocco in Diplomacy* (London, 1912); VICTOR PIQUET, *Le Maroc: Géographie; Histoire; Mise en Valeur* (Paris, 1920); ALFRED DE TARDE, "The Work of France in Morocco," *Geogr. Rev.*, Vol. 8, 1919, pp. 1–30. See also pp. 56–58 of the last-named volume for a note on the progress of French occupation. E. F. GAUTIER, *L'Algérie et la Métropole* (Paris, 1920), offers a good brief outline of Algerian life and problems. HENRI LE POINTE, *La Colonisation Française au Pays des Somalis* (Paris, 1917?), explains the value of Somaliland's position on the Red Sea and as a point of exit for the Abyssinian hinterland. A convenient guide to the literature of Syria is to be found in a large work by PAUL MASSON, *Éléments d'une Bibliographie Française de la Syrie*, 2 vols. (Marseilles, 1919).

CHAPTER IV. BELGIUM

La Belgique, published for the Liége Exposition of 1905 by the Belgian government, contains a survey of the country's resources and its industrial situation. H. GEHRIG and H. WÄUTIG, *Belgiens Volkswirtschaft* (Berlin, 1918), covers the economic situation in the light of the German occupation. V. BIERKENS, "Le Port d'Anvers: Son Avenir, son Importance Économique pour la Suisse," *Bull. Soc. Neuchâteloise de Géogr.*, Vol. 28, 1919, pp. 5–208, describes the port and its relations to Swiss trade. For a brief history of Belgium consult R. C. K. ENSOR, *Belgium*, in Home University Library (London and New York, 1915); a short bibliography is given. RAOUL BLANCHARD, *La Flandre* (Paris, 1906), is a regional geographical study of the Flemish plain in France, Belgium, and Holland. The books by E. D. MOREL on the Congo have had great influence in the reorganization of that region. A. B. KEITH, *The Belgian Congo and the Berlin Act* (London, 1919), is a historical study.

CHAPTER V. ITALY

Among volumes on the political and economic situation before the outbreak of the World War may be mentioned: F. M. UNDERWOOD, *United Italy* (London, 1912); W. K. WALLACE, *Greater Italy* (New York, 1917). E. M. JAMISON, C. M. ADY, K. D. VERNON, C. S. TERRY, *Italy, Mediaeval and Modern* (Oxford, 1917), is a convenient presentation of the essential facts of Italian history. OLINTO MARINELLI, "The Regions of Mixed Populations in Northern Italy," *Geogr. Rev.*, Vol. 7, 1919, pp. 129–148, deals with the mixed language zones on Italy's frontier, in former Austria, Switzerland, and France. It represents the Italian scientific viewpoint and is conservative in form. CESARE BATTISTI, *Il Trentino*, 2d ed. (Novara, 1917), contains 19 maps, and outlines the Italian claims in the Tyrol. ATTILIO TAMARO, *La Vénétie Julienne et la Dalmatie: Histoire de la nation italienne sur ses frontières orientales*, 3 vols. (Rome, 1918), is the most comprehensive work on the subject, with abundant references to sources, and, although Italian in point of view, it is a basic reference. (See also references under Jugo-Slavia on the subject of Italy's claims in Istria and Dalmatia.) ATTILIO BRUNIALTI, *Trento e Trieste dal Brennero alle Rive dell' Adriatico* (Turin, 1916), is profusely illustrated, has many maps, and covers all the Italian claims from the Trentino to Dalmatia. GUIDO ASSERETO, *L'Italia e le sue Colonie* (Novara, 1913), contains many maps and diagrams illustrating the economic and political conditions of both Italy and her colonies. G. BEVIONE, *L'Asie Minore e l'Italia* (Turin, 1914), sets forth the Italian view of the Turkish situation and the claims of Italy, especially in the Adalia region. The *Annnario Statistico Italiano* publishes each year a series of demographic maps and charts.

CHAPTER VI. SPAIN

C. E. CHAPMAN, *A History of Spain* (New York, 1918), is a brief history of Spain based largely upon the comprehensive work of the Spanish historian, Altamira. EDUARDO REYES PRÓSPER, *Las Estepas de España y su Vegetación* (Madrid, 1915), describes the physical character of the drier portions of Spain. J. DANTÍN CERECEDA, *Resumen fisiográfica de la península ibérica* (Madrid, 1912), supplies the best available general view of the physiographic conditions in the natural regions of the Spanish peninsula. DON ALFONSO MERRY DEL VAL, "The Spanish Zones in Morocco," *Geogr. Journ.*, Vol. 55, 1920, pp. 319–349, 409–422, discusses Spanish interests in Morocco at the present time. JULIUS KLEIN, *The Mesta* (Cambridge, 1920), is a thorough study of the institution of that name, which was developed by the grazing interests and dominated the economic life of portions of Spain for several centuries. For general references on subjects indicated in the respective titles, see: I. M. COLMEIRO, *La Historia de la Economía Política en España* (Madrid, 1863); MARTIN HUME, *Spain, 1479–1788* (Cambridge, 1913); R. B. MERRIMAN, *The Rise of the Spanish Empire in the Old World and in the New*, 4 vols., of which 2 are published (New York, 1918).

CHAPTER VII. PORTUGAL

GEORGE YOUNG, *Portugal Old and Young: An Historical Study* (Oxford, 1917), deals with the history and the present problems of Portugal. W. H. KOEBEL, *Portugal: Its Land and People* (London, 1909), and A. F. G. BELL, *Portugal of the Portuguese* (New York, 1915), are general references. ANGEL MARVAUD, *Le Portugal et ses colonies* (Paris, 1912), is a political and economic study. LUIS SCHWALBACH, *Emigração e colonização* (Lisbon, 1914), deals with the problems of colonization from the Portuguese standpoint.

CHAPTER VIII. SCANDINAVIA AND HOLLAND

For a summary presentation of the history of the Scandinavian countries see R. N. BAIN, *Scandinavia: A Political History of Denmark, Norway, and Sweden, 1515–1900* (Cambridge,

1905). PAUL DRACHMANN, *The Industrial Development and Commercial Policies of the Three Scandinavian Countries* (Oxford, 1915), reviews the interesting economic history of these lands. Among books on Denmark the following should be consulted: H. RIDER HAGGARD, *Rural Denmark and Its Lessons* (New York, 1913); W. J. HARVEY and CHRISTIAN REPPIEN, *Denmark and the Danes: A Survey of Danish Life, Institutions and Culture* (London, 1915). *Norway* (Kristiania, 1900), a work prepared for the Paris Exposition, contains an interesting survey of the country. KNUT GJERSET, *History of the Norwegian People*, 2 vols. (New York, 1915), is concerned chiefly with history prior to the 19th century. J. GUINCHARD, editor, *Sweden: Historical and Statistical Handbook*, 2d ed., 2 vols. (Stockholm, 1914), is issued under the direction of the government; it contains excellent articles on the present life of Sweden and is well illustrated with photographs and maps. STEN DE GEER, *Befolkingens Fördelning i Sverige* (Stockholm, 1919), is accompanied by a large map (1 : 500,000) showing by a dot and shaded circle method the exact distribution of population, as well as the distribution of forests, industrial enterprises, etc., — a model treatment. HELMER KEY, *La Vie Économique de la Suède* (Paris, 1913), is a competent analysis of Sweden's economic life. The following references treat of Spitsbergen: R. N. RUDMOSE BROWN, *Spitsbergen* (London, 1920); R. N. RUDMOSE BROWN, "Spitsbergen, Terra Nullius," *Geogr. Rev.*, Vol. 7, 1919, pp. 311–321; CHARLES RABOT, "The Norwegians in Spitsbergen," *Geogr. Rev.*, Vol. 8, 1919, pp. 209–226. R. SCHUILING, *Nederland: Handboek der Aardrijkskunde*, 5th ed. (Zwolle, 1915), is the standard geographical work on Holland; it is amply supplied with statistical tables and extremely valuable maps and plans, many of them in color. K. ZEEMAN, *Moderne Geographie van Nederland*, 3d ed. (Amsterdam, 1917), relates the physiography to the economic and industrial geography. A. A. BEERMAN, *Nederland als Polderland*, 2d ed. (Zutphen, 1915), is an excellent detailed treatise on Holland's reclaimed areas. *Yearbook of the Netherlands East Indies*, English ed. (Batavia, 1920), is a well illustrated survey of the region. The following works will also be found useful, the first-named being the standard reference on the subject: CLIVE DAY, *The Policy and Administration of the Dutch in Java* (New York, 1904); A. CABATON, *Java and the Dutch East Indies* (New York, 1911).

CHAPTER IX. SWITZERLAND

Dictionnaire Géographique de la Suisse, 6 vols. and atlas (Neuchâtel, 1902–1910), published under the auspices of La Société Neuchâteloise de Géographie, is the standard treatment of the subject. *Atlas Graphique et Statistique de la Suisse* (Berne, 1914), is published by the Bureau of Statistics of the Swiss Department of the Interior, and contains a series of beautifully printed and authoritative maps. R. C. BROOKS, *Government and Politics of Switzerland* (Yonkers, 1918), is a well-ordered treatment of its subject. HENRI HAUSER, "La Position Géographique de la Suisse: Étude de Géographie Politique," *Ann. de Géogr.*, 15 Nov. 1911, pp. 413–429, deals with Switzerland's relations to Europe's navigable waterways. See also E. J. CLAPP, *The Navigable Rhine* (New York, 1911). HEKTOR AMMANN, *Die Italiener in der Schweiz* (Basle, 1917), studies the problems arising from the increase of Italian population in Switzerland.

CHAPTER X. GERMANY

JOSEPH PARTSCH, *Central Europe* (New York, 1903), is a scientific geographical survey of Germany, Austria-Hungary, Belgium, the Netherlands, Serbia, Rumania, and Bulgaria. FRIEDRICH NAUMANN, *Central Europe*, trans. by C. M. MEREDITH (London, 1916), deals with the political and economic phases of the German imperial project from the German point of view and was especially influential during the war period. J. A. R. MARRIOTT and C. G. ROBERTSON, *The Evolution of Prussia: The Making of an Empire* (Oxford, 1917), traces the growth of the German Empire. JEAN BRUNHES and CAMILLE VALLAUX, "German Colonization in Eastern Europe," *Geogr. Rev.*, Vol. 6, pp. 465–480, contains valuable historical and statistical information; it gives the number of Ukrainians in the various governments of southern Russia. For Germany after the revolution of 1918 and the treaty of Versailles, see GEORGE YOUNG, *The New Germany* (London, 1920). L. GALLOIS, "La Paix de Versailles: Les nouvelles frontières de l'Allemagne," *Ann. de Géogr.*, Vol. 28, 1919, pp. 241–248. *Das Deutsche Kolonialreich*, 2 vols. (Leipzig and Vienna, 1909), by Hans Meyers and others, is the standard reference on former German colonies; it is elaborately illustrated with photographs and colored maps. On the same subject see EVANS LEWIN, *The Germans and Africa* (New York, 1915), and WILLIAM EVELEIGH, *Southwest Africa* (London, 1915); the latter discusses the suitability of the colony for white settlement. On Germany's former colonies in the Pacific see WILLIAM CHURCHILL, "Germany's Lost Pacific Empire," *Geogr. Rev.*, Vol. 10, 1920, pp. 84–90. *Handbuch des Wirtschaftskunde Deutschlands*, 4 vols. (Leipzig, 1901–1904), published by the Deutschen Verbandes für das Kaufmannische Unterrichtswesen, is valuable, though based on the census of 1895. JOSEPH PARTSCH, *Schlesien, Eine Landeskunde für das deutsche Volk*, 2 vols. (Breslau, 1896), is a detailed regional geographical study of German Silesia. It is accompanied by colored maps and sketches, and though now somewhat out of date, it is still one of the best regional studies in the field of modern geography.

CHAPTER XI.   AUSTRIA

Die Österreichisch-Ungarnische Monarchie in Wort und Bild, 24 vols. (Vienna, 1886–1902), contains a detailed survey of the former empire by provinces. The following contain studies of the national and other problems of Austria before the World War: VIRGINIO GAYDA, *Modern Austria: Her Racial and Social Problems* (London, 1915); H. W. STEED, *The Hapsburg Monarchy*, 3d ed. (London, 1914); the various books of R. W. SETON-WATSON; B. C. WALLIS, "The Peoples of Austria," *Geogr. Rev.*, Vol. 6, 1918, pp. 52–65. E. DE MARTONNE, "Le traité de Saint-Germain et le démembrement de l'Autriche," *Ann. de Géogr.*, Vol. 29, 1920, pp. 1–11, pictures the present situation.

CHAPTER XII.   HUNGARY

L. EISENMANN, "La Nouvelle Hongrie," *Ann. de Géogr.*, Sept. 1920, pp. 321–333, discusses Hungary within its new boundaries; valuable especially for its statistical material and its outline of geographical conditions. For discussions of former Hungary's national problems see: A. HEVESY, *Nationalities in Hungary* (London, 1919); B. C. WALLIS, "The Peoples of Hungary," *Geogr. Rev.*, Vol. 4, 1917, pp. 465–481; and by the same author, "Central Hungary: Magyars and Germans," *Geogr. Rev.*, Vol. 6, 1918, pp. 421–435. *Magyarország Gazdasági Térképekben* (The Economics of Hungary in Maps), edited by GUSTAVUS DE EMICH, prepared by ALADÁR DE E. ILLÉS and ALBERT HALÁSZ (Budapest, 1920), contains 74 maps, 6 diagrams, and in the preface a list of references to sources; the several maps give a complete picture of the economic elements of Hungary before the World War; almost every map is accompanied by a transparency of present and former boundaries, thus making it possible to see at a glance just what Hungary has lost as a consequence of the war.

CHAPTER XIII.   CZECHO-SLOVAKIA

E. BENEŠ, *Bohemia's Case for Independence* (London, 1916), and VLADIMIR NOSEK, *Independent Bohemia: An Account of the Czecho-Slovak Struggle for Liberty* (London, 1918), outline the arguments for the formation of the Czecho-Slovak state. *Manuel statistique de la République tchéco-slovaque* (Prague, 1920) gives the latest available statistics on the area, population, size of farm holdings, and resources of the various main political divisions of the state.   B. C. WALLIS, "The Slavs of Northern Hungary," *Geogr. Rev.*, Vol. 6, 1918, pp. 268–281, presents the demographic facts and the national and economic problems connected with the Slovaks and Ruthenians of Hungary.   E. DE MARTONNE, "L'État Tchécoslovaque," *Ann. de Géogr.*, May, 1920, pp. 161–181, discusses the territorial limits and economic situation of the state as determined at Paris in 1919–1920.

CHAPTER XIV.   JUGO–SLAVIA [1]

JOVAN CVIJIĆ, *La Peninsule Balkanique* (Paris, 1918), is a thorough geographical treatment of the Balkan region and especially of the territory inhabited by the Jugo-Slavs. M. I. NEWBIGIN, *Geographical Aspects of Balkan Problems in their Relation to the Great European War* (London, 1915), deals in an exceptionally clear manner with the political geography of the region.   M. I. NEWBIGIN, "The Geographical Factor in Balkan Questions," *Scientia*, Jan. 1921, pp. 41–50, is a short but competent treatment of the subject. The Commission de Géographie of the Service Géographique de l'Armée has published a number of geographical booklets on various parts of the Balkans, illustrated with maps and diagrams.   R. W. SETON-WATSON, *The Rise of Nationality in the Balkans* (London, 1917), is a survey of the nationality problem in the Balkans.   J. A. R. MARRIOTT, *The Eastern Question: An Historical Study in European Diplomacy* (Oxford, 1917), presents briefly the recent history of the Balkans.   J. G. SCHURMAN, *The Balkan Wars*, 3d ed. (Princeton, 1916), is a short but useful presentation of the subject.   R. W. SETON-WATSON, *The Southern Slav Question and the Hapsburg Monarchy* (London, 1911), and A. H. E. TAYLOR, *The Future of the Southern Slavs* (New York, 1917), are excellent treatises.   B. C. WALLIS, "The Slavs of Southern Hungary," *Geogr. Rev.*, Vol. 6, 1918, pp. 341–353, is useful for its maps and statistical analyses.   CLIVE DAY, "The Pre-war Commerce and the Commercial Approaches of the Balkan Peninsula," *Geogr. Rev.*, Vol. 9, 1920, pp. 277–298, describes the backward economic conditions of the Balkans and the pre-war commercial pathways.

H. W. V. TEMPERLEY, *History of Serbia* (London, 1917), presents essential facts. F. S. STEVENSON, *A History of Montenegro* (London, no date), is convenient.   For a presentation of recent events by a partisan of the late ex-King Nicholas see A. DEVINE, *Montenegro in History, Politics, and War* (London, 1918).   *Report of the International Commission to Inquire into the Causes and Conduct of the Balkan Wars* (Washington, 1914), is a valuable impartial account on the basis of field investigations.   ATTILIO TAMARO, *La Vénétie Julienne et la Dalmatie: Histoire de la nation italienne sur ses frontières orientales*, 3 vols. (Rome, 1918–1919); see comment on this work in the section of this bibliography dealing with Italy.   GIOTTO DAINELLI, *La Dalmazia: Cenni Geografici e Statistici* (Novara, 1918), consists of an atlas with accompanying text, and presents the Italian claim to Dalmatia, with full cartographic treatment of the demographic facts.   A. G. OGILVIE, "A Contribution to the Geography of Macedonia," *Geogr. Journ.*, Vol. 55, 1920, pp. 1–34, explains the physiographic character of the region and the chief aspects of the human geography as well.   The following books deal with the Macedonian problem: H. N. BRAILSFORD, *Macedonia: Its Races and Their Future* (London, 1906); D. M. BRANCOFF, *La Macédoine et sa Population Chrétienne* (Paris, 1905), a statistical study from the Bulgarian point of view; T. R. GEORGEVITCH, *Macedonia* (New York, 1918), from the Serbian standpoint.   WACE and THOMPSON, *The Nomads of the Balkans* (London, 1914), is concerned with the Vlach settlements in the Balkans.

R. J. KERNER, *Slavic Europe: A Selected Bibliography in the Western European Languages* (Cambridge, 1918), is a scientific bibliography, brought down to the beginning of the World War; the works cited deal with the Russians, Poles, Czecho-Slovaks, Jugo-Slavs, and Bulgarians.

---

[1] Including general references to the Balkans.

CHAPTER XV. RUMANIA

For a discussion of the Rumanian national problem see R. W. Seton-Watson, *Roumania and the Great War* (London, 1915), and Eugène Pittard, *La Roumanie* (Paris, 1917). N. P. Commène, *La Dobrogea: Essai Historique, Économique, Ethnographique et Politique* (Paris, 1918), is a treatment of the Dobrudja problem from the Rumanian point of view. E. de Martonne, *La Valachie: Essai de Monographie Géographique* (Paris, 1902), is a thorough geographical treatment with excellent maps and illustrations. See also the same author's "Essai de carte ethnographique des pays roumains," *Ann. de Géogr.*, Vol. 29, 1920, pp. 81–98, which combines upon one colored map the density of population and the ethnic composition; and "La Nouvelle Roumanie," *Ann. de Géogr.*, Vol. 30, 1921, pp. 1–31, containing a description of the natural regions and the economic life.

CHAPTER XVI. BULGARIA

Bulgaria of Today (London, 1907), by the Bulgarian Ministry of Commerce and Agriculture, describes the country, and is still useful in many particulars, though it was compiled before the Balkan wars. For presentations of the claims of Bulgaria see the following: Balkanicus, *The Aspirations of Bulgaria* (London, 1915); A. Ishirkoff, *Bulgarien: Land und Leute* (Leipzig, 1917). For presentations of Jugo-Slav claims, see other references above. J. Ivanoff, *Les Bulgares devant le Congrès de la Paix*, 2d ed. (Berne, 1919), outlines the Bulgarian position in relation to the peace settlement.

CHAPTER XVII. ALBANIA

Miss Edith Durham, *High Albania* (London, 1909), and *The Struggle for Scutari* (London, 1914), give vivid and intimate pictures of Albanian life and problems. G. Louis-Jaray, *L'Albanie Inconnue* (Paris, 1913), is a more scientific survey of the country. Among other works may be mentioned Wadham Peacock, *Albania: The Foundling State of Europe* (London, 1914); C. A. Chekrezi, *Albania, Past and Present* (New York, 1919); C. A. Dako, *Albania: The Master Key to the Near East* (Boston, 1919). The last two are by Albanians.

CHAPTER XVIII. GREECE

H. Lefeuvre-Méaulle, *La Grèce économique et financière* (Paris, 1916), outlines Greece's position in the eastern Mediterranean. J. P. Mahaffy, *Rambles and Studies in Greece*, 7th ed. (New York, 1913), is a well-tried volume by a noted classical scholar. See also W. Miller, *Greek Life in Town and Country* (London, 1905). A. G. Keller, *Homeric Society* (New York, 1906), presents not only a picture of early Greek life but also the beginnings of colonization. Otto Maull, "Kultur- und Politischgeographische Entwicklung und Aufgaben des Heutigen Griechenlands," *Mitteilungen der Geographischen Gesellschaft in München*, Vol. 2, Dec. 1915, pp. 91–171, is a comprehensive paper on the political and economic geography of the southwestern Balkans and is illustrated by a map representing the commercial routes, the chief belts of production and trade, the main climatic elements, the ecclesiastical boundaries, etc.

CHAPTER XIX. POLAND

Eugeniusz Romer, *Atlas Géographique et Statistique de la Pologne* (Warsaw, 1916), is indispensable for a thorough understanding of Polish problems. It contains 32 colored plates with explanatory text in French, Polish, and German. The same author has a brilliant article entitled "Poland: The Land and the State" in the *Geogr. Rev.*, Vol. 4, 1917, pp. 6–25. Vol. 1 of the *Polish Encyclopædia* (Warsaw, 1912) contains a treatment of the physical geography of the Polish region and the physical characteristics of its inhabitants. E. WUNDERLICH, editor, *Handbuch von Polen* (*Kongress-Polen*): *Beiträge zu einer Allgemeinen Landeskunde*, 2d ed. (Berlin, 1918), is a broad geographical survey prepared under the direction of the German governor-general of Warsaw after the occupation of Russian Poland during the World War. *Handbuch des Oberschlesischen Industriebezirks*, Vol. 2 of *Festschrift zum XII. Allgemeinen Deutschen Bergmannstage in Breslau*, 1913, is accompanied by a number of large-scale maps of the Silesian industrial region. For the history of Poland see H. E. LEWINSKI-KORWIN, *The Political History of Poland* (New York, 1917). R. H. LORD, *The Second Partition of Poland, a Study in Diplomatic History* (Cambridge, 1915), is a thorough piece of historical research and is fundamental to a study of Polish national character and problems in the period of decline that ended with the fall of the Republic. E. ROMER, "Statistics of the Languages of the Provinces being under the Polish Civil Administration of the Eastern Lands (December 1919)," (Warsaw, 1920), gives the statistical results and an analysis of them, of a census taken in the governments of Minsk, Vilna, and Brest-Litovsk; the data relate to the disputed zone about Minsk, where the Soviet government made concessions to the Poles in the final treaty of peace signed early in 1921, and the disputed zone about Vilna, where Polish troops are in occupation pending the final settlement; the title given above is taken verbatim from the title page of the publication, which is printed in Polish and English in parallel columns.

CHAPTERS XX, XXI. BALTIC STATES

L. M. LARSON, "Territorial Problems of the Baltic Basin," *Univ. of Illinois Bull.*, Vol. 16, No. 18, 1918, deals with Slesvig, Finland, the Baltic Provinces, and Danzig. In *Meereskunde*, No. 152, 1919, RICHARD POHLE sketches the growth of Riga; his paper is illustrated by several interesting maps. M. MARTNA, *L'Esthonie; Les Esthoniens et la Question Esthonienne* (Paris, 1920), covers the problems of Esthonia from the national point of view. A concise article on "The Peoples of the Baltic Provinces and Lithuania" is to be found in the *Round Table*, March 1918, pp. 293–307. OTTO KESSLER, *Die Baltenländer und Litauen* (Berlin, 1916), contains statistical material of value. See also K. A. JUSAITIS, *The History of the Lithuanian Nation and its Present National Aspirations* (Philadelphia, 1918).

CHAPTER XXII. FINLAND

Atlas de Finlande, 1910, atlas and 2 vols. of text (Helsingfors, 1911), together with the earlier *Atlas de Statistique Sociale sur les Communes Rurates de Finlande en 1901* (Helsingfors, 1908), were published by the Finnish Geographical Society, and constitute the best existing survey, along the lines of scientific geography, of the social and political conditions of the country. *Finnland im Anfang des XX. Jahrhunderts* (Helsingfors, 1920), published by the Finnish Ministry for Foreign Affairs, despite its title has been brought down to 1919; it contains many maps. For descriptions of the country and the people consult: ARTHUR READE, *Finland and the Finns* (London, 1914); WERNER SÖDERJHELM, editor, *Finlande et Finlandais* (Paris, 1913); ERNEST YOUNG, *Finland: The Land of a Thousand Lakes* (London, 1912); ERLAND NORDENSKIOLD, "Finland: The Land and the People," *Geogr. Rev.*, Vol. 7, 1919, pp. 361–379.

CHAPTER XXIII. RUSSIA

GREGOR ALEXINSKY, *Modern Russia* (London, 1913), is a general treatment of the historical and economic development of Russia, the constitutional situation before the

World War, Russia's literature, and the problems of nationality and religion. The following works on the history of Russia may be recommended: R. BEAZLEY, N. FORBES, and G. A. BIRKETT, *Russia from the Varangians to the Bolsheviks* (Oxford, 1918); F. H. SKRINE, *The Expansion of Russia*, 1815–1900 (Cambridge, 1904). The *Russian Almanac* (annual, London) continues the *Russian Year Book* and contains much statistical and other information. M. J. OLGIN, *The Soul of the Russian Revolution* (New York, 1917), is an intimate and detailed view, chiefly social and political, but containing also valuable sections on land tenure and local village or community government. J. M. CRAWFORD, editor, *The Industries of Russia*, 5 vols. (St. Petersburg, 1893), prepared by the Russian government for the World's Fair at Chicago, and W. DE KOVALEVSKY, editor, *La Russie à la Fin du 19ᵉ Siècle* (Paris, 1900), published for the Paris Exposition, contain many useful maps and much statistical material, and will be found especially useful in comparative studies. For a statistical treatment of the Russian population by nationalities, see RUDOLF CLAUS, "Die Zusammensetzung der Bevölkerung Russlands nach Nationalitäten," *Zeitschrift des Königlich Preussischen Statistischen Landesamts*, Vol. 55, 1915, pp. 1–12. The same number of this publication, pp. 13–22, contains a valuable article with statistical material on agricultural and industrial production, "Die russische landwirtschaftliche und industrielle Produktion," by C. BALLOD. T. H. ENGELBRECHT, *Landwirtschaftlicher Atlas des Russischen Reiches in Europa und Asien* (Berlin, 1916), contains an excellent series of maps displaying the economic resources of the Russian Empire. WALTHER TUCKERMANN, *Verkehrsgeographie der Eisenbahnen des Europäischen Russland* (Essen, 1916), includes a history of Russian railroads and a survey of their present economic and strategic importance. The two following works treat of the commercial importance of Russia: W. H. BEABLE, *Commercial Russia* (New York, 1919); ARTHUR RAFFALOVICH, editor, *Russia: Its Trade and Commerce* (London, 1918). Among other important works on Russia in the last few years see: E. ANTONELLI, *Bolshevist Russia* (London, 1920); T. G. MASARYK, *The Spirit of Russia*, 2 vols. (London, 1919); E. A. ROSS, *Russia in Upheaval* (New York, 1919); CHARLES SAROLEA, *Great Russia: Her Achievement and Promise* (New York, 1916); H. W. WILLIAMS, *Russia of the Russians* (New York, 1915). STEPHEN RUDNITSKY, *Ukraine: The Land and Its People* (New York, 1918), is published by the Ukrainian Alliance of America; it had previously appeared in German under the title *Ukraina — Land und Volk: Eine Gemeinfassliche Landeskunde* (Vienna, 1916). Foremost among works on Siberia is the *Atlas of Asiatic Russia*, published in Russian in 1914 by the Colonization Bureau; it contains an excellent series of maps and is accompanied by descriptive text in three volumes. The following additional volumes may be noted: M. A. CZAPLICKA, *Aboriginal Siberia* (Oxford, 1914); FRIDTJOF NANSEN, *Through Siberia* (New York, 1914); M. P. PRICE, *Siberia* (London, 1912).

CHAPTER XXIV. CONSTANTINOPLE

PAUL MASSON, "Constantinople et les détroits," *Ann. de Géogr.*, Vol. 28, 1919, pp. 121–142, is a thorough statistical study of the commerce of the Straits. C. PHILLIPSON and N. BUXTON, *The Question of the Bosphorus and the Dardanelles* (London, 1917), contains a well-rounded and scholarly treatment of the problem. The handbook on the Dardanelles and the Bosporus, published by the French Commission de Géographie of the Service Géographique de l'Armée (Paris, 1915), should also be consulted; it contains a relief map and a plan of the city of Constantinople. For the relation of the Hellespont to the Greek world, and especially its place in Greek commerce and politics, see G. NEILSON, "The Hellespont in Retrospect," *Proc. Royal Philos. Soc.* (Glasgow), Vol. 47, 1915–16, pp. 1–24. H. C. DWIGHT, *Constantinople, Old and New* (London, 1915), treats of the life of the city and to some degree of its recent history.

CHAPTER XXV. PALESTINE

G. A. SMITH, *The Historical Geography of the Holy Land*, 13th ed. (London, 1907), is a classic work, and is now admirably supplemented by the same author's *Atlas of the Historical Geography of the Holy Land* (London, 1915). ELLSWORTH HUNTINGTON, *Palestine and Its Transformation* (Boston, 1911), is a suggestive treatment of the influence of climatic factors in the Holy Land. See also "The Future of Palestine" by the same author, *Geogr. Rev.*, Vol. 7, 1919, pp. 24–35. ISIDORE SINGER, editor, *The Jewish Encyclopedia*, 12 vols. (New York, 1901–1906), should be consulted upon problems connected with the Jews which had taken shape before its publication. Among recent works on the Jewish people may be cited: ARTHUR RUPPIN, *The Jews of Today* (New York, 1913); NORMAN BENTWICK, *Palestine of the Jews, Past, Present, and Future* (London, 1919). ALBERT T. CLAY, "Political Zionism," *Atlantic Monthly*, Feb. 1921, discusses the political phases of the Zionist movement and of the Palestinian mandate. Mention may be made of *Palestine*, a small weekly published at London which chronicles events in Palestine from the Zionist standpoint.

CHAPTER XXVI. ANATOLIA

D. G. HOGARTH, *The Nearer East* (New York, 1902), covers the region at the eastern end of the Mediterranean and beyond to Persia and Arabia, and contains many maps and diagrams. VITAL CUINET, *La Turquie d'Asie*, 4 vols. (Paris, 1900), has been the standard work on Asiatic Turkey, though it is now unreliable because of the great shifting of population due to war and forced migration; it discusses each vilayet systematically. Among other geographical works which may be mentioned are: EWALD BANSE, *Die Türkei: Eine Moderne Geographie* (Brunswick, 1915); ALFRED PHILIPPSON, *Das Türkische Reich* (Weimar, 1916). WILLIAM MILLER, *The Ottoman Empire, 1801–1913* (Cambridge, 1913), is a useful volume with extensive bibliographies, but it does not carry the story through the Balkan wars. Other historical works of note are: W. E. D. ALLEN, *The Turks in Europe: A Sketch Study* (London, 1919); LORD EVERSLEY, *The Turkish Empire: Its Growth and Decay* (London, 1917). M. A. CZAPLICKA, *The Turks of Central Asia in History and at the Present Day* (London, 1918), is "an ethnological inquiry into the Pan-Turanian problem." The *Handbook* on the Bagdad Railway published by the Commission de Géographie of the Service Géographique de l'Armée (Paris, 1916), describes in detail the route traversed by this important line.

CHAPTERS XXVII, XXVIII. TRANSCAUCASIA

NOEL and HAROLD BUXTON, *Travel and Politics in Armenia* (London, 1914), is noteworthy. H. F. B. LYNCH, *Armenia: Travels and Studies*, 2 vols. (London, 1901); Vol. 1 deals with the Russian provinces and Vol. 2 with the Turkish provinces. D. GHAMBASHIDZE, *Mineral Resources of Georgia and Caucasia* (London, 1919), though brief, is a useful treatise. A valuable reference is *Conditions in the Near East*, the report of the American Military Mission to Armenia, MAJOR GENERAL J. G. HARBORD, 1919, published as Senate Document No. 266. RICHARD COTTHEIL, "Armenia and the Armenians. A List of References in the New York Public Library," Bell. N. Y. Publ. Lib., Vol. 23, 1919, pp. 123–143, 251–277, 303–336. W. L. WILLIAMS, *Armenia: Past and Present* (London, 1916), is almost wholly concerned with Turkish Armenia. J. D. HENRY, *Baku: An Eventful History* (London, 1906), gives an account of the oil region,

CHAPTER XXIX. PERSIA

P. M. SYKES, *A History of Persia*, 2 vols. (London, 1915), carries the story of Persian history down to 1905. W. MORGAN SHUSTER, *The Strangling of Persia* (New York, 1912), is an account of the author's experiences as Treasurer-General of Persia. J. DeMorgan, *Mission Scientifique en Perse*, 5 vols. (Paris, 1894–1905), is the basis of a large part of our geographical knowledge of Persia. A. V. W. Jackson, *Persia Past and Present: A Book of Travel and Research* (New York, 1906), contains useful material. G. N. Curzon (Lord Curzon), *Persia and the Persian Question* (London, 1892), is a general treatise with the emphasis chiefly upon political questions; there is an abundance of geographical data; the point of view is frankly British and imperial.

CHAPTER XXX. INNER ASIA

H. H. Howorth, *History of the Mongols*, 4 vols. (London, 1876–1888), is a standard work on the Mongol invasions. It covers the period from the 9th century. Ellsworth Huntington, *The Pulse of Asia* (Boston, 1907), is a study in geographic environment and the influence of climate on history; the claim is made that the drier phases of climatic cycles account for the Mongol invasions of Europe. Arved Schultz, *Die Natürlichen Landschaften von Russisch-Turkestan* (Hamburg, 1920), is a geographical work on Russian Inner Asia. Other works on the same region are: W. E. Curtis, *Turkestan: The Heart of Asia* (New York, 1911); A. Woeikof, *Le Turkestan Russe* (Paris, 1914). E. N. Fell, *Russian and Nomad: Tales of the Kirghiz Steppes* (New York, 1916), gives an interesting account of travel and life in central Siberia about Lake Balkash. Standard references on geographical and archæological subjects are the recent articles or books, published variously, by Sven Hedin, Sir Aurel Stein, Holdich, and Younghusband.

CHAPTER XXXI. THE FAR EAST

A. Little, *The Far East* (Oxford, 1905), is a geographic treatment by a scholar long resident in China. Sir Robert K. Douglas, *Europe and the Far East, 1506–1912* (New York, 1913), deals with the interaction of Orient and Occident. S. K. Hornbeck, *Contemporary Politics in the Far East* (New York, 1916), covers events leading up to the presentation of the Twenty-One Demands by Japan. See also K. S. Latourette, *The Development of China* (New York, 1918). Hosea Ballou Morse, *The International Relations of the Chinese Empire*, 3 vols. (London, 1910–1918), surveys comprehensively the period from 1834 to 1911. See also the same author's *The Trade and Administration of China* (London, 1913). Samuel Couling, editor, *The Encyclopedia Sinica* (London, 1918), is a general reference. E. J. Dingle, editor, *The New Atlas and Commercial Gazetteer of China* (Shanghai, 1918); the text contains a comprehensive treatment of the economic resources, means of transportation, principal cities, etc., of the various provinces of China. G. Maspero, *La Chine* (Paris, 1918), has a useful account of the geography, history, and political and social structure of China, together with the history of Chino-Japanese relations and the various treaties that affect the present political situation. *The China Year Book*, 5th ed. (London, 1920) and *The Japan Year Book* (published annually at Tokio) are useful as general references. *Japan: Trade During the War*, United States Tariff Commission Report (Washington, 1921), is a study of Japanese trade from 1913 to 1917 with special reference to the trade of Japan with the United States. The following works should also be consulted upon the subjects indicated by their titles: T. W. Overlach, *Foreign Financial Control in China* (New York, 1919); Mongton Chih Hsu, *Railway Problems in China* (New York, 1915); E. T. Williams, "The Open Ports of China," *Geogr. Rev.*, Vol. 9, 1920, pp. 306–334. E. A. Ross, *The Changing Chinese* (New York, 1911), describes China as seen by a sociologist.

The three following works are recommended for a survey of contemporary Japanese history (the last two are by Japanese): K. S. Latourette, *The Development of Japan*, (New York, 1918); Count S. Okuma, *Fifty Years of New Japan*, 2 vols. (New York, 1909); G. E. Uyehara, *The Political Development of Japan, 1867–1909* (London, 1910). For a study of Japanese emigration statistics see Ernst Schultze, "Die Japanische Auswanderung," *Peter. Mitt.*, Vol. 61, 1915, pp. 129–133, 175–179, 270–276, 301–308, and the note by R. Biasutti, "L'Emigrazione Giapponese," *Rivista Geogr. Italiana*, Vol. 61, 1916, pp. 210–216. K. K. Kawakami, *Asia at the Door: A Study of the Japanese Question in Continental United States, Hawaii, and Canada* (New York, 1914), is written by an assimilated (Americanized) Japanese. R. Malcolm Keir, "Modern Korea," *Bull. Amer. Geogr. Soc.*, Vol. 46, 1914, pp. 756–769, 817–830, discusses the resources and problems of the region. Alleyne Ireland, *The Far Eastern Tropics* (Boston, 1905), consists of a group of studies of the administration of Hongkong, Malay States, French Indo-China, Java, the Philippine Islands, etc.

CHAPTER XXXII. AUSTRALIA

Among a number of important works by Griffith Taylor may be mentioned the following: *A Geography of Australasia* (Oxford, 1914); *The Australian Environment* (Melbourne, 1918); "The Settlement of Tropical Australia," *Geogr. Rev.*, Vol. 8, 1919, pp. 84–115. G. H. Scholefield, *The Pacific: Its Past and Future* (London, 1919), is an excellent general work. Among others may be mentioned: H. H. Bancroft, *The New Pacific* (New York, 1912; first publ. 1899); James Colwell, editor, *A Century in the Pacific* (London, 1914), "a review of the developments in the South Pacific during the past hundred years"; it has an extensive bibliography. On the history of Australia see: A. Wyatt Tilby, *Australasia, 1688–1911* (London, 1912); T. A. Coghlan, *Labour and Industry in Australia from the First Settlement in 1788 to the Establishment of the Commonwealth in 1901*, 4 vols. (London, 1918), a somewhat encyclopedic industrial history of Australia. The Commonwealth of Australia publishes an exceptionally valuable *Yearbook* compiled under the direction of the Commonwealth Statistician, G. H. Knibbs.

CHAPTER XXXIII. AFRICA

Acquaintance with the work done by Sir Harry Johnston is absolutely necessary for any one interested in African problems. Among his many published works may be mentioned the following: *The Opening Up of Africa* (1911); *A History of the Colonization of Africa by Alien Races* (Cambridge, 1913); *British Central Africa* (London, 1897); *George Grenfell and the Congo*, 2 vols. (1908); *Liberia*, 2 vols. (1906); *The Uganda Protectorate*, 2 vols. (1902). J. S. Keltie, *The Partition of Africa*, 2d ed. (London, 1895), gives an excellent statement of the problems of political geography as they presented themselves in Africa during the nineteenth century. N. D. Harris, *Intervention and Colonization in Africa* (New York, 1914), contains a history of the continent since the beginning of white exploitation. The treaty documents for the period up to the end of 1908 are to be found in Sir Edward Hertslet, *The Map of Africa by Treaty*, 3 vols., with a portfolio of maps, 3d ed. (London, 1909). C. H. Stigand, *Administration in Tropical Africa* (London, 1914), outlines the problems connected with the government of African tropical dependencies. Sir Patrick Manson, *Tropical Diseases: A Manual of the Diseases of Warm Climates*, 5th ed. (London, 1914). For a brief but detailed description of the resources, trade routes, and future value of eastern tropical Africa, with special reference to white settlement, see G. F. Scott-Elliot, *Journ. Royal Soc. of Arts*, Vol. 68, 1920, pp. 315–329. Sir Charles Metcalfe, "Railway Development of Africa, Present and Future," *Geogr. Journ.*, Vol. 47, 1916, pp. 3–21, contains a history of early railroad projects and a record of achievements to date.

CHAPTER XXXIV. LATIN AMERICA

Wilhelm Sievers, *Süd- und Mittelamerika*, 3d ed. (Leipzig and Vienna, 1914), is the best general geographical reference work on the subject. For a historical background the best reference is E. G. BOURNE, *Spain in America, 1450–1580* (New York, 1904); it also contains an exceptionally valuable critical essay on authorities. F. GARCÍA CALDERÓN, *Latin America: Its Rise and Progress* (New York, 1913), is written by a Peruvian diplomat; it discusses "the German, North American, and Japanese perils," and other problems of Latin America. VISCOUNT BRYCE, *Observations and Impressions* (New York, 1912), presents a closely interwoven account of the historical setting of the Latin-American peoples and present economic, social, and political conditions. E. A. ROSS, *South of Panama* (New York, 1915), is a survey of the peoples of Latin America by an observant sociologist. The volume on *Colombia* by EDER, in Scribner's South American Series, is an authoritative work. W. R. SHEPHERD, *Latin America* (New York, 1914), is a concise treatment of the essential historical facts and contains a useful bibliography. A. B. HART, *The Monroe Doctrine: An Interpretation* (Boston, 1916), traces the historical development of the doctrine since its proclamation. PIERRE BERNE, *L'Immigration Européenne en Argentine* (Paris, 1915), is an account of the European settlements. Among works on Argentina the following are noteworthy: PIERRE DENIS, *La République Argentine: La Mise en Valeur du Pays* (Paris, 1920); JULES HURET, *En Argentine*, 2 vols. (Paris, 1912–1913). W. S. TOWER, "The Pampa of Argentina," *Geogr. Rev.*, Vol. 5, 1918, pp. 293–315, is an informing article with maps. *The Boundary between Bolivia and Peru* (London, 1918), treats of the newly surveyed zone north of Titicaca long in dispute between these two republics; it contains recent and valuable maps. SIR THOMAS H. HOLDICH, *The Countries of the King's Award* (London, 1904), describes the Andes of Argentina and Chile, and the boundary settlement made there by the award of the King of England after a field study under the auspices of the Royal Geographical Society. PIERRE DENIS, *Brazil in the Twentieth Century* (New York, 1910), is one of the best books yet published on any South American subject. B. L. MILLER and J. T. SINGEWALD, *The Mineral Deposits of South America* (New York, 1919), is one of the most recent and comprehensive works of its kind. *The South American Year Book* (London), deals especially with the railroads of the continent. *The Argentine Year Book* (Buenos Aires), though dealing primarily with Argentina, also contains chapters on Uruguay, Paraguay, and Chile.

APPENDIX

PRINCIPAL TREATIES AND AGREEMENTS, 1814–1920

THE list includes chiefly those treaties and agreements that are mentioned in the text. For detailed lists of treaties and agreements, with texts and maps, see SIR EDWARD HERTSLET, *The Map of Europe by Treaty*, in four volumes, of which volumes 1–3 were published in 1875, volume 4 in 1891. See also the same author's *The Map of Africa by Treaty*, in three volumes, with portfolio of maps (1909). An indispensable reference for the student of political geography is ANDERSON and HERSHEY, *Handbook for the Diplomatic History of Europe, Asia and Africa, 1870–1914* (1918); in one hundred and sixty main sections with several subdivisions each, are listed practically all the international acts essential to a knowledge of territorial problems. The introduction, the running text-comment, and the convenient and logical arrangement of the whole make it unusually valuable in spite of the absence of an index.

DATE	NAME	SIGNATORIES	TERMS OF IMPORTANCE IN THIS BOOK
1814	First Treaty of Paris (following deportation of Napoleon to Elba)	Austria, France, Great Britain, Portugal, Prussia, Russia, Spain, Sweden	Provided for calling of Vienna Congress
1814–1815	Congress of Vienna	As above	Determined the main lines of the map of Europe as they stood in the 19th century
1815	Second Treaty of Paris (following Waterloo)	As above	France ceded certain bits of territory on her eastern frontier and paid an indemnity
1839	Treaty of London (the "scrap of paper")	Austria, Belgium, France, Great Britain, Netherlands, Prussia, Russia	Belgium's neutrality guaranteed
1856	Treaty of Paris (close of Crimean War)	Austria, France, Great Britain, Prussia, Russia, Sardinia, Turkey	Independence and integrity of Turkey guaranteed. Danube internationalized. Bessarabia annexed to Russia. Rumania under Turkish suzerainty. Serbia given a large degree of autonomy. Åland Islands to be unfortified.
1859	Zurich	Austria, France, Sardinia	Beginning of unification of Italy
1864	Vienna	Austria, Denmark, Prussia	Cession of Slesvig-Holstein to Prussia and Austria
1866	Prague	Austria, Prussia	German Confederation dissolved. Austria renounced rights to Slesvig-Holstein, and consented to union of Lombardy and Venetia with Italian kingdom

599

DATE	NAME	SIGNATORIES	TERMS
1871	Frankfort (close of Franco-Prussian War)	France, Germany	Cession of Alsace-Lorraine to Germany. Indemnity of 5,000,000,000 francs paid by France
1878	San Stefano	Russia, Turkey	Serbia, Montenegro, and Bulgaria enlarged. Russia obtained Bessarabia and Transcaucasian territory. The opposition of the powers led to the Congress of Berlin and the modification of the treaty of San Stefano
1878	Congress of Berlin	Austria-Hungary, France, Germany, Great Britain, Italy, Russia, Turkey	Eastern Rumelia formed. Austro-Hungarian occupation of Bosnia and Herzegovina authorized. Independence of Montenegro and of Serbia recognized under enlarged boundaries. Rumanian independence recognized. Districts of Ardahan, Kars, and Batum ceded to Russia. Turkey promised reforms in Armenia
1879	Formation of Dual Alliance	Germany and Austria	
1882	Formation of Triple Alliance	Germany, Austria, Italy	
1885	Berlin Act	Austria-Hungary, Belgium, Denmark, France, Germany, Great Britain, Italy, Netherlands, Portugal, Russia, Spain, Sweden, Turkey, United States	Spheres of influence in Africa laid down. Formation of neutral Congo Free State. Free trade area in Africa defined. Declaration prohibiting the slave trade
1898	Paris (close of Spanish-American War)	Spain, United States	Independence of Cuba recognized. Porto Rico, Guam, and the Philippines ceded to the United States
1904	Anglo-French Convention	Basis of the Entente Cordiale	
1905	London	Alliance between Great Britain and Japan	
1907	The Hague	Delegates of 44 countries	Second Hague Conference[1] for the peaceful settlement of international disputes
1912	Lausanne	Italy, Turkey	Annexation of Tripoli (Libya) by Italy. Occupation of Dodecanese by Italy

[1] The first Hague Conference (1899) had a similar though more restricted program.

DATE	NAME	SIGNATORIES	TERMS
1913	London	Bulgaria, Greece, Montenegro, Serbia, Turkey	Cession by Turkey to the Balkan allies of all territory (except Albania) west of the Enos-Midia line. Autonomous Albania to be created.
1913	Bucarest	As above, with Rumania added, and without Turkey	Frontiers as shown in Fig. 150
1915	Secret Treaty of London	France, Great Britain, Italy, Russia	Italy to enter the war, and to receive the Trentino, Istria, a large part of Dalmatia and the Adriatic islands, Valona in Albania, a sphere of influence in Turkey, and territory in Africa if the other signatories made gains there
1916	Sykes-Picot Agreement	France, Great Britain	Provided for spheres of influence in Turkey. Later a new agreement included Italy, and provision was made for Russia (Fig. 47)
1918	Treaty of Brest-Litovsk	Central Powers, Russia	Russia withdrew from the war and renounced her right to Baltic Provinces, Poland, and certain districts in the Caucasus
1918	Bucarest	Central Powers, Rumania	Rumania to withdraw from the war, and to cede certain districts to Austria-Hungary. Treaty was never ratified
1919	Versailles	Allied and Associated Powers, Germany	See chapter on Germany
1919	St. Germain-en-Laye	Allied and Associated Powers, Austria	See chapter on Austria
1919	Neuilly	Allied and Associated Powers, Bulgaria	See chapter on Bulgaria
1920	Trianon	Allied and Associated Powers, Hungary	See chapter on Hungary
1920	Sèvres	Allied Powers, Turkey	See chapter on Turkey
1920	Tripartite Agreement	France, Great Britain, Italy	Determined spheres of influence in Turkey (Fig. 48)
1920	Agreement among Allied Powers whereby Rumania receives Bessarabia, subject to later discussion by Russia		
1920	Riga	Poland, Russia	Eastern boundary of Poland and Polish control of Eastern Galicia
1920	Rapallo	Italy Jugo-Slavia	Settlement of Adriatic question. See chapter on Jugo-Slavia
1920	Franco-British Agreement	France, Great Britain	Division of mandated territory in Syria. See chapter on Palestine

The Russian Soviet (Bolshevist) government has concluded, among others, the following treaties of peace with former parts of the Russian Empire:[1]

COUNTRY	DATE	PLACE
Esthonia	2 February 1920	Dorpat
Lithuania	12 July 1920	Moscow
Latvia	11 August 1920	Moscow
Poland	12 October 1920	Riga
Finland	14 October 1920	Dorpat

Each treaty recognizes the territorial limits of the state in question or provides for future settlement.

[1] For details see the chapters on the respective countries in the list.

INDEX

INDEX

Abadan, 74, 468
A B C powers, 562
Abdul Hamid II, 432
Åbo, 373
Abyssinia, 532, 555, 557; Italy and, 140; unique position, 557
Acknowledgments, ii
Acre River, 570
Ada-Kalessi, 287
Adalia, 140, 321, 434
Adana, 434; massacres, 433
Adde (ill.), 170
Aden, 29, 72, 160, 555; region (map), 556
Adowa, 140
Adrianople, 221, 251, 296, 298, 318, 320, 327, 440; treaty of, 278, 314
Adriatic Sea, Austria and, 207, 215; differences between the two sides, 263; in Pact of Corfu, 258; Italy's claim, 259, 261; Italy's control, 270
Adriatic Sea, east coast, ethnic elements (map), 260; final settlement of disputed territory, 269; harbors, character, 266; Italian culture, 262; Italy and, 131; rival claims, 259
Ægean coast, 304
Ægean Islands, 417
Ægean Sea, Greeks and, 313, 321
Afghanistan, 465, 470, 483; British policy in, 484; independence movement, 484; Kabul wall (ill.), 486; near Baluchistan border (ill.), 487; Russian and Indian railways, proposed connections (map), 485
Africa, Belgium's gains by the war, 124; bibliography, 597; British possessions (map), 42; colonial expansion and struggle for raw materials, 532; colonies loyal in the war, 532–533; early colonial rivalry, 540; former German colonies, 541, 199 (map); French interests in northern, 105, 551; French possessions (map), 106; germ diseases and insects, 538; German ambitions, 199–200; German colonial expansion, 198; international regulations, 548, 550 (map); Islamism in, 534; Islamism versus Christianity in northern, 535;

Africa (*continued*)
Italian colonies, 140; mandate principle in settlement of problems, 546; minor interests and problems, 552; native welfare and control, 548; negroes, 533; negroes, conversion to Islam, 54, 56; partition by great powers, 540; population density in central (map), 538; Portuguese colonies, 159, 160 (map); races and cultures, 533; slave and liquor traffic, 548; sleeping sickness localities (map), 539; Spanish possessions (map), 153; Stanley's explorations, 540; threat to peace of the world, 541; trade policies, 547; tropical products, 537; Turkey and northern, 113; Uganda region (map), 538; white control, effect on natives, 535; white penetration, history, 539; white man's lands in central, 536, 537 (map)
Africa, West, 553, 554 (map); British in, 553, 554; commercial rivalry, 554; resources, 555
Africans, growing self-consciousness, 532
Agadir, 107, 541, 545, 553
Agram, 257
Agriculture, nomads' idea of, 474
Al Hasa, 68
Åland Islands, 173, 374, 375
Alaska, 520
Albania, 132, 249, 317; Austrian and Serbian rivalry, 308; bibliography, 592; boundaries, various proposed (map), 307; brigandage, 311; centers of interest, 310; character of country, 306; division proposed, 308, 309 (map); ethnography, religions, and boundaries (map), 310; feuds, 306; foreign control, 309; Italy's interest, 144, 306, 309; Jugo-Slavia and, 257; mountaineers, 306; people, distribution, 310; union, plan of, 311
Albania, southern. *See* Epirus, northern
Albanians, Serbs and, 257; view of Greek control, 325
Albert, Bishop, 362
Albertville, 128
Aleppo, 70, 102, 412, 429

605